The Coming WITHDRAWN

of the

Civil War

The Coming

of the

Civil War

By

AVERY CRAVEN

THE UNIVERSITY OF CHICAGO PRESS

CHICAGO & LONDON

THE UNIVERSITY OF CHICAGO PRESS, CHICAGO 60637
The University of Chicago Press, Ltd., London

*Copyright 1942 by Charles Scribner's Sons; Second Edition ©
1957 by Avery Craven. All rights reserved. Published 1957.
Printed in the United States of America*

05 04 03 02 01 00 99 98 97 96   12 13 14 15 16

ISBN: 0-226-11894-0 (paperbound)
LCN: 57-8572

PREFACE TO THE 1966 PRINTING

In reissuing a book written more than thirty years ago the author faces certain difficulties. Extensive revisions are not possible and whatever changes are permitted must be confined to a word or to a sentence here and there. The book must, therefore, remain essentially as first published.

In this case the difficulties are greater than usual. The book was something of a pioneer in a field where revision was just beginning. Much has since been done to secure a better balanced story and the author himself has had a part in that work. The question, therefore, arises as to just what changes he would make in this volume were he to rewrite it at this time.

Since he believes that the book was, and is, essentially sound, such changes would be largely in a shift of emphasis. Some things that needed to be stressed thirty years ago are now taken for granted. Other things are now more important and would need enlarged treatment. Changes would be largely in sections having to do with slavery and with the South. The reason for this is quite simple. Thirty years ago the Civil War story was written almost exclusively as a Northern story and with slavery as the sole cause of the conflict. The effort in this work was to balance the picture, not to present a Southern point of view or to defend slavery.

The emphasis could now be shifted, for most historians agree that there were two groups of Americans involved in that war, and it can be viewed as a national tragedy without the charge of revealing a Southern bias. It is not possible, however, even yet, to say that slavery was basically a labor system and should be equated with labor in Northern factories. Even one who is a Quaker with five generations of antislavery Quakers behind him, and who attended school from kindergarten through college in Iowa, is called "a defender of Slavery" for doing so. He is even charged with being "educated in the South."

Nor is it yet possible to say that such material interests as homesteads, tariffs, internal improvements, and even slavery, had to be emotionalized before they became "war measures" without the charge being made of believing it was all an abstraction and therefore "a needless war."

For these reasons the author has given his consent to have the book, in practically the original form, made more available to those who are interested in a more balanced view of a nation's tragedy.

PREFACE TO THE SECOND EDITION

WHEN this volume appeared fourteen years ago historians, as a rule, still viewed the Civil War much as the victors had pictured it. Little effort at an objective approach had been taken. That this was a Civil War and that there were two sides to the quarrel seemed to have been forgotten. In spite of all that Lincoln had said to the contrary, slavery alone was credited with causing the war. Many even insisted that war between North and South had been foreordained from colonial days.

The author of this volume, working from a suggestion made by Professor Carleton J. Hayes to the effect that there was no history of American democracy, had begun research with the idea of producing such a study. Early in his work he realized that one of the most significant things about the democratic process in the United States was that it completely failed in the critical period that culminated in the Civil War. His efforts to answer the questions as to *why* the democratic process so signally failed, and *how* issues got into such shape that they would not yield to that process, resulted in this volume. He was not interested in trying to untangle the complex factors that are supposed to have caused the war, nor did he intend to say that one factor was more important in producing war than were others. Most certainly he had no intention of saying categorically that the war was a "needless war"—a term he has never used at any time. And even more certainly he had no desire to defend slavery.

The approach taken, however, was somewhat new and, like most ideas, was not widely understood. All kinds of interpretations, for which the book gave no foundations, were ascribed to it, until it is questionable whether many of the historians who write glibly about it know what the book actually says. Yet the writing of Civil War history has changed profoundly since the book appeared, and most scholars have accepted the general point of view that it suggests. In the new edition an effort has been made to make some points more clear, and the entire text has been proofread—a task which was prevented in the first edition by the absence of the author on a government project.

PREFACE

IT IS not easy to write the story of the coming of the American Civil War. The three decades of bitter sectional strife which preceded open warfare left little in the way of historical material that was free from bias and distortion. The propaganda of war days still further damaged truth. It gave official sanction to the wildest assertions of pre-war extremists and completed the false impressions which each section had been slowly forming of its rival. Then men could kill their fellow countrymen with clear consciences. The hating and romancing of postwar times did almost as much damage. The prerogatives of the victor at the North and the certainty of superhuman ef-

fort against great odds at the South, justified continued sec-
tional pride and prompted elaborate defenses of the attitudes
and actions which had been taken during the recent war. A
Northern interpretation of the causes of the Civil War and a
Southern interpretation of the struggle quickly developed.
The Southern "point of view" served only local needs; the
Northern explanation of events, as evolved by Von Holst,
Schouler and McMaster, became the orthodox history of the
period. Textbooks followed their interpretation and gradually
even the South itself accepted them as "sound" and "un-
biased." What Jefferson Davis had said would constitute the
South's most serious loss became a reality; the victor was
writing the history of the War for future generations.

In recent years scholars have returned to a study of the
Civil War as scientists and not as partisans. They have come
to view the struggle as a national disaster. They have lost
respect for simple explanations of the growth of sectional
consciousness and sectional hatreds. Economic and social forces
as well as political ones have been considered and the effort to
fix blame has yielded to a desire to know why Americans only
two generations away from the formation of their Union
should have held positions so uncompromisable that only a
war could alter them. Much progress has been made toward a
sounder understanding of problems; much remains to be done.
Because new findings have and must upset the "orthodox" or
Northern interpretations, those who go back to the sources in
this field are still called "revisionists" and their interpretations
are too often charged with being "pro-Southern."

For these reasons the author of this volume must say that
he has not been interested in defending or attacking any
section. He has examined every document bearing on the complex problems of sectional consciousness and sectional distrust
that he could find in years of patient research. Every important collection in the country has been worked; newspaper

offices and court houses all over the South have been searched
for the uncollected files of ante-bellum newspapers; manuscripts in public depositories and in private hands have been
examined. Wherever possible in the writing of the story, contemporaries, men and documents alike, have been permitted
to speak for themselves. Even where "quotes" have not been
used the words of contemporaries have often been allowed to
take the place of those more natural to the author. The effort,
at least, has been to come as near to the truth as possible regardless of personal and sectional interests.

The approach from the angle of the South was deliberate.
Since that section's ways and institutions were under fire, it
was thought necessary to understand its position before that
of the North was studied. In that way realities could be more
easily distinguished from distortions; mere defenses and unfair attacks could be more easily recognized for what they were
worth. The very fact that the narrative ultimately shifted to
the Northwest seems to justify the procedure. The final es-
timates were always national. At any rate, the conclusions
reached, many of them tentative, seem to point out the
tragedy of being human rather than of being either Southern
or Northern.

The author's debts are numerous. His graduate students at
the University of Chicago, Northwestern University and the
University of California have made many contributions to this
book. They have also patiently tested his many theories and
pointed out both the strength and the weaknesses in them,
Many of them will recognize their own contributions to the
work. Mrs. Helen Van de Woestyne has read and criticized
the entire manuscript. She has given me the benefit of her
many unusual abilities. My gratitude cannot be expressed in
formal words. Librarians everywhere have served with the
kindness characteristic of the profession and placed me under
obligation at all times. My colleague, William T. Hutchinson,

has patiently accepted numerous interruptions and listened as patiently to my discussion of problems. His criticisms and his suggestions were invaluable. Fortunate indeed are those of us who toil at his side. And last, but not least, Jack and Ruth and Georgia have listened to the reading of each and every chapter and have made valuable, if not always serious, comment. To all of these I am deeply grateful.

A. C.

CONTENTS

I. THE NATIONAL SETTING 1

II. A WAY OF LIFE 17

III. THE RURAL DEPRESSION, 1800–1832 39

IV. BY THE SWEAT OF THEIR FACES 67

V. THE COTTON KINGDOM RISES 94

VI. THE NORTHERN ATTACK ON SLAVERY 117

VII. THE SOUTHERN DEFENSE OF SLAVERY 151

VIII. SLAVERY AND EXPANSION 175

IX. THE POLITICIANS AND SLAVERY 200

X. POLITICAL REVOLT 220

XI. THE FIRST CRISIS 241

XII. THE UNION ON TRIAL 272

XIII. THE NORTHWEST GETS EXCITED 303

XIV. SECTIONAL REACTIONS TO EVENTS 332

XV. BUILDING THE REPUBLICAN PARTY 361

XVI. THE LAST CRISIS 394

XVII. THE BREAKUP OF THE UNION 428

NOTES 441

INDEX 481

xiii

THE COMING OF THE CIVIL WAR

CHAPTER ONE

THE NATIONAL SETTING

W HEN Lee surrendered at Appomattox a tall, gaunt North Carolinian stolidly stacked arms and fell back into line. He was worn, hungry, and dirty. The insistent Yankees had granted him little time during the past weeks for relaxation. Food had been scarce; opportunities for cleanliness lacking. He had gone on fighting more from habit than purpose. He had quit because the orders were to that effect. Suddenly, with a sharp realization of what was taking place around him, he turned to his neighbor and drawled: "Damn me if I ever love another country."

In these words the disheartened Tarheel passed judgment on a generation.

In 1820 there was no "united North" or no "self-conscious South." These sections differed in climate, in economic interests, and in those intangible things which go to make a way of life. But differences were of long standing. They were not on the increase. They were not much greater than those existing between East and West. The Revolutionary and Constitutional fathers had recognized them and had not found them antagonistic to unity. In fact, the chief merit of the federal system, which the founders had adopted, lay in its ability to accept variations in component parts. The Colonies had revolted from England for this very principle and the Mother Country was already acknowledging the merit of their contentions by adjusting the federal system to an empire composed of entities as scattered and divergent as Canada and Australia. Physical and social differences between North and South did not in themselves necessarily imply an irrepressible conflict. They did not mean that civil war had been decreed from the beginning by

Fate. It came when problems arising from rapid growth and expansion got into such shape that they could not be solved by discussion, tolerance, and compromise. Where sections differed in interests, social patterns, and even in moral values, and all looked to a common central government for legislation, conflict was inevitable. It was not easy to satisfy industrial and agricultural areas on the tariff or to please old and new regions on lands and internal improvements. It was next to impossible to reach satisfactory agreement on territories where conflicting social-economic systems would gain or lose strength through expansion.

The most serious difficulty came over slavery, which, by the 1820's, had become localized to the South and which had gained a new hold with the spread of cotton. As a purely social or moral question to be faced and dealt with as such, slavery might not have proved a national tragedy. As a sectional issue linked to sectional rivalry and territorial expansion, it produced an "irrepressible conflict."

How this happened is not entirely clear. We only know that sectional rivalry in the nation turned into a struggle between North and South and that slavery became the symbol of all the differences between them. And, more important, slavery became the symbol of a conflict between "civilizations," between progress and backwardness, between right and wrong. Men ceased to reason, to tolerate, to accept compromise. Good men then had no choice but to kill and to be killed.

The process by which a repressible conflict was being made into an irrepressible one was closely seen and described by a thoughtful Georgia editor in 1858.[1] "A catastrophe," he said, "will never occur as the result of a settled conclusion or by the willful and deliberate forcing of one party by the other to the mutually understood and clearly recognized extremity. It will probably come at last like all family breaches, by surprise and in part accidentally. Every day, week, month and year brings an increasing alienation of feeling between the two sections. Northern injustice, insult and domination are rankling with every sun, deeper and deeper in the Southern breast. Almost every feeling of national consanguinity between the two sections is gone, and in its place is arising a sentiment of actual hostility. Thus it will continue, until it shall find a head most probably on the floor of Congress, on some comparatively trifling occasion which shall develop this feeling in full force by actual collision, and (it may be to the astonishment of the actors themselves) show that the Union is already gone irrecoverably,—gone through an intensity of mutual hatred which renders even its name intolerable. . . . Disunion will come . . . as the inevitable fruition of an uncompromising hatred, rankling and deepening through years of insult and wrong, itself the result of a belief that it can be *safely* inflicted. . . ."

In 1861 the crisis which this editor feared was reached. The legal election of a President set two peoples, who knew little of each other as realities, at each other's throats. Each side fought against mythical devils. Each struggled for honor, for civilization, for high principles, and for the glory of God. The cost was more than five billion dollars and more than a half million human lives. When the struggle was over few vital problems other than those dealing with nationalism and slavery had been solved, and others equally vexing had been created. Later historians would talk about "a blundering generation."

*　*　*　*

The period in United States history from 1820 to 1860 had three major characteristics. The first of these was rapid growth and expansion. Population doubled in nearly every decade, and the frontier of settlement, which in 1820 touched Lake Erie, ran thinly in a wedge across Ohio, southern Indiana and Illinois into Missouri, and then back sharply to middle Tennessee and Alabama, had by 1860 reached Minnesota, Kansas, Nebraska, Arkansas, and the newly acquired Texas. It had jumped to the Pacific, scattering human islands, where fertile soils or gold and silver lured. One generation had peopled an empire—yes, several of them—and had advanced life therein from simple to complex forms.

They were a sweaty people, that generation. They not only broke a hundred million acres to the plow but produced, with only the crudest tools, ten million bales of cotton, a billion bushels of wheat, and nearly two billion bushels of corn. They raised a dozen cities to metropolitan proportions and set the Industrial Revolution going in one corner of the nation. When they started out, the Indian still held his ground in Georgia, Alabama, Mississippi, Indiana, Illinois, and Wisconsin; the Mexican possessed Texas, New Mexico, and California; the British claims in Oregon sometimes ran well back to the Great Salt Lake. When the Civil War began, the Indian's fate on the continent had been sealed, England had granted the present northern boundary, and the worried Mexican had yielded up a Southwestern empire. That the American was a trifle buoyant, self-confident, intolerant, and aggressive, should hardly create wonder. Cuba, Central America, and even Canada might lie within his sphere of interest. Spacious days, indeed!

A second characteristic of this period, closely related to the rapid growth, was the sharp development of sectionalism. Expansion across a continent, in size and variety surpassing the one which held the European nations and all their quarrels, tended to create great provinces of differing economic, social, and mental outlook. Population, as a rule, moved in lines directly westward from the older portions of the nation. The New England stream poured into upper New York, Ohio, Michigan, and Wisconsin, following the lakes and forests, and then spreading out into the oak openings and prairie lands of the farther West. The Southern states sent their floods out through Nature's gateway at Cumberland Gap into the bluegrass regions of Kentucky and Tennessee, and then across the Ohio River into the hilly, wooded portions of the Old Northwest, or southward around the mountains into the "deep South" along the Gulf. The Middle States, always more American than their neighbors, overflowed to mingle with Northern and Southern streams and to give flavor to many a region where their settlers predominated. New states in the West in turn became hives to send swarms to lands nearer the setting sun— lands which changed sharply in physical character as rainfall lessened and vegetation grew sparse.

From the Canadian border, where the winters were long and severe, to the Gulf lands with their semitropical conditions, from the Allegheny Mountains to the Great Plains and the desert, one generation built provinces whose economic efforts and interests, whose social ideals, and whose political purposes differed from one another in large or small degree: The Greater New England, The Ohio Valley, The Old Northwest, The Blue Grass regions, The Lower South, The Southwest, and The Prairies. All of these were in more or less contrast with the earlier New England, The Middle States, and The Old South. The very fact of a steady advance into a wilderness meant modifications in economic life. Men who pioneered "began over again." They went back to first processes. They hunted pelts; they plundered the forests; they tended flocks and herds; they mined with pick and pan and shovel; they exploited the soils. They did most things for themselves because their social order could not as yet support the specialist. Their interests were primarily to secure easy access to lands and to find a cheap way to markets with the surplus wastefully wrung from nature. These people wanted to be let alone. Freedom was, with them, the path to equality.

Behind the pioneer, American life grew increasingly complex and interdependent. Shading back irregularly from frontier simplicity, it ended along the eastern seaboard, in cities and factories, in well-tended farms, and in plantations capable of supporting Old World ways. Specialization and localization of economic effort made one region the center of the Industrial Revolution; another, of staple crops and Negro slavery; another, of food stuffs sufficient for an empire's needs. Capital played a growing part in these developments, and capital gave economic advantage and social prestige to those who controlled it. Individual equality, therefore, gradually weakened, and the "living of the many" tended to pass "into the keeping of the few." Government grew in importance as a means of protecting rights and interests or as a means of securing favors. . . . The American provinces differed in age as well as in physical environments.

Four major sections emerged in this period: The Northeast, The Old South, The Northwest, and The Southwest. They were not entirely unique or entirely separate. Each held within itself regions quite distinct and often antagonistic. Boundaries were vague and elastic, varying with time or the point of view in classification. Neutral regions, such as the so-called Middle States, which lay between the main divisions, sometimes served as battlegrounds for rivals, and sometimes allied themselves definitely with one section or the other.[2]

Cohesion in the Northeast, born of early associations and traditions, was altered and expanded after 1815 by new commercial and industrial interests. Colonial New England had stood off alone, but the influence of the economic forces of the nineteenth century ran well beyond Puritan borders. From the edges of Maine and New Hampshire to the busy factory towns about Philadelphia a common purpose was early felt and a common program desired. The city and the factory had taken charge. Dominance, once in commercial hands, now passed into the hands of those connected with manufacturing. Spokesmen in legislative halls pressed for protective tariffs, centralized banking and "sound, honest" financial policies—meaning, of course, those which favored the creditor. Ambitious young men moved to the growing cities and trimmed their ideas, as did Daniel Webster, to fit the prevailing temper. Opposition to liberal land legislation and to free-trade doctrines indicated a degree of respectability not shared by the restless farmer, who turned westward in search of more fertile lands and more congenial society, or by the weakening commercial group, who sought the aid of Robert Y. Hayne of South Carolina in pressing their claims on Congress. Economic consciousness was the basis of sectional consciousness.[3]

The Northwest, on the other hand, was ever primarily a farming area. A few cities, especially Cincinnati, and later Chicago, arose to supply forwarding agents for a growing surplus and to distribute imported and locally made goods. But the great majority of the Northwest settlers lived and thought as rural people. The region along the Ohio, early settled by "upland Southerners" and men from the Middle States, passed out of the home-market stage in the 1820's and adjusted itself to the larger national economic pattern. The rich valleys in Ohio fattened stock on their grass and corn; Cincinnati became the packing center of the nation. Elsewhere on both sides of the Ohio River the products of general farming were supplemented by sheep, hemp, tobacco, mules, and horses, which served as "cash crops," but which found only partially satisfactory markets.[4]

Henry Clay and his American system represented the desire of this region for internal improvements at federal expense and for protective tariffs to bring greater diversification and build better markets. The graduation system and the distribution of sale proceeds to the states expressed its idea of just land legislation. The Ohio Valley was an "old West" before the panic of 1837 sharply emphasized the end of the national economic cycle.

That portion of the Northwest which lay along the Great Lakes and spread out onto the prairies was settled some two decades later than the Ohio Valley. It received heavy migrations from New England and her "colonies" in New York. Germans, Irish, Canadians, and the ever-present Middle States element soon mixed with these, to form, after an early period of misunderstanding and conflict, something of a unity based on common experiences and sectional needs.

The lands of this region were easily occupied. Their average fertility was high. The central government inaugurated a program of regional planning in the Northwest Ordinance and the systematic land surveys, and Federal troops crowded the Indian into submission. The settler was thus given both a national and social outlook. He might well believe that there was a preordained course which western regions ought to travel in the interests of poor white men. Kansas and Nebraska, as children of this region, were thus destined for freedom even before they existed as territories![5]

By 1860 the varied settlements along the Lakes had grown old enough to want homestead legislation for their poorer elements, railroads to carry their goods to the outside world, and tariffs to aid their rising industries and build better home markets. They had come, in part, to common ground with the older Northwest in the Ohio Valley. Lincoln, Douglas, and Chase were ready to play their parts on the national stage.

The Old South was traditionally a distinct section. Staple crops, the plantation system, and Negro slavery had combined with weather and peculiar social ideals to set this region apart both in its own thinking and in that of its neighbors. Its unity, however, had been largely exaggerated, and the wide variations within the section, between the tobacco and the rice areas, between the coastal plain and the up-country, had been overlooked. Yet in colonial and early national days, Southern leaders had acted with enough accord on occasion to justify the expression The South.[6]

Under the conditions prevalent from 1820 to 1860, this section grew increasingly self-conscious. Until near the end of the period, economic disaster was the common lot. Soils weakened under poor farming methods; markets failed; emigration, of serious proportions, went on unceasingly carrying off whites and blacks alike. In wealth and population these Southern states soon found themselves outdistanced by their rivals and face to face with the danger of becoming a permanent minority in the councils of the nation. Internal conflicts between tidewater and up-country added to the political problems. Constitutions were revamped under pressure, and property interests felt the strong hand of King Numbers. Sectional spokesmen, meanwhile, explained these evils as results of the protective tariff system, the Missouri Compromise, the attacks on slavery, and the Northern refusal to abide by the Constitution. The Old South was on the defensive. Calhoun strove to weld it into a solid political bloc with the Lower South; Rhett and Ruffin sought to give it greater self-consciousness.[7]

The Southwest was, as its name implies, both Southern and Western. Its settlers had come largely from the Old South and had brought with them the economic and social patterns of that section. Most of them were yeoman—middle-class farmers— men on the make, who migrated to secure fresher and cheaper lands. They differed little from their fellows in the Northwest. Some had slaves; many had none. But each settler hoped for a plantation and a "parcel of Negroes." Cotton promised to gratify their wishes. Large planters, in far less numbers, also moved with cotton westward. They carried their slaves with them and had some capital with which to escape part of the drudgery of pioneering.[8] But they too were beginning over again and the frontier imposed both its hardships and its spirit upon them. Outside the sugar-bowl area, where conditions were as unusual as California weather, only a few were able to build the traditional Southern home or to reproduce the Old World gentleman's way of life. The Southwest was as buoyant and aggressive as the Northwest. Its outlook and interests were largely the same. Yet it was not entirely like the other American West. Its climate and physical environment, its crops and methods, the social patterns it chose to follow, and the human values it admired—these were, in some degree at least, more Southern than Western. Furthermore, the central government had left the Southwest pioneers alone to settle their lands, fight their Indians, and establish their own political systems. Government gave them no Northwest Ordinance, no official land survey, no regular army campaigns. Men of the Southwest did things for themselves. If individualism is the great American virtue, then these pioneers were the finest fruits of our westward movement. One scholar has described their temperament as turned toward "the religious rather than the ethical, the intuitive rather than the logical, or, if you please, toward humor rather than wit." He is saying only that they added to a Southern base all the truly Western qualities. As cotton set its kingdom up among them and made tributary the lands of hemp and mules, they revealed something new in both Southern and Western sectionalism. Their Yanceys, Quitmans, Soulés, Benjamins, and Davises added a new note to the already confusing babel of American voices.[9]

* * * *

Throughout the middle period of American life, these four sections struggled to secure, from a common central government, legislation favorable to their varied and conflicting interests and to escape measures harmful to these interests. Their leaders, with an eye often on the presidency, sought combinations with other sections and fanned sectional consciousness to new heat. The Northeast often gave up opposition to liberal land policies which might draw its potential workers away, in order that it might secure Western support for protective tariffs. Webster was inclined even to emotionalize the issue by an appeal to the strong national sentiments of a people who needed federal aid in lands and internal improvements. The Old South, likewise, yielded on lesser issues when such a course seemed necessary to avoid the tariffs or to protect peculiar local institutions from a too active central authority. Calhoun, at one time, made a bid for Western support by arguing the right of Congress to improve the Mississippi River under the same powers used to build lighthouses, beacons, and buoys. A harbor might extend far up an inland river when Calhoun wanted to be president!

Few of these issues reached final settlement. The farmers of West and South destroyed the central bank, kept the tariff within limits, but most of the battles ended in compromise—which meant that they could not be settled. Bitterness increased with each sectional brush; feelings grew more intense. Hatreds and loyalties gradually made compromise neither possible nor desirable. In the end, brothers went to war.[10]

A third characteristic of this period arose from the democratic and humanitarian stirrings which swept the nation in every decade. Some came from the West where the frontier generated new faith in common men and revived old dreams of a more perfect society. Some drifted across from the Old World, where those capable of disinterested thinking had begun the fight to free men from wars and poverty and slavery. Most of them arose out of the ills of a re-forming economic and social order at home and became vocal through the evangelical churches of plain unimaginative people. They found largest response in the rural belts. They took form in the phrases of the Declaration of Independence or the Scriptures. They produced a strange tangle of dreaming and practical effort. They left few things not classified as right or wrong.[11]

In the 1820's Andrew Jackson symbolized the longings of common men for political equality and plunder, and their resentment against what they did not share or understand— designated as privilege and aristocracy. Western and Southern men, aided by the lesser coast and back-country people of the Northeast, made him president and he in turn struck down the bank, humbled the proud, and distributed spoils to the people's delight. Recurring waves of Jackson's brand of democracy continued to beat against things established to the end of the period.[12]

More significant than positive attitudes were the defensive expressions of democracy in this period. In the vast growth and expansion of the day, the wealth and power of the few grew disproportionately to that of the many. Liberty was putting an end to equality. If some were content with progress, others thought that the American dream of a social order more perfect than that of Europe was being lost. Some felt the danger of wars which burdened the masses with taxes and death. They struggled to establish peace to the ends of the earth. A few carried this doctrine to the extreme of non-resistance. Some feared the evils of intemperance; some those of ignorance; some those of a permanent, down-trodden laboring element. One group wanted to give woman her legal and political rights. Another resented the materialism of the day and sought the reality which transcends that of the senses. Idealistic societies sprang up here and there in which all were to share in lighter burdens of production and all were to receive more abundant riches, material and spiritual. Sometimes the struggle took the form of rural-opposition to a rising urban life; sometimes it expressed itself in deep resentment of the poor against the increasing wealth of the few. Gradually the effort to free the Negro slaves on Southern plantations brought to a focus most of the sentiments engendered by all injustice and set the reformer at the task of bringing low the perfect aristocrat who held these slaves in bondage.[13]

Emerson looked back at it all to exclaim, "What a fertility of projects for the salvation of the world!" And Lowell declared that "all stood ready at a moment's notice to reform everything but themselves."

Even more important than these protests against inequality, because it touched the great American masses, was the new fervor which took hold of the evangelical churches and manifested its extreme qualities in periodic revival meetings throughout the back country. The theology of most Americans was that of John Calvin, and the American preacher revealed surprising ability to cast and recast Calvinistic tenets to more satisfactory form. The New England group reached its climax in Jonathan Edwards and his praise of damnation when endured for the glory of a stern unbending God. But abstract speculation was not a frontier trait, and in the newer sections emphasis shifted to conduct as a manifestation of salvation. More and more the back-country preacher pictured the world as a field fertile for Christian effort and stressed the obligation of the elect to transform it into the kingdom of heaven. The frontiersman was practical even in matters of religion. With the wider expansion of this period and the new simplification of thought and forms which it produced, the religious leaders of the Greater New England stirred and accepted much more of emotion than had their forebears. Their revivals burned more brightly and more often, and the theology necessary to plain wilderness conditions underwent great change at the hands of such a leader as Charles Grandison Finney. Where before the emphasis in Calvinism had been on "a painful quest for a safe escape from life" and salvation had been the end of that quest, Finney saw conversion as but the beginning of "being useful in the highest degree possible." His converts, and they were legion, went to work in the Lord's vineyard 'round about them. As they understood the new life, a moral obligation rested on every Christian to rid the world of sin. Sin consisted both of personal indulgence and of social wrongs. The whole program of the humanitarian reformer became a church program. Social evils were somebody's sins. There should be a law against them.

The state was but the agent of good men for the doing of justice and the ending of evil.[14]

The fight for democracy and the fight for morality were, therefore, one and the same. The kingdom of heaven on earth was a part of the American political purpose. The Constitution, the Declaration of Independence, and the Scriptures were all in accord. The Christian reformer thus entered the political world in an era of sectional controversies and placed a halo of righteousness over sectional attitudes, even as they related to material things.

While such ideas were developing in the North, the Methodist, Baptist, Presbyterian, and Quaker at the South made heavy inroads on the prestige which the Episcopal Church had long enjoyed and crowded the unbeliever out to the very edges of respectability. As prosperity declined in older coastal regions, the up-country peoples, strong in numbers if not in tradition, slowly impressed their point of view on public affairs. Since churches and denominational schools were the dominant influences in their emotional lives, theological and moral beliefs colored all attitudes. A staunch orthodoxy, not unlike that preached by Finney, took deep hold on the section. Thomas Jefferson found this out when he attempted unsuccessfully to add the learned Doctor Thomas Cooper to the faculty of his new state university.

Cooper, as a Deist, had some grave misgivings regarding the accuracy of the story of creation as found in Genesis. He was a great scholar—greater than the American order could have produced or even attracted if the repressions of Europe had not assisted. The people, however, would not accept his unorthodox opinions. Jefferson, nearing permanent "bed-time" and bent on giving democracy a leadership fit to lead, had overlooked the realities of the new situation in Virginia. He might sit on his hilltop and watch the Grecian-pillared halls and the rows of unadorned student cloisters rise down at Charlottesville with the tolerant hopeful eyes of a democratic philosopher, but his neighbors, feeling that religion, not philosophy, held the future, could not accept scholarship which lacked faith. Reluc-

tantly Cooper was passed on to the more liberal College of
South Carolina, there further to enrich American thought, but
soon to face again the rising tide of Southern up-country orthodoxy.[15]

The College of South Carolina, located at Columbia, was
no ordinary institution. No college which, in a series of years,
claimed a Cooper, a Lieber, and a LeConte could be ordinary.
Under the influence of the Charleston area, the most civilized
spot on the continent, the school had been great even as it had
been aristocratic. And it had been liberal also. Academic freedom was its boast. With the spread of cotton, however, and
with the weakening of those economic foundations on which
"the kingdom of rice" had been built, the lesser groups above
the fall-line came to new influence in South Carolina, as they
had earlier done in Virginia. New wealth from a superior staple
made education possible for common men who turned critical
eyes upon the unorthodox ways of those whom gentlemen had
permitted to teach the youth. Under the leadership of the
Reverend J. H. Thornwell, who "really had scruples about
associating with" the faculty and trustees of Harvard because
they were Unitarians, "the Christian people of the state rose
up to defend the altars" which Cooper and his kind "proposed
to subvert." They too turned Jefferson's scholar adrift "for
poisoning the very fountains of knowledge in the State." They
cleansed the Augean stables so that Presbyterian, Methodist,
and Baptist sons might go to college and remain untouched in
matters of belief. Fundamentalism began its reign in the Old
South.

The evangelical groups of the South were not entirely untouched by the great democratic humanitarian stirrings of the
day. The temperance cause took firm hold in widely scattered
corners—even in colleges and universities. "Signing the pledge"
and "pinning the ribbon" became matters of major interest.
There were peace men, anti-dueling advocates, and even an
anti-slavery element, which adjusted its protests to the necessity
produced by Northern extremists. But group effort was always
weak among these rural individualists. Both sin and reform
were primarily personal matters to them. Separated from the

living, breathing entities comprehended by the words, uncle, brother, cousin, or neighbor, good and evil had little reality and no appeal. These men could follow a leader blindly to death itself; they could not be inspired by an abstraction. That is one reason why the other great movements, which so deeply affected New England and the West, did not take hold. Yet this people had a sharp sense of right and wrong and a firm intolerance of those who differed with their convictions. Their church leaders, diverted by no sharp changes, such as industry produced, kept largely to the task of individual salvation from self-indulgence and turned aside only when the abolition efforts threatened the stability of society, and when the divinity they could confer was needed to bolster up slavery and the Southern way of life. Then they did yeoman service in the interest of things established.

*   *   *   *

Out of this national setting, the War between the States evolved. By the strange twistings of Fate, the three great strands of development, in the life span of a generation of Americans, were tangled together in such ways as to push reason aside and to give emotion full sway. Unparalleled expansion only served to magnify and intensify sectional differences and raise the question of Constitutional rights in the spread of institutions and peoples to new territory. Growth shifted the old balances of power and posed anew the insoluble problem of minority and majority rights. Intense humanitarian impulses and awakened religious feelings supplied the emotions with which sectional positions and sectional interests could be glorified. All contests became part of the eternal struggle between right and wrong. This caused the break-up of national political parties which had constituted the main element in American nationalism. For party unity men had been willing to sacrifice sectional interests and to yield personal principles. Membership in the party organization and allegiance to its platform was in itself a compromise and the party could yield where the individual could not. As long as the national parties held firm, conflicting principles were not dangerous to national unity; men with principles could belong to parties which did not have them. Political compromise was thus always possible. But when right and wrong came into politics then parties had to become sectional and the sectional party could be based on principles. That lifted politics to new levels and put an end to compromise. What were but normal differences in the beginning of the period thus gradually became principles. The maintenance of principle became a matter of honor, of sacred duty. The conflict was then irrepressible. Only the God of battles could judge.

The old North Carolina soldier at Appomattox was right. It is a serious thing to love a country!

CHAPTER TWO

A WAY OF LIFE

THE ante-bellum South is shrouded in romance and hidden by the lingering clouds of abolition propaganda. Friends and foes have conspired to distort realities. Circumstances have abetted them. In colonial days opportunities in tobacco and land permitted a few families to approximate the English country gentleman's way of life and to form ruling cliques in the simple governments of Virginia and South Carolina. In national days the longing of democratic peoples for equality magnified this homespun approximation into genuine blue-blooded aristocracy and royal living. What a few partially enjoyed, in spite of the overbearing influence of frontier conditions, was ascribed to large numbers. What existed in limited corners was spread out, in imagination, over wide areas. The gay Cavalier of the South, dwelling in luxury in a mellow clime, was created to contrast with the stern Puritan of stingy-soiled New England.

This, however, was only the beginning of distortion. The bitter sectional struggles of the middle period in American history and the introduction of moral factors into the slavery controversy, combined to develop the idea of basic unity in the region and peoples, and to evolve the charge that Southern people, as a class, were indolent, licentious, intemperate, and overbearing. Southerners, regardless of locality, were supposed to think and act alike. There were Southern attitudes on all social and political questions. There were distinct moral codes and well-defined philosophies common to all.

Institutions were treated in like manner. Slavery was imagined, not investigated. Its practice was assumed to accord with the depravity of human nature and the possibilities inherent in such a relationship. The slaveholder—and all Southerners, or most of them, were assumed to hold slaves—was shaped into a monster capable of enjoying the plunder and indulgence for which mastery over other human beings gave opportunity. His days were spent in sexual irregularity at the expense of Negro women. He was snobbish in his relations with lesser whites. He drank to excess, quarreled at the slightest provocation, despised those who toiled.

From decade to decade details were added to the fiction and the pattern stereotyped. The desire of Southern leaders to break up the Union, which God Himself had given to down-trodden humanity, was accepted as final proof of all charges. The current Northern picture of those who lived "down South" became one of haughty nabobs, intemperate and lax in morals, dwelling in great white-pillared houses, wringing wealth from those in bondage and sorrow, and seeking to destroy the best government on the face of the earth. Sinners and aristocrats *par excellence!*

The fact that Southerners retaliated by the ultimate assumption that all men in the North were Yankees, and that all Yankees were John Browns, did not help matters. Incrimination bred incrimination. Gradually the South was assigned the role of Devil in the old Puritan conflict to establish the Holy Commonwealth. Southern life and institutions were twisted to fit the part. What the abolitionists wanted the section to be, that it came to be in their thinking. When actual war broke in 1861, the material was thus at hand for Northern propaganda against "ignoble foes." The necessities of strife made "truth," for those yet unborn, of the wildest imaginings of a generation's extremists.

The sunset glory of a lost cause added the final touch to the picture. The war between the states ended in bitter defeat for the section, but it became a glorious tradition—the end of golden days never to come again. Thomas Nelson Page and others took up where Harriet Beecher Stowe and her kind had left off. Romancing completed the damage. A South that never was dominated the minds of a generation. The historian has only begun to clear the vines from ancient ruins. A true picture of the section has not yet been drawn.

* * * *

Any study of the South must begin with geography. Nature has always been close to this people. Fertility of soils or its absence has largely conditioned their economic well-being; mountains and valleys and fall-lines have divided them physically and socially as well; great rivers have run through their lives as through their lands; and weather has crept into their very souls and shaped their destiny both in things material and in things of the spirit. "Ninety degrees in the shade" is an historical fact.

And geography denies the first of the popular assumptions regarding the section: that the South was a natural entity which always thought and felt as one because of common foundations and common interests. The land which sweeps from the Maryland shore south and west to Arkansas and Texas is, in reality, anything but a unity. It is made up of coastal plains, some facing the Atlantic, some the Gulf, all varied and divided; of a great, red-soiled Piedmont plateau stretching from Pennsylvania to the "deep South," more of a unity in itself than a part of the states which cut it into segments; of mountain ridges, with valleys great and small in between, swinging south and west and spreading out into a veritable chaos in the Carolinas and Tennessee and bending sharply across northern Alabama. Beyond the mountains to the north, lies a highland rim studded with islands of blue grass, and to the south are black prairie lands and clay hills, with "Ole Man River" cutting the whole west into two parts and creating a world of his own of flood plains and bluffs which give way near the Gulf to swamps and bayous and delta lands. Across the Mississippi, adding more of variety, lies all that is comprehended in the interior plains of Texas, Louisiana, and Arkansas, the Ozarks, the black waxy belts, and the semi-desert stretches at the southern end of the Great Plains.[1]

If enough of unity ever existed amid such diversity to justify the term "the South," obviously it was achieved in spite of geographic conditions rather than because of them.

Nor did human experience in the region justify the assumption of sectional coherence in 1820. In Virginia, for example, sharp sectional lines were early drawn. The coastal regions, settled directly from England, were kept in close contact with the mother land by great bays and rivers, which reached far to the interior, and which permitted ocean-going vessels to anchor at private wharfs to the fall-line. Prospering with tobacco, these tidewater Virginians quickly reproduced in homespun fashion the Old World country way of life. Some became gentlemen. Others merely acquired wealth. The less fortunate moved farther out to join the hordes of plain folk who were swarming south along the Piedmont out of Pennsylvania—America's first great melting pot. On rolling uplands they cleared their farms, built their simple cabins, and ignored the comments of coastal visitors who thought them little above the Indians. Neither tobacco nor English ways disturbed their lives.[2]

From two such separate beginnings and from the two entirely different ways of living, two distinct economic-social orders evolved to contend for control in a common government. With Bacon's Rebellion Virginians began a sectional conflict which moved their capital westward, subjected their Constitution to perpetual strain and readjustment, and in the end separated West Virginia from the parent state.

The story in South Carolina is much the same. Charleston, in time to be almost a city-state, early became a social and political center for the rice and indigo plantations which lay along an island-studded coast but which could not expand far inland. Her wealth and culture set new levels for colonial America and her stately homes, theatres, clubs, and racecourses indicated the realization of genteel society. There was substance to the boast: "See Charleston and forever envy her citizens." To be buried in St. Philip's or St. Michael's softened even the sting of death.

But behind the fall-line and sand hills which marked the Piedmont's beginning, the sons of Pennsylvania migrants and of lesser men from the Carolina coast lived in self-sufficing simplicity. They were numerous but not cultured. A traveller through the region in 1800 found log houses and "a gouging, biting, kicking" people. They had started their first newspaper only five years earlier. Their rudeness to genteel persons was a matter for comment. They were typical frontiersmen. One day, years later, their sons would go trudging back in gray uniforms past the graves of their ancestors scattered all the way from Ninety-six to Gettysburg.

Charleston was slow to grant these people an equal share in the government. They complained increasingly of unfair representation, too limited franchise, the absence of courts and local administration. The eve of the American Revolution found them in open resistance against the low country.

They gained some ground in the Constitution of 1790 but even then reformers protested that one fifth of the population were the rulers of four fifths. "Charleston with . . . less than one ninth of the population . . . elected more than one third of the legislature." And, it might be added, the legislature almost completely ruled the state, even in matters purely local.[3]

In 1790, Columbia took the capital away from Charleston. But this was accomplished only by permitting some officials and departments to remain behind or to be duplicated in the coastal city. Property could not yield to numbers until economic and social security had been assured. Only when cotton brought slaves and conservative ideas to the red hills could Western men hope for equal rights. In spite of the boast made in 1852 that the people of South Carolina had come more and more to regard the state as a unit, the old hostility between up-country and coast lived on to the very outbreak of the War between the States.

In North Carolina, the internal strife was as much more intense as were the qualities and achievements of her people more modest. Actual warfare between east and west climaxed the colonial struggle in the so-called Regulation movement, and hostility was not allayed until the Constitutional Convention of 1835 righted the balance between coast and interior. Even then the long and bitter struggle left its scars, and sectional cleavage cropped out constantly in all political contests.[4]

The newer Southern states repeated this story in varying degree as streams of settlers out of different states poured into their diverse geographic areas. Alabama and Mississippi early revealed marked antagonisms, not only between districts settled by the larger slaveholders and planters and those occupied by the lesser farmers, but also between regions inhabited by emigrants from different states, such as Tennessee and South Carolina. The distribution of offices according to degrees of latitude in the former was matched in the latter by "the spirit of sectionalism, of jealousy and want of unity of sentiment which induce us in our State Conventions to draw lines throughout the State in the selection of candidates. . . ." In Louisiana the French element, Catholic in religion, long remained aloof amid the swirling tide of American expansion. In 1836 New Orleans was divided into three distinct municipalities in order to end the bitter conflicts of Creole and American.[5]

Indeed, taken as a whole, a section which contained social and political elements as diverse as Arkansas and Charleston, eastern Tennessee and tidewater Virginia, upland North Carolina and western Texas, can hardly be thought of as forming a solid block of interests or ideas. There were units which were old; others which were frontier; some which contained wealth and refinement; others whose people rightly carried the word "poor" even before the designation of their race. Conflict and strife characterized the relationships among these units from early until late. How they were, even temporarily, welded into a working unity is one of the major problems of American history.

*   *   *   *

The second erroneous assumption regarding the South has to do with the make-up of its people and with their way of life. Fortunately, the notion that early Virginia settlers were all Cavaliers has been largely dispelled.[6] We now recognize the scarcity of blue blood among them and the prevalence of both middle-class origins and middle-class attitudes. But the idea that gentlemen and poor whites were the sole elements of Southern society still persists. The number of stately mansions, wherein dwelt gentle folk and about which grew up elegance and culture, is far too great in both fiction and history. Even careful writers are wont to assume chivalry and gallantry in most Southern men and studied charm in most Southern women. The rest are dismissed as white trash and Negroes.

The charge made by a seventeenth-century English observer that the people who went to the American Colonies "were the very scum and off-scouring of our nation" is as false as Doctor Johnson's famous remark that "they are a race of convicts." They were, in fact, with a few exceptions, of the vigorous middle-class stock and ever manifested in their greed for land and office and wealth the typical bourgeois traits—they consti- tuted "a little world of London burgesses new seated on the banks of the James and the Rappahannock."[7]

Yet in a few years, out of the opportunities afforded by abundant lands and their exploitation with cheap labor in to- bacco cultivation, such families as the Carters, the Lees, the Fitzhughs, the Byrds, etc., were able to establish country seat- ings up and down the great tidal rivers. To these estates they gave names as they would have done had conditions in old England permitted such advancement: Nomini Hall, Shirley, Westover, Stratford, Curles. They adorned themselves and their houses with English goods and reproduced the country gentleman's way of life from a political office close to the gov- ernor, to the wine cellar, the library, and the fox hunt. The significant thing is not Cavalier blood, for none of those here listed had it, but the fact that middle-class men carried with them to the New World a pattern for society long developing among the successful in England and found in America the chance to reproduce it more or less completely. In time, agri- cultural maturity and pressure for economy forced the substitu- tion of Negro slaves for white indentured servants. Then the peculiarly Southern version of that pattern was completed.

Late in the eighteenth century pious old Devereaux Jarratt could write of the "ideas of the difference between gentle and simple" folks being "universal among all my rank and age" and tell of the fear which smote his heart, as a boy, when a periwig appeared.[8] About the same time one Humphry Chamberlaine, "a person of low rank," was fined and jailed for "offering to fight a gentleman"; and one James Bullock, "a taylor," was given like treatment for racing his horse—"a sport only for gentlemen."[9]

But the self-made aristocrat constituted always a small minority in the South. The great majority, crowded to the ridges between the great rivers or sent westward to the Piedmont, found in America only opportunity to make a better living. They hunted, farmed, reared their numerous progeny, squatted on the speculator's lands or secured a small tract of their own and, on occasion, rose to declare the rights of numbers as above those of property.

Bacon's Rebellion had something of that flavor about it. The Revolution in Virginia may have been in part a struggle for home rule but it was certainly also an effort to determine who should rule at home. Patrick Henry was not merely a patriot; he was also a democrat. And when independence had been won, Thomas Jefferson successfully gathered the lesser men of coast and interior into a political party to challenge the rule of "their betters." Even at that time, though handicapped by property requirements for voting and a system of representation which Jefferson said gave nineteen thousand tidewater men equal voice with thirty thousand Westerners, common men were numerous enough to cut state support from the aristocrat's church and to set aside primogeniture and entail. Then they began steps to force a more liberal franchise and a more just representation. For the next fifty years the fight went on to reveal, in spite of the use of all the clever tricks which privileged minorities have ever tried, the growing strength of plain middle-class citizens, whose interests were in persons, not in accumulated property.

In the colonial Carolinas, common men were just as numerous as in Virginia. At Cape Fear, in the northern colony, the Moores, the Moseleys, the Howes, the Ashes, and the Harnetts may have lived somewhat like "the ancient feudal barons . . . dispensing a noble hospitality to the worthy," proud of a coat of arms and boastful of "gentle manners and cultivated minds," but "the great mass of people," outside this district, "were the common small farming type. . . ." They signed their names, when they could sign them, with such words appended as farmer and yeoman. They were strong, fearless, independent, provincial in outlook, democratic in social attitudes, tenacious of their rights, and, if interested in religion, earnest, narrow, and dogmatic. Some were as worthless as those Colonel William Byrd found leaning with both arms upon a cornfield fence, and generally finding reasons for putting off till another time the much-needed plowing. Others deserved Brickell's description of "a straight, tall, well-limbed and active people," the "women often very fair" and "the young men . . . generally of a bashful, sober Behavior, few proving Prodigals." Nearly all were of that sturdy yeoman class, who wore deep the pioneer trails to the Old Northwest and to the lower South in the early nineteenth century, or remained behind to follow Lee and Jackson in the 1860's with courage seldom equalled by human beings.[10]

In South Carolina few among the settlers, even in Charleston, could claim noble descent. The English planters who came by way of the West Indies were of the same sort as those who sought to better their material lot in early Virginia. The French Huguenots and the New England migrants who made up the larger part of the remaining element on the coast were thoroughly middle-class. Gentility in Charleston society was achieved, not inherited.

Even when rice and indigo had wrought their miracles and Negro slaves outnumbered the whites in favored districts, a Christopher Gadsden, an Alexander Gillon, or a James Fallon could gather the unpropertied classes together in such numbers as to dominate public action. Under pressure from these common people, reluctant conservatives accepted independence from the Mother Country, permitted paper-money issues, and at length even yielded to the passage of stay laws in the interest of debtors.

Meanwhile the Irish at Port Royal, the Swiss at Purrysburg, the Germans in Orangeburg, the Welsh on the Pedee formed, with the Scotch-Irish and other lesser people who came plodding down the Piedmont, a great raw mass, as thoroughly American in hopes and fears as any group on the continent.

Some of them were to rise to the status of great planters; most of them were to remain sturdy farmers. Their very number frightened aristocrats into support of a stronger central government and into tenacious defense of property interests in state government. One "gentleman" wrote in 1785: "Our governments tend too much to Democracy. A handicraftsman thinks an apprenticeship necessary to make him acquainted with his business. But our back-countrymen are of the opinion that a politician may be born such, as well as a poet." Common men answered by talk of a "despotic aristocracy" composed of "a few able and designing men" determined to "enslave the rest."[11]

Westward expansion in the first half of the nineteenth century, when cotton came to build its kingdom in the wider South and West, swung the balance even more definitely in favor of the middle class. The lowly back-country always gave far greater numbers to the new lands just beyond than did the tidewater areas. After 1800 Piedmont Virginia and the Carolinas sent restless foot-free farmers into central Georgia, and after 1830, when the Indians had been removed, on into the northern corners where gold and fresh lands attracted. This latter region was still in the frontier-farming stage of development in 1850, as was the whole southeastern part of the state. Georgia, with debtor-class beginnings, retained her yeoman qualities throughout the ante-bellum period. The census of 1850 listed only nineteen hundred planters as against some eighty-one thousand farmers. The term Yankee state, sometimes applied to Georgia, referred in part to the presence there of many New Englanders, but it was used also to describe the aggressive, acquisitive temper which characterized her citizens and made her progress equal that of her Northern rivals.[12]

Tennessee frontiersmen early followed the path into Alabama cut by Andrew Jackson in his campaigns against the Indians, and after 1830 the same groups which had peopled central Georgia carried cotton in a great crescent sweep across the deep South. Only one generation matured in the Cotton Kingdom. Save where a limited number of planters from the old rice and tobacco regions moved their establishments full blown into the new lands, the usual American type of pioneer led the way and continued to predominate to the beginning of the Civil War. Land speculation, lawlessness, hard driving of selves and dependents, characterized the economic efforts of these men; emotionalism and the multiplication of sects, their religious life. Times were flush. Men were on the make. Their West, as Wests were wont to do all over America, set things back a bit toward the primitive and added a touch of coarseness and aggression. The thirty years before war intervened were not enough to alter the general flavor.[13]

In the sugar bowl about New Orleans, a favored staple and protective tariffs enabled planters to move more rapidly. During the 'thirties and again a decade later, profits permitted the erection of great houses and the development of a social life which flowered in New Orleans and Natchez. Old World beginnings gave both an added charm and a better opportunity for rapid growth; yet the pattern, except in one section of New Orleans, was distinctly American. A few Creole planters built houses reminiscent of old France, one at least with its rampart and moat. The great majority, however, followed the classical pattern which Thomas Jefferson had popularized, and some planters, new-rich, revealed the raw frontier spirit by placing silver doorknobs where the entering guest might be properly impressed. At Oak Alley, Rosedown, Belle Grove, The Shadows, Stanton Hall, or Greenwood a way of life fashioned after the recognized Southern pattern was soon in full swing. Sulley painted family portraits. Sons went back to Yale and Princeton and to the University of Virginia. Families travelled abroad, to the Northern watering places, and to the Virginia springs. The theatre and a gay social life attracted them to New Orleans. Some even built town houses there and went down for the season which climaxed in Mardi Gras. An aristocracy below that of Virginia and Charleston only in age grew up amid the turmoil of a river life which reflected the temper of the whole busy West and the pushing quality of the young cotton world.[14]

The usual test for measuring the amount of gentry in the ante-bellum South is slaveholding. Here again the evidence is all against the planter-poor-white interpretation. In 1860, when slavery had reached its widest point of diffusion, after two centuries of growth, there were only 383,637 slaveholders in a total white population of over eight million. The number of persons in any way connected with the institution by family or direct interest could not have reached two millions. Three fourths of the white people in the South were, therefore, outside the favored circle. Of those who held slaves only 48,566 held twenty or more —a number sufficient to have constituted a plantation force or to have required an overseer. Nearly half the slaveholders held fewer than five, and nearly one third held but one or two—a Negro family, a domestic, an artisan, or a field hand. Most white men and women must have toiled in field and home alongside their slaves. They must have slept in the same houses or at least in the same yard with their servants, and eaten the same hog and hominy. As Hundley says of the Southern yeomen: ". . . when they are slaveholders, they seem to exercise but few of the rights of ownership over their human chattels, making so little distinction between master and man, that their Negroes invariably become spoiled . . . never receiving a stripe unless some one of their young masters is stout enough to give them a lamming in a regular fisticuffs fight, and in all things treated more like equals than slaves. . . ."[15]

* * * *

If aristocrats, either completed or on the make, were scarce in the Old South and even scarcer in the days of King Cotton, genuine poor whites were equally few in number. Vague as the term has become, it still implies ignorance, shiftlessness, poverty, and depravity, and brings up pictures of tumble-down shanties, a few rows of tattered corn, hogs ranging the pines, sodden men and women, weakened by pellagra and hookworm, much given to hunting and fishing, and well deserving the names of hill-billies, crackers, or clay eaters.

Such people there were in widely scattered localities of the ante-bellum South. They lived in definite areas—especially in the pine barrens of the coastal plain, the sand hills at the Carolina fall-line, the wire-grass regions of Georgia and the pine barrens in eastern Alabama and western and northern Mississippi. Their number probably never exceeded a few thousand.

Travellers commented on their sickly sallow complexions, their
slovenly appearance, their intemperance in the use of tobacco
and corn liquor, and their utter ignorance. Modern writers have
called them "the slum element of the South" and reached such
absurd conclusions as that "the plantation system by virtually
monopolizing industry rendered superfluous the potential contribution of the poor white, consigning him to a life of useless-
ness so far as productive society was concerned." Such statements exaggerate the number of those deserving the name, miss
the real factors which produced them, and ignore the great
proportion of Southerners not on plantations who toiled pro-
ductively. There were probably no more people with poor white
qualities in the South than in any other section of the nation.
Persons who elsewhere would have lived on charity, in alms-
houses, or in prison, or who were habitual ne'er-do-wells, were
in the simple rural Southern structure merely crowded into the
undesirable corners to shift for themselves. Poor health added
to characteristics already predominant. The firm lines of physical environment held tightly when once effective, and inbreed-
ing, social as well as physical, strengthened their hold. Habitual
poverty, "enjoyed" through several generations, did the rest.
The poor white was simply the lowest element of this rural
society, exaggerated and given his peculiar characteristics by
physical and social forces operating in his surroundings. The
presence of industry or the absence of Negroes might have
altered his form or life, but would not have greatly influenced
his numbers.[16]

The great body of Southerners belonged to the middle class
in both an economic and a social sense. Some were near the top,
about ready to enter the aristocracy; some were as near the
poor white at the other end of the scale. It is not far wrong to
think of them as the counterpart of Northern pioneer farmers,
small rural residents of the older sections, professional men
and those who hired out for a time in the hope of some day
becoming independently established. They owned or rented
farms of moderate size; less than 3 per cent of all farms in
the South in 1860 contained five hundred acres. They and their
families, women as well as men, worked the usual rural hours

from sun to sun most of the year. Some acquired a few slaves to help them get ahead and used these slaves much as hired help was used elsewhere.[17]

One of these independent farmers, William Carrigan, wrote from Alamance County, North Carolina, in 1851, of his 150 acres "in corn" worked "with eleven horses, some of them little, some blind, and some very old"; of 250 acres in wheat and oats; of 30 slaves, a cotton manufacturing plant, a store, 50 head of cattle, and a goodly parcel of hogs much depleted "by a disease cald Quinsy." He had just subscribed "$4000 stock" to help bring a railroad through his county seat, and had rented to a relative another farm he owned. Yet his son Alfred, a graduate of the State University at Chapel Hill, had "most of the charge of the farm," and another son, John, who had spent two years at a classical school "without much profit (his health gave way & he dislikes to study)," and a younger son, James, were "plowing and farming when we have no school." The "baby," James, "ten years old the last day of Jany.," was "a regular plower in the field with the Negroes and larger brothers." In fact, there were only "four grown men" in the entire working force, black and white, "the balance boys and women" —all toiling together.

On another occasion, when "under the Divine blessing of our All-wise God" he was "permitted" on "His Holy Sabbath to write" a letter, Carrigan pictured himself with his sons having "just quit reading in the Bible, verse about." On another, after speaking of sickness among his Negroes, he revealed his attitude toward them by a side reference to "my white family." Most else in his simple pages had to do with the difficulties of making farming pay, with health, weather, and the harshness of fate which permits men to grow old and lose close contact with those who in youth were dear. An Illinois farmer could have written every line—not excepting even those which dealt with farm labor if the word Negro were omitted.[18]

Another yeoman, whose grandson in the twentieth century was to be one of the nation's most illustrious divines, wrote in 1850 from northwest Georgia of clearing land with the aid of Albert, the only slave he possessed, and a white man hired. A neighbor told of chills always contracted when one "overdone himself" in the fields, and invited friends from "back home" to "come and take a shake with us." Olmsted found blacks and whites at work together in Alabama and Mississippi; and Ingraham, at Natchez, in 1835, described a "cheek by jowl" familiarity between the yeoman and Negroes, "with good will and a mutual contempt for the nicer distinctions of color."[19]

Edward Hale, in 1853, declared that in his neighborhood few wealthy men had inherited slaves or other property and many had begun with nothing. Ebenezer Pettigrew insisted that if he had not "in early times" spent all his hours on the plantation, "from the first of January to the last day in December, hot or cold, sick or well . . . [his] children would now in all probability be where [their] father was when a boy, with a hoe in the cornfield and where [their] aunts were, at the spinning wheel."[20]

Most of the professional men and all of the white artisans, laborers and tradesmen belonged to this middle class. Successful lawyers, doctors, teachers, and preachers usually entered the upper social levels after a time, if they had not started there; but the great majority who toiled among the lesser rural groups remained at the level of their constituents. A Thornwell, a Palmer, a Jeter, a Bachman, a Capers, or a Polk might associate with gentlemen but not the humbler clergyman who ministered to a flock in northwest Georgia and prayed, as one did, that the Lord would remove two Baptist families and send in Presbyterians. Lawyers, especially, found the road from obscurity to gentility easy, and men of the Joe Brown, Zeb Vance, B. F. Perry, H. S. Foote type reached high office if not always recognized social standing. Even Charleston opened wide her doors to talent and strengthened her blood with the best that the hinterland and Europe could offer. The success of a Calhoun, a Hayne, a Petigru, a King, or an Aiken goes far to deny the long-held opinion of her exclusiveness.

Southern doctors, like Richard D. Arnold or the learned Josiah Nott, who pioneered the theory of insect transmission of both malaria and yellow fever and helped to found the science of ethnology, moved in the best social circles, whether in Georgia, South Carolina, or Alabama. But those who, like William Walker, although trained in the same medical center with Nott, chose to work among the common folk of the interior, lived their days out quite unknown to aristocracy. Walker, with Doctors Campbell and Montgomery, eased the pain of those in northern Georgia and Alabama who had the chills and more than their share of typhoid and childbirth.[21]

To the same group belonged the so-called mountain whites. Though of like blood to the other southward-drifting peoples, they had been caught and held in the coves and valleys of the Appalachians and checked both in their wanderings and in their social-economic development. They were proud and quarrelsome, suspicious of strange persons and things, loyal to friends and family, ignorant in the sense that they knew not the ways of complex society. Untouched by developments brought by expansion and cotton culture, they remained to become "contemporary ancestors" to generations yet unborn.[22]

*   *   *   *

Such were two thirds of the Southern peoples: not squires, certainly not poor whites, but rather middle-class Americans bent on getting on in a land of opportunity! The great tragedy of the ante-bellum South lies in the fact that this group failed to assert itself or to greatly influence trends in the section. Gradually, under Northern attack on slavery and slaveholder, it came to defend the interests and institutions of the few aristocrats at the top and to permit them to symbolize all Southern values. For this mistake the middle class eliminated itself from the thinking of most Southern spokesmen and from the attention of Northern enemies. They were thereby lost to a generation of historians and have only been rediscovered in our own time.

*   *   *   *

These physical and social factors gave more of variety to Southern life and attitudes than was to be found in any other American section. But they did not destroy the possibility or fact of unity. Material things never made up the whole of any ante-bellum Southern story. Ideals were often more important. Tradition had a way of ignoring impudent realities. Influence and power were not fixed by mere numbers. Three great forces always worked toward a common Southern pattern. They were a rural way of life capped by an English gentleman ideal, a climate in part more mellow than other sections enjoyed, and the presence of the Negro race in quantity. More than any other forces these things made the South Southern.

The gentleman and the way of life for which he stood constituted the highest good of which the South was conscious, and, amid the coarser reaching for physical things which land and cotton and slaves produced, there was some recognition of living as an art. There was, as one writer has put it, "more interest in being than in becoming," more concern "with conserving than with acquiring." A way of life, begun back in rural England and made American in Virginia and Charleston, and to a degree in Mobile and New Orleans, took form wherever economic returns permitted. Only the few built great houses, planted their gardens, hung their family portraits, and found time for "gentleness" and the classics. Fewer still cultivated the poise of the self-sufficient and the good manners of the born gentleman. Gallantry and honor too often received more of lip service than of practice. Yet the standards were recognized and flagrant violations quickly resented. It was an up-country Southerner who defined politeness as "nothing more than habitual consideration for the feelings of those we converse with and the making it a rule never to give ourselves the preference."[23]

At least it can be asserted with confidence that men and women in the region had a more leisurely outlook on life than did their fellows to the north and west and less concern about changing themselves and nature and other men. Life was more than bread and gain; nature was something to accept, not something always to be fought. The obligation to public service and the responsibility for lesser folk bore heavily upon them. Southern gentlemen, like English squires, early became J. P.'s, County Lieutenants, and members of the Council or Assembly. The spirit of *noblesse oblige* marked their social relationships.

Paternalism was more than a gesture; it was a tradition. In the ante-bellum South the mere acquisition of property did not make a full and successful life.

In 1846, when Francis Lieber had described "The Gentleman" to a group of college students, a thoughtful citizen of Mobile wrote him as follows:[24]

. . . I fear that 'The Character of the Gentleman'—that calm, forebearing, self-possessed and gentle disposition which you describe is very rare in any part of our country—out of South Carolina. . . . In Virginia, where the pretension to it is greatest it is mixed with more or less swagger, tobacco juice, or horse racing fancy. In North Carolina, where perhaps there is less moral contamination than in any other state, there is not enough of education. In Georgia I don't think they know what a gentleman is, the ideal of rural perfection being a smart lawyer who unites with a loud voice and extravagant elocution, the profusion of a Methodist parson. In the West, Northwest and Southwest, there is no public opinion and no standard of anything, and as a mass the population is semi-barbarous, illiterate, coarse, violent and unscrupulous. Yet in no country on earth, conceding the full truth of all this, is the foundation of a fine character better. Generosity, magnanimity and courage are pervading elements, and when this is the case no character is bad and is always admirable.

The force of the ideal, in spite of weakness in practice, gave trend to Southern life. Planting outranked all other forms of endeavor and the rural home became an institution as potent as was the church in New England. "A plantation, well stocked with hands, is the *ne plus ultra* of every man's ambition who resides at the South," was one man's comment. "Planting . . . in this country," said another, "is the only independent and really honorable occupation. . . . The planters here are essentially what the nobility are in other countries."[25] The gentleman was thus a planter, and the planter was under obligation to assume the ways of a gentleman. Amid rural surroundings Southern purposes were to be sought and the good life erected. Hospitality, individualism, self-reliance, orthodoxy, and all the other rural qualities, personal and social, became Southern traits. Attachment to land and locality grew strong. Life could be lived to fullness in one place, and, when life ended, it was well to mingle the body with the good earth of one's own plantation. The country-gentleman ideal became a part of the South and was a vital element in its make-up.

Nor was the pattern entirely altered by the rise of Southern cities, most of which grew and flourished throughout the antebellum period. Always the urban peoples depended upon the rural hinterland for the commerce and trading and financing on which they prospered. Unconsciously they took their values from the country gentleman who came down to his town house for the season. Even when industry developed, markets for manufactured goods remained in the rural South and the wishes of the planter class influenced attitudes on public questions. The rapid increase of an entrepreneur class, trading peoples and urban workers after 1840 slowly weakened the tie. Richmond, Mobile, New Orleans, Memphis, and even Charleston lost step, to a degree, with the rural order. Yet Southern tradition still held when King Cotton dictated secession. The country-gentleman ideal remained intact.

* * * *

Southern weather was always something to be reckoned with. While not tropical, save at the tip of Florida and in the Rio Grande Valley of Texas, heat and high humidity were its chief characteristics. Summers were long, with a growing season from six months in Maryland to nine in Charleston, Montgomery, and Galveston. From late June until September, the temperature could be trusted to rise above 90° F. on fifty or more afternoons, and long-continued hot spells, when, as the old Negro said, "you could just touch the sun," were the rule. The annual rainfall, except in West Texas, averaged over forty inches for the entire South, and in some parts it was double that amount. Storms were violent, rains came in concentrated showers, and the run-off was enormous where the luxurious vegetation had been cleared. Yet summer droughts, when shallow-rooted vegetation perished, were common, and in severe winters frosts visited even the deep corners of the section. Sub-zero weather and traffic-blocking snows were not unknown, and most up-country Southern rivers froze solid from bank to bank. The records prove that at some time or other men froze to death in every Southern state.

Such weather lifted Southern ceilings and adorned Southern homes with piazzas, verandas, and balconies. It permitted the growing of staple crops and gave abundant returns from none-too-fertile soils. It relieved man of some effort in finding food and shelter, but caused him to suffer unduly at times. The relentless force of heat and storm slowed down the tempo of life and tended to encourage a Calvinistic outlook. One may as well accept what one cannot resist. The quick reaction of emotions probably also, in some measure, reflected the unstable weather. Health may have been weakened by indifference to shifting climatic conditions and improvidence against extremes. Heat excused, even if it did not force, the employment of Negroes in rice and cotton fields. The peculiar character of rain and heat made the problem of retaining fertility in soils certainly greater here than in any other part of the nation. Erosion and harmful micro-organisms had wider play, and the effects of careless cultivation were more devastating.

From land to labor, and perhaps also to human tempers, weather takes its place among the things which made the South Southern. "The mellow clime" has a part in the story even when the "gay Cavalier" has been sent back into romance.

* * * *

The third important factor in Southern life was the Negro. The fact of his status as a slave may, in the main, be ignored. He should be thought of, first, only as a different racial element in this society, a human being of another color and with another cultural background. His very numbers made him important. In 1860 there were 4,215,614 blacks in a total population of slightly over twelve and a third million. His personal qualities made him even more significant.

The color of the Negro's skin set him apart in an already stratified society. Because he was black, white skins, regardless of what they covered, were enhanced in value. The presence of so large a mass of foreign material, undigested and purposely

kept so, created a race problem and made the determination
to keep this region a white man's country the central theme
of Southern history. The section was ever race-conscious.[26]

The presence of Negroes in the South checked the inflow of
other foreign groups which might have furnished a crude labor
supply. The black-skinned workers gave to some white men
and women freedom from drudgery, time for more of pleasure,
and close association between elders and youth. They afforded
the opportunity, sometimes accepted, for culture and refinement. Furthermore, the Negro, with real talent for flattery,
may have added something more of self-assurance and may
have encouraged the bent to paternalism. Unquestionably, he
imparted something of superstition and happy-go-lucky attitudes to Southern children. His exact influence on Southern
life cannot be completely defined, but the Negro, as a Negro,
was beyond doubt one of the vital factors which gave to this
section whatever of unique character and quality it possessed.

* * * *

In such a varied physical environment, common men from
all western European groups, leavened a bit by Old World
gentlemen, slowly fashioned, with staple crops sold in world
markets, a way of life soon designated as Southern. The pressure of weather, the tuggings of the country-gentleman ideal,
and the subtle influence of a host of unsuspecting Africans,
furnished what Doctor Phillips once called "the climate of
coherence." Slowly but surely, these factors, operating in a
society kept primarily rural by opportunities and ideals, fashioned the dominant character of Southern life. A sense of
stability and continuity came into being. In a hurrying, rest-
lessly-moving-about America, some Southern men slowed down,
lost their zest for changes, and became attached to places and
persons and to their own pasts. Roots sunk deeply into black
and red soils and love of locality and familiar things quieted
the urge toward what others called, perhaps mistakenly, progress. Life became more a matter of folks than of things. Men
knew that they belonged to families—a tie that ran backward
as well as forward and included often vague and distant rela-

tionships. Houses were built to endure and to serve best the accidents of climate and good living. Lands were not for sale and did not constitute a capital investment on which a known percentage of interest had to be realized. They were merely foundations on which a home, a way of life, was to be erected, a source from which a living, on established levels, might be expected without too much worry and without an undue amount of fighting. Men and families knew kinship with things and persons and gained the poise and self-contained serenity of those who have come to terms with both the human and the physical world of which they are a part.

CHAPTER THREE

THE RURAL DEPRESSION, 1800–1832

THE way of the farmer, like that of the transgressor, is hard. He must ever plant and await his harvest amid the uncertainties of weather, pests, and markets. His hopes must always be tempered with fears. His brightest prospects may at any moment turn to utter ruin. Heat and cold, rain and sun are at once his fickle friends and his brutal enemies. If he succeeds, a thousand other living things must perish. Abundant harvests ruin prices; crop failures leave nothing to sell. One may well sympathize with the beaten tiller of stubborn soils who quit farming with the declaration that he was going to get into some business with which the Lord had less to do.

But the farmer's troubles are not all with a willful Nature. The isolated character of his occupation and the wide variety of tasks he must perform encourage a rugged individualism which makes him a poor co-operator and weakens the power of his group in dealing with rivals. His efforts at social and political reform are often spasmodic and disjointed. The promise of a good harvest is usually sufficient to cool his ardor for change.

Furthermore, constant dealing with the fixed forces of nature develops reliance on rule-of-thumb methods which tend to make the farmer conservative. He cannot quickly adjust his practices or his ideas to new conditions. He is ever at a disadvantage when he confronts manipulation and efficiency of organization. When urban-industrial groups arise and contend for political control and a larger share of the returns of economic endeavor, the agricultural groups lag behind and place and profits pass to others. Gradually farmers sink to the level of serfs or peasants while men of commerce, finance, and industry thrive and shape governmental machinery and policies to their own benefit. Such has been the history of those who have fed mankind throughout the centuries.

The Southern planter began his career at one of the few periods in the history of the western world when agriculture was in the ascendancy. He was heir to the station and prestige of the English country gentleman. He could proclaim with wide approval the superiority of his calling. It was basic to human well-being and it added something unique to character and to the development of a sound social order. Thomas Jefferson was wont to speak of "those who labor in the earth" as "the chosen people of God . . . whose breasts He has made His peculiar deposit for substantial and genuine virtue." John Taylor of Caroline once boasted that "the divine intelligence which selected an agricultural state as a paradise for his first favorites, has again prescribed the agricultural virtues as the means for the admission of their posterity into heaven." Both Jefferson and Taylor were certain that democratic government could endure only so long as the great majority of its people were farmers.[1]

Modern capitalism enhanced the superiority which physiocratic doctrine granted to agriculture. Gentlemen who farmed might, under the spread of a new spirit of acquisitive individualism, speculate in lands, exploit the natural resources of new continents, and enslave black men for private gain. Profits were no longer beneath the notice of a country squire. He might even praise the doctrines of *laissez faire* and insist that natural law alone could give the greatest happiness to the greatest number. Frontiers could produce gentleman farmers.

Those who planted tobacco and rice in Virginia and the Carolinas appeared to prosper under this philosophy. The plantation with its great house, its quarters, its gardens, and its far-flung acres indicated wealth; life upon the plantation bore the marks of culture and refinement. Planters sat in legislative halls and made laws satisfactory to their own interests. Lesser men envied them, and those who overcame poverty and rose in the economic scale quickly adopted the accepted pattern. Planting and gentility went hand in hand.

This agricultural paradise, however, was, after an early period of widespread prosperity, more apparent than real. The methods used to secure the single cash crop depleted soils and wasted other resources, physical and human. Cultivation was shallow, and heavy rains cut rolling lands into deep gullies and splashed them with galled and barren patches. Harmful micro-organisms added their part to the ruin, forcing the abandonment of wasted lands and a constant search for fresh ones. Sedge and briers and pine soon took the place of staples, and old fields became a familiar part of every landscape. After a time wild animals came back to establish themselves in places from which they had been driven a century earlier.[2]

Under such conditions the weak and most inefficient farmers slowly sank to wretched poverty. Sagging roofs and broken windowpanes proclaimed their hopeless condition. The more energetic gathered their few belongings and turned wearily toward the West and a chance to begin over again. By 1830 nearly one third of those born in Virginia and Maryland were living in other states, while the white population of the Carolinas remained almost stationary. Mount Vernon, which Washington had developed with skill and affection, stood a "perfect agricultural ruin," and Monticello, which had benefited by Jefferson's agricultural experiences on two continents, could not keep its master from economic distress. Travellers described the region as a "scene of desolation that baffles description," a land of "dreary and uncultivated wastes . . . lean and hungry stock . . . houses falling to decay, and fences wind shaken and dilapidated." An agricultural convention meeting in Richmond informed the legislature of Virginia that "extensive neighborhoods, once . . . garden spots" were threatened with "almost entire depopulation." The planter was facing destruction.[3]

Some blamed the soils for their troubles. More spent their bitterness on the policies of government, which in colonial days restricted markets and taxed the colonists, and which, after independence, neglected the welfare of those who farmed. A few realized that the Revolution itself had brought much physical ruin where armies had passed, and that independence had lost markets essential to American produce. The Virginia statesmen, after 1789, increasingly turned against the policies of the Federalists and saw in the rise of banks and tariffs the real factors in their decline. All agreed with William Strickland that "land in America affords little pleasure or profit, and appears in a progress of continually affording less."

There were, of course, in this general decline, some periods of improvement and optimism. The second century of colonial life had been sprinkled with a number of years when prospects were good and a few in which they were realized. These periods of good times had, however, only served to keep the farmer at his tasks and gave no permanent relief. The Revolution, therefore, found progressive planters shifting crops, experimenting with new methods, and seeking new markets—while streams of emigration ran always at flood tide. The establishment of a new government, even though it was supposed to be blessed with the smile of heaven, brought little improvement. During the next three decades only brief periods of relief came with the intermittent calls from Europe for food when the French Revolution and its great exploiter had upset the usual course of supply and demand. The War of 1812 and the general world peace which followed took the bottom out of the farmer's world and brought to a sharp end the old agricultural order which had existed for a century and a half.[4]

In the attempt to remedy conditions so out of place in a society where farmers were supposed to be a chosen people, Virginia spokesmen took the lead. They boldly struck at the program launched by Alexander Hamilton and carried forward to new heights by John Marshall. They insisted that the assumption of the national debt, the laying of protective tariffs, and the establishment of a national bank, forecasting extended credit and paper money, were creating an artificial aristocracy. When John Marshall's great decisions declared all this to be in accord with the Constitution and went so far as to subject state legislation and state court decisions to federal judicial review, the Virginia statesmen saw a consolidated government in the making which threatened to destroy local democracy. Thomas Jefferson, John Taylor, Spencer Roane, and other loyal agrarians rose in protest to defend both their class and their state.[5]

The struggle which followed has too long been viewed as a contest between abstract political theories. It was instead a class conflict—the beginning of the great struggle between rural-agricultural America and the new rising urban-industrial order. True, the principle of local self-government, based on a strict interpretation of the Constitution, was defended by appeal to every ancient theory and practice. But behind that conflict of ideas lay more fundamental economic and social antagonisms. A strong central government, achieved through what contemporaries called consolidation, meant the rise of a new group hostile in purposes to the agricultural order praised by physiocrats and practised on Southern plantations. Only by the creation and constant favoring of new financial and industrial groups could central government flourish. Those interests, in turn, could not arise without artificial stimulation. There was thus a direct relationship between the growth of urban-industrial life and the development of a central government strong in its ability to create and fund debts, to grant bounties and tariffs, and to confer perpetual charters. If true democracy was to live and flourish in the open fields, it must check central power and the resulting influence of city and factory and financial groups.[6]

Virginia leaders, as spokesmen for all farmers, set about to stem the rise of "an order of stock-jobbers in loans, banks, manufactories, contracts, rivers, roads, houses, ships, lotteries, and an infinite number of inferior tricks to get money. . . ." They saw clearly that if governments were given or could usurp the power to distribute wealth by law, this artificial aristocracy would soon destroy the natural order of things. As John Taylor put it:[7]

The device of protecting duties, under the pretext of encouraging manufactures, operates like its kindred, by creating a capitalist interest, which instantly seizes upon the bounty taken by law from agriculture; and instead of doing any good to the actual workers in wood, metals, cotton, or other substances, it helps to rear up an aristocratical order, at the expense of the workers in earth, to unite with governments in oppressing every species of useful industry.

Such thinking, of course, implied the belief that, in a true republic, the majority of the citizens would always be agriculturalists and the mass of wealth would always be in their hands. On the backs of the farmers would rest the burden of government. Its weight would in large degree determine their well-being. "Agriculture," said Taylor, "pays and must forever pay most of whatever is collected by taxes, by charters, by protecting duties, by paper systems of every kind, for armies, for navies, and though last, not the least of its losses, of whatever the nation is defrauded by a treasury system operating in darkness." Farmers were "like the ox who tills the crop to be eaten by others. . . ."[8]

It could be assumed, therefore, that, wherever officeholders, speculators and industrialists prospered above agriculturalists, they "filched" wealth from its real producers and that an artificial economic life was being developed. Such had long been the condition in the Old World. In America, under Hamilton and Marshall, "the laws [had already] established a thousand modes by which capital would produce quicker and larger profits, than when employed in the slow improvements of agriculture." Thus "a legal faction . . . pretending to no religion, to no morality, to no patriotism, except to the religion, morality and patriotism of making itself daily richer . . ." was already established. The farmers of the nation must bestir themselves or others would "monopolize the sweets of life, which . . . [they] sweat for. . . ."[9]

In the 1790's conflict raged about the bank and the unwarranted extension of central powers in the passage of the Alien and Sedition Acts. The basic issues, because the relation to agriculture was indirect, were not always clearly stated, and fundamental social-economic attitudes were often confused with party purposes and political ends. Local cleavage added to the tangle and divided those whose interests should have been one. Jefferson, Madison, and John Taylor took the lead. Their first great stroke came in the Virginia and Kentucky resolutions,

which declared that the central government had been established for special purposes and had only delegated powers.
Heavy emphasis was placed on local democracy functioning
through the states. These resolutions gave Jefferson, especially,
the reputation of being primarily a States' rights man and
clouded his more vital interest in the agrarian order. The concessions which he, as a practical statesman, later made to "manufactures, sufficient for our own consumption . . . [and] commerce sufficient to carry the surplus produce of agriculture . . ."
still further hid his interest in the clash between the planters
and the urban groups. Yet Jefferson's all-pervading fear of
the growth of a capitalistic class and his ruling passion for the
maintenance of those who worked in the earth determined his
stand on most important issues. To view Jefferson as merely
a Southern provincial is to miss one of America's greatest agricultural nationalists.[10]

The clear-cut statements of John Taylor, in *Arator* and *An
Inquiry into the Principles and Tendencies of Certain Public
Measures,* leave no doubt as to *his* understanding of the issues
involved. His battle was ever with class rivals. He insisted on
the supremacy of local institutions, not only because the Fathers
planned it that way, but because through these institutions the
planter class might dominate and the nation's economic life be
kept natural. "The plough can have little success," he said,
"until the laws are altered which obstruct it." "So long as the
laws make it more profitable to invest capital in speculations
without labor, than in agriculture with labor . . . a love of
wealth, and a love of ease" will make agricultural improvement
impossible. Farmers "had become political slaves" because they
were "political fools." The weight in Congress was "very visably
against the agriculturalists" not because of "popular folly in
elections," as some thought, but because of "the transit of
wealth, and of course wisdom, from agriculture to its natural
enemies, charter and privilege."

Looking ahead, Taylor saw the danger in such developments.
At first he spoke of the usurpation "of constitutional principles
. . . if allowed to acquire maturity . . . yield[ing] to the
dreadful remedy of civil war." The combatants would be the

agricultural and the industrial groups of the nation. Later he saw that the antagonistic interests tended to be sectionalized into North and South, and he declared that "if either can acquire local advantages from national supremacy, it will aggravate . . . a perpetual warfare of intrigue and a disolation of the Union will result."[11]

With a clear conviction that economic advantage was the key to this conflict between two ways of life, Taylor set himself to the task of establishing agriculture upon foundations sound and enduring. On his plantation, Hazelwood, near the town of Port Royal, he experimented with the use of fertilizers, crop rotation, and improved plowing, and created, in the midst of general decline, "a farm . . . distinguished by the verdure of its fields . . . and the abundance of [its] crops." He wrote papers and books on agricultural problems, discussing farm labor, soil fertility, crops best suited to the day and region, methods of plowing, and evils to be eliminated. He evolved a system called enclosing, which embraced all he had discovered by theory and practice. It included a great deal that has been thought modern in erosion control, the use of gypsum, lime and marl as fertilizers, a three-shift system of crop rotation with corn, wheat and pasture in order, the growth of clover on every spot where it could be prevailed upon to exist both as a soil binder and an improver, and much else which marks him as a truly great scientific farmer. But the significant thing about this phase of his work is that it was but a part of his fight against Alexander Hamilton and John Marshall. He was trying to establish a firm and enduring economic base from which the farmer might wage his battle for the preservation of the country-gentleman ideal. Democracy was worth preserving only because it gave dominance to planters; and planters could preserve their superiority only when given a just share of what they produced. Such conditions could exist only where local governments exercised wide powers and central governments did not have the right to grant economic favors. John Taylor was forging a single program of political philosophy and agricultural practice to prevent the American government from becoming an agent for the plundering of the many by the few;

and to keep peasantry from developing on this side of the Atlantic.

The next stage in the struggle, roughly covering the years 1814–24, came with certain decisions of the Supreme Court under John Marshall and the passage of protective tariff legislation by Congress. Marshall was also a Virginian. He represented a Federalist group in Richmond which had been heavily interested in speculations in paper and lands and which looked forward to industrial development. It constituted the party of opposition to Jefferson, and John Adams had rewarded faithful support by appointing one of its most aggressive members to the Chief Justiceship of the Supreme Court. From this office John Marshall continued the local fight of urban interests against the planter. A surprising number of his decisions struck at the men and the party which controlled his native state. Many Virginians believed that they were dictated by personal, party, and economic interests.

Three court decisions in particular stirred Virginia—that of McCulloch *vs.* Maryland, Martin *vs.* Hunter's Lessee, and Cohens *vs.* Virginia. The first upheld the constitutionality of the bank act and thereby approved Hamilton's doctrine of implied powers. The other two asserted the superiority of federal courts and their right to review and reverse, if necessary, state court decisions.[12]

Equally disturbing was the new enthusiasm for tariffs which began in 1816 and continued through the twenties. Tariffs gave direct federal assistance to manufactures. They added to the cost of everything the planters purchased. Combined with Marshall's decisions they indicated an increase of federal activity which threatened the planter and his local government. Judge Spencer Roane of the state Supreme Court of Appeals and John Taylor, vigorous as ever, accepted the challenge.

Roane flatly denied the claims made by Judges Marshall and Story. He warned Republicans that they had been found sleeping at their posts. "The hair of the federal Samson . . . [had] again begun to grow and with it, strength and power." He and his associates refused to obey the mandamus of the United States Supreme Court and declared that this Court could not constitutionally interfere with the decisions of state tribunals acting within their jurisdiction. The state was sovereign within the sphere of powers not specifically granted away and "the rights and freedom of the people of the state" would be defended by physical force if necessary. The efforts of the Supreme Court "to control the operations of the co-ordinate departments of its own government" and "to settle exclusively the chartered rights of the states" would be "no less disastrous in its consequences" than the "memorable judgments of the courts of Charles I."[18]

From the pen of John Taylor, meanwhile (1819–23), came three profound treatises on the nature of sovereignty and of our constitutional government. For searching historical statement and for clear-cut theoretical exposition, they have never been surpassed by any American political writings. Thomas Jefferson spoke of one of these treatises as "the most effectual retraction of our government to its original principles, which has ever yet been sent by Heaven to our aid."

Taylor offered a completed States' rights argument. He held that the Union was a union of States, not people. The term "the people," as used in the Constitution, referred to the people of each state. Had they not been represented by States in the Convention which framed that document? Had they not voted by States? "No people or community has ever been composed in the United States, except by the inhabitants of each State, associating distinctly from every other State, by their own separate consent." The States had never dissolved their own people and formed them into "one great people." They formed a central government, not a *Union*. And sovereignty, an indivisible thing, rested with the people—that is, with the States, or people as a state. Sound theory and history both supported this conclusion.[14]

Furthermore, Taylor asserted, the powers of the central government and of its different departments were strictly limited. The Supreme Court, for instance, was supreme only in the federal judicial system. The Constitution, in vesting federal judicial powers, speaks of "supreme" and "inferior courts as Congress may from time to time establish." It has no reference whatever to supremacy over state courts—an entirely different system. The Supreme Court of the United States had, therefore, no more power to enjoin or abrogate the decisions of the state courts than Congress had to repeal or enjoin the acts of state legislatures! Its judges took no oath to support state constitutions! What was to prevent, under such a distorted interpretation, the invasion and destruction of the legislative rights of the States?

Nor was the implied power idea any more sound. "There is no phrase in the Constitution," Taylor declared, "which even insinuates that the actual divisions of power should be altered or impaired by incidental or implied powers." "If a delegation of powers implies a delegation of an unrestrained choice of means for the execution of these powers . . ." the central government can "impair or destroy the powers of the state governments. . . ." As to the statement that if the end is constitutional the means to that end is also constitutional, he said:[15]

As ends may be made to beget means, so means may be made to beget ends, until the co-habitation shall rear a progeny of unconstitutional bastards, which were not begotten by the people. . . .

That "the means were not intended to be unlimited" is shown by the fact that, in some cases, there is in the Constitution "a specification of . . . means for the attainment of ends."

Regarding the "supreme law of the land clause," by which the courts elevated federal power, Taylor contended that laws and treaties were supreme only when "made in conformity with the powers bestowed, limited and reserved by the constitution." Thus the States, acting within that vast sphere reserved for them, are not "subjected to the impediments of" the federal government, nor is the power of the federal government enlarged one iota. In fact, "the Constitution has invested the States with a complete, and the State governments with a limited, supremacy, over the federal government and expressly subjected its *operations to the influence* of the latter in sundry instances." They may even "alter or dissolve the union" if they desire.[16]

It is not necessary to follow farther the fact and logic by

which John Taylor attempted to demonstrate that the United States had not formed a government endowed with "the power of distributing property, able to gratify avarice and monopoly," or one whose great purpose was to "foster a fanaticism for wealth." It need only be noted that the interests he was attempting to defend from the ills of a bad government continued to lag behind and planters continued to believe that their trouble came from unconstitutional advantages granted to their enemies through tariff legislation.

Taylor wrote his pamphlet, *Tyranny Unmasked,* to deny the right of the central government "to distribute wealth and property" and to show the fallacy of all the arguments used to support protection. Governor Giles declared that "never before were any people subjected to such plunder and degradation." He suggested "an internal excise upon domestic manufactures brought within the limits of the plundered states" and "an excise upon all animals on foot, driven within the same limits" to "teach the western people their dependence upon the Southern people for a market."[17] From the agricultural societies of Virginia protests and criticisms issued, pointing out the need for all of the nation's capital in agricultural improvements, the danger to agricultural markets from tariffs and the unsound character of the claims made for protection. One such petition bore the name of "Edmund Ruffin, Sec'y." Before long this progressive young farmer would be dressed in homespuns and would be preaching a self-sufficiency economy. His neighbor, James M. Garnett, in an address to the Fredericksburg Agricultural Society, would discuss the diminution of agricultural enterprise and conclude that "weavers and spinners, therefore, our children must become however reluctant." These men plainly saw the struggle in which they were engaged in terms of a conflict of interests. They were fighting the planters' battle.[18]

Some of this group viewed the Missouri Compromise from the same angle. They believed that "the idea of a balance of powers between two combinations of states, and not the existence of slavery" lay back of the whole affair. Such a balance, forced by differences on the slavery issue, would develop constant friction in Congress between North and South and thus enable those desiring "exclusive advantage" and motivated only by "ambition and avarice" to fish in troubled waters with greater success. "Bounties, pensions and corporations" were again seeking to dwarf the rights of a state, by restrictions placed on Missouri, and to further consolidation in their own interests. Slavery was but "a cunning device to draw . . . attention from home." It was a local question on which "each state [had] . . . a right to think for itself." To invest Congress "with supreme power over State rights" and then set the sections against each other would "endanger the Union." For "if either [section could] . . . acquire local advantages from national supremacy, it [would] . . . aggravate . . . a perpetual warfare of intrigue and a dissolution of the Union. . . ."[19]

The planter's struggle against his foes, however, never acquired the unity and efficiency necessary for success. All the weaknesses common to farmers' movements early manifested themselves in this one. Vital issues became tangled and confused with extraneous matters, to be either lost or never faced at all. Immediate problems crowded aside long-time values. Personalities prevented the consideration of principles on their own merits. Fleeting periods of prosperity, or the hope of them, weakened cooperation and prevented sustained effort.

Then in 1820 a half century of conflict between the eastern and the western parts of Virginia over representation, suffrage, and abuses in local government came to a head in a demand for constitutional reform. The contest which ensued shifted emphases so radically that the earlier issues became confused and lost ground. Leaders turned from national to local affairs; interest shifted to domestic problems. The eastern part of Virginia, with its numerous counties and with three-fifths of its slaves counting as population, held a disproportionate amount of power in the House of Delegates. Property qualifications for voting, although not severe, added to this inequality and suggested the undemocratic character of the system. The appointive powers of the governor's council and the closed-corporation character of the county courts, with their hold on local offices, gave added cause for complaint.

These long-discussed problems might not have provoked a

struggle, had not immediate social-economic conditions pressed. For several years, under expansion and growing complexity, western Virginia had been demanding increased funds for internal improvements and schools. Some of the citizens even wished to develop manufactories about their iron and salt deposits. A few favored government aid for these enterprises. They had been casting favorable eyes toward Washington. Eastern Virginians realized that, if constitutional changes added to the West's power in government, their weary plantation lands and even their unprofitable slave property might be further taxed or perhaps destroyed. It was not impossible that Richmond capitalists, friends of John Marshall, might combine with Western forces. Consolidation threatened even at home.

The two factions in Virginia, although both were primarily agriculturalists, had never been really united in the struggle against industry and high finance. The agrarian philosophy had been monopolized by planters to the neglect of farmers; by slaveholders, as contrasted with the yeomen of the West who held few slaves; by those whose natural means of communication were unusually good, as against those whose markets were generally inaccessible. The planter's conception of democratic society had not always taken into consideration the peculiar force of the frontier in producing a practical equality among men and a stronger interest in things national. Consequently, where the agriculturalists of a great commonwealth should have stood shoulder to shoulder against the forces of an advancing new age, they were sharply divided among themselves and ready to fight out, in their own local arena, the great issues which had begun to vex a whole nation and which one day would divide North and South into hostile camps. They were weighing the benefits of an active government, taxing and spending for complex social improvements, against the benefits of a government which let alone; the advantages of a dominant planter economy against the advantages of diversified economic effort developed with government aid. They were facing the problems of the rights of majorities and minorities; of the rights of property against numbers; of the benefits of slavery and its enjoyment of special protection and consideration. In the convention called to meet in Richmond in October, 1829, Virginians battled with Virginians over these problems. Every argument later to be used in the national conflict, both *pro* and *con*, on each and every question, was offered. They achieved a working compromise and gained a temporary peace; but they neglected the larger agrarian problem and the local democracy it required. They ultimately surrendered leadership in the greater cause to a neighbor farther south.[20]

The long debates in the Virginia Convention need not be followed in detail. The standards were high. Few assemblages on the American continent have ever exhibited more of ability. Issues were faced honestly and opinions voiced fearlessly. The views expressed appear strangely like those which men of the deep South and men of the Northwest used decades later when civil war was imminent.

Speaking on the rights of property in government, Judge Upshur declared that "there is a majority in *interest*, as well as a majority in numbers." He was willing to adjust representation only in such a way as to give to those "who have the greatest stake in the government . . . the greatest share of power in the administration of it." He spoke of "our property" in slaves as "peculiar" both because of "its imposing magnitude" and because of the hazards to which it was exposed. He accused the West of hostility to the institution and asked for "*that kind of protection* which flows from the possession of power." Prophetic words from a slaveholder in 1829![21]

John Randolph, in like vein, spoke contemptuously of King Numbers and went back to the French Revolution for comparisons. He called the West alien to the East and declared that if the three-fifths rule were surrendered emancipation would follow. He "would as soon trust the Quakers of Pennsylvania as the Quakers of any county of Virginia. . . . Fanatics—like madmen—are on a par. . . ."[22]

His opponent from the West took up Randolph's reference to King Numbers and called that good king "the legitimate sovereign of all this country." "There is none . . . so august . . . I love King Numbers," he continued. "I wish to live, and I hope to die, under the government of this majestic personage. He is, Sir, a wise, benevolent, patriotic and powerful prince. . . ."[23]

When appeal was made to the supposedly sacred Declaration of Rights to support the equality of men and the rights of the majority, slaveholders called its principles wild and visionary, abstractions and metaphysical subtleties. In the face of "the most crying injustice ever attempted in any land," only practical considerations applied. Men would one day talk that way about the Declaration of Independence.[24]

Back of the struggle between numbers and property, lay the matter of taxes and the proper scope of government activity. The non-Freeholders of Richmond, debarred from the right of suffrage, dared, in a petition to the Convention, to question the superiority of agriculturalists "in moral or intellectual endowments," and scoffed at the danger "from large manufacturing establishments in Virginia." The fact that they gave assurance that "such establishments must, for an indefinite period, be at the mercy of those who affect to dread them," showed the interest they represented and their ideas of why change was resisted.[25]

Mr. Gree left no room for doubt as to the relation of internal improvements to the question. "The gentleman asks us," he said, "what *motives* the people of the West can have to misuse their power. . . . They have one great object of desire . . . and that is the construction of roads and canals. The desire for roads and canals has of late years grown into an enthusiastic passion among them. . . . Here, then, is an inducement, and here are actual efforts, to tax the lowlands for the benefit of western interests."[26]

The institution of slavery also came in for a thorough discussion in the Convention. James Monroe said: "I am satisfied, if no such thing as slavery existed, that the people of our Atlantic border would meet their brethren of the West upon the basis of a majority of the free white population." But the concentration of slave property made for divided interest. Of the 447,000 slaves in Virginia, nearly 400,000 were held east of the Blue Ridge. Many Western men had, moreover, begun to question the value of the institution. Judge Upshur accused them of having "a rooted antipathy to this species of population." Their spokesmen, however, attempting to avoid unnecessary irritations, held back their true opinions. Only now and then did they indicate hostility by assertions that slavery in part accounted for tumble-down conditions in the East and that it prevented the development of white laboring classes. One speaker warned the East that, if it were "once openly avowed and adopted as a principle of your Constitution, that the price which the western people must pay for the protection of your slaves is the surrender of their power in government, you render that property hateful to them in the extreme, and hold out to them the strongest of all possible temptations to make constant war upon it. . . ." Two years later, in the State Legislature, they made good the threat. At their hands slavery received such blows as it never before had received and it seldom would receive again.[27]

The slavery debates of 1832 in the Virginia Assembly were part and parcel of the same struggle. The Nat Turner Insurrection hastened this local irrepressible conflict but it did not create it, nor did it originate the opinions expressed in the Assembly. Western men, who brought the question to open discussion there for the first time in twenty-seven years, were only completing a task in which they had long been engaged. The positive convictions they revealed had not been developed in two years' time.[28]

The attack on slavery took lines soon to be familiar enough in another portion of the nation. It began when Thomas Jefferson Randolph proposed an inquiry into the expediency of submitting to the voters the propriety of a law by which slaves born after July 4, 1840, should, on reaching maturity, become the property of the State and their earnings, for a time, be used to transport them from the country. During the discussion of this proposal men questioned the justice of slavery, blamed it for the weakened condition of agriculture, and declared that it drove lesser white men from the community, made labor a disgrace, and prevented the rise of a diversified economic life. One speaker called it "a mildew which has blighted . . . every region it has touched from the creation of the world." Another called it "a blighting, withering curse" and insisted that "gentlemen would not, could not, justify traffic in human beings. High minded men," he thought, "ought to disdain to hold their fellow creatures as articles of traffic . . . dividing husbands and wives, parents and children, as they would cut asunder a piece of cotton cloth." "How many a Rachel mourns because her house is left unto her desolate," he cried. "Slavery was, and had long been, offensive to the moral feelings of a large portion of the community. . . ."[29]

In like vein, another assemblyman noted that "no gentleman has yet risen in this hall, the avowed advocate of slavery." He insisted that the day had gone by "when such a voice could be listened to with patience, or even forbearance." One of his colleagues declared that there was not a man in the body "who would not have thanked the generations . . . gone before . . . if, acting as public men, they had brought this bondage to a close. . . ."

One speaker said that slavery was "ruinous to the whites" —retarded "improvement—root[ed] out an industrious population, banish[ed] the yeomanry of the country—depriv[ed] the spinner, the weaver, the smith, the shoemaker, the carpenter, of employment and support." "Labor of every species," he said, "is disreputable, because performed mostly by slaves." Another saw the "division, discontent, indolence and poverty of the southern country" as results of slavery, and contrasted such conditions with "the happiness and contentment" of the northern States—"the busy and cheerful sounds of industry— the rapid and swelling growth of their population—their means and institutions of education—their skill and proficiency in the useful arts—their enterprise and public spirit—the monuments of their commercial and manufacturing industry." He closed with the significant statement: "Sir, the evils of slavery stand confessed before us."

Some in the Assembly pointed out the danger to Virginia of "nourishing within her bosom half a million bondsmen, alien to her interests, hostile to her feelings, and prepared at any favorable moment to deluge the country in blood, and dance upon the ruins of public liberty." Others noted the tendency of slavery to create "a political interest in the Union, which is, of all others, the most positive; an interest, which in relation to those who do not possess it, is adversary and exclusive." This speaker thought it produced "unkindness and suspicion," created "geographical parties" and unending conflict between them. He saw in this inevitable clash danger to the Union, and he foretold "a ruptured brotherhood" and the formation of two hating nations. He saw that, in this struggle, slavery would be the cementing force in the South, and that the section would therefore be subjected to "a crusade, in the name of liberty but with the purpose of plunder." Its people would be "held up as common enemies of man whom it will be a duty to overthrow and justice to despoil. . . ." For clear understanding and prophetic vision, James M'Dowell, Jr., was never surpassed by any one who opposed the holding of Negroes in bondage![30]

*   *   *   *

Here in the Virginia Assembly of 1832 was the anti-slavery argument in surprising fullness. In the next three decades the most rabid New England reformers would be able to add little to it. Virginians contending with Virginians for political justice and the well-being of their own State had gone to the bottom of a serious social problem. Of course, their opponents answered. The tone of the rebuttal was not as positive as it later became, but the practical difficulty of turning loose "four hundred thousand . . . of poor, without one cent of property" and the dangers to society of a race war between whites and blacks were not overlooked. Not satisfied with their own efforts, the defenders of slavery turned for assistance to young Thomas Dew down at the College of William and Mary. Dew had only recently returned from the German universities, where the idea of "the inequality of men was fundamental to all social organizations." He could speak on the subject as a trained political scientist. The *Review of the Debates in the Virginia Legislature,* in which Professor Dew discussed and defended slavery, is a masterpiece. He proclaimed the difficulties of abolition and the benefits of bondage. Calling history and experience to his support, he justified existing conditions and showed the impossibility of change without ruin. His statement became a classic with those who sought to find justification for continuing things as they were.[31]

Thus ended Virginia's part in the first agrarian struggle. All issues had been localized. The larger problem of the relative place of planting and capitalism in American life had been lost sight of amid the factions and sectionalism of state affairs. Slavery had come in to color attitudes and, in the end, to exclude most other considerations. Symbols had taken the place of realities.

* * * *

The basic struggle in which Jefferson and Taylor had been engaged did not end, however, with Virginia's desertion. The planters of the Carolinas had also been experiencing poverty and ruin. That mattered little in North Carolina, where such conditions were more or less normal and where there were few voices which could be heard beyond the state's own borders. Economic hardships, however, operated to make the Old North State the greatest center of southern emigration and eventually produced a Convention in which eastern and western men struggled to compromise much as they had done in Virginia; yet that was a local situation, to be passed over as such. But in South Carolina economic decline was a matter of national concern. When South Carolinians talked, even about their local affairs, it was well to listen. And they were in a mood to talk at the end of the 1820's, even more than usual.

The Revolution had left South Carolina in desperate straits —money scarce, men unable to pay their debts, indigo and naval stores profitless without British bounties, and the markets for rice sadly crippled. Merchants failed, ships rotted at the wharfs and rents fell to "one-third" their former level. Relief was sought in paper money and stay laws for debtors, but little help came until the middle of the '90's when cotton began its spectacular rise to economic control. Even then the first cotton crops were of the "sea-island" variety and the area where this plant could grow was limited. Not until Eli Whitney had produced a gin capable of removing seeds from the short staple plant did cotton spread to the up-country where wheat and general farming had predominated. That was an important step toward the building of a greater South, but it soon spelled ruin for those along the coast whose worn and limited soils had raised the first crops. Competition with cheaper, fresher, and ever-widening lands quickly lowered prices and drew slaves westward. Charleston merchants encountered rivals first at Savannah and then in towns along the Gulf Coast as cotton reached the rivers whose courses were north and south. A prolonged depression set in. The 1820's found conditions in agriculture even worse in South Carolina than in Virginia. James Hamilton, Jr., saw "the melancholy signs of coming decay," "the wilderness regaining her empire. . . ." "On the very hearthstones where hospitality once kindled the most genial fires . . .," he said, "the fox may lie down in security and peace, and from the mouldering casement . . . the owl sends forth to the listening solitude of the surrounding waste her melancholy discant to mark the spot where desolation has come. . . ."

Senator Robert Y. Hayne drew an even more distressing picture. He declared that Charleston's commerce was completely lost—her "shipyards broken up, . . . the very last" ship sold, "mechanics in despair, the very grass growing in our streets, and houses falling into ruins." In the country, fields were abandoned and agriculture was drooping. Slaves were working harder and the "once thriving planter, reduced to despair, cursing this hard fate, [was] gathering up the small remnants of his broken fortune, and, with his wife and little ones, tearing himself from the scenes of his childhood, and the bones of his ancestors, to seek, in the wilderness . . . [the] reward for his industry."[32]

To explain this deplorable condition, the Carolina spokesmen turned to the policy of protective tariffs—"the tax[ing] of agriculture and commerce for the benefit of manufactures." They saw their interest, because of these tariffs, paying more than its proportion of taxes.[33] George McDuffie told them that exports paid for imports and since southern agricultural prod-

uce made up more than half of the nation's export, the southern farmers who constituted about one fifth of the total population, paid more than half of the Federal taxes. On that basis,
forty out of every hundred bales of cotton raised went to the
government. Whether this was sound economic doctrine or
not, the planters knew that the prices of what they produced
were falling, and the prices of what they purchased were going
up. They were convinced that, unless they were willing to
accept an inferior place in the nation's life, the policies which
were producing this ruin must be checked. Jefferson and Taylor had already pointed the way.

Historians have generally ignored the fact that the South
Carolina statesmen, in the so-called Nullification Controversy,
were struggling against a practical situation. They have con-
jured up a great struggle between nationalism and States'
rights and described these men as theorists revelling in constitutional refinements for the mere sake of logic. Yet here was
a clear case of commercial and agricultural depression. Charleston's trade disappeared and no Lowells and Bostons rose behind her; plantations gave way to "loblolly pine, half choked
with brown grass and dog-fennel," and no new market gardens
to feed industrial centers took their places. The cause of their
depression, as the Southern farmers saw it, lay in favors granted
by government to Northern industrialists. The course to be
taken to save the situation was clearly indicated by all that had
been said and done by distressed planters for more than three
decades. If the South Carolinians carried theory and action to
more practical and extreme conclusions than others had done,
the reasons must be sought in the character and history of their
locality, not in some peculiar bent for logic!

Political developments in South Carolina in the next few
years revealed only the hostility to industrialism normal to a
highly individualistic and self-reliant agricultural state long accustomed to fight its own battles in its own way against the
Spaniards, the Indians, the tempests and the sea; a state which
included, not only Charleston, but also a sharply differentiated
interior, peopled by the same kind of small farmers, facing the
same kind of economic problems, as those who had fought the

tidewater gentlemen in the Virginia Constitutional Convention of 1828–1829. The struggle against consolidation in South Carolina was also tangled with a domestic conflict between coast and up-country. A series of concessions on primogeniture, representation, courts, etc., made by Charleston in the period when cotton and slavery were spreading to the up-country, softened the local conflict. Yet these changes had not prevented the political alliance of the interior of the state with The Greater South which had arisen in Tennessee and Kentucky and which was composed largely of small farmers who had migrated from the up-country of Virginia and the Carolinas. Together they formed a great new West whose power was rapidly upsetting old balances. Tariffs and internal improvements appealed to these pioneers; they wanted the Indians removed from prospective cotton lands; they would gladly see the National Bank destroyed. They found in Charleston, as the Virginia consolidationists had found in Richmond, a body of allies. Andrew Jackson of Tennessee and John C. Calhoun from the Abbeville district of South Carolina were the great leaders of this new West. Jackson had won his way by crowding the Indians back in Alabama and by sterling deeds against the Spanish in Florida and the British at New Orleans. Calhoun had also risen because of his ardent expansionist attitudes and his loyalty to Western principles. In 1828 the combination of West and South made Jackson President of the United States and Calhoun Vice-President and heir apparent to the Presidency. But Jackson and Calhoun, with the aid of Benton and Van Buren, had quarrelled. The South Carolina leader found himself rudely thrust aside in Washington at the very moment his up-country constituency was being sharply changed by cotton and slaves and some of his supporters in Charleston were beginning to resent the growing burden of protective tariffs.

Fortunately, Calhoun was not entirely unprepared to meet this emergency. From 1817 to 1829 he had held public offices which freed him from active participation in state politics. As a Cabinet member and then as Vice-President, he had been able to watch developments and to form independent opinions on important issues. He was therefore in a position to assume leadership in the new South Carolina when that was required of him. The tariff issue now made such a demand.

Some South Carolinians had opposed the Tariff of 1816. John C. Calhoun was not one of them. Representing the western part of his state, which needed everything which any government could give to hurry development, he had approved of the measure. Two years earlier he had declared in Congress that he did not "represent my own State alone" but contended "for the interests of the whole people of this community." He had, on another occasion, expressed contempt for "a low, sordid, selfish and sectional spirit" and pictured a "great organic nation, every part responsive to the other, sacrificing local interests for the good of the whole." John Randolph sneeringly charged him with "tendencies to consolidation and to destroy state government." That was unfair. Calhoun valued the Union, not a centralized government.[34]

From 1816 forward, however, South Carolina's opposition to tariff legislation steadily increased. This opposition centered first in Charleston and in the southern part of the state. By 1824, when duties on hemp, cotton bagging and cheap woolens, used for slave clothing, were proposed, cries of "injustice" and "unconstitutionality" echoed throughout the state. Memorials and protests went off to Congress. Non-consumption agreements were launched against those responsible for protection demands. Homespuns returned to favor and many a puzzled Kentuckian with his customary droves of hogs and mules found no buyers in South Carolina.

In Congress Robert Y. Hayne proclaimed the injustice of making the planting section pay the costs of protection, and George McDuffie talked of "tributary states." John Randolph called the Constitution a dead letter. "I have no faith in parchment, sirs," he said. "I have faith in the power of the commonwealth, of which I am an unworthy son. . . . If, under the power to regulate trade, you prevent exportation; if, with the most approved spring lancet you draw the last drop of blood from our veins; if, *secundum artum*, you draw the last shilling from our pockets, what are the checks of the Constitution to us? A fig for the Constitution! When the scorpion's sting is

probing us to the quick, shall we stop to chop logic? There is
no magic in the word *Union*."[35]

The tariff debates of 1827 aroused even more bitter opposition and helped to create a greater unity at home. James
Hamilton, Robert Turnbull and other Calhoun supporters
joined the movement, and Calhoun himself, as Vice-President,
gave the deciding vote in the Senate against the bill. The following year a scheme to defeat tariff measures by lifting rates
on both raw and finished goods to absurd heights failed when
tariff advocates suddenly accepted—"abominations" and all—
an act which brought South Carolina to the verge of open revolt. Only the belief that Calhoun would soon be President
kept the opposition to words instead of deeds.

The words, however, were sharp and significant. Robert J.
Turnbull published *The Crisis or Essays on the Usurpations
of the Federal Government,* in which he declared that "the
subject which ought at this moment to claim the attention of
every South Carolinian . . . [was] the tendency of the government toward *consolidated* national government." He
thought the Supreme Court doctrine of "means to an end,"
while good for manufacturers, would only be "a means to the
end of Our Prosperity in the South." Congress had no power
to encourage either cotton planting or manufactures because
both were local interests. This was a federal, not a national,
union. Turnbull counselled resistance. And if resistance brought
"Disunion [he spelled it with capital letters], better that it
should come now, than some twenty years hence when *our trade*
shall have been destroyed, our policy *crumbled* to *ruins,* our
citizens *ruined,* and our *spirits broken down* by wrongs upon
wrongs heaped upon us, by a Government in the hands of manufacturers, fanatics and abolitionists."[36]

Then in June, 1828, from Walterboro in Colleton district,
came a sharper and clearer note of protest saying: "The day of
open opposition to the pretended powers of the Constitution
cannot be far off; and it is that it may not go down in blood
that we now call upon you to resist." "If you are doubtful of
yourselves," it ran on, "if you are not prepared to follow up
your principles wherever they may lead, to their very last con-

sequence—if you love life better than honor—prefer ease to perilous liberty and glory, awake not! stir not! Impotent resistance will add vengeance to your ruin. Live in smiling peace with your insatiable oppressors, and die with the noble consolation that your submissive patience will survive triumphant your beggary and despair." Honor! principles! blood! The tariff had produced a fire-eater. Robert Barnwell Rhett had begun his public career.[37]

Such radicalism threatened Calhoun's beloved Union and his political plans as well. Immediate action was necessary. Until now he had remained noncommittal except for his vote on the tariff bill of 1827. His position as Vice-President did not require a public statement on the issue. But the break-up of the old political alignments in South Carolina and the growing hostility to the tariff on the part of many of his supporters forced him to act. Both the Union and the rights of his state must be preserved. Both disunion and revolution must be avoided. He must hold onto as much of his West as possible and yet appease his Eastern followers. Accepting ideas already expressed by James Hamilton, Jr., Calhoun wrote, at the request of William C. Preston, a report to be presented by the Committee on Federal Relations to the state legislature. It was his great *Exposition*. The solution he offered was nullification—a constitutional way to protect the minority from the unconstitutional acts of the majority. It was based on the compact conception of the central government and the theory of indivisible, indestructible sovereignty. Through it the sovereign people of a state in convention assembled might declare an act of Congress null and void and appeal to their fellow sovereigns to uphold or reject their action. The amending process, whereby three fourths of the states might approve or refuse constitutional changes, authorized this plan. South Carolina could thus be rid of the hated tariff; revolution could be prevented.

The South Carolina legislature approved this procedure and in 1832 applied it. The story of President Jackson's brusque answer and the final adjustment by which both parties could claim the victory need not be told. The important fact, revealed from beginning to end, was that the conflict was, in large part, a strictly local affair. Again, as in the case of Virginia and John Marshall, this struggle was between fellow South Carolinians. Personalities dominated; local sectional enmities colored every phase. The quarrel between Jackson and Calhoun unquestionably played its part in precipitating hostilities and in shaping the course of action. The sectional quarrel within the state was equally important. Western South Carolina was still a part of the greater West and if Calhoun deserted its people they would not desert Jackson. They, therefore, joined with Joel Poinsett and his group in Charleston and gave Jackson loyal support to the very end.[38] The local fight over Nullification was sharp and bitter. The forces were nearly equally divided. This contest was no more a National North against a States'-right South than the early conflict in Virginia had been. Calhoun's conduct was certainly as national in its import as was that of his fellow South Carolinian, Andrew Jackson. Furthermore, South Carolina failed to receive support from the other Southern states and stood alone in her defiance of the central government. Hayne's great effort to unite the farmers of the West with those of the South, in his debates with Webster, had failed. Jackson still represented a dominant Southern attitude. Calhoun had offered a political device for which the people of the section as a whole were not yet ready. The lure of internal improvements and home markets through national aid proved stronger than the appeal to local pride. Virginia had enough troubles of her own. The Richmond *Enquirer* said frankly that the Old Dominion was "opposed to nullification" and "objected to the manner in which the citizens" were being "precipitated into the measure."[39] The Raleigh *Register* spoke for North Carolina in declaring that "the violent spirits of South Carolina are completely deluded"; and the Savannah *Georgian,* while insisting that the Georgians were "as much opposed to the tariff as those in any other state," made it clear that they were "unwilling to resort to such measures. . . ." Andrew Jackson had permitted the people of Georgia too much freedom with Indians to be greatly opposed by them on other policies. Besides, as the Augusta *Constitutionalist* said: "The dissolution of our

Union would be one of the heaviest blows ever struck at the happiness of the human race." It does, indeed, take a wild stretch of the imagination to interpret what happened in the Southern states in 1832 as "a manifestation of Southern sectionalism," "the beginning of secession."[40] Some sectional elements were, indeed, present. But the larger forces had to do with agriculture and its fear of consolidation as a step toward economic favors to urban-industrial rivals. Personal and purely local conflicts, closely related to these larger national interests, determined the course and color of every struggle. The South as a conscious section did not exist. The Civil War was yet a generation ahead.

*   *   *   *

When emotions had subsided and the interests of the people had shifted to the bank and toward Texas, the thoughtful investigator might have found two comments made on affairs during the struggle of far-reaching significance. One came from the pen of Chancellor Harper. He said:

> It is useless and impracticable to disguise the fact that the South is in a permanent minority, and that there is a *sectional* majority against it—a majority of different views and interests and little common sympathy. This is the origin of the evil and the great fountain of the waters of bitterness. We are divided into slave-holding and non-slave-holding states; and this difference creates the necessity for a different mode of labour, different interests and different feelings: and however particular states or sections on either side may have started from their proper spheres, this is the broad and marked distinction that must separate us at last. . . .

The other comment, made by a loyal Charlestonian, was to the effect that South Carolina might nullify the tariff, but she could not nullify the climate and soils of Alabama and Mississippi, which had more to do with her agricultural poverty than all the tariffs ever passed.

CHAPTER FOUR

BY THE SWEAT OF THEIR FACES

PHYSICAL work has a bad reputation in history. It began, according to one version, as a curse inflicted on man with his expulsion from the Garden of Eden. For centuries thereafter slaves and serfs, "by the sweat of their faces," carried the burden of toil that enabled the few to enjoy the luxury of leisure. Not until Luther and Calvin, facing the hard facts of a new economic day, found work a blessing and lifted the individual's task to the dignity of a "calling," was respectability conferred upon labor. Even then, some men sought the "blessing" for others but not for themselves, and contrived new methods of human exploitation by which they could avoid disagreeable effort and take the returns of other men's toil. The term "dignity of labor" still lacks something of sincerity.

Slavery, as a stage in these developments, had largely passed in western Europe before the discovery of America. The frontier, however, turned life back toward the primitive on the new continent and permitted the old system to be introduced and to spread. With an abundance of cheap lands and natural resources, favorable to the production of things much desired in the markets of the Old World, the real problem of those who would overcome the wilderness and enjoy a quick prosperity was one of securing labor. Few who came out to the colonies even with scanty funds found it necessary to remain long in the employ of others. The door of opportunity was too wide open. If English ways were to be resumed some form of forced labor was necessary. The heavy displacement of European rural peoples under commercial expansion provided the labor supply; the system of indenture furnished transportation and the means of control. White men and women, mostly English, Scotch-Irish, and German, bound themselves to service in America in payment for their passage to the land of opportunity. For a period of years their efforts went to enrich the planter who purchased their time from the ship captain. They learned the ways of the New World and earned the right, at the end of service of varying duration, to such varying goods as a new suit, some bedding, a few tools, a horse or a cow, or even a parcel of land. Then all that America offered was theirs.[1]

The superiority of tobacco as a colonial surplus soon turned this labor stream heavily toward Virginia and Maryland. Planters vied with each other for desirable workers. The Government gave lands to those who imported them. The cargoes of "filthy weed" grew heavier. Plantations spread up and down the tidewater valleys; English country ways appeared in houses and manners. Patient men and women cleared the land, planted and harvested other men's crops, and eagerly awaited the day of freedom. A wilderness offering advantages in rapid exploitation had again brought human beings into temporary bondage.

For three quarters of a century the tobacco crop, by which Virginia and Maryland successfully solved the problem of frontier living and progress to comfort and luxury, was produced primarily by the aid of indentured servants. For another similar period, such servants played a lesser part. The labor codes and practices of the colonies took their form and purposes from the problems of indenture. As a normal consequence of the scarcity of men, the hard, grinding toil required by the frontier and the frontiersmen, and the opportunities wide open to all in the vast continent beyond, difficulties quickly appeared which required solution. A distinctive set of laws came into being, whose aims were to insure justice to the servant, a full measure of work to the planter, and security to the community. In the light of all that was later to be ascribed to slavery, these laws, shaped by necessity, deserve notice.

A frontier flavor characterized all relationships. The planter, in spite of growing pretensions to gentility, showed a hard, grasping spirit, aggressively driving toward more land and influence. Having paid in advance for the servant's labor, he was generally inclined to collect all he could and to assert his full right to control. The idea of private ownership of the servant's time, as a thing to be sold at will or left as part of an estate at death, was early incorporated into the law. Then the right of corporal punishment by the Assembly or the Court was asserted. Since the laborer could not be discharged or fined for neglect of duty, only the threat of pain or of the extension of his time of bondage would influence him. In 1619, the Virginia law provided that, "If a servant wilfully neglect his master's commands, he shall suffer bodily punishment." Later, offenses against the dignity, status, and interest of the planter were included, and the inflicting of punishment by the planter himself was accepted in practice if not in law. In 1639, Virginia restricted the servant's right to trade, to sell articles without his master's consent, and then his right to marriage. First, females were forbidden to marry without the permission of parents or master; later, men servants were punished for this offense by the addition of a year to their bondage. Perhaps as a consequence of these restrictions, it was soon found necessary to punish servants for the birth of illegitimate children. Additional penalties were imposed in cases where the father was a Negro.[2]

Almost from the beginning, the law forbade the "seducing" of servants from their masters or the employing of those who could not show a certificate of freedom. Runaways were whipped and sometimes branded. The Government, in time, assumed partial responsibility for the capture of fugitives, offering rewards and making it the duty of its officials to assist in their capture. As the number of servants increased, fear of the danger incurred by having so large a group of under-privileged persons about led to harsh restrictions. Unauthorized meetings of servants were forbidden. Masters were urged to exercise closer supervision over their activities, to keep them at home on Sundays and to furnish them with "lycences" when they went abroad on other days. In 1699, when the question of arming and drilling servants was being discussed, the Virginia House of Burgesses resolved that such action was unsafe because servants "for the most consist of the worser Sort of the people of Europe," and to arm them and give them "the opportunity of meeting together by muster" would give "just reason to fear they may rise upon us."[3]

Outside the law a softer note appears in the ease with which "maid-servants" found husbands even among the more prosperous settlers, and in the steady recognition of human rights, regardless of economic and social status. The servant was protected in his person and property, and a surprisingly large number of obligations to society were imposed upon him. That he was a human being, with rights and duties as such, was never questioned.

Indenture, however, had serious drawbacks. It was a comparatively expensive system. The initial outlay, when spread over a rather short term of service, amounted to from £2 to £4 per year, and the keep for white men and often families was high. Time lost in becoming adjusted to American conditions and in learning plantation routine could not be recovered; the freedom dues required at the end of service took profits from the most valuable year of control. Furthermore, the keen competition for labor beat prices upward and gave the servant advantages in bargaining. As frontier conditions passed, harsh legislation lost its force. Public opinion checked "pushing" tendencies and unfair advantages. Labor held the whip hand and was bound to do so in a system where seasoned workers were being constantly pushed out at one end and a fresh supply was always being required at the other.

British taxes and regulations on the tobacco trade added the final straw to the planter's burdens. Markets were limited and those which remained were soon glutted. Prices fell and the middleman seemed to consume more than his share of the returns. Pinch and poverty became the lot of the planter. Expansion to larger-scale production in the plantation system gave some relief; the breaking of the Dutch monopoly over the African Negro supply offered more. Black men began to appear in the tobacco fields and in domestic and artisan service alongside the whites.

The first Negroes apparently worked under the system of

indenture. Some went free at the end of a period of servitude; some even acquired fellow Africans as servants. Anthony Johnson (Negro) was sued, in 1653, by John Casor (Negro) for holding him beyond his term of indenture. Later the said Anthony Johnson sued a white man who had employed Casor, and the Court, reversing its first decision, returned Casor to his original Negro owner as a "servant for life." Discrimination against the Negro as such, however, began early. Slowly his term was lengthened, and his condition came to be viewed as a permanent one. Vague misgivings regarding the duty to Christianize the heathen and the wrong of holding the Negro in bondage after he became a Christian complicated matters and caused men to hide race discrimination behind the term "servant for life." Yet indenture, under which white men labored, and a separate and more permanent system under which the Negro was increasingly held, were soon distinguishable even though the term servant applied to both blacks and whites. Gradually the Negro became a slave.[4]

The bases for slavery were both traditional and practical. The Negro had known it in Africa and in most of the countries of Europe to which he had been carried. More recently he had toiled as a slave in the sugar colonies of the New World. Few thought of him as a laborer in any other condition. The trader who secured him in Africa and brought him to America sold him outright for a purchase price. The contract idea inherent in indenture was nowhere present. Moreover, the Negro brought directly from Africa was quite unfitted for the liberal nature of indenture. Strange to it all, he needed a longer period for adjustment and for the acquiring of skills; he reached a fitness for freedom much more slowly than the white European. Even when he was ready for liberty, his absorption into society was difficult because of his race. There is some evidence that freed bondsmen sometimes returned voluntarily to service after one trial at making their own way. For his own best welfare, the Negro seemed to need a system different from indenture; for its own security, society demanded a different system. Slavery, as the traditional institution under which Negroes had long worked, offered a solution to both the economic and the social problems. Human selfishness and economic pressure continued the practice long after the first excuses were no longer valid. Law and conscience soon accepted what practice had begun.

The rise of the plantation system hastened this development and the slave, in turn, hurried forward the plantation. In large-scale production, with its division and supervision of labor, opportunity for ignorant and inexperienced workers was greatest. The Negro, regardless of background and intelligence, could, under an overseer, carry his share of the agricultural load. If he showed special ability, his skill could be utilized in the attainment of plantation self-sufficiency. There was work on the plantation for the children, for the aged, for the skilled and for the unskilled. Domestics and field hands, mechanics and artisans, all found a place in the varied tasks required to keep the great agricultural factory going. Here, better than in any other place in the life of the South, the Negro found his opportunity for service.

Virginians, however, did not always welcome the Negro. Discrimination was evident in such acts as that of the Assembly of 1630 which resolved that a white man should be "soundly whipped before an assembly of Negroes and others, for abusing himself to the dishonor of God and the shame of Christians, by defiling his body in lying with a negro. . . ."[5] This assembly, as one writer said, "forseeing the evil consequences of importing such numbers [of slaves] hath often attempted to lay a duty upon them which would amount to a prohibition . . . but no governor dare pass such a law, having instructions to the contrary from the Board of Trade at home. . . ." On the very eve of the American Revolution, the House of Burgesses implored "your Majesty's paternal assistance in averting a calamity of a most alarming nature." "The importation of slaves," it said, "hath long been considered a trade of great inhumanity, and under its present encouragement we have too great reason to fear it will endanger the very existence of your Majesty's American dominions. We are sensible that some of your Majesty's subjects may reap emoluments from this sort of traffic, but when we consider that it greatly retards the settlement of the colonies with more useful inhabitants and may in time have the most destructive influence, we presume to hope that the interest of the few will be disregarded when placed in competition with the security and happiness of such numbers of your Majesty's dutiful and loyal subjects."[6]

The appeal fell on deaf ears. Against the wishes of the Virginians, the number of Negroes increased. By the end of the eighteenth century, Negro slaves equalled the white indentured servants in the tobacco colonies and dominated the rice and indigo fields of South Carolina. When the Revolution came, they monopolized most of the Southern plantation areas. They had entered all the American colonies, but nowhere had they found such advantages as in the South. Out of a total of 485,000 slaves in the entire country in 1775, only 45,000 were in New England and the Middle Colonies. Slavery was being localized. The liberal doctrines of the American Revolution hastened this process; economic unprofitableness completed it. The hold of slavery had never been strong in the North, where families supplied enough labor for limited and concentrated efforts and indentured servants sufficed for extra needs. Now Northerners were ready to dispense with it entirely. One by one Northern states abolished "the evil practice." By the second decade of the nineteenth century, slavery had become an institution peculiar to the South.

When sectional conflict developed, with the War of 1812 and afterward, the fact that the South still held slaves proved a vulnerable spot in her armour. In the Missouri Compromise struggle the politician attacked it; then the abolitionist made it the chief object of Northern reform effort. Because slavery could be called undemocratic and immoral, enemies of the South quickly magnified it into the distinguishing feature of Southern life. In time they sought to explain all Southern differences and all the peculiar features of the section in terms of slavery. Slavery, they said, was responsible for the single-crop system, for exhausted farm lands, poor roads, lack of common schools, absence of manufacturing, lack of large cities, the presence of poor whites, great houses, good manners, high-strung temperaments, and a thousand and one other things that were or were not a part of Southern civilization.

They assumed, in like manner, that the institution of slavery, and that alone, determined the Negro's way of life—his manner of working, his treatment in and out of the fields, his domestic life, and even his relations with his God. Slavery was believed to be as precise and as all-inclusive for the Negro as it was for the section in which he dwelt.

Because of this magnifying of slavery to make it the symbol of all things Southern, it is very difficult to understand the more modest place it occupied in the actual life of the section and of the Negro. It was not the distinguishing feature of the South; nor was it the thing which gave the region a sectional flavor. The South had been Southern in its basic traits long before the slave became important; it remained a unique section after slavery had ceased to exist. The Negro discovered, to his sorrow, that his troubles did not all come to an end when war made him free. Most of his ways were unchanged; the burdens of labor and of race were still heavy on his shoulders. Being free as a bird did not put an end to hunger nor change the kind of tasks which his neighbors required. It somehow failed to alter the color of his skin.

In the first place, it must be clearly understood that the Negro was desired because of the work he could perform. He was in the South as a *laborer*. As such he shared the lot of all Americans who accepted the task of conquering a wilderness, creating a surplus, and developing a more complex social-economic order. That meant back-breaking toil, abuse by the tough, aggressive leaders who were able to command the services of others, much of privation and more of primitiveness. Regardless of the system under which the American labored, his lot was not easy. The indentured servant had early found that out; wives and children and hired hands all knew it equally well.

Slavery as a labor system, however, was characterized by certain features which distinguished it from other labor systems. Under it, the worker was owned. That is, a price had been paid for his life-time service and for that of his descendants, or he had been inherited along with other property. His status and that of his children were permanent unless the master chose to terminate his bondage. He could be sold, hired out, given away, or left as an inheritance. He had no legal right to choose or to refuse a master. He was property, yet a peculiar kind of property—he had certain rights and obligations.

Slavery, as it developed in the United States, did not give to the master absolute, arbitrary, despotic power over his slave. It was not the Roman type of slavery. The legal theory of slavery, as expounded by Southern lawyers, clergymen, and politicians—the three great spokesmen of the section—generally held that the slave was in all ways a human being with the right to life, livelihood, and "anything else not inconsistent with the services he was obligated to render." He was held and controlled only for the purpose of securing his labor. The master's rights did not extend beyond the bounds necessary for this end. For violence against the person of the slave, the master was amenable to the State. For brutality or for overworking his slaves, the owner met the disapproval of public opinion. Sometimes the law regulated the food and care which the master was expected to provide. The slave, on the other hand, could be arrested and tried in the courts of the state for his crimes. He found his freedom, on and off the plantation, restricted by the Black Codes passed by the state legislatures. Patrols ranged the countryside to regulate his conduct where slavery failed to give complete security. Three fifths of his number counted as population in determining representation. Some masters provided churches and hospitals for his care. Edward Bryan summed up the whole tangled relationship by saying: "Our slave property lies only *incidently* in the *person* of the slave; but *essentially* in his *labor*."[7]

What owning and being owned added to the usual relationship between employer and employee, it is difficult to say. Rugged individualism seems to have characterized most of those who got ahead in young America and the ability to accumulate property and to employ others was usually ascribed to superior industry and intelligence. Employers, whether in New England factories or in Southern cotton fields, easily fell into attitudes of exploitation and paternalism. Practices varied with individuals rather than with systems. Factory relations differed

with each employer, each town, and each decade. Slavery implied uniform practices and attitudes no more than did the
factory system. The man with only a few slaves was generally
inclined to fraternize with his men and to deal with them much
as a Northern farmer dealt with his hired help. The plantation
owner, with his larger force and his overseer, was, of necessity,
on less intimate terms with his slaves, but his attitude toward
them did not necessarily differ from those between factory
owner and factory workers. Slave relationships were one thing
in the older regions where Negroes and masters had grown up
together and quite a different thing on the frontier where slaves
had been recently purchased, where the push to get ahead was
strong, and where practices had not been standardized. Some
masters were naturally kind and careful; some slaves were in-
herently industrious and docile. Other masters were harsh and
indifferent; and other slaves were lazy and provoking. From
place to place, from period to period, from person to person,
slave-master relationships varied in about the same ways and in
about the same degrees as did the employer-labor relations at
Lowell or Chicopee or Waltham. Such basic differences as appeared were primarily due to the difference between rural-agricultural effort and urban-industrial effort. Southerners were
wont to say that the master, living among his slaves, felt a
deeper responsibility for the welfare of his workers than did the
factory owner; that paternalism and the spirit of *noblesse oblige*
were stronger. Yet many manufacturers provided dormitories
for their girls and regulated hours for retirement, kinds of
amusements, and even places of worship for them. Northerners
asserted that the slavemaster grew haughty and overbearing
and that the tendency to exploit was untempered by the slave's
ability to quit and find a new job. Yet black lists and agreements between capitalists not to employ one another's workers
even when they were laid off temporarily, gave them nearly
equal control. In fact, it may be said with much truth that some
factory owners manifested all the attitudes of ownership toward
their workers and that some masters of slaves manifested few
of them. The opposite might be asserted with equal truth.

As to the effects which being owned had on the slave, the

matter was again an individual one. The records show that some slaves were resentful and rebellious. They ran away and sulked in the swamps or found their way to free territory. Unquestionably they resented the fact as well as the idea of slavery. The great majority, however, seem to have accepted their status, as most human beings do, with only occasional complaint. Slavery was their lot. Life was made to endure and to enjoy. Why quarrel with fate? They found little to envy in the condition of the poor whites or the free Negroes round about. Life was hard but the humble rewards of those who serve were not absent in slavery Praise for loyalty and service was as abundant and as gratifying here as elsewhere This simple entry in a plantation diary tells an important story: "Old Daniel has disgraced himself and has become a field negro again, which has sunk his spirits very low." Special abilities found opportunity and rewards. The mason, the carpenter, the blacksmith, the domestic, the nurse, and the cook knew the instinct of workmanship and gained privileges by its expression. The Negro Mammy exercised an authority and enjoyed an influence which became a Southern tradition. She claimed in life all that love and loyalty can give and often found her last sleep in the family graveyard with her white folk. The Negro foreman and overseer sometimes had complete charge of the plantation and received the respect due his talents. Such slaves must have known the feelings of pride and satisfaction mixed, perhaps, with a realization of the limitations imposed by slavery.[8]

Nor was the slave necessarily broken in spirit. Many of the so-called Negro insurrections were nothing more than labor strikes. Many of the runaways were revolts against the attempt to speed up activity. The fact that they increased during the periods of planting and harvesting indicates as much. The genuine slave insurrection, and there were many of them, showed all the daring and all the drive which have made men free throughout the ages. The mad rage with which white men crushed out all participants in such uprisings proved the genuineness of the threat they carried. Day-by-day plantation happenings also revealed the normal character of the Negro's reactions. Under most circumstances, he acted as any other worker would have acted under like conditions. Thrown together in a lone-some rural world, whites and blacks, masters, overseers, and slaves tended to forget the finer distinctions of station and of race. Human traits came to the surface. Mulatto children were born to white women and to black women alike. Negro men committed rape and were lynched for it. White men committed the same crime and escaped punishment save where some Negro took it upon himself to avenge the wrong. Life-long friendships developed between children, black and white, who played together and learned to appreciate each others' virtues. More than one Southern lady came to love some Negro child as did the good Rachel O'Connor who wrote from Louisiana in 1830 of[9]

sixteen little Negro children arising . . . all very healthy . . . ex-cepting my little favorite Isaac. He is subject to a cough, but seldom sick enough to lay up. The poor little fellow is laying at my feet sound asleep. I wish I did not love him as I do, but it is so, and I cannot help it. . . .

Whites and blacks quarrelled and fought over the same things and in the same ways that they would have done had their skins been of the same color and their stations equal. They developed the same high *esprit de corps* for the making of good crops and took equal pride in the results. Things went well most of the time. Trouble came only at rare intervals. A typical plantation letter written from Barrens, Mississippi, in 1852, reads:[10]

The servants have all enjoyed good health, the teams have kept in good order, the weather, until the first of the month, was favorable for cultivation and everything has gone smoothly, evenly and quietly,—no jars, no fuss, no runaways, no quarreling, no fighting,—and with few exceptions, all hands seem to have striven to see who could best work or best agree. . . .

When troubles developed, they tended to take a very normal course and resulted in an exchange of words and actions char-acteristic of bosses and workers. One overseer on a Louisiana plantation told the story of his troubles with a slave in the fol-lowing manner:[11]

. . . As to the difficulty with Summer, it arose from my having hit his wife a few light licks when backward to procede to work. after which I proceded to the field where Summer left his work to the distance of 20 or 30 yards with his Cane knife in his hand & very much inraged, and said that I had abused his wife & that he was not going to put up with it & that I was an unjust man, and that I might go get my gun, kill him and bury him but that he was not a going to put up with any other punishment to himself or family, and that he was instructed by his master Alfred & yourself that if his family was punished unjustly that he must report it to one of you. and that his master Alfred told him to see to the business that it went right and if any of the hands were lying up & he thought they were not sick, that he must make them go to work. I then told him that he must be the manager & I his driver & had nothing to do in the management of the business, and that I knew what he was after which was to get 8 or 10 of the hands to run away with him that I might be blamed when Mr. Conrad returned. he said not but that he intended to stay and work. . . . since which time I have not seen him. . . . John Dickerson has also disappear'd. . . .

Not all cases of slave resentment and resistance ended with talk or even with running away. Sometimes slaves "assaulted" their masters or overseers, and, in what appears to be a normal number of cases, they killed them. "On Tuesday last," reported the Baton Rouge *Gazette* (June 17, 1848), "the overseer of Col. Philip Hicky on Hope Plantation was severely cut with a cane-knife, by a negro named Jim, belonging to the plantation." In a neighboring household a slave girl "returned the blows" of her mistress, "threw her down and beat her unmercifully on the head and face." A few years earlier, in the same community, the slave "Zac" was executed for the murder of "Mr. John Whitten, overseer." At one time in 1854, two Negroes were confined to the Natchez jail for the murder of their masters and a third for the murder of his overseer. In the latter case, the slave had resisted punishment "then shot" the overseer, "then strangled him and then stabbed him." A few days earlier in Montgomery County, Alabama, a Negro slave had beaten Doctor McDonald to death with a club, and a short time later another had fatally stabbed "Mr. James Stubbs, overseer for Nathan Bass," on a plantation near Macon, Georgia.[12] These incidents could be duplicated in every slave community for every period. They offer convincing evidence of the human nature found under black skins and the institution of slavery. They were not unrelated to the revolts taking place in New England factories against long hours, the speed-up of machinery, and the reduction of wages, which sent "solemn columns" of girls marching down the streets waving "their kerchiefs to the girls in the other mills to join them."[13]

* * * *

Slavery offered some advantages and disadvantages to both employer and worker that were not found in other labor systems. The master was forced to compete with others for the possession of labor and to pay in proportion to the demand. That required a heavy initial outlay. But, once he had builded his force, the problem of a labor supply was permanently solved. Births more than balanced deaths and replenished invested capital. A surplus at any time constituted a marketable commodity. So obvious were the possibilities for gain from this source that critics of the system early brought the charge of slave breeding. Concrete evidence for a single case of forced child-bearing, however, has never come to light, in spite of the historian's patient search through all available materials. Some cases may have occurred, but artificial stimulation does not seem to have been necessary. Rural conditions, ignorance of contraceptives, and commonly held attitudes, were sufficient forces among all Americans, regardless of race or station, to give a steady production of that valuable asset, children. Slave records, as will be shown later, vary little in this regard from those of the free whites.[14]

Another advantage to the slave owner lay in the matter of labor control. Slave workers, theoretically at least, were subject to closer supervision than freemen. Their entire way of life was determined by the master's wishes and their days were lived in close association with him. A wise master might use this control to increase the health and general efficiency of his force. Labor turnover was almost entirely eliminated. Workers could not shift to another employer nor quit the tasks to which they were assigned except by running away. Furthermore, the master held the dubious right of inflicting physical punishment. If fear supplied a superior incentive to hard and efficient exertion, then the master of slaves stood to benefit. Such advantages, however, were more theoretical than real. Few masters made the most of their opportunities, and Northern employers developed methods of control equally effective. A wise overseer from Georgia spoke for the better men of both groups when he wrote: "I have killed twenty-eight head of beef for the people's Christmas dinner. I can do more with them in this way than if all the hides of the cattle were made into lashes." And again: "You justly observe that if punishment is in one hand, reward should be in the other."[15]

The disadvantages in slavery to the master are obvious. His capital, so necessary for large-scale effort and marketing abroad, was tied up in labor. Funds that might have lessened dependence on the hated factor were frozen in workers. The planter was thus always at a disadvantage in financing and disposing of his crops. He was from the beginning cast for the debtor's role. Furthermore, his kind of property, in a climate where cholera, yellow fever, and smallpox became regional epidemics, was not always the safest of investments. It was even less so in neighborhoods where abolition propaganda flourished. Nor was this all. Under slavery, the size of the working force, and consequently the size of the economic undertaking, were to a large degree fixed. It was not easy to vary production with changing demands or to shift types of endeavor. Costs remained steady regardless of the price of the staple produced. The master did not pay wages, but he did provide permanent support for his workers. He contributed the quarters in which they lived; he gave them food and sometimes bore the added expense of cooking and housekeeping for them. He furnished medical care and often hospital facilities for the sick. He supplied nurses for the children, took care of the halt and blind; he cared for the aged and kept his people from suffering in depression periods. He took over most of the functions of local government for the lowest, and hence the most troublesome, element in the population; kept peace and order and meted out punishments which courts and magistrates inflicted elsewhere. The work of relief and charity was his. The education of Negro children for their life tasks fell to his household. If he failed, the woes and sufferings of the whole body of his dependents were on his conscience. If he held property in the slave, the slave, just as truly, held property in his head and heart and hand.

For the slave also there were both advantages and disadvantages in his lot, not to be found in other labor systems. Of most importance was the fact that he was relieved of all personal direction and material care. He was a soldier without the brass buttons. Responsibility for his care and well-being and for the direction of his efforts was assumed by his master. The slave had no worries about loss of time or unemployment. Against losses from sickness, injury, and old age, he was secure. Worry about weather, crops, and prices belonged to others. As long as his white folks ate, he too would have his rations. He could be confident that the morrow would take care of itself. Life could be serene and unhurried. The acquisitive drive neither corrupted him nor rushed him about. Fear of losses did not disturb his slumbers.

But he had surrendered, with his physical freedom, the right to drift about from employer to employer, or from place to place. He was robbed of the dignity of responsibility and the stimulation of worry. He was subject to the humiliation of corporal punishment. Any formal education which he might acquire was accidental and soon became illegal. The number of those from whom he might choose a wife was often limited to a single plantation force or, at best, to the members of a single neighborhood. Even then his life partner was often selected for him. His plight in this respect was as bad as that of European royalty but only a trifle worse than that of the rural whites, whose acquaintances seldom ran beyond a few families and whose parents often engineered all "matches." At least, the system under which the slave "suffered" seems to have produced a rather normal number of happy families and loyal husbands and wives. White comment on the slave's marital standards differs little from that current today concerning the free Negro's.

*   *   *   *

The size of families and the age at which Negro women began bearing children do not seem to have been greatly affected by slavery. As has been said, the charge of deliberate breeding for legal sale and polyandry between black women and selected men on plantations to improve the human stock has been widely circulated. The Negro writer, DuBois, bluntly asserts that the planters viewed Negro women as brood mares and black children as puppies. Bancroft naively confuses rearing with breeding. Both have ignored the simple fact that most American girls in that period, black and white, married early and as often as necessary to be ever in wedlock. Most of them early accepted what a Virginia tombstone inscription called maternal duty. They brought children into the world with a terrifying regularity. One foreign traveller declared that children came in litters and another insisted that North Carolina parents never had less than twelve. "Every man feels the increase of his family to be the increase of his riches," was Thomas Cooper's comment. To be unmarried at twenty was a misfortune. Not to bear children was a disgrace. In the sense that the critics of slavery charged, all Americans were equally guilty of breeding. The raw continent required it.[16]

In Massachusetts the incomplete records for three years beginning in 1856 show one bride of thirteen, thirty-two of fourteen, 124 of fifteen, 469 of sixteen, and 976 of seventeen. In a list of seventy white families given in the manuscript census of Hinds County, Mississippi, for 1850, one woman bore her first child at twelve years of age; four at thirteen; four at fourteen; fifteen at fifteen; twelve at sixteen; twelve at seventeen; eight at eighteen; four at nineteen; three at twenty; and the remaining seven after that age. In 1859 over 24 per cent of the girls married in Rhode Island, 38 per cent of those in South Carolina, and 42 per cent of those in Kentucky were in their teens.[17]

Once begun, child-bearing went on uninterruptedly. George

Mason humorously remarked that his wife always had one child in arms, one in hand, one at dress-tail, and one on the way. Robert Y. Hayne, of debate fame, was one of fourteen children; Robert Barnwell Rhett, one of fifteen; the notorious John Brown, one of sixteen. Professor Stillwell tells of eight families in one New England community whose offspring totalled 113. He finds repeated accounts of families of ten, twelve, and fifteen children. Nor were these all among the lower classes. Boston aristocrats did as well as their lesser folks. Russel Sturges had sixteen children; Thomas Winthrop and John Balch, fourteen each; Benjamin Balch, thirteen; Stephen Higginson and John Carter, twelve each; and Robert Shaw, eleven. Southern gentlemen could match such records. Edwin Holt, the richest man in North Carolina, had ten children; Thomas Ruffin, Chief Justice of the same state, had twelve; Thomas Dabney, the famous Mississippi planter, had ten. Of the seventy Mississippi families mentioned above, two had thirteen children, one had twelve, four had ten, and seven had nine. Only nine of the mothers had reached the age of forty.

Negro slaves differed little from the whites in these matters. Girls became mothers at about the same age. They bore about the same number of children and lost them at about the same fearful rate. Negro children, like white ones on Northern farms, were always welcome as potential laborers. The slave girl's value to her master, like that of the white girl to her husband, was, in part, measured by her capacity for motherhood. She was encouraged to bear children and sometimes rewarded with a new dress. In the matter of the dress she probably had an advantage over most of her equally fruitful white sisters.

Plantation records are notoriously vague and incomplete in regard to the Negro's personal affairs. Data on marriages and births are not always what the historian might wish either in quality or in quantity. Yet some information is available. On the Edgewood Plantation of F. W. Pickens, in South Carolina, there were in 1840, thirty-nine families. One family had nine children; one had eight; one had seven; three others had six each. The others ranged between one and four. Of the twenty-four mothers whom we can identify, thirteen were past twenty years of age when their first living child was born; three were nineteen; four were eighteen; and two were seventeen. On the John E. Fripp plantation, St. Helena Island, over a period of fifty-eight years, two Negro women bore ten children each; one, nine; two, eight; three, seven; one, five; four, four; and three, two. Only four mothers were under nineteen years of age when their first child arrived. The records of the J. W. Fowler plantation, in Louisiana, show that one slave was the mother of ten children; another of nine; a third, of seven; and three, of five. In twenty-four families owned by William F. Palfrey in the same state, two had eleven children; two had ten; four had eight; three had seven; one had six; three had five; and nine had from one to four.[18]

Newspaper advertisements of slave sales sometimes listed a mother with her children. It is, of course, impossible to know whether the oldest child sold with the mother was her first-born. Yet where the mother was comparatively young the assumption seems fair. If this premise is granted, in seventy families so advertised in a New Orleans newspaper in the mid-1850's, one girl had become a mother at thirteen years, one at fourteen, ten at sixteen, seven at seventeen, eight at eighteen, nine at nineteen, eight at twenty, and thirty after that age. These ages it will be noticed, do not differ materially from those given for the same number of white girls in the Mississippi census of 1850. The similarity certainly raises some doubts as to the soundness of the unsupported assertions regarding slavery and child-bearing which have so long been circulated as history.[19]

In most other ways, also, the life and labor of the slave were much like those of other American workers. Race and economic station determined the greater part of his everyday affairs. The slave's working hours were the usual rural ones, from sunrise to sunset. Occasionally some master, especially in the older regions, adopted the task system, in which a certain amount of work was assigned for a day. Travellers reported that the better workers often finished their assignments by mid-afternoon and might be seen leisurely making their way back to the quarters. But this was not the rule, and only the accidents of weather and off seasons shortened working hours. It should be remembered, however, that long hours also characterized the New England factories, where rural hours came into the villages with rural operatives. At Chicopee, in the 1830's "work started at five o'clock in the morning and lasted through until half past seven in the evening with two half-hour breaks for breakfast and dinner, making the actual working time 13½ hours per day." Even in later times, at Holyoke, children worked "nearly seventy hours a week," and the law "of 1842, which forbade the employment of children under twelve . . . for more than ten hours in any one day" was evaded "through inadvertence or intention." The mills at Griswold, Connecticut, kept their machines going fifteen hours and ten minutes per day, and women and children in those mills "were urged on by the use of the cowhide." Our fathers, whether they lived North or South, accepted the Calvinistic doctrine that work was a "blessing," and they were inclined to bestow it generously.[20]

The slave's living quarters compared favorably with those of Northern workers and were certainly as good as those of the freedmen in post-war days. They varied greatly with individuals and localities. Some masters built substantial quarters of brick and stone with tile roofs; some were content with crude log cabins. One master wrote:[21]

> My first care has been to select a proper place for my quarters, well protected by the shade of forest trees sufficiently thinned out to admit a free circulation of air, so situated as to be free from impurities of stagnant water, and to erect comfortable houses for my negroes. . . . There being upward to 150 negroes on the plantation, I provide them 24 houses made of hewn post oak, covered with cypress, 16 by 18 with plank floors and good chimneys and situated two feet from the ground. . . .

Another praised the virtues of "a coat of whitewash inside and out, every summer," and recommended a "row of mulberries . . . planted in front, and so as to protect the houses [16 × 18 is a convenient size for a small family] on the south and southwest." Lyell described "the Quarters" on a South Carolina plantation as "neat and whitewashed, all floored with wood, each with an apartment called the hall, two sleeping-rooms, and a loft for the children. . . ." Some masters built double cabins with fireplaces in the center and placed two families together. Others insisted that "in no case should two families be allowed to occupy the same house"—"it was unhealthy"; "it bred contention"; "it was destructive of delicacy of feeling"; it promoted "immorality between the sexes."[22]

There were meaner quarters, of course, tumble-down and dirty. They corresponded to the equally inferior big houses of their owners. Yet it is doubtful whether living conditions anywhere among the slaves were worse than in the overcrowded New England factory tenements where, according to a local historian, "six girls often slept in one room," where the pig pens and the wells were close enough together to produce epidemics of typhoid fever, and where "many families were huddled into low, damp and filthy cellars, and others in attics which were but little if any better, with scarcely a particle of what might be called air to sustain life." Adequate housing for laborers was an American problem, not one confined to a section or determined by one labor system.[23]

The slave's food and clothing were coarse but adequate to his needs. Masters furnished the larger part of these necessities, but the slave's own gardens, chicken houses and pig pens often supplemented regular rations and the skill of his own hands added to the garments imported from Old or New England. Rations usually included "clear meat," meal and molasses, with vegetables and fruit in season. Clothing consisted of two or three suits, four or five shirts, and a pair of shoes each year for the men, and a corresponding quantity of dresses, petticoats, and other clothing for the women. Cotton goods sufficed in the summer, but woolens were generally supplied for the winter months. Some masters furnished a garment waterproofed with oil to be worn in wet weather. Some permitted the Negroes to cook all of their own food. Others, who thought the matter of good cooking too important to be left to the slave, maintained a central kitchen and a regular staff of cooks. They required that there be "stated hours for the negroes to breakfast and dine and that those hours . . . be regularly observed." "The master cannot expect full work from one who is but partially fed," wrote one Mississippi planter in 1851. ". . . Good, sufficient and comfortable clothing, a sufficiency of good, wholesome and nutricious food," wrote another, are "indispensably necessary to successful planting, as well as for reasonable dividends for the amount of capital invested, without saying anything about the Master's duty to his dependents, to himself, and his God. . . ."[24]

* * * *

Any survey of plantation records will show that many of the rules and regulations laid down by the masters had nothing to do with the fact that the workers were slaves, but were instituted because they were Negroes. Such rules represented the white man's notions of Negro character and his understanding of how best to handle the race and the race problem which the Negro's presence created. "They should be treated like children," ran one comment, "they break, waste, and destroy everything they handle, abuse horses and cattle, tear, burn and rend their clothing." "When at work," wrote another, "I have no objection to their whistling or singing some lively tune, but no drawling tunes are allowed in the field, for their motions are almost certain to keep time with the music." "As to their habits of amalgamation and intercourse," wrote a third, "I know of no means whereby to regulate them or to restrain them; I attempted it for many years by preaching virtue and decency, encouraging marriages, and by punishing with some severity departures from marital obligations; but it was all in vain." Record after record comments on the Negro's reluctance to go to bed on time and on the desirability of seeing that he did so; on his unusual sense of rhythm and his weakness "for a good fiddler" which might be used to make him more contented with his lot; on his inclination to take what did not belong to him and on the resulting necessity for forbidding him "to sell anything off the plantation"; on his weakness for ceremony and show and his quick acceptance of present enjoyment in preference to greater future pleasures, which made it impossible to trust him at any one time with supplies more than sufficient for his immediate needs.[25]

The harsh regulations against teaching the Negro to read and write, against his absence from the house of the master without a pass, against his congregating with his fellows, were born of race fears, not of slavery. The presence of so great a mass of "undigested foreigners" in the community called for regulations such as had been earlier made against the indentured servants. The Black Codes and the patrols of ante-bellum days were the product of a race question. They were the result of a section's workers being Negroes, and not an inherent part of the institution of slavery.[26]

Another factor which shaped Negro life almost as much as slavery itself was the plantation. The fact that some Negroes lived in quarters, arose to the sound of a bell or a horn, worked in gangs in the field under the supervision of an overseer, performed standardized tasks with tools provided for them, was due to their residence on a plantation. They were the laborers in large-scale agriculture. Greater capital, mass production, division and supervision of routine effort went with the plantation as it went with the factory. More efficient management brought more minute and careful regulation and direction of labor and added something to slavery. Even a larger interest in the worker's personal and home life came with factory methods in farming. The workers took on all the characteristics of factory hands. They standardized the rate of production and protected themselves against labor sweating in orthodox fashion. When contests between gangs were arranged, the usual amount of cotton picked was easily doubled. They found out how to rid themselves of unpopular foremen, and overseers generally constituted the only changing personnel on the plantation. It was indeed an unusual overseer who remained on the same plantation more than one year. Slaves taught more than one master that practices once established constituted rights which could not be easily taken away. In fact, the plantation so nearly determined the life and labor of its workers that, when slavery ended and the plantation continued under the wage system, neither the Negro nor his white friends could detect any major changes. They could not believe that slavery had ceased until the plantations were broken up, the quarters scattered, and each individual Negro had his own tract of land.[27]

One final question remains to be answered regarding slavery as a labor system: Did it pay? Was it responsible for the oft-described backward and tumble-down conditions of the ante-bellum South? To begin with, it must be understood that the Old South did not always value all things in terms of dollars and cents. Pay might be taken in satisfaction and comfort and human relationships. Percentages, important as they were, did not always measure the good life. It was something to succeed according to the accepted standards, which included holding slaves. Dependents, by being dependent, paid dividends. The pious old slave, whose prayers for the master met a good-natured chuckle, more than paid his way even though he had long ceased to toil. Attention to things which enriched every-day living more than compensated for the gates that might have been repaired in the time such attention took, or the weeds pulled, or the slaves driven. The traveller Olmsted, who laughed at the foolish Southerners because they dropped their hoes and stood at the fence as long as he was willing to talk to them, could not understand the riches he brought or how much they exceeded the gain which busy hoes might have given.

This, however, begs the question. The larger fact is that the North, which did not have slaves, had more flourishing cities, a more diversified economic life, more rich people. Its factories, its railroads, and its public schools were not matched in the slave-holding South. Southern planters were dependent on Northern bankers for financial accommodations and some people were already talking about its colonial status. If one were to assume that slavery was the only real difference between the sections and the only cause of economic variations, the conclusion that slavery did not pay would be inevitable. If slavery alone determined whether Southern agriculture prospered and plant-ers became wealthy, then the answer is the same. The matter, however, is not so simple. The South lacked some things in the Northern pattern because her values and her ideals had been taken from rural England. Southerners did not always want a diversified economic life or a public school system or a great number of large cities. The South often deliberately chose rural backwardness.

A far more intelligent question is: *Does agriculture ever pay?* And if it does, *When and Why?* Thoughtful scholars will hesitate to answer. Unquestionably the greater profits from American agriculture have come from increasing values of land, from the exploitation of virgin soils, and from low standards of rural living in which every member of the family has toiled long and hard. Even under these conditions, depression has ever been a normal part of the farm story and farmers have constituted one of America's major protest groups. In a general way, it may be said that, in the early periods when lands were cheap and rapidly rising in value, when soils were fresh and fertile, some men at the South were able to set up establishments considerably above the average American farm level. Even in later days, some planters in that section made a reasonable amount of money. Historians have overlooked the fact that most planters secured the major part of their laboring force before prices were high, or raised that force themselves; that the inflationary effect of California gold on land and slave prices in the 1850's magnified the capital invested but did not actually affect the real profits; that depreciation on this investment was constantly being offset by births. They have ignored the lower costs of local government resulting from the slave-system handling of petty crime, care of the poor, and support of the defective. When these things are taken into consideration, the 2 and 3 per cent profits suggested by the few writers who have chanced an estimate are boosted to 10 to 15 per cent. That may or may not be a fair guess, but most certainly there is nothing in the gloomy story of present-day Southern agriculture to indicate great advances in profits because slavery has ended. There is almost as little in the record of Northern agriculture to warrant the assumption that the absence of profits in the agriculture of the ante-bellum South was due entirely to its labor system. Even today, scholars write of the colonial status of South and West; of their condition of dependency on the industrial East.

Rural scattering of population also played a part in preventing the rapid development of roads, schools and other social accumulations. The Southern population of 6.4 persons to the square mile in 1830 and 12.5 in 1860, when contrasted with the 31.5 and 50.6 of New England for the same periods, suggests that differences in social complexity were not entirely a matter of a difference in labor systems. Southern rivers provided rather adequate ways to market for a crop which kept well and was relatively bulky. The South had a larger percentage of its youth in college in 1860 than did either the North or the West. That merely represented a difference in social emphasis, for North and West both surpassed the South in facilities and number of elementary schools.[28]

Nor should it be forgotten that destructive methods characterized agriculture in most parts of the nation. The single-crop type of production, poor plowing, failure to fertilize—these evils and others were as common in the North and West as in the South. Southern soils suffered more from nature but no more from man. All but a few American farmers, and those few mostly Germans and Scandinavians, were spending their soils as rapidly as possible. That was the normal frontier way of doing things. When reform was required, Virginians and Carolinians took the lead. By 1860, they had learned more about restoring fertility, good plowing, the use of legumes, marl, ground bone, dried blood, and other fertilizers, than any other farmers in the nation. They led in the invention of farm machinery, the diversification of crops, and the draining of lands. They had achieved a degree of prosperity greater than any they had known since early colonial days. And they did it with slave labor. The slave proved himself as efficient in the use of machinery, the application of fertilizers, the production of diversified crops as he had been in the destruction of soils and the production of a single great staple. He had also made his way into the new manufacturing establishments of the communities which diversified. There he worked alongside of free whites and blacks, found his own rooming and boarding places, and was often permitted to keep what he earned above a specified amount. The outbreak of civil war prevented the South from demonstrating what American Negro slavery might have become in a more complex social-economic order.[29]

* * * *

It is thus perfectly clear that slavery did not work alone in changing the life of the South and of the Negro. Much that has been ascribed to its influence should be credited to labor, race, agriculture, and ordinary human nature.

Yet, in a period of sectional rivalry and bitterness, slavery became the symbol of all sectional differences and the cause of all sectional hatred. The Abolitionist first and then the politician made slavery the object of an attack that in the end became an attack on the South as a section. Slavery was held responsible for all the things that Northerners disliked about the South. It explained matters political, economic, and social. It was the reason why the South prevented the North from securing the legislation needed to build internal improvements, to encourage manufactures, and to secure homesteads.

Southerners in turn accepted this magnified and distorted conception of the institution and came to view it as the cornerstone of what was a unique culture based on rural values. In the end they were willing to stake their all for its preservation.

But if slavery was somewhat less important in the life of the Negro and the South as a whole, the idea of holding men in bondage and buying and selling them as property was one that was sadly out of line with the democratic and Christian ideal of the modern world. The fact that it could be as bad as was possible where the worst white man could own the best Negro cancelled all that its defenders could say in its defense. It was a poor foundation on which to erect a civilization.

CHAPTER FIVE

THE COTTON KINGDOM RISES

TO MOVE west is a normal experience for American men and institutions. From earliest days the trek has been on. Before roots have firmly taken hold in one place the urge to press farther out has driven the settler to new frontiers, robbed him of all place attachment and made him a wanderer on the face of his native land. Year in and out, the setting sun has cast its fading light into the tired, hopeful faces of rugged pioneers seeking fresher lands and new places in which to begin over again. America has bred a race of migrants.

At times the westward flow from older regions has reached flood tide. The normal steady movement of restless and rebellious souls has been augmented by new pressures behind and new lures ahead. New Wests have sprung up as by magic and a new balance in national life has resulted. Such a period came after 1815. The second war with England had reached its dubious close and with it a lingering colonial life had abruptly ended. Until then America had faced eastward. As colonies, the settlements along the coast had been a part of Europe. Even with political independence the ties, based on markets and supplies for both mind and body, weakened only gradually. European quarrels still involved the young republic and problems of neutrality lifted leaders to prominence. Splendid isolation had not been achieved.

With the heavy migrations of the new period, however, all was changed. Henceforward the major interests of American men and government lay in the vast interior of the continent. Domestic affairs—problems of land, finances, internal improvements, and markets—absorbed attention and furnished political leaders with their programs. The Monroe Doctrine was but public notice of an outlook already generally accepted. The West had begun its domination in American life.

The Southern phase of this expansion created the Cotton Kingdom. Under the push of hard conditions in tobacco and rice fields and the pull of opportunity in the territories which faced the Gulf, men from Virginia and Tennessee, the Carolinas and Georgia thronged the ways which led south and west. Soon, with cotton, in virgin lands they built a new and greater South which, in wealth and power, dwarfed the mother sections. In the decades immediately preceding the War Between the States men often spoke of the Cotton Kingdom as though it constituted the whole of the South.

Another stream out of the Old South ran north and west. Pioneers had early found their way out of Virginia and North and South Carolina into Tennessee and Kentucky. Some had crossed the Ohio and not a few had gone on into Missouri. Old foundations thus laid were strengthened in the period after 1815, and an upland Southern flavor was added to the wooded and hilly portions of the old Northwest and even to southern Iowa across the Mississippi. Quakers, Methodists, and Baptists they were, used to toil and unacquainted with luxury. Many disliked slavery and had left their old homes more willingly because of its spread to their neighborhoods. They knew, moreover, that the worn red-and-yellow soils of their homeland contrasted sharply with the rich black lands above the Ohio. They were glad to leave behind the poverty and social conflicts of the South. But memories of home in a warmer clime, church ties, and distrust of the "queer ways" of new neighbors in the Northwest still bound them together. Something in habits and outlook born in the South clung to their persons. The food on their tables and the covers on their beds, like certain expressions in their speech, bore the mark of their origin. The Greater South reached well beyond Mason and Dixon's Line.[1]

* * * *

The story of the Cotton Kingdom begins with the agricultural depression which settled down like a permanent shadow over the Old South in the period following the War of 1812. Under the burden of taxes, competition with fresher lands, and poor farming methods, vast regions, where tobacco had once grown in Virginia, were being recommitted to the forests and their original inhabitants, the beasts; broom sedge and stunted pine, abandoned houses, half-clothed Negroes, lean and hungry stock indicated the hopelessness which drove young men, despairing of success, rapidly from the state. The failure of first efforts at improvement only deepened the gloom.[2]

Conditions were no better in the rice and sea-island cotton area of South Carolina. There "commerce, which once poured its treasures at . . . [men's] feet . . . [was] now driven from [their] . . . shores. Agriculture . . . scarcely afford[ed] . . . a bare subsistence." Plantations were "deserted and abandoned"; "poverty and embarrassment universally prevail[ed] and nothing . . . [was] seen or heard, from the seaboard to the mountains, but the signs of decay and the language of despair."[3]

In more modest North Carolina decline began at a lower level and sank to greater depths. Farmers there had never known completely satisfactory markets and the merchants at Norfolk and Charleston had taken commissions which might have builded home towns had nature given harbors. The state always boasted more of agricultural self-sufficiency and less of plantation economy. Slaves were confined to quite limited areas, home manufactories supplied most needs, and men and women were more inclined to superstition, assault and battery, and religious extravagances. "Hard times" had become chronic in the old North State since the Revolution, and citizens, little encumbered with worldly belongings, had been drifting westward at an alarming rate. "Times" grew even worse after 1815. Travellers saw lands "scarcely half under cultivation" worked only by black women and "faded mules." A legislative committee in 1833 declared "that agriculture [had] . . . ceased to yield to the landowner a compensation equivalent to the expense attending the transportation . . . to market." It reported that "the land of nine-tenths of the farmers of the State [were] . . . actually in market," and concluded that *Something Ought, Something Can . . . Something Must Be Done* to arrest the progress of our down hill march." The stage was set for North

Carolina to become a center of emigration comparable only to Connecticut in New England and Iowa in the later Northwest.[4]

But bad conditions in these older states were not the only forces operating to build the Deep South. The Gulf regions had a drawing power equalled by few Wests. Climate and soil, indeed, were strong magnets in days when a craze for cotton cloth had taken hold of Europe and she in turn had set about clothing the peoples of distant lands in her own fashion. Just what a peculiar fitness for cotton meant to this section, to the nation, and to the whole Western world few men could have dreamed. Yet the course of the Industrial Revolution in Europe and America was wrapped up in the forest-clad sweeps of central Georgia, Alabama, Mississippi, and the regions beyond. Potential cotton fields ready to feed the hungry new spindles and looms of rising factory towns! Arkwright, the English barber, Ross and his Cherokee Indians, plain farmers of the up-country South, rural peoples of old England crowded from their lands into new-forming towns—all tied together by the strange thread of fate. Great and little things about to make over much of the Western world.

* * * *

In 1815, the Cotton Kingdom-to-be was largely an untamed wilderness. The four civilized tribes—Cherokee, Creek, Chickasaw, and Choctaw—still held their lands against the press of advancing pioneers, and the scattered American settlements which were hurrying forward political organization, represented the frontier at its worst and best. The region was highly varied. Its coastal plain, cut by numerous alluvial valleys, was more fertile than that on the Atlantic side. The rolling Piedmont, broken by stretches of black-soiled prairies, offered its usual advantages under climatic conditions more favorable to vegetation. The valleys, plateaus, and ridges of the Appalachian system, which reached central Alabama and then melted into the clay hills and rich delta lands of the Mississippi, varied greatly in resources but contained valuable mineral deposits and numerous areas of fertile soils. Barren stretches of sand and pine, a goodly supply of tangled swamps, and an unusual number of great rivers carrying amazing quantities of water, completed the picture and suggested the possibilities for cultural development.

Into this great crescent-shaped region, its points in Virginia and Arkansas Territory, the restless American had already penetrated. The vanguard were men of the usual frontier type—a strange breed, at home only on the move, as crude as Indians and as capable of caring for themselves in the rugged fashion which the wilderness required. One hesitates to call them shiftless, because there was no need for sustained effort; or to praise their dogged advance, lest it consisted of nothing more than a desire to escape adjustments to a new social order. They squatted on public lands, traded illegally with Indians, hunted, and drank when possible. Shadows on the wilderness, they left only slight mark of their having entered it and even less record of themselves.

Behind them came the true pioneers, driven as often by poverty as by a restless spirit of adventure or a desire to better themselves by being early on the ground. They planted fields, pastured their cattle on convenient lands regardless of ownership, and moved about in quicksilver fashion in response to each new opportunity. They were eager for lands and always tempted by those which lay just ahead. The frontier humorist has told how their chickens, when they saw the wagons being made ready, would lie down on their backs with their feet in the air ready to be tied for the journey.[5]

Fresh land, or at least cheaper land, was the attraction which usually set them in motion, but, now and then, the chance of finding gold in the rugged up-country drew them on. In 1829 and '30 veritable "gold rushes" took place in North Carolina and Georgia. Their flavor was that of any mining advance. "I have heard scarce anything since my arrival, except gold," wrote a traveller from western North Carolina in 1829. "Nothing before has ever so completely engrossed the attention of all classes of the community in this section, since my earliest recollection. . . . Those who have been esteemed prudent and cautious, embarked in speculation with the greatest enthusiasm—bankrupts have been restored to affluence, and paupers turned nabobs." Boom towns sprang up overnight around a diggings and disappeared almost as quickly when strikes failed or news of richer ones came. Law was weak and temptation strong. The miners in one place were described as "a set of cutthroats and savages, with some exceptions." Gambling, fighting and even murder rendered the state of morals, according to a contemporary writer, deplorably bad. Foreigners were resented at the mines but Negro slaves toiled side by side with the once lazy, lounging whites, now stirred into active and manly exertion by the gold fever. Small farmers, raising a surplus of pork and corn for sale to miners, made the scene complete and as typically western as anything in American history.[6]

Gold was weak as a lure on this frontier, however, compared with lands fitted to produce the new staple which had already established its claims on the edges of the Piedmont. Cotton was everywhere proving its ability to produce wealth. It had already, in 1815, begun its westward trek.

The story of cotton must begin at the other side of the world. Cotton goods had been known in medieval Europe but were never widely used. The Moors in Spain had raised a limited supply and manufactured it into cloth, and Italian traders had brought small quantities back from the East to be made into coarse fabrics, usually mixed with linen. Such manufacturing had moved northward to Austria and Switzerland and had even found its way to England. But the output was never large. Woolens and linens dominated the Western textile industry and the production and use of the types of cotton goods now familiar were left to the peoples of India and the East.

English ships in the East India trade sometimes accepted cotton goods in exchange for their wares and carried them farther on to the Spice Islands, where they found ready sale. In time this became a recognized procedure and quantities of calico, purchased but not resold, began to find their way back to England, first as a superior kind of ballast, then as a regular part of the return cargo. Poor people found this material a cheap and satisfactory substitute for the more expensive woolens and linens. So wide was its adoption that by the end of the seventeenth century the older industries were demanding protection against cotton invasion. In 1721 the Calico Act prohibited the use of all printed, painted or dyed calicoes in apparel, household stuffs, furniture or otherwise.

That should have been the end of cotton in England. But it was more nearly the beginning. For cotton, always a great democrat, had allied itself with the masses of common men whose station and outlook in the Western world had slowly but steadily begun to alter. Signs of change were everywhere. Production, other than agriculture, was mounting. People, once more or less stationary, were shifting about so rapidly that they gave the impression of serious over-population. New mechanical contrivances, drawing labor to new centers, added to this impression and, on the other hand, emphasized the *new* things being done and the *new* ways in which they were being done. In a land where class and habit were strong, where sons followed fathers into business and custom fixed their ways, opportunities were unfolding for those who had long been outside the favored groups. Common men were finding open doors to wealth and influence.

Cotton cloth, as has been said, had first been worn in England by the poorer people. Its chief users in the early part of this new era were those who were rising in the economic scale. They, in turn, were able to seize the opportunities which cotton production, unfettered by all the traditions which surrounded woolen and linen manufacturing, offered in a period when the Industrial Revolution was about to reach its most spectacular expression in the making of cloth. Men unknown to the older capitalistic groups, unacquainted with those who dominated the economic order of old England, found in cotton textiles the chance to become captains of industry and possessors of fortunes. New techniques were here readily adopted—spindles, looms, new methods of printing, and the use of power. Methods in the manufacture of cotton cloth came gradually to typify the entire Revolution. The advances made in quality and economy broke down the barriers of caste in clothing and introduced a vogue for cotton cloth among all classes. This, in turn, reordered the whole market. And, as if this were not enough, Englishmen, building a far-flung empire and a world-wide commerce, carried European habits of dress widely about the earth.[7]

The call for raw cotton to support this social-economic revolution in the Western world fell on the ears of the restless upland southerner in far-off America. England's importation, largely from Brazil, the Levant, and the West Indies, had risen from about five million pounds at the beginning of the American Revolution to fifty-six millions by 1800, and was mounting rapidly. A few planters along the Carolina coast had raised cotton at least as early as 1778. The questions, yet unsettled, as to who planted the first seed and where it was planted, are not important; the significant fact is that the industry spread rapidly along the island section of the coast, giving an export of nearly eight and a third million pounds by 1801. By that time an improved strain from the Bahamas was producing a larger plant than had at first been raised. It yielded fibers some two inches long, easily cleaned from the black glossy seed. The profits were large. At a price of fifty cents per pound a single hand was at times able to clear $500 in a season. An average of from $170 to $260 might be expected.[8]

But the area in which sea-island cotton could be grown was limited. The islands off the Southern coast were not large and the plants would not grow far inland. Cotton which would grow in the interior was known, but the fiber was short and clung so tenaciously to the green seeds that it could not be cleaned for profitable sale. Inland farmers depended on corn and wheat and stock. They might have a few cotton plants in the family garden, but it was not worth while to raise more.

Eli Whitney completely altered this situation with his cotton gin, and a half dozen others were soon producing machines at a rate which destroyed any and every chance of a monopoly or the opportunity to keep prices high. Cotton once more offered its profits to common men. The short-staple variety would grow widely throughout the sections where small Southern farmers lived and on the newer lands of the Deep South toward which their faces were set. In the four years after the gin appeared the United States production of cotton doubled. The crop of 1804 was eight times as great as that of a decade earlier. The following year a traveller declared that a Tennessee family on four acres had cleared $212—more actual cash than most frontier families had formerly seen in a lifetime. South Carolina led production in 1801 with twenty million pounds; Georgia came next with half that amount. By 1811 both states had doubled these figures and had cut the price by more than half.

Most of this cotton came at first from smaller farms. White men, not slaves, produced it. Planters with fixed investments and established routine were slow to make changes. Even when they did, cotton seemed to give plantation economy less of advantage over the farm than did the older staples. Cotton again proved its democratic character. Tobacco, rice, and sugar had usually been associated with gentlemen. The areas in which they had been grown were limited and they had early been monopolized by the plantations with their slave labor. Cotton was no such snob. It shared the fields with plebeian corn and wheat. A few bales, sent off to a distant market, gave ready cash but did not quickly eliminate other products. Cotton fitted into any system and yielded profits impartially. It went along with pioneers or remained behind to widen its acreage. Such adaptability was essential, for the people among whom it had taken up its abode were a restless lot, bent on the gains to be secured by expansion in familiar neighborhoods or emigration to new ones. While cotton soon revealed its fitness for plantation economy with Negro slaves, it also continued to be grown successfully by small farmers in both the older and the newer corners of the section.

Three distinct developments were, therefore, under way in the great human reservoirs about to overflow, in 1815, toward the Southwest, from which the Government's Indian policy alone held back settlement. In the first place, the planters in older neighborhoods, employing slave labor, were turning more and more to cotton as a major crop. A few had even shifted location to gain the advantages it offered. Secondly, small farmers in the interior, once indifferent or even hostile to slavery, were now purchasing slaves in increasing numbers as they widened the acreage given the new staple. Cotton culture was enlarging the black belt and strengthening its hold in older regions. And, lastly, lesser men in the older states were selling out to those who could expand their efforts and were drifting westward. They kept to self-sufficient agriculture, but raised a few bales of cotton wherever they stopped, and thus unwittingly revealed the fitness of Western lands for its production.[9]

The important events which opened the way for cotton's complete occupation of the Deep South are linked with the name of Andrew Jackson. From Tennessee in 1813, he had launched his great drive against the Creek Indians which carried him into the very heart of Mississippi Territory and brought the cession of lands along the Coosa, the Alabama, and the northern border of Florida. Men from Tennessee and Georgia who took part in the campaign saw the rich soils in what was to be the state of Alabama. Many of them returned later as settlers. The land cessions drove in wedges from both north and east forming crevasses through which the rising flood might run. One day, in the United States Senate, twenty-four years later, a spokesman for the West, striving to expunge the record of censure entered against his hero at the time of the bank conflict, pointed to the almost unbelievable development of the South and Southwest, and asked what it was before "the victorious arms" and "the still more victorious policy" of General Jackson had done their work. He pictured vast cotton fields, an export "only limited by the wants of Europe, Asia, Africa, and the two Americas," an augmented shipping interest, manufactories scattering Manchesters and Birminghams over the Old and New World alike, an agricultural interest sweeping across the Mississippi Valley, all because of the cotton lands which Jackson had added.[10]

Jackson's "still more victorious policy," to which this speaker referred, had to do with the removal of the Indians from the region. When the state of Georgia ceded her western lands to the United States Government, the latter promised to remove the Indians as quickly as possible, but it did not make this clear to the Indians. Some of them actually thought they had been guaranteed permanent occupation. Efforts to teach them farming and to civilize them only strengthened this belief. The state,

meanwhile, adopted a liberal land policy, designed to hurry settlement, and set about organizing western counties with customary frontier haste. Conflict was inevitable. In the next two decades
Georgia constantly denounced the central government for its
delays. The Indians at first reluctantly ceded lands and then
refused to negotiate. Sharp disputes developed between the
President of the United States and the governor of Georgia,
heading up, after President Monroe had failed to adjust matters, in the state's open defiance of the orders of John Quincy
Adams. Governor Troup talked of the sovereignty of Georgia
and his duty to resist to the utmost any military attack which
might be made. There was talk of disunion, but Adams gave
ground, and the Creeks, the cause of immediate irritation, were
pushed aside.

The Cherokees, however, continued the struggle. When
Jackson became President, Georgia was trying to extend her
law over their territory while the Supreme Court of the United
States was inclined to take the position that the Cherokees were
a nation subject to the authority of the central government.
The discovery of gold in the region still further complicated
matters. It brought other court decisions declaring Georgia
laws void, and forced the state again into open defiance.

Jackson sympathized with Georgia. The case was quite like
the nullification fight in South Carolina, but a Western man
could not assert abstract principles when Indian rights were
involved! His terse comment, "John Marshall has made his
decision; now let him enforce it," was, in large part, responsible
for the frantic efforts for new treaties and the rapid removal
of the Indians to lands beyond the Mississippi. A state had,
with a President's connivance, defied the central government.
The last Indian barrier to the Deep South was removed. The
way for cotton was open.[11]

* * * *

When, in 1797, Spain evacuated the disputed area between
the Mississippi and the Chattahoochee rivers and the United
States began the organization of the original Mississippi Ter-

ritory, there were but two white settlements in the entire region. One centered about the village of St. Stephens on the Tombigbee, the other around Natchez on the Mississippi. The first contained, in 1800, some 1250 souls; the second, 7600. Both raised cotton and both had a goodly parcel of Negro slaves in their fields. They were, however, isolated communities, closer to the foreign ports of Mobile and New Orleans than to the nearest Americans in Tennessee. They were, of necessity, largely self-sufficing and somewhat primitive. The acquisition by the United States of Louisiana (1803) and West Florida (1810) improved their markets and stimulated their growth. So rapid was the increase in population that, in 1817, the territory was divided and Mississippi was admitted to the Union as a state. Alabama followed two years later. By 1820, Mississippi had a population of over 75,000 and Alabama of over 127,000.

Settlers poured in from the south Atlantic states along the old Federal Road which followed the fall-line through Columbia, Augusta, and Milledgeville to middle Georgia and lower Alabama. Some turned northwest at Augusta to enter the rich valley in the bend of the Tennessee from the north or to follow the Natchez Trail farther west. The Mississippi River carried its share from Kentucky and Tennessee and not a few who had come down the Ohio from the North and East. Some came by water from seaboard states to Mobile and New Orleans and then sought the interior. But, however they came, they tended to settle in neighborhoods already pioneered by people from their own localities and to give something of sectionalism to the new states from the very beginning.[12]

Natchez and vicinity, older and with more Northern blood, was always at odds with the lesser, but more populous, region to the east of it. Jealousy as much as convenience was back of the removal of the Mississippi state capital, first to Washington, and then to Jackson. North Alabama, about Huntsville, with Tennessee and Georgia beginnings, often took sides against the central areas of that state, where the Carolina-Virginia flavor dominated the Warrior-Tombigbee region, and the later Georgia migration colored the Montgomery neighborhoood. Geography and source of settlers were both factors in shaping the political story of later years.

Early settlers, as has been said, were usually small farmers from the Piedmont section of the older states. Even the first slave-owning planters seem to have come from that area and not from the coast. In 1817 a citizen from western North Carolina wrote of "the anxiety and confusion that pervades all ranks of people . . . to remove to Alabama" and again that "the Alabama Feaver rages here with great violence and has carried off vast numbers of our citizens. . . ." Western newspapers reported that, whereas the tide of emigration had formerly been "periodical" it had now "become constant and flow[ed] with increasing magnitude." Sometimes settlers went in caravans of covered wagons, eight, ten or fifteen close together; sometimes a lean horse pulling the single cart wended a lonely way. A few stopped several times before they finally located, cleared a patch, planted food crops and built a rude loghouse. Then they were ready to raise cotton.[13]

An interesting example of the early Southern migrant was Gideon Lincecum.[14] His family began its American career in North Carolina but drifted into Georgia before 1800, settling near enough to the frontier to find the Indians troublesome and retreat necessary. Gideon's father raised the first crop of cotton in Hancock County and carried it in a meal sack to the local store where he sold it for fifty cents a pound. He then began dreaming of better things to be had in Tennessee. Selling everything that he could not easily carry along, he started west with his family, now augmented by four Negro children. Twice he stopped for a season and raised cotton, the second time in the Abbeville district of South Carolina. Then he about-faced into Georgia, where the cotton crop was large and where little Gideon learned to pick the fleecy harvest, presumably alongside the Negro children.

A third attempt of the Lincecums to reach Tennessee ended at the Saluda River, where "strong drink" produced a runaway and enough damage to the caravan to necessitate the purchase of a farm and settlement for another season. The next move took the family back to Georgia, where they waited impatiently on the edges of lands just ceded by the Indians but not yet abandoned by them under the terms of treaty. Then a rush with "great numbers of people" as the Indians withdrew, the clearing of lands and more cotton, then another move farther south and another crop!

A little schooling, a quarrel with the father, a turn in the War of 1812, and marriage, brought Gideon to maturity and independent effort. He "planted 60 acres of cotton and 40 in corn" and, with cotton selling at thirty-one and a half cents a pound, had excellent prospects. But the Alabama, Black Warrior, Tombechee and Chattahoochee counties had all been acquired by conquest, so the promising crop was sold before harvest, and Gideon and his father were soon on their way west again. A short distance out the father, when "tight," bought lands and cattle. The family paused and pastured their herd, as did their neighbors, across the river on Indian lands. Meanwhile, Gideon, with better physical than mental equipment, taught school for the "children . . . born and raised . . . among the cows and drunken cowdrivers . . ." The Oklahoma "Sooner" was in the making.

The next season found the Lincecums on their way to the heart of Alabama. The father now had six Negroes; a brother-in-law, two; and Gideon himself, a like number. In six weeks they covered five hundred miles of wilderness and reached the log-cabin village of Tuscaloosa. Gideon sawed lumber and worked in a billiard room until his father pointed out the greater desirability of lands farther west. Then, blazing a trail through the woods and floating down the streams, they reached the Tombigbee River, built their cabins and began life anew among the few half-civilized whites and Indians settled there. They planted corn with a sharpened stick, sawed lumber for new settlers, traded whiskey, cloth, and trinkets to the Indians, and speculated in lands. They saw farms slowly appear about them and then small towns. Alabama was attaining stability. But Gideon was not content. After a few years he caught the Western fever and drifted off to Texas, there to end his days.

As typical of the westward movement into the Deep South

is the very different story of Thomas Dabney of Virginia.[16] He lived much later than Gideon Lincecum, in the period around 1835, when a great many Virginians were induced to remove with their families to the far South. He had been one of the most successful wheat and tobacco farmers in his part of the state. But the cost of living in the Old Dominion, for a man with a growing family and many slaves, was too heavy. Therefore, Thomas made a trip through a large part of Alabama, Louisiana and Mississippi, and finally bought from a half dozen small farmers a tract of four thousand acres in Hinds County, Mississippi. Returning home, he called his Negroes about him and offered to buy or sell where intermarriage on neighboring estates threatened to divide families. No one, he announced, was to leave Virginia who did not wish to do so. Such careful preparations for the removal were made that the long trip was completed in comfort and health. Old lands were planted at once and a hundred new acres cleared each year. Cotton crops ran a bale and a half to the acre. The Dabney plantation, with a well-organized labor force competing for prizes and assigned to tasks according to ability, raising its own stock and provision, and widening its acres as opportunity offered, became a model in the kingdom of cotton.

To settlers of the Dabney and Lincecum types must be added a third class, which constituted the largest group of all. It consisted of men who moved westward with their families to carve out of the wilderness a home for themselves and to rise on the opportunities offered to whatever of affluence their abilities or good fortune permitted. They moved about much less than the Lincecum family and somewhat more often than the Dabneys. They worked hard, acquired land and slaves, and knew an average prosperity greater than they had experienced in older regions. Some of them grew rich; some merely held their own. They constituted the great yeoman class who planted cotton when it paid, and who curtailed their crops in the interests of self-sufficiency when prices were low. Sometimes they were the bane of the great planter's life because he, with his larger capital investment, was forced to carry the load in lean years and meet their competition in fat ones. They built small but comfortable houses and often sold their improved acres at a profit to the planter who was expanding his undertakings. Then they moved along to lands less favorable for cotton, or sought a new frontier where they could start over with superior advantages.[16]

This process of consolidation produced what have been called the black belts. These were regions where Negroes, because of the dominance of large plantations on which there were many slaves, outnumbered the whites. Representing large-scale production, with larger capital investment and the economies of division and supervision of labor, the plantation tended to be more efficient than the independent small farm. When competition drove profits per unit downward in cotton (and other staples as well), or when soil depletion threatened, the plantation owners were able to monopolize the more favorable lands. Competing against farmers, they took the field; competing against each other, they tended to prevent diversification and to maintain an unbroken agricultural front. Where soils or transportation were unusually favorable, and those already in possession did not resist, the cotton plantation tended to shoulder the less efficient farmer aside and to absorb his lands. Some hardy farmers rose to the planting status. The wealthy slave-owning immigrant bought and consolidated farms. In time the traveller would be told that the first settlers had taken "the cream off their lands" and, being "unable to restore them by rest, manure, or otherwise," were selling out to the "wealthier planters" who were "able to live on smaller profits. . . ." He would hear that "the white yeomen . . . are driven west to clear and prepare the soil for the army of Negroes and Negro-drivers which forever presses on their heels, to make their industry unprofitable, and their life intolerable."[17]

* * * *

In such manner population spread from middle Georgia to the edge of Arkansas. By 1840, at least a million and a half people lived in the region where cotton would grow. They were, however, not all cotton farmers. The sugar industry prospered in lower Louisiana and corn and wheat and self-sufficing agriculture still played a vital part in the life of the section. But, in fact and in imagination, cotton was the great staple of the new day of expansion. Its kingdom lay without question across the Deep South. To the middle of the 1820's the old Atlantic coastal states led in production. In 1821 they raised a hundred and seventeen million pounds as against sixty million for the six Western states. In 1826, the figures stood at a hundred and eighty million as against a hundred and fifty and a half million. By 1834 the balance had been completely overturned. The older states had fallen to one hundred and sixty million pounds; the newer ones were producing two hundred and ninety-seven and a half million. Never again was the East to approach its rival in production. Cotton, in its new home, with Texas yet ahead, was entering the dizzy period when the output would double and treble, reaching at length the astonishing figure of more than two billion three hundred million pounds! By 1850, nearly 60 per cent of the slaves in the United States were employed in cotton fields.[18]

American cotton made up an increasing percentage of Great Britain's growing consumption. Whereas in the period from 1816 to 1820, the United States had furnished less than half her supply, by 1840 this country was providing more than 82 per cent of a vastly increased total. About three fourths of the raw cotton used in Europe came from the American South. Such demands swung the balance of national exports heavily to the Southern side. Men could soon exclaim: Cotton is king!

At the same time, home consumption grew rapidly as the mills at Lowell and Lawrence and Pawtucket increased their output. In 1831 they took less than seventy-eight million pounds. By 1850 they were using over two hundred and seventy-six million. Southern cotton was playing its part in altering the face of New England. Factory villages sprang up along her tumbling streams to furnish work for surplus children and markets for a sluggish agriculture. Black wagons roamed the countryside to carry girls down to the mills. Wealth fell into unaccustomed hands. The city came to rival the West as a land of opportunity. The Industrial Revolution took long quick strides to completion, its ominous shadow falling darkly across New England fields and harbors.[19]

The playing of such a role in remaking the Western world could hardly have left the Cotton Kingdom with normal attitudes. Even more than most frontiers it had cause for optimism, self-assurance, and a general disregard for the past. It was literally demonstrating a theory not found in the works on political economy. "Every cross-road and every avocation presented an opening—through which a fortune was seen by the adventurer in near prospective." Flush times were the rule, not the exception.[20]

Settlers wrote of cotton "nearly avaridge shoulder high," of loans bringing in "40 & 50 per cent," of weather "not warmer . . . than old Va." and requiring a blanket *always* at night! A traveller from Charleston to New Orleans and up-river saw "mountains of *cotton* on the wharves," "stores, ships, steam and canal boats, crammed with and groaning under the weight of *cotton*," the streets in the towns and the roads in the country crowded with *cotton* wagons, and *cotton* fields, white with harvest, stretching endlessly in every direction. Conversation everywhere was on the price of *cotton* lands or the staple itself. He was awakened at night by the talk of two young clerks who expected to win a lottery and invest the whole proceeds in warehouses and *cotton* to fill them. He could not escape the sight of *cotton* or the hearing of the word until he took passage on a northern boat bound for St. Louis. Even then his dreams were about *cotton*.[21]

The intense frontier spirit was even more manifest in matters of lands and finances. In the land sales of 1817–18 in Alabama, companies of speculators struggled madly for choice sites. Prices were run up to figures ranging from fifty to a hundred dollars an acre, with average cotton land bringing from twenty to thirty dollars. Intimidation was freely used and huge profits realized on resale to those not able to bid. In Mississippi, Robert J. Walker, soon to be secretary of the United States Treasury, openly bargained with squatters to refrain from bidding, so that prices would be kept down, promising them the chance to repurchase their improvements at low rates.

Those who refused were forced to pay as high as ten dollars an acre for their lands. In one case, at least, the public crier admonished the bidders to compromise among themselves and to stop fooling away their money![22]

Banking revealed the same temper. Both Mississippi and Alabama braved constitutional obstacles and economic dangers to charter more banks than conditions warranted and to take a hand in the business themselves. Bonds were issued without sufficient backing, loans made on frail security, and notes poured out with reckless abandon. A New Orleans paper later described the period as one in which:[23]

the poor man of yesterday was worth his thousands today; and the beggar of the morning retired to his straw pallet at night, burdened with the cares of a fortune acquired between the rising and the setting of the sun. While this saturnalia continued, no undertaking was deemed too gigantic, no enterprise beyond the accomplishment of men who had engraved plates, paper in abundance, and credulity to operate on. . . .

Under such conditions debts piled high and crashes brought repudiation and bitter condemnation of capitalists and investors. When outside creditors attempted to recover losses and throw them back on those whose optimism had blown the bubbles, one Mississippi newspaper showed its good Western debtor attitudes by saying:

The beds on which your wives and children sleep, the tables on which you eat your daily bread will be taken by the excise men for the benefit of those who [live] in splendid brick palaces, who sleep in mahogany bedsteads, eat with gold knives and forks, and drink champagne as the ordinary beverage of the day.

The governor of the same state condemned, in no uncertain terms, Baron Rothschild who held Union Bank bonds. He charged him, in whose veins "the blood of Judas and Shylock" flowed, of advancing "money to the Sublime Port" and taking "as security a mortgage upon the Holy City of Jerusalem and the Sepulchre of our Saviour." Scornfully he declared that it was "for the people to say whether he . . . [would] have a mortgage on our cotton fields and make serfs of our children."[24]

The Western character of the Cotton Kingdom manifested itself also in other ways. David Clark at Natchez, unashamed, wrote: "I have sprain'd my right wrist, and dislocated my left thumb in a hard fought battle with Mr. Daniel Hickey, whose Eye by the Bye I completely closed."[25] Street fights were sometimes even more serious. A running gun battle between two citizens on the streets of Cahaba, Alabama, led the editor of the local paper to address a "few plain words to the people" to the general effect that "guns and pistols . . . [were being] fired in and from the alley ways and streets of the town" so much of late that it was "hardly safe to go from house to house." Assault and battery were as common in this section as in any other West, and for the same reasons.[26]

Nor was the democratic spirit, so characteristic of all Wests, lacking here. When Thomas Dabney took his slaves to work at a house-raising in Mississippi the people resented the action. He was sent for no more. When these slaves were used to get a neighbor's cotton "out of the grass," that, too, was an offense. The recipient of the good deed explained that if Colonel Dabney had taken hold of a plough, and worked by his side he would have been glad to have his help, but to see him sitting up on his horse with his gloves on directing his Negroes how to work was not to his taste.[27]

Bitter dislike of speculators and complete approval of squatters on public lands were especially noticeable in this section. An Alabama senator asserted: "Those who settle upon the public lands . . . are not violators of law, nor trespassers. And I declare further, sir, that they are meritorious individuals, because they have been the pioneers to all the new settlements in the West and Southwest. . . ." The legislature of his state agreed with him, and prayed for a law which would protect the settler in the enjoyment of his crop and save him from the "Tender Mercies of the Unfeeling Speculator."[28]

Institutions, as well as persons, felt the force of frontier conditions. Slavery itself altered under their influence. The same factors which tended to "select" certain types of white men for westward migration operated with equal force on Negro slaves. The restless or rebellious slaves who refused to conform in the

older states, who showed the strong bent of their spirits by running away, were promptly sold down river to keep company
with the equally restless and non-conforming whites who had
preceded them. Early newspapers in the cotton belt are filled
with descriptions of runaway slaves whose backs were scarred,
whose cheeks and breasts were branded, and whose ears were
cropped. These were habitual runaways who were in the West
for precisely that reason! The abnormal number of cases in
which overseers and masters were assaulted or killed by slaves
in the new cotton states, and the existence of so many well-
known hideouts where fugitives congregated and maintained
themselves on the country for years at a time were also, in part,
the results of these causes. New arrivals, for reasons of experience, were generally viewed with suspicion by "home-grown
slaves" up to the very beginning of civil war.[29]

The hard task of clearing new ground and the lonesome
character of life in strange crude neighborhoods, moreover,
bore heavily on those who pioneered, whether masters or slaves.
Ambition, which sent men west to gain a quick fortune, caused
them to drive themselves and their dependents with abnormal
severity. Slaves found life and labor in new districts far more
severe than in the older ones because the master trying to get
rich was more pushing. Statistics are not available, but a comparison of advertisements for runaway slaves in early newspapers with those in later ones seems to indicate that attempts
to escape were far more frequent in the period 1825–35
than in the period 1850–60. Some of these papers printed three
times as many such notices in the early years as they did in the
years just preceding the war. The increasing standardization
of agricultural effort and the growing proportion of slaves
born in the region and associated through their lives with the
same group, black and white, probably account for the changed
conditions which these advertisements suggest. The difference
between the institution of slavery under frontier conditions
and the same institution in a mature society are also indicated
in this record.[30]

The Church in the Southwest also altered under frontier
pressure.[31] Methodists, Baptists, and Presbyterian groups pre-

dominated; Episcopalians took root in favored corners, and Catholics held on where the French and Spanish had controlled. Much of the early religious work was done by missionaries from the older South, but here and there some rugged pioneer assumed responsibility for breaking the spiritual darkness of the wilderness. Itinerant preachers and camp meetings characterized the earlier period; rural churches, where emotions found outlet, the later one. The Methodists, for instance, had, even in 1849, one thousand four hundred and seventy-six travelling preachers as against three thousand and twenty-six local ones. Primitive religious conditions existed in parts of every cotton state up to 1860, and the evangelical flavor characterized even the oldest centers. Conversion was a thing to be talked about on all occasions, discussed in letters; its exact date and place were remembered as one would remember the day and place of his birth. Preachers, as a rule, were unlettered men. Mutual intolerance among denominations was intense. New sects sprang up easily. Doctrinal conflicts flourished. Yet these struggling church groups early established academies and colleges to carry on the Southern educational tradition. They paralleled the developments going on north of the Ohio. They gave something of unity to a rising social order and linked it to the larger South of which they were a part.

Other institutions need not be considered in detail in order to emphasize the strictly Western form and flavor they assumed. Here was a region going through the typical Western experience of evolution out of frontier conditions into a more complex life. The mature pattern toward which this particular section moved was Southern. The ideal which it held and for which it struggled had been evolved in the tidewater valleys of Virginia and the fresh water swamps about Charleston. Its emphasis was on a rural way of life in which those who succeeded became country gentlemen. This social-economic evolution took place, moreover, under Southern weather, and the staple crop was one well fitted to both plantation and slavery economy. The result—a Western region slowly becoming Southern.

For one portion of the South that meant a new baptism of

self-confidence, a new aggressiveness, the addition of a coarser and more material outlook. It meant also a new rawness and crudeness. The decades which elapsed before war brought ruin were too few to produce maturity. The Southwest remained half-finished to the end. Yet the very speed and magnitude of these developments shifted the balance of influence in the South and changed drastically the whole Southern pattern. The older states, overshadowed by this greater region and drained for its building, tended to become over-sensitive and somewhat defeatist in attitude. They could not compete in production, in returns from labor units, in the use of capital. They had either to sink to a meager self-sufficiency or to follow the course already adopted in the Northern states. They could diversify and improve their economic efforts, raising special crops for definite markets, building factories and expanding their commerce in such ways as would weaken slavery and, in general, turn from accepted Southern ways; or they could accept a minor place in a South dominated by the Cotton Kingdom.

The years ahead would find the problem of sectional unity strangely complicated. Portions of Virginia and North Carolina would become far more like Pennsylvania and New York than like Alabama and Mississippi. Towns in the Old South would veer sharply away from the agrarian opinion. The Old South and the Lower South would differ as Easts and Wests were wont to do. Fireater and conservative, separate state actionist and co-operationist, Southern nationalist and Southern unionist would contend for leadership because a new South, a greater South, was rising to control.

CHAPTER SIX

THE NORTHERN ATTACK ON SLAVERY

REMOVING motes from a brother's eye is an ancient practice. The urge to make over other individuals and to correct real or fancied evils in society operates with unusual force in certain individuals. This used to be ascribed to a peculiar sensitiveness to wrongdoing—a willingness to sacrifice personal comfort for a larger good. Perpetual reformers, though resented as meddlers by those they disturbed, have been hailed as pioneers and martyrs who have unselfishly helped to usher in new eras and a better world.

The modern psychologist is somewhat skeptical of such explanations. He talks of youthful experiences, maladjustments, inferiority complexes, and repressed desires. He is not so sure about the sources of the reform impulse or the unselfish character of the reformer. The student of social affairs is likewise less inclined to grant unstinted praise to the fanatic and is not certain about the value of the contribution. He views him as a normal product of social phenomena acting on certain types of personality. He sees the triumph of emotion over reason in the extremist's course and sometimes wonders if the developments of history might not have been more sound without him. He talks with less assurance about "progress" in human affairs.

At all events, recent historians have been inclined to reconsider the part played by the abolitionists in the coming of the War Between the States. They have judged the reformer and his efforts to be open fields for new study. The old assumptions that the movements against slavery arose entirely from a disinterested hatred of injustice and that their results were good beyond question can no longer be accepted without reservations. Those who force the settlement of human problems by war can expect only an unsympathetic hearing from the future. Mere desire to do "right" is no defense at the bar of history.

* * * *

Slavery as a reality and slavery as the symbol about which sectional conflict raged for a generation were two different things. The first was a very ancient labor system, drastically adjusted to local American conditions, and one which may have been almost ready to break down of its own weight in one of the last corners left to it on the face of the earth; the second was the creation of inflamed imaginations which endowed the institution with all the ills possible in its theory and assigned to the slave-owner all the qualities and characteristics desirable in a bitter rival. The first was not a major economic factor in Southern life, as the record of free Negroes since the war has amply demonstrated. The second was an emotional influence which left few pages in the nation's history untouched from 1820 to 1860.

In the period before 1820 slavery had been sharply criticized by far-seeing men in all parts of the nation. Quaker groups, especially in Pennsylvania, Virginia, and the Carolinas, early and late quietly insisted on its moral weakness. The doctrines of natural rights and individual equality emphasized by the American Revolution increased the opposition, and unprofitableness in periods of depression after independence was won permitted open condemnation. In the Northern states, where slaves were too few to create a race problem and where white families were usually large enough to furnish a labor supply for small-scale effort, slavery was gradually abolished. Even in the South, where the institution was then localized, Washington apologized for it and Jefferson roundly denounced it. Teachers in Southern colleges questioned its economic value and its ethical foundations. Most Southern men spoke of it as an institution which they confidently expected to disappear in due season. They helped to check the slave trade and to keep slavery from the Northwest Territory. Many freed their own slaves; more hoped to do so at a later time.[1]

The much abused American Colonization movement was a sane effort to give practical expression to these sentiments. It recognized the race problem produced by manumission as the one serious difficulty in the way. It proposed to transport out of the country all slaves whom masters might free. That would solve the social problem and encourage further grants of freedom. The assumption, clearly implied, was that all fair men recognized the evil in slavery and that human beings could be relied upon to act justly in regard to it. Cooperation was a better way of getting results than angry attack.

The success anticipated for the movement was never realized. A few Southern states made generous contributions and prominent men lent their names to the cause. But only 11,909 immigrants went out to Africa and only 6,000 of these were freed for that purpose. Soon restless critics, impatient of slow progress and the lack of moral fervor, withdrew their support, and enthusiasm was further dampened when the spread of cotton took up the slack in the Southern labor supply. Enemies charged that the movement had degenerated into an effort to rid the country of free Negroes. A few denounced it as a proslavery program. Gradually colonization lost ground. A temperate policy which respected property rights and which at the same time pressed for freedom was open to attack from both front and rear. The slavery question was not to be approached with either sanity or moderation. The abolitionist and the extreme defender of "the peculiar institution" were to have their way with it.[2]

The abolition movement in the period before 1830 found its chief support among the evangelical church members of the older Southern states. As large numbers of these people migrated to western Virginia, Tennessee, Kentucky, and the southern part of the Old Northwest, anti-slavery sentiment tended to center in that region. In 1827, one hundred and six of the one hundred and thirty abolition societies in the nation were located there. They had 5,125 of the 6,625 members in all anti-slavery organizations.

The first periodical established primarily to discuss slavery was published by Charles Osborne, a North Carolina Quaker who had moved first to Tennessee and later to southern Ohio. The second was published in Tennessee; and the third, first issued in southern Ohio, early moved to that state. Benjamin Lundy began his work with the first of these publications and was the editor of the third, which had on its staff, after its removal to Baltimore in 1824, one William Lloyd Garrison.[3]

The Southern abolition movement, however, soon lost its force. The extreme position taken by Northern reformers in the 1830's stirred hostility and discouraged its supporters. Appeal to reason and conscience for freedom by gradual emancipation could be tolerated within one's own household; the denunciation of slavery as a sin, and the demand for immediate abolition, which Northern reformers were now making, could be met only by equal unreason. The effect of Northern interference on the Southern anti-slavery groups was shown when the Friends' Yearly Meeting in Virginia (1836) declared that such extreme attitudes as those being voiced in the North "had closed the doors of usefulness" to them in behalf of the slave, and that, while they could bear witness that a desire to emancipate was becoming more general in Virginia, they must now warn all Quakers against the abolitionists. A non-Quaker Virginian of the same period protested that the extremists had "created new difficulties in the way of all judicious schemes of emancipation, by prejudicing the minds of slaveholders, and by compelling us to combat their false principles and rash schemes. . . ."[4]

Such statements, however, should not be over-emphasized. The Denmark Vesey slave insurrection in South Carolina in 1822 and the Nat Turner uprising in Virginia in 1831 had greatly alarmed Southern slaveholders and non-slaveholders alike. Many associated these disturbances with the organization of abolition societies. Southern members of such societies, therefore, drew back, and resorted to condemnation of Northern extremists partly as a means of self-defense. After Garrison began his crusade from Boston, the Southern opponents of slavery grew increasingly silent. Only on rare occasions was a critical voice to be heard.

* * * *

Northern hostility to slavery was not widespread until after its abolition from that section in the period 1780-1804. A few critics had early spoken boldly against it, but there had been defenders as well. As early as 1700, Judge Samuel Sewall of Massachusetts had written a pamphlet entitled *The Selling of Joseph,* in which he drew on both the Bible and the doctrine of natural rights to condemn the practice of slavery. "He that stealeth a man and Selleth him," he quoted, ". . . shall surely be put to death." "Therefore all things whatsoever ye would that men should do to you, do ye even so to them. . . ." Arguments followed based on the fact that "since Liberty is in real value next to Life; none ought to part with it themselves, or deprive others of it, but upon most mature considerations." Sewall questioned whether the province was safe with so many restless slaves in it and closed his argument by declaring that "originally and naturally there was no slavery." The Ethiopians, "black as they are," are the "Sons and Daughters of the First Adam, the Brethren and Sisters of the Last Adam, and the Offspring of God; they ought to be treated with Respect agreeable."[5]

The following year brought *A Brief and Candid Answer* by one John Saffin, lawyer and slaveholder. He matched Scripture with Scripture, then asked:[6]

. . . What is all this to the purpose, to prove that all men have equal right to Liberty, and all outward comforts of this life; which Position seems to invert the order that God hath set in the world, who hath ordained different degrees and orders of men, some to be High and honorable, some to be Low and Despicable; some to be Monarchs . . . Masters . . . others to be subjects, and to be Commanded; Servants of sundry sorts and degrees, bound to obey, yea some to be born Slaves, and so remain during their lives, as hath been proved.

He argued that if slaves were to be freed

then the Negroes must all be sent out of the country, or else the remedy would be worse than the Disease; and it is to be feared that those Negroes that are free, if there be not some strict course taken with them by Authority will be a plague to this country. . . .

He concluded by saying:

It doth evidently appear both by Scriptures and Reason, the practice of the People of God in all Ages, both before and after the giving of the Law, and in the times of the Gospel, that there were Bond men, women and Children commonly kept by holy and good men, and improved in Service: and therefore, by the command of God, Lev. 25.44, and their venerable Example, we may keep Bond men and use them in our service still.

Here was the pro-slavery argument from the Bible, from nature, and from history. Evidently if New England was to be rid of slavery, climate would work the change, not principle alone nor the inability of logic to support the institution.

By the time of the American Revolution, for reasons economic and moral, the Northern states were ready to free their slaves. The movements toward abolition were always local in character; each state furnished its own reformers and made its own provisions according to its own best interests. Some provided for gradual emancipation; some, for immediate freedom. None of them faced either a social or an economic problem by its action.

These early anti-slavery movements had run their course largely before 1820 and were not to be directly connected with the Abolition Movement of Garrison and Weld. That effort had its origins in a later period and represented a far more complex set of forces.

*   *   *   *

The first indication that slavery might become a sectional issue appeared in the Congressional debates over the Missouri Compromise. Livermore of New Hampshire asked:[7]

How will the desire for wealth render us blind to sin of holding both the bodies and souls of our fellow men in chains. . . . Do not, for the sake of cotton and tobacco, let it be told to future ages that, while pretending to love liberty, we have purchased an extensive country to disgrace it with the foulest reproach to nations!

Senator King of New York went so far as to insist that "no human law, compact, or compromise can establish or continue slavery. . . . There is no such thing as a slave." His assault was so vicious that one senator alleged that King would not dare publish it "in the naked ugliness of its original deformity."

Southern men in turn defended their institution. Most of them could have said with Reid of Georgia: "Believe me, sir, I am not a panegyrist of slavery. It is an unnatural state: a dark cloud which obscures half the lustre of our free institutions." All agreed with Barbour of Virginia that the opponents of slavery exaggerated the evils in the system and knew all too little about it. "He has shaded it too deeply, with the coloring of his own imagination," Barbour said of one speaker. But a few men, like William Smith of South Carolina, "justified slavery on the broadest principles, without qualification or reserve." Smith declared that it was right and viewed it as a benefit which should be perpetuated.

Thomas Jefferson, from the seclusion of his mountain, viewed the controversy as "a fire-bell in the night." The use to which politicians in sectional conflict could put slavery had been clearly revealed. A grave national crisis had been averted only because the public mind was not as yet inflamed on the subject and complete sectional cleavage did not yet exist. It was perfectly clear, however, that back of the attack on slavery lay Northern resentment of Southern strength in national affairs. The three-fifths rule gave the South an advantage and the steady addition of new states from Jefferson's Louisiana Purchase added to it. The Virginia dynasty held on to its control while the Federal Party steadily crumbled. The panic of 1819 bore heavily on commerce and industry, while slave-manned plantations, seen from a distance, seemed to continue prosperous. Tariff legislation, designed to remedy such disparity, met increasing opposition from the South. Reprisal was in order.

When Missouri asked for the right to join the opposition as a state, the opportunity was presented to strike back, and that opportunity could not be overlooked. Well might the Fathers view the future with alarm.[8]

The politicians, however, were not destined to be the leaders in the great fight against slavery about to be launched in the North. Nor were the forces behind the Missouri struggle those which were to lift an abolition crusade to national importance and ultimately to precipitate a civil war. The new abolition movement was to be born out of an entirely different set of conditions, and expressed a far more profound set of attitudes. To understand it, a whole series of fundamental changes going on in the northeastern corner of the United States must be considered.

In the decades immediately after 1800 parts of New England and neighboring states underwent profound alteration under the impact of the Industrial Revolution. Up to that time the region had been made up of coastal towns, inhabited by venturous merchants and hardy fishermen, and self-sufficing farms, whose owners tilled the rugged hillsides and the more fertile hinterland. They supplemented agriculture with domestic manufacturing. Now the factory made its appearance. The making of cloth, and later of shoes and implements, passed gradually out of the home and into the hastily built towns which sprang up wherever water power could be found. Here and there industry invaded old urban centers, but people and capital tended to shift as needed to the places more favorable to new types of economic effort. The early New England factories centered about Providence, Rhode Island, but the center of industry soon shifted northward into Massachusetts, where Lowell and Lawrence and Waltham rose to compete with Salem and Newburyport, and where Boston took her place in the minds of New Englanders as the Hub of the Universe.[9]

In 1810, less than seven per cent of the people in this section lived in cities of 10,000 and over; by 1860, more than thirty-six per cent lived in such cities and the region could be described as one in which most people through investments, labor and consumption were linked to industry. Improved transportation and banking facilities, necessary for the production and distribution of goods in mass, helped give numbers and power to the urban centers. A new group of businessmen found opportunities in these new enterprises to reap fortunes soon large enough to permit them to intermarry with the aristocracy which trade in wines and slaves and other very commonplace things had earlier created.

The growth of finance-industrial cities, largely dependent on the outside for food and raw materials, opened markets for the farmers who in earlier days had had little incentive for improved methods and surplus production. An agricultural revolution followed. Farmers of enterprise and capital began to specialize their crops. Near the factory towns they produced increasing quantities of vegetables, fruits, and dairy produce. Travelers noted a greater beauty of farms and a higher state of cultivation in such neighborhoods. Improved breeds of stock were introduced and better farm machinery came into use.[10]

On the hillsides, farther away, beef cattle were fattened and driven to the Brighton market in such numbers as to excite the protest of clergymen whose services on the once quiet Sabbath were interrupted by the constant passing of great "phalanxes of horned cattle."[11] The sheep industry flourished in parts of the hill country less favorably situated. Men of capital bought the lands of the unfortunate and enclosed them for their flocks. By 1835 Vermont boasted more than a million head of sheep; half her people had turned shepherd. Western Massachusetts was not far behind. In some places there the farmers had so completely gone over to sheep raising that they were dependent on other states for their bread and pork. With these changes, the agricultural society prospered and the agricultural periodical made its appearance. The factory had remade New England's agriculture.[12]

These revolutionary developments, however, did not come without suffering. Many were crowded aside; others were crushed. The shift of activity centers and the increased use of capital in both industry and agriculture left old towns and isolated rural communities outside the benefits of the new developments. Even where old levels were maintained, people once influential found themselves overshadowed by the greater men and institutions produced by the new day. Thousands turned their faces westward toward upper New York, Ohio, and Michigan where lands were cheap and old crops and methods would still yield sufficient returns. Thousands entered the new urban centers where opportunity for energy and talent was equally great. Young people went first; their elders followed. Boston not only lured the ambitious youth, but soon drew the old aristocratic families of Salem, Beverly, and Newburyport as well. The West took few of wealth and fewer of high social standing, but it did, in some cases, persuade whole communities to abandon their native section. Parent towns suffered heavily and their bitterness and resentment kept pace with their losses. The coming of industry was not an unmixed blessing.[13]

Nor was all permanently satisfactory in the factory or on the new type of farm. Opportunity in textile manufacture led to overexpansion, and the panic of 1837 brought ruin to the weaker units. The reorganization and consolidation which followed, placed control in the hands of a relatively few capitalists. Favored communities outstripped their rivals. Labor everywhere lost ground. Wages were lowered, and when labor troubles followed, foreigners in large numbers found their way into the factories. The Lowell girl, who had excited the admiration of many a traveller, was replaced by the Irish woman or by an inferior type of native worker. Strikes and lockouts were of frequent occurrence. Paternalism passed. Capital and labor began to assume their modern attitudes and relationships. The politicians, meanwhile, both at the state capitals and in Washington, looked after the interests of the favored few and glorified the political policies which favored industry and urban development.[14]

Agricultural expansion brought even greater disappointments. Canals and railroads, which in the beginning promised only wider access to expanding markets, soon reached out into the rich, cheap lands of New York, Ohio, and Michigan. At first they brought back supplies of wheat and flour to help complete the agricultural specialization in New England. But the pioneer, carrying wheat, the first great frontier crop, ever farther west, was constantly forcing those immediately behind him into other lines of production. Before long the New York farmer had turned to beef cattle, sheep, hogs, and dairy products. He poured his surplus back upon the Atlantic coast in quantity great enough to satisfy all demands and at prices below those at which the stingy soils of New England could compete. Step by step the New England farmer yielded ground. He shifted crops. He tried new methods. He mortgaged his lands to the Boston insurance companies to get new capital. But his fight was a losing one. Only those unusually well situated as to markets for perishable supplies could hold out against the constant changes required by the continued spread of wheat into the farther West. A new restlessness developed. Writers spoke of the "moving, nomadic character of our population"; one of them insisted that "you will not find one in twenty who lives where his fathers lived or does as his fathers have done." The *New England Farmer* declared that it was "perfectly evident that farmers, with moderate means, must go down under this burden. They do go down by the thousands. And what is infinitely the most to be regretted, they go down in poverty. . . ." The city and the West enlisted new recruits. The abandoned farm became a permanent part of the New England countryside.[15]

Those who moved west to form a Greater New England in upper New York and along the Great Lakes also met conditions less than satisfactory. The frontier was harsh and exacting. Tasks were arduous; rewards not always in proportion to efforts. The restless pioneer, filled with hopes and dreams which he expected to realize by the exploitation of fresh resources and the development of a new society, found himself forced to return to a more or less primitive way of living and to fight his way slowly back to comfort and security. Legislation framed to give easy access to lands and to profitable markets met opposition from the older sections. New Wests, forming constantly out ahead in the wilderness, quickly threw their first surpluses back eastward, forcing agricultural readjustments upon those who had only just begun to prosper. Then the panic of 1837 struck. In regions where overexpansion had taken place the suffering was acute and long continued. In the late 1830's and early 1840's New York experienced all the ills of Western competition and production shifts which New England had known earlier. Prosperity came only at infrequent intervals. After 1845 Ohio and Michigan were in the same plight.[16]

Such were the economic conditions which combined with a stern and forbidding Calvinism to interfere with the pursuit of happiness in both the New Englands. Together these factors constituted a somber background against which sharp reactions now developed. These sometimes took the form of violent protest against existing conditions; sometimes of fantastic schemes by which perfection of society might be achieved. It was a day of ideals in every camp, of high-flying souls, of keener scrutiny of institutions and domestic life. Lowell humorously described the situation as one in which[17]

every possible form of intellectual and physical dyspepsia brought forth its gospel. Bran had its prophets. . . . Plainness of speech was carried to a pitch that would have taken away the breath of George Fox. . . . Everybody had a mission (with a capital M) to attend to everybody-else's business. No brain but had its private maggot. . . . Not a few impecunious zealots abjured the use of money . . . professing to live on the internal revenues of the spirit. Some had an assurance of instant millennium so soon as hooks and eyes should be substituted for buttons. Communities were established where everything was to be common but common sense. . . .

These stirrings were, no doubt, partly the result of spiritual forces; they could not have been unrelated to the great economic and social changes which were so fundamentally altering the lives and thwarting the purposes of this people. Filtering in from the Old World, transcendental thinking and humanitarian impulses furnished forms of expression to American spokesmen, but they did not supply the motives which made them speak. The injustice and inequality against which these men reacted existed in their own immediate environment. A reactionary Federalism and a repressive theocracy had long held the stream of New England thought within safe and accepted banks. The dawn of the new economic day, however, thawed out the frozen social-intellectual landscape. Every phase of life became more fluid. People moved about, ideas changed, forms altered. Old impediments and new ones felt the pressure of flood waters which left their banks and spread out into every lowland. Both destruction and new life were the result.

Reactions and reform efforts varied sharply according to the regions in which they developed. Near Boston, where the Unitarian revolt had already made liberals out of conservatives, the tone was decidedly philosophical. The emphasis was on man's innate goodness and his capacity for improvement. Sometimes the movement took the form of revolt against reason and asserted that truth is known by intuition and introspection, not by contact with material things. Sometimes it was highly individualistic, becoming anti-social and anti-governmental. At other times, it expressed itself in bitter hatred of the injustices and restrictions which increasingly plagued the individual. It set earnest men and women at the tasks of ending war, achieving temperance, winning women's rights, and building new communities where greater opportunities for self-expression and social justice might be found. Emerson, Channing, Parker, Garrison, Ladd, Thoreau, Alcott, and their kind were the leaders. A social order, sane and just enough to permit men to realize their potentialities, was the end sought by them all.[18]

A second type of expression developed in the rural sections and ran back from New England into the farther West where many lesser persons, carrying the imprint of Puritan training, had settled in the wilderness and had met there the streams of emigrants from other sections. In line with frontier ways of thinking, the purpose here was the practical one of bolstering up and restoring a faltering American Democracy. This included the destruction of all special privileges and a restoration of prosperity. It implied an acceptance of the Declaration of Independence as an integral part of the American political system and a recognition of the teachings of Christianity as binding on the government. Because it operated in frontier and rural surroundings, it moved much of the time through

religious channels. It was closely associated with the spread
of the Methodist and Baptist denominations in New England,
where the revival meetings lingered on in the regions in which
Jonathan Edwards had labored, and in New York and Ohio
where Charles Grandison Finney had given Calvinism a
warmer and more practical social turn.

For the same reason it became tangled with politics. Western men, especially, believed in the efficacy of governmental
action for the achievement of social and moral ends. Both
Church and State ought to serve democracy. Democracy was
one with the will of God and the natural law. It guaranteed
a moral order and when men or the misinterpretation of constitutions violated that order appeal to the higher law might
be made. Reform movements in such an atmosphere became
crusades. Even material problems had their moral aspects.[19]

Variations in regional and group expression, however, should
not obscure the larger fact of unity in the whole great reform
impulse, nor hide the fact that it arose out of apprehension
engendered by changes going on in the immediate environment of the reformers. The underlying idea, common to all
moves and found in all places, was that something hoped for
in American life was not being realized; that democracy—
meaning everything from the Holy Commonwealth and men
free from all kinds of unpleasant restraints to a high degree of
material prosperity for all Americans—was being threatened
by the rise of new and greater aristocrats and the imposition of
new and harsher restraints. The Industrial Revolution was
creating a new rich group and reducing labor to a new degree
of dependence. The spread of cotton was bringing into existence
a new and overshadowing power in a rival section. The urban
center, differing from the farm in material standards and moral
codes, lured the rural youth and exercised an increasing influence
in legislative halls. The Southern plantation seemed even more
extravagant and foreign. The acquisitive drive was growing
stronger, and the world and the flesh more enticing. Inequality
was becoming everywhere more apparent. The purposes of God
and of the Founding Fathers were in grave danger.

Men took part in a half dozen different crusades at the same time. It is sometimes difficult to tell whether Garrison was more interested in the abolition of slavery, or in peace, or in women's rights. The appeal made by a single crusade might be at once moral, social, and material. Gerrit Smith insisted that no man's religion was better than his politics. The course of development in different movements and the technique of propaganda employed by different groups were strikingly similar. The possibility of the fusion of them all into one great drive which fully expressed the determination to rescue American democracy from some all-embracing evil was present from the beginning.

The thoroughly local and immediate character of early resentments and reform efforts and their relation to democratic appeal needs further emphasis. As has been said, the aristocracy which was threatening American freedom and equality had been produced largely by the new economic shifts in the Northeast itself. The cotton planter was much more a symbol than a reality to most of them. The New England farmer saw, as the "only legitimate and fruitful parent of [his] ruinous debts and mortgages," "the excessive accumulations of property in the hands of a limited number of individuals." He bitterly complained that life in his own section was made up of "industry on the part of the farmer and pleasure on the part of the aristocracy." He rejected utterly the suggestion that his daughters help relieve the strain by turning to domestic service and declared that he would "sooner, infinitely sooner, follow [his] daughters to the grave than see them go out to service in the kitchens of those who by successful industry, by good luck, or possibly fraud, were in a situation to make hewers of wood and drawers of water out of their less fortunate sisters and brethren." A thoughtful observer in a neighboring state sensed a feeling of "envy and even hatred . . . in persons [against merchants] as strong as those of serfs in Europe against the privileged classes."[20]

Professor Darling, discussing Massachusetts politics from 1824 to 1848, says that

Jacksonian Democracy was essentially a rural party in rebellion against the domination of urban wealth and social position. . . .

Antagonism toward the city of Boston had existed from colonial times, but as manufacturing developed and the wealth of such financiers as the Lawrences and Appletons increased, hostility between country and city heightened. As these capitalists acquired commanding positions in the conservative party, rural elements which were irked by such accumulations of wealth gathered in the opposition and protested against "corporations" and exclusive privileges.

He also says that the Workingmen's Movement in Massachusetts was almost exclusively a farmers' effort—"a protest against the 'accumulations' in Boston society, the assault of 'country folk' on the exclusive privileges of the wealthy." Even in New York and Philadelphia the labor movements were class struggles —the poor against the rich. When the Journeymen Mechanics of Philadelphia organized, it was to ward off "from ourselves and families those numerous evils which result from an unequal and very excessive accumulation of wealth and power into the hands of a few. . . ." A New York group resolved that "the greatest knaves, imposters, and paupers of the age, are our bankers. . . ."[21]

The locofoco movement, which found its support among New York farmers and mechanics, was even more deeply concerned about inequality and privilege. Philip Hone once said that this group waged its fight entirely "upon . . . the grounds of the poor against the rich" and that its cry was: Down with the aristocracy.[22] A locofoco convention, held in Utica, New York, in 1836, condemned the Banking System because it was a "plan by which the idle few live by the labor of the many"; because it was an effort to "fill the coffers of the already wealthy" at the expense of the poor. It denounced the practices of the courts of law as aristocratic and declared, in a form consciously modelled after the Declaration of Independence, that "the foundations of Republican Government are in the equal rights of every citizen in his person and property, and in their management." The following year a locofoco committee declared that "at present, although we may live under the *cloak* of republicanism, we are in reality subjected to the worst of all tyrannies—an aristocracy of wealth. Our actual government, our real regulator of social rights and social intercourse, is *money*—the greater heaps ruling the less. . . ."[23]

Close association of democratic ends with morality and religion also characterized locofocoism. One contemporary called its devotees "these Methodists of Democracy" and insisted that they had "introduced no new doctrines . . . into the true creed" but had "only revived these heaven-born principles which had been so long trodden under the foot of Monopoly. . . ." The historian of the movement dedicated his volume "To a Believer who has rejoiced in the light of Locofocoism, as an outward sign of the inward light of Christianity." The *Democratic Review* declared that "democracy is the cause of Humanity. . . . It is essentially involved in Christianity, of which it has been well said that its pervading spirit of democratic equality among men is its highest fact."[24] Gerrit Smith's congregation at Peterboro in December, 1840, resolved, among other things, that:[25]

Whereas there is, even amongst professors of religion, a prevailing opinion that it is wrong to preach politics on the Sabbath. *Resolved,* That the correctness of this opinion turns wholly on the character of the politics which are preached: for whilst it is clearly wrong to preach anti-Bible or unrighteous politics on the Sabbath or any other day, nothing can be clearer than that no day is too holy to be used in preaching the politics which are inculcated in the Bible.

Smith himself believed that sound government depended on "the prevalence of [a] Christianity" which kept from office "anti-abolitionists, and land-monopolists and other enemies of human rights." To leave God out of a moral reformation was like enacting the play of Othello and leaving out the part of Othello. To Smith civil government was of God.

In the farther West this temper was revealed most clearly in the condemnation of speculators in public lands. A Missouri Assembly voiced a common opinion when it said that "Our Country is peculiarly the asylum of the oppressed and emphatically the poor man's home." One of its resolutions declared that "Every law . . . which opens to the poor man the way to independence . . . not only subserves the cause of

Humanity but advances and maintains the fundamental principles of our Government." Another Western spokesman assailed the speculators who were establishing a petty aristocracy
and choking the "tree of Liberty . . . so that her sons [could]
no more recline under her balmy shadows, but [were forced to]
. . . endure the scorching rays and blasting influences of the
slavery making idol of money tyrants." Yet another compared
them to the flies which came "upon the borders of Egypt."
Senator Lewis Cass of Michigan added the moral note by declaring that Americans should forget the profits to be made
from lands and "look to our duty as a Christian people." One
of Cass's colleagues in the House argued that the public lands
should go, as "God intended, and as good government and
good men desire they should go, into the hands of the people."[26]

* * * *

The abolition movement was part and parcel of this whole
great stirring. It was closely related in origins, leadership,
and expression to the peace movement, the temperance crusade,
the struggles for women's rights, prison and Sabbath reform,
and the improvement of education. It was not unrelated to the
efforts to establish communities where social-economic justice
and high thinking might prevail. It was part of the drive to
unseat aristocrats and re-establish American democracy according to the Declaration of Independence. It was a clear-cut
effort to apply Christianity to the American social order.

The anti-slavery effort was at first merely one among many.
It rose to dominance only gradually. Fortunate from the beginning in leadership, it was always more fortunate in appeal.
Human slavery more obviously violated democratic institutions
than any other evil of the day; it was close enough to irritate
and to inflame sensitive minds, yet far enough removed that
reformers need have few personal relations with those whose
interests were affected. It rasped most severely upon the moral
senses of a people whose ideas of sin were comprehended largely
in terms of self-indulgence and whose religious doctrines laid
emphasis on social usefulness as the proper manifestation of
salvation. And, what was more important, slavery was now

confined to a section whose economic interests, and hence political attitudes, conflicted sharply with those of the Northeast
and upper Northwest.

Almost from the beginning of the new anti-slavery movement, two distinct centers of action appeared, each with its distinct and individual approach to the problem. One developed
in the industrial areas of New England. Its most important
spokesman was William Lloyd Garrison, founder and editor
of a Boston abolition paper called the *Liberator.* Garrison at
first accepted the old idea that slavery was an *evil* to be pointed
out and gradually eradicated by those among whom it existed,
but he shifted his position in the early 1830's and denounced
slavery as a damning crime to be unremittingly assailed and
immediately destroyed. The first issue of his paper announced
a program from which he never deviated: ". . . *I do not wish
to think or speak or write with moderation.* I will not retreat
a single inch, and I will be heard." The problem, as Garrison
saw it, was one of abstract right and wrong. The Scriptures
and the Declaration of Independence had already settled the
issue. Slavery could have no legal status in a Christian democracy. If the Constitution recognized it, then the Constitution
should be destroyed. Slaveholders were both sinners and criminals. They could lay no claim to immunity from any mode of
attack.

The character of this movement and its leadership is strikingly revealed in an incident related by one of Garrison's travel-
ing companions:[27]

As we rode through the [Franconia] Notch after friends Beach and
Rogers, we were alarmed at seeing smoke issue from their chaise-top,
and we cried out to them that their chaise was afire! We were more
than suspicious that it was something worse than that, and that the
smoke came out of friend Rogers' mouth. And so it turned out. This
was before we reached the Notch tavern. Alighting there to water our
beasts, we gave him, all round a faithful admonition. For anti-slavery
does not fail to spend its intervals of public service in mutual and
searching correction of the faults of its friends. We gave it soundly to
friend Rogers—that he, an abolitionist, on his way to an anti-slavery
meeting, should desecrate his anti-slavery mouth . . . with a stupefy-

ing weed. We had halted at the Iron Works tavern to refresh our horses, and while they were eating walked to view the Furnace. As we crossed the little bridge, friend Rogers took out another cigar, as if to light it when we should reach the fire! "Is it any malady you have got, brother Rogers," said we to him, "that you smoke that thing, or is it habit and indulgence merely?" "It is nothing but habit," said he gravely; "or I would say, it was nothing else," and he significantly cast the little roll over the railing into the Ammonoosuck.

"A Revolution!" exclaimed Garrison, "a glorious revolution without noise or smoke," and he swung his hat cheerily about his head. It was a pretty incident. . . . It was a vice abandoned, a self indulgence denied, and from principle. It was quietly and beautifully done. . . . Anti-slavery wants her mouths for other uses than to be flues for besotting tobacco-smoke. They may as well almost be rum-ducts as tobacco-funnels. . . . Abolitionists are generally as *crazy* in regard to rum and tobacco as in regard to slavery. Some of them refrain from eating flesh and drinking tea and coffee. Some of them are so bewildered that they want in the way of Christian retaliation . . . they are getting to be monomoniacs, as the Reverend Punchard called us, on *every* subject.

The extreme and impractical nature of the Garrison anti-slavery drive served to attract attention and arouse antagonism rather than to solve the problem. It did, however, show how profoundly the conditions of the time had stirred the reform spirit and how wide the door had been opened to the professional reformers—men to whom the question was not so much "how shall we abolish slavery, as how shall we best discharge our duty . . . to ourselves."[28] Garrison may be taken as typical of the group. His temperament and experiences had combined to set him in most relationships against the accepted order of things. His life would probably have been spent in protesting even if slavery had never existed. From childhood he had waged a bitter fight *against* obstacles and *for* a due recognition of his abilities. A drunken father had abandoned the family to extreme poverty before William was three years old, and the boy, denied all but the rudiments of an education, had first been placed under the care of Deacon Bartlett, and then apprenticed for seven years to one Ephraim Allen to learn the printing trade. His first venture after his apprenticeship was over failed. His second gave him the opportunity to strike back at an unfair world. He became an editor of the *National Philanthropist,* a paper devoted to the suppression of "intemperance and its Kindred vices." This publication served also as a medium through which to attack lotteries, Sabbath-breaking, and war. A new Garrison began to emerge. His personality, given opportunity for expression, asserted itself. Attending a nominating caucus in Boston, he made bold to speak, and, being resented as an upstart, he replied to his critic in a letter to the Boston *Courier*:

It is true my acquaintance in this city is limited. . . . Let me assure him, however, that if my life be spared, my name shall one day be known to the world—at least to such an extent that common inquiry shall be unnecessary.

To another critic he reiterated this statement, adding these significant words: "I speak in the spirit of prophecy, not of vainglory—with a strong pulse, a flashing eye, and a glow of the heart. The task may be yours to write my biography."[29]

Anti-slavery efforts entered the Garrison program when Benjamin Lundy, the pioneer abolitionist, invited him to help edit the *Genius of Universal Emancipation* in Baltimore. Hostile treatment there, climaxed by imprisonment for libel, together with the influence of extreme British opinion, changed a moderate attitude which admitted "that immediate and complete emancipation is not desirable . . . no rational man cherishes so wild a vision," into the extreme and uncompromising fanaticism expressed only two years later in the *Liberator*.[30] From that time on Garrison was bothered only by the fact that the English language was inadequate for the expression of his violent opinions. Southerners in Congress were desperados.

We would sooner trust the honor of the country . . . in the hands of the inmates of our penitentiaries and prisons than in their hands . . . they are the meanest of thieves and the worst of robbers. . . . We do

not acknowledge them to be within the pale of Christianity, or republicanism, or humanity!

Hatred of the South had supplanted love for the Negro![31]

In such an approach as this, there could be no delay, no
moderation. Right was right, and wrong was wrong. The Slaveholder could not be spared or given time to learn the evil of
his ways. Action immediate and untempered was demanded.
Yet this was the same William Lloyd Garrison who, in 1877,
replied to Susan B. Anthony's request for aid to Women's
Suffrage:[32]

You desire me to send you a letter, to be read at the Washington
Convention of the National Woman Suffrage Association, in favor
of a petition to Congress, asking that body to submit to the several States
a 16th Amendment for the Constitution of the United States, securing
suffrage for all, irrespective of sex. On fully considering the subject,
I must decline doing so, because such a petition I deem to be quite
premature. If its request were complied with by the present Congress
—a supposition simply preposterous—the proposed Amendment would be
rejected by every State in the Union, and in nearly every instance by
such an overwhelming majority as to bring the movement into needless
contempt. Even as a matter of "agitation," I do not think it would
pay. Look over the whole country, and see in the present state of public
sentiment on the question of woman suffrage what a mighty primary
work remains to be done in enlightening the masses, who know nothing
and care nothing about it, and consequently are not at all prepared to
cast their votes for any such thing. . . .

Evidently circumstances alter cases in reform as drastically
as in other lines of human endeavor!

The second center of anti-slavery effort was in upper New
York and the farther Northwest. Influences from this center
included in their sweep, however, much of rural New England
and the Middle States and the movement found liberal financial help in New York City. Benjamin Lundy and other
Quaker leaders started the crusade, but it did not come to full
and wide expression until Theodore Weld, already the ablest
temperance orator in the Northwest, set about cultivating the
great field prepared for social reform by the Finney revivals.

Weld was, like Garrison, unusual both in abilities and in personal characteristics. He was much given to "anti-meat, -butter, -tea, and -coffee, etc. -ism[s]." He indulged in excessive self-effacement and in extravagant confessions of selfishness, pride, impatience of contradiction, personal recklessness, and "a bad, unlovely temper." Of his pride, "the great besetment of my soul," he wrote:[33]

I am too proud to be ambitious, too proud to seek applause, too proud to tolerate it when lavished upon me, proud as Lucifer that I can and do scorn applause and spurn flattery, and indignantly dash down and shiver to atoms the censer in which others would burn incense to me; too proud to betray emotions, too proud ever for an instant to lose my self possession whatever the peril, too proud to ever move a hair for personal interest, too proud ever to defend my character when assailed or my motives when impeached, too proud ever to wince when the hot iron enters my soul and passes thro it.

He wrote also of his contempt of opponents—"one of the *trade* winds of my nature [which] very often . . . *blows a hurricane*," and he listed by name those "who strangely and stupidly idolize me , . . and yield themselves to my sway in all confidence and love." He boasted of his daring and told of how as a child a tremendous thunderstorm would send him whooping and hallooing through the fields like a wild Indian. He had the Puritan's love of enduring; the saint's "right" to intolerance. He was, in fact, always a revivalist—a man with a mission to perform in the great West—"the battlefield of the World."

The campaign which he launched was but an expansion of the benevolence crusade already a part of the Western revival effort. As W. C. Preston said: "Weld's agents made the antislavery cause 'identical with religion,' and urged men, by all they esteem[ed] holy, by all the high and exciting obligations of duty to man and God . . . to join the pious work of purging the sin of slavery from the land."[34] The movement, as it developed, was generally temperate in tone, and tended to function through the existing agencies of religion and politics. Lane Theological Seminary, founded in Cincinnati to train leaders in the Finney tradition, became the center from which Weld worked. Here, in a series of debates, he shaped the doctrine of gradual immediatism which by insisting that *gradual emancipation* begin *at once,* saved the movement from Garrison's extremes; from here he went out to win a group of converts which included James G. Birney, Joshua Giddings, Edwin M. Stanton, Elizur Wright, and Beriah Green; and here he adapted the revival technique to the abolition crusade and prepared the way for his loyal band of Seventy to carry that crusade throughout the whole Northwest.[35]

There was, however, another aspect to the movement in this region—a very hard-headed practical aspect. Its leaders believed in action as well as agitation. And action here meant political action. Western men had a way of viewing evil as something there ought to be a law against. They thought it was the business of government to secure morality as well as prosperity. They were even inclined to regard the absence of prosperity as the result of the existence of evil. Naturally, therefore, in spite of the revival-meeting procedure used to spread the gospel of abolition, action against slavery followed political precedent. This action began with petitions to Congress for such a practical end as the abolition of slavery in the District of Columbia. When Southern resentment of such a measure brought the adoption of gag rule methods, the contest was broadened into a fight on the floors of Congress for the constitutional rights of petition and free speech. This proved to be an excellent way to keep the slavery question before the public and to force slaveholders to reveal their undemocratic attitudes. Petitions arrived in such quantities as to clog the work of Congress. A Washington organization for agitation and lobbying became necessary. Weld himself went to Washington to advise with John Quincy Adams and his fellow workers. Slavery thus again entered national politics, this time by way of the Northwest. Anti-slavery politicians, such as Joshua Giddings and Salmon P. Chase of Ohio, quickly proved the value of the cause as a stepping-stone to public office.[36]

James Birney took the next step. The indifference of old political parties to petitions and abolition demands gave rise to the belief that the slave interest controlled their programs. The conviction that the welfare of other sections was being neglected for the advancement of the South followed logically upon this premise. The slave power, said the abolitionists, had already destroyed the protective system "at the hazard, if not with the intention" of breaking up the manufacturing interests of the free states. The federal government had developed and protected markets for cotton "in all parts of the known world, while it studiously avoided doing anything to procure a market for the free products of the grain-growing Northwest." As a result wheat had been stacked seven successive years in the fields, and none sold. The United States had sent

six expensive embassies to make markets for tobacco. We had one embassy six years to get money for a few slaves wrecked on a British colony; but not one to find a market for the astonishing produce of the great Northwest. We've been thirty years toiling to keep a market for cotton; but not an hour for wheat. If our government was honest; if our statesmen had eyes, they would see that the most important benefit they could render this country would be to find a market for the produce of the Northwest. . . .

Anti-slavery must organize a political party.[37]

The Liberty Party entered the national field in 1840 with James G. Birney as its candidate. It was a protest party. In his acceptance letter, Birney declared that the country was in the hands of the slave power—"the North . . . a conquered province." Its honor, its influence and the real prosperity of the nation had declined in proportion to Southern rule. Tariffs, beneficial to free labor, had been abandoned; monetary affairs had become deranged; commercial opportunities had been neglected. Abolitionists could vote for neither Van Buren nor Harrison.[38]

Having issued this statement, the Liberty Party candidate set out for London to attend the General Anti-Slavery Convention of 1840. He carried with him to the English Anti-Corn Law League a mass of propaganda designed to aid in opening the English markets for the wheat crops of the Old Northwest. His general purpose was to secure the withdrawal of all British restrictions on American wheat and to encourage the growth in India of cotton for English factories. English commercial interests would thus be shifted from the South to the North and slavery in American cotton fields would be rendered unprofitable. Throughout the summer and fall, Birney waged his presidential campaign on British soil. Back home the dejected wheat farmers of the Northwest organized Anti-Corn Law Societies to help influence the course of English politics![39]

As economic rivalry between North and South increased, the anti-slavery movement gained strength and began to emerge as the dominant reform effort of the period. The motives underlying this development are partly revealed by a letter written by Joshua Leavitt to his friend Joshua Giddings in October, 1841. Leavitt spoke of Giddings' belief that the best policy for action was to aim "at specific points . . . which you deem beneficial to free labor or rather to the North, as a bank, tariff, etc." and then declared that his own purpose was to make opposition to slavery the *leading object* of public policy. "We must have a leading object," he continued,[40]

in which we can all harmonize, and to which we shall agree to defer all other favorite objects. It is vain to think of harmonizing the North in favor of a restrictive policy or an artificial credit system. . . . There is no object but slavery that can serve our turn . . . it is the greatest of evils and the prime cause of other evils. . . .

With the new growth and new importance of the movement, the technique of its propaganda also reached new efficiency. Never before or since has a cause been urged upon the American people with such consummate skill and such lasting effects. Every agency possible in that day was brought into use; even now the predominating opinions of most of the American people regarding the ante-bellum South and its ways are the product of that campaign of education.

Indoctrination began with the child's A B C's which were learned from booklets containing verses like the following:[41]

A is an Abolitionist
A man who wants to free
The wretched slave, and give to all
An equal liberty.

B is a Brother with a skin
Of somewhat darker hue,
But in our Heavenly Father's sight,
He is as dear as you.

C is the Cotton field, to which
This injured brother's driven,
When, as the white man's *slave*, he toils
From early morn till even.

D is the Driver, cold and stern,
Who follows, whip in hand,
To punish those who dare to rest,
Or disobey command.

. . . .

I is the Infant, from the arms
Of its fond mother torn,
And at a public auction sold
With horses, cows, and corn.

. . . .

Q is the Quarter, where the slave
On coarsest food is fed
And where, with toil and sorrow worn
He seeks his wretched bed.

. . . .

W is the Whipping post,
To which the slave is bound,
While on his naked back, the lash
Makes many a bleeding wound.

Z is a Zealous man, sincere,
Faithful, and just, and true;
An earnest pleader for the slave—
Will you not be so too?

For children able to read, a wider variety of literature was written. One volume in verse urged "little children" to "plead with men, that they buy not slaves again" and called attention to the fact that[42]

They may harken what *you* say,
Though from *us* they turn away.

Another verse suggested that:

Sometimes when from school you walk,
You can with your playmates talk,
Tell them of the slave child's fate,
Motherless and desolate.
And you can refuse to take
Candy, sweetmeat, pie or cake,
Saying "No"—unless 'tis free—
"The slave shall not work for me."

Juvenile story books, with some parts written in verse and printed in large and bold type and the rest written in prose and set in smaller type, were issued with the explanation that the verses were adapted to the capacity of the youngest reader, while the prose was well suited for being read aloud in the family circle. "It is presumed," said the preface, "that [with the prose] our younger friends will claim the assistance of their older brothers and sisters, or appeal to the ready aid of their mamma." Such volumes might contain pictures and stories from *Uncle Tom's Cabin* or they might consist of equally appealing tales of slave children cruelly torn from their parents or tortured by ingenious methods.[43]

For adults the appeal was widened. No approach was neglected. Hymn books offered abolition songs set to familiar tunes.[44] To the strains of "Old Hundred" eager voices invited "ye Yeomen brave" to rescue "the bleeding slave," or, to the "Missionary Hymn," asked them to consider

> The frantic mother
> Lamenting for her child,
> Till falling lashes smother
> Her cries of anguish wild!

Almanacs, carrying the usual information about weather and crops, filled their other pages with abolition propaganda. In one of these, readers found the story of Liburn Lewis, who, for a trifling offense, bound his slave, George, to a meat block and then, while all the other slaves looked on, proceeded slowly to chop him to pieces with a broad ax, and to cast the parts into a fire.[45] Local, state, and national societies were organized for more efficient action in petitioning, presenting public speakers, distributing tracts, and publishing anti-slavery periodicals. The American Anti-Slavery Society "in the year 1837–38, published 7,877 bound volumes, 47,256 tracts and pamphlets, 4,100 circulars, and 10,490 prints. Its quarterly *Anti-Slavery Magazine* had an annual circulation of 9,000; the *Slave Friend*, for children, had 131,050; the monthly *Human Rights*, 189,-400, and the weekly *Emancipator*, 217,000." From 1854 to 1858 it spent $3281 on a series of tracts discussing every phase of slavery, under such suggestive titles as "Disunion, our Wisdom and our Duty," "Relations of Anti-Slavery to Religion," and "To Mothers in the Free States." Its "several corps of lecturers of the highest ability and worth . . . occupied the field" every year in different states. Its Annual Reports, with their stories of atrocities and their biased discussion of issues, constituted a veritable arsenal from which weapons of attack could be drawn. Like other anti-slavery societies, it maintained an official organ, issued weekly, and held its regular conventions for the generation of greater force.[46]

Where argument and appeal to reason failed, the abolitionists tried entertainment and appeal to emotion. *Uncle Tom's Cabin* was written because its author, "as a woman, as a mother," was "oppressed and broken hearted, with the sorrows & injustice" seen, and "because as a Christian" she "felt the dishonor to Christianity—because as a lover of [her] country, [she] trembled at the coming day of wrath." It became a best seller in the most complete sense. Only the Bible exceeded it in numbers sold and in the thoroughness with which it was read in England and America. Editions were adapted to every pocketbook, and translations carried it throughout the world. Dramatized and put on the stage, it did more to make the theatre respectable in rural America than any other single influence. The fictitious Uncle Tom became the stereotype of all American Negro slaves; Simon Legree became the typical slaveholder. A generation and more formed its ideas of Southern life and labor from the pages of this novel. A romantic South, of planter-gentlemen and poor whites, of chivalry and dissipation, of "sweet but worthless" women, was given an imaginative reality so wide and so gripping that no amount of patient research and sane history writing could alter it.[47] Other novels, such as *Our World: or the Slaveholder's Daughter,* built their plots about the love affairs of Southern planters with their Negro slaves. Jealousies between wives and mistresses, struggles between brothers for the possession of some particularly desirable wench, or the inner conflict of a master over his obligation to his mulatto bastards, constituted the main appeal in such works. The object was always the same: to reveal the licentious character of Southern men, the unhappy status of Southern homes, and the horrible violation of Negro chastity everywhere existing under slavery.[48]

Reformed slaveholders and escaped slaves were especially valuable in the crusade. Under the warming influence of sympathetic audiences their stories of cruelty and depravity grew apace. Persecution and contempt from old friends increased their zeal. Birney, the Grimké sisters, Frederick Douglass, and many others influenced the movement and were influenced by it in a way comparable only to the relation of reformed drunkards to the temperance cause.

By means of such agencies and methods a well-defined picture of the South and slavery became slowly fixed in Northern minds. The Southern people were divided into two distinct classes—slaveholders and poor whites. The former constituted

an aristocracy, living in great white-pillared houses on extended plantations. The latter, ignorant and impotent, made
up a rural slum which clung hopelessly to the pine barrens or
the worn-out acres on the fringes of the plantations. Planters,
who lived by the theft of Negro labor, completely dominated
the section. They alone were educated; they alone held office.
Non-slaveholders were too poor to "buy an education for themselves and their children," and the planters, not wishing to
"endanger their supremacy," refused to establish public schools.
Few poor whites could either read or write. They gained their
opinions and their principles from "stump speeches and tavern
conversations." They were "absolutely in the slaveholder's
power." He sent "them to the polls to vote him into office and
in so doing to vote down their own rights and interests. . . ."
They knew "no more what they [were] about, than so many
children or so many Russian serfs. . . ."[49]

Social-economic conditions in the South were described as
tumble-down and backward. The slave, lacking the incentive
of personal gain, was inefficient. The master, ruined by power,
self-indulgence, and laziness, was incapable of sound management. James Birney described the section as one[50]

whose Agriculture is desolation—whose Commerce is mainly confined
to a crazy wagon and half fed team of oxen or mules as a means of
carrying it on—whose manufacturing "Machinery" is limited to the
bones and sinews of reluctant slaves—whose currency is individual notes
always to *be* paid (it may be at some broken bank) and mortgages on
men and women and children who may run away or die, and on land,
which without them is of little value. . . .

Others went so far as to charge the panic of 1837 to Southern
profligacy. "The existence of Slavery," resolved the American
Anti-Slavery Society in 1840, "is the grand cause of the pecuniary embarrassments of the country; and . . . no real or permanent relief is to be expected . . . until the total abolition of that
execrable system." Joshua Leavitt called the slave system
"a bottomless gulf of extravagance and thriftlessness." Another explained its "withering and impoverishing effect by
the fact that it was the "rule of violence and arbitrary will.

... It would be quite in character with its theory and practice," he said, "if slave-drivers should refuse to pay their debts and meet the sheriff with dirk and pistol." Leavitt estimated that the South had "taken from the North, within five years, more than $100,000,000, by notes which will never be paid," and quoted an English writer to the effect that "planters are always in debt. The system of society in a slaveholding community is such as to lead to the contraction of debt, which the system itself does not furnish the means of paying. . . ."[51]

Nor did the Southern shortcomings, according to the anti-slavery view, end with things material. Moral weaknesses were even more offensive. Sexual virtue was scarcely known. "The Slave States," wrote an abolitionist, "are Sodoms, and almost every village family is a brothel." Another writer declared that "in the slaveholding settlements of Middle and Southern Mississippi . . . there [was] not a virtuous young man of twenty years of age." "To send a lad to a male academy in Mississippi," he said, "is moral murder."[52] An anti-slavery pamphlet told of "a million and a half of slave women, some of them without even the tinge of African blood . . . given up a lawful prey to the unbridled lusts of their masters." Another widely circulated tract described a slave market in which one dealer "devoted himself exclusively to the sale of young mulatto women." The author pictured the sale of "the most beautiful woman I ever saw," without "*a single trace of the African about her features*" and with "a pair of eyes that pierced one through and through" to "one of the most lecherous-looking old brutes" that he had ever seen. The narrative closed with the shrieking appeal: "God shield the helpless victim of that bad man's power—it may be, ere now, that bad man's lust!" The conclusion was inescapable. Slavery and unrestrained sexual indulgence at Negro expense were inseparable.[53]

In such a section and in the hands of such men, abolitionists assumed that slavery realized its most vicious possibilities. Anti-slavery men early set themselves to the task of collecting stories of cruelty. These were passed about from one to another, often gaining in ferocity as they travelled. Weld gathered them together in a volume entitled *American Slavery As It Is* and scattered them broadcast over the North. The annual reports of the anti-slavery societies, their tracts and periodicals, also revelled in atrocities, asking no more proof of their absolute truth than the word of a fellow fanatic.[54]

The attempt to picture slavery "as it was," therefore, came to consist almost entirely of a recital of brutalities. Now and then a kind master and seemingly contented slaves were introduced for the purpose of contrast—as a device to deepen shadows. But, as a rule, Southerners, according to these tracts, spent their time in idleness broken only by brutal cock-fights, gander pullings, and horse races so barbarous that "the blood of the tortured animal drips from the lash and flies at every leap from the stroke of the rowel." Slavery was one continual round of abuse. The killing of a slave was a matter of no consequence. Even respectable ladies might cause "several to be *whipped to death*." Brandings, ear cropping, and body-maiming were the rule. David L. Child honestly declared: "From all that I have read and heard upon the subject of whipping done by masters and overseers to slaves . . . 1 have come to the conclusion that some hundreds of *cart whips* and cowskin instruments, which I am told make the skin fly like feathers, and cut frequently to the bone, are in *perpetual daily motion* in the slave states." John Rankin told of Negroes stripped, hung up and stretched and then "whipped until their bodies [were] covered with blood and mangled flesh," some dying "under the lash, others linger[ing] about for a time, and at length die[ing] of their *wounds*. . . ."[55] The recital was indeed one of "*groans, tears, and blood.*"

To abuse was added other great wrongs. Everywhere slaves were overworked, underfed, and insufficiently clothed and sheltered. Family ties were cut without the slightest regard for Negro feelings—infants were torn from the mother's breast, husbands separated from their wives and families. Marriage was unknown among slaves, and the right to worship God generally denied. Strangely enough, little was said of slave-breeding for market. That charge was largely left to the politicians of the next decades and to the historians of a later day.

Two principal assumptions stood out in this anti-slavery indictment of the slaveholder. He was, in the first place, the arch-aristocrat. He was the great enemy of democracy. He was un-American, the oppressor of his fellow men, the exploiter of a weaker brother. Against him could be directed all the complaints and fears engendered by industrial captains and land speculators. He, more than any other aristocrat, threatened to destroy the American democratic dream.

In the second place, he was a flagrant sinner. His self-indulgence was unmatched. His licentious conduct with Negro women, his intemperance in the use of intoxicating liquors, his mad dueling, and his passion for war against the weak were enough to mark him as the nation's moral enemy number one! The time for dealing moderately had passed. Immediate reform was imperative.

Thus it was that the slaveholder began to do scapegoat service for all aristocrats and all sinners. To him were transferred resentments and fears born out of local conditions. Because it combined in itself both the moral and the democratic appeal, and because it coincided with sectional rivalry, the abolition movement gradually swallowed up all other reforms. The South became the great object of all efforts to remake American society. Against early indifference and later persecution, a handful of deadly-in-earnest men and women slowly built into a section's consciousness the belief in a Slave Power. To the normal strength of sectional ignorance and distrust they added all the force of Calvinistic morality and American democracy and thereby surrounded every Northern interest and contention with holy sanction and reduced all opposition to abject depravity. When the politician, playing his risky game, linked expansion and slavery, Christian common folk by the thousands, with no great personal urge for reforming, accepted the Abolition attitudes toward both the South and slavery. Civil war was then in the making.

CHAPTER SEVEN

THE SOUTHERN DEFENSE OF SLAVERY

AMERICAN Negro slavery was first justified on the grounds of necessity. Opportunity on the American continent encouraged men to strike out for themselves. Few were willing to work for others. Without forced labor, slavery advocates insisted, progress was impossible. Free men could not push back the wilderness single-handed. Swamp and heat increased the difficulties and encouraged the use of Negroes. The black man was immune to malaria and flourished under a blazing sun. The production of tobacco, rice, cotton, and sugar required more of grinding toil than white settlers could endure. If men were to enjoy the great blessings which America had to bestow, it seemed that they must acquire Negroes and use them under the traditional system of slavery. The opportunity to receive Christian instruction and to come in touch with a higher civilization was compensation enough to the slave for his temporary loss of freedom.

Such a justification lost its force when economic pressure lessened. In periods of depression the institution of slavery was vulnerable to the moral thrusts of the Quakers and to the political arguments of those who emphasized the natural rights philosophy. Anthony Benezet insisted that those who bore in mind the Golden Rule could "never think of bereaving [their] fellow creatures of that valuable blessing, liberty, nor endure to grow rich by their bondage." Arthur Lee declared "that the bondage . . . imposed on the Africans [was] absolutely repugnant to justice . . . inconsistent with civil policy . . . shocking to humanity . . . [and] abhorrent utterly from the Christian religion." Jefferson thought its "abolition . . . the greatest object of desire . . ." and Thomas Paine believed that the government "should, in justice, set [slaves] free and punish those who [held] them in slavery."[1]

The reply to such early criticism was halting and somewhat vague. It consisted of references to the Scriptures and to Bible times when Abraham and other worthies held slaves, and of a "realistic statement of the observable facts which demonstrated an actual inequality in nature." The Declaration of Independence was dismissed as an overindulgence in French philosophy by the youthful and too enthusiastic Jefferson; it had no application to social realities. The charge that "holding . . . human flesh in bondage" was a crime met flat denial and a quick insistence that slavery was nothing more than a political evil. Even at that time it was permissible to point out the fact that New England traders had brought the slaves and English laws had forced their retention. Senator Smith of South Carolina observed that no persons were "more apt to remonstrate against the crying sin, slavery, than such as [had] just sold off their stock of Negroes, and vested the price in bank stock."[2]

The defense continued to be half apologetic as long as the attack was not aggressive. The few who chose to speak in slavery's favor were wont to tell of the great benefits bestowed on the Negro and of their own worries as masters. Sympathy, they implied, was deserved by the owner rather than the slave. Most slave-owners, meanwhile, went on undisturbed by questionings about their institution, accepting it as a matter of course and probably thinking it a practical good regardless of what their religion or their patriotism required them to say on Sunday or on the Fourth of July.

A turning point came, however, with the 1820's. The Vesey uprising in South Carolina and the Northern attacks on slavery in the Missouri Compromise debates unquestionably brought home to Southern men the dangers lurking in unrestrained criticism. The open hostility to slavery within the Southern states themselves was even more alarming. Generally combined with political unrest and sectional bitterness, it threatened to produce serious consequences in the form of unfriendly taxation if not of gradual emancipation. Long before the Northern attack on slavery required an answer, the situation at home demanded action. Serious agricultural depression, with resulting heavy emigration, combined with dissatisfaction over representation, the franchise, and inadequate transportation and educational facilities to produce, in areas where slaves were few, serious unrest and open censure of existing controls. The old order, political and social, was required to justify itself. Slavery was the obviously weak point in its armor.

To check local aggression, even more than to meet Northern criticism, the pro-slavery argument was thus begun. Hostility at home made outside attacks dangerous. South Carolinians, who were the first to speak, struck at Northern opposition, but answered Carolina opponents as well. Professor Thomas Dew's great defense of slavery, which came a decade later, was produced at the request of the Virginia legislature whose Western members had just given "the peculiar institution" an unmerciful drubbing. Dew framed his argument to check his fellow Virginians, not to refute William Lloyd Garrison, as writers have usually assumed. Dew, in turn, was answered by "A Virginian." The struggle was strictly a family affair.[3]

The Virginia dispute was more extreme than that in other Southern states, but it was not unique. The North Carolina attack on slavery was just as harsh and even more open and widespread. Quakers and Methodists, of whom the modest Old North State had many, early denounced the holding of men in bondage. Thousands of the members of these denominations moved to Western states but opposition did not end with their departure. In 1816 the Legislature called upon Congress to set aside territory on the Pacific coast as a colony for emancipated "persons of colour," and soon after that date the American Colonization Society had eleven auxiliary societies in the state. Agitation increased steadily throughout the '20's. It was frequently tangled with the sectional grievances which culminated in the Constitutional Convention of 1835. Dennis Heartt spoke of the deteriorating effects of slavery and called it "a misfortune of greatest magnitude." Doctor R. H. Helme ascribed the backward condition of agriculture to its presence and Judge William Gaston, addressing the graduating class of the University of North Carolina in 1832, told his listeners that they could not with impunity longer neglect the "extirpation of the worst evil that affects the southern part of our Confederacy." Anti-slavery lecturers went about the state reasoning with slaveholders on the great evil. Large assemblies listened to "the testimony of Truths proclaimed against it." Congressman J. H. Bryan even "cherished the hope" that he might "settle in some more healthful clime & out of the reach of the moral contagion & danger of slavery...."[4]

Criticism in South Carolina at this time was less open. It cropped up occasionally in the long and savage conflict over restricting the slave trade. Its existence was clearly implied in the aggressive hostility shown toward the Colonization Society. There was more than a hint of it in the sharp lines drawn between the nullifiers, who came from parishes having a majority of slaves, and their opponents, who lived in districts where the small white farmers predominated. Theodore D. Jervey, after a careful study of the field, concludes that criticism of slavery was deliberately omitted from the published reports of speeches made by such leaders as Robert Barnwell and insists that, in the "thirty years of unavailing effort" against importing slaves, a "strong minority" opposed "Calhoun's most unwise view that the blacks furnished 'the best substratum of population, upon which great and flourishing Commonwealths may be most easily and safely reared.' "[5]

Anti-slavery sentiment in Georgia advanced steadily from the adoption of the Federal Constitution through the 1820's. Not even the expansion of cotton production affected it. One of Georgia's congressmen publicly expressed himself as "desirous of seeing the Negroes set free" and the strongest newspaper in the Commonwealth declared: "There is not a single editor in the State who dares advocate slavery as a principle." Colonization efforts met generous response in the early period and four branches of the American Colonization Society were still in existence in the state in 1832. There was need in Georgia, as in the other states of the Old South, for stubborn defense of the peculiar institution.[6]

The defense of slavery which developed in the South in the 1820's came, consequently, from the coastal sections of the older states. Since its purpose was, in part, to bolster up a slipping political-social order, justification for the slave system was found in the Constitution, in nature, and in the moral law. The tone of argument was moderate; its appeal was to reason rather than to emotion. Sectional hostility, while present, did not constitute a major weapon. Race fears and the assumption of a superior Southern civilization were only mildly suggested.

Senator William Smith of South Carolina launched this defense movement with his speeches on the Missouri question. He justified slavery on the broadest principles, without qualification or reserve, and said that he expected it to be perpetuated. In a speech on the recovery of fugitives, he ascribed Negro slavery to the curse of Ham and declared that Thomas Jefferson's hostility to the institution belonged to his youth and passed with his maturity. Others, in the Missouri debates, denied that Congress had the Constitutional right to legislate on the subject of slavery. A few even ventured a comparison of slave and free societies, favorable to the former. All except Senator Smith permitted a note of apology to creep into their statements. The opponents of slavery appeared to be far more certain of their position and far more confident of general approval than its defenders.[7]

But this apologetic tone disappeared abruptly when Edwin C. Holland and a group of South Carolina planters issued "A Refutation of the Calumnies against the Southern and Western States Respecting the Institution and Existence of Slavery among Them" (1822).[8] These writers lashed out sharply at those "Northern and Eastern Sections" which had grown rich on the slave trade and which now misrepresented the condition of the slave. They denounced the "hostile and unfriendly spirit with which the most vital interests of the people of the South and West were canvassed and discussed." They ascribed the attack on established constitutional rights to the "intemperate zeal of a few, or the profligate ambition of the many." With rising emotion, they asked: Why should a people so "totally ignorant of the actual state and character of [the] Negro Population" as to "represent the condition of their bondage as a perpetual revolution of labor and severity" be permitted to visit the South "with the Sacred Volume of God in one hand" and with "the fire-brands of discord and destruction" in the other?

Holland and his collaborators presented a straightforward statement of facts. Slavery was a very old institution. It had existed among the Romans and the Jews. It had played its part in those "bright and sunny periods of history when literature and science poured out their full radiance . . ." and it had been sanctioned by the Word of God. The hot climate and swampy character of the South Carolina and Georgia low country, where rice and sea-island cotton were grown, were "inconceivably hostile" to the white man's constitution. The African throve under these conditions and his immunity to malarial diseases made possible the production of these "useful article[s] of food and commerce."

To the "foul slander" of abuse and "total disregard . . . to [the Negro's] physical comforts and general happiness," an indignant denial was entered. Southerners were both Christian and humane. The slave was fully protected from abuse both by law and by public sentiment. He was far better off than "the poor laboring class of people of any Government on earth. . . ." That there might be no room for doubt on this point a group of planters, whose veracity could not be questioned, had been asked to describe the management and treatment of slaves on their own plantations. The information thus secured and presented in the tract showed that the slaves were well fed, abundantly clothed and sheltered, were not overworked, and were not abused.

The striking thing about Holland's pamphlet is its tone. The writers were indignant at false accusations. Those who had spoken before them were ignorant of the facts. They should be checked. Honest and reasonable people needed only to be told the truth. In this spirit sound and reliable information was provided.

The following year, 1823, Richard Furman, as president of the Baptist State Convention, addressed the governor of South Carolina on the subject.[9] The Convention was obviously stirred by the recent slave insurrection and prefaced its communication with a warning to Negroes regarding the certain failure of all revolts. It spoke because "certain writers on politics, morals and religion, and some of them highly respectable," had "advanced positions, and inculcated sentiments, very unfriendly to the principles and practice of holding slaves. . . ." This, the Convention held, disturbed the peace, infringed on rights, and produced greater severity in the treatment of Negroes. The Church should speak out and clarify issues. The right of holding slaves was "clearly established in the Holy Scripture, both by precept and example." History demonstrated its value. The polished Greeks and the powerful Romans who succeeded them held slaves, and when many of the latter were converted to Christianity by the Apostles themselves the relationship, as masters and slaves, was not dissolved. Slavery did not necessarily imply injustice and cruelty. A bond-servant might be treated with justice and humanity; the master might be the guardian and even father of his slaves. Whereas, in a "free community by taxes, benevolent institutions, lettering houses and penitentiaries," the poor, the children, the aged, the sick, the disabled, and the unruly were objects of public care, they were, under slavery, the responsibility of those who benefited by their future or past labor.

As to the injustice of depriving the Negro of his freedom, the Convention pointed out that many had been slaves in Africa before coming to America. They were ignorant and unfitted "in their present state . . . to enjoy liberty." As slaves in America, they could be, and were being, Christianized. Their social-economic status was equal if not superior to that of the poor "in countries reported free." True, some masters were cruel. So were some magistrates, husbands and fathers. But this did "not prove that magistracy, the husband's right to govern, and parental authority [were] unlawful and wicked." Some day also the state of the poor, the ignorant and the oppressed of every description and of every country might be meliorated —the free might be free indeed, and happy.

The next few years brought more pamphlets and a broadening defense. Whitemarsh Seabrook and Robert Turnbull both condemned the Colonization Society's efforts and urged slaveholders to correct the false impressions of slave practices circulated by its agents. The venerable Thomas Cooper, contributed by English oppression to America and by Virginia orthodoxy to South Carolina, added the great weight of his prestige to the argument. He asserted frankly that slavery was nowhere forbidden in the Bible, and insisted that the slave's condition in America compared most favorably with that of natives in Africa or laborers in industrial England. Freedom would only bring idleness. Edmund Brown went a step further and called slavery "the stepping ladder by which countries have passed from barbarism to civilization." "It appears," he said, "to be the only state capable of bringing the love of independence and of ease, inherent in man, to the discipline and shelter necessary to his physical wants. . . . Hence the division of mankind into grades, and the mutual dependence and relations which result from them, constitute the very soul of civilization." He was certain that, in a new country, a cultured class could not be developed without forced laborers to support it.

The final step, that of declaring slavery a positive good, was now possible. In 1829, C. C. Pinckney denied that slavery, as it existed in South Carolina, was a greater or more unusual evil than was the lot of the poor in general, and Governor Stephen D. Miller went the whole way by saying that "slavery is not a national evil; on the contrary it is a national benefit." He called attention to the fact that "the agricultural wealth of the country . . . [was] found in those states owning slaves, and a great portion of the revenue of the government . . . [was] derived from the products of slave labor." He warned his fellow slaveholders that it did not become them "to speak in a whisper, betray fear, or feign philanthropy" on this subject. By July, 1833, the Charleston *Courier* could notify critics that they were "utterly mistaken in supposing that the people of the South regard[ed] slavery, as it exist[ed] among them, in the light of a curse." Their curse was a climate, not slavery. Slavery was absolutely necessary to the proper cultivation of the soil and was the great source of their prosperity, wealth and happiness. It was not even a curse to the Negroes themselves.[10]

South Carolinians had thus rounded out their defense of

slavery long before the Garrison movement had got under way. With the Virginians who, during the 1820's, had, through almost constant debate, clarified their opinions and positions, they were now ready for a thorough well-reasoned summary of conclusions. Professor Thomas Dew of William and Mary College supplied that summary. In answer to a request from the Virginia legislature he brought forth the first of the "classic statements" on slavery. He added little to the sum total of ideas already presented by other writers. He did, however, give to the pro-slavery argument a more closely woven and more polished form. The Southern scholar, heretofore a rather harsh critic of slavery, had begun to shift his ground.

Professor Dew took a thoroughly realistic approach. He looked back into history to find not a race of freemen, but of slaves. From earliest times, through misfortune, crime, and economic necessity, men were in bondage—in Israel, in Greece, and in Rome. In fact, the progress of mankind from savagery to civilization began when captives in war were put to work instead of to death. Then permanent abodes, private property, freedom and respect for women, leisure, and culture became possible. Where slavery was, there civilization flowered.

Modern slavery, Dew said, had benefited the Negro even as the Negro had benefited civilization. It had taken him out of the horror that was Africa—starvation, disease, ignorance—made him economically valuable and hence assured of kind treatment and excellent care. Unfitted by nature for freedom, the Negro found in slavery that security and direction which was more than an equivalent for the liberty enjoyed by half-starved and exploited free laborers. The Scriptures did not condemn such an institution or indicate that the master committed any offense in holding slaves. New England traders had bought them; English regulations had forced their retention. The still small voice of conscience need not disturb Virginians.

Practical considerations reinforced theory and history. To free the slaves and send them away would bankrupt the state, nearly one third of whose wealth was in such property. To export only the annual increase would not affect the basic stock or reduce its numbers. To remove "the breeding portion of the

slaves to Africa" or to "carry away the sexes in such dispropor-
tions" as to check breeding would mean a relentless division of
families. No humane person would agree to that. And, besides,
the sending of American-born and American-reared Negroes to
Liberia would be cruelty itself. They were now unfitted to
such an environment. Quick death would be the only outcome
of such misguided philanthropy. On the other hand, if Negroes
were freed to remain in the United States, freedom would not
"alter their condition—they would still be virtually slaves;
talent, habit, and wealth would make the white the master still,
and the emancipation would only have the tendency to deprive
him of those sympathies and kind feelings for the black which
now characterize him. Liberty has been the heaviest curse to
the slave, when given too soon."

The evils charged against slavery were, Dew believed, greatly
exaggerated. Tariffs and emigration, not unproductive labor,
accounted for the depressed state of Southern life. Slaveholding did not debase the whites. "Look to the slaveholding population of our country," said the good Professor, "and you will
find them characterized by noble and elevated sentiments, by
humane and virtuous feelings." "That cold, contracted, calculating *selfishness*," which, by inference, marked the peoples of
some other sections, was nowhere to be found among the Southern slaveholders. Thomas Jefferson had been mistaken.

Nor did slavery interfere with the republican spirit and form
of government. Instead, it made democracy possible by bringing all white men "to one common level." "We believe," Dew
wrote, "slavery in the U. States has accomplished this, in
regard to the whites, as nearly as can be expected or even desired in this world. The menial and low offices being all performed by the blacks, there is at once taken away the greatest
cause of distinction and separation of the ranks of society."

Dew's statement brought to a close the first phase of pro-
slavery thought. This phase had been characterized by moderation and the appeal to reason. Bitterness was absent. The
tone was one of defense against misunderstanding. Indignation
against ignorance was sometimes present, but the general purpose seems to have been to convey sound information to a well-

intentioned audience. Sectional feeling was evident only to a minor degree, and nowhere did it degenerate into hatred. The impartial observer might have prophesied a peaceful solution of the problem because of the absence of dogmatic opinions and the presence of a vague undercurrent of belief in the ultimate extinction of the evil.

From this point forward, however, the defense of slavery sharply changed in tone if not in content. Garrison and Weld had launched their crusades. Under the stimulation of their activities, Congress was flooded with anti-slavery petitions and the mails were filled with abolition propaganda on its way to the South. An attack "as harsh as truth" had begun. Like the hated tariff, this assault came out of the North—positive and fanatical. The Southern defense became as extreme, as aggressive, and as uncompromising. Uncertainty passed. Emotion matched emotion. Sectional criticism brought sectional reaction. As Calhoun said: "It has compelled us to the South to look into the nature and character of this great institution, and to correct many false impressions that even we had entertained in relation to it. Many in the South once believed that it was a moral and political evil; that folly and delusion are gone; we see it now in its true light, and regard it as the most safe and stable basis for free institutions in the world." He pronounced it a positive good.[12]

With this impetus, pro-slavery effort increased at an astonishing rate. Pamphlets and books by the score came from the press. Novels, essays, poems, sermons, and scientific treatises justified the institution and explained its benefits. Newspapers and periodicals published countless articles, some written by the greatest thinkers in the section, some by those unknown outside their own neighborhoods. Professors lectured to their classes on the subject. Organizations offered prizes for essays written in slavery's defense. Publications dedicated to commercial interests, literary pursuits, religious efforts, or scientific endeavors sprinkled their columns with propaganda. The agricultural periodical crowded to one side articles on soil restoration or crop rotation in order to give space to pro-slavery argument. Speakers at farm meetings forgot their primary interest to extol the virtues of Negroes in bondage. When *Uncle Tom's Cabin* appeared, Southern writers produced fifteen novels in answer. When a Northern congressman attacked slavery, a half dozen indignant Southerners were instantly on their feet to reply. One might say with considerable truth that the talents of a section—literary, scientific and political—were sidetracked for a greater part of a generation by the slavery controversy. A region's intellectual life was almost frozen, not so much to justify a questionable labor system as to repel a fanatical attack!

Such a movement inevitably produced its fire eaters to match the abolitionists. Defending slavery and Southern civilization became an obsession with those whose peculiar natures needed such an outlet. The "lonely," "nervous and mercurial" Barnwell Rhett, "all passion, excitement and fire"; the timid, yet bold, Edmund Ruffin, resentful and eager for notice; the more "convivial" George Fitzhugh, relative of Gerrit Smith: these and others of their kind can be explained only in part by the justice of the cause they espoused. The great enemies against which they spent their force were not all blundering Yankees. They were, unconsciously, strangely akin to Garrison and Weld.[13]

The completed pro-slavery apologia, hurled back by irate Southerners as a direct answer to Northern attacks, included much that was old and some that was new. It elaborated the Biblical statement and called on the past with new enthusiasm to witness to the superiority of slaveholding civilizations. The abolitionist was now proclaiming that slavery was a sin. To a people as deeply religious as ante-bellum Southerners no charge could be more serious. The Scriptures were searched with a diligence and thoroughness worthy of the holiest cause. Few writers on slavery failed to quote chapter and verse in complete vindication of the institution. Dew, Harper, Hammond, Cobb, and even Jefferson Davis included the Biblical defense along with their more practical arguments. Many writers made it the sole object of their efforts. John Fletcher, in his *Studies on Slavery,* gave one of the most elaborate of these Scriptural justifications. He answered Wayland, Barnes, Channing, and other Northern clerics with unmatched "bulk and erudition," citing most of the books of the Bible and many of the Latin church fathers, to prove the curse on Ham and the justice of holding inferior races in bondage. With an astonishing display of Greek and Hebrew philology, he argued that the word "servant" in the King James version of the Bible should have been translated "slave," and that the Northern position was thereby completely invalidated.[14]

Clergymen, as a rule, followed this general line. A dozen or more, of whom Stuart Robinson, George D. Armstrong, Richard Fuller, Josiah Priest, and Thornton Stringfellow were typical, made the region familiar with the stock quotations: "And he said, Cursed be Canaan; a servant of servants shall he be unto his brethren"; "Both thy bondmen, and thy bondmaids . . . shall be of the heathen that are round about you"; "And he shall take them as an inheritance, for your children after you, to inherit them for a possession, and they shall be your bondmen forever."

The Reverend J. H. Thornwell took a slightly different tack. In complete contradiction to the Finney-Weld teachings regarding the relation of church and society, he insisted that the church had "no commission to construct society afresh, to adjust its elements in different proportions, to rearrange the distribution of its classes, or to change the forms of its political constitutions." He did not believe that the great purpose of the church was to promote universal good. He did not hope or expect that the world would be converted into a paradise. God had permitted such evils as poverty, sickness, and slavery. The business of Christian people was to ease their harshness and to wring a blessing from each curse. Slavery should be made patriarchal and humane. The Negro should be Christianized and trained for greater usefulness.[15]

Thus by a literal interpretation, and by a strict adherence to the letter of "The Word," paralleled only by Calhoun's handling of the Constitution, the Southern clergy made their position the conservative orthodox stand. To dislodge them, Northern preachers were forced to exalt "human reason above the Scriptures" and to bend it "to their preconceived notions of what a revelation ought to be. . . ." To condemn slavery,

Southerners said, such churchmen had to distort and abandon the Bible because it did not sustain their opinions. The abolitionist was an infidel. His spirit was undeniably atheistic. Like the Jacobin of the French Revolution, he worshipped at the feet of his own falsehood. The humor of the situation was lost on Southern seriousness!

The next step required was a defense against the charge that slavery was un-American. The abolitionists were taking the Declaration of Independence seriously and making it an integral part of the American system of government. They talked much about the natural right of man to his freedom. They asked pointedly just where the slave fitted into the democratic pattern. On what legal or political basis could slavery be justified?

The Southern defender made short work of such talk. He bluntly denied the soundness of the premise. The Declaration of Independence was not a part of the American political system. Its talk about equality was ridiculously absurd. As Chancellor Harper said, it was nearer the truth to assert that "no man was ever born free and that no two men were ever born equal." He insisted that it was "as much in the order of nature, that men should enslave each other, as that other animals should prey upon each other."[16] Edmund Ruffin proclaimed Jefferson's statements both false and foolish and the Rev. Fred A. Ross, pastor of the Presbyterian Church in Huntsville, Alabama, ventured the opinion that the much-quoted "self-evident truths" were "denied and upset by the Bible, by the natural history of man and by Providence in every age of the world. . . ."[17]

Regarding the relation of slavery to the American system of government, some of the apologists ingeniously argued that a true republican system was impossible where all men were free. The majority in such a society would ever be ignorant and poor. The many at the bottom who performed menial tasks would sooner or later become class conscious. Knavish demagogues would use them to overthrow the existing order and to rear a despotism on the ruins. History revealed no instance where a republic, "unless a large proportion of the population [were] . . . slaves," had survived for any length of time. By uniting capital and labor, by curtailing the franchise at a natural point, "the institution of slavery ever [had] been and ever [would] be the only sure foundation of all republican governments. . . ."[18]

This was true, they insisted, not only because slaves took the place of the rabble in free society, but because all free white men were "elevated above the mass" and were "higher toned and more deeply interested in preserving a stable and well ordered government." From which J. H. Hammond concluded that "slavery is truly the 'corner-stone' and foundation of every well-designed and durable 'republican edifice.'" In war days the Reverend B. M. Palmer told the General Assembly of South Carolina that the maintenance of republican institutions was "bound up in the fate of our own Confederacy." The Northern people had "failed to seize the idea of a republic." They "confounded it with democracy . . . a merely mechanical device for condensing the masses, and rendering practicable the government of the mob." Palmer charged them with pushing "the doctrine to the verge of ungodliness and atheism, in making the voice of the people the voice of God; in exalting the will of the numerical majority above the force of constitution and covenants, and [in] creating . . . the vilest tyranny known in the annals of the world." The North lacked a united conservative class with which to check this "vulgar fanaticism." Wherefore "the same grave in which this Confederacy shall be buried will prove the sepulchre of republicanism upon this continent."[19]

A third line of defense had to be thrown up against the charge of injustice to the Negro. Abolitionists, who had extended to him the benefits of the Declaration of Independence, had forgotten that the Negro was a Negro. The fact of his inferiority had to be recalled. One group of writers turned to history and science to demonstrate what most Southerners accepted as an obvious fact. "In no age or condition," one of them wrote,

[had] the real negro shown a capacity to throw off the chains of barbarism and brutality that [had] long bound down the nations of that race. . . . In no quarter of the globe [had] the energies of the human mind been so long locked up in the dungeon of despair. While in other nations its elastic energies [had] burst up like the heavings of a volcano . . . the barbarous negro nations of Africa [had] quietly rested in their

unalloyed barbarism for thousands of years, exhibiting no more evidence of a capacity for native born advancement than the baboons and orangoutangs that people[d] the forest.

Another pointed out the Negro's want of judgment and lack of thrift and foresight. This writer credited him with the ability to "imitate with ludicrous nicety" but declared that he could not originate or invent even in the lines in which he excelled. His capacity to learn stopped abruptly where reason and judgment and reflection were required.[20]

The conclusion was obvious. The Negro, while exceptionally well fitted for slavery by his "heat resisting skin," his immunity to tropical diseases, and his "absence of nervous irritability," was a total loss to mankind as a freeman. If proof were wanted and history did not satisfy, it was only necessary to take one glance at the "degraded, underfoot, downtrodden . . . wretchedness" of the free Negro in the United States or at the miserable state to which those taken to Liberia had sunk. In the North, freedom had only turned "a contented and cheerful peasantry" into a "horde of outlaws" and "a multitude of paupers whom the white population could never amalgamate, and who must forever feel themselves degraded and outcast. . . ." In Liberia, a comparatively healthy place, deaths exceeded births, and the colonists had never become self-supporting. Freedom everywhere had proved such a curse to the Negro that men like George Fitzhugh and Edmund Ruffin were soon advocating the return of all free blacks to bondage. "Humanity, self-interest, consistency all require" it, said Fitzhugh. "Why peril, then, the Negro's humble joys, why make him free, if freedom but destroys?" asked the poetic William Grayson.[21]

If such evidence did not wholly convince, science also had something to offer. Writers had early commented on the Negro's slanting forehead, the depressed summit, and the increased size of the back of his head. Some had insisted that this meant a smaller brain than that of the white man, smallest in the front where intellectual faculties were located and largest in the rear where animal propensities developed. Some thought that the Negro had a peculiar backbone and even nervous system. A few believed that his eye was equipped with an additional "membraneous wing" which enabled him to gaze into the brightest sun.

A more scientific group raised the question as to whether the Negro had originated at the same time as the white man. The idea of plural origin had long been speculated upon by naturalists. Here was a practical use to which the theory could be put. It might be made to prove that the inferiority of the Negro was innate and not the result of environment or slavery. Southern naturalists were not slow to accept the suggestion. Richard Colfax and J. J. Flournoy pioneered the course, but Dr. Josiah Nott of Mobile, building upon the ethnological work of Samuel G. Morton, brought it to fullest expression.[22] From his medical practice among Negroes, Nott was convinced that the black man was a separate species from the white man. He could not believe that the two had sprung from a single pair of progenitors. With a full realization of the implications of his statements, he asserted that "the Mosaic account [of creation] sheds no satisfactory light on this question." The Doctors of Divinity, he found, after two thousand years of discussion had only proved "that they [knew] nothing about it." Natural history, therefore, should "be left open to fair and honest investigations" of the subject. "My object is truth," he said, "and I care not which way the question is decided, providing the decision is a correct one."[23]

In two lectures delivered in his home city, Nott offered evidence to show that there had been many creations instead of one. Some animals on the present earth were different from those existing before the flood and must, therefore, have been created since Noah gathered the few from his own locality into the Ark. New lands, rising out of the sea, produced their own peculiar vegetation. Physical forces did not change one species into another. They could not turn a white man into a Negro. The two races had existed, without change in physical characteristics, for thousands of years and nowhere could relationship be shown between them. Since man in body is an animal, it was logical to suppose that there might be different species in the human race. The marked moral and intellectual disparity between whites and blacks indicated separate origins. The Negro was of a different and inferior creation!

Later, with an elaborate set of plates and diagrams, Nott developed his theory and piled up his evidence, in a volume entitled *Types of Mankind*. Doctor J. H. Van Evrie brought the discussion to bear more directly on the pro-slavery issue in his work, *Negroes and Negro "Slavery": the first an inferior race: the latter its normal condition*. Both Nott and Van Evrie argued for creations "in different places and of different forms to fit the needs of locality." "Commencing with the simple forms of organized existence, and ascending the scale till reaching the Caucasian man (the most elaborate in his structure, and therefore the highest endowed in his faculties)," nature had produced her different species with their varying organizations and functions. Somewhere in this series of creations the Negro appeared. His equipment destined him to servitude. To consider him the white man's equal, and to ask him to perform the white man's duties and share his responsibilities would be an outrage upon nature. It would destroy both the Negro and the society which placed him in this unnatural position.

From such bold thinking the clergy drew back. After all, there were limits beyond which it was not wise to go even in the defense of slavery. Did not the Bible offer sufficient justification when "correctly" interpreted? Could a society which prized stability above all else tolerate unorthodoxy in any realm of thought? The South would have to choose between the scientist and the preacher. The Richmond *Enquirer* quickly let it be known that those who followed Dr. Nott could not also retain Moses and Paul. It feared even more serious consequences. "The Bible," the editor wrote,[24]

is now the grand object of attack from the Abolitionists, because they know it is the bulwark of Southern principles. . . . Destroy the Bible, and lay bare the very citadel of our strength to our foes. This they well know, and hence, the Parkers and Garrisons and Pillsburys, are almost as bitter against the Bible and the Churches as they are against Slavery. Let us not then allow this shield of strength to be torn from us until we have something to put in its place.

With the inferiority of the Negro firmly established, the benefits of slavery to him were taken for granted. John C. Calhoun early told his fellows in the Senate that the South had taken "a low, degraded and savage" people and improved them far beyond any condition their race had attained "from the dawn of history to the present day." Chancellor Harper, in his *Memoir* on slavery, asserted that if the fate of the Negroes "were at the absolute disposal of a council of the most enlightened philanthropists in Christendom, with unlimited resources, they could place them in no situation so favorable to themselves. . . ." He thought slavery had done more "to elevate a degraded race . . . to civilize the barbarous . . . to enlighten the ignorant, and to spread the blessings of Christianity among the heathen, than all the missionaries that philanthropy and religion had ever sent forth." Edmund Ruffin pointed out the fact that in 1855 the "heathen churches" of the world had only 180,000 members, while in the Methodist Church South alone, there were 175,000 Negroes. An enthusiastic clergyman saw the hand of God using the Puritan love of gain to "force slaves upon the Cavaliers of the South"; for by this means African heathen were brought into direct contact with the finest "gentlemen and ladies of England and France, born to command, and softened and refined under [the] Southern sky." No other road could lead the Negro so quickly to civilization![25]

The defenders of slavery crowned their argument by asserting the superiority of Southern civilization. Abolitionists had charged that slavery corrupted morals, destroyed enterprise, and produced an inferior tumble-down social-economic order. They had assumed that free societies had every advantage in both men and conditions. Early Southern writers had been inclined to grant the correctness of this assumption to some degree at least. They now completely changed their position. In 1837, Calhoun insisted that the South was "equal [to] the North in virtue, intelligence, patriotism, courage, disinterestedness, and all the high qualities which adorn our nature." She had furnished her "full share of talents and political wisdom in forming and sustaining [the] political fabric." In only one thing was she inferior to the North—"the arts of gain." Calhoun did not hesitate to say that where two races, with marked differences, were thrown together as in this country, "the relations . . . existing in the slaveholding States between the two" was "a positive good." In all wealthy and civilized societies, one portion of the community always lived on the labor of the other. If one device was not used to turn the greater share of wealth to the non-producing classes, another was. As a matter of fact, there were few countries in which so much was "left to the share of the laborer, and so little exacted from him," or where as much kind attention was paid to him in sickness or infirmities of age as in the South. The result was a society without a labor problem —yes, without even a race problem. In stability and peace the South stood alone.[26]

Others carried this argument further and made more elaborate comparisons between slave and free societies. George Fitzhugh took the lead.[27] His basic premise was "that *Labor makes values, and Wit exploitates* and accumulates them." The many toil; the few consume the greater part of that which is produced. *Cannibals All or, Slaves without Masters*, Fitzhugh called one of his volumes. Modern free society, as he viewed it, had glorified the practice of human exploitation with its economic doctrine of *laisser faire*, which, when properly understood, meant only "every man for himself, and the Devil take the hindmost." Free competition begat a war of wits in which the weak, simple and guileless were steadily reduced to a position where they struggled against each other for the chance to work for a bare sustenance. Control of machines and raw materials, through superior intelligence or guile, gave the employer complete mastery. The economic theories of the day freed him from all social responsibility. He achieved success by piling up wealth and power; his workers fell back on charity when sickness and old age became their lot. All free society tended toward "robber barons" and "pauper slavery."

Such were the conditions already reached in England under the Industrial Revolution, Fitzhugh asserted. Such were the conditions toward which the North was moving. The final stages in the United States were being postponed only by the abundance of free lands in the West. Surplus workers were being drawn off and wages thereby kept up. But, as one of Fitzhugh's followers wrote:

Whenever the valuable vacant lands shall have been all settled upon . . . and when by the returning and crowding of population, the supply of labor shall (as is inevitable) greatly exceed the demand, then in New England, as already . . . in Old England, *slavery to want* will be established rigidly, and in the form most oppressive and destructive to the laborers, but the most profitable of all slavery to the employers, to capitalists.

In this critique, the principal charge lodged against free society was disregard of its obligations to its real producers. "The free laborer rarely [had] a house and home of his own; he [was] insecure of employment; sickness [might] overtake him at any time and deprive him of the means of support; old age [was] certain and generally [found] him without the means of subsistence. . . ." This situation was already producing unrest and the threat of social revolution. It was responsible for the rapid growth of socialism and all the other wild isms of the day. Men were demanding greater security and well-being for the workers. They were realizing that these things must come through a surrender of individual freedom and a greater interest of man in his fellow men. "Dives and Lazarus [were] elbowing one another in the street, *and [the] political economist [had selected] Dives as the sole type of the nation.*" A new social deal was required. The forgotten man—the slave without a master—must be considered.

What a contrast to all of this slave society offered! Its laborers were conscious of security, freed of "all corroding cares and anxieties," protected in sickness and old age, happy and contented, free from jealousy, malignity, and envy, and at peace with all the world. The slave system provided the very best form of socialism without any of its drawbacks. To be the slave of one owner was better than to be the slave of society. Slavery gave the slave the protection which came of interest in property. It gave him the rights of a dependent to well-being and care under adversity. The master had property in the slave's labor; the slave had "the most invaluable property" in the master's obligations to care for him throughout life. In the sense that society should cooperate for greatest economic effort and that it should be responsible for the highest social well-being of its weaker elements, slavery was socialism in all save the master.

Edmund Ruffin argued that farmers in free society were destined to peasantry. Gain was their sole object of endeavor. Their wives and children were drudges. The city drew the more energetic and intelligent away from the farms, and industry shaped governmental policies toward its own interests and to the destruction of rural independence. Only with slavery could farmers escape the "brutalizing effects of continued toil" and retain the intelligence and spirit with which to defend their rights. Only in the American South could a man be both a farmer and a gentleman.[28]

Elwood Fisher followed this up with the assertion that a rural way of life, based on slavery, produced finer individual character and action than came out of free urban-industrial society. "For a warm heart and open hand, for sympathy of feeling, fidelity of friendship, and a high sense of honor; for knowledge of the sublime mechanism of man, and reason and eloquence to delight, to instruct, and to direct him, the South [was] superior." The logic was simple: slavery made possible a superior agricultural life; that way of life produced the finest type of American citizen.[29]

Thus by ingenious use of theory and fact the South and its institutions were justified and set over against the persons and practice of its critics. Adequate weapons had been forged for combat. Men could go forward with easy conscience and renewed confidence. The section had been forced to create a picture of itself, to rationalize its practices, and to have in hand a ready answer to each and every criticism. It had, in the process, also created a picture of Northern men and their society as positive and simple as that which the abolitionists had drawn of the South.

The whole North, according to Southern extremists, had submitted to *Yankee* influence. That implied the dominance of certain definite sectional traits. Just what the average Southern extremist thought these were was shown in a pamphlet published in 1832 under the title, *Memoirs of a Nullifier by Himself*. The author described his imaginary journey to Hell where he witnessed the trial of a recently arrived Yankee. The charges against him were for selling "in the course of one peddling expedition, 497,368 wooden nutmegs, 281,532 Spanish cigars made of oak leaves, and 647 wooden clocks"; and on other occasions, "stealing an old grindstone, smearing it over with butter, and then selling it as a cheese"; "taking a worn pair of shoes . . . and selling them to a pious old lady, as being actually the shoes of Saint Paul"; and, at the age of six, "making a counterfeit dollar of pewter" and cheating his own father with it. To which charges the astonished Yankee could only reply that, where he came from, these were considered "the cutest tricks" and that his father had been delighted at his son's show of genius. Even the Devil was disgusted, and declared that New England gave him more trouble than all the rest of the world![30]

Later, on a trip to Washington, the author met other Yankees simply obsessed with "a sacred desire of propagating everywhere" the New England "virtues," and "improving" those around them: lawyers, doctors, clergymen, moving South and West to lift the darkness there, but always taking along a wagon load "of checked handkerchiefs and tin ware." Prophets and profits! Keepers of unwilling brothers!

Such, the South came to believe, were the people of a free competitive order. And the social conditions of this people were just as bad. The vagaries in moral and political philosophy which characterized New England bred anarchy. The colleges were unsafe for young people. The churches had forgotten Christ and had gone in for free thinking. Agrarianism and socialism, free love and spirit-rapping, Mormonism, Millerism, and a dozen and one other "isms" testified to their lack of stability. Only the one thing was permanent—"the fierce idolatry . . . of the *eternal* dollar." Well could J. H. Thornwell say in 1860, when war had come between North and South:

The parties in this conflict are not merely abolitionists and slaveholders—they are atheists, socialists, communists, red republicans, jacobins on one side, and the friends of order and regulated freedom on the other. In one word, the world is the battle-ground. Christianity and atheism the combatants, and the progress of humanity the stake.

The extremists of the South, like their fellows of the North, stood thus self-convinced of their own righteousness and of the depravity of their opponents. Argument had deepened prejudices. Unreason had engendered unreason. Emphasis on faults had obliterated all understanding of virtues in other ways of life. The purposes of men had become the purposes of God. They, too, could be as harsh as truth and as uncompromising as justice!

CHAPTER EIGHT

SLAVERY AND EXPANSION

A S LONG as the slavery controversy remained out of politics it did not portend national disaster. Most Americans of the mid-nineteenth century were inclined to explain social misfortune as the result of personal shortcomings. They were not generally aroused by questions of abstract justice, unconnected with concrete situations. The masses, especially in the West, were politically minded. Democratic government was supposed to take care of injustice, and until a problem was important enough to attract party attention it was not regarded as pressing. For that reason, problems of social reform tended, sooner or later, to become political. And for the same reason, any political question might become a moral issue and the most ordinary material interest be tangled and confused with those involving basic human rights.

It was inevitable, therefore, that slavery should become a political issue. It was equally inevitable that its high moral and emotional appeal should, in due time, be used to strengthen the claims of many a lesser cause. A drift in these directions started in the late 'twenties when the abolition societies, following an old Quaker practice, began a direct assault on Congress with anti-slavery petitions. These were, at first, directed mainly at slavery in the District of Columbia. Later they referred to every possible phase of the subject. By the middle of the 'thirties, the volume of petitions, "from soured and agitated communities," had become great enough to disturb John C. Calhoun, who denounced them as instruments of a Northern conspiracy and moved for their rejection. Under the impulse given by Theodore Weld and his Seventy during the next few years, the flow of appeals reached flood stage and threatened to clog the whole machinery of government. Whig minority leaders seized upon them as a means of checking Democratic party legislation, and John Quincy Adams won the sobriquet "Old Man Eloquent" in their defense.

The conflict which raged in Congress over petitions was as vicious a mixture of sham and duplicity and high purposes as can be found in American history. Congress was already struggling with the problem of getting an increasing load of business done in the face of antiquated rules and interminable oratory. If all the petitions which abolition presses could print and "inspired" agents could get signed were to be received and dealt with in the accustomed way, no time would be left for other pressing work. A constant stirring up of passions made harmonious action impossible. From 1830 to 1840, both Houses faced the problem and solved it by what came to be known as the gag resolutions. The first of these resolutions in the House was introduced by Henry L. Pinckney of South Carolina. They denied to Congress any powers over slavery in the states, questioned the wisdom of interference with it in the District of Columbia, and established the rule that all petitions on the subject should be laid on the table without being printed, referred, or further acted upon. Senate procedure differed slightly and the House varied its regulations somewhat from year to year until 1840 when the practice advocated by Pinckney was made a standing rule. Moderate men viewed the procedure as a temporary expedient made necessary by the action of overzealous fanatics. The abolitionists seized upon the gag rules as an opportunity to link their cause with the sacred right of petition.

John Quincy Adams, a thoroughgoing abolitionist who concealed the fact in order to increase his effectiveness, led the way. When the Pinckney resolutions were presented, he denounced them as "a direct violation of the Constitution . . . the rules of this House, and the rights of my constituents." He constantly refused to obey the rule, insolently defied his colleagues, and found ways to provoke Southern leaders to extremes in speech and action. In the end, he became the spearhead of an avowed anti-slavery lobby, with Leavitt and Weld as his assistants and Giddings as his chief ally. But always he hid these connections, avoided all unpopular extremes, and sheltered his moves behind the abstract right of petition. With a daring unmatched in the annals of congressional debate, and with a mastery of rules and logic unequalled in his day, "he lifted his voice like a trumpet, till slaveholding, slave trading and slave breeding quailed and howled under his dissecting knife." With a skill entirely lacking in his presidential days, he played on men's emotions as a means to practical accomplishment. He made the cause of the despised abolitionists the cause of democratic government. Through his efforts the right to denounce slavery on the floor of the House was won.[1]

In spite of Adams' courageous fight and its effects on the American people, the justice of his cause is rather doubtful. The right of the people to petition the government for a redress of grievances was no more explicit than the right of each House to make its own rules and the obligation of legislators to see that legislation went forward smoothly. Furthermore, the right-of-petition move was based on the assumption that all anti-slavery petitions were private—an assumption which a hundred thousand repetitions and the practice of pasting lists of names to printed forms constantly denied. Petitions were, in fact, only instruments of agitation. John Quincy Adams' purpose, in spite of much constitutional talk, was to stimulate anti-slavery feeling in the North.

Perhaps also the violent reactions of Southerners to the Northern attacks were aimed primarily at the consolidation of Southern opinion and the development of a political bloc. James L. Petigru, in 1833, had said:[2]

> It is clear that our Nullifiers mean to pick a quarrel with the North about Negroes. It will take some time and many things may turn up in the meanwhile that we can't foresee either to favor or to destroy their hopes. But Nullification has done its work: it has prepared the minds of men for a separation of the States, and when the question is mooted again it will be distinctly union or disunion.

Calhoun's demands for a Southern convention, in 1835 and 1837, for the implied purpose of securing permanent protection for the South, were directly in line with Petigru's charge. His famous resolutions on the nature of the Federal Union and the rights of slavery in it were another step in the same direction. The Southern politician, as well as the Northern, was fishing in troubled waters.[3]

The fact that issues were confused and true motives hidden in the petition controversy did not, however, lessen the effect it produced on the country at large. Until the passage of the gag rule and the impassioned attacks of John Quincy Adams, the North had been overwhelmingly indifferent or hostile to the abolitionists. Substantial citizens generally had viewed the cause as visionary and extreme; the leaders as fanatics and dreamers. Now that the question had been made one of slavery, —"a good," and beyond Federal control—*versus* the right of petition, the whole situation was altered. Thousands moved toward greater toleration for the abolition cause and even rallied to its support. When the Whigs censured Joshua Giddings for party irregularity in the interests of anti-slavery, his Ohio constituents returned him to Congress as an unfettered free lance. When the impression became general that Southern leaders would sacrifice sacred constitutional rights for slavery, a deep distrust of the South developed. Politics and sectionalism and slavery became hopelessly tangled. Respectability began to clothe a once despised reform movement.[4]

The effects of the petition fight on the South and her leaders were even more significant. The Nullification controversy had forced Calhoun and South Carolina more or less to one side in the sweep of national life. Calhoun had broken with the Democratic Party, and had failed to secure the support of the other Southern states for the formation of a solid bloc devoted to his political theories. While he sought his bearings, Jackson and Clay completely occupied the stage. The Bank question absorbed public interest. Nicholas Biddle took over the villain's role opposite Old Hickory.[5]

Calhoun, meanwhile, gave half-hearted support to Whig measures and sought to reestablish his prestige. Avoiding nullification mistakes, he fostered the idea of the entire South united in defense of "the liberty and the constitution of the country"— meaning, of course, States' rights. The appeal was rather abstract; the response was correspondingly weak. Then came the petition conflict. It was a godsend. It furnished concrete occasion for united Southern action and a chance to force political parties back into orthodox positions. Seizing the opportunity presented by the Independent Treasury Bill, Calhoun swung over to Van Buren's support and, with Barnwell Rhett's help, began his effort for a Southern convention and his drive to make the Democratic Party accept the Southern political doctrines. Moderate Southerners, controlling the meetings he called, checked his schemes temporarily, but they could not prevent him from presenting and putting through the Senate a series of strong States' rights resolutions in answer to a Vermont memorial against slavery in the District of Columbia and the annexation of Texas. One of these resolutions declared that the states, when they formed the Constitution, ". . . retained control over their domestic institutions" and that "any inter-meddling" with slavery was unconstitutional and tended "to destroy the Union." Another spoke of the Union as the common agent of the states and as resting upon an equality of rights and advantages. Others condemned the attacks on slavery as violations of the solemn pledge of mutual protection, and denounced "attempts to discriminate between states in extending the benefits of the government . . . by the annexation of new territories, or states. . . ." Taken as a whole, Calhoun's resolutions constituted a platform upon which the radical Southern groups might stand and defy Northern aggressors. Evidently James L. Petigru was not far wrong when he wrote a few weeks after their passage, ". . . The spirit of disunion is very general in the State, and if it suited Calhoun to take that ground there would hardly be a rally."[6]

Rhett went even further in the House. He talked enough about the best means of dissolving the Union to force his colleagues virtually to accept the Southern position. By 1840, both he and Calhoun were confident that the Democratic Party would take the proper stand on both slavery and the tariff. They could even hope that Virginia would soon be in line with the other Southern states. The petition struggle had put new foundations under their feet. They had found in the defense of slavery the true basis for a Southern movement. Calhoun began to hope again for the presidency.

* * * *

Into such a situation, serious enough in itself, a far more serious factor was now injected. The restless American pioneer in his westward thrust had reached the Pacific on the Northwest and had crossed the border into Texas. Englishmen and Mexicans alike learned anew the meaning of Manifest Destiny. Men talked of reannexing Texas and of taking all Oregon. On either border, war was more than a remote possibility as an aggressive expansionist sentiment swept the Midwestern states from which the majority of the settlers in the new lands had come. The people were restless. Economic disaster, under the panic of 1837, sharpened resentments and justified aggressions. Other issues were pushed aside. Western leaders again took charge. Faced with ruin, the most astute politicians shifted their ground and the more clever agitators turned about to search for new allies. In the midst of this confusion, the exponents of slavery and anti-slavery suddenly discovered that their programs might be linked with the most powerful national interest of the day and thereby given greater force and appeal. Expansion and slavery might be joined. Much might thus be gained. Danger lay in surrender to the politician and in the shifting of emphasis from slavery *per se* to slavery extension. But they accepted the risk and their choice brought the first phase of the slavery controversy to an end.

The actual pushes into Texas and Oregon had nothing to do with slavery.[7] They were normal American drives, originating from normal pressures and lures. In the period of 1820–40, conditions were particularly favorable to expansion. In the first decade the home market, which had supported the economic life of the older Middle West along the Ohio, began to weaken. Overbuying of public lands and the introduction of a new cash policy by the government in 1820 added financial difficulties to glutted markets and set the less well established and the more restless again in motion. The trans-Mississippi West called.

Already the traders and trappers, together with the government military explorers, had opened the way and made known both the riches and the adventure which awaited the settler. The Santa Fé trail had begun to yield its silver harvest. Missouri had become the jumping-off place for a steady stream of intrepid frontiersmen who knew rest only in motion, and who found companionship only in solitude. By 1830, settlement had crept well out to the great bend of the Far West's river highway. The trapper and the trader were out on the Bighorn, the Green and the Great Salt Lake, in quest of pelts. The more prosaic farmer, in turn, had begun to look hopefully down the fast deepening trails and up the muddy streams for new plow lands.[8]

Under the land laws which held from 1800 to 1820, the minimum price of two dollars per acre paid in installments amounted virtually to a credit system. Speculation had been heavy. Evils, inherent in the American belief in the natural rights of possession and exploitation, had developed, and the government had been forced to adopt a new policy. After 1820, under this policy, tracts were smaller, cash was required, and the price of the land was lowered to $1.25 per acre. Sales dropped rapidly, from 5,110,000 acres in 1819 to 781,000 in 1821. Debtors, throughout the West, demanded relief from payment. At the same time, the National Bank, under new management, clamped down on wildcat banking and the ruin of Western plungers was complete. The so-called panic of 1819 struck with sudden fury and then settled down on the land as a lingering depression.[9]

Soon the roads from the southern parts of Ohio, Indiana, and Illinois were crowded with covered wagons filled with farm implements, household goods, women and children. The caravans were headed westward. Another parcel of Americans was beginning over again. Stolid grownups, unconscious of dust and the smell of sweaty harness, occupied the spring seat in front, their hopes and fears well hidden behind immobile weather-beaten countenances; but the eager faces of children, peering out from under canvas flaps, betrayed the optimism and dreams in cargo. A traveler wrote of as many as thirty or forty prairie schooners moving in sight of each other. At one point on the

Missouri, two hundred and seventy-one wagons and carriages, fifty-five two-wheeled carts, and as many pack horses passed in a single month, headed for the interior. Congressmen declared that the Pacific Ocean was our natural western boundary and defied the government to attempt to set limits to a westward march which moved with the increasing rapidity of fire.[10]

In the next few years, settlement moved up the streams which run into the Mississippi from the west—the Red, the Arkansas, the Missouri, and the Des Moines. There it halted for a period as if gathering strength to make the next great leap into Utah, California, and Oregon. Population also widened in the newer counties of the Old Northwest; and, down along the Gulf, the old crowding of Spanish peoples began again. In the latter area occurred the first important crisis produced by the renewed expansion.

Soon after the passage of the new cash land law, a St. Louis newspaper had contrasted its provisions with Mexico's land policy in the following significant language:[11]

The difference is too great not to produce its effect between a republic which gives first rate land gratis, and a republic which will not sell inferior land for what it is worth. . . . Mexico does not think of getting rich by *land speculation,* digging for lead, or boiling salt water, but by increasing the number and wealth of her citizens.

The inference was perfectly clear. Hard-pressed citizens, who had once known prosperity in Missouri when it was under Spanish control, might again find similar advantages across the Mexican border.

At least that was the way one Moses Austin felt. Born in Connecticut in 1765, he had, as a young man, gone first to Pennsylvania and then to Virginia to engage in lead mining. Greater opportunities in the same field later took him to the District of Saint Genevieve in what is now Missouri but what was then Spanish Louisiana. He made a fortune. The panic of 1819 destroyed it. The next year he turned his face, as he had done in 1798, toward Spanish territory, with the idea of securing government land and leading other men like himself to a region where beginning over again was easy. December, 1820, found him in conference with Colonel Don Antonia Martinez, Governor of the Province of Texas.

Austin's first efforts were unsuccessful, but finally, through the assistance of a German baron in Spanish employ, he received a grant to bring three hundred settlers. But revolution and independence for Mexico in 1821 delayed the project and made necessary the re-confirmation of his grants. Moses Austin was dead before the work of colonization could get under way. The task of leading out the first restless band of Americans, stirred by the announcement of generous land grants at nominal prices and easy terms, fell to his son Stephen.[12]

How ready the Southwest was for swarming was shown by the flood of applications which poured in on the Austins as soon as news of their undertaking became known. Even before the grant had been made, enough *"names* of respectable families" to "make up the Number" had been received. Nearly a hundred letters of inquiry from Missouri and many from Kentucky awaited Stephen Austin on his return northward in 1821. He assured Governor Martinez that he could take on fifteen hundred families as easily as three hundred if permitted to do so. A resident of Arkansas Territory wrote that *"the Spanish Country"* was all the rage in his neighborhood, and another prophesied an immense emigration the following spring. Inquiries came from Louisiana, Ohio, and Illinois. Missouri considered the project especially her own. Mrs. Austin wrote that "nothing was talked of but the province of Texas and she thought a third of the population of Missouri would move in another year, if reports continued favorable." Some adventurers did not wait to make inquiry. They packed their worldly goods and headed toward the Southwest. Fifty families arrived before Austin left Texas, and by 1824 some 272 titles had been granted to Americans by local officials. By 1825 the immigrants numbered 1,800 and in the next six years they increased to 5,665. The lure was land in tracts of 640 acres at twelve and a half cents per acre! The force behind was panic and depression. The story was an old one. Its features were normal in every way! Certainly slavery was not its author.[13]

Nor were the events which later led to revolution and the

independence of Texas the product of the social conflict developing in the United States. American pioneers had never been
inclined to snatch other people's chestnuts out of the fire. They
were emphatically provincial and self-centered. Immediate
material gain, not sectional or national interest, prompted them.
They had not hesitated to expatriate themselves when personal
benefit lay in that direction. When necessary, they had claimed
as natural rights everything, material and spiritual, which they
considered conducive to individual happiness. They were not,
as Nathaniel Macon observed, "your easy-going, chimney-corner
people . . . the timid and fearful. . . ." They were a restless
race and they were always resentful of restraints and impatient
under failure to make rapid progress. More than once in the
occupation of the West they had rudely taken matters into their
own hands and acted with violence in the interests of greater
freedom. Their methods were direct; their faith in themselves
unbounded.

It was, therefore, to be expected that, when such a people
entered Mexican territory, some misunderstanding, and even
strife, would occur. Spanish American governments were none
too stable and their politics were correspondingly shifting. They
had every reason, in the light of the past, to distrust American
immigration. Their traditions did not guarantee all the freedom
to which the Western pioneer had been wont to lay claim.

Under such conditions four points of irritation soon developed
between Americans and the Mexican government. The first
came from the uncertain and shifting policy in regard to colonization. A more or less favorable act was passed in January, 1823,
suspended in April of that year, and recast in 1824 so as to give
Mexicans preference on the coast and on foreign borders. Then
followed more liberal legislation, which was altered in 1828 to
prohibit the settlement of Americans in Mexico along their own
border and revised again in 1830 so as to prevent further colonization by adjacent nationalities.

Uncertain legislation regarding slaveholding was a second
source of trouble. The first settlers, the majority of whom came
from the neighboring Southern states, were permitted to retain
their slaves, at least temporarily, but were soon forbidden to

traffic in that species of property (1824). An act of 1827, freeing the children of slaves and forbidding the further introduction of slaves after a six months' period, was followed by another in 1829 abolishing the institution entirely and by still another in 1830 checking all slave importations. Exceptions and suspensions limited the damage done by these laws largely to irritation. But Americans felt with keen dissatisfaction the unstable character of Mexican procedure.

The insecurity of landholding added its part to the growing irritation and, in Edward's colony, led to open rebellion and the setting up of the temporary Fredonian Republic. Political uncertainty, produced by Spain's refusal to recognize Mexican independence and by a series of revolutions which magnified the evils resulting from the union of Texas with Coahuila, added the final pressure which drove the distressed Texans to revolt and independence. Their course was entirely normal. It was in no way inspired by outside interests for outside purposes. "The government and people of the United States," says a careful scholar of the movement, "appear to stand acquitted of serious blame" for what happened in Texas.[14]

American occupation of Oregon was another normal phase of this same expansion movement into the Trans-Mississippi West. Discovery of the mouth of the Columbia had given the United States its claims in the region, and the expeditions of Lewis and Clark had stirred the interest of John Jacob Astor in the possibilities of fur-trading in the Valley of the Columbia. The post Astor built and called Astoria gave Englishmen and Americans a subject for dispute for nearly two decades. Their quarrel, soon official, ended in a series of agreements by which all the territory claimed by England or by the United States should be indefinitely open to the citizens or subjects of both nations. Joint occupation should, however, be ended by a twelve-month notice from either party. After 1828, Oregon was in a position to rival Texas for settlers.

A New England schoolteacher, named Hall Jackson Kelley, popularized the region with his *Geographical Sketches of Oregon* and by an enthusiasm seldom matched in the annals of American promotion. The cry of the Western Indian for religious instruction and the economic disasters of the upper portion of the Old Northwest, however, provided most of the emigrants. Hall made great plans for trade and settlement but in the end set out alone for the promised land. Only one of his converts, Nathaniel Wyeth, Harvard graduate and ice-dealer of Cambridge, Massachusetts, took practical steps to make dreams come true. Collecting a band of some thirty-one men, Wyeth toughened them on an island in Boston harbor, clothed them like frontiersmen with bayonet, knife, and ax at belt, and taught them the intricate uses of an amphibious machine which was to serve them as wagon on land and boat on river or lake. In March, 1831, his expedition began the long overland trip to Oregon, its wagons cutting the first faint traces of a new transcontinental trail. Groups of pious missionaries, intent on service to the Nez Percé, Cayuse, or Walla Walla Indians, followed in his wake, but the Oregon valleys were not destined to be filled until the home market broke in the Lakes portion of the Old Northwest in the 1840's, and that region began to suffer from what contemporaries called the Oregon fever. Then Manifest Destiny embraced the Northwest as well as the Southwest.[15]

Interest in the acquisition of both Texas and Oregon had early been manifested by American statesmen. John Quincy Adams, in 1825, and Andrew Jackson, in 1829, had made unsuccessful attempts to purchase Texas. After the declaration of independence of Texas in 1836, many Americans favored early recognition and not a few desired to see her annexed to the United States. Even after annexation efforts failed, the activities of European governments in Texas, or the fear of such activities, kept the question alive in the minds of such men as Hunter and Calhoun.

Traders from the Middle West had been as much concerned about Oregon. Senator Lewis F. Linn of Missouri seldom missed the opportunity to press the subject of American rights in that region. He was aided, in 1840, by the publication of Greenbow's *History of Oregon and California* as a government document, and by the discussion of the Oregon boundary line in the negotiations preceding the Webster-Ashburton Treaty of 1842. The appointment of Doctor Elijah White as Indian Agent for Oregon in that year and the setting up of a provisional government in 1843, definitely raised the question of control and brought an open demand for the whole territory.[16]

The steps by which this expansion movement became tangled with the slavery controversy are not entirely understood. One thing, however, seems to be quite clear: the combining of these issues was the product of political scheming, not of inherent forces. The political ambitions of John C. Calhoun and the reforming zeal of his abolition rivals were, in part at least, responsible. Both had seen slavery implications in annexation when it had been advocated in the period of 1836–40. Calhoun, just after Texas had won her independence, had favored annexation to avoid annoyance to the slave states, and the American Anti-Slavery Society had circulated petitions against annexation on grounds that it would increase Southern strength against free speech, and the right of petition. The two groups had, at that time, given the issue a pro-slavery and an anti-slavery twist. Then, for a few years, interest had waned and the issue had lost both sectional and party appeal. But the necessity for political weapons had not lessened.

* * * *

Because of the intensity of personal and sectional rivalry, the three great politicians of the period, 1815–50, Clay, Webster, and Calhoun, found it necessary to take a stand on every important issue.[17] Each had to hold his own section and to win as much favor as possible in others. Clay, with his American System and his proposal for distributing the revenue from the public lands to the states in proportion to membership in the electoral college, made his bid for favor in the older sections where tariffs and internal improvements were needed and where the supply of public lands was largely exhausted. He aimed to keep lands high and the treasury empty. That would make tariffs doubly desirable. Webster more or less followed Clay's lead, showing more interest in tariffs than in lands and furnishing eloquent national and constitutional justification for the whole new urban-industrial expansion. The Northeastern in-dustrialists gave him unwavering financial and political sup-port, and Western men applauded his views even if they did not always vote in his favor. Calhoun, with less of party strength and with more vulnerable sectional interests to defend, was forced to emphasize the doctrine of States' rights, the good of slavery, and the evils of protective tariff. It was a less popular program and he, even more than the others, had to trim his sails and widen the bases of his appeal. Democratic support in the border states, especially Virginia, was hard to hold; the West was considerably more difficult to attract.

Calhoun made his great bid for Southern support in the 'thir-ties by defending slavery in the petition struggle. He sought wider favor by accepting the Independent Treasury. In 1837, and again in 1840, he countered Clay's land policy with bills providing for the cession of all public lands to the states in which they were located with half the proceeds of sale reverting to the federal government. That would enable the states to pro-vide their own internal improvements and, at the same time, keep treasury funds at a point where a higher tariff could not be justified. In 1842, he went so far as to assure Eastern Whigs that he would support a moderate tariff in return for aid against Clay's distribution schemes. The proposal was ignored, but neither he nor his state threatened action when the act, as passed, set rates well above the "moderate" level. Again in 1844, he acquiesced when the Democrats failed to fulfill their promise of tariff reform and squashed Rhett's Bluffton Move-ment for separate state action when Polk wrote a pussyfooting letter on the tariff to Kane of Pennsylvania. He climaxed his conciliatory efforts at the Memphis Convention in 1845 by asserting the right of Congress to improve the Mississippi River under the same grant of powers by which it improved seaboard harbors![18]

The approach of the presidential year, 1844, found these great leaders again in the foreground. Webster had just com-pleted the treaty with England which bears his name with that of Lord Ashburton. Some thought he deserved the Whig nomi-nation. Clay too had added to his strength by opposing Tyler and by advocating old Whig policies. The rank and file of the party viewed him as their leader and the party organization favored him to lead. Calhoun's problems, as usual, were more serious. His hold on the South and his concessions to the West strengthened the belief of his followers that he was the most popular man in the Democratic Party. But Van Buren controlled the machine. If delegates were chosen by the states he would control the Convention. Hope for Calhoun depended on delay so that public opinion could assert itself and on shifting the choice of delegates closer to the people. In both of these matters he failed. In spite of desperate effort on the part of Rhett, Hunter, and others to have delegates to the national convention elected by the districts and to delay the meeting until this was accomplished, the party machine, with Ritchie of Virginia cooperating, steam rolled Van Buren to the front. By the autumn of 1843, Calhoun supporters knew that some more dynamic issue was necessary if success was to be won.[19]

The suggestion that Texas might furnish just such an issue seems to have occurred to several politicians at about the same time. On October 10, 1843, R. M. T. Hunter informed Calhoun that, for Virginia, he regarded "the issues which we now have *and the Texas question* (should it become one of present or immediate interest) as the best for us that could be presented." He believed that the Texas question would be urged upon the South and West with great effect. The "combinations in Christendom against the slaveholding interests, the course of English diplomacy abroad, the state of Northern feeling at home and the present necessity for maintaining the balance of power between the free and the slaveholding states constitute[d] a crisis" which gave importance to the question. He said that Rhett and Upshur agreed with him in raising the issue in spite of the fact that it would divide the parties sectionally.[20] Early in December, Virgil Maxcy wrote that a rally "against Mr. V. B." on the tariff alone was hopeless and that the "more exciting topic . . . the Annexation of Texas was the only matter that [would] take sufficient hold of the feelings of the South."[21]

That these suggestions were not lost on Calhoun is shown

by a letter written to him a few weeks later by F. W. Pickens. It was evidently a reply to one from Calhoun. It said:[22]

I fully agree as to the importance of the Texas question in all its bearings. I think we are bound to take the highest and most decided grounds. I think the possession of Texas as a British colony would be just cause of war, and if the non-slaveholding states oppose its admission upon the ground of its strengthening the slave holding interests etc., we will be bound in self respect and self preservation to join Texas with or without the Union. . . . I am sure it is our policy to unite [Oregon and Texas] together, and thus separate the non slaveholding N.West states from the Northern states.

By December, 1843, Calhoun was out openly for the immediate annexation of Texas. On the 4th he wrote George McDuffie:[23]

I see the subject of Texas is destined to be one of the first magnitude. The interference there by Great Britain in order to act on our Southern institutions has presented it in a new and most important aspect, and so changed it, that those who were formerly opposed to the annexation, may well support it now.

On the 25th, in a letter to Thomas W. Gilmer, he went the whole way, declaring that the annexation of Texas was necessary to the peace and security of both countries and beneficial to the rest of the civilized world. He stressed the peculiar interest of "the Southern portion of our Union" in the matter and declared that opposition on the grounds of slavery extension ought to be met as a direct attack on the compromise of the Constitution.[24]

The important point in Calhoun's statements was the fact that he had adopted the Texas issue on sectional grounds. The great reason for annexation was the protection of slavery. Great Britain was promoting abolition. Duff Green, writing from Europe, had already warned Calhoun of England's intentions: Under the pressure of public debt she was unable "to maintain her commercial and manufacturing superiority, because she [could] not raise cotton, sugar &c as cheap in India as it [could] be raised in the United States." By making war on slavery, she could so hamper the Southern planter as to force prices upward, thus enabling the East Indies to compete and her monopoly in the manufacturing field to continue.[25]

Northern opposition to slavery extension also influenced Calhoun. In May, 1836, he had spoken in the Senate of "powerful reasons why Texas should be a part of this Union" and had gone on to say that "the Southern States, owning a slave population, were deeply interested in preventing that country from having the power to annoy them." Again, in 1837, as already noted, he had introduced resolutions denouncing Vermont's attempts to have the government declare against the extension of slavery by the annexation of new territories or states. He had called it "a new bold step, from a higher quarter" and had declared that "the subject [had] now assumed an aspect, in which it must be met by the South." "It is time the issue should be met," he said, "and it shall not be my fault if it is not."[26]

The long speech of John Quincy Adams, in July, 1838, denouncing resolutions for the annexation of Texas, and the charge, made in March, 1843, by Adams and twelve associates, that annexation was a pro-slavery scheme, may well have convinced Calhoun that the annexation of Texas and the security of slavery were one and the same. He may also have seen a pamphlet, published in 1836 by Benjamin Lundy, entitled *The War in Texas: a review of facts and circumstances, showing that this contest is the result of a long premeditated crusade against the government set on foot by slaveholders, land speculators, etc. with the view of re-establishing, extending and perpetuating the system of slavery and slave trade in the Republic of Mexico.* If he did, he read the bold statement that

the leading object of this contest originated in a settled design among the slaveholders of this country . . . to wrest the large and valuable territory of Texas from the Mexican Republic in order to reestablish the system of slavery, to open a vast and profitable slave market therein, and ultimately, to annex it to the United States.

The abolitionist had prepared the way for Calhoun. He could continue his fight against anti-slavery and at the same time capitalize on the latent enthusiasm for expansion. That might give him the presidency; it would at least do what R. M. T. Hunter had desired—make an issue with the anti-slavery feeling and arouse the public mind to its importance. If that could be done, the constitutional rights of the South might be preserved and the nation saved from disruption.[27]

Response to the Texas appeal, which the Calhoun forces launched in the early months of 1844, was immediate. Soon coupled with the demand for all of Oregon, it overshadowed all other issues and threatened to upset the best of political plans. West and South were in an expanding mood. The Northwest, although more interested in Oregon than in Texas, supported both moves; the South showed more interest in the acquisition of Texas and quickly stirred to the slavery appeal with which Calhoun endowed it. British interference in Texas, said the Jacksonville (Alabama) *Republican*, was "a subject of fearful interest to the people." "There is no question," it said a few months later,[28]

the tariff scarcely excepted, in which we think the people of the South are more interested. . . . Our peculiar institution of slavery is already boldly menaced by a strong and numerous band of fanatics in the North. Indeed the whole of the non-slaveholding states have manifested a great disposition to trample upon and disregard the rights of the Southern, as slaveholding states. . . . The balance of power is already against us. . . . The admission into the Union of all Oregon Territory . . . will perhaps make six large [free] states . . . added to those already existing. . . . Under these circumstances the addition of Texas with its slaves · is the only possible means of saving the South.

"That Texas question," wrote a citizen of Macon, Mississippi, "is one that has wakened up the South to a sense of her danger."

Calhoun, however, was not the only man with presidential ambitions who saw the opportunities in the Texas question. As early as October, 1841, John Tyler, unexpectedly President of the United States through Whig party strategy and the death of Harrison, had suggested to his new Secretary of State, Daniel Webster, the bright luster which might be shed upon the administration through acquiring Texas by treaty. The great secretary, however, was kept busy with other negotiations, and the matter lay neglected until his resignation in May, 1843.

By that time, the cleavage between Tyler and his fellow Whigs was complete and he had already begun the effort to build up independent political support. The Texas question promised to be useful in this endeavor. Properly handled, it might enable Tyler, in his own right, to retain the presidency. The first step in the program, as planned, was to get rid of Webster by sending him as ambassador to the Court of St. James. Everett, who was being replaced, was to go to China on special mission. A. P. Upshur, friend of Calhoun and advocate of the annexation of Texas, could then be appointed Secretary of State. Everett blocked the plan by refusing to resign, but Webster, well satisfied with the reputation already assured to him by the settlement of the northeast boundary, stepped aside without further pressure. The way to action was at last clear in official circles.[29]

Affairs in Texas also seemed to be more satisfactory. Lamar, who, after the United States had rejected annexation in 1837, had opposed all further efforts, retired from the presidency in 1841. Houston, his successor, was more friendly. He did not, however, take an aggressive stand. During the first three years of his administration, he gave "all the prominence possible to the alleged intrigues of Great Britain with Texas" but, after early overtures for annexation, appeared unconcerned about the matter. Throughout his administration Texas played the part of the coy maiden. European states were encouraged to hope that she might remain an independent state, thereby increasing their economic advantages; ardent advocates of annexation in the United States, meanwhile, were given every possible cause for alarm by her seeming indifference. Whether intended for that purpose or not, it was a splendid way to bring about renewed efforts for annexation.

Events now moved rapidly. After Webster's resignation, Legaré held the office of Secretary of State for a few months and then Upshur took possession. Spurred on by Duff Green's excited correspondence from abroad and the equally alarming reports sent by William S. Murphy, the American Chargé in

Texas, Upshur quickly reopened negotiations and made ready to annex Texas by treaty. His avowed reason for quick and positive action was his desire to protect slavery from British interference. Whether he represented Tyler's interests or those of Calhoun is a question. Certain it is that Calhoun was secretly informed of every move long before it was made. Equally certain is it that the Tyler administration, through Upshur, had given official sanction to the whole Calhoun approach to the Texas question. "For the first time in its history," says Professor Reeves, "the government deliberately assumed a position to the world that, in international relations, the United States stood for slavery; that the United States was nationally a slave power and opposed to abolition in a neighboring state as a menace to its own interests."[30]

The sudden death of Upshur, caused by an explosion on the gunboat *Princeton* in February, 1844, brought Calhoun directly to the center of action. His hopes for the Democratic nomination were now completely gone. The Van Buren machine had wrecked what he had believed were excellent prospects. For a time, he even thought of a party revolt. Then he decided to wait in private life for 1848. Upshur's death changed the situation abruptly. Friends in Washington at once urged his appointment to the vacant post. As the great friend of Texas annexation and the chief defender of slavery, Calhoun must be made Secretary of State to complete the negotiations already under way. Before Tyler could move, Virginia friends had committed him to the appointment against his own interests and wishes, and Calhoun, professing reluctance, but bowing to duty, had given his consent. Tyler accepted a bad situation with what grace he could command and Calhoun returned to Washington.[31]

The grim old South Carolinian, who thus again took the center of the stage, is one of the most difficult of all American leaders to understand. He was a nationalist who wrecked a nation in defense of sectionalism. He was a democrat who defended Negro slavery as an essential to liberty and equality. He was a legalist who understood the law only as a defense against majorities. In singleness of purpose and cold-blooded devotion to his duty, Calhoun was matched only by Jackson

and Polk—his fellow Scotch-Irish Presbyterians. Yet the political motives and methods of no other statesman of the day
were questioned by so large a number of honest men.

In private life, Calhoun was ever the austere Puritan. His
conduct, even by the strictest Calvinistic code, was above reproach. He neither drank, nor gambled, nor indulged in riot-
ous living. In youth, he scattered no wild oats; in maturity,
he "needed the forgiveness of neither man nor woman." He
was righteous and he knew it. Perhaps, as Gerald Johnson says,
his very virtues, when accompanied by the total absence of a
sense of humor, made for a self-righteous intolerance—an overbearing self-assurance, which could admit of no error and of no
compromise. When such intolerance was joined to a mind which
always reasoned closely and logically, quickly detected errors
in others' thinking, and reached only "sound and final" conclusions, the combination offered to a stumbling, blundering,
half-formed nation poor leadership for the solution of its many
problems.

In office, Calhoun lost no time in getting to work. He reached
Washington on the twenty-ninth of March; the treaty of annexation was signed on the twelfth of April. It went to the
Senate accompanied by correspondence which emphasized the
decisive importance of the slavery angle. Then, as the country
settled down to face the question of ratification, Calhoun presented his own version of the issues involved in a letter addressed to Pakenham, the British minister at Washington. The
excuse for this letter was found in a communication written by
Lord Aberdeen and presented to Calhoun's predecessor only
a few days before his death. It was a protest against the distortion of England's attitudes and explained carefully that, while
Her Majesty's Government desired the general abolition of
slavery throughout the world, she would not interfere unduly,
or with an improper assumption of authority. England had no
selfish interest in Texas, except "such as attached to the extension of her commercial dealings abroad." Emphatically,
Aberdeen denied any intention of seeking to act directly or
indirectly, in a political sense, on the United States through
Texas. "We shall neither openly or secretly resort to any

measure which can tend to disturb their internal tranquility, or thereby to affect the prosperity of the American Union."[32]

This letter required no answer. It most certainly was not a declaration of anti-slavery sentiments intended to disturb the people of the United States. Yet Calhoun's reply assumed exactly that intention. He expressed the President's deep concern over this first avowal of desire and effort for universal emancipation. He affirmed the still deeper concern over England's wish to see slavery uprooted in Texas and declared that the prosperity and safety of the United States were endangered by such attitudes. Abolition would place Texas under England's protection, and thus "expose our weakest frontier to inroads" from which emancipation would result in adjacent states. His letter closed with an announcement of the annexation treaty and a defense of slavery as a wise and humane institution.

Here was the whole story. Calhoun wished, and said the President wished, to annex Texas for the preservation of slavery and the Southern political power based largely upon it. The entire country was asked to defend such a course on such grounds.

The strictly sectional character of this letter to Pakenham caused many to believe that Calhoun was attempting to defeat the treaty he had just made, and thereby create an excuse for Southern secession. His private correspondence, however, shows that his larger aims were to vindicate and maintain the existing relation between the two races in the South, to secure greater unity among the Southern states and to unite them more strongly with the West. Expansion, he knew, was a desirable thing in most Western eyes. The annexation of Texas, the country to which so many men of the Middle West had gone, was an object of especial desire. Even Andrew Jackson, from retirement at the Hermitage, had written enthusiastically in favor of annexation. The South, Calhoun also knew, was both anxious for expansion and apprehensive regarding the security of her peculiar institution. Calhoun was moving on solid ground, even though he had overstressed the slave interest.[33]

Thus was the annexation issue thrust into the political arena where Clay and Van Buren confidently awaited nomination by the approaching party conventions. Certain of their control over party machinery, both hesitated to touch an issue so clouded with sectional hostilities. Perhaps they had even, on Van Buren's recent visit to Ashland, agreed to avoid the question. At any rate, on April 27 there appeared in the *National Intelligencer* a letter by Henry Clay written from Raleigh, North Carolina, a few days before, in which he "opposed at the present time" the acquisition of Texas; and, on the same day in the *Globe,* was published a letter of similar import from Martin Van Buren. Clay's letter was clear and concise; Van Buren's "ambiguous enough 'to preclude 96 out of 100 electors from ever acquiring a knowledge of its contents, except at second hand.'" The effect in both cases, however, was the same. Both candidates had misjudged the force of expansion appeal. Both had underestimated the strength of Calhoun's following and had ignored an abolition convention, that had met in Buffalo in August of the preceding year and nominated James G. Birney for President. Revolt began almost at once. The Whig Convention, meeting only a few days after Clay's Raleigh letter, unanimously gave him the nomination. But his attempt to wage the campaign on the domestic issues of tariff, the Bank, lands, and limitations on the President, fell flat before the flood of letters demanding that he make clearer his attitude on annexation. His Raleigh letter had been an attempted straddle. His efforts to repair the damage by insisting that he had no personal objection to annexation, but was unwilling to see the Union dissolved for the sake of acquiring Texas, only added to Southern distrust and aroused new apprehensions in the Northeast. He lost strength with every passing day.[34]

Van Buren fared even worse. The Democratic Convention did not meet until the twenty-seventh of May. By that time, although a clear majority of delegates were pledged to the former President, his enemies had gained enough ground to push him aside. For some, his annexation letter was enough reason for revolt; for others, it was a welcome pretext. Even Jackson now doubted his availability. By use of the two-thirds rule, the machine was completely blocked; shrewd leaders, like Gideon J. Pillow and George Bancroft, were able to bring forward to success the first dark horse in American party history. James K. Polk, groomed originally for the vice-presidency, received the nomination on a platform asserting our title to the whole of the Territory of Oregon and our wish for the reannexation of Texas at the earliest practicable period. And Polk was not one to take a party platform lightly. Bluntly honest and devotedly loyal, he accepted responsibility with a grim Scotch-Irish lack of imagination. When, therefore, in November his popular vote stood at 1,337,243, as against Clay's 1,299,062 and Birney's 62,300, it meant that the questions of Texas and Oregon were on their way to solution.[35]

It would be claiming too much to ascribe Polk's election entirely to his unquestioned support of the expansion program. That was, of course, a real factor in the West and South. His Kane letter, offering mild assurance to Pennsylvania on the tariff issue, influenced that important state, and the force of party loyalty assisted in all sections. Of greater significance, however, even if of less immediate importance, was the shift to the Liberty Party which took place in New England and New York. Clay suffered most, but votes given to Birney played their part in making Polk a minority President. Slavery and expansion had united to produce a major political upset. What that combination might mean to the future no one could have surmised.

To John C. Calhoun and President Tyler, the election of Polk meant but one thing: expansion had been approved. They might now complete their task. In his December message to Congress, Tyler spoke of the "instructions . . . most emphatic" which had "come up to both branches of Congress from their constituents" for the prompt and immediate annexation of Texas. He demanded action.

Up to that time Congress had been hostile to Tyler and Calhoun, if not to Texas. Throughout the days of party convention, the Senate had played politics with ratification and then had sharply rejected the treaty. The senators were now in a different mood. Expecting Tyler to leave action to his successor, they granted the President the choice of action by a new treaty or by joint resolution. Tyler did not hesitate. On the day before he left office, he despatched a special messenger to Texas to carry the joint resolutions and to urge Texas to accede to the terms required. On July 4, a Texas convention agreed, and in December President Polk approved the Congressional resolutions admitting Texas as a state.

Meanwhile, the West awaited action in regard to Oregon; the abolitionists sullenly repeated the old charge of slave-power dominance; the warring factions of the Democratic Party waited to see to which side James K. Polk would throw his favors. Few, if any, were conscious that a new day had dawned in the life of the nation.

CHAPTER NINE

THE POLITICIANS AND SLAVERY

IN May, 1844, while Whigs and Democrats, in party convention, struggled over candidates and platforms, another gathering, perhaps more representative and more significant in the larger balance of everyday American life, was in session in New York City. From thirty-three annual conferences all over the United States, one hundred and eighty delegates had come to attend the General Convention of the Methodist Church. Most of them belonged to the middle class. Many of them were from rural areas. As a cross section of the American people, they were probably no more typical than the politicians. They did, however, afford a better glimpse of the moral attitudes of the average man, a clearer expression of the American conscience stirred by the fundamental issues of the day.

Assembled for the general work of church business, the Conference was almost at once drawn off into a bitter conflict over slavery. First the delegates discussed the case of a slaveholding minister who had been suspended from the Baltimore conference for refusing to free his slaves. Then they turned to the more troublesome case of a Georgia bishop who, by a second marriage, had become a slaveholder. What should the church do when justification for slaveholding was based on the age and infirmity of Negroes who constituted a responsibility, rather than an asset? On what charge could such a slaveholder be tried? The Conference could only answer, after eleven days of debate, by asking the good bishop to desist from his episcopal labors until he had rid himself of his slaves. Compromise had failed. Slaveholding had been accepted as a moral issue. Slaveholders and non-slaveholders could not dwell longer in peace together in the House of the Lord. The closing days of the Conference were occupied with plans for separation. A year later, the *Methodist Episcopal Church South* came into being. A great American institution had broken along sectional lines.[1]

The Baptist missionary groups also divided in 1845 on the slavery issue, and the Presbyterians soon began an internal struggle which lasted until the opening of the Civil War. Thoughtful Americans viewed these happenings with genuine alarm. The slavery struggle, strangely connected as it was with almost every basic fear, interest, and dream in national life, had passed out of the realm of abstract discussion and had begun to influence the everyday affairs of men and institutions. When churches divided, how long could political parties withstand the disrupting force of an issue which had already influenced the outcome of a presidential campaign? Could politicians refrain from the use of a weapon which carried so much of moral force to the support of material interests? Here were many "fire bells" ringing in the night.

* * * *

The political maneuvering which gave James K. Polk the presidency widened rifts in an already badly divided Democratic Party. Calhoun had withdrawn from the presidential contest with none too good grace and had seemed to give only lukewarm support to the party candidate. The Van Buren faction was even less acquiescent to the party will. Blair's indifference was marked enough to draw complaint from Polk and reproof from Jackson. For a time it was feared that Benton might bolt the party; and Van Buren made no effort to check open revolt among his New York followers.[2]

The seriousness of the schism became apparent as Polk's administration got under way. One group of his advisers set to work immediately to destroy Blair and his *Globe* and to establish another paper, under another editor, as the official organ of the party. This was a bold move. Blair was close to Jackson. He had been a member of the famous Kitchen Cabinet. Under two presidents, the *Globe* had been the voice of the administration. Whenever actions or characters needed defense, Old Hickory had been wont to exclaim: "Send it to Bla-ar!" And "Bla-ar" had done so well that many considered him the real power behind the Jackson throne.

He had been even closer to Van Buren. The *Globe* had

wielded greater power after Jackson's departure because it spoke for both Jackson and the new administration. Even when the Whigs triumphed in 1840, and government patronage was withdrawn, the *Globe* continued powerful, for it was in a splendid position to point out the reasons for defeat and to shape issues for the next campaign. Its support of Van Buren for the Democratic nomination in 1844 very nearly carried the day for the crafty old New Yorker. The candidate's own failure to follow Blair's advice on Texas and Abolitionism greatly embarrassed the editor but did not weaken his influence to the point where Polk could dispense with his support in the campaign. Few, therefore, thought that the new administration would dare attempt to get on without Blair and the *Globe*.

But Polk had ideas of his own, and the influence of Rhett and Calhoun, Cave Johnson and Robert Walker was strong. On March 24, Blair was summoned to the President's office. Bluntly he was informed that he must step aside. The *Globe*, if it continued, must have a new editor. That failing, another paper would be established. Bitterly Francis Blair accepted his fate. A few months later, Thomas Ritchie came up from Virginia to edit the *Union*, the new official organ.

Polk attempted to soften the blow by offering the deposed editor the mission to Madrid, but Blair, as one of his supporters said, "on account of his honor, & the honor & interest of his friends" could "take no office from Mr. Polk." He retired to his country estate to brood over injustice and to find consolation through correspondence with the equally mistreated Benton and Van Buren. Jackson stood by his friend as well as he could, but the old General had lost much of his accustomed fire and he was too much in accord with the Western influences back of Polk to be entirely comforting. Blair was angry. Corruption and other sinister influences were at work in the party he had served and loved so well. He began to wonder whether the defense of his principles might require of him revolt from the party.[3]

Van Buren was treated as badly as Blair and liked it no better. His supporters in New York had come home from the Democratic Convention of 1844 certain that they had been betrayed. Against Cass in particular they were enraged, and against him they vowed vengeance. Silas Wright, the outstanding leader in the state, sharply refused the nomination for the vice-presidency and accepted the nomination for Governor only because he believed such action alone could prevent the complete disruption of the party. Two factions, differing on canal and taxation policies, were already in bitter conflict in New York. One group, more or less *locofoco* in sympathies, had allied itself with liberal movements and a few of its members had leanings toward the anti-slavery cause. The other group was more conservative and tended to follow the old political ways and policies of the past. Van Buren's friends were among the liberals. When their leader was dropped from the presidential race, many of them lost interest and some of them actually signed a document in which they pledged themselves not to vote for the party nominee. Van Buren himself, too much of a politician to engage in open revolt, held his peace but did little to insure party success.[4]

If the Van Buren element expected Polk to overlook such conduct when he distributed the spoils of office, they were badly mistaken. The President consulted briefly with Van Buren, and then offered Wright a place in his cabinet as Secretary of the Treasury, knowing almost certainly that the offer would be refused. He then made William L. Marcy of the opposing faction Secretary of War. A few lesser appointments fell to the liberals but thereafter administration influence was thought to favor the conservative faction.

Van Buren felt humiliated and irritated. Even Wright began to talk of the imbecility and roguery which held sway. Bitterness increased throughout Wright's term as governor, and the liberals drifted toward open revolt in alliance with the Liberty Party men who already were in arms against both the Hunkers and the administration in Washington. Soon they had become Barnburners, and in 1848 they were ready to settle scores with all regular Democrats.[5]

A third Democratic leader estranged through the election of 1844 was Thomas Hart Benton. Closely allied to Blair and Van Buren, Benton had been one of the important figures in the Jackson period. Prime spokesman of the West, staunch nationalist, and loyal Democrat, he stood with Webster, Clay, and Calhoun in party influence, and throughout the 'thirties, he dominated the party struggles. He had led the forces in Congress against the Bank. Almost single-handed, he had carried the fight to expunge from the record the resolutions of censure passed in the Senate against Jackson. So vehemently did he struggle for "hard money" and the Independent Treasury that he ever afterward carried the nickname, "Old Bullion."[6]

But Benton had not favored the immediate annexation of Texas. His interest in the trade which ran south and west from Missouri and his even greater interest in the silver bullion which came back from Mexican sources made him reluctant to favor steps which might lead to war with our southern neighbor. "Policy and interest if not justice and honor," he said, "should make us refrain from this war." Perhaps also, his hatred of Calhoun helped determine his attitude. The two men had differed on practically every issue since the first Jackson administration and harsh words had passed between them on more than one occasion. They both disliked and distrusted each other.[7]

Benton had enthusiastically supported Van Buren for the Democratic nomination of 1844, and he was bitterly disappointed when Polk was chosen. He turned on A. V. Brown, who had obtained and used to good effect a letter from Jackson approving the annexation of Texas, and accused him of playing the game unfairly. He charged the friends of annexation with being "tainted with a desire to dissolve the Union and speculate in land." He denounced Tyler; he flayed Calhoun. The Texas treaty, to his mind was "but the final act of a long conspiracy in which the sacrifice of Van Buren had been previously agreed upon." "The intrigue for the presidency was the first act in the drama: the dissolution of the Union the second." "Under the pretext of getting Texas into the Union, the scheme was to get the South out of it." So rabid did Benton become that even Jackson was ready to believe that he had joined hands with the despised John Quincy Adams.[8]

In the Senate, Benton took the lead against ratification of the annexation treaty. Without the consent of Mexico, he would have nothing to do with Texas. Later he changed his mind, but he almost blocked annexation by demanding a new treaty, which, presumably, would be drawn by the Polk administration after Tyler and Calhoun were out of the way. Francis Wharton charged that Benton had formed a coalition with the Whigs and was using the Texas question to spite Calhoun. "He will not brook your superior genius," he wrote to the Carolinian. Political and personal jealousy, he thought, lay back of the Missourian's actions.[9]

Such stepping over the traces would have been politically dangerous under any circumstances. With a revolt already brewing in Missouri, it was doubly so. Benton's hard money ideas had for some time been under fire at home. He had opposed the use of bank paper and had favored the chartering of but one state bank, whose issue would be confined to notes of large denomination. He had also limited the activity of insurance companies and had checked the use of small notes from banks outside of St. Louis. These policies had offended merchants and soft money advocates. Benton's refusal to support a new constitutional convention to reform representation evils and to do away with life tenure for judges had alienated another element. When, therefore, in Congress, the senator from Missouri opposed the good Western policy of annexation, the storm broke with renewed fury. In May, 1844, the Missouri *Register* spoke of the unnatural coalition of Van Buren, Clay, and Benton which opposed "the veteran heroes, Jackson, Johnson, and Cass" and "the sage politicians and statesmen, Calhoun, Walker, Polk, and Ritchie." The paper concluded that "Van Buren stands in awe of the infernal abolitionists of the North, and Benton is merely actuated by contemptible jealousy of Calhoun. They must not be permitted to stand in the way of the onward and upward march of our country to those high and holy destinies to which God and nature seem to have designed. May a dishonorable grave and a name forever infamous be the fate of him who will thus sacrifice the highest hopes and the dearest interest of our native land."

The fight had begun which was to ruin any chance Benton had for the presidential nomination in 1848; which was to prevent him from playing a hero's part in the Mexican war; and which was, in the end, to deprive him of his seat in the Senate.

Like Blair and Van Buren, he was to turn toward anti-slavery and to know the bitterness of political exile.[10]

* * * *

Out of such personal and political conflicts developed serious consequences for the nation. Historians are generally agreed that civil war between the sections became practically inevitable when the Northern and Southern wings of the Democratic Party split in 1860. They have not always understood that this break had its origin in the rift between the great party leaders of the Polk era. Scholars are further agreed that the Republican Party, which came into being in 1854, owed much of its early strength and more of its principles to dissenting Democrats who joined it. They have been inclined, however, to emphasize Whig influence and to seek the beginnings of the movement in the immediate period. Yet in the Polk campaign, years before the new party was born, the slavery question was for the first time phrased in terms of expansion—the issue on which the Republican Party was to be founded. In that struggle, too, appeared the first leaders in party revolt. Four years later Van Buren would head the Free Soil ticket. A few years after that Blair would preside at the preliminary convention which launched the Republican Party on a national career. In 1850, Benton would go down fighting in defense of anti-slavery in Missouri, and soon his son-in-law, Frémont, would become the first candidate for the presidency on the Republican ticket. The conflicts of the early 'forties thus marked the beginning of a new political era for an unsuspecting nation.[11]

Calhoun had started the trouble by his handling of the Texas question. He had not, unaided, made annexation and slavery a single issue. The abolitionists and other political schemers had already linked the two together before Calhoun brought them into the political arena. But Calhoun had made it appear that the South, more than any other section, was interested in the acquisition of Texas and that her great reason for this interest lay in the necessity for protecting slavery. He had, moreover, seized the occasion for again defending slavery in the abstract. His opponents were, therefore, perfectly justified in charging him, first as a presidential aspirant and then as a public official, with keeping the Texas issue constantly in the foreground and with giving it a Southern slant. They had good reason to believe that he was responsible in large degree for all the disasters which had befallen them; that he was unscrupulous; that he was wholly selfish; that his Southern bloc was the tool of slave interests determined to rule or to ruin the Democratic Party.

Sectional consciousness and sectional distrust were greatly augmented by these developments. Slavery became the symbol of Southern interests. Calhoun was increasingly thought of as the Southern spokesman. Other leaders and other Southern interests were overshadowed by the one man and the one concern. Opposing politicians, using fire against fire, began to adopt the emotional and moral attitudes of abolitionists. Anti-slavery became a weapon with which to fight a political foe and a rival section. Growing distrust of Calhoun meant growing distrust of the South. An increasing number at the North were ready to believe that the moral standards of neither this man nor his section were higher than those involved in Negro slavery as they understood it.

Both Blair and Van Buren shared this belief. In March, 1844, Blair had written of Calhoun's efforts "to give new features to the contemplated Treaty calculated to defeat it for the present & make it a main question for the next canvass." He had reference to "stipulations on the negro question, calculated to make it odious in the North & practically a Southern question." "Perfect Union in the South," Blair added, "has long been a favorite idea with Mr. C. no matter at the expense of a break with the Northern Democracy."[12]

After Polk's nomination, Blair complained of "the corrupt intriguers," who had taken Polk, "infinitely more disagreeable to them," for the sole purpose of "killing off" Van Buren for the present and "Benton for '48." Blair and Van Buren were both certain that the whole thing was a "war waged for the acknowledged or known purpose of extending or perpetuating slavery." It seemed obvious to them that a group of "despicable conspirators" promoting their presidential aims were determined "to make a crisis of this Texas business." Calhoun, of course, was branded as the arch-conspirator. He was regarded as the destroyer of Van Buren, the one who "decided the late controversy . . . in favor of Polk." The South, at his bidding, had betrayed the authentic leader of the party. Even Southern Whigs had gone over to the opposition through his influence. Calhoun was held chiefly responsible for the destruction of the *Globe*. In February, 1845, Jackson wrote to Blair:[18]

> Our mutual friend, General Robert Armstrong, spent part of yesterday with me, from whom I confidentially learned some movements of some of our Democratic friends, not of wisdom but of folly, that would separate the Democratic party and destroy Polk, and should of course drive you from the support of Polk's administration and separate the Democratic party. I forthwith wrote Col. Polk upon the subject and am sure he will view it as I do, a wicked and concerted movement for Mr. Calhoun's and Mr. Tyler's political benefit. It is this, to amalgamate the *Madisonian* and what was the *Spectator* and make that paper the organ of the Government to the exclusion of the *Globe*. I am sure that Polk, when he hears it, will feel as indignant at the plot as I do. . . .

But the *Globe*, notwithstanding, was destroyed, and Jackson could only conclude that the President had "been listening to the secret counsels of some political cliques, such as Calhoun or Tyler cliques" who had "gotten hold of his ear and spoiled his common sense." Polk had thereby called "down upon himself suspicions . . . of secretly favoring some of the . . . cliques who are looking to the succession of some favorite."[14]

Blair was sure he knew which of these cliques had influenced the President. Describing his interview with Polk regarding the *Globe*, he later declared that he had given the President ample warning of the failure which would come from helping "Calhoun & his emmessaries." He had told him that it would "lose him Van Buren, Allen, Benton, Wright—all the honest & truly patriotic statesmen of the party . . ."; that it was evidence of a policy "to sacrifice the honest to the perfidious."[15]

Benton likewise saw the hand of Calhoun and the slave interests back of the misfortunes which were befalling him. He was certain that the newspaper attack which followed his opposition to the annexation treaty was inspired by the Secretary of State and carried on through control of government printing. "Every Calhoun man and every Calhoun newspaper in the State, and in the United States," he declared, supported the move; three hundred editors were ordered to confine themselves to attacks upon Benton. And all of this because he had desired the peaceful annexation of Texas.[16]

Benton believed also that Calhoun was the author of the unfortunate war with Mexico which followed the ill-advised treaty efforts. Calhoun's friends, Marcy, Walker, and Buchanan, were, in his mind, responsible for the defeat of the bill which created the office of lieutenant-general for the more efficient execution of that war—"the appointment, it being well known, intended for Senator Benton, who had been a colonel in the army before either of the present generals held that rank." Calhoun had undoubtedly also influenced Polk to approve the court-martial of John Fremont, Benton's son-in-law. Calhoun was obviously the moving force behind the "soft" revolt in Missouri which later brought Atchison forward to contest with Benton for control of the state.[17]

Speaking, in September, 1849, of his political troubles during the past year, Benton said:[18]

Calhoun started it all. . . . I know of no cause for this conspiracy against me except that I am the natural enemy of all rotten politicians, and since the death of General Jackson, the chief obstacle to Mr. Calhoun's schemes of a Southern confederacy. I am for the Union as it is, and for that cause Mr. Calhoun denounced me in his own state, for a traitor to the South—a denunciation which gave the cue, and the signal to all his followers in Missouri to go to work upon me. Out of that came the conspiracy. My assailants here are his subalterns. He has but one code of acting against those who are in his way; and that is . . . assassination of character through subalterns while he lies behind the hedge, directing the operation and affecting to be above it.

Some of the charges which Blair, Benton, and Van Buren placed against Calhoun were well founded. The stern old South Carolinian was capable of considerable malice and his political ambitions were now rationalized into sectional necessity. He wanted to be President and he had convinced himself that the security of constitutional government, as well as the security of slavery, depended upon the realization of this ambition. The old Democratic leadership must be pushed aside. Duff Green had told him that if Blair, Benton, and Wright were given "three years to organize and pack another convention . . . there will be an end of the matter. Whoever the *Globe* nominates will be the Democratic candidate and that candidate will be defeated." Green called this "the crisis of the slaveholding interest" and added that "to hesitate now is to be lost." Lewis Coryell had been even more active. He, with John P. Heiss, checked the last-minute effort to select the *Globe* as the official organ of the Polk administration, and then pledged the funds to establish a new press. Still not satisfied, the Calhoun group, according to their own statement, continued to work upon the newly elected President until they had convinced him that he had "everything to fear and nothing to hope by identifying himself further with" the Blair-Van Buren crowd.[19]

Calhoun himself worked toward the same ends. He rejoiced at the overthrow of the *Globe* and declared that it was "a great point to get clear of Blair and his filthy sheet." He avowed his intention to support the new administration in all ways unless "forced by its acts to believe that they are resolved to restore to power the miserable clique, which was overthrown at Baltimore; and on the overthrow of which Mr. Polk was raised to Power." He dismissed Benton's charges as "light as air—old and stale, without even plausibility," but the famous Jackson Resolutions passed by the Missouri Assembly, and on which Benton refused to be instructed, were but a restatement of Calhoun's own words and were pushed forward by a group whom Frank Blair, Jr., called "the field marshals and devotees of Calhoun." Benton had good reason to devote nearly four fifths of his appeal to the People of Missouri to a discussion of Calhoun and his base influence.[20]

* * * *

The Polk administration, which was getting under way while these personal and sectional conflicts were developing, promised unusual activity and vigor. After a long period of deadlock, restraints were suddenly loosed and national problems were faced with a directness unknown since the days of Andrew Jackson. Expansion, tariffs, lands, and internal improvements, one after the other, were taken up in a manner which indicated a desire to solve the problems involved and not merely to play politics with them. After years in the shallows and eddies of idle talk and compromises, the nation had swung out into the main current and was moving forward toward its larger destiny.

This very activity tended to widen personal, party, and sectional cleavage and to force all issues, as they developed, into the sectional-slavery mould. In his Inaugural Address, Polk asserted the clear and unquestionable title of the United States to Oregon and recommended the extension of American laws to the settlers there.[21] He and his cabinet approved the Tyler invitation to Texas and the President agreed to protect the Texan claims to territory up to the Rio Grande. Early in the administration, the American consul at Monterey in California was instructed to discover and defeat attempts of foreign governments to establish themselves there and told to assure the Californians of the desire of the United States to render them "all the kind offices in our power" and of this nation's willingness to receive them into the Union when it could be done without offense to Mexico.

The sending of troops to support the boundary guarantees given to Texas and the refusal of Mexico to receive Slidell as minister, led to the outbreak of war with Mexico in May, 1846. The assertions of the United States in regard to Oregon led, first, to a brusque refusal of compromise on the forty-ninth parallel by Great Britain, and then to the termination of joint occupation. The Mexican war brought victory and the acquisition of a vast new territory which included California. The Oregon controversy ended in a compromise boundary line which followed the forty-ninth parallel from the Rocky Mountains, through the Strait of Juan de Fuca to the sea. Polk's "bold & firm course" had taken all of Texas and more, but had, in Oregon, fallen far short of the much shouted 54° 40'. The statesmanship involved in both controversies may have been sound; the political acumen revealed in the handling of neither was of such high order.[22]

Calhoun, of course, was eager for the completion of the Texas annexation even if it provoked a war of "little trouble" with Mexico. He did not, however, want a war and did not think that one was required. He was later certain that only "the great mismanagement by the Executive" brought the Mexican struggle. As to Oregon, he pretended at least to want the whole territory if it could be secured by being "quiet," doing "*nothing to excite attention, and leav[ing] time to operate.*" He believed that joint occupation was our trump card. It should be held until its playing would clinch the game. But when Polk wasted his trump and began to look John Bull straight in the eye, Calhoun quickly favored compromise and took the lead for a peaceful settlement. He later claimed the credit for saving the day in the face of Polk's blunders. To the very end, he insisted that if the Oregon question had been taken up first and handled with gentleness, but firmness at the same time, we might have had "*the whole Territory.*" With Oregon secured, we could have then taken all of Texas without a war with Mexico.[28]

Calhoun's desire for peace was due in part at least to his plans for the campaign of 1848. He knew that nomination by the Democratic Convention depended on adopting a program satisfactory to both South and West. With slavery and Texas he had already made certain of Southern support; his problem now was largely one of winning the West. The way to do this had already been pointed out by Hannegan of Indiana. Duff Green reported him as saying that[24]

> The West will be united and will demand funds for the improvement of their harbours, rivers and the Cumberland road, and the graduation of the price of public lands, and that if the South will give these to the West, the West will go with the South on the tariff. . . .

With this Western temper in mind, in November, 1845, Calhoun attended a convention at Memphis, Tennessee, to promote Western trade and internal improvements. He acted as presiding officer and, on June 26 of the following year, presented to the Senate a report on the Memorial of the Memphis Convention.

Both at the meeting and in the report, Calhoun argued that, under the power to regulate commerce, the central government could remove "obstructions from the western waters" as well as build "lighthouses, buoys, beacons, and public piers for the increased safety and facility of the commerce" of the Atlantic coast. He discovered, as some one said, that the Mississippi River was "a great inland sea." This was strange doctrine to come from the great champion of strict construction. Even the Charleston *Mercury* drew back with the terse comment that "if the federal government may do all that the resolutions of the convention propose, we can see no limit whatever to its power of engaging in internal improvements." The New York *Evening Express*, in the same frame of mind, wondered "at the liberality of Mr. Calhoun's views."[25]

Calhoun was, of course, not interested primarily in removing obstructions from the Mississippi. He hoped to "remove the only barrier, that remain[ed] between the Union of the South and West." As he wrote to his son-in-law:[26]

> The improvement of the navigation of the Mississippi was the great barrier, which kept them asunder and threw the West into the arms of the East. I hope I have forever removed it, by showing that the power is clearly embraced by that of regulating commerce among the states.

He followed this action by giving his support for graduation and reduction of the price of public lands, and by hinting that he favored such financial policies as Western men desired. Even Robert Barnwell Rhett was brought into line on these measures, consoling himself that all would be righted when Calhoun became President in 1848.[27]

The outbreak of war and the necessity of taking a position on the Oregon question were disturbing matters to Calhoun and his supporters. They had strained their principles if not their consciences to gain Western support. Now the turn of events opened the way for their enemies to strike. The best laid plans were in danger.

The reaction was not long in coming. "Fifty-four forty or fight" had been more than a slogan to men of the Northwest.

With home markets sagging and yields of grain increasing, Oregon had become a test of government sincerity—an issue in which the central government might prove that it had the interests of Western men at heart. Westerners had been willing, even eager, to fight for Texas; they viewed compromise on the Oregon boundary as nothing short of betrayal. They began talking about a bargain of 1844 which Calhoun and his South had not kept.[28]

Suspicion of bad faith became open protest when Calhoun took the lead against "the notice to Great Britain resolutions." Hannegan sullenly reminded the Senate that, "Texas and Oregon were born the same instant, nurtured and cradled in the same cradle—the Baltimore Convention—and they were at the same instant adopted by the democracy throughout the land. There was not a moment's hesitation until Texas was admitted; but the moment she was admitted the peculiar friends of Texas turned and were doing all they could to strangle Oregon."[29]

In the House, a like outburst occurred. When Rhett, Yancey, and other Southern leaders took the Calhoun grounds in regard to Oregon, Douglas of Illinois at first intimated and subsequently boldly charged the Southern members with an attempt "to play a game treacherous to the West." "He asserted distinctly that the Oregon and Texas annexation projects had their birth in the Baltimore convention . . . [that] they were 'cradled together' with a distinct understanding that if the West sustained the South in securing Texas, the South would sustain the West in her claims to Oregon." Wentworth of Illinois was even more blunt in his charges. He declared that the South had used the West to get Texas and had then abandoned it to oppose Oregon. Other Northwestern men, such as Brinkerhoff and McDowell of Ohio, and Ficklin of Illinois, reiterated the charge in equally plain language.[30]

Convincing evidence of an actual bargain between the politicians of the sections has never come to light. There is, however, no question about the bitterness and distrust which the Oregon matter stirred. Men of the Northwest more and more often spoke of the South as hostile to their interests—perhaps even responsible, through its control of Democratic officials, for the disasters and thwarted hopes of their section. More and more, they saw the reason for this hostility in the existence of slavery. They began to think that perhaps, after all, the abolitionist was right.

Joshua Giddings was quick to seize the opportunity to plant seed in fertile soil. He had earlier "voted against terminating our joint occupation of Oregon and against all political association with Texas." But, he declared, the annexation of Texas carried out "obviously to enhance the price of human flesh in our slave-breeding states, by opening a slave-market in Texas" had "dissolved" the "Union formed by our venerated predecessors" and had instituted a "new slave-holding confederacy, with a foreign government" in its place. "The whole of Oregon" was, therefore, "necessary to restore that balance of power," and to free the North which was "politically bound, hand and foot, and surrendered to the rule and government of a slave-holding oligarchy."

The people, Giddings believed, had "had abundant demonstrations of Southern feelings in regard to northern interests." "We know," he said, "it is vain for us to talk of maintaining the interests of the manufacturers of Pennsylvania, New York, and New England, while the political power of the nation is swayed by those who have always been inexorably opposed to them. No man of reflection can for a moment believe that southern statesmen, who have from time immemorial striven to destroy all protection to northern labor, will now turn around . . . and . . . lend their aid to sustain northern industry." A war with England would be preferable to acquiescence to Southern rule, for the "laborers of the free States would suffer less, in a pecuniary point of view, by a war with England, than . . . by a quiet surrender of their interests to the control of the slave power of the South." "I mention the laborers of the free States, including the agricultural interests of the West," he said, "as well as the manufacturing interests of New England and Pennsylvania."[31] He had already, in an earlier speech, discussed the "harbor improvements, and the improvements of our river navigation, as other measures in which the Northwest and West have felt great interest, and to which the South have been constantly opposed."[32]

Controversy over tariffs helped widen the party and sectional rift. And here also the slavery question thrust its ugly head into the conflict. Robert J. Walker, Polk's Secretary of the Treasury from Mississippi, an avowed free trader, presented, on December 3, 1845, a report which pointed out the nation's abundance of raw materials and its need for foreign markets. He prophesied the repeal of England's corn laws if the United States would reduce its duties; he advocated a series of tariff schedules to fit differing kinds of goods, and recommended the discontinuance of all specific duties and all minimums. A bill, following his proposals in most ways, was framed and, after sharp debate and some amendments, passed by both houses and signed by the President.[33]

This bill did not establish free trade. It only instituted tariffs for revenue—a rather imperative matter with war on hand. It was, furthermore, a scientific measure, quite superior to most tariff laws which have graced our records. Yet, in the House, the Northeast, except for portions of New York, New Hampshire, and Maine, where industry did not exist, opposed it regardless of party; Massachusetts, Connecticut, Rhode Island, and New Jersey gave not one vote in its favor. Only one member from Pennsylvania voted for it; his name was David Wilmot. Southern Democrats, on the other hand, gave fifty-seven votes in favor of the bill and only one against it. The North Central politicians, still relying on Southern support for more vital measures, remained loyal to the administration. But it was quite evident, from Whig speeches, that self-interest, not desire to aid the South, dictated the section's course. The Senate vote was closer, but just as sectional. The measure carried, twenty-eight to twenty-seven, and every one noted that the two senators from Texas voted for it. As Pennsylvania papers appeared in mourning and her leaders shouted "Repeal," many recalled the bitter words of Giddings in 1844:[34]

Are the liberty-loving democrats of Pennsylvania ready to give up the tariff? To strike off all protection from the articles of iron and coal and other productions of that state, in order to purchase a slave market for their neighbors who . . . breed men for the market like oxen for the shambles?

More directly of interest to the Northwest and consequently more provocative of sectional distrust was the question of internal improvements. Because the upper Northwest was facing an economic crisis, the old Western doctrines of easier access to lands, better ways to market, and more profitable markets were being agitated with renewed vigor as home markets broke and restless citizens began migrating toward the farther West. Something was evidently wrong with the democratic system. It was the duty of government to act quickly and positively to correct evils and to restore prosperity, the right of all good Western citizens.

Calhoun's Memphis doctrine had stirred hopes of Southern support which would ensure the desired legislation. A river and harbor bill, with generous provisions for the Great Lakes and the rivers of the adjacent territory, had passed Congress in the summer of 1846. To the surprise of many, Southern opposition to this measure had developed and Rhett and his South Carolina friends had led this opposition. Then, to cap the climax, Polk had vetoed the measure on constitutional grounds. The general impression was that the South and Southern attitudes were responsible. The West was furious. On April 7, the Chicago *Democrat* commented on the House vote, saying:[85]

> No man in Louisiana voted for it. No one in Mississippi. Only one in Tennessee. . . . Only two of the five Missouri members and only four of the seven Illinois members. No one in South Carolina or Alabama. Only one in North Carolina. Only one in Georgia. So much for the Memphis Convention.

In November, the same paper declared that "this harbor question is not a political one, but a sectional one. It is one between the North and the South. . . . Politics have nothing to do with the matter." By July of the next year, it was saying that, "Hereafter, the West must be respected, and her commerce must be protected as well as that of other portions of the Union: and the iron rod wielded over her by Southern despots must be broken. . . ."[36]

Throughout the remainder of Polk's administration, Western men "fumed and fussed." A Chicago citizen wrote to a friend:[37]

Chicago is prospering as usual. Lots continue to sell, houses to be built, & people to die as formerly, and our magnificent Lake frets, and foams, and storms this winter, more wrathily than even Ocean herself; and all because she can't get into the harbors. . . . We have a new defense to the entrance of our *harbor*, by either friend or foe. In its center stands the celebrated "Mount Polk," frowning, stationary & from its commanding position, hurling defiance to all who may approach our widespreading City, & should all the fleets in the world run butt up against *it, it* would not "budge a hair." . . . I suppose all the money is wanted in that friendly undertaking of ours, of civilizing barbarous Mexico, and when that is done, to introduce into the country that most princely & chivalrous avocation of raising, by some national process, *large crops of curled hair*. . . .

The Chicago *Daily Journal* stated the case more bluntly.[38] It declared that "the lives and property of the freemen of the North, her free laborers, sailors, and those passing to and fro upon her Great Lakes and Rivers" had ceased to concern the government because they lived "*in a portion of the country which [was] out of the pale of its care and protection.*" Northern lives "weighed against a Virginia abstraction, or that idol of the South, *negro slavery*," were nothing in the sight of James K. Polk. Southern jealousy of Northern progress was the sole reason for all objections to the Harbor Bill. The government's policies were being constantly changed at the command of the South. The *Journal's* protest ended on a rising sectional-slavery note:

The North can and will be no longer hoodwinked. If no measures for the protection and improvement of anything North or West are to be suffered by our Southern masters, if we are to be downtrodden, and all our cherished interests crushed by them, a signal revolution will inevitably ensue. The same spirit and energy that forced emancipation for a whole country from Great Britain will throw off the Southern yoke. The North and West will look to and take care of their own interests henceforth. They will deal justly with the South, but at the same time they will see that they have equal justice, and that the power to oppress shall not again be entrusted to men *who have shown themselves to be slave-holders, but not Americans,*

. . . The spirit of freedom yet lingers around Bunker Hill, Bennington, and Saratoga, and there are children yet living, of the fathers whose bones are bleaching there. They have ever been willing to allow more than justice to their Southern brethren, but they will not allow them to be their masters—they will have justice. The fiat has gone forth—*Southern rule is at an end.*

* * * *

Meanwhile the Mexican War moved on to its inevitable conclusion. The abolitionists, now reinforced by those whose economic and political toes had been trampled, endlessly harped upon the charge that it was an unjust war—a war of conquest waged solely for the extension of slavery. Thomas Corwin of Ohio declared that if he were a Mexican he would greet the Americans "with bloody hands" and welcome them "to hospitable graves." The legislature of Massachusetts called it a war to strengthen the slave power—one which could not be supported by honest men. James Russell Lowell broke into poetry to insist that

> They may talk o' Freedom's airy
> Till they're pupple in the face;
> It's a grand gret cemetary
> Fer the barthrights of our race. . . .

Sectional consciousness and sectional hostility colored every issue. Slavery and freedom were coming to be regarded as the distinguishing features of a South and of a North. The rift in the Democratic Party was widening. The politicians had begun to follow the course already trod by the Methodist and Baptist churchmen.

CHAPTER TEN

POLITICAL REVOLT

O N August 10, 1846, James K. Polk wrote in his diary: "Late in the evening of Saturday the 8th, I learned that after an exciting debate in the House a bill passed that body, but with a mischievous and foolish amendment to the effect that no territory which might be acquired by treaty from Mexico should ever be a slaveholding country. What connection slavery had with making peace with Mexico it is difficult to conceive." On January 4th of the next year, he again wrote: "The slavery question is assuming a fearful and a most important aspect. The movement of Mr. King today [the reintroduction of the same resolutions], if persisted in, will be attended with terrible consequences to the country, and cannot fail to destroy the Democratic Party, if it does not ultimately threaten the Union itself. Slavery was one of the questions adjusted in the compromises of the Constitution. It has, and can have, no legitimate connection with the war with Mexico, or the terms of a peace which may be concluded with that country. . . . To connect it with the appropriations for prosecuting the war, or with the two million appropriation with a view to obtain peace, can result in no good, but must divide the country by a sectional line and lead to the worst consequences." He concluded by declaring that slavery could never exist in any territory acquired from Mexico. Neither New Mexico nor California, the only regions in which the United States had any direct interest, was fitted for it. Agitation on the subject was, therefore, "not only unwise, but wicked."[1]

In these brief entries, the President of the United States revealed his reactions to a measure which became known as the Wilmot Proviso. He noted its irrelevance to the problems in hand. He forecast its dire consequences to party and nation. But he did not clearly understand that the endeavor of politicians to prevent the spread of slavery into new territory was the logical development from Calhoun's insistent but unnecessary use of the sectional appeal in slavery to gain personal and party advantage. Southern chickens were coming home to roost. The move to build a Southern bloc or party was beginning to produce a Northern counter-effort. The Proviso gave the North a perfect rallying point. So well did it serve the needs of Western and Northern politicians, just then a little uncertain of themselves, that it was soon attached to every bill which had the slightest sectional flavor. The Wilmot Proviso became the symbol of Northern interests in conflict with the interests of the South.

David Wilmot, who gave a name if not substance to the Proviso, was a rather insignificant country lawyer from a backward corner of Pennsylvania. He seems to have stumbled into history and then to have slumped back into a well-deserved obscurity lighted only by the afterglow of his one great moment. Contemporaries noted his slovenly dress, his unkempt hair, his constant use of profanity, and the ever-present quid of tobacco. They praised his eloquence and made especial mention of his ambition. They noted that Martin Van Buren was his hero; that party regularity was his greatest virtue.[2]

He had come to Congress in December, 1845, and had at once voted for the restoration of the rule which forbade the receiving of petitions asking "the abolition of slavery in the District of Columbia or any State or territory or of the slave trade between the States and territories." He had favored the annexation of Texas, opposed the River and Harbor Bill, supported the resolutions for notice to Great Britain on Oregon, and voted with the regular Democrats on the Walker Tariff. In the case of Texas, he had helped vote down an amendment offered by Julius Rockwell, a Massachusetts Whig, "which would have recommitted the resolution to committee on the Territories with instructions to add a proviso 'that within the State by this resolution admitted into the Union, slavery and involuntary servitude (except for crime) shall be prohibited, and all provisions of the said (State) constitution inconsistent with this proviso shall be null and void.' "[3]

Throughout the early part of 1846, Wilmot was a regular party man, loyal to the administration even when the pressure of local interests was strongly against such a course. Then suddenly, on August 8, when the request of the President for an appropriation of $2,000,000 for the purpose of terminating the Mexican War and adjusting the boundaries between the two republics was under consideration, he offered an amendment to that bill in the strangely familiar words that "neither slavery nor involuntary servitude shall ever exist in any part of the territory [acquired from Mexico], except for crime, whereof the party shall first be duly convicted." The public stirred. North and West responded as to a clarion call. The name of David Wilmot became a household word to the farthest corners of the nation.

* * * *

On the origins of the Wilmot Proviso and the reasons for its introduction, there has been much speculation.[4] Some early writers were inclined to view Wilmot as merely the spokesman of a group of disgruntled Northern and Western men, bent on showing their disapproval of Southern conduct. The bargain of 1844 regarding Texas and Oregon had been broken. Southern men had interpreted the Baltimore Convention resolutions "to mean all of Texas and the half of Oregon" and for that breach of faith they were being punished. The South had also proved faithless on harbor and river improvements. The real author of the Proviso, according to these scholars, was Jacob Brinkerhoff of Ohio. Believing that he could not secure the floor, Brinkerhoff had entrusted the amendment to Wilmot, whose friendship for the South was at that time taken for granted. Brinkerhoff, himself, claimed to be the author, and the original document in his handwriting was supposed to be among his papers. Wilmot's biographer would have us believe that this claim was not made until years later, but the facts do not bear out this contention. Gideon Welles states in his diary that he heard Brinkerhoff say on the day after the resolutions were first introduced that they were in his [Brinkerhoff's] writing. He also says that "while most of the originators of this measure were influenced by the purest and best of motives, there [was] no doubt [that] some . . . had vindictive feelings to gratify." Brinkerhoff later told Henry Wilson that the idea of a proviso arose simultaneously in the minds of several members and implied that other drafts were prepared by others of the group.

David Wilmot, however, always claimed exclusive authorship and the copy recovered in 1923 from the files of the Twenty-ninth Congress was most certainly in his handwriting. But he admitted that a group of men, including Preston King and Jacob Brinkerhoff, "were engaged in drafting an amendment, myself among the number, and several were submitted, all of which underwent more or less alterations at the suggestion of those standing around and taking part in the business going on. After various drafts had been drawn and altered, the language in which the amendment was offered was finally agreed on." Since this language was almost a direct quotation from Thomas Jefferson and since like provisos had already been offered by Julius Rockwell for Texas and by James Thomson for Oregon, the so-called authorship of the Proviso is not nearly so important as the fact that it was the work, not of one man, but of a group.[5]

More difficult to analyze are the motives behind the measure. Why did Wilmot, or any other man, introduce this Proviso at this particular time? Why did it create a national stir when other similar efforts had fallen dead? Convincing answers to these queries are not easy to find.

Wilmot's biographer implies that Wilmot acted solely because of his deep hatred of slavery and love of freedom. Most historians have rejected this explanation as too simple and too out of harmony with Wilmot's earlier record. Yet it must be remembered that, when Calhoun turned what had been an abstract constitutional question into a concrete moral one, many men were ready to act who earlier had been completely indifferent. It is quite conceivable that Wilmot should have acted as a loyal party man up to this point and then, quite suddenly, should have acquired conscientious scruples when brought face to face with the concrete question of extending slavery into a definite territory. Others might have undergone the same transformation of attitude.

Shifts in conscience, however, are often greatly aided by interest pressure. The political game is highly complex. The politician, forced to indulge in much of talk and always to justify his every act, may often be quite unconscious of his own deeper motives. Wilmot had greatly offended his Pennsylvania friends by his vote on the Walker Tariff. Did he now seek to regain their favor by catering to the well-known anti-slavery sentiment of the state?[6]

That he had been mercilessly criticized in Pennsylvania for his tariff vote there can be no question. Newspapers in the state called him "this recreant son, who basely betrayed her interests" and suggested that he "be banished from her territory." They declared that "his name and his deeds will stink in the nostrils of every true-hearted Pennsylvanian forever." This criticism did not come, however, from Wilmot's own district. His immediate constituents were not protectionists. A former governor once said that the only things they manufactured were shingles for which they stole the lumber, and that their only interest in *protection* "was protection from the officers of justice." Wilmot was reelected the following November by a comfortable majority. The efforts of outside Democrats to defeat him because of his tariff attitudes failed. The Proviso, moreover, was scarcely mentioned in the contest and did not, according to the local newspapers, add one vote to Wilmot's majority. The tariff vote may have played some part in Wilmot's decision. It hardly seems to have been the dominant factor.[7]

The general political disruption of the period suggests a better key to Wilmot's motives. Economic conditions were not satisfactory, and restlessness and distrust were developing on all sides. Appointments and policies were being determined by sectional and interest combinations and the compromises they permitted. Whether Western men had a hand in framing the Proviso or not, the support which they gave to it in the years following proved it to be a perfect expression of their sentiments. If Wilmot had not introduced his Proviso, some Western man would surely have presented one like it.[8]

Wilmot, as an individual, had suffered all the ills of the situation. In spite of his loyalty to the Polk administration, Pennsylvania patronage was controlled by Buchanan, and "discouragement" seemed "to surround all [Wilmot's] efforts in behalf of . . . friends." Even when his tariff vote brought assurance that he was "strong with the Administration," he "received no evidence that such was the case," and could only hope "that by and by [he would] be able to get something done." He therefore consoled himself with the thought that "it does require . . . some time, before a man can accomplish much here," and registered his determination "to give no rest to the President until he does in some proper manner recognize the strong claims of my district."[9]

But patience seemed unavailing. His friend George W. Woodward, selected by a caucus of more than two thirds of the Democratic members of the legislature to fill a vacant seat in the Senate, was shelved in favor of Simon Cameron. His constituent, Colonel Piollet, was passed over for a paymastership in the Army to give place to a Buchanan nominee. Wilmot had enough in common with neglected Western men to understand their discontent. He was close enough to Van Buren and Preston King in New York to share their spirit of revolt. Both his ideals and his resentments, like theirs, could best be expressed in terms of opposition to the spread of slavery into territory acquired by "Mr. Polk's war." Those who had made *expansion and slavery* the test of Democratic party regularity had also inevitably made opposition to *slavery extension* the accepted mode of party revolt. They enabled David Wilmot, politician, without change of character, to become David Wilmot, the moral crusader.[10]

This peculiar turning brought the politician and the social reformer together and wrapped the mantle of unselfish devotion to humanity, long worn by the abolitionists, about the shoulders of the party man. The movement against slavery was taken out of the hands of those idealists who had begun and developed it, and given into the keeping of the politician. The anti-slavery impulse, as a pure reform movement, came almost abruptly to an end. Its efforts at independent political action lost their force. Opposition to *the expansion of slavery* began to replace opposition to slavery *per se*. The issue became a practical one to be dealt with by practical men. It altered its whole character, but it lost neither emotional nor moral force.

The consequences of these developments were of greatest importance. The politician could now be a practical abolitionist and yet deny the charge that he was one. He could draw to his support all the moral forces behind the opposition to slavery and phrase his political programs in terms of right and wrong. The way was clear for the creation of a new type of political organization, one which would carry all the high and noble purposes of the Liberty Party, yet which would also represent the material interests of the sections now in conflict with the South. All that was needed was some event which would crystallize sentiment and precipitate action. The foundations of the Republican Party were securely laid.

*   *   *   *

Wilmot himself fired only the first gun in the new conflict. His Proviso soon became common property. "The North," wrote Alexander H. Stephens in January, 1847, "is going to stick the Wilmot amendment to every appropriation and then all the South will vote against any measure thus clogged. Finally a tremendous struggle will take place and perhaps Polk in starting one war may find half a dozen on his hands. I tell you the prospect ahead is dark, cloudy, thick and gloomy."[11]

Stephens was right. The struggle had only begun. The organization of government in Oregon and soon in California and New Mexico prolonged the conflict almost without interruption to 1850. In each of these cases, Congress entirely disregarded the provision in the resolutions for the annexation of Texas, which had drawn the Missouri Compromise line across the northern part of that territory and declared that states formed above it should be free and those to the south of it should decide the matter for themselves. Every foot of the new territory was thereby made a subject for dispute. Twice the

House passed bills for the organization of Oregon with the Wilmot Proviso. Southern men opposed with increasing bitterness. Jefferson Davis, Barnwell Rhett, and other leaders denied that Congress had any right to act on such matters. They did not expect slavery to go into Oregon, but they knew that a principle vital to the South was involved. In the end they offered to accept the extension of the Missouri Compromise line to the Pacific as a way to peace. But the Senate checked all measures and produced a deadlock. Oregon remained unorganized. Ultimately, when local government and the prohibition of slavery were accomplished facts, the opposition gave way. Even then, the South, as will be seen, accepted the reality with a sharp statement of principles, pregnant with danger for California and New Mexico.[12]

The reactions to the Proviso and the conflict it had stirred showed how fundamentally vital interests had been touched. Its introduction had cleared men's thinking. It had brought the basic issues into the open. For the first time the two great sections of the nation faced each other with something like a clear understanding of what was at stake. Must Congress make freedom national and slavery sectional, or must it keep its hands off except to protect? Was sole regard for Southern interests the price of political unity and national harmony? These questions must be answered even though the answers to them shake the foundations of the nation.

In the North, belief in the Slave Power suddenly sprang up in strange new places. "Respectable people" no longer shunned the idea. Resistance to slavery in the form of a positive refusal to permit its extension, became good political doctrine. Compromise lost its appeal. "We are against . . . any new slave territory . . . and against extending the constitutional inequality in favor of slaveholders beyond the states already in the Union," said the Cincinnati *Gazette*.[13] "It is time that the lovers of freedom should unite in opposing the common enemy by fixing bounds to their aggression," echoed the Cleveland *Plain Dealer*. On August 8, 1846, before news of the Wilmot Proviso had reached it, this latter paper had said, "Another four years will add slave territory enough to the South to for-

ever over-balance the free representatives from the North.
. . . Let the boundaries of Slavery be set!"[14]

The Ann Arbor *True Democrat* was even more emphatic.
"The North," it said, "is strong enough to submit no longer
like Southern slaves to the dictation of the South, especially
when it is asked to extend slavery beyond its natural boundaries." The *Daily Sanduskian* was ready to dissolve the Union
rather than to permit slavery to "pollute the soil of lands now
free," and the Chicago *Democrat*, galled by the treatment
which the West had received in the rejection of River and Harbor bills and in the failure to secure all of Oregon, added a
new note by opposing slavery in that territory because it was
"wrong," not because "it was above 36° 30'."[15]

The legislatures of both Ohio and Michigan passed resolutions against slavery extension in 1847—a thing which all
except one Northern legislature would ultimately do. In
1848, the Ohio State Democratic Convention resolved "that
the people of Ohio look upon slavery as an evil in any part of
the Union, and feel it their duty to prevent its increase, to
mitigate and finally to eradicate the evil." That was a new
way for Ohio Democrats to talk! Chase had been right when
he had insisted that the political views of the Democrats were
in the main sound.[16]

How closely all this was connected with Southern opposition
to Western interests is shown by the comment of the Detroit
Daily Advertiser:[17] "Millions may constitutionally be ex-
pended in the acquisition of southern slave territory, and in the
improvement of southern rivers and harbors, but not a cent on
the great avenues of northern commerce." The Chicago *Journal* complained that "the Treasury doors" were "unbarred
whenever the *'open sesame'* is whispered by a slave driver,"
and the *Daily Sanduskian* insisted that "we have an administration that knows no country but the South, and pursues no
object but the perpetuation of slavery." The Chicago Convention of July, 1847, called to consider the matter of internal
improvements, became a veritable anti-Southern meeting, and
played no little part in shifting the market-hungry eyes of the
Northwest toward the Atlantic seaboard. New Orleans had

good reason for her fear that the contest "between North and South [was] not limited to slavery or no slavery" but was "a contest for the wealth and commerce of the great valley of the Mississippi"—one which was to decide "whether the growing commerce of the great west [should] . . . be thrown upon New Orleans, or given to the Atlantic cities."[18]

Economic neglect and moral indignation begat political discontent. Throughout the Northwest, local groups in both major parties hastened to proclaim themselves the champions of free soil. A few men shifted sides; others set to work to alter the attitude of their own party on important measures. Unrest was particularly noticeable in Ohio. Giddings, as has been said, boldly changed his earlier position in regard to Oregon and urged its admission with the Proviso as a check on the Slave Power. Soon he broke openly with his party and was ready to support the free-soilers. Salmon P. Chase, first Whig and then Liberty leader, began to view the Democratic Party as the logical carrier of free-soil doctrines, and to urge that Liberty men affiliate themselves with any non-partisan group which would oppose the extension of slavery. This liberal attitude of Chase and other leaders who desired to unite all those who "prefer free territory to slave territory and are resolved to act and vote accordingly," alarmed the party regulars and caused them to view the Ohio Liberty group with much suspicion. They were getting too much like "other men."[19]

For six years, Chase had been conscious that the existing political structure did not rest upon solid foundations. Party ideals and party practices were not in harmony. He had already expressed his conviction that the people of Ohio revered "the maxims of true Democracy [which were] identical with those of true Christianity in relation to the rights and duties of men as citizens." Christianity and Democracy, to his mind, were both "founded on the love of mankind and the immutable principles of equality and justice." "Ignorance of the proper application of these principles to slavery as it exist[ed] in this country" alone permitted that institution to continue. "Once enlightened on this subject," Democrats, even "multitudes in slave states . . . would hail with joy . . . a movement . . . to restore the government to its original principles," these principles being that this was "a non-slaveholding government" and "a non-slaveholding nation."

Soon afterward, Chase assured his friend Giddings that: "The country [was] beginning to awaken at length to the danger of slaveholding encroachments, and the time [was] rapidly drawing on . . . when the champions of freedom [would] have the place which of right belong[ed] to them in the confidence & favor of a long deceived & oppressed . . . people." He felt that there was "now a glorious opportunity to restore the government to its original principles," and he urged Giddings and his associates "to take the position of leaders of the Liberty party and *issue an address to the People which will be responded to throughout the land.*"[20]

These were prophetic words! A decade later Chase would act upon his own advice and a new party would rise into being. One free-soiler, at least, had shrewd political sense.

Meanwhile, Chase seized upon the case of one John Van Zandt, charged with aiding in the escape of fugitive slaves, as an opportunity to clear up clouded Democratic minds. A recent Court decision (Prigg *vs.* Pennsylvania) had held that the States could not be compelled to enforce fugitive slave laws but that such enforcement was a function of the federal authorities. Chase questioned the constitutionality of the act of 1793 on which the decision was based. He declared it subversive of the sovereignty and independence of the States and repugnant to the feelings of men. Both natural law and the Constitution were against it. The Courts were not bound to enforce it. With the aid of his associate, William H. Seward, he went over the whole constitutional ground, and found there no support for slavery.[21]

While Chase labored in Ohio, political dissension broke out anew in New York State and became a matter of national importance. The "sacrifice" of Van Buren in 1844 had left its scars. The Texas question opened old wounds. Preston King, close friend of Van Buren, broke away from the administration, and back in Albany the old factions renewed their struggles in ways which showed how deeply "the Free-Soil sentiment had . . . taken root among the Radicals. . . ." When Silas Wright insisted on running for reelection as governor, the Hunkers deserted in such numbers as to cause his defeat. Wright's death a few months later made him a martyr and left his supporters vowing "to do justice to his murderers."[22]

The Wilmot Proviso brought about new clashes. King was close to its author and zealous in its reintroduction. Hunker representatives, such as Selah B. Strong, denounced him, and Hunker counties were soon passing resolutions calling him an enemy to his party and his country. Then Martin Van Buren let it be known that he favored the Proviso. Charges of treason to satisfy personal grudges flew thick and fast. His friends countered with charges of subservience to slave domination. The refusal of the state Democratic Convention of 1847 to declare opposition to slavery extension "sound Democratic doctrine," brought an open split. The Radicals became Barnburners and walked out of the Convention. Meeting at Herkimer a short time later, they declared their belief "in the dignity and rights of free labor; resolved that free white labor cannot thrive upon the same soil as slave labor; and that it would be neither right nor wise to devote new territory to the slave labor of a part of the States, to the exclusion of the free labor of all the States." The Democrats of New York were hopelessly divided.[23]

* * * *

Southern reaction to the Wilmot Proviso developed more slowly. Congressmen answered quickly enough, but the people were not greatly disturbed. Even Calhoun at first viewed the battle as one to be fought out between Northern factions. "It has been forced into politics with you," he told a Northern correspondent, "and it must now be put down politically, or triumph with you, with all the inevitable consequences that will follow—disunion among others." But he was greatly disturbed when Congress met in December, 1846. The future never looked darker or more uncertain. Rhett was equally alarmed. In his speech of January 15, 1847, he clearly stated the constitutional theory of property rights which Calhoun, a month later in the

Senate, elaborated as the Southern answer to the Proviso and the basis for a proposed new Southern political party.[24]

Alluding to the expressed determination of Northern states to exclude slavery from the territories and to prevent the further admission of slave states, Calhoun prophesied the reduction of the South, as an artificially created minority, to the position of an economic and political dependency. He stated the federal theory of government and declared the States, not the people, to be the constituents of the American federation. He insisted that the territories were "the common property of the States" and that the settlers could establish "what government they may think proper for themselves."

He followed these statements with resolutions asserting common ownership of territories and denying the right of Congress to pass any laws which "make any discrimination between the States" or deprive any citizen of any state from emigrating with his property into any of the territories. These resolutions closed with the declaration that a people, forming a constitution, have a right to make a government according to their own wishes and without conditions being imposed by Congress.[25]

The Southern States awoke. On February 18, the Richmond *Enquirer* announced: "The tocsin, 'the firebell at night,' is now sounding in our ears; the madmen of the North and Northwest have, we fear, cast the die, and numbered the days of this glorious Union." "Do the wicked men of the North imagine," it asked, "that we will be silent or inactive when enactments are proposed incompatible with our existence as freemen?" "Men of the South!" it continued, "the danger which threatens you is imminent! Speak forth, then, and warn those who would violate your rights . . . of the fate which will await them."[26]

A few days later, the legislature of Virginia adopted a series of resolutions, similar to those of Calhoun but even more emphatic. They denied the right of the federal government to control slavery and agreed to resist the Proviso at all hazards and to the last extremity. They urged all Southern men, as they valued "their dearest privileges, their sovereignty, their independence, their rights of property, to take firm, united and concerted action in this emergency." Duty required that every man to whom the Union was dear should vigorously oppose the application of the Proviso to territories.[27]

Governor Brown of Mississippi praised these resolutions and assured the governor of Virginia that his people, regardless of party, would support them. The South, he said, must "first exhaust all the sources of reason and argument in exhorting our Northern brethren to let us alone on this subject," but if persuasion failed they must "feel prepared . . . to become enemies and defend [their] rights with those means which God and Nature [had] placed in [their] hands. . . . The South must be united."[28]

Alabama, likewise, endorsed Virginia's action, and her State Democratic Convention echoed the Calhoun resolutions. North Carolina was less excited, yet her newspapers talked of ending party distinctions and taking the final stand. A local meeting denounced the "audacious outrage upon Southern rights," and the State Democratic Convention (1848) agreed to oppose the Proviso in "whatever shape it may be presented." The Texas legislature declared that "we will never submit to a usurpation of power which robs us of our rights." Georgia was, as usual, moderate. Robert Toombs had warned his colleagues in the House that the South would stay in the Union on grounds of perfect equality, or not stay at all, but Alexander H. Stephens and J. M. Berrien had headed a move to eliminate the whole issue by a pledge not to acquire territory as a result of the Mexican War. The same conflict of opinion was revealed in the Georgia State Democratic Convention where, only after the most bitter debate, the delegates declared that no Proviso legislation could be recognized as binding, that slavery had a right to enter all territories and that they could vote for no presidential candidate who did not "unquestionably declare his opposition to the Principles and Provisions of the Wilmot Proviso."[29]

South Carolina, meanwhile, became the center of opposition. Her newspapers vigorously denounced the Proviso and heartily approved of Virginia's action. When Calhoun stopped over in Charleston on his way home from Washington in March, the citizens gave him a warm and even enthusiastic welcome—the occasion, of course, for a speech. In it, Calhoun "dwelt wholly on the slave question, its dangers and our means for resisting it." When he had finished, the meeting adopted the Virginia resolutions verbatim and declared that submission to the Proviso "would be unwise, dangerous, dishonorable, and debasing." Other communities throughout the state followed in the Charleston wake, holding "the Union as dust in the balance," requesting representatives in Congress to return home, and pledging resistance "although a dissolution of the Union be the result."

Even B. F. Perry and Waddy Thomson were caught in the excitement. Perry declared that the issue was one of life and death and that the passage of the Proviso was "tantamount to a dissolution of the Union." Thomson advised resistance at all hazards and to every extremity to this act which would convert "the South into black provinces." He too was ready to dissolve the Union if the hated Proviso passed.[30]

*   *   *   *

Under such emotional strain, the people of the United States approached the presidential campaign of 1848. Both parties had been badly shattered in the past four years; both were hard pressed to find new leaders who would replace the old without creating too much hard feeling. On the basis of accomplishment, Polk deserved consideration from the Democrats, but his enemies were many and his chances hopeless. Calhoun had long looked forward to 1848, but the Mexican War, Oregon, and Ritchie had ruined his chances and even he recognized the fact. Van Buren and Blair had long planned that Benton should head the ticket that year, but his military career had failed to materialize, his old fight with Calhoun had again broken out in open warfare, and the Wilmot Proviso had put him completely out of the running. Even in Missouri, he faced rebellion. Blair, therefore, turned to Zachary Taylor. The simple-minded old general, however, refused to come over to the Democrats and they could not "go in for him" even though Jefferson Davis assured them that he had "always claimed to be a Jefferson Democrat."[31]

The situation was not improved by the sharp development of party factions in the Northwest and especially in New York, where the Barnburners had revolted and chosen their own delegation to the National Convention. It grew worse when that convention met. When a rule was passed requiring all delegates to support any candidate nominated, the New York liberals walked out; when a resolution favoring "non-intervention with the rights of property of any portion of this Confederacy . . . in the States or in the territories, by any other than the parties interested," was voted down, William Lowndes Yancey and one of his fellow Alabamians also withdrew. Availability became the one test of a candidate. William Allen of Ohio was offered the nomination. He refused. Then the choice fell on Lewis Cass of Michigan, whose place of residence and whose recent Nicholson Letter, favoring squatter sovereignty in the territories, constituted his chief claims to support.[32]

The Whigs were more fortunate. Under the clever guidance of Thurlow Weed, Simon Cameron, and J. J. Crittenden, they did what the Democrats had not done—"went in for" Taylor, who was ready and willing to accept the nomination from either or both parties.[33] Rudely, but wisely, they rejected Henry Clay, best loved and most deserving of all their number, and, with the scent of victory in their nostrils, achieved a unity quite out of keeping with their actual condition. A Clay supporter summed up the situation thus:[34]

I have voted for Mr. Clay all the time, have *bet* on him, and lost, until I am tired, and have finally concluded that Mr. Clay is *too pure a patriot* to win in these *demagogueing* times— We must mix up a little *"Humbugging"* with our glorious Whig creed, before we can expect a victory—and Gen Taylor's *military fame* is about the best we can make use of at present. . . .

The nomination of neither convention satisfied those who had risen above party to face the vital issues of the day. Taylor was a Southern man and a slaveholder. The Proviso conflict had caused many men at the North to declare that they would never again "vote for a President . . . from a slaveholding state." This sentiment was so strong among Indiana Whigs that leaders feared that they would bolt the party and nominate a Northern candidate.[35] The *Lafayette Journal* called Taylor's nomination "an insult to the intelligence and virtue of the American people"—"a disgrace to the Convention." In Ohio, "many Whigs became incorrigible fanaticky—mad men upon the subject of electing a slaveholding President"— "goaded on," as one of the party leaders said, "by as graceless demagogues as ever roamed unhung."[36] Giddings left the party declaring: "Sooner shall this right arm fall from its socket and my tongue cleave to the roof of my mouth than I will vote for Zach Taylor for President." The Western Reserve was full of rebellion. "And this is the cup offered by slaveholders for us to drink," cried the Cleveland *True Democrat*, "We loathe the sight. We will neither touch, taste, nor handle the unclean thing."[37]

Cass was received with even less grace by disgruntled Democrats. Calhoun had kept South Carolina out of the convention and he now urged that state to remain neutral. If a choice must be made, he preferred Taylor to Cass. Rhett hesitated. He had early approved of Taylor but he had been angered by the recent Whig defeat of the Clayton Compromise, which organized Oregon without slavery but left final settlement in other territories to the Courts. He decided to remain loyal to the party and support Cass, but the city of Charleston refused to follow his lead. Calhoun men in Georgia also deserted the Democratic nominee, and up-country farmers fell in behind them in surprising numbers. It became evident that Cass could not carry the older South.[38]

Wentworth out in Illinois resentfully remembered that Cass had not attended the Chicago River and Harbor Convention in 1847. When the Democratic platform approved Polk's internal improvement veto and ignored the public land question, Wentworth was certain that his section could expect nothing from the candidate of that convention. Throughout the campaign his efforts for party success were only halfhearted. Even in Michigan all was not well. The Nicholson letter displeased a legislature which had only recently endorsed the Wilmot Proviso. Wisconsin papers spoke of subservience to the South, called Cass unfit to represent Democratic principles and declared that he "ought to have the reprobation of men of all parties."[39]

The real center of revolt, however, was in New York. The "arbitrary and insulting exclusion" of the Barnburner delegation from the Baltimore Convention completed the division of the party in that state. The nomination of Cass opened the way for the calling of a separate convention and the selection of another candidate. Instinctively disaffected New Yorkers turned toward Van Buren. He had already endorsed the Wilmot Proviso, and his son John had been a leader of the Barnburner faction from the beginning. Van Buren had always believed that Cass' desertion in 1844 had been a deciding factor in his own rejection by the convention of that year. He considered the Hunkers henchmen of what Blair called "the bastard dynasty at Washington," which had permitted Calhoun to dominate. The time had come when "the party & the country [might] be more effectually served by putting a wall between [the true Democrats] . . . & the persons who now but pretend[ed] to represent the Democracy."[40]

On June 16, a committee, complying with their own feelings, and with those of their constituents, addressed the ex-President with an inquiry regarding his willingness to accept the nomination of a new party eager to preserve "the great Jeffersonian doctrine now boldly repudiated in the South, and by too many tamely surrendered in the North—that slavery, or involuntary service should not, by an action of the Federal Government, be extended to the Free Territories of this union. . . ." Blair urged him to accept. He was certain "that a general revolt [was] possible," and "the defeat of Cass inevitable." But Van Buren hesitated. Not until a convention meeting at Utica on June 22 nominated him in the face of his first refusal did he acquiesce. For the first time in American history an ex-President had revolted against his party! The nation was dumb-founded![41]

Late in August, the bolting elements from the whole Great Lakes region, augmented by a New England group, met at Buffalo in a convention which, for seriousness and almost religious enthusiasm, was not to be matched until the day when Theodore Roosevelt marshalled his forces "at Armageddon." Men sang and prayed. They called themselves a union of free men, resolved to maintain the rights of free labor against the aggression of the Slave Power. They labelled their platform a second Declaration of Independence.

The platform so designated was an interesting combination of moral indignation and shrewd political insight. Offered as a national platform of freedom, in opposition to the sectional platform of slavery, it declared that Jefferson's proviso had prohibited slavery after 1800 in all the territories of the United States, Southern and Northern; that slavery depended on state laws and that Congress had no power to institute or establish it but should relieve itself of all responsibility for its existence or continuance. There must be no more slave states and no more slave territory.

The practical program set up by the convention might have been drawn by John Wentworth or any other grumbling Northwestern man. It included freedom and established institutions in Oregon, California, and New Mexico, cheap postage, a frugal government, river and harbor improvement, free lands to actual settlers, and a protective tariff! Not a sectional interest was overlooked. All that Western Christianity and democracy considered essential for genuine progress was to come to pass. The needs of the nation's most rapidly growing section had at last been recognized by a political party. The cry of fanaticism could not cover so cold a fact!

Of the campaign it is not necessary to speak. In November, Taylor was elected President, and the Whigs, again without a program, were in power. The Van Buren-Free-Soil defection had broken the Democrats in New York and weakened them in the wider Northwest. Great numbers of Southern Democrats had deserted the party. "Is it not extraordinary," wrote James Cooper to Howell Cobb, "that so large a wing of the Democratic Party has deserted without a solitary leader at their head? The rank and file have rebelled by regiments. . . . We have been stabbed in the dark." "It is with pain," wailed the Raleigh *Standard*, "that we confess the mortifying fact that . . . we have lost hundreds of votes, solely on the ground that Gen. Cass was a Northerner and Gen. Taylor a Southern man."[42]

Sectional vituperation began at once. The Illinois *State Register* spoke of "the lamentable defection of the South in the crisis." Wentworth's Chicago *Democrat*, in a thoroughly "I-told-you-so" mood, pointed out the fact that General Cass had not carried "a single Southern State except . . . [those] he could have carried without that Nicholson letter which proved so fatal to him in the North." "The Union is still ruled by the capitalists of the South . . . who by their slave representation overrule the North and continually seek to bring it to their feet. . . ." The same paper warned its readers that the South would never be satisfied "until slavery is extended in all the territories . . . and free labor is entirely degraded there. . . ." Doctor Graham Fitch of Indiana soundly expressed the general feelings of the section when he declared that:[43]

We of the North were willing to make a partial sacrifice of feeling to preserve our ranks unbroken, and thus continue the supremacy in our national councils of those great principles for which we have ever contended. But how with the South? Professed Democrats there deserted us by the thousands, permitting us to be defeated in States upon which we surely relied, and giving us others by such meager majorities that the moral effect was that of defeat. And why this desertion? Not because the political principles of the opposing candidate, General Taylor, were more consonant with their views, but because he was one of themselves, a slaveholder; and they knew that under his administration their "peculiar institution" would be fostered and extended. They sacrificed principles to slavery. . . .

Here was the whole story. Southerners had proved themselves to be slaveholders first, and Democrats afterward. They had acted as sectionalists. The North, therefore, must also forget party and advance with the firm determination to check all schemes to extend slavery.

* * * *

Immediately after the election, Francis Preston Blair sat down to console his old friend Martin Van Buren. "The election," he wrote, "has eventuated as well as possible. Our forlorn hope has accomplished all that was wished & more than we had any right to expect for the free soil party." He noted that every Cass and Taylor man in the North had been compelled to assert the adhesion of his candidate to "the principle of no new Territory to be annexed to our Africa." He was convinced that, if there "should be an equivocation in giving effect to this absolute interdict," the Free-Soil Party would "grow to a power which [would] shake from their lofty pedestals those who gained them by hollow professions."

Van Buren replied that of the 121,000 votes he had received in New York, "more than 100,000 were those of out and out & incorruptible Radical Democrats, who [could] neither be bought, forced or driven by any power on earth." Parties were forming along sectional lines! A new political day was dawning.[44]

CHAPTER ELEVEN

THE FIRST CRISIS

THE election of 1848 only intensified the sectional conflict. The short session of Congress which convened a few weeks later was less than ten days old when the slavery issue made its appearance. Senators tried to avoid a struggle; Representatives seemed to court trouble on every possible occasion. To the last sessions of the House the issue remained a smouldering fire which broke intermittently into flame. "From morning to night, day after day and week after week," said a member, "nothing can get a hearing that will not afford an opportunity to lug in something about negro slavery. . . . Sir, I am heartily tired of this nigger business. I want a change. I beg gentlemen to remember there are some white people in this country, and that these white people are entitled to some consideration. . . . Yet, a stranger . . . on listening to the debates on this floor would consider . . . that Congress was instituted mainly for the benefit of negroes."[1]

Dissatisfaction over political irregularity was in part responsible for this condition. The more positive attitudes taken toward slavery by both sides was a more important factor. Robinson, a Democrat from Indiana, boldly charged that slavery had determined the result of the late presidential election and that henceforth he intended to support the Wilmot Proviso regardless of party pressure. Brown of Mississippi, an equally good Democrat, complained that "thousands and tens of thousands of voters in the North [had] been brought to General Taylor's support on the Free-Soil issue." Hereafter he intended to vote on all occasions "to maintain the rights of the South in their broadest latitude."[2] Extremists saw the opportunity to press issues with greater effect and to keep political waters troubled. In that spirit, Root of Ohio asked that the Committee on Territories be instructed to report a bill providing a territorial government for each of the Territories of New Mexico and California, and excluding slavery therefrom. Giddings then tried to secure an act by which the citizens of the District of Columbia, black and white, should choose between slavery and liberty. Gott of New York brought the attack to a climax by declaring that "the traffic now prosecuted in this metropolis of the Republic in human beings, as chattels, is contrary to natural justice and the fundamental principles of our political system, and is notoriously a reproach to our country throughout Christendom, and a serious hindrance to the progress of republican liberty among the nations of the earth." He offered a resolution for the prohibition of the slave trade in the District of Columbia.[8]

Southern reaction to these efforts was quick and positive. Calhoun took the lead. He saw more clearly than others the dangers involved. More than a year earlier he had surveyed Northern attitudes and acts, and had predicted for the South a fate in comparison to which "the conditions of Poland would be a state of bliss." He had tried to stir his section to action. Benton even charged him with attempting to create issues in order to bring about secession.[4] In August, before the short session, Calhoun had addressed a meeting in Charleston. He had measured the value of the Union against "our honor and our liberty" and declared that Southern generalship and soldiership were equal to those of the North. In closing, he had urged the calling of a Southern Convention to consider a program of action. Rhett was willing then to withdraw the state's representatives from Congress and to stand unaided and alone. Response, however, had been slow. A few local groups answered, but the legislature of South Carolina was not ready for separate action. Other Southern states had been even more conservative. In the proposals of Gott, Giddings, and their fellows, however, men of the South saw new concrete evidence of Northern aggression. If such legislation were passed, their section would indeed be reduced to the status of an inferior. Amid great excitement the Southern congressmen met in caucus and instructed a committee to prepare a statement of position. The result was Calhoun's "Address of the Southern Delegates in Congress to their Constituents."[5]

The Address surveyed the whole unconstitutional invasion of Southern rights and concluded that aggression had followed aggression until the section could no longer remain silent. It asserted that every single provision, stipulation, or guaranty of the Constitution intended for the security of the South had been "rendered almost perfectly nugatory." It prophesied that abolition would be certain if the North were permitted to monopolize the territories, and thus acquire a three-fourths majority in Congress. It foretold a struggle between the races which would result in the prostration of the white race. It begged for Southern unity.[6]

Meanwhile the governor of Virginia, in his message to the legislature, had declared that if Proviso measures passed Congress, "then indeed the day of compromise will have passed, and the dissolution of our great and glorious Union will become necessary and inevitable." The legislature, in response, had reaffirmed its earlier resolutions against the Proviso and had authorized the governor to convene the legislature in extra session to consider modes of redress if the suggested legislation were passed by Congress.[7] In South Carolina, committees of Safety and Correspondence were formed in most of the districts and parishes, and in May a state convention was held in Columbia to approve the Southern Address and to concur in the Virginia resolutions. The Florida, North Carolina, and Mississippi legislatures also took action looking toward the defense of slave interests, and meetings or conventions in Alabama, Mississippi, Tennessee, and Georgia revealed a strong sentiment in favor of cooperation and resistance. A Southern Movement had been launched.[8]

Much extreme talk had accompanied these developments. Calhoun expressed fear that "the alienation between the two sections [had] . . . already gone too far to save the union." He saw "an increasing disposition to resist all compromises and concessions and to agree to nothing." "Disunion [was] the only alternative." J. H. Hammond found the conviction "growing rapidly . . . that the union . . . always [had] been and always

. . . [would] be a disadvantage to . . . [the South] and . . . the sooner . . . [she could] get rid of it the better." The Mississippi *Free Trader* declared "the time for talking or threatening . . . past; we must lay down our platform broadly and openly, and say to our Northern brethren, 'thus far and no further.'" The *Sumter Banner* (S. C.) insisted that "the only remedy which [would] free . . . [the South] from Northern oppression, from the Wilmot Proviso and all its evil results [was] the SECESSION OF THE SLAVEHOLDING STATES IN A BODY FROM THE UNION AND THEIR FORMATION INTO A SEPARATE REPUBLIC."[9]

Conservative voices, however, could still be heard. The Whigs generally minimized the danger and even questioned the value to the South of New Mexico and California. Only two Southern Whigs supported "Calhoun's Address" in the Congressional caucus. Both Cobb and Berrien of Georgia issued minority addresses to their constituents and urged quiet and compromise.[10] Cobb, writing to his wife, referred to Calhoun as the old reprobate, and added: "If it would please our Heavenly Father to take Calhoun and Benton *home*, I should look upon it as a national blessing."[11] B. F. Perry, although he supported a Southern convention, wrote: "I love the Union of these States, & look upon their dissolution with horror approaching despair." The Richmond *Times* believed that nine tenths of the Southern people distrusted Calhoun's judgment and the Savannah *Republican* stated in no uncertain terms that it was not yet tired of the Union and intended to stand by it.[12]

Northern reactions were as intense as those of the South. Political truancy became the order of the day. Blair talked of "the Free Democracy standing aloof."[13] Others were ready to drop party leaders who did not agree with the Cleveland *Plain Dealer* that: "Rather than see slavery extended one inch beyond its present limits we would see this Union rent asunder!"[14] Letters from the Northwest spoke of the fusion of Free-Soilers and Democrats and the rapid decline of Whig power. "Men who last fall proved the Wilmot proviso a humbug & unconstitutional," wrote one Indianan, ". . . are now hugging the proviso as a darling." Another spoke of "the bargain and sale . . .

going on between locos and free soilers"; and yet another declared that "*all* factions are beginning to fraternize throughout the land."[15] In Ohio, Chase was chosen senator over Allen by a combination of Free Soil and Democrat votes. Illinois and Indiana both replaced conservative senators with men of more pronounced Free-Soil views. The refusal of Thomas H. Benton to receive instructions from the Missouri legislature on slavery in the territories sealed his fate. Early the following year he found himself again in the company of Blair and Van Buren with free-soil his only hope of return to power. The threat made by Congressman Delano of Ohio two years before was being carried out. "Conquer Mexico," he had cried, "and add the territory but we will make it free; if not with the politicians we have now, the people of the North will bury these and send honest men in their places. If you drive on the bloody war of conquest to annexation, we will establish a cordon of free States that shall surround you; and then we will light up the fires of liberty on every side until they melt your present chains and render all your people free."[16]

* * * *

When the new Congress assembled early in December, 1849, sectional feeling was at white heat. In October, a Mississippi state convention had issued a call to all the slaveholding states to send delegates to a Southern convention at Nashville, Tennessee, "on the 1st MONDAY IN JUNE next, to devise and adopt some mode of resistance to [Northern] . . . aggressions. . . ."[17] Thoughtful men believed that this was the first step toward the break-up of the Union. Many Northerners were ready to accept it as such if that were the price required to stop the spread of slavery. "The North is determined that slavery shall not pollute the soil of lands now free . . . even if it should come to a dissolution of the Union," said an Ohio newspaper.[18]

To make matters worse a series of events during the past year had turned some rather remote abstract questions into very immediate concrete ones. On a March morning in 1848, a San Francisco newspaper had carried the following bit of news:

"Gold mines found. In the newly-made race-way of the Saw Mill recently erected by Captain Sutter, on the American Fork, gold has been found in considerable quantities."[19] A restless people stirred. The slow westward American trek became a series of mad rushes. Eighty thousand persons reached California in one year. As many more were on their way. The Mormon, Marshall, had begun the transformation of the vague, unreal California of the Mexican treaty into a rugged social-economic reality in which ten thousand homes back east felt a close personal interest. The year 1849 quickly earned the sobriquet, the days of gold. Horizons lifted. California presented everything Western in exaggerated degree and form—greater opportunity, more rapid settlement, easier wealth. Lawlessness matched other extravagances. The frontier urge to self-government, in turn, more quickly asserted itself. Without consent or assistance from Congress, the people of California met in September, 1849, and formed themselves into a state, framed a constitution, elected senators, prohibited slavery, and now stood, hat in hand, asking admission.[20]

The year had also seen the problem of the fugitive slave greatly magnified. Since the Court had decided that federal authorities must enforce the law, some Northern states had shed their responsibility in ways which made recovery of runaways exceedingly difficult. In a few cases, citizens of such states resisted the slaveowner with impunity and accepted the abolition opinion that slavery was "a state of war, and escape from its battle-fields both justifiable and meritorious." The recent publication in Virginia of Doctor Ruffner's pamphlet against slaveholding and similar writings by C. M. Clay and Thomas Marshall in Kentucky had produced in the Cotton Kingdom distrust of the border states, and had caused steps to be taken against the further importation of slaves from the border. Texas had become alarmed by the demands for the organization of New Mexico where her boundary claims had not been satisfied. She too was ready to add something to the determination, distrust, and bitterness which surrounded the gathering of the thirty-first Congress.[21]

Trouble began at once in the House. The Democrats and Whigs were so nearly equal in number that a handful of Free-Soilers held the balance of power. The attempt to elect a speaker produced a deadlock. Cobb of Georgia and Winthrop of Massachusetts were the strongest candidates, but neither could muster the required majority as long.as the Free-Soil members scattered their votes among other candidates. Day after day the voting went on. Behind the scenes pledges were demanded and bargains attempted. On the floor of the House, speakers increasingly revealed their stubborn resolve to express the tense and uncompromising attitudes of their sections. Sharp passages between members became more frequent as the days became weeks and attempts at organization failed. The votes scattered, and again concentrated. Brown of Indiana took the lead. Southerners gave him ready support. Then debate showed that he had given some assurance to the Free-Soilers regarding the appointment of committees. The price for organization was to be the Wilmot Proviso. Bedlam broke loose. Meade of Virginia declared that "if the organization of this House is to be followed by the passage of these bills, [abolition of slavery in the District of Columbia and in the territories]—if these outrages are to be committed upon my people, I trust in God, sir, that my eyes have rested upon the last Speaker of the House of Representatives. . . . If these be passed, there will be but one determination at the South—one solemn resolve to defend their homes and maintain their honor." Duer of New York called him a "disunionist." "It is false," Meade retorted. "You are a liar, sir," Duer snapped back. Meade rushed toward him. Friends intervened. Even the dull reporter for the *Congressional Globe* was caught in the excitement and for once dropped his plodding:[22]

Indescribable confusion followed—threats, violent gesticulations, calls to order, and demands for adjournment were mingled together. The House was like a heaving billow.

The CLERK called to order, but there was none to heed him.

Some time elapsed.

The Sergeant-at-arms of the late House of Representatives . . . now took the mace in his hand, and descending among the crowd of members held it up on high.

Cries of "Take away the mace; it has no authority here."

When some semblance of order was restored, members realized that a crisis had been reached. The mock innocence with which Wilmot had insisted that all he had demanded was a majority of fair Northern men on committees and the irritating humor with which Root had justified Free-Soil tactics now seemed out of place. Some wished to adjourn; others attempted to press an immediate election of a Speaker. Then Toombs of Georgia, a Southern conservative, who, only a few months before, had foiled Calhoun's "miserable attempt to form a Southern party," took the floor. His black, uncombed hair stood "out from his massive head," his eyes glowed "like coals of fire," and his sentences rattled "like volleys of musketry." Bluntly he went to the heart of the matter. "A great sectional question [lay] at the foundation of all these troubles." By a "discreditable trick" Northern members had attempted to gain an advantage in the formation of important committees. The interests of the South were in danger. No longer was he interested in organizing a body from whose legislation his section could hope for nothing. To organize would open the treasury to the use of one half the nation. It would bestow the territories, won by common blood and effort, upon the same half. The rights of a minority section would end. "Sir," he said, "I have as much attachment to the Union of these States, under the Constitution of our fathers, as any freeman ought to have. I am ready to concede and sacrifice for it whatever a just and honorable man ought to sacrifice . . . [but] I do not . . . hesitate to avow before this House and the Country, and in the presence of the living God, that if by your legislation you seek to drive us from the territories of California and New Mexico . . . and to abolish slavery in this District, thereby attempting to fix a national degradation upon half the States of this Confederacy, *I am for disunion;* and if my physical courage be equal to the maintenance of my convictions of right and duty, I will devote all I am and all I have on earth to its consummation."[23]

The effect of these words was sobering. Debate was suspended for continuous voting. At length, on December 23, Cobb of Georgia was made Speaker by a plurality vote. When the result was announced, according to the *Congressional Globe,* "a slight murmur of approbation, not amounting to a distinct expression, passed over parts of the Hall."[24]

* * * *

Meanwhile the Senate had assembled and adjourned day after day. It contained, this session, an unusually large number of outstanding men. Henry Clay had come back. He was a bit pinched and sunken but as human and open-minded as ever. Calhoun was there—sick unto death, yet always grim and certain of the rightness of his position. The more earthy Webster, solid, stolid, and brilliant by turns, rounded out the triumvirate of great leaders who had fought together and against each other through the long years since the young nation, emerging from the War of 1812, had begun its giant strides across a continent and toward social-economic maturity. Then there was Cass, who, with good reason, thought himself the most abused man in the land, and Benton, who was about to take over that title. They were old men. Their ambitions for high office were dulled, if not completely gone. They carried many scars and a few grudges, but they loved the Union which they had helped over so many rough places, and they could distinguish between fundamentals and the temporary emotions of the hour. They were the last gift of a passing generation to a new day.

A younger group, to whom the future belonged, showed promise of matching their elders. Some were partly seasoned, others had been thrown forward by the recent political upheavals. Seward of New York, Chase of Ohio, and Hale of New Hampshire, represented the strong Wilmot Proviso sentiment which had developed in the "Greater New England" lying north and west of the Old and rapidly spreading out along the Great Lakes. They typified the new moral attitudes toward slavery; they questioned its rights in a democracy where the Declaration of Independence formed an essential part of political dogma. They were in earnest about a better order of things.

They did not intend to sacrifice principle to expediency. Douglas of Illinois represented the Older Northwest—the upland Southern, corn-and-hog area bordering the Ohio River, where economic interest suggested fairness to Southern constitutional rights along with a goodly recognition of Western needs and the national harmony necessary for their satisfaction. Douglas saw no moral issues in the conflict, only political questions which the people had a right to determine as their own well-being dictated. Davis of Mississippi and Clemens of Alabama spoke for the Cotton Kingdom, now confident of its strength and sure of its rights. They were as uncompromising of principle as their fellows from the North, as certain of the course to be followed as Calhoun himself.

The slavery issue was raised in the Senate almost at once and would not down. Every proposal seemed somehow to have a relationship to it. The question of permitting a foreign visitor to sit within the bar of the Senate brought out his anti-slavery leanings and thus led to strife over the institution itself. The customary resolutions from the legislature of Vermont, calling slavery "a crime against humanity, and a sore evil in the body politic," brought Southern senators angrily to their feet to denounce the promptings of fanaticism, and to set the stage for impassioned debate over the return of fugitive slaves and the organization of California and New Mexico. The Senate seemed about to follow the course already taken in the House. "The Southern members are more determined and bold than I ever saw them," wrote Calhoun. "Many avow themselves to be disunionists, and a still greater number admit, that there is little hope of any remedy short of it." Chase, as spokesman for the North, declared that "no menace of disunion, no resolves tending towards disunion, no intimations of the probability of disunion, in any form, will move us from the path which in our judgment it is due to ourselves and the people whom we represent to pursue."[25]

As passions mounted Henry Clay evolved his plan. On the evening of January 21, in spite of a cruel cough, he braved the stormy weather and knocked at Webster's door. For an hour, he outlined his ideas, and Webster, deeply moved, promised support.[26] Eight days later, the tired old man, who had earlier begged that he might be relieved from any arduous duties, rose in the Senate chamber and began his last great effort to save the beloved Union. "I hold in my hand," Clay said, "a series of resolutions which I desire to submit to the consideration of this body. Taken together, in combination, they propose an amicable arrangement of all questions in controversy between the free and slave states, growing out of the subject of Slavery." By these proposals California would be admitted as a state without Congressional action on the matter of slavery. A territorial government would be set up in the remaining part of the region acquired from Mexico without provision either for the introduction or exclusion of slavery. Somewhat restricted boundaries would be drawn for Texas, but that state would be compensated by the federal assumption of her debts. Slave trade in the District of Columbia would be abolished, but slavery itself would be allowed there as long as it continued in Maryland, or until her people and those of the District itself should accept compensation for abolition. A new and more effective fugitive slave law would be passed and the principle that Congress had no power over the domestic slave trade would be recognized.[27]

On February 5, Clay defended these resolutions. He pleaded for moderation and for unselfish, non-partisan devotion to the Union. One by one, he took up his resolutions and asked for thoughtful consideration of each. Was there any concession to either section in the California proposal? The people themselves, not Congress, had already chosen freedom. Was the Wilmot Proviso necessary in the organization of the other territories? No. By law slavery nowhere existed, and nature, more powerful than a thousand provisos, forbade its introduction. Congress might have the power either to introduce or to exclude slavery, but patriotism demanded that the abstract principle be not pressed. The proposed boundaries of Texas were liberal and just. The assumption of her debts was a fair compensation for the loss of her right as an independent nation to collect duties. The resolutions affecting slavery and slave trade in the District of Columbia were equally just. What more could the South ask than absolute security for property in slaves? Did not the Southern States themselves prohibit the introduction of slaves within their limits as merchandise? An effective fugitive slave act was a constitutional requirement, not a Northern concession; the acknowledgment that Congress had no right to interfere with the domestic slave trade was a concession, not a constitutional requirement!

Here was compromise. Its spirit had made possible a glorious past. Kindness, forbearance, and concessions would still enable the sections to live in happiness and peace. Disunion would solve no problems. The dissolution of the Union and war were identical and inseparable. "Conjure . . . at the edge of the precipice," Clay begged both North and South, "before the fearful and disastrous leap is taken in the yawning abyss below. . . . I implore, as the best blessing which Heaven can bestow upon me upon earth, that if the direful and sad event of the dissolution of the Union shall happen, I may not survive to behold the sad and heart-rending spectacle."[28]

A month later Calhoun took the floor. He had been too ill to hear Clay's speech or to attend the regular sessions of the Senate. This day, wrapped in flannels, he tottered to his chair and sat with sunken eyes half closed until the consideration of the special order brought Clay's resolutions up for discussion. Then he arose, explained his inability to speak, and asked his friend, Senator Mason of Virginia, to read the speech he had carefully prepared. Another old man would make a last attempt to save the Union.

The speech which Mason read was that of a realist. "I have . . . believed from the first," it began, "that the agitation of the subject of slavery would, if not prevented by some timely and effective measure, end in disunion." That measure had not come. The Union was now imperilled. The danger grew out of Southern discontent and belief that they could not, consistently with honor and safety, remain in the Union. That attitude was due to the long-continued agitation of the slavery question and to the upsetting of the equilibrium between the sections. The South had lost ground by constant surrender of territory to the North—in the Northwest Ordinance, the Missouri Compromise, Oregon, and now in the greater Southwest. The result had been a complete change in our form of government—the substitution of a consolidated union for the old confederation, and the passage of tariffs and other legislation favorable to commerce and industry and harmful to agriculture. Government by and for one section had been established.

Under such distortion the cords of Union were snapping. The Churches had already divided. The parties were now practically sectionalized. The Union could not be saved by eulogies, by Clay's proposals, or the administration's efforts to encourage the people to act for themselves in California. Congress must exercise its powers in the territories and give the South justice. The South could accept no compromise but the Constitution. The North, the aggressor, must grant equal rights in the territories, cease to agitate the slavery question, faithfully observe the fugitive slave laws, and grant Constitutional amendments which would restore sectional equilibrium. If the North would not do this, California was the test question, and the Union was at an end![29]

Here was an ultimatum. It explained the errors of the past. It should have made clear to both North and South the necessities of the future. The nation stood at the crossroads. Vital decisions had to be made.

Back of Calhoun's position lay three basic and yet tragic assumptions, in part implied and in part stated. In the first place, he assumed, as had John Taylor, that a rural-agricultural order was the natural one; that it would prosper and dominate unless, through political trickery and legislative favors and advantages, the commercial-industrial interests were artificially built up. The South had achieved the good life and the superior order. She would have held her own and given direction to national legislation if fairness and honesty had prevailed. But she had fallen behind, was outnumbered in the House, and was threatened, by the refusal of the North to share the territories with slaveholders, with similar loss of power in the Senate. That could only mean sectional exploitation and ultimately a state of dependency. In the second place, he assumed the inferiority of the Negro—slavery as a necessity for the black man's welfare and for the safety of society. Slavery was a natural condition, and the peculiar superiority of the Southern rural-agricultural order rested in part on this institution. Without it, neither the race question nor the labor problem could be solved. Lastly, he assumed that the Fathers had established a confederate form of government, not a consolidated Union. The national government had delegated powers only; the States retained their sovereignty. True democracy was local democracy. The Constitution, as the framers intended it, was the basis of government—the rock against abuses from both sides. When the Constitution no longer protected all, and government became the agent of one interest to oppress the citizens of a state, secession was a right.

Much can be said for these assumptions. Neither history nor experience was entirely against them. Urban-industrialism and finance-capitalism have yet to prove their soundness and their superiority in producing a way of life. The evils of consolidation are only too evident in a world of dictators and Fascists. The importance of regionalism in social-economic planning is becoming more apparent every day. We have never succeeded in ridding ourselves of human exploitation, even though we have changed its forms and altered its names. The Negro has yet to achieve equality; the race question is yet unsolved. Calhoun's assumptions, however, were completely out of line with the whole trend of affairs in the United States and in the Western world of his day. His South and its values were out of date and he did not know it. The Industrial Revolution was in the ascendancy. The future belonged to the city, to the financier and the industrialist. Agriculture was declining to inferiority and dependency; farmers might no longer aspire to the status of gentlemen. A new kind of peasantry was developing. Lands were becoming a market commodity, not just a place where a home and a way of life were to be builded. Great technical changes in communication and production were cutting down space, increasing interdependence and calling for an efficiency and uniformity which only strong centralized government and dominant nationalism could give. And lastly a wave of humanitarianism and a new enthusiasm for democracy had come to help clear the way for the new economic forces. Old restraints and forms had to be broken; freedom had to be reemphasized, opportunity exalted. New forms of human exploitation were required. Slavery, too old even when America began, had no place in a world of factories, railroads, science, and democratic symbols. Calhoun's assumptions were already invalidated by what men, a bit blind perhaps, called progress.

Daniel Webster, who spoke three days later, understood these facts. He spoke as a nationalist—as an American. The Union, he declared, could no more be peacefully dissolved than could the "heavenly bodies rush from their spheres." Secession was an utter impossibility. Extremists on both sides were wrong. Northern supremacy in population, and growth, and wealth was not the result of government action. When had the government given the North any favor comparable to the purchase of Louisiana or the annexation of Texas?—both slave areas. Superiority was the product of "the operations of time." And time, he knew, had been, and would be, with the North. She could, therefore, afford to be generous and patient. The sincere, but mistaken, abolitionist, and his harmful societies, need not press the Wilmot Proviso. There was not "within the United States, or any territory of the United States, a single foot of land" where "some irrepealable law" did not forbid slavery. Nature need not be reenacted by legislation. Webster saw that slavery was doomed. The Fathers had expected it soon to run out. Cotton had given it temporarily a new lease of life, but time was against it. Webster was willing, therefore, in spite of his belief that slavery was a moral and political evil, to give it full constitutional rights. He would agree to support all that Henry Clay had proposed. The Union was worth temporary concessions.[30]

Moderation and generosity characterized every paragraph of Webster's great national appeal. Yet underneath was the calm and cruel confidence which belongs to those who are in step with time. Contemporaries, at first, missed that undercurrent. New England radicals could scarcely find words in which to express their wrath. Webster was "a recreant son," misrepresenting Massachusetts, a "Benedict Arnold," "Lucifer descending from heaven," a man whose honor was dead! Southerners, on the other hand, saw in Webster's speech a guarantee that Clay's compromises would be passed. They began to hesitate. Soon a change in public opinion manifested itself, first among Southern Whigs and then among moderates throughout the section. "Our politicians have gone over to the compromisers," wrote a Virginian late in March. "We have a tolerable prospect for a proper settlement of the slavery question," was Toombs' comment. A few saw deeper. They realized that Webster had, indeed, shown a friendly spirit but that he had given no approval of the basic assumptions on which the ways of the Old South rested. They guessed that New England industrialists had good reason for applauding him.[31]

The speech of William H. Seward, given a few days after Webster's, was even more to the point and, in some ways, more significant. Seward expressed current attitudes. He revealed future trends. He would have nothing to do with the Compromise: all compromises meant the surrender of the exercise of judgment and conscience. He would admit California at once on merit alone, and settle the other issues in like manner as a majority wished. The United States, he declared, was a consolidated Union. "The States [were] not parties to the Constitution as States; it [was] the Constitution of the people of the United States." The States had "surrendered their equality as States, and submitted themselves to the sway of the numerical majority without qualifications or checks." Sections as sections had no standing in such a government. Seward could not recognize any rights of a slave-section as such, or give it favors. The unequal, the minority, could not have the advantages of the majority, even though that minority constituted a section.

The issues before Congress were moral, Seward asserted. Slavery was a sin and Americans could not "be either true Christians or real freemen, if [they] impose[d] on another a chain [they] defi[ed] all human power to fasten on [themselves]." Southern demands for the extradition of fugitive slaves smacked of the Dark Ages. The modern conscience was against them. Human law "must be brought to the standard of the law of God . . . and must stand or fall by it." The Constitution did not recognize property in man and if it did there was a higher law than the Constitution. A Christian democracy must give freedom to its territories![32]

Here were the fundamental attitudes of Webster, without his spirit of tolerance, moderation, and compromise. Seward's proposals were as blunt and positive as anything Calhoun had offered. They emphasized an "irrepressible conflict" with bloodshed or submission at the end.

Fortunately for the immediate safety of the nation, not many members of Congress understood the assumptions behind Calhoun's statements and the conflict they implied with all that Seward had just uttered. Few would have been willing to follow them to their logical conclusions if they had understood. Fewer would have shared Calhoun's pessimistic realism regarding the necessity for immediate and final action. Even Seward saw no great impending disaster and no reason for physical strife. Lesser men saw and thought even less clearly than he. Most of them expected and favored compromise after they had talked their bit. The risk they ran was that something would happen to require them to line their action up with their talk.

Thus, in spite of the fact that Davis and Chase, Brown and Wilmot, and other young leaders, expressed opinions even more dogmatic than those of Calhoun and Seward, the trend of opinion slowly turned in favor of Clay and Webster. Northern merchants anxious for peace and prosperity threw their weight in that direction; Northern conservatives were even more weary of strife than were the Southern planters. Debate went on throughout the spring and summer, but the advocates of compromise gained ground. Bell of Tennessee supplemented Clay with further resolutions. Cass and Douglas brought the force of the optimistic, democratic West to the side of peace. A Committee of Thirteen took the bills in hand. After March, a settlement was definitely in sight.

Circumstances favored. Late in March, Blair went down to the capital city to see what progress the various intrigues had made since his last visit there two weeks earlier. He hunted up his friend, "the Colo.", meaning Benton, and asked him the state of the Republic. Benton gave him interesting information regarding the old enemy, John C. Calhoun. Calhoun, he said, was " 'possumming of it' "—feigning deathly sickness for fear of an encounter in the Senate with Webster. Some said he was writing a speech or speaking it to one of his mouthpieces to be read in the Senate. Others said that he was getting ready a constitution for the Southern Confederacy to be issued from the Nashville Convention. Only close friends were allowed to see him, but a plain man had got in a private interview and reported that he "seemed almost demented—talked of nothing but first seceding the District to Maryland—then letting Maryland go & making the Potomac the boundary & monopolizing the blessings of Negro slavery between that latitude & the tropics across the Continent." "This is his euthanasia," added Blair, "for 'tis given out that having completed this ground work he does not look to live to enjoy it—poor old man, he resolved to die in giving birth to the Southern Confederacy. . . ."[33]

Five days later Calhoun was dead. He left behind only a fragmentary document which proposed a constitutional amendment by which he hoped the Union and Southern rights could be saved. It provided for the election of two Presidents, one from the free States and one from the slave States; either could veto all Congressional legislation.

The removal of the great South Carolinian from the scene hastened the disintegration of the Southern forces. Already a few had broken away. Foote of Mississippi, perhaps influenced by an old quarrel with Jefferson Davis, had early pledged support to Henry Clay. He had quickly dissented from Calhoun's statement that California was a test case and had forwarded the Committee of Thirteen. Blair reported in late March that "Southern men (Foote and others of his stripe) who [had] aspirations, [had] seized the occasion to secede from South Carolina instead of the Union" and had developed "quite a counter movement." Even in South Carolina many felt in regard to Calhoun's passing as did B. F. Perry, who confided to his Journal that: "I regard his death as fortunate for the country & his own fame. The slavery question will now be settled. He would have been an obstacle in the way. . . . His death has relieved South Carolina of political despotism. Every man may now breathe more freely as England did after the death of

Henry the Eighth." Preston and Poinsett agreed; Preston called Calhoun's death "the interposition of God to save the country."[34]

President Taylor had been another obstacle to compromise. Before his election he had said that the "South must resist boldly and decisively the encroachments of the North." But once in office he proved himself considerably more the soldier than the slaveholder. He sent a personal representative to California to help establish order there; and, in his first message, he recommended to Congress the favorable consideration of the new state's request for admission. Quickly falling under Weed's and Seward's influence, he assured the people of the North that they need have no apprehension of the farther extension of slavery, and made it quite clear to Southern Whigs who called on him in February, 1850, that he would approve any constitutional bill that Congress might pass, regardless of the slavery issue, and hang any traitors who might rebel against the Union. He held out stubbornly against Clay's proposals, derided them as an omnibus bill, and advised his friends to make open, undisguised war on them.[35]

Suddenly the whole scene changed. On July 4, the President attended patriotic exercises at the Washington Monument. He sat long exposed to a blistering sun and drank great quantities of iced water. On his return home he ate freely of cherries and followed them with cold milk. Five days later he was dead of a violent form of cholera morbus! Millard Fillmore, bitter enemy of Seward, became President![36]

Even more important for compromise and peace were the changing attitudes in the South. Throughout December and January it seemed that the Nashville Convention, when it met in June, might precipitate a secession movement. Radical talk was common. Democrats, as a rule, were more extreme than Whigs, less inclined to waver and more willing to threaten disunion. Yet here and there a radical Whig editor was to be found and an occasional dropping of party attitudes. In Virginia, men like Edmund Ruffin, John B. Floyd, and Beverley Tucker advocated "separation from, and independence of, the present Union." The Richmond *Enquirer* was only a trifle less emphatic.

The destiny of the Union, it insisted, depended upon the present decision. Only by a strict observance of all the guarantees of the Constitution could the Union be preserved. "The only Union we love is a confederacy of equals . . . we will remain in it on no other condition." "Let us show, by assembling at the Nashville Convention, that we are prepared to meet the consequences whatever they may be. . . ."[37]

The New Orleans *True Delta* advocated the formulation of a Southern creed, upon the violation of which the slave state delegations in Congress should retire. The *Daily Delta* averred that, should the South "be reduced to the alternative of subjection in [its] dearest right, to Northern domination, or a dissolution of the Union," her people would not hesitate to secede. Even the *Daily Crescent* was for calm but firm action.[38]

In Georgia, Governor Towns proclaimed that further aggression was not to be endured and the legislature responded with an act providing for a state convention to consider the mode and measure of redress in case Congress should pass any of the contemplated acts affecting slavery. All Georgia, save perhaps some mountain districts in Cherokee, was ready for final resistance to the Proviso. Even in North Carolina, usually moderate, men talked of secession. "Unless there is reform, and that speedily," said the Wilmington *Commercial* (Whig), "there will be found an immense majority in all the Southern States who will very readily entertain a proposition for disunion." The North Carolina *Standard* urged a united front at Nashville and action in place of talk. A Wilmington States' rights meeting boldly declared that the South could not "yield up principle and honor, even if the maintenance of them involved the sacrifice of . . . political and individual existence, in the dissolution of the Union and the bloody consequences likely to flow therefrom."[39]

In December, Governor Collier of Alabama recommended that the General Assembly "announce the ultimatum . . . [of the state] upon the grave question which now convulses the Union." He assured the nation that Alabama would be at Nashville "with her persecuted sisters . . . [to] present an unbroken front to insult and usurpation." For some time the Montgomery *Advertiser and Gazette* had been urging "a general convention . . . and preparation . . . to withdraw from the Union before Congress" could pass acts depriving the South of its just share of the territories. Even the moderate Mobile *Daily Register* was inclined strongly to the opinion that the causes of difference would be "pushed to the catastrophe of a dissolution of the Union."[40]

South Carolina and Mississippi were surprisingly quiet. The call to Nashville, however, had originated with them. Their governors, Seabrook and Quitman, were outspoken States' rights men. Both accepted the possibility of secession and each made radical recommendations to his legislature. But these bodies were content to reaffirm their earlier positions and to await the Nashville Convention. The Natchez *Free Trader* and the Charleston *Mercury*, meanwhile, kept the issues before their readers. They did not openly advocate the breaking up of the Union, but neither were they willing to compromise Southern rights. Now and then, however, some local editor proclaimed it "the sacred duty of the South, enjoined by every sentiment of patriotism, honor and interest, to demand a dissolution of the Union."[41]

Retreat from extreme positions was discernible quite early. The Whigs were not eager for a break which would rob them of the fruits of their late victory. They found it difficult not to make political capital out of the Democratic radicalism. After the first reluctant denunciation of "Northern aggressions," they hesitated. The Richmond *Republican and General Advertiser*, which in January had warned the North that attachment to the independence and institutions of the Southern States was equal to the love of the Union, was soon praising Northern enterprise and energy and denying that there were any inherent differences between the sections. Other papers took a similar stand and some began denouncing the Nashville Convention as a move "to familiarize the public mind with the idea of dissolution." The New Orleans *Daily Crescent* spoke of "the wildness, not to say silliness, of this project" and expressed a doubt whether the convention would ever meet. The New Orleans *Bee* thought it a "work of supererogation to argue against" a movement which was about to "die a natural death."[42]

North Carolina Whigs soon fell in behind Edward Stanly, who hoped that "the citizens of Nashville [would] drive every traitor of them into the Cumberland River." Georgia Whigs, meanwhile, realizing that compromise was a possibility, opposed the holding of both state and sectional conventions. After Toombs and Stephens came out in favor of Clay's proposals, these two men were able to destroy almost completely all interest in the movement. Leading Whigs in Alabama soon began asserting that the convention should not meet unless Congress passed anti-slavery measures, and their friends in Mississippi declared they saw nothing in the admission of California as a state to warrant action. While still supporting the Nashville Convention, both groups steadily insisted on its Union purpose.[43]

Whig opposition put the Democrats on the defensive. Gradually they too began to retreat. Long before June they were denying that any purpose of disunion was at the bottom of the movement for the Nashville Convention. All they were asking was Southern organization to match that of the North. "There are no disunionists at the South," declared the Richmond *Enquirer* on April 17. "Now we deny that any proposition or memorial for disunion has emanated from the South," echoed the New Orleans *Delta*. "Such a sad alternative has never been contemplated." The Nashville Convention was planned only as a family meeting to consult together as to the best means of "allaying the agitation, which is continually imperilling the friendly relations of these states and seriously affecting the peace and prosperity of the South." The primary object of the convention was to take steps to make the Union one of safety and permanency. "To defend the Constitution inviolate and to MAINTAIN THE UNION is the great purpose" said the Mobile *Daily Register*. "The objects of the Nashville Convention," said a Mississippi Democrat, "are to call the Northern States, the Northern people, and the Congress and Government of the United States *back to the Union* . . . and to prevent the calamities of *secession and* disunion."[44]

As compromise sentiment increased, interest in the convention dwindled. Outside of South Carolina and Mississippi the people showed startling indifference to the selection of delegates. The April election in Georgia was a farce and the Democrats themselves admitted that the movement was dead and buried. When Father Ritchie and his Washington *Union* decided for the compromise measures, even the Richmond *Enquirer* began to weaken. It hailed Webster's speech as a masterly production, showing "his determination . . . to do justice to the aggrieved South." Soon it was publishing articles supporting representation at Nashville primarily for the purpose of checking radicals from the lower South! More than half the Virginia counties refused to select delegates; only six of the fourteen men finally chosen were willing to go to Nashville. In Alabama, resolutions passed by county conventions made it clear that delegates were being sent to preserve, not to dissolve, the Union. A few important leaders, such as Henry W. Hilliard, questioned the right of the legislature to appoint delegates. So uncertain had opinion become by May that delegates were being asked to make known publicly whether they intended to go to Nashville or not. North Carolina and Louisiana failed to select delegates and the Tennessee legislature and many of the counties refused to act. The New Orleans *Delta* called Webster's speech a godsend—"the trident of Old Neptune, calming the excited sea and soothing the raging billows." "Of the eight millions of people in the Southern States, not ten thousand" took any part in "the appointments of the delegates . . . who will attend the Nashville Convention," said the *Delta's* neighbor, the *Daily Crescent*.[45]

The great Southern Convention was thus foredoomed to failure. On June 3, delegates from only nine states appeared at Nashville. The atmosphere in the Tennessee capital was anything but friendly. Most people in the South, like the editor of the *Columbus* (Miss.) *Whig*, attached little or no importance to the meeting. It was, he said, incapable of harm or of good.[46]

The sessions of the convention brought a few fiery speeches, a series of resolutions affirming the Southern position as taken by Jefferson Davis in Congress, and an Address to the Southern people written by Robert Barnwell Rhett. Nothing was done about "the methods suitable for a resistance" to Northern aggression. These were not necessary when Congress was making such rapid strides toward compromise. The convention, therefore, adjourned to meet again in six weeks.[47]

The resolutions passed were notable for their acceptance of an extension of the line 36° 30' to the Pacific; Rhett's address, for the lecture it gave the South against forbearance and submission, its criticism of the Clay proposals, and its final plea for Southern nationalism. Rhett believed that North and South were now two distinct peoples. The South must determine its own internal policies or perish. Neither resolutions nor address attracted much attention in the section.

The sharp changes in Southern sentiment and the complete failure of the Nashville Convention removed the last serious barrier to compromise. Measures were crowded to final acceptance during the summer months, with Stephen A. Douglas taking the lead. One by one the bills were debated, often bitterly, and ultimately passed. September saw the task completed. The Southern States must now accept or take steps toward secession.[48]

Southern opinion on the Compromise was badly divided. There was, of course, no great enthusiasm over the admission of California, the Texas boundary, and the abolition of the slave trade in the District of Columbia, but there was a general feeling that the Compromise was the best that could be secured without radical action. Only the few were ready for that. The struggle, therefore, was completely localized again. It had to be fought out by groups within the separate states. All hope for one great sectional movement was gone. The second session of the Nashville Convention offered tragic proof of that fact. Its membership was more irregular and less official than that of the first. Its resolutions, asserting the sovereignty of the States, the right of secession, and the unsatisfactory character of the Compromise measures, attracted little attention and had even less influence.[49]

What the States would do was soon indicated by the action of Georgia. The passage of the California measure obligated Governor Towns to call a state convention "to deliberate, and counsel together for . . . mutual protection and safety." The election of delegates on November 26 brought a Union majority greater than any party had ever rolled up in the history of the state. When the Convention assembled in December, it drew up the famous "Georgia Platform" which said, in effect, that Georgia accepted the present Compromise but expected the North faithfully to maintain its provisions. One is reminded of an individual in one of the local meetings who violently urged resistance and who, when pressed for a program of action, said he would petition.[50]

The effect of such action by the state which was expected to lead off in the secession movement was decisive. The Virginia Assembly quickly answered South Carolina's appeal for another Southern Convention by declaring that the people of the state were "unwilling to take any action . . . calculated to destroy the integrity of this Union." North Carolinians also generally accepted the Compromise measures, but her legislature and her public press both stated emphatically that the Fugitive Slave Law must be enforced. "Let this question of Slavery alone," warned the North Carolina *Standard*, "take it out and keep it out of Congress; and respect and enforce the Fugitive Slave Law as it stands. If not, *we leave you!* Before God and man . . . if you fail in this simple act of justice, *the bonds will be dissolved!*" The people of Louisiana, with like warning, fell into line. The interests of the state were too closely allied with those of the Northwest to make disunion attractive. Alabama was more divided. A majority, unquestionably, doubted the merits of the Compromise and believed in the right of secession. They were not, however, ready to accept the injury done as cause enough for action. A few saw "justice, wisdom and national equity in the bills passed by Congress." More recognized the lack of unity in the South and the heavy cost of breaking up the Union. But the balance was a delicate one. Radicals, under the lead of William Lowndes Yancey, began the formation of Southern Rights Associations whose definite purposes were agitation and preparation for secession. Those who accepted the Compromise were of one opinion as to any further encroachments. The Fugitive Slave Law "must be enforced . . . no matter what may be the consequences." They were willing to put the Union on probation. Meanwhile they would prepare the "capacities" of the South—military, agricultural, and commercial—for successful defense when compromise failed.[51]

Left alone, Mississippi and South Carolina were seriously handicapped. In the former state, the legislature, on Governor Quitman's advice, called a state convention "to consider the then existing relations between the Government of the United States and people of the state of Mississippi, to devise and carry into effect the best means of redress for the past, and obtain certain security for the future. . . ." Significantly, this convention approved the position taken by Jefferson Davis in Congress. A Union meeting, which had assembled in Jackson at the same time, considered and endorsed Senator Foote's conduct, organized a Union Party, and accepted the Compromise as final *if their rights were not farther invaded.* Soon afterward the Central Southern Rights Association issued a radical platform asking for constitutional amendments to prevent unequal sectional taxation, and to insure the return of fugitive slaves. It insisted that the only compromise which the South could accept was the extension of the Missouri Compromise line to the Pacific. Unless these demands were granted, the South must sink into a position of inferiority or look out for her own rights outside the Union. The Association failed, however, to demand separate state action. It asked only for a new Southern Convention.[52]

Meanwhile the Mississippi party conventions met to choose candidates for state office. Senator Foote accepted nomination for the governorship on the Clay Compromise platform. Governor Quitman was renominated by the States' rights Democrats, but later withdrew in favor of Jefferson Davis. With Foote and Davis as candidates, all the personal hatred engendered in the late Congress became part of the struggle. A bitter campaign ensued. The Mississippi *Free Trader* saw, in the acceptance of the Compromise, immediate political inferiority and the ultimate abolition of slavery. To acquiesce was to agree to "the unmeasurable numerical, commercial and territorial aggrandizement of the North." All that section's cravings of interest, her hatred of slavery and slaveowner, and her most baneful spirit of jealousy and rivalry would then be free to render Southern fields waste and desolate and to drive her children from their homes.

The border states, the *Free Trader* warned, were fast giving up slavery. If the South acted at once, these states might cast in their lot with the South. A few years' delay and they would certainly stay in the Union. The Woodville *Republican* saw but one issue—slavery *versus* abolition. The opposing Natchez *Courier*, on the other hand, counted the Union of priceless value and endorsed the proposition of the Port Gibson *Herald* that "the secession of the State of Mississippi from the Union should be immediately followed by the secession of the Southwestern submission counties from the State."[53]

In September, compromise candidates for the state convention swept all but eighteen counties, and in November, Foote triumphed over Davis. Mississippi had acquiesced. Its convention resolved to consider the compromise measures as permanent adjustment of the sectional controversy. It declared "the asserted right of secession from the Union . . . utterly unsanctioned by the Federal Constitution," yet issued a solemn warning that further pressing of the slavery issue might lead to measures of resistance. South Carolina was thus left standing alone.

To be abandoned and to face grave danger without allies was not a new or a terrifying experience for South Carolina. As a colony, she had, unaided, opposed the Spanish Empire. In nullification days, she had defied the United States Government and the far more terrifying Andrew Jackson. What others might now decide did not make her decision. At the very suggestion of such a thing the Charleston *Mercury* exclaimed:[54] "What! is it come to this, that the State whose talk of chivalry has passed into a proverb—whose creed of State Sovereignty has been proclaimed for half a century, henceforth looks for redress in the courage and swords of others? Does South Carolina hold her rights by so feeble a tenure as this? Is she so crippled that she must hobble about on crutches imploring the protection of others? . . . History, honor and our own consistency force upon us what some may think the terrible alternative of *separate state action*."

To those who felt this way, the passage of the Compromise

measures was a signal for immediate secession. "No earthly power can save this confederacy from dissolution," said the *Mercury*. "We must give up the Union or give up slavery," responded the *Spartan*. "Give us SLAVERY, *or* give us death," concluded the pamphleteer, Edward B. Bryan.[55]

The Governor's decision to await Georgia's move proved fatal. Slowly, sentiment began to shift toward cooperation, and a few citizens, such as Poinsett, Perry, Thomson, and Grayson, even dared to avow their attachment to the Union.[56] The issue gradually came to be clearly defined as between those who would act only in unison with the other Southern States and those who would accept separate state action. After a desperate struggle, the legislature agreed to a compromise, calling both for a state convention and for a Southern Congress which it suggested should meet at Montgomery, Alabama, on January 2, 1852. The vote for delegates to the state convention was light. The separate state secessionists secured a majority. The convention, however, was not to meet for more than a year— a year in which the other Southern States one by one dropped all plans for resistance and acquiesced in the compromise measures. The election of delegates to the proposed Montgomery Convention held in October showed the effect of these developments on opinion in South Carolina. The cooperationists scored a decided victory. They secured a majority in twenty-five of the forty-four districts and a total vote of 25,045 to their opponents' 17,710. The Montgomery Convention never met. The State Convention ended in an empty assertion of rights. "We have been saved," wrote Francis Lieber. "The match, the powder horn, has been wrested out of the hands of daring fools and maniac demagogues . . . I thank Thee, O Lord!"[57]

A few weeks later the editor of the Black River *Watchman* wrote: ". . . It may look like sacrilege, at this late hour of the day, to call in question the chivalry of our people. Yet, the truth must be confessed, the spirit and pride of the state have undergone a wonderful declension in the last twenty years.

"The fact stares us in the face that we have submitted to wrongs which we solemnly—and wisely—resolved, a free people could never submit to, without a loss of honor, and of self-respect. . . . We have submitted, ingloriously submitted!"[58]

* * * *

The crisis had passed. The Southern movement had collapsed. Had secession ever been a real danger? Were the *fighting* resolves of the legislatures and associations "nothing but gasconade put forth by partisan leaders for partisan effect?" The facts do not warrant such a conclusion. Intelligent Union men in the South everywhere testified to the genuine seriousness of the crisis, and came out of it with *Te Deums* on their lips. Then why had the movement weakened and finally collapsed? The answer must be found in temporary conditions, not in any basic weakness of the radical contentions or in any misjudgment of inevitable trends. The parties had started toward permanent sectionalization. The North had altered its position on slavery and had, by checking its expansion, begun to place it on the road to ultimate extinction. The South was taking up the role of permanent minority. The Higher Law was already rendering the Constitution frail protection against the "sweep of time." If the South was to hold firmly all she had once enjoyed, the hour for action had struck. Ten years' delay would only make ruin more certain.[59]

That she did not act was due, in the first place, to "the cursed Bonds of party," as James A. Seddon called them. The Whigs, flushed with the victory of 1848, had acted reluctantly in the beginning, and, when their great heroes, Clay and Webster, moved toward compromise, the rank and file stirred again with all the old dislike of Democrats. Partisanship obscured sectional dangers; it dictated Union sentiment.[60] In the second place, the South was enjoying a period of prosperity. "Thirteen cents a pound for cotton . . . make[s] civil war and revolution exceedingly distasteful . . .," wrote General James Hamilton after a trip across central Georgia. "Prosperity makes the masses indifferent to the crisis," was the comment of Governor Seabrook. The *Spirit of the South* enlarged on the theme:[61]

The present apparent prosperity of the South is one of the causes of whatever there may be of reluctance among her people to advocate resistance; because there is plenty to live on, because we are out of debt, and cotton brings a good price, many are in so good a humor and so well satisfied with themselves and things around them as to shut their eyes to the future in the consoling reflection that the future cannot hurt them.

The cities were especially prosperous, and therefore out of step with the radicals. Richmond, Charleston, Savannah, Mobile, New Orleans, Natchez, and Memphis were all compromise centers. References to their Yankee flavor and their unsound and uncertain character were often on the lips of the States' rights enthusiasts.[62] Furthermore, the masses "refused to throw up their caps and shout for the dissolution of the Union." "You cannot imagine how perfectly quiet the whole people are on the subject of all the stir and fuss at Washington," wrote a Georgian. "Nobody at home, Whig or Democrat, believes that any man there feels what he expresses of ultraism." A traveller through the countryside found that "more than 4/5 of the people" in North Carolina would sustain the Union, the same for Tennessee, and he considered the Virginians in favor of the Compromise to a man. "The people—those for whose protection the government exist[ed], and who [had] a stake in it as a *government*, not as a milch cow—[had] . . . by a united vote said: Not yet." Herschel V. Johnson had been right when he had warned Calhoun more than a year earlier "that the people of the South [were] not properly awake to the danger—not thoroughly nerved to united resistance."[63]

* * * *

In September, 1852, when the country had settled down with the comfortable feeling that the Compromise had brought a final settlement of all sectional troubles, clear-thinking, far-sighted Henry L. Benning wrote his friend Howell Cobb the following letter:[64]

You know well that it has been my conviction for the last two or three years that nothing we could do, short of general emancipation,

would satisfy the North. Your idea was that the measures of the Compromise would substantially effect that object, and you went for them
for that reason chiefly, I think. Should it turn out that I am right and
you are wrong it will not be long before it must be known. And it is,
therefore, now time for you to be making up your mind for the new
"crisis." Suppose the Whig party shall be beaten [in the presidential
election of 1852], and especially at the North, will not that disband
it and send the elements of which it has been composed into union
with the late Pittsburg free-soil anti-slavery concern? Manifestly.
What then? That concern takes the North. The Democratic party
there, in conjunction with pretty much the whole South, may be able
to make one fight, say in 1856—a grand Union rally—but then the
thing will be out. Is it not so? You must have thought of all this. Have
you made up your mind as to what is to be done?

The North and the Constitution were to be given one more
hopeless trial.

CHAPTER TWELVE

THE UNION ON TRIAL

A S WAS to have been expected," observed the Columbus, Georgia, *Sentinel* in January, 1851, "the storm which has just passed . . . has been succeeded by a calm. It is the calm of preparation, and not of peace; a cessation, not an end of the controversy. . . . The elements of that controversy are yet alive and they are destined to outlive the government. There is a feud between North and South which may be smothered, but never overcome."[1]

Not every one in the South took this gloomy view. Some regarded "the late compromise measures as the recognition of those great constitutional principles for which the South [had] always contended. In the repudiation of the Wilmot Proviso, and the enforcement of the Constitutional obligation to deliver up fugitive slaves, the North [had] given practical evidence of their intention to stand, in good faith, by the Constitutional Union of their fathers—recognizing and enforcing all the rights guaranteed by that solemn compact to their brethren of the South." The Union, they thought, deserved further trial.[2]

Events were soon to show that the *Sentinel* was right and the compromisers entirely mistaken. The sectional conflict was not over. The radicals of neither section had changed their attitudes or their purposes in the slightest degree. They had not lost ground. In spite of the collapse of secession threats, sectional fears and resentments had been heightened. Each section had become more self-conscious and more certain that it differed in fundamental values from its rival. The crisis had been passed only because issues were still largely political rather than moral, and because sectional symbols and stereotypes were not completed. The term "Slave-power" did not, in 1850, conjure up before Northern minds the image of a single, great brutal force bent on destruction and evil doing. Until "Black Republicanism" made its appearance, Southern common folk could not whole-heartedly believe that the North wanted to reduce their section to dependence and social ruin. Until Uncle Tom, Bleeding Kansas, "Bully" Brooks, Dred Scott, and John Brown had done their work, the emotional force necessary to complete the distortions was not present. The next crisis would have a different outcome.

Southern radicals, soon to be known as "fire-eaters," early understood the reasons for their failure to secure united and positive action in 1850, and set about to remedy conditions. The Southern people, they were convinced, had not been thoroughly aroused to the danger. The masses had not realized that their section was hopelessly different from the North in values and interests, that its purposes could never be realized in the present Union. The Southern people had not seen the North in its true light as the determined enemy of Southern life and labor—selfish, grasping, and unscrupulous. They must be made to realize that the abolition of slavery and the economic plunder of their section were imminent. The South must achieve economic, social, and intellectual independence. That was a necessary preliminary step toward the inevitable break-up of the Union. The time was ripe for beginning.

The movement toward Southern self-sufficiency was not entirely new. The extreme Southern nationalist was already a familiar figure. For the past five or six years a few bold spirits in most of the Southern States had been openly advocating secession and boasting of the supremacy of Southern culture. Some of them were already working closely with a more conservative and practical group who were attempting to improve agriculture, develop and extend commerce, improve Southern education, and develop a sectional literature.

The crisis of 1850 strengthened their hands. Under the text, "It is an ill wind that blows nobody good," the Mobile *Daily Register* noted that the Pandora box of slavery agitation had set the South to seeking economic independence. "We scarcely open one of our Southern exchanges," it said,[3]

without seeing an account of some new manufactory of cotton, iron, or wood, springing up in our midst. . . . But this is not all. Since the North has become expert at kidnapping our negroes, our people have learned to stay at home. Not one in ten of those among us, who spent their summers at the North ten years ago, now show their faces there. Mineral waters in many localities have been discovered. Bathing and other places of recreation, have sprung up among us, where, with the luxuries of life in profusion, our people of leisure and of means spend their summers, secure from the insolent sneers of fanatics. . . . The deep-seated determination of the South to become independent cannot be arrested.

The leaders of the movement were men of pronounced opinions and strong emotions. Conservatives were inclined to view them as extremists until the drift of events brought war near and turned them into prophets. Northern writers treated them as villains, and history has rewarded them with undeserved neglect. Their part in dividing a nation, however, was an important one, and Rhett, Yancey, Ruffin, and their fellow workers cannot be ignored in any attempt to understand how civil strife came to the United States.

Robert Barnwell Rhett, born Smith, came of New England forebears who had settled in the southernmost corner of South Carolina. He was one of fifteen children, and, for that reason, was early placed in the care of a grandmother who undertook his education. His father was an accomplished scholar—barrister from Middle Temple Bar in London—whose failures as a planter shunted him back and forth between the two Carolinas and kept him poor. His mother was a distant relative of John Quincy Adams!

We know little of Rhett's youth except that he was high-strung and without vices great or small. He studied law and, at the age of twenty-six, entered public life as the representative of his parish in the state legislature. Two years later [1828], in the tariff struggle, he revealed the temper and qualities which were to characterize his entire public life. While others hesitated, he spoke sharply for open resistance and rejoiced at the glorious inalienable right of a people to throw off an oppressive government. He praised revolution as "the dearest and holiest word to the brave and the free." The spirit of

'76, he declared, was not dead in Carolina. By the late 'thirties, he was asking: "If a Confederacy of the Southern States could now be obtained, should we not deem it a happy termination?" He then offered a series of resolutions to the effect that the Constitution had proved inadequate to protect the Southern States in the peaceful enjoyment of their rights and property and should be amended "or the Union of the States dissolved."[4]

As an editor of the Charleston *Mercury* and then as a representative in Congress, Rhett loyally supported Calhoun in his efforts to create a Southern bloc and to reach the presidency. Only once did he falter. When the great Carolinian acquiesced in the tariff of 1842, Rhett drew back and, at Bluffton, sounded the cry for a state convention and separate state action. But Calhoun kept developments in hand, and Rhett, eager to see his old chief secure the Democratic nomination in 1844, allowed his movement to become only another episode which enemies might cite as evidence of South Carolina's disloyalty.[5]

While hope for Calhoun's success remained, Rhett curbed his feelings; but after 1848 he prayed that the North would go the whole distance in abolishing slavery in the territories and the District of Columbia, so that the final contest would come and the South be set free. "You have tamely acquiesced," he chided his people, "until to hate and persecute the South has become a high passport to honor and power in the Union." He was convinced that North and South constituted two different peoples. Climate, crops, and slavery set the South apart. She must rule herself or perish.

After the Nashville Convention, he cast all restraint aside and openly and without reservation proclaimed himself a disunionist.[6]

Let it be, that I am a Traitor. The word has no terrors for me. . . . I have been born of Traitors, but thank God, they have been Traitors in the great cause of liberty, fighting against tyranny and oppression. Such treason will ever be mine whilst true to my lineage. . . . No, no, my friends! Smaller States before us struggled successfully, for their independence and freedom against far greater odds; and if it must be, we can make one brave, long, last, desperate struggle, for our rights

and honor, ere the black pall of tyranny is stretched over the bier of
our dead liberties. To meet death a little sooner or a little later, can be
of consequence to very few of us. . . .

Other South Carolinians of the day, however, held life a
trifle dearer than Rhett and viewed treason with more concern.
They sent Rhett to the Senate in 1851, but they almost immediately thereafter gave the cooperationists control of the state.
Sensing this reaction at home and hostility among his fellows
in the Senate, Rhett resigned before the end of the session. He
was convinced that his place was in the South; his task, that of
stirring the whole section to a realization of its danger. While
James L. Orr and other conservatives took charge in South Carolina, Rhett joined with Yancey in "preparation of the Southern
mind." Throughout the 'fifties, he labored to reopen the slave
trade, to organize committees of safety, and to devise a program
on which the South could unite for independence. Year in and
year out, he talked of Southern rights and Northern hostility.
Well does he deserve the title, Father of Secession.

William Lowndes Yancey contributed even more than Rhett
to the Southern movement. He was less forceful with his pen,
but he excelled as an orator. Few Americans, even in a period
which produced most of our great public speakers, were as
effective in swaying audiences. Whenever Yancey spoke, and
he was in constant demand throughout the 'fifties, great crowds
gathered and stood at rapt attention for hours. History has
designated him: The Orator of Secession.

Yancey's father, a lawyer friend of John C. Calhoun in Abbeville, South Carolina, died when his son was but three years
of age [1817]. His mother remarried soon afterward [1822]
and the new head of the family, Nathan Beman, called to the
pastorate of the First Presbyterian Church of Troy, New York,
carried the Yanceys northward. There, in a region of rapid
economic change and intense social-intellectual ferment, young
Yancey grew to manhood, obtained his early education, and
prepared for Williams College. Troy was interesting training
ground for a high-spirited youth. The Erie Canal was just being completed; factories, here and there, were opening their

doors; the first of several agricultural revolutions, forced by Western competition, was under way. Near by, the Mormons had established anew direct contact with God, and the Locofocos were attempting to give the democratic dogmas a real social-economic significance. To Beman's church, in 1826, came Charles Grandison Finney to preach the great revival. Weld and Tappan and Leavitt were friends of the family and Beman himself soon accepted the abolition doctrine. The region between Albany and Buffalo was just entering the era of isms, revivals, and reforms which was to make it the most vigorous and lively spot on the American continent during the next two decades.

For twelve impressionable years, three of them at Williams College, Yancey lived in this aggressively Northern environment. Then he returned to South Carolina and took up the study of law in the office of Benjamin F. Perry in Greenville. Two years later he married the daughter of a wealthy planter and moved to Dallas County, Alabama, then something of a frontier, and began the career of planter, editor, lawyer, and politician. At first he combined planting with the editing of a Wetumpka newspaper but, when his slaves were accidentally poisoned, he turned to the law and politics. From 1841 to 1846, he served his district first in the state legislature and then in Congress, resigning the latter office because of the "foul spell of party which binds and divides and distracts the South."

Yancey's return to private life, as a lawyer, launched him on his true public career. His magic gift of oratory turned his every appearance at court into an occasion and brought calls from far and wide to speak before political, agricultural, and sectional gatherings. Few peoples have ever matched those of the antebellum South in their devotion to oratory; Yancey, in the opinion of these seasoned critics, stood out like Saul of old above all who spoke.[7]

After the introduction of the Wilmot Proviso, the invariable theme of all Yancey's orations became Southern wrongs and Southern rights. As he later put it:

All my aims and objects are to cast before the people of the South as great a mass of wrongs committed on them, injuries and insults that have been done, as I possibly can. One thing will catch our eye here and determine our hearts; another thing elsewhere; all united may yet produce spirit enough to lead us forward, to call forth a Lexington, to fight a Bunker's Hill, to drive the foe from the city of our rights.

His first move was to persuade the Alabama State Democratic Convention of 1848 to adopt a series of resolutions asserting the duty of the federal government to protect slave property in the territories and pledging the Alabama delegates to the National Convention to vote for no presidential or vice-presidential candidate who favored restrictions on slavery. Armed with his platform and the answers to a questionnaire he had addressed to all prospective candidates, he set out for Baltimore to attempt to shape the national party platform and candidates to its demands. Failing in this, he and one companion bolted the convention.

From that hour until the fateful day at Charleston in 1860 when he led the delegates of the Lower South out of the Democratic Convention and into civil war, Yancey labored for Southern unity and independence. Something about his zeal recalls the statement once made to a friend: "Twelve years of my life spent among New England farmers were not thrown away. Come see what a Yankee I am around my cattle sheds." With Edmund Ruffin, he organized *Southern Rights Associations* and then the *Leagues of United Southerners* in the hope that the dissemination of truth might help "true hearted son[s] of the South" to "know each other" and to "know too [their] foes." At home and throughout the South, his eloquence intensified the fears and deepened the hatreds of things Northern.[8]

The third of this triumvirate was Edmund Ruffin of Virginia.[9] Slight and frail, shy and hesitant, he lacked the personality and oratorical ability essential to political success in his section. Yet pride and ambition and certainty of intellectual superiority had pushed him early into public life and consequent failure. That failure made him seek compensations and develop an alertness against suspected foes. He turned his talents to agriculture and worked out a theory of soil fertility which, in practice, transformed the face of his native state and brought increased prosperity and improved methods to much of the South. His agricultural periodical, *The Farmers' Register*, judged from any angle, was superior to any other publication of the kind in the United States. His *Essay on Calcareous Manures* has been called by a recent government expert "the most thorough piece of work on a special agricultural subject ever published in the English language."[10] He taught and practised deeper and horizontal plowing, the growing of legumes, the rotation of crops, underground drainage, and the use of all kinds of fertilizers from calcareous matter to dried blood and ground bone. He doubled and quadrupled yields of wheat and corn and lifted real-estate values in Virginia by the millions of dollars. The agricultural renaissance which he inaugurated is, even today, a matter for astonishment.

But Ruffin was more than a progressive farmer in a frontier-wrecked agricultural world. He early became an intense Southern nationalist. His purpose in restoring soils was thereafter to check emigration and to create a prosperity which would enable the South to hold her own in population and representation, or to achieve her independence.

Ruffin's whole life, up to this time, had been a bitter fight against ill health, economic disasters, an indifferent public and cunning politicians. He now found in the Yankee a substitute for all foes and thwartings. His adversary was the enemy of farmers, enemy of slaveholders, enemy of gentlemen, enemy of a superior way of life, enemy of the South! All the force of bitter, pent-up emotions found outlet. Calm and satisfaction came to a troubled soul.

The Wilmot Proviso deeply stirred him. In it he thought he saw complete proof of Northern determination to destroy slavery and the civilization builded upon it. He was convinced that the time had come for "separation from and independence of, the present Union." Another Haiti was preparing. The "degradation and final prostration" of his section were near at hand. The South must be aroused.

Ruffin's pen, so prolific in the production of agricultural advice, now turned to the service of slavery and sectional rights.

Soon he gave up farming that he might better serve. Pamphlets, books, newspaper articles, and personal letters, in astonishing quantity and quality, carried his message. He travelled widely throughout the South, consulting with Rhett and Yancey and Hammond, attending meetings and conventions like a veritable Peter the Hermit, organizing Associations and Leagues, and always preaching the gospel of secession. When John Brown went to Harpers Ferry, Ruffin hurried there to gather up the pikes, "designed to slaughter sleeping Southern men and their awakened wives and children," and scattered them about the South where they would best teach their lesson. When the guns turned on Sumter, Ruffin was permitted to pull the first lanyard.

What Ruffin was to Southern agricultural improvement and independence, the more calm and conservative William Gregg was to manufactures.[11] He was not, strictly speaking, a fire-eater, but no story of the efforts at Southern self-sufficiency would be complete without mention of his contribution. He was born in Virginia, but spent the greater part of his mature life in South Carolina. At Columbia and later at Charleston, he carried on the business of jeweler and silversmith. Then in the mid-'forties, he suddenly became an industrial enthusiast. With utter disregard for contemporary Southern opinion, he published a series of newspaper articles in praise of manufacturing and of Northern energy in its development. "It would indeed be well for us," he wrote, "if we were not so refined in politics—if the talent, which has been, for years past, and is now engaged in embittering our indolent people against their industrious neighbors of the North, had been with the same zeal engaged in promoting domestic industry and the encouragement of the mechanical arts." He urged his fellow Southerners to invite capital to come to the South, put the "poor, ignorant, degraded white people" to work and scatter a few Lowells and Lawrences about the Southern countryside.

Example followed precept. In 1845, he organized the Graniteville (S. C.) Manufacturing Company and developed what was undoubtedly the most successful concern of the kind in the section. It became a model widely discussed and frequently copied. Gregg viewed it as a demonstration of Southern opportunities. Though he denounced the movement toward political independence, he labored as ardently as Ruffin himself for economic liberation. Without condemning the North, whose activity and enterprise he warmly admired, he sought the well-being of the lesser Southern whites and the wide prosperity of the section of his birth. In the end, he too became a Southern nationalist.

Rhett, Yancey, Ruffin, and Gregg were the great leaders, who during the stirring 'fifties were preparing the South for her attempt at independence. They were not, however, working alone. In every state they had able allies. James H. Hammond, son of a New England schoolteacher lodged in South Carolina, provided much of skill and industry toward economic diversification and especially the improvement of agriculture. By 1850, he had lost all faith in "any Constitutional Compact with the North" and declared that: "If we do not act now, we deliberately consign our children, not our posterity, but *our children* to the flames." "We must act *now*, and *decisively*," he said. James D. B. DeBow, whose father had come from New Jersey to South Carolina, made the commercial and industrial development of the South his special concern. In the 'fifties, his *Review*, published at New Orleans, was the outstanding medium for the expression of extreme Southern opinion. It attained a circulation greater than that of any other magazine published in the section. DeBow's constant cry was, "action, Action, ACTION!!! —not in the rhetoric of Congress, but in the busy hum of mechanism, and in the thrifty operations of the hammer and the anvil." "Light up the torches [of industry]" he urged, "on every hill top, by the side of every stream, from the shores of the Delaware to the farthest extremes of the Rio Grande—from the Ohio to the capes of Florida. Before heaven! we have work before us now." Roger Pryor of Virginia, William C. Dawson and Henry L. Benning of Georgia, and the editors of such newspapers as the Richmond *Enquirer*, the Raleigh *Standard*, the Mississippi *Free Trader*, the New Orleans *Daily Crescent*, and the *Southern Literary Messenger*—the list could be indefinitely extended—preached economic or political preparedness through the development of complete self-sufficiency. Slowly into Southern consciousness they wove the idea of an irrepressible conflict and the necessity for Southern strength with which to meet it.[12]

* * * *

The general call to action and renewed action along these lines was sounded in DeBow's *Review*, January, 1851:[13]

. . . There are two things upon which the whole South seems now agreed, *as one man,* whatever minor points may separate us:—and these are, *that grievous wrongs have been done, as well as gratuitous insults offered us, by the free States of the North, and the Congress of the Union, and that the cup of forebearance or endurance is so full that a single drop shall make it overflow.* . . . The cup of endurance is full! Are we in earnest, men of the South, in this declaration, and do we realize in all its force how much is involved in it? *Is this the Southern platform?* Thank God, if we had such a platform to stand upon and unite together upon, we could then be respectable, could be feared, could present an unbroken phalanx to the invader, and bid him move and die. . . .

Then followed a program aimed to check future dangers and to prepare the South to meet them in case "the remaining drop . . . be poured out to swell over the already brimming cup." It proposed:

(1) A Southern Convention, not like that at Nashville, but one elected by all the people of the South, which was to demand "like the Barons of Runnymead, the *great Charter* of their liberties."

(2) A Southern Mercantile Convention to consider means by which the people might own their own ships and conduct their own trade with foreign nations.

(3) A Southern Manufacturing Convention where the people should agree "to manufacture at home every bale of cotton that we eventually consume and pay no more tribute to northern looms."

(4) The diversification of industry to the point where nothing

would be purchased outside which could be made at home. The building of railroads and plank roads.

(5) The ending of annual vacation migrations to the North and the squandering of millions; the developing of Southern watering places; the education of children at home in the South; and the encouragement of a Southern literature.

Over and over again in the next few years these proposals were echoed throughout the South with local variations and shifting emphasis. In 1855, the Richmond *Enquirer* demanded "the declaration of our independence of the North in commercial, literary and other matters of equal importance." It rejoiced at the absence of Southern beaux and belles from Saratoga, Newport and other fashionable summer resorts at the North. It proclaimed the superiority of Southern schools and colleges, especially the University of Virginia and the Virginia Medical College, and denounced the sending of Southern youth to Northern schools where their minds were "poisoned by the incendiary teachings of fanatical professors . . . ,—implacable enemies of the South and of its patriarchal institutions." It wanted the South to build its own ships, carry its own trade, and manufacture for itself. But its goal was only self-sufficiency; it had no desire that men of the South should become "hucksters and cobblers, shop-keepers and common carriers for mankind." For, it added: "It is reputable, honorable and desirable to build our own ships, carry our own trade, and manufacture for ourselves; but not for other people."[14]

Three years later the *Southern Dial* (Wetumpka, Ala.) commented on the stupidity of quarrelling "with the North for political offices and bounties, and then spend[ing] . . . precious energies in legislating ourselves, in our State halls, free and independent States, while we feed our minds on her literature, and our bodies on her luxuries, and clothe them in her manufactured goods, make her vessels the carriers of our foreign trade, and her merchants our financial agents."

The *Dial* editor urged that the South stop "the drain of millions" paid to "northern schools and presses; stop the cost of travel among them; end all . . . trade there, and commercial and financial agencies." He advocated the building up of direct

trade with Europe, Africa and China and South America. He
wanted New Orleans, Mobile, Pensacola, Brunswick, Savannah,
Charleston, Norfolk, Petersburg, Richmond and Baltimore to
develop themselves into great thriving commercial and industrial centers, where a million new voters would dwell. Then
indeed would Cotton be King and "educational independence"
and "commercial independence . . . bring the North into political dependence upon the South."[15]

Practical programs and steps toward the realization of these
suggestions did not always follow impassioned utterance. Rural
worlds are not much given to innovations and quick changes.
Southern values had long been fixed by a widespread belief in
the superiority of the agricultural way of life. The spell of
cotton was still great. The capital necessary for new enterprise
was already tied up in land and labor, the directing ability
already employed in planting and politics. The first problem
was, therefore, to create an interest in, and a sentiment in favor
of, new types of economic endeavor and new methods in the old
ones. A program of education had to precede a program of action.

Talk and action, therefore, must both be considered in discussing developments in this period. And each movement must,
moreover, be seen both as part of a series of changes normally
due in the section and as part of a new drive toward sectional
independence.

Agricultural reform came first. It was already widespread
and successful before the sectional flavor was added. John Taylor
had led the way in Virginia back in the 1820's, when plows and
plowing were poor, when the rotation of crops was difficult because of the failure of clover and other legumes, and when
exhausted lands were being abandoned by the thousands who
trekked westward. Edmund Ruffin had carried the work forward
with his theory of soil acidity and the benefits to be derived
by the application of calcareous materials. A new era had
dawned. Agricultural societies had reorganized and agricultural
periodicals had been established. New tools and new methods
and new crops had appeared, and Virginians, who had earlier
migrated from poverty-stricken fields, returned to find luxuriant
corn in place of scanty hen's-grass. "Mother Earth has changed

her face," one of them wrote. "Verdant fields," "luxuriant clover" and "abundant harvests have taken the place of broom-straw and poverty grass." The truck gardens around Norfolk sent great quantities of peas, strawberries, tomatoes, potatoes, cabbages, to Baltimore, Philadelphia, New York, and Boston. By 1860, profits in the Virginia-Maryland gardens passed the million-dollar mark. Dairy farmers, tobacco farmers, stock raisers, and general diversified farmers could match in their prosperity the cotton growers of the Deep South.[16]

From Virginia the move spread southward. Ruffin went to South Carolina on Hammond's invitation to conduct an agricultural survey, and together, Hammond and Ruffin preached the restoration of soils, the diversification of crops, and even the introduction of manufacturing in the interest of improved markets. Soon J. D. Legaré and G. R. Carroll were publishing the *Southern Agriculturalist* in Charleston, and just across the border in Augusta, their friends, J. W. Jones, James Camak, Daniel Lee, and D. Redmond were issuing the far more important *Southern Cultivator*. Even cotton planters on fresher lands, rice planters along the river swamps, and sugar planters in Louisiana were talking of better tools and better methods of raising their crops. Each group had its own agricultural paper and its recognized leaders. The South understood that its early years of careless, carefree exploitive agriculture were ended, and it was ready for a more scientific era. The accepted notion that Southern agriculture was a more tumble-down affair than was agriculture in other parts of the America of that day is the worst of myths. Only differing physical conditions made its problems greater and its appearance, in some places, more ragged.[17]

How much did the new self-conscious drive toward Southern independence accelerate and intensify the agricultural efforts already under way? No final answer can be given to that question. Most of the leaders in agricultural reform became ardent Southern nationalists and increased their zeal and scope of action as they adopted this purpose for their endeavor. Ruffin travelled more widely and presented his agricultural program as a means of increasing the strength of the South "against the plundering and oppression of tariffs to protect Northern interest, compromises (so-called) to swell Northern power, pensions and bounty laws for the same purpose." He drew stirring pictures of an independent South, freed from paying tribute to Northern manufactories, carrying its own produce, buying and selling in markets of its own choosing, and keeping for itself the wealth which in the past had gone to build New York and Boston. He was certain that a revived agriculture would either right political balances or prepare the way for a new nation.[18]

DeBow was particularly eager to make the Southern planter independent of all outside supplies. "Let the farmer . . . make his bread, his meat, raise a few colts and hay to feed them," he wrote. "Let him increase the quantity of corn and forage until he can spare a little; . . . let him remember the old saying, 'a master's footsteps are manure to his land.' " J. H. Hammond in South Carolina, M. W. Philips in Mississippi, and N. B. Cloud in Alabama preached and practised the same doctrine. They were not able to entirely remake Southern agriculture before 1860, but they did bring improvement and enough of agricultural independence so that the food problem of the Confederate States in war days was reduced to a minimum. What was most important, they created confidence. "Let it be understood," said the *American Farmer* in 1859, "that there is no such thing as worn-out land; that expression conveys a falsehood. . . ." "A new era has dawned. . . . The noblest victory of modern times has been achieved," echoed a plain farmer.[19]

The drive for sectional economic independence also included the stimulation of Southern manufactures. DeBow led off, saying:[20]

Let the South but adopt a system of manufactures and internal improvements to the extent which her interests require, her danger demands, and her ability is able to accomplish, and in a few years northern fanaticism and abolitionism may rave, gnash their teeth, and howl in vain.

A South Carolina editor urged "the necessity of bringing up the rising generation to MECHANICAL BUSINESS." In thoroughly un-Southern fashion, he spoke of the mechanic arts as

the arm of civilization and urged the people to do away with the
foolish pride or objection to such measures. "If we educate one
generation in the useful arts," he added, "we will soon free ourselves from our Northern foes. . . . The mechanic arts are the
bone and sinew of the country and we can never be a *free* people
unless we recognize them."[21]

Like sentiments began to appear in newspapers throughout
the South. All Southern editors regretted the slavish dependence
upon the North. A few dared to denounce the "lack of enterprise and skill of our people" and even dared to assert that the
tariff was not at all responsible for Southern ills. Here and
there some editor contrasted the sleepy character of the Southern white and the wide-awake and busy temper of the Yankee.
"There is nothing like the clattering of the busy looms, the
scream of the steam horse, the incessant tink, tink, tink of the
Tinker's hammer, and the ring of old Vulcan's anvil, to put
springs into the heels of the multitude," said the Augusta
Chronicle and Sentinel. "Let us build then," it continued, "our
Woolen and Cotton mills, and beside the cotton mill erect the
paper mill . . . and the lately invented rope machine. . . .
Besides our Tanneries let us have boot and shoe factories, and
. . . saw-mills, and . . . our own sash and blind and furniture
manufactories. . . ."[22]

The New Orleans *Daily Crescent* emphasized the fact that
the "superlatively pious, Christian, philanthropic, generous and
charitable commonwealth [of Massachusetts], the people of
which [had] recently voted for a free-soil-abolition candidate
for the Presidency to spite and insult the South, [made] . . .
more money by the manufacture of the products of slave labor
than [did] . . . any slave state from the growth of the raw
material." This paper advocated true and complete independence by the manufacture of all clothing, by the raising of all
foodstuffs, and the rearing of flocks and herds. "It is to our
deficiencies in these respects," it concluded, "that most of the
outrages perpetrated upon us by the fanatics of the North are
to be attributed. Were we practically independent we could
afford to laugh to scorn their ravings and their threats. But we
are not. . . ." In the same vein, the *Southern Literary Mes-*

senger remarked that "men curse the Yankees as a pack of rogues, when they are clothed from head to foot in fabrics made on Yankee land. . . ."[23]

Again it is impossible to say how much the sectional impulse added to the practical steps already being taken toward industrial development. Better cotton prices throughout the 1850's unquestionably strengthened the normal tendency to plant. Some leaders felt that the South owed its superior position to the great staple crops and to the agricultural virtues of the people. They did not take kindly to talk of imitating the Yankee world and of giving up King Cotton. But here and there we find planters who had resolved to buy "no Northern Cloth for . . . Negro's clothing, no Northern shoes, if others can be obtained, no Northern soap, candles, flour, or (Ohio) bacon, no Northern potatoes, cabbage, fish, or hay, no Northern butter, cheese or preserved fish, and no Northern refined sugar!" Items appear quite regularly in widely scattered newspapers, reporting the purchase by local planters of shoes in Petersburg, Virginia, or Mobile, Alabama, "in place of New York, Boston, or Philadelphia as heretofore"; of cloth at Graniteville, South Carolina, Prattville, Alabama, or Athens or Columbus, Georgia, instead of at Lowell or Lawrence.[24]

Sectional patriotism, moreover, clearly weakened the old prejudice against industry in many centers and helped to account for its rapid growth in the period from 1850 to 1860 when the value of Southern manufactures increased 96.5 per cent; the capital invested, 73.6 per cent; and the labor employed, 25.3 per cent. That this growth indicated a desire to end dependence on the North is shown by the fact that the largest increases were in industries competing with the North. Woolen manufactures increased 143.55 per cent; men's clothing, 65.76 per cent; and boots and shoes, 89.9 per cent. The production of paper and coal, meanwhile, trebled; flour, lumber, and tobacco more than doubled; and the value of bar, sheet, and railroad iron increased by more than half (63 per cent). Georgia took the lead but Tennessee and Alabama also made rapid gains, and Richmond and Petersburg in Virginia were rightly designated as industrial towns. Graniteville, where Gregg labored, and Prattville, where

Daniel Pratt invested his capital and genius, were typical mill villages. The iron works at Richmond and the shipyards in Norfolk grew on Southern patronage and soon found staunch supporters in their own neighborhoods. The change being wrought was both material and mental.[25]

* * * *

The ante-bellum Southerner held a convention on the slightest provocation. This was partly due to his eagerness, as a rural man, for social relationships, and partly to his inclination to be busy about public affairs. As a part of this general conventioning habit, Commercial Conventions had been held in various Southern cities since 1837. From the very beginning, these assemblies had manifested interest in economic independence. "We ought to be our own importers and exporters, for the very best reason, that we furnish nearly all the articles of export in the great staples of cotton, rice and tobacco," read the call issued for the first of such gatherings. In the meetings of the 1840 period the idea of direct trade with Europe was emphasized more and more, references to the "abject state of colonial vassalage" into which the South had fallen became increasingly frequent, and the encouragement of general internal improvements, sometimes with a view of closer relationship with the West, was discussed with growing eagerness. Open hostility to the North was rapidly emerging.[26]

After 1850, the drift toward such hostility was unmistakable. The radicals attended more frequently. Ruffin, Yancey, Pryor, Dawson, and DeBow were now to be seen and heard at the sessions. The thought that the South might some day become a separate Republic dominated the programs. The Louisville *Journal* charged that the membership of the Savannah Convention of 1856 consisted of "blazing fire-eaters,"—a group "as thoroughly treasonable as the vilest conclave that ever polluted the soil of South Carolina. . . ." The address which called the New Orleans Convention in 1852 spoke of the interest which the Southern States had in each other's prosperity, founded upon common hopes, and fears, and dangers, and that for the Knoxville Convention in 1857 stated that its purpose was "to spread far and wide, correct and enlarged and faithful views of our rights and obligations, and to unite us together by the most sacred bonds to maintain them inviolate to ourselves and our posterity." The subjects discussed at the later conventions also indicated a growing sectional objective. The delegates urged, not only the building of Southern railroads, local and transcontinental, and the encouragement of direct trade with Europe and South America, from Southern ports in Southern-owned and -built ships, but also the stimulation of manufacturing, the establishment of free schools, the production of Southern textbooks, the acquisition of Cuba and the opening of the slave trade. At one such meeting, DeBow pointed out the completely non-reciprocal character of North-South relations, and declared that a tribute of one hundred million dollars was paid each year on trade, travel, books, and education, to those who denounced Southerners as slaveholders and robbed them of their slaves! "Great Gods!" he cried. "Does Ireland sustain a more degrading relation to Great Britain?"[27]

Just how much the Commercial Convention stimulated establishment and building of ships and railway lines, it is impossible to say. Projects for the creation of steamship lines were advanced in Virginia, South Carolina, Alabama, and Louisiana at various times in the period; legislatures granted charters; subscription books were opened; and one or two boats were built; but no great revolution in Southern trade resulted. Railroad building moved forward more successfully. Under the push of coastal cities, such as Richmond, Charleston, Mobile, and New Orleans, a network of lines slowly began to spread out into the interior, much as they had earlier from Boston, Philadelphia, Baltimore, and New York. Charleston promoters dreamed of tapping the great Northwest and turning its trade and loyalties in the direction of their city. New Orleans and Mobile reached northward for the same purposes. The absence of thriving inland centers was a serious handicap, but Memphis, Jackson, Chattanooga, Augusta, and Atlanta furnished some aid and grew in corresponding importance. Considering the abundance of river highways, always certain to be navigable at floodtime, the splendid keeping quality of cotton and the great supply of idle labor between harvest and planting which might better be employed in hauling crops than in idleness—the section made, by 1860, highly satisfactory progress. Richmond was tied to Chattanooga through the Valley and to Wilmington along the coast; Charleston and Savannah reached through Atlanta to Memphis and Vicksburg and to the Ohio River through Nashville; Mobile was connected with Cairo in Illinois; and New Orleans, through Memphis, with Louisville in Kentucky. Some states, notably South Carolina and Virginia, supplemented these main systems with numerous local branches and short independent lines. The transportation problem was either adequately solved or on its way to solution. The enthusiasm of the Southern nationalist had played some part in the accomplishment.[28]

Northern reaction to these Southern efforts was confined largely to centers where Southerners had long purchased their supplies and where Southern enterprises were financed. The merchants of New York City and Philadelphia, once open in their opposition to slavery expansion, now suddenly began to draw back in alarm. Valiantly they strove for the finality of the Compromise of 1850. As Whigs, then as independents, they threw their influence against their fellow-citizens of the interior who threatened Southern institutions. In no uncertain terms they let it be known that the Northern merchant was the friend of his Southern customer. Elections throughout the 'fifties in Pennsylvania and New York revealed sharp cleavage between city and country. After the panic of 1857 had weakened Western trade the trend was even stronger. Not a few were inclined to contrast the steady demands of the South with the shifting character of trade in other sections. Under such conditions the threat of Southern economic independence was not to be taken too lightly.

* * * *

The campaign for intellectual independence was equally vigorous. Every agency enlisted in the various drives, at some time or other, made its appeal for keeping children in Southern schools, supplying them with "home-grown" textbooks and their parents with Southern reading matter. Orators harangued conventions, editors scolded their readers, and fire-eaters railed at all who would listen. The general character of the appeal is shown by one of DeBow's editorials, March, 1851. It read:[29]

An important part of the reform now being preached on the house-tops in every part of the South, must be considered the subject of Home Education. If the child be "father to the man," it ought assuredly to be our care to protect him from influences which the man may here-after deprecate. But what . . . is the fact? We find throughout the Northern States a current of popular opinion, extending throughout all classes, gaining every day in intensity, attacking and dividing the Churches, developing itself in literature, presiding over the press, dis-cussed in the schools, argued in the forum, potent at the polls. Clam-ourous and inveterate in the national halls, threatening annihilation to the South . . .; and it is just precisely into this hot-bed of political heresy and "higher law," that we are hurrying our children . . . to be trained to the duties of manhood . . . and the defenses of their fire-sides, their altars and their homes. There they go, crowding Dartmouth and Harvard, and Brown and Yale, and Amherst and Middlebury, and Hamilton,—the sons of the men who have raised throughout all the South a storm they cannot still, and carried into Africa a war to be ended God only knows when. . . .

Granted that our institutions of learning are inferior in endowment and celebrity, and for argument, even inferior in scholastic attain-ments and merit . . ., better would it be for us that our sons remained in honest ignorance and at the plough-handle, than that their plastic minds be imbued with doctrines subversive of their country's peace and honor, and at war with the very fundamental principles upon which the whole superstructure of the society they find *at home* is based. . . .

Many writers complained of the folly of employing Yankee teachers in the South and hoped for the not "far distant" day when no person would "be employed to teach and instruct . . . unless he [was] . . . of the 'Manor born.' " Others pointed out that not "a single textbook of the schools [was] published or printed south of Mason and Dixson's line" and insisted that "Southern booksellers [were] . . . literally in a state of peon-age" to the "barons of Cliff Street" and "others of that ilk." Northern texts, "prepared by Northern men often without practical knowledge of teaching [and] untraveled in the United States," were, they complained, arranged in sets so that when one volume found its way into the classroom all the rest followed. These books taught that the States were divided into towns and counties; devoted two pages to Connecticut onions and broom-corn, and ten lines to Louisiana and sugar; were silent about Texas. Some were filled with "abolitionism, insidiously inculcated, and [with] the religious, political and social heresies of which that quarter of the Union is so rife." DeBow summed up the whole matter by saying:[30]

> Should that unhappy time ever arrive when the whole South must rally as one man and resist or perish, we may rely upon it that the "man of the hour" will not be found among the "curled darlings" who have imbibed their education at the feet of some abolition Gamaliel of the North, but the true man will arise from the working classes of brains and hands; he will be some one who sat on the bench of the free school, and obtained his first ideas of the world, and the rights of man in the world from noting and mingling with representatives of all classes . . . and from books and teachers that taught him the history of the South and the destiny of the South. . . .

Along with the condemnation of Southern patronage of Northern schools went a complaint equally bitter against complete dependence on Northern books and magazines. Young and old, one writer asserted, were obliged to read Northern books for want of something better. They were becoming "more familiar with such abominable works as Mrs. Stowe's 'Uncle Tom's Cabin,' and with the abolition sermons of Theodore Parker than with the constitutionalism which has rendered us a nation." Harper's "semi-English" magazine and Putnam's "free-soil" magazine, not to mention the openly abolition "Saturday Evening Post," had large circulations in the South, whereas Southern writers and editors, "who for years [had] been laboring for the honor and prosperity of the South . . . [had] grown gray . . . and grown poorer as they grew older." "Why should Southern men patronize these mammoth literary journals in the North, whose tendency in abolitionism and morals [was] so often detestable, to the exclusion of their own excellent periodicals?" The only answer any one could give was that the North had "more business enterprise in everything from a rocking chair to a review." That certainly was a poor reason for the South to accept "intellectual vassalage."[31]

The rather unusual developments along educational lines in the 'fifties, no doubt, were in part due to this campaign. Newspapers spoke of "a great change in respect to . . . school teachers and school teaching" which marked the period. In states which once were "filled with indifferent Yankee school teachers" and "you could scarcely find a school master who occupied an influential position in society," the jobs were being taken by "native born," and "the profession of teaching [had] . . . become one of the most important, lucrative, and respectable of pursuits."[32] That claim was extravagant, but steps were unquestionably being taken in every Southern state to improve the common schools, and higher education was making more rapid strides in that section than in any other part of the nation. Academies sprang up on all sides and most of the State universities enjoyed a new prosperity. Soon a larger percentage of Southern youth was enrolled in college than in either North or West. The University of Virginia, with a faculty graced by such eminent men as Gildersleeve, Bledsoe, McGuffey, Holmes, Minor, and Holcombe, outdistanced Harvard and Yale in size of student body. Its enrollment rose above the six hundred mark in 1859–60 and it boasted registrations from every Southern state.[33] The University of North Carolina was not far behind in either numbers or recognition. Even in the Lower South, where Western conditions predominated, the Universities of Alabama and Mississippi experienced modest revivals. What was more significant from the sectional point of view, the new University of the South, at Sewanee, Tennessee, laid the cornerstone of its main building in 1860 and began to collect its five-million-dollar endowment. The forces behind its founding were primarily those born of the new desire for Southern intellectual independence.[34]

The production of Southern textbooks lagged. One "Doctor" McCormick of the College of Opelika brought out an arithmetic printed in Charleston and intended to replace books "bearing

the names of Gregg and Elliott . . . Harper or Appleton."
Professor F. M. Hubbard of the Language and Literature Department of the University of North Carolina published a series
of readers, written "with special reference to the wants and
interests of North Carolina." This series, along with Mitchell's
*Intermediate Geography . . . designed for the Schools of North
Carolina alone,* was expected to supplant the texts "heretofore
in use [which] were calculated to instil into the minds of our
youth a dislike of their own State, and an improper estimate
of its resources."[35] D. H. Hill, professor of mathematics at
Davidson College, capped the climax with his *Elements of
Algebra* in which problems of the following kind were used:[36]

A Yankee mixes a certain number of wooden nutmegs, which cost
him ¼ cent apiece, with a quantity of real nutmegs, worth 4 cents
apiece and sells the whole assortment for $44; and gains $3.75 by the
fraud. How many wooden nutmegs were there?

The Buena Vista battlefield is 6½ miles from Saltillo. Two Indiana
volunteers ran away from the battle at the same time; one ran half a
mile faster than the other, and reached Saltillo 5 minutes and 54 6/11
seconds sooner than the other. Required: their respective rates of travel.

But these were about all the notable efforts at the making of
Southern texts. In 1858, history classes at the Citadel, in
Charleston, were using *Wilson's United States History,* which
denounced the "manners and morals" of the Southern States
where "the upper classes . . . [were] distinguished for a luxurious and expensive hospitality" but were "too generally addicted to the vices of card-playing, gambling and intemperance,
while hunting and cock-fighting [were] favorite amusements of
all ranks." Wilson concluded by saying: "It cannot be denied
that New England's colonial character and colonial New England history furnish, on the whole, the most agreeable reminiscences . . . for the historian." Evidently agitation alone could
not bring about sectional freedom in this field.[37]

Nor did the drive for Southern patronage of Southern authors
and periodicals yield entirely satisfactory results. The *Southern*

Literary Messenger, which had been founded back in 1834, was "almost gone" in 1851, its editor "up to the armpits in mud." Four years later this editor complained that "*Harpers Magazine* has probably five times as many subscribers south of the Potomac . . . and even *Putnam's Monthly,* which has recently outraged the entire slaveholding portion of the Union by lending itself to the extremist views of the abolitionists, has a larger circulation among slaveholders. . . ." His appeal for the payment of arrearages brought enough response to enable him to continue publication, but his periodical was never financially successful. The *Southern Quarterly Review,* begun in New Orleans in 1842 and moved to Charleston a year later, came under the editorship of William Gilmore Simms in 1849. If literary ability and devotion to things Southern could have given success, the magazine should have flourished. But unpaid subscriptions brought about its failure and suspension in 1857. *Russell's Magazine,* founded in Charleston in 1857 "to give utterance and circulation to the opinions, doctrines and arguments of the educated mind of the South," fared no better. In 1860, it "struck upon breakers and sank." A few agricultural and religious periodicals and *DeBow's Review,* which represented varied interests, managed to survive. Most of these became ardent defenders of Southern institutions and, in the end, advocated secession.[38]

A group of writers attempted to supply other types of reading matter. But most of the novels, even though "buttered by flattery" were weak and trashy and even such ardent patriots as Edmund Ruffin could not finish them. Sir Walter Scott supplied enough of the romantic, and the best Southern writers, like William Gilmore Simms, soon found their talent required for sectional defense.[39]

*   *   *   *

Editors, meanwhile, waxed eloquent in denunciation of Southern men and women who spent their summers and their money at Northern summer resorts. They contrasted the peace and quiet of Southern mountains or the coolness of "breezes fresh from ocean or prairie" with "the rustling of silk, the noise of

the piano, . . . the small rooms, bad cooking, and constant
dressing" at Newport, Saratoga, or Niagara. They insisted that
Biloxi, Pass Christian, Point Clear, Cullum's Springs, Hot
Springs, Cooper's Well, or the Carolina and Virginia mountains offered more of relaxation and better associations. They
wanted to build up "Southern retreats" which "in their day
[would] become more famous than Saratoga or Newport, and
hereafter draw from the North as the North now draws from
us." In this way, "the fashionable folly" and "ridiculous snob-
bery that [carried] . . . so many to the crowded pleasure places
of the Northern States" would be ended.[40]

To what extent Southern men and women responded, we do
not know. Numerous references to the decline of "Northern
sojourns" are to be found in the press, but condemnation of the
practice continued to the very outbreak of the war. That some
"good" was accomplished can be inferred from a society note
written from Saratoga in 1855 to the New York *Evening Mirror*
and copied enthusiastically by Southern editors:[41]

> "Warmer clime that lies
> In ten degrees of more effulgent skies."

The rose of Florida, the magnolia of Alabama, are not here. The
sunny-eyed daughter of Carolina, graceful as the palms that shade her
native plains; the stately Kentuckian, as fair and fresh as streams that
run laughing through her vales; the warm and frank-hearted Mississippian, as sweet and exuberant as her own sugar cane,—they are not here!

And why? The Northern Abolitionists who steal the nurses, body
servants, and coachmen from Southern families, are cheating our hotels
and merchants of Southern custom, and our watering place society of
the beaux and belles who were wont to grace it. We learn that all the
popular summer resorts south of Mason and Dickson's line, are full
this season to overflowing. Such is the effect of fanaticism.

*   *   *   *

An exact appraisal of the role which Southern nationalist
leaders, and the various movements they originated or helped to
forward, played, in preparing the Southern mind for the great
national crisis of 1860, is difficult. Many other forces were

working in the same direction. Since 1844, some religious denominations had become entirely sectional and, along the border, members fought for possession of church property. Separate publishing houses had been set up and loyalty to sectional religious organizations was being developed. Political quarrels over expansion, land legislation, and internal improvements added yearly to sectional consciousness and hostility, Even though actual gains along some lines were slight, the constant discussion of Southern independence in things economic, of self-sufficiency in agriculture, education and amusements, must have added something to the idea of distinct Southern interests and purposes. Achievement in any of these areas increased sectional confidence. When this confidence was accompanied by the suggestion of hostility to the North and the inference of unfair advantages enjoyed by Northerners, its effect was heightened. A great background was gradually created against which the movement of events and particularly the slavery controversy took on new meaning. An aroused section, taking conscious strides toward economic and social and intellectual independ-, ence, was unconsciously making ready for political independence. The stuff out of which a nation could be fashioned was being woven. The South needed only clearer mental pictures of itself and of its great rival, to be ready for the coming struggle. The outlines of these pictures had already been drawn while the South worked out its defense of slavery. The movement toward self-sufficiency now added new details. Praise of Southern ways and recognition of her inherent superiority had been part of the reformers' technique. The fire-eater used this technique even more effectively. He used both the need of greater sectional security and the progress made toward it to emphasize differences and to assert Southern superiority. He based that claim to superiority on the unique stability of the Southern way of life.

"In the people of the North and of the South," said a Charleston *Mercury* editorial, "there were original specific differences of character. . . . The peoples of both sections were largely imbued with the blood of England. They were, however, of a somewhat different stock. Each derived its mental habitude and tone of thought from a different class of society and a different side in politics. The Puritanic element existing in the substratum of English society, gave cast of character to New England and the Northern States. The spirit of the Cavalier predominated at the South." The writer then pictured the Northerners as possessed of a "hard practical shrewdness," an "utter disregard of persons," a "stern proscriptive disposition," "a cold calculation of means to ends." He described them as "grasping and unyielding in the advancement of their pecuniary and political advantages," their statesmen always sectional.[42]

Southerners, on the other hand, were, in his estimate, "warmer and more generous in their appreciation of all that is high in intellect, morals and sentiments." They had always sacrificed material interests to the general welfare of the whole country. They had thus become the victims of treachery. North and South were "two nations . . . as distinct as the English and the French; [their] annual meetings at Washington [were] not Congresses to discuss common interests, but conventions to contest antagonistic opinions, and to proclaim mutual grievances, and utter hostile threats."[43]

Southern superiority was implicit in such differences. Proudly the Richmond *Enquirer* contrasted "one of our fine old country gentlemen, who lives ten hours a day in the open air superintending his plantation, who rides a high-mettled horse as if he were a part of him, follows the fox-hounds in spite of fences and ditches, brings down a partridge on the wing with each barrel, and when the day is over returns to a home characterized by comfort without luxury, and simplicity without meanness," with the New York "gentleman who winters in a Parisian house on Fifth Avenue, and summers at Newport or Saratoga, whose greatest feat of strength and skill is to drive a fast horse on a smooth road, who copies assiduously European luxury, European manners and European morals, and anxiously escapes from all contact with . . . his own countrymen." This writer saw Southern granaries full and the jails empty, while in that *free* Europe which the *free* North aped famine stalked about, religious faith had departed, and jails and poorhouses were filled to repletion. Because of her slavish following of an unworthy example, the North was a land of "riots, trades-unions, strikes,

and socialistic infidel philosophy." Food was scarce. Every one
was trying to live by his wits. Even the North's own people had
passed the sentence of condemnation on it as shown by the fact
that "the rich and the learned" were "Socialists, the poor . . .
revolutionists, rioters, anti-renters, Infidels, Mormons, Shakers,
Greeleyites, Fusionists, Owenites, Free Lovers, etc., etc." They
had all given up the cause of democracy and were "trying dis-
gusting experiments in new forms of society."[44]

The spread of isms in the North received much attention.
Isms revealed the lack of *stability*—the *summum bonum* of
all society! "Take these ism-smitten people of Massachusetts,"
wrote one editor, "whole classes of them, factories of them.
Counties of them. Cities full of them, and they crowd to hear
a Bloomer-clad unsexed lecturer, who has left her husband at
home to take care of the children,—she being strong minded.
. . ." Abolitionism, said another, was but "the head and front
of the family of *isms* as numerous as the catalogues of folly and
wickedness [were] capable of containing." All were intent on
overthrowing existing social systems, uprooting religion and re-
modelling the world on some utopian and impracticable basis.
All tended toward anarchy. All followed the direct and short
road to infidelity.[45]

In sharp contrast to such chaos was the stable Southern social
order founded on slavery. It was entirely exempt "from all
those distresses which periodically affect[ed] the Northern and
English communities,—labor riots in which the masses [arose]
. . . with a rallying shout for bread . . . strikes of vast bodies
of operators, who thus protest[ed] against the tyranny which
[ground] . . . them down to crushing toil for a mere pittance,
[and] 'bad seasons' or 'hard times' . . . when the community
seem[ed] disorganized [and] its equilibrium destroyed. . . ."
These things could not exist where "the bondsmen, as a lower
class, as the substratum of society, constitut[ed] an always reliable, never wavering foundation, whereon the social fabric
rest[ed] securely, rooted and grounded in stability, and entirely
beyond the reach of agitation by such causes as [shook] . . .
other communities to their center."[46]

Another argument used to prove the greater stability of the

South was the number of landowners. Senator Dawson of Georgia combed the census to discover that slaveholding states were also the landholding states. Nearly one half of the adult whites in South Carolina owned land and only one fifth of those in Massachusetts. The same group in Virginia were twice as numerous as those in New York. Kentucky had a third more than Ohio, and Mississippi more than Indiana or Illinois. The senator concluded that farms and plantations were "the great nurseries . . . of liberty, of valor, of patriotism, of morals."[47]

The Southern university was recognized as another great force working toward the stable order. In earlier days, students, in a few institutions, might have met disturbing ideas from the lips of a Thomas Cooper or a Horace Holley, but the day of unorthodoxy had passed, as Professor B. S. Hedrick at the University of North Carolina was soon to learn. A superior civilization could not permit the fountains to be poisoned at the source. Un-Southern thinking could not be permitted to youth and professors. The following editorial, modern in its ring, tells an old and a new story as well. It was published in the Richmond *Enquirer*, December 29, 1855:

Young men at College in the North are constantly exposed to the danger of imbibing doctrines subversive of all old institutions, and of all the established tenets respecting religion, law, morality, property, and government. Every village has its press and its lecture room, and each lecturer and editor, unchecked by a healthy public opinion, opens up for discussion all the received dogmas of faith. Nothing is considered as settled, nothing too venerable or sacred to be controverted. The intellectual rashness of Youth, and their love of novelty, predisposes them to reject old opinions, and accept, without sufficient investigation, what is novel and startling. It is not safe or prudent to expose young minds to the contagion of the conventions, the lectures, and the press of the Northern Isms. They naturally hate restraint and gradually embrace doctrines which teach them that to throw aside all restraint, and give free reins to inclination, appetite and passion, is the highest virtue.

The great movement at the North, the great lesson, taught everywhere now in free society is that "Passional Attraction," "Free Love," "attractive Labor," and "the Voluntary Principle," are to be substituted for Law, Religion, and Government. It is but the failure and breaking up of free society, and may be all right and proper *there,* but would be quite out of place at the South, where society is healthy, vigorous and flourishing.

The North fifty years ago, was eminently religious and conservative. Then it was well to send Southern youth to her Colleges. She is now the land of heresies, infidelities, and superstitions, and not fit to be trusted with the education of our sons and daughters.

As institutions of learning, the colleges of the South are equal to those of the North—the University of Virginia probably superior to any in the Union. Under these circumstances, it surprises us, that moral, conservative and religious men at the North, who can afford it, do not send their sons to Southern schools. Their training would be moral, religious and conservative, and they would never learn, or read a word in school or out of school, inconsistent with orthodox Christianity, pure morality, the right of property, the sacredness of marriage, the obligations of law, the duty of obedience to government.

*　*　*　*

Thus through the decade of the 'fifties, the few labored to prepare the way for a Southern nation. In season and out, they strove to build self-sufficiency and self-consciousness. While they prepared the ground, others were scattering seeds which in time would yield a harvest. Truly the calm which followed the Compromise of 1850 had been "the calm of preparation, and not of peace; a cessation, not an end of the controversy. . . ."

CHAPTER THIRTEEN

THE NORTHWEST GETS EXCITED

T HE history of the progress of the institution of slavery in America, should not be wholly lost upon the more Southern and Cotton growing States, nor should they fail to profit by its teachings. That history teaches that it was introduced by the early settlers of the North and East, who continued to foster the institution as long as it was advantageous and then profited by its emancipation, by sending their slaves to the South and selling them at high prices. . . . The past foreshadows the future. By degrees the spirit of emancipation has ever progressed and is progressing south. Maryland, Kentucky, and Virginia are [now] discussing its practicability, and the extent of the benefits that will accrue to them thereby."[1]

Thus wrote a Georgia editor in January, 1849. Unwittingly he suggested that, while the few labored to make the South ready for unity and independence, other forces were pulling in quite the opposite direction. The changing economic life of the older seaboard and border states was rendering slavery less advantageous and slowly cutting ties with the Lower South. The new agriculture was requiring fewer workers. Markets for their surpluses were being found in the free states, and an increasing quantity of flour, garden truck, and stock was turning in that direction. Methods and attitudes in the region came more and more to resemble those of Pennsylvania, New York, and Ohio. The old notion of Southern isolation and uniqueness was passing.

The rise of industrial interests in the cities of these areas contributed to the same end. Already, in some instances, the citizens of Richmond and Charleston, Memphis and St. Louis, had aligned themselves against the surrounding rural areas. Advocates of protective tariffs and larger national cooperation were reappearing and those who praised Yankee thrift and energy were by no means unknown.

These developments, together with the rise of the great Cotton Kingdom to dominance in Southern life, had already started a heavy black stream of surplus labor running south and westward. As the price of slaves soared under cotton's demands and as their own new efforts required less of unskilled labor, border farmers were selling their surplus workers to the once despised slave trader or to the Southwestern planter who came back east to increase the force on his hungry sugar or cotton lands. Many in the older states were finding the price of slaves too high for profitable use on worn lands and themselves in the unhappy position where the increase of Negroes provided one of their best crops. The effect was to break all the artificial restraints which slavery, up to this time, had placed on the normal westward migration of Negroes and to send this Southern group pell-mell along the usual American trail.

The charge of slave-breeding, which the abolitionist now hurled at the border states, can be dismissed until some evidence other than gossip has been found to support it. The fact of heavy sales, however, did indicate a comparative decrease in the importance of slave labor to the region. Regular laboring forces had to be reduced and supplemented in time of pressure with slaves hired from owners or through commission men. Slaves who remained behind had to be made more efficient and given a wider scope of freedom. Soon the slave was performing all the steps in improved agriculture. Soon he was toiling in the factories and upon the spreading railway lines. Often he selected his own employer and employment, found his own meals and sleeping quarters. Occasionally he was permitted to keep all he might earn beyond a specified amount. Border-state slavery, especially in urban centers, was becoming quite a new thing. Well might the Cotton South take notice.[2]

Of more immediate importance as a hindrance to the Southern unity and independence movement was the conservative reaction which followed the high tension of 1850 in the more radical states. In Georgia, where the conservatives, according to Henry Clay, had "crushed the spirit of discord, disunion and Civil

War," Compromise Whigs and Democrats formed the Constitutional Union Party and, in 1851, elected Cobb governor by a majority of 18,000 votes. Some thought that a new political era had dawned; that the old parties were doomed. The coalition, however, was based on a local situation and could become permanent only if a national organization were formed. The Whigs, whose union with their Northern element had been hopelessly strained by Taylor's affiliation with Seward, were anxious for such a result, and began at once to work for its attainment. Even the Democrats, whose Northern wing was comparatively safe, gave halfhearted assistance. But the approach of the national presidential campaign of 1852 confronted both factions with the dilemma of impotent state action or a return to the old party affiliations. The Democrats generally fell back into line, with a more or less positive assertion that their national organization stood for union and the finality of the Compromise. The Whigs were forced to do the same thing, but one group rejected the party nominee and cast their vote for Daniel Webster, who, by election day, was in his grave. The old political order was thus re-established in Georgia, but on what was admittedly a rather infirm national basis.[3]

Virginia's conservative reaction was even more marked. The Whigs, disorganized and uncertain, flatly denied the right of secession in 1851, and a Richmond faction under John M. Botts henceforward took positive national ground. The Democrats were only a trifle less conservative. At the very outset, through the retirement of Thomas Ritchie from public life, the conservatives had lost the great leader who had checked the Nashville Convention move and made the state safe on the Compromise measure. Robert M. T. Hunter's extreme Southern faction, however, failed to profit from this circumstance because of strife in its own ranks which immediately developed around Henry A. Wise and his ambitions. The doctrine of States' rights was lost in the scuffle. Virginia drifted into what her own radicals and other Southern nationalists spoke of as supreme indifference. Edmund Ruffin was soon certain that "talk of secession would ruin any man with political aims."[4]

In Alabama also, the Union Party, after carrying the state

for the Compromise, continued to dominate. In the legislature of 1851, it held a majority of nearly two to one; and, in the Congressional elections, it carried five out of seven districts. In the Montgomery district, the candidate backed by Yancey was soundly beaten by an opponent who declared: "If this Union, and the South too, is broken into fragments by the secession of any one, two, or three Southern states, I could but view it as the greatest possible calamity to human liberty." So scattered to the four winds of heaven was the Southern rights party, that the Montgomery *Advertiser* announced its determination "to offer no further opposition. . . ."

Gradually, however, old party animosities reappeared. Whigs and Democrats found it difficult to work together after the crisis had passed and when cooperation with national parties was required. As the election of 1852 came on, the Democrats began to reorganize. A few extreme States'-rights men in the Black Belt counties held out and nominated third-party candidates, but the rank and file gave Pierce and King an overwhelming majority. Even Yancey advised the people to accept the principles of the Georgia Platform and declared that he would not support the third-party candidates if Pierce's success were endangered. Under such circumstances, the Whigs had no choice but to return to their original party associations. An effort to revive the Union Party by calling it the States Rights Union Party failed, and most Alabama Whigs voted for Scott in the national election. Alabama, too, was politically back where she had started, but with both parties under conservative control.[5]

The reaction in Mississippi followed only a slightly different course. In November, 1851, a convention of the people denied the constitutional right of secession. In February, following, two Union Democrats were elected to the Senate, and Albert Gallatin Brown, once a rabid secessionist, declared "the Southern movement . . . dead" and himself the best of Union men. Governor Foote summed up the situation by saying: "I always told you that Mississippi was one of the most reliable Union States in the Confederacy. . . . Quitman and Quitmanism are dead in Mississippi forever."[6]

The pronouncement was a trifle premature. Brown was soon

in the Senate and Davis in the Cabinet. Even Quitman went to the House of Representatives in 1855. But the sharp conservative reaction of the Compromise period had taught its lessons. Mississippi politicians, while ardent in defense of Southern rights, talked little of secession during the next few years.

More surprising than any of these developments was the turn of affairs in South Carolina. The reaction against the "near-secession" episode was violent. In 1851, cooperationists talked of "the disgrace our mad politicians have involved us in" and expressed the belief that "our madness is almost at an end. . . ." They hoped that "the good & true men of the country . . . [would] place our state in the enviable position she once occupied in our glorious Union," and that "not a vestige of our folly [would] remain." "Single isolated secession" was now viewed as "the greatest humbug of the age." Where in the beginning "Union men, men proper," had formed a "very small minority," "the Ultras" had "overdone the matter and reaction [had to] take place." As one writer has observed, the men of South Carolina "in sheer exhaustion . . . sank into political apathy. Old issues and old leaders now met no response. Calhoun's works, published after his death by order of the legislature and distributed in large numbers to every section of the state, lay on the shelves unsold, and in three successive sessions of the legislature the proposal to erect a monument in his honor was defeated. Why erect a monument to a man whose principles had been abandoned?"

A new set of leaders now came to the fore in the Old Palmetto State. James L. Orr and Benjamin F. Perry, from the western counties, quickly crowded the secessionists aside. They picked J. J. Evans to succeed Rhett in the Senate, and soon controlled a solid political bloc which *The Mercury,* in derision, dubbed The National Democrats. Frankly repudiating his earlier position, Orr in particular advocated the abandonment of the policy of isolation and the reconciliation of South Carolina to the Union. He urged the Democrats to send delegates to the National Conventions and to help shape party policies. He dismissed disunion as the agitation of radicals and presented a series of demands for the democratizing of the state through the choice of presidential electors by the people instead of by the legislature, the establishment of a system of common public schools, and a more equitable distribution of representation than had existed under the old parish-district system. The *Mercury* saw in such demands the beginning of a "reign of mediocrities and cliques," the supplanting of "planter-parish control" by "the same mob spirit, the same tyranny of the majority" as in "the Northern democracies." A writer in the *Courier*, however, insisted that the state was "arousing herself like a strong man after sleep."

The fight was a bitter one. Only slight gains were made in political and educational reform. But South Carolina sent her delegation to the National Democratic Convention of 1856 in Cincinnati, where Orr proved a conspicuous leader in the Stephen A. Douglas camp. The Convention, impressed by the new spirit and purposes at work in South Carolina, awarded the next national Democratic Convention to the city of Charleston! Little did they dream what a tragic commitment they had made![7]

* * * *

While the great majority of Southerners temporarily settled back into inaction and indifference, largely ignoring the fire-eaters and proclaiming the Compromise of 1850 a permanent and final settlement of sectional differences, extremists in other parts of the nation found new causes for alarm.[8] The Northeast was particularly disturbed. The new fugitive-slave law was the immediate object of wrath and cause of confusion. But the roots of unrest lay deeper and, in part at least, grew out of reactions to fundamental changes in the social-economic order at home. As has already been said, industrial capitalism had by this time come to dominance in the section and the factory system had reached a high degree of maturity. After a series of bitter conflicts, the native laborers had, to some degree, been replaced by the recently arrived and more submissive foreigners, and the smaller and less efficient manufacturers had been crowded out of competition. Profits were now more satisfactory and a firm control over legislative bodies insured stability. The merchants of Boston and New York had expanded their businesses with the growth of Southern trade and the opening of new markets in California, South America, and the farther corners of the earth. Boston had become the Hub of the Universe, New York City, the Wonder of the Western World.

With these developments, a conservative capitalist class had appeared. Its members were intensely confident of themselves and equally certain of the inferiority of those who tended their machines or who toiled in their countinghouses. They had become strangely tolerant of, if not entirely sympathetic with, the Southern planters whose cotton they spun and wove, whose markets they enjoyed, and whose social philosophy they shared. In politics they were staunchly Whig—Cotton Whigs, said their critics, bound by a thread of cotton to fellow aristocrats and labor exploiters. They, too, had had enough of turmoil and strife. Greater prosperity lay just around the corner, if only agitation would cease and business interests would replace politics in the public mind. These men had approved of Webster's great speech; now they thought of the Compromise as final. Soon they would come to terms with the Southern planter even on the tariff schedules, and together the two groups would seek that peace and quiet in which property would be secure and privilege would be respectable.

But there were others who were deeply concerned at the drift of events and more suspicious than ever of the South and "her ways." Lesser men of the towns and country, already rudely awakened by economic changes, saw in the fugitive slave law and its acceptance by industrial aristocrats, positive proof of the triumph of sin and the defeat of democracy. They made ready to resist. The Higher Law removed all legal restraint. Disobedience became a moral duty; nullification, sound doctrine. "I will not obey it, by God," said Emerson.[9]

In Boston a Vigilance Committee, with Samuel Gridley Howe and Theodore Parker at its head, hurried fugitives on toward Canada and intimidated masters who sought to recover their property. Late in October of 1850, they "rescued" Ellen and William Craft. In February following, they broke open the jail to liberate the fugitive Shadrach and to carry him safely out of the country. "The noblest deed done in Boston since the destruction of the tea in 1773," said Parker. "We enjoy ourselves richly," wrote Wendell Phillips, "and I doubt whether more laughing is done anywhere than in anti-slavery parlors." "We have some hundreds of fugitives among us," he added.[10]

President Fillmore's proclamation against such "aiders and abettors" had no effect. Judge Curtis, who attempted to enforce the law, was denounced as a public enemy and held up "to receive the hootings and rotten eggs of the advancing generation." Webster was arraigned anew. "No living man," said Parker, "has done so much to debauch the conscience of the nation, to debauch the press, the pulpit, the forum, and the bar. . . . He poisoned the moral wells of society . . . and men's consciences died of the murrain of beasts, which came because they drank thereat." Freesoilers and Democrats combined to elect the abolitionist, Charles Sumner, to the Senate, where almost immediately he moved for the repeal of the Fugitive Slave Act. Caleb Cushing, meanwhile, was cruelly attacked as an unprincipled politician for opposing Sumner's election and charged with unduly hurrying his dead sister to her grave in order to cast his vote.[11]

In Central New York, a like spirit prevailed. On the passage of the "infernal Fugitive Slave Bill," the "country flamed with excitement." Meetings, "great and good," were held to protest, and "the boldest denunciations . . . called out the loudest applause." "It would be almost certain death to a slave-catcher," wrote W. H. Burligh from Syracuse, "to appear, on his infernal mission, in our streets. No fugitive can be taken from our midst."[12]

A chance to make good that boast came on October 1, 1851, when a Missouri fugitive, William Henry, popularly known as Jerry, was arrested by a United States deputy marshal and brought before the commissioners of the United States Circuit Court. A mob, urged on by Gerrit Smith and the Reverend Samuel J. May, forcibly entered the official's office and, after one failure, effected Jerry's escape across the border to Kingston, Ontario. Some of the rescuers were indicted, but not the ringleaders. After two years of delay, Senator William H.

Seward going bond, one man was convicted; all the others were acquitted or their cases dropped. Not content with even so complete a victory, the rescuers then secured the indictment of the United States Deputy Marshal who had arrested Jerry, and forced him to stand trial on the charge of kidnapping! The leaders were determined to bring the people into direct conflict with the government so that the government might "be made to understand that it [had] transcended its limits. . . ." As Gerrit Smith put it: "If the rescue of Jerry was not a work of justice and mercy, then there is no justice, no mercy, no God!" The reign of the "Higher Law" had begun.[13]

The conservatives made far less noise. They constituted, however, a majority. Few of them doubted the great evils of slavery and most of them would have rejoiced at its destruction. But they would not threaten the Union to accomplish that end. Obedience to law and respect for authority were more important than reform; quiet and prosperity more to be desired. Caleb Cushing spoke for them when he declared:[14]

> We reject and repel the doctrine that it is the duty of the citizens of Massachusetts to give themselves up to the agitation of the question of slavery abolition in the South. On the contrary, we insist that it is the duty of every good citizen and every good man to leave the subject . . . where Washington and Madison, Morris, Hamilton and Jay, the framers of the Constitution, placed it, namely, with the domestic legislation of each of the several states respectively concerned.

Benjamin R. Curtis was even more emphatic. He reminded his friends of the solemn pledge Massachusetts had taken in accepting the Constitution and warned them that she had nothing to do with the rights of fugitives. "It is enough for us that they have no right to be here," he said. ". . . Whatever natural rights they have, and I admit these rights to their fullest extent, *this* is not the *soil* on which to vindicate them." He challenged any reformer "to show that the moral duty which we owe to the fugitive slave, when in conflict with the moral duty we owe to our country and its laws, is so plainly superior thereto, that we ought to engage in a revolution on account of it."[15]

The advocacy of similar principles and the necessity for securing the support of this conservative element in the Northeast, made Franklin Pierce of New Hampshire available as the
Democratic candidate in the election of 1852. Except for residence in New England and a firm insistence on the finality of
the Compromise of 1850 as a settlement of sectional differences, Pierce had few qualifications for the rôle. Even his most
ardent supporters had thought of him, in the beginning, only
as the vice-presidential candidate. Yet the tide of reaction was
strong enough to bring such consummate mediocrity to the
highest office in the land. Even New England was not ready
to follow her radicals.[16]

Shortly after Pierce's inauguration and his first message con-
gratulating the country on "a sense of repose and security to the
public mind," Parker and Dana and Phillips led a Boston mob
in the attempted rescue of the Negro, Anthony Burns. They
failed, but neither repose nor serenity ensued. Eleven days
before the fugitive walked back to slavery along Boston streets
draped in black and hung with flags at half-mast, the Kansas-
Nebraska Act had passed the House and had gone to the President for his signature. A new storm of greater fury had broken.
This time, however, the storm center lay in the Old Northwest,
not in the Northeast. With this shift, the sectional conflict entered a new phase.

*   *   *   *

The part played by the Northwest in the final break-up of
the Union was to be of major importance. The attitudes developed in that region during the 'fifties made the conflict of
sections irrepressible. There the Republican Party was born
and the struggle over slavery developed into its final form.
Uncle Tom and Dred Scott and John Brown became national
figures on that stage. Abraham Lincoln stepped from its rural-
ness to become, as wartime President, the symbol of American democracy, to phrase a people's innermost thoughts and
aspirations, and to hold their strength together for victory.

In early days, the entire Middle West, from Canada to the
Gulf, was something of a unity. The Mississippi River system

gave it physical foundations. Trade, which followed the water-ways, strengthened the ties, and common origins and coexisting frontier conditions made outlooks and values everywhere very much alike. As time went on, social economic patterns in the northern parts of the Mississippi Valley slowly diverged from those to the south, but the differences which developed before the 1840's were far less than those existing between most American sections. The West had still to be reckoned with as a unity where national issues touched expansion, lands, internal improvements, and financial policies. The sharp revolt of the Northwest over measures in Polk's administration had, therefore, marked a new trend in Western affairs. For the first time, the Northwest had reacted as a North and not as a West.

* * * *

The first settlers on the north side of the Ohio River came predominantly from the upland South. They were a plain people—sallow, lean, restless woodsmen who had, in earlier days, hewn clearings out of the forest and builded cabin-homes in the Carolinas, Virginia, and Tennessee. Some of them had drifted along through the mountain gaps with the frontier, stopping for a time at one place or another; some had moved directly to the Northwest to get a better farm or to escape the spread of slavery. They were a homely people in their vices and their virtues and their persons. Drunkenness was all too common among them, and assault and battery all too frequent. But they were a generous people, kindly, and honest as they understood the term. They worked hard and lived simply. The home and the church constituted about all in their lives which might be thought of as social institutions. Education was scant and illiteracy high. But they were not ignorant of nature nor of people. Religion, indulged in according to Quaker, Methodist, Baptist, or Presbyterian forms, afforded the major outlet for their half-starved emotions; going a-visiting, trading at the country store, attending court, political speakings, or religious meetings occupied their time when the fields did not require their attention. An independent spirit and a neighborly attitude characterized their relations with one another.

These early Ohio River Valley settlers were mainly farmers of the corn and hog type. They were, however, soon augmented, first by a growing group of merchants in the towns, who forwarded their surpluses to distant markets and sold them store goods, and then by a few manufacturers who processed their raw materials. Cincinnati and St. Louis were their greatest urban centers, but New Orleans, to which most of their pork, whiskey, corn, and wheat went, was equally near and important in their thoughts. Rivers and river towns controlled their destinies and stirred their ambitions. In 1845, the Secretary of the Treasury reported over $250,000,000 worth of property afloat on the Mississippi and its tributaries. Nearly one half of this was employed in the sugar and cotton trade about New Orleans; almost all of the other half passed to and from the ports of Cincinnati, St. Louis and other neighboring towns interested in the trade of the lower West and South. In 1844, 90 per cent of the Northwest's entire corn export of a million and a half bushels, 81 per cent of its eight hundred thousand barrels of pork and bacon, and 95 per cent of its one hundred thousand barrels of whiskey went down the rivers flowing toward the Crescent City.[17]

There were human beings as well as cargoes on the river boats. The young Abraham Lincoln, and hundreds of young frontiersmen like him, floated their rafts, loaded with a neighborhood's produce, down muddy northern streams to get their first taste of the larger world on the great Mississippi highway and in the great turbulent cosmopolitan New Orleans. Mark Twain as a boy played along the river's banks and as a young man became a river pilot. He found Huck Finn and Tom Sawyer in that half-lazy, half-hurried world.

In politics the early Northwest was Democratic. Andrew Jackson was its hero. Few of its citizens questioned the capacity of common men for self-government; fewer doubted the value of individual freedom and initiative. The great majority were positive that virtue resided in the breasts of farmers and mechanics; that the United States represented God's own experiment in good government. The need for internal improvements and better markets, however, made Henry Clay's American System popular and Whigs more numerous in the older sections when immigration from the East fell off and home markets declined. Many voted for Harrison in 1840, both as a Western man and as an advocate of government assistance to economic improvements. But the majority, throughout the decade, still found in the party of Jefferson and Jackson the better expression of their notions of the nation's destiny, the individual's rights, and the common man's place in society and government.

Such were the main features of the people and their outlook in the lower Northwest up through the 1840's. Fundamental changes, however, were already taking place. After 1830, a new stream of population had begun to move westward along the Lakes from New England and New York. It was made up of the human surplus which had resulted as social-economic conditions in those sections matured. It carried with it the values and habits which characterized New England and her children. In the town form of local government he established, in the Puritan desire to be his brother's keeper, and in other institutions and attitudes he brought with him, the settler carried the stamp of his origin. Sometimes a whole congregation, preacher and all, made a pious migration to Ohio or Michigan, drawing up a compact before their departure like that which came out of the cabin of the *Mayflower;* sometimes a group of serious college boys bound themselves together as a band to carry light by preaching and teaching in the Western field. More often the individual or family group turned westward under economic necessity or dissatisfaction with social pressures to harvest the timber, to break the prairie soils, or to practice some profession for which thrifty parents had provided training. Opportunity lured a surprisingly large number of young lawyers, doctors, printers, teachers, and preachers. Quickly they sprinkled the countryside with Congregational spires, opened the doors of "little Yales," and hopefully planted the elms along the streets of towns-to-be. Usually they voted Whig, and they furnished a large part of the Liberty and Free Soil support in the section. By 1850, more than a half million persons of New England and New York birth lived in Ohio and in the states to her west. Most of them were to be found in what was coming to be known as the Great Lakes region.[18]

A second element came to this region from abroad. Englishmen and Germans had entered the Ohio Valley at an early date, but after 1840 a new flow set in from Germany, Ireland, and Canada great enough to give a foreign tinge to many a locality. Within ten years, there were some 640,000 foreign-born in the North Central region. The Irishmen, usually Catholic in faith, helped to build the canals and railroads and then settled down on near-by farms or in the new towns which sprang up along the lines of transportation. The plain Germans occupied the less favorably located lands or those most encumbered with timber, or found places as butchers, shopkeepers, or bakers in the rising urban centers. Some were Lutherans, some were Catholics. Most were poor and had only toil and faith to give. The more cultured Forty-eighters found larger opportunities, but most of them also settled in communities where men of their own nationality already predominated. Both groups tended at first to associate themselves with the Democratic Party, whose principles at least seemed to be in accord with the desire for equality and freedom which had brought them to America. All found some difficulty in adjusting themselves to the Greater New England element which surrounded them, but common trials and experiences soon made the Irishman's Church and the German's "beer and Beethoven" part of the accepted community pattern. Throughout the 'fifties, the Northwest along the Great Lakes grew more rapidly than did the region along the Ohio and moved steadily toward greater unity of interest and outlook.[19]

The rise of the upper Northwest, with its new peoples and differing values, upset old balances. As a surplus developed in the region, it naturally turned back along the Lakes toward the Northeast. Canals and railroads quickly supplemented natural highways, and markets along the Atlantic seaboard from Boston to Baltimore opened to Western wheat, beef, and pork. Shipments increased largely in proportion to the growth of the Lake regions, but even those who lived in the Ohio Valley could now choose whether they ship by river to the South; by the Lakes, canals, and rail to Boston and New York; or by rail to Philadelphia and Baltimore. After 1853, although more and more produce was sent down river, the percentage of such shipments to the total export steadily declined and the percentage which went eastward steadily increased. The building of the Illinois Central and the pushing forward of railroad lines from Mobile and New Orleans, did not alter the situation. In 1860, the East took 62 per cent of the Northwest's flour, nearly all its wheat, 80 per cent of its corn, 61 per cent of its salt meat, and some 52 per cent of its whiskey. This was 5 to 15 per cent more than the shipments of 1857. Thus, while the South in each year took more of everything except flour, the relative proportion of each product which it received declined. The Lakes region was outstripping the Ohio Valley. Economic and political dominance was shifting northward to where Chicago, Milwaukee, Cleveland, Detroit, and Toledo were dropping clumsy frontier ways and taking on metropolitan airs. Stephen A. Douglas, spokesman for the Valley, paid tribute to that fact when, in 1847, he moved to Chicago.[20]

New social attitudes came with the peoples who settled the Lake region. Their demand for the prohibition of traffic in alcoholic liquors reached crusade proportions after 1847 and the legislatures of most of the states were henceforth under constant pressure for legislation of the Maine law variety. Local and state organizations, temperance periodicals, petition signing, oratory, mob assaults, and political action all played a part in the movement. Its strongholds were the neighborhoods in Ohio, Michigan, Indiana, Illinois, and Iowa where New Englanders predominated, but even in Missouri the pressure was great enough to secure the enactment of mild legislation.

This movement, like the women's rights movement and the efforts toward more strict Sabbath observance, which flourished at the same time, met bitter opposition from the Southern counties of the Old Northwest, and, of course, from most of the foreign groups along the Lakes. They gradually defeated legislation and held the movement in check until the anti-slavery controversy brushed it aside. The temperance crusade, however, served to emphasize a sharp cleavage between the attitudes of those who were building up the Lakes district and those who lived in the Ohio Valley. It lent color to the charge that the Democratic Party, now designated as the whiskey party, could not be counted on for reform. It enabled the New England element to talk about the moral and intellectual darkness which enshrouded the older and southern Northwest. It paved the way for and contributed to the birth and extension of the Republican Party.[21]

But more important than differences and conflicts between the upper and lower parts of the Northwest was the fact of their basic common interests and attitudes. Lakes region and Ohio Valley alike were Western. Both were interested primarily in their own development and well-being. On the larger issues of lands, internal improvements, expansion, and finance, they generally stood on common ground and revealed a sectional flavor quite their own. In spite of serious surface differences, Douglas and Lincoln and Vallandigham were never very far apart in objectives.[22] The old charge that the Ohio Valley was pro-Southern in its purposes is not supported by the facts. That accusation was raised to blacken rivals in a domestic conflict. It was pure distortion. The region, no doubt, had a greater liking for the South than it had for New England, but its first thought was always for its own welfare. Throughout the ante-bellum period it showed far more dislike for the Lakes area than it did devotion to the South. It valued Southern markets, but not necessarily Southern institutions and programs. Political control at home was always a more vital matter than the interests of some outside group. Opposition first to Whigs and later to Republicans was a party matter, not a sectional one. From the necessity which grew out of its physical location, the region was national. As the editor of a Cincinnati newspaper said in 1857:[23]

The West does not recognize itself as belonging to what are regarded as the Northern and Southern Sections of this Union. . . . [It has] set up for itself a politically distinct, independent, self-reliant community, which recognizes as its chief basis the Union of these States, and is resolved to maintain that Union against North and South.

This basic unity of self-interest and nationalism in the Old Northwest, which by 1860 was to make Douglas as objectionable to most Southern men as Lincoln himself, and both of them unacceptable to William Lloyd Garrison, must be understood as clearly as the fact of a distinct cleavage within the section. The two tendencies were never separated, and they shaped a West and a Western mind which had no small share in determining the fate of a nation.

Like most men who went west, those who settled the Old Northwest expected to better themselves by the move. They were men of faith and hope—idealists, no matter how material their ambitions or how coarse their personal qualities. They believed that America promised, probably owed, them a chance to get ahead, which most of them interpreted as the ownership of land, a reasonable degree of prosperity, and perhaps even a public office. They talked much of equality of opportunity; they bitterly complained of privileges to the few.

Because this people held such views, Benton's efforts in behalf of pre-emption and graduation and Henry Clay's American System had gained wide support, the annexation of Texas had been popular, the demand for all of Oregon had been generally approved. For the same reasons, a deep undercurrent of resentment and unrest had developed. Under the emphasis given to freedom, speculators monopolized the lands and prevented developments. Eastern politicians opposed liberal legislation of all kinds and Western dreams remained half-realized. Poverty and hard times were the usual lot where markets were glutted and freight rates were high. The West was ever a potential rebel. Revolts here were ever potential crusades for democracy.

While the Ohio Valley dominated the Northwest, Stephen A. Douglas was its outstanding spokesman. New England origins had not handicapped a rugged, aggressive personality in Springfield, Illinois, and Douglas had risen steadily from local office holding to the United States Senatorship in 1846. His political principles were typically Western. They reflected the attitudes and needs of the Ohio Valley. As a member of the House of Representatives in the early 'forties, he served as

Chairman of the Committee on Territories and was consistently an ardent expansionist. He favored the annexation of Texas and took the extreme position in regard to Oregon that England should not hold one acre on the Northwest coast of America. When Polk accepted compromise, Douglas was one of the radical group who marched by the House teller shouting: "fifty-four, forty forever!"[24]

Yet he did not allow his disappointment over Oregon to weaken his loyalty to national interests. He ardently defended the War with Mexico, viewed the Wilmot Proviso as an act of folly, and soon was recognized as the outstanding advocate of the good Western doctrine of Squatter Sovereignty which Lewis Cass had expounded in his Nicholson letter. That doctrine denied that Congress might exercise political control in a territory after organization and left the people to regulate their own internal affairs as they saw fit. That was practical democracy.

Douglas was primarily interested always in seeing new territory added to the national domain and in having democratic self-government quickly established therein. He had worked for this in Oregon; he now pressed for it in California and New Mexico. As the representative of an older West, already sending its more restless peoples on to newer pastures, he could favor no other policy. Nor could he accept the extreme anti-slavery demands of the abolitionists or the purely sectional appeal of John C. Calhoun. His upland-Southern constituents had no particular affection for Negroes; they had to pass through and to other sections for markets. "I have no sympathy," said Douglas, "for Abolitionism on the one side, or that extreme course on the other which is akin to Abolitionism." Calhoun denounced him, and Senator Foote of Mississippi answered him with the language of just indignation. But Douglas stood his ground, insisting that "if slavery be a blessing, it is your blessing." The North had moulded her own institutions to her own needs and could grant the South assistance only "in the maintenance of all [her] Constitutional rights."[25]

Here was a new and independent kind of Democracy. It was *national*, yet it was *Western*. Vallandigham of Ohio spoke of it as that approach "sometimes sneeringly called the 'progressive school of politics.' " It was loyal to the party and to the fundamental doctrines for which it stood, yet it had its own understanding of the tangible benefits which good democratic practice ought to yield. Politicians should be practical and tolerant. They should know how to compromise. Petty whims and selfish desires should not interfere with manifest destiny.[26]

Acting on such principles, Douglas had not hesitated to quarrel with Polk about Oregon and with Southern Democrats about California. He had supported the Whig moves, under Clay and Webster, to compromise sectional difficulties in 1850. He was now intent on the building of railroads in the West which would make Chicago and St. Louis greater centers of wider trade. In most of these efforts he had received loyal support from Allen of Ohio, Hannegan of Indiana, and Dodge and Jones of Iowa. For his irregularity and theirs, he and his section had been ignored when the Cabinets of recent Democratic administrations had been formed.

The rapid development of the Lakes region added heavily to Douglas's difficulties. The votes of the new element had to be won, and that element was just then in serious trouble. Its home market had broken in the early 'forties and suffering was acute and widespread. Corn sold for eight and ten cents a bushel and "wheat [did] not bring 25 cts. a bushel in . . . the best markets." "Where is a market for our surplus?" queried *The Prairie Farmer.* "We have just commenced exporting . . . [and] the home market is even now completely glutted. . . ." "Where shall we find a market for our surplus grain," echoed *The Western Journal* of St. Louis. "We want a foreign market for our produce, which is now rotting in our granaries," Breese of Illinois told the Senate. "We need annexation to the lakes; some access to the markets of the great world," declared a Wisconsin editor.[27]

Proposals for relief ranged from improved transportation facilities and land reform to protective tariffs and government assistance in foreign markets. The Walker tariff, with its free-trade features, and Polk's veto of the River and Harbor Bill, therefore, aroused bitter protest in the region and loosed a storm of abuse, first upon the Democratic administration and then upon the slaveholding South which was thought to dominate it. John Wentworth of Chicago called the tariff a superior tax paid by the Western pioneers "to this Southern nabob who has countless slaves to watch him when he sleeps and fan him when he wakes!" Brinkerhoff of Ohio objected to it as taxes designed "to support an exclusive Southern chivalry, taxes to support a government which gave no significant offices to the Northwest, a government which sacrificed Northern territory in Oregon but added new taxes to carry on a 'war for southern conquest.' " In speaking of the Administration's war on Mexico, another Ohioan, Thomas Corwin, declared that our Democracy preferred "to pay money for blowing out brains, rather than blowing up and getting round rocks that impede the progress of the most efficient civilizer of our Barberous race—commerce. . . ." *The Chicago Democrat* blamed the failure to secure land legislation favorable to actual settlers onto Southern fears that such legislation would inevitably extinguish slavery. *The Detroit Daily Advertiser* insisted that the Democrats' whole program was designed "to break down the prosperity of the North for the benefit of the slave interests."[28]

The region grew increasingly restless. The Wilmot Proviso became a basic doctrine. Homestead legislation won new supporters. The size of the Whig and Free Soil vote increased alarmingly and party coalition became frequent. The cleavage between the Lakes region and the Ohio Valley widened. Discontented farmers, receiving only thirty-five cents a bushel for wheat on the Chicago market in June and July, 1846, were inclined to classify all Democrats as pro-Southern and pro-slavery. Consistently, from 1847 to 1854, the representatives of the northern districts voted against those of the Ohio Valley. They had decided to set the boundaries of slavery. A major political revolt was in the making. Stephen A. Douglas no longer spoke for the men of the upper West.[29]

To economic ills was added, after 1850, the offensive fugitive slave law. Its passage was the signal for almost immediate opposition throughout the upper West. The Common Council of Chicago, by a vote of 10 to 3, adopted resolutions denouncing the act and declaring those Northern Senators and Representatives who had supported it, "fit only to be ranked with the traitors, Benedict Arnold and Judas Iscariot." The Council refused to require the city police to render any assistance for the arrest of fugitive slaves, and expressed confidence that this action would not cause "our Harbor appropriations [to be] withheld, our railroads injured, our commerce destroyed. . . ."[30] An Ottawa, Illinois, convention resolved: "That no legislative enactments can make it wrong to aid in the escape of fugitive slaves from bondage." Similar sentiments were expressed in Indiana, where one meeting insisted that its members would not assist in the capture of fugitives even though refusal should "deprive us of our possessions and incarcerate us between dungeon walls." The arrest of one Giles Rose as a fugitive in Detroit was followed by a spirited assembly of citizens who denounced the law as a violation of the manifest principles of Justice and humanity.[31] Ohio men talked in the same rabid fashion. One meeting, at Columbus, declared that any one who aided in the enforcement of the law, "whether as a magistrate, officer or citizen," was "an enemy of the human race, a criminal of the deepest dye. . . ." Another, at Ravenna, asserted that any person who accepted the office of commissioner or marshal under the bill would prove himself "to be a man utterly heartless and devoid of humanity and a fit associate of hangmen." "Come imprisonment, come fine, come death, we will neither aid or assist in the return of any fugitive slave," said a group assembled at Canfield. Benjamin F. Wade, soon to be chosen United States Senator from Ohio, was one of this Canfield group and supported these resolutions. Senator Chase managed the meeting in Highland County which resolved that "Disobedience to the enactment is obedience to God." The Higher Law was making real progress in the Northwest.[32]

Throughout the next three years excitement continued. Late in 1852, Harriet Beecher Stowe published her nation-shaking, melodramatic *Uncle Tom's Cabin*, which supplied something heretofore lacking in the anti-slavery crusade. Vague generalities of past decades took on intimate reality. Uncle Tom became a living person, beloved and admired, the symbol of all slaves. His sufferings could be shared and his abuses resented. He took his place in the hearts of a generation along side of Oliver Twist, Tiny Tim, and Little Nell. The evils of slavery, like those of industrial England, became distressingly real. They were something to be excited about, to be acted upon. For a thwarted world, the slave had been stereotyped.

Meanwhile, the Free Soil Party, which had been weakened by the anti-slavery extension attitudes of both old parties in the Compromise period, revived as a pure anti-slavery movement. "Genuine, good, old-fashioned Conventions" began to be held again. The underground railroad showed new life. Revolt was in the air.[33]

Salmon P. Chase fought earnestly to confine the political movement to the liberalizing of the Democratic Party. He succeeded in substituting the name Free Democracy for anti-slavery in the call for a national convention in 1852. He broadened the appeal to include economic interests and tried to attract Whigs and Democrats as well as Free Soilers. His efforts, together with the utter collapse of the Whig Party after the November election, prepared the way for the ultimate formation of a broader-based new party which would capitalize on the unsettled state of Northwestern public opinion. *The Lafayette* (Ind.) *Courier* forecast such a party as early as October, 1852:[34]

We have heard it estimated that in the event of the defeat of General Scott the Whig party will be disbanded, and of the fragments will be formed a grand National anti-slavery party, which, by including the Liberty party, the Free Soil party, the abolitionists, and that portion of the Democrats who sustain the nominees but not the finality resolutions of the platform, may be able to control the national elections of the future. That such a party will be organized we have good reason to believe.

* * * *

In spite of all these signs of political discontent, the three years following the Compromise of 1850 had not brought any great upheaval. On the contrary, some things on the surface seemed to indicate a gradual return to political normalcy. Except in a few notable cases, Southerners had, by 1852, returned to the old party folds. Many had done so half-heartedly and were willing to scratch the ticket if suitable candidates were not offered. Whigs were particularly unsettled because of the growing influence of anti-slavery men in the party, but only the few had found the courage necessary to go over to the Democrats. Northerners, especially in the upper Northwest, were seemingly even more disturbed. Yet they too had left the third party to the pure reformers and had tried to get back some of the old enthusiasm for the regular organizations. Neither party had, in 1852, dared to nominate one of its real leaders. Both had accepted the finality of the Compromise of 1850 on the one issue to which there was no finality. Thousands of voters stayed home, and thousands cast meaningless votes. General Scott, the Whig candidate, carried only four states— Vermont and Massachusetts in the North, and Kentucky and Tennessee in the South. Pierce became President by virtue of the conservative reaction and desire for quiet which characterized the planting South, dominated the industrial Northeast, and still held sway in the Ohio Valley. The Whigs were badly disorganized, perhaps completely broken; the Democrats, however, might be on their way back to unity and strength, if only quiet and national prosperity could be maintained.

*   *   *   *

Into this atmosphere of uncertainty underlaid by unrest and revolt came, on January 23, 1854, the announcement that Stephen A. Douglas had introduced in the Senate a bill for the organization of the territories of Kansas and Nebraska in which "all questions pertaining to slavery in the Territories, and in the new States to be formed therefrom" was "left to the decision of the people residing therein, through their appropriate representatives." To this bill was appended a section specifically declaring the Missouri Compromise measure of 1820 inoperative and superseded "by the principles of legislation of 1850, commonly called the compromise measures." The bill climaxed a series of efforts earlier made by Senator Douglas and later by Senator Dodge of Iowa and Representatives Hall and Miller of Missouri, to organize this territory in the interests of railroads and settlers. The section of the bill dealing with slavery followed the notice, served on January 16 by Senator Dixon of Kentucky, to the effect that he would offer an amendment for the repeal of the Missouri Compromise to any territorial bill presented.[35]

Reaction to Douglas's bill was immediate and violent. He had announced his intention to introduce the bill on January 4, and, even before debate began in the Senate, anti-slavery politicians had seized upon the bill with fiendish glee. Here was the great opportunity for which Chase and Giddings and Seward and Sumner had been waiting. For four years and more, the upper North and West had been preparing for political revolt. All that had been lacking was some dramatic pro-slavery step which would crystallize wavering opinion and precipitate action. Chase in particular had sensed the situation. In February, 1853, he had prophesied that there would "be in Ohio, in less than two years a united Democracy, united upon principle and determined to maintain their principles everywhere. . . ." In December of the same year he had asked his friend Hamlin: "Is there any prospect of division among the democrats of the old line . . . ? Cannot enough of them be induced to unite with us & the liberal Whigs to carry the state next fall . . . ?" He now saw the chance to answer his own question.[36]

On the morning of January 24, 1854, there appeared in the *National Era,* under the date line, January 19, a public letter headed, *Appeal of the Independent Democrats in Congress to the People of the United States.* It was written by Salmon P. Chase, but the text, as republished in the *Congressional Globe,* was signed by Chase, Wade, Smith, Sumner, and DeWitt (Mass.). In the next few days, this *Appeal* was printed in newspapers all over the North and reprinted on circulars for wider distribution. It opened with the warning that "the freedom of our institutions" and "the permanency of our Union" were in imminent danger. It stated, without qualifications, that the passage of Douglas's bill would "open all the unorganized territory to the ingress of slavery." It arraigned the bill "as a gross violation of a sacred pledge; as a criminal betrayal of precious rights; as part and parcel of an atrocious plot to exclude from a vast unoccupied region immigrants from the Old World, and free laborers from our own states, and to convert it into a dreary region of despotism, inhabited by masters and slaves." Then followed a glowing description of this vast territory and a studied recital of its dedication to freedom under the Missouri Compromise. With a keen understanding of the Lakes region's interests, it asserted that, should this bill become law, the building of Pacific Railroads would be checked and the expectation of profitable returns ended. A homestead law would be worthless. Westward expansion for the Northwest would be impossible because of a great slave territory stretching along its border from Canada to the Gulf. Only by resisting the demands of slavery could "the Union formed to establish justice and secure the blessings of liberty" be saved![37]

The political shrewdness of the *Appeal* was matched only by its dishonesty. No interest, no fear of the restless upper North and Northwest was neglected. Homesteads, railroads, and markets were at stake. An aggressive slave power, with the hated Douglas at its head, was on the march against morality and democracy. A well-worked-out plot was about to succeed. All good citizens who wanted prosperity and a square deal must join hands with the Free Democrats!

The falsity of the *Appeal* was apparent to any one not swept away by his emotions. The facts were easily available. Douglas had not originally intended to repeal the Missouri Compromise but to limit it to the territorial period. Repeal developed even after the bill had been proposed to the Senate on January 4. The South had not been the least bit interested in the organization of this territory, nor had it shown the slightest inclination to interfere with the Missouri Compromise. For a decade, its leading spokesmen had advocated the extension of the line 36° 30' to the Pacific as a means of permanently settling the slavery issue. Northern votes had defeated such proposals. Only a short time before Douglas made his move, Senator Atchison of Missouri had solemnly stated "that there was no prospect, no hope of the repeal of the Missouri Compromise excluding slavery from that territory. . . ." Until Northern radicals made the Douglas bill a sectional issue, few Southerners manifested any enthusiasm for it.[38]

Furthermore, the principles for dealing with slavery contained in the bill did not imply the creation of new slave territory. Most thoughtful Southerners saw that at once. Douglas himself neither expected nor wished slavery to expand. He called slavery a curse beyond computation to both white and black and frankly declared that "all candid men who understand the subject admit that the laws of climate, and production, and of physical geography . . . have excluded slavery from that country." ". . . It is worse than folly to think of it being a slaveholding country. . . . I have no idea that it could." "The cry of the extension of slavery has been raised," he said, "for mere party purposes. . . ." The real principle involved in his bill was the great democratic one of the right of self-government.[39]

Chase more or less admitted Douglas's charge when he urged his friend Hamlin to keep the anti-slavery idea paramount. He wrote, on November 21, 1854:

> . . . Anti-slavery men should be constantly warned of the importance of keeping the anti-slavery idea paramount. There is *danger* of its being shoved aside. They must see that it is not lost sight of. Now more than ever it is essential that an earnest anti-slavery tone should be maintained by our men & that the fire should be sustained.

The soundest explanation of Douglas's action is to be found in the needs and the ambitions of the Northwest itself. The Ohio Valley had not shared in the unrest and revolt which had characterized the Lakes region. It had accepted the Compromise of 1850 as final and the fugitive slave law as one to be obeyed. It had stood loyally by the old parties and had enabled the Democrats especially to regain much of their old solidarity. It looked forward in 1850 hopefully to a new era of quiet and substantial growth.

To Douglas the realization of the Northwest's hopes lay in the building of railroads. Since 1836 he had been active in promoting lines and much that had been accomplished in his own state must be credited to him. He originated the movements for both the Illinois Central and the Northern Cross railroads and was instrumental in securing federal land grants for their building. In his first term in the House he introduced a bill for the organization of Nebraska (1844), and, when Asa Whitney proposed a railroad to the Pacific in 1845, Douglas issued an eight-page pamphlet favoring the idea but substituting a railroad plan of his own which included the organization of the same territory as a necessary step.[40]

After he went to the Senate and moved to Chicago (1847), Douglas became even more active. Missouri and Iowa groups were busy with schemes for local lines and were on the watch for profit that would accrue from connections with the proposed railroad to the Pacific. Douglas worked with Hall and Atchison of Missouri and Leffler of Iowa for the success of their moves and again introduced his Nebraska bill (1848). In 1849, Chicago sent him to a St. Louis Railroad Convention where he advocated a western line from Chicago to Council Bluffs and then by South Pass to the coast. The next year he secured land grants for the Illinois Central and included also a grant for the Mobile and Ohio line which would connect it with Chicago instead of St. Louis as originally intended. Meanwhile he invested heavily in lands at the head of Lake Superior and in Chicago real estate. His investments stood to profit largely as railways would reach from Superior to the Gulf and the Northwest Coast, and from Chicago to the Pacific.

At this stage, Douglas's plans were threatened from two directions.[41] In Missouri, Thomas Hart Benton, fighting hard to regain his slipping political power, continued to agitate a central railroad route to the Pacific with the eastern terminal at St. Louis. He had advocated this program first in the St. Louis Railroad Convention of 1849. After his defeat for the Senate in 1850, he seized upon it again as a popular issue which might help him stage a rapid recovery. He added to it an effort to organize the Nebraska territory under the provisions of the Missouri Compromise. A group of Missouri Whigs soon joined forces with him, both to forward his railroad schemes and to secure the organization of a free territory. Hall and Atchison again got busy. In 1852, they secured a land grant for the

Hannibal and St. Joe railroad, and Hall reintroduced his bill for the organization of the Territory of the Platte. The Committee on Territories reported a substitute bill for the organization of Nebraska. These moves, if carried out, would bridge the gap between existing mid-Western lines and the proposed central route to the Pacific and effect the organization of the territory through which it would pass. Chicago might not become the great terminal city if Douglas did not watch out!

A second series of developments was even more threatening. A movement to build the Pacific line along a Southern route had been discussed at the close of the Mexican War. When Congress met in 1853, this plan received new attention. Jefferson Davis, as Secretary of War, took over the proposal, hurried forward the treaty with Mexico to secure territory south of the Gila River across which to construct the road, and advocated building it under the war powers. The territories through which the remainder of the road would pass were already organized. The last impediment was now removed. Since no one expected that more than one road to the Pacific would ever be built, these advantages, combined with the Administration's official interest in the Southern route, seemed about to blast all of Douglas's best-laid plans![42]

If the South Pass route and Chicago were to have a chance, the Nebraska territory must be immediately organized. Persons from Iowa and Missouri were already taking steps of their own in that direction. Douglas could delay no longer. His bill of January, 1854, was the answer. Since the support of the advocates both of the Central route and of the South Pass route was necessary to pass the bill, the territory was divided into Kansas and Nebraska. That would at least give both routes a future chance. Dixon's threat to amend the bill by a provision repealing the Missouri Compromise, backed by Atchison, who had to meet Benton's efforts to make Kansas-Nebraska free territory, forced the addition of the repeal section. Perhaps also, the arguments of Representative Philip Phillips of Alabama in favor of the move had some effect. More basic than such pressures, however, was the consideration, always important to Douglas, that to permit the people of a territory to decide domestic matters for themselves was genuine democratic doctrine. He had acted on that consideration.[43]

Some scholars have recently suggested that Douglas had less to do with the shaping of the Kansas-Nebraska bill than has been thought. They point to the political chaos that had been developing ever since the Compromise of 1850 struggle and suggest that various groups were now using the situation to further their own ends. Professor Rory Nichols has argued in brilliant fashion that the Kansas-Nebraska bill was not the work of one man but was the product of bargaining and manipulating that went on between conflicting and designing groups in Congress. He thinks that Douglas, under threats that went as far as removing him from his chairmanship of the Committee on Territories, was forced to go along with men behind the scenes who were shaping territorial policy.

Professor James Malin, on the other hand, insists that Douglas feared the creation of a permanent Indian territory in Kansas and Nebraska and knew that this would destroy his great dream of a Mid-American empire stretching from the Alleghenies to the Rockies and bound together by rail and water transportation. He even argues that Douglas had accepted the idea of self-determination on slavery well before he introduced his bill and that the people of Missouri, even in slave territory, were opposed to raising the slavery issue for fear it would delay organization.

Yet the fact remains that motives made little difference in 1854. The drift of events had sharpened their fears; antagonisms had grown. Some Northern men were ready to believe that Douglas, in conjunction with the slave-holding South, was plotting the ruination of all they held dear. The time had come to leave futile compromises and hesitating old parties behind.

CHAPTER FOURTEEN

SECTIONAL REACTIONS TO EVENTS

W HEN Stephen A. Douglas introduced his Kansas-Nebraska bill and Chase answered with his *Appeal*, the sectional conflict stirred by slavery reached new levels of fury. The bill did not come from the South nor in response to her demands. It was born of *Western* politics and railroads. Its basic principle was perfectly good *Western* doctrine. The South stood to gain little by its passage. Few thoughtful men expected slavery to be extended by its provisions. Subsequent events proved squatter sovereignty a practical abolition measure. There were only two slaves in Kansas in 1860. Yet the *Appeal*, shouted forth in the strained atmosphere of the upper North and West, twisted the whole move into the base schemings of a Southern Slaveocracy. "Its inflammable sentences fell like sprays of oil upon the fires" which economic discontent and slavery agitation had lighted. The conflict between North and South was entering that tragic stage where the realities of events had little relationship to the reactions which they produced.

Distortion began almost at once. Protest meetings, often strangely non-partisan in character, resolved and petitioned; excited editors took up their pens and enlarged on the sentiments of the *Appeal*. Everywhere the fight was against "the extension of slavery into territory now free."[1] "REPEAL! is the cry," said the *Commercial Register* of Sandusky, Ohio. "With almost one voice the true Northern press is echoing the word, and the people are gathering to the call. . . . This measure—the scheme of a weak and imbecile administration; of a corrupt and ambitious demagogue; of grasping, dishonorable Slaveholders—has filled the cup of bitterness which has been pressed to Northern lips so long. . . . The triumph of the measure is a triumph of Slavery [and] Aristocracy, over Liberty and Republicanism. . . ."[2] Representative E. B. Washburne of Illinois described the move as ". . . the last attempt of the slave power (aided by its northern allies) to break the old landmarks of freedom, so as to eventually give to that power the entire control of Government. . . ."[3] The *Ohio State Journal* referred to the bill as "the issue now tendered by the South," and the *Free West* denounced Douglas as "the tool of southern slave drivers." In Douglas's own state, a Putnam County meeting called his measure "the foul fraud of the Slave Power . . . perpetrat[ing] its black designs"; *The Alton Telegraph* accused him of catering to the slave power, and charged that "his bill, in whatever light it may be viewed, practically contemplates the introduction of human slavery into that territory, and proves beyond a peradventure, that the Illinois Senator, although pretending to represent a free State, is wedded to slavery, and is using his influence for its extension. . . ."[4]

The moral issue was quickly raised. Chase in the *Appeal* had especially "implore[d] Christians and Christian ministers to interpose" in behalf of humanity. A group of New England clergymen, numbering more than three thousand, responded, on March 1, with a protest to Congress issued "in the name of Almighty God, and in his presence." They denounced the Nebraska bill as "a great moral wrong, as a breach of faith eminently unjust to the moral principles of the community. . . ." A few weeks later, some twenty-five Chicago ministers approved these resolutions and declared it their duty "to recognize the moral bearing of such questions . . . and to proclaim . . . the principles of inspired truth and obligation." Numerous rural preachers followed the example of their urban colleagues, and church periodicals did their part "to cause the wrath of men to praise Him." The combined efforts of these agencies gave to the anti-Nebraska movement a crusading flavor which both added to and profited from a strong revival effort then sweeping the West.[5]

The next step was to twist Douglas himself into a slaveholder. Seizing upon the circumstance that his first wife, Martha Martin of North Carolina, had inherited a plantation and slaves from her father, but ignoring the more important truth that Douglas had refused this same property as a wedding present, enemies now boldly charged him with slaveholding. The *Free West* led off with this quip: "We know of no more fit man to present such an infamous proposition than Senator Douglas, a North Carolina slaveholder, who represents the State of Illinois in the Senate." *The New York Tribune* referred to him as "the Mississippi slaveholder, Douglas," and *The St. Louis Intelligencer* printed a list of his slaves, analyzed their value, and said the repeal of the Missouri Compromise would add ten thousand dollars to their cash value. Even the *Illinois Journal* commented on the Senator's slaves and his peculiar interest in the institution. Reports were circulated that Douglas intended, in due time, to become a citizen of the South.[6]

Opposition in Congress also followed the general line suggested by the *Appeal*. In the Senate, Chase defended that document and insisted that: "It is Slavery that renews the strife. It is Slavery that again wants room. It is Slavery, with its insatiate demands for more slave territory and more slave States."[7] Seward saw in the Nebraska movement "slavery and freedom . . . seeking for ascendancy in this Union." The contest would be the "great feature of our national hereafter." It was no struggle over abstractions; it would determine the practical question whether we resign all that vast region to the blighting threat of race and caste wars such as Egypt and Spain and San Domingo had known; or whether they would be occupied by non-slaveholders whose representatives would uphold and protect the interests of freemen and the Union. The conflict was irrepressible. "Say what you will, here, the interests of the non-slaveholding States and of the slaveholding States remain just the same; and they will remain just the same, until you shall cease to cherish and defend slavery, or we shall cease to honor and love freedom! You will not cease to cherish slavery. Do you see any signs that we are becoming indifferent to freedom? On the contrary, that old, traditional, hereditary sentiment of the North is more profound and more universal now than it ever was before. The slavery agitation you deprecate so much, is an eternal struggle between conservatism and progress, between truth and error, between right and wrong. . . ." The result was foreordained. "The non-slaveholding States [were] teeming with an increase of freemen, educated, vigorous, enlightened, enterprising freemen; such freemen as England, nor Rome, nor even Athens ever reared." Millions from Europe yearly augmented their number. The South might temporarily turn them from Nebraska, but it could not "pour forth its blackened tide in volumes" sufficient to stem the flood. When North and South met in contest for territories, there could be but one outcome! Seward was back where he had stood in 1850! Freedom and progress were one and the same.[8]

Wade and Sumner savagely assailed Douglas for attempting to repeal a sacred compact but added little except bitterness to the struggle. Sumner was particularly offensive. His reference to Douglas as *a Northern man with Southern principles* furnished a badly needed catch-phrase to the rising opposition, but it misrepresented fact. If the Missouri Compromise were overthrown, Sumner asserted, then the spread of slavery was clear, beyond dispute; the territory would "be smitten with sterility." As "a blade of grass would not grow where the horse of Attila had trod," so true prosperity would not spring up "in the footprints of the slaves."[9]

Such unfair distortion of the Nebraska bill aroused Douglas's wrath. On January 30, he took the floor to explain and to defend. With biting sarcasm, he turned on Chase and Sumner. Mercilessly he flayed their treacherous methods and their dishonest statements. He had only fulfilled his duty as Chairman of the Committee on Territories; he had accepted the nation's decision in regard to slavery as given in the Compromise of 1850; he had been more loyal to the Missouri Compromise than any of his critics. They or their friends had defeated that compromise in 1848 and forced the adoption of a new principle—the principle of self-determination. That was the great democratic principle for which he now contended. That was the heart of the Nebraska bill. Chase had raised a false issue. Legislation had nowhere extended or restricted slavery. The will of the people alone was responsible for the spread of free institutions.[10]

Throughout February, week after week, the debate con-

tinued. The Ohio Valley and the South generally supported the
measure; the Lakes area and the Northeast generally opposed
it. Then, on March 3, near midnight, Douglas took the floor to
bring the contest to a close and the bill to a vote. He spoke until
nearly dawn. Over the old arguments he went, defending himself against inconsistency and tearing to shreds the flimsy charges
of Chase and Sumner. Never was he more forceful; never did
his critics receive such telling blows. They had called the Missouri Compromise a sacred compact. If it were a compact,
Douglas declared, the North, as a party to it, had never signed.
When it had come to a vote Northern men had opposed it more
than four to one. When the resolution to admit Missouri as a
state under the Compromise was presented, the North rejected it.
Her representatives had even favored, by a vote of two to one,
an amendment to admit Missouri as a free state in the face of
the Compromise. A few years later, forty-nine Northern votes
had been registered against the admission of Arkansas as a slave
state under its terms!

Yet Chase and Sumner and Seward now called that Compromise "a sacred and irrevocable compact, binding in honor, in
conscience, and morals. . . ." These men were merely playing
politics, declared Douglas. All the troubles the country had
ever known over slavery had resulted from Congressional interference with the institution in the territories and in the new
states formed therefrom. His committee had now removed the
issue from Congress by applying to Nebraska the new principle
of local self-determination. At last there could be peace.[11]

When Douglas had finished, the gnarled old Texan, Sam
Houston, insisted on a final word. Significantly, he declared that
the South had not asked for the repeal, nor would she gain by
it. "Will it secure these Territories to the South?" he asked.
"No sir, not at all. . . . I think the measure itself would be
useless. . . . But what will be the consequences in the minds
of the people? They have a veneration for that compromise. . . .
Abrogate it . . . and you exasperate the public mind. . . .
My word for it, we shall realize scenes of agitation which are
rumbling in the distance now. . . . It will convulse the country from Maine to the Rio Grande. . . . I, as the most extreme

Southern Senator upon this floor, do not desire it. If it is a boon that is offered to propitiate the South, I, as a Southern man, repudiate it. I reject it. I will have none of it."[12]

At twelve minutes after five o'clock the vote was taken. The bill passed by nearly three to one. The Senators filed out into the gray of the morning. They were weary and ready for rest. The workaday world, however, was just beginning to stir. Its voice was yet to be heard.

The bill did not pass the House until May 22. Confusion and strife marked its course. Only the parliamentary skill of W. A. Richardson and the constant drive of Alexander H. Stephens and Douglas himself made progress possible. Cutting of New York attempted to check all action by referring the bill to the committee of the whole, whose calendar was already overfull. President Pierce, in alarm, brought executive pressure to bear on editors and Congressmen and actually used the patronage to swing recalcitrant members into line. He assured the country that the bill was in the interest of freedom; that not another slave state would ever come into the Union. Prominent leaders in the House gave the same assurance. Bell of Tennessee canvassed the opinion of members with some diligence, and found that the greater number agreed that extension to Kansas was out of the question. The acceptance of this point of view probably turned the tide. Gradually the majority which had passed the Cutting motion melted away. Debate began. In two weeks the struggle was over. On May 30, Franklin Pierce affixed his signature to the fateful measure.[13]

That the alarmed North and West had put little faith in Douglas's impassioned speeches and the assurance given by Congressmen that slavery would not be extended, was quickly apparent. The New York *Tribune* spoke of "these falsifiers and dodgers" and declared that slavery was already in the territories. Administration supporters were merely trying "to put the North to sleep . . . so that the peculiar institution [might] establish itself there without opposition." "Freemen must go to Kansas resolved to sustain their rights and exclude slavery," it said. "Anti-Slavery emigrants, Anti-Slavery ministers, and Anti-Slavery newspapers are wanted there with the smallest

possible delay." Western newspapers also insisted that assurance
of freedom was offered "for the express purpose of giving [the
South] a preponderance over the North in the government."
They too had remedies to suggest. "Shall the North lie supinely
down and await the welding of chains already forged for its
subjection?" one of them asked, and then added: "There are
worse evils than dissolution [of the Union]. . . . If our fate is
either to be Slaves or members of a Northern Free Confederacy,
we choose the latter." Another paper was of the opinion that the
old parties should be abandoned and that all men opposed to the
expansion of slavery, should join hands in a new organization.
"Let us unite on a common principle," it urged, and "we shall
soon find a common name in the pure Republicanism of our
object." Let "able and true *Northernmen*" be sent to Congress
to decide "the great issue thrust upon us—Slavery or Freedom,"
said a third.[14]

Few men were prepared for the suggested dissolution of the
Union. Great numbers, however, were ready for political revolt,
and some were willing to emigrate to Kansas. Fear and dissatisfaction were rife. The repeal of the Missouri Compromise
was increasingly viewed as only the last link of a chain long in
forging: one of many evidences of Southern aggression. For a
decade the feeling had been growing that Northern and Western welfare was being sacrificed. Territory in Oregon had been
surrendered because the South was not interested in it; the
tariffs had been lowered and homestead legislation defeated for
the same reason; the rivers and harbors of the Lakes region
had been neglected and its wheat crops had brought little profit
because the government, under Southern domination, had failed
to encourage markets. Political parties had felt the strain of
mounting indignation in every election between 1844 and 1854.
Third parties had, more than once, upset the calculations of
both Democrats and Whigs because sectional hostilities had
crept in to weaken party loyalties. The Whigs had suffered most.
After the election of 1852, they appeared to have reached the
end of their trail as one of the great national parties. The vague
principles by which Northern and Southern wings had been held
together up to this time proved frail bonds under the stress of

the violent slavery conflict. The Democratic Party, on the surface, seemed to have been less disturbed, but underneath the current of revolt was running almost as strongly.

The Nebraska bill brought matters to a head but it did not work alone. The efforts of the Pierce Administration to continue the expansionist program inaugurated under Polk by acquiring Cuba was at once suspected of being a pro-slavery move which would involve the nation in another aggressive war. Filibustering expeditions out of Louisiana and the swashbuckling tactics of Soulé in Spain seemed to confirm the suspicion. Giddings bitterly denounced the movement as an effort "to meanly and piratically steal Cuba, in order that the chains of slavery [might] . . . be more securely riveted upon her bondsmen." "Sir," he cried, ". . . I tell you there is a spirit in the North which will set at defiance all the low and unworthy machinations of this Executive, and of the minions of its power."[15]

The defeat of the homestead bill in this same session, with representatives of the Old South taking the lead in opposition, and Pierce's veto of another River and Harbor bill on the Constitutional grounds advanced by Toombs of Georgia, particularly incensed the West. As Senator Dodge of Iowa remarked, nothing the West desired had been passed—homesteads, railroads, river and harbor improvements had been urged in vain. "Why treat with utter neglect those vast arteries of national commerce in the interior?" asked Campbell of Ohio. "I say to the House, and to gentlemen, that the time has come for making the rights of the great interior of this nation . . . a *test*. . . ." Henceforward, Campbell declared, he was willing to stand shoulder to shoulder with other Western men against parties, against all influences, in the interest of his section.[16]

Out of this tangle and mixture of economic, political, and moral discontent, accumulating for a decade or more, came the new attitudes toward the South and slavery which were to give rise to the Republican Party and to the struggle for Kansas. Up to this point, the abolitionists, fighting slavery *per se*, had been generally viewed as crackpots. They had not achieved respectability. The great masses of common men, though disapproving of slavery on both practical and moral grounds, had no great interest in the institution as it existed in the South, nor any grave apprehensions regarding its influence in the nation. They were willing to allow it to remain where it was and to enjoy such rights as it had under the Constitution. They vaguely hoped that it would disappear in time, but their strength and their emotions were consumed in getting ahead in their own communities. They had little time or effort left to bother about the labor system of the South.

Gradually, however, this attitude had been undergoing change. The Nebraska bill completed its transformation. Seward and others had made a new kind of moral appeal, quite unlike that of Garrison, Weld, and the other abolitionists. Slavery was not just a personal sin, it was a barrier to *progress*. It was impeding Manifest Destiny. It was in conflict with the great fundamental moral concepts on which American democracy was established. It held back the white man of the North and interfered with his "God-intended" well-being. As a recent writer has said: "The basic postulate of the democratic faith of the nineteenth century affirmed that God, the creator of man, had also created a moral law for his government, and had endowed him with a conscience with which to apprehend it. Underneath and supporting human society, as the basic rock supported the hills, was a moral order which was the abiding place of the eternal principles of truth and righteousness." This was the appeal in Seward's Higher Law, it would be the appeal in Lincoln's "house divided against itself." This basic assumption made the *contest* between freedom and slavery irrepressible—a part of "the *eternal* struggle between right and wrong." Common men who had no scruples against slavery in the South and little interest in the sinfulness of Southern planters, could grasp this moral concept and react to it as democrats, not as abolitionists. They could enlist wholeheartedly in a great moral crusade against the further extension of a blighting institution! They could share all the moral indignation of the abolitionist and still retain their contempt for the petty personal character of abolitionism![17]

Something more had happened. The question of slavery extension had become *the slavery issue*. Opposition to extension was the new anti-slavery attitude. First vaguely in California and New Mexico, now inescapably in Kansas-Nebraska, the common man of the upper North and West had to face the institution of slavery as a matter in which he had a personal stake. It was no longer an abstract problem of practical import only to Southerners. It was not just a question for professional reformers. It was an issue on which the common man of the North had to make a choice—a choice which might directly affect him or his neighbors who were steadily drifting westward. He had to decide whether he wanted freedom or slavery established in a *definite* and *neighboring* territory. In making such a choice he had to look squarely at slavery and decide what he thought about it. Consciously and unconsciously, he accepted the whole abolition picture. The campaign of education which the abolitionist had waged for two decades had done its work for a whole great region. The average man in that region, regardless of his past attitudes toward slavery in the South, could no more choose slavery as a part of the life of the new territories than could the most rabid abolitionist. Even against his will, he was forced to take the abolitionist's views and attitudes. For all practical purposes he became an abolitionist even though he retained all his contempt for and his hostility toward "abolitionists." Soon his talk, like that of his great spokesman, Lincoln, would become so confused and contradictory that historians for generations would quarrel among themselves as to the threat he carried to the South.[18]

How completely the non-extensionist had taken over the abolitionists' cause, bag and baggage, and how fully non-extension had become *the abolition movement* was quickly revealed. In the common man's newspapers over a wide area a strangely familiar attack on the South and slavery began as if spontaneously. The New York *Tribune,* soon to be known as the Northwest's political bible, led the way. The South, it insisted, was backward and brutal. She lacked schools, her fields were in ruins, her people were without enterprise or self-restraint. Slavery had so stagnated "her life blood that she [could] not support good schools even for the children of the wealthy." Young Southerners, therefore, crowded Northern schools where

some of them learned that "there is a better and decenter state
of society than that which renders concubinage not an uncom-
mon evil in the households of slave plantations." Virginia, according to the *Tribune*, was in a sad state of decay. "Norfolk,"
it reported, "is commercially a ruin. Mount Vernon domestically
another ruin, and Richmond, if not a ruin, might as well be one
as to be sustained by the trade in human flesh. The fields of
Virginia, too, are ruined: pride and folly, and tobacco raising,
chewing and spitting have contributed to wear them out and
drive the Chivalry to new lands. The people, too, are intel-
lectually ruined. There are eighty thousand white human ruins
who can neither read nor write, and there are some hundreds
of thousands of illegitimate mulatto ruins without the position
of manhood and womanhood, liable to be sold by their white
parents or brothers and sisters at any moment, to make up for
real estate ruins. . . ." South Carolina was in equally bad shape.
Her people were ignorant and poor. Too long had she been
ruled by "a few college-bred men, readers of English political
economy, written to suit the oligarchic markets of Europe."
Immigrants shunned her, "because the laboring man [was]
despised" by the "chivalry-ridden inhabitants of the Palmetto
state." Even Calhoun's own son had been forced to emigrate to
Alabama in order to retrieve his fortune.[19]

The South, declared the *Tribune*, was contributing nothing to
the upbuilding of the nation. If activity were discovered anywhere in the section, it was sure to be due "to the stimulus and
men . . . derived from the North." Any man found with "a
pen behind his ear" would prove to be from New York or Boston. Southern engineers were Yankee-born; mechanics were
from Lowell or Lawrence. A single literary agency in Boston
or New York was worth more than any whole state at the South.
In all the South, the *Tribune* could not find ingenuity enough
to invent a labor-saving machine. "Where are her chemistry,
geology, mechanics, engineering, esthetics . . . her steam en-
gines, locomotives, timber bending or planing or sewing or
washing machines. . . ." "Why," the paper exclaimed, "she is
full a thousand years behind the North in civilization . . . !"
And "the sad, the deplorable error of the South [was] that it

[did] not, or rather [would] not, see how all its inferiority [sprang] from this single cause of slavery. . . ."[20]

Character was at an equally low ebb in that section. The *Tribune* pictured "Southern plantations [as] little else than negro harems," and declared that "the best recommendation to a slave girl [was] . . . that she [be] handsome enough to please the eye of her master." "Of all the Southern Presidents," it gossiped on, "hardly one has failed to leave his mulatto children. Amalgamation! Why the South is a perfect puddle of amalgamation!" Southerners "habitually" went around "armed like assassins." Lynch law prevailed because slavery forced a "hideous savageism worthy of original Africa in crime and punishment." The South had fewer churches and fewer religious people than the North. Without Northern help, the religion of the South would face "sheer bankruptcy." Even the Southern boast of having fewer insane people indicated a weakness, not a strength. "Fools never become insane and slaves seldom," said the *Tribune*. "It is the more active, ardent, impulsive, creative imaginations that become disordered. . . ."[21]

Lesser papers all over the North and West followed the *Tribune's* lead. Unconsciously they repeated the charges shouted through the years by the abolitionists: *The South was aristocratic and immoral*. It was filled with planters, politicians, and professional men, but contained only "a very small proportion of laboring men . . . because labor is there contemned." Southern gentlemen, keeping an office, but unable to own a slave found "no difficulty in hiring one from planters or farmers for purposes of prostitution." So "nightly at twilight, there [were] to be seen, passing from some suburban retreat, colored or black women, to the office of a Colonel in one street; a Doctor in another; a Lawyer in another; and an Editor in another street; and on the following morning, until approaching midday the streets [were] streaked with ebony-hued divinities, passing from the caresses of 'gentlemen' of the first families." Later these "gentlemen" "would visit in the homes of the elite." "The mothers [would] applaud their chivalry and admire their swaggers; the daughters smile in adoration at their captivations, while the matron and the child [would] witness their intellectual and physical faculties diseased from excessive applications of bad rum and corroded by low lustful indulgences . . . and dote upon their sickly sensibilities, languid laziness, slovenliness, and bully propensities as features of character."[22]

With such pictures before them, the youth of the nation, looking toward Kansas, were asked to decide "whether they wished their country to become more like the North, with all its institutions of freedom, with its active pulsating commercial life, with its intelligence and free schools—with all the avenues of labor open to generous strife, respected and crowned with the rewards of vigorous but honest toil," or whether they wished it to become more like the South, with its oppression of "aristocratic pride" and "degraded labor."[23]

* * * *

The first practical result of these new developments was the birth of the Republican Party. The movement toward a new party had its actual beginnings in the summer and fall of 1854 and resulted directly from the reaction against the Nebraska bill. It expressed, however, the deep unrest and reforming spirit of a decade. In its first phases the movement was generally non-partisan. Local protest meetings found restless Whigs and Democrats standing together. Their resolutions often spoke of the necessity for dropping old party ties and combining in a new, perhaps temporary, political organization. Democrats who took part objected violently to "the prevailing tendency to Whig-ize every anti-Nebraska movement, and to claim every anti-Nebraska triumph as a Whig victory." Both Whigs and Democrats protested against being labelled abolitionists because of their hostility to slavery expansion. Only now and then did local groups, as at Ripon, Wisconsin, and Jackson, Michigan, take on the name Republican and think of themselves as a separate and permanent party.[24]

Efforts of the Administration to make support of the Nebraska bill the test of party loyalty still further complicated matters. "It is not true that we have joined the opponents of Democracy, and it is still more notoriously untrue that we have done anything to injure the Democratic party," wrote an Illinois editor. He had merely joined the opponents of the Douglas-Nebraska party. "I am and ever have been, a Democrat of the Jackson and Benton school," said Frank Blair, Jr., "and I do not intend to abandon that faith or surrender that proud title. . . . I am well aware that the servile tools of the present administration, have sought to proscribe every Democrat who opposes its dogmas upon the question of slavery in the Territories, and on the Kansas act. . . . I have, [however], no hesitation in avowing that I am opposed to the repeal of the Missouri Compromise. . . ."

Such leaders believed that it was "the dictate of common sense and patriotism to welcome all—from whatever party or sect, country or color—whose views in this particular [were] congenial—who had hearts that vibrate[d] with want and woe, the cruelty and oppression, under which millions of our race, in our free land—this boasted democratic government—suffer[ed] and groan[ed]."[25]

Local elections soon showed how great was the political force of this single appeal. Anti-Nebraska candidates swept the spring elections in New Hampshire, Rhode Island, and Connecticut, and the early fall elections in Vermont and Maine. In August, James W. Grimes, Whig with free-soil backing, was elected Governor of Iowa. In October, fusion candidates triumphed in Indiana and Ohio, winning seven out of eleven Congressional seats in Indiana and all of the twenty-one filled in Ohio. In November, New Jersey Anti-Nebraska Whigs carried the state and a fusion of Whigs and Americans in Pennsylvania elected a governor and reduced the Democrats in Congress to six. New Republican organizations in Michigan and Wisconsin achieved notable victories:—the first for the party as such. The Anti-Nebraska men of Illinois secured five out of nine congressional seats and dominated the legislature, which soon chose an outstanding Anti-Nebraska leader, Lyman Trumbull, to the Senate. Political fusion had "literally slaughtered" the administration Democrats in the Northern, Middle and Western States. Desertions from their ranks were growing in number and importance. They would be the minority party in the next Congress.[26]

Anti-Nebraskaism had proved a powerful political weapon. Could it be used as a tool to build solid foundations for a new national party? The answer was by no means certain even in the face of recent victories. Too many other interests were competing for support. The Whig Party still had many loyal followers who expected it to be revived as the carrier of anti-slavery sentiment. Seward and his New York supporters were especially eager for this outcome. The New York Senator was boasting that he would die a Whig. New England Whigs were equally certain that the party could take a new lease of life. Then there was the strong anti-foreign, anti-Catholic sentiment which had developed into a political movement under the name of Americanism or Know-Nothingism. It had spread, not only into those regions where the foreign-born were numerous, but also into the South. It had caught the drifting Whigs and the disgruntled Democrats and had been one of the factors in the fusionist movements of the late elections. The Americans had elected the governor in Massachusetts and had won eleven seats in Congress. They were especially strong in southern New England and the Middle States. They had made considerable headway in the South where the Whigs were badly shattered. Gradually their party was achieving national proportions, but was sadly handicapped because it had within it a strong Anti-Nebraska element which refused to accept the demands of the Southern group that the party declare that Congress had no right to legislate on slavery in the states and ought not to legislate on it in the territories. Nevertheless, Know-Nothings talked much of saving the Union and of making Americanism the great national issue on which all sections could unite. The Americans were definitely in the field as a party by 1855 and they made a far better showing in that year than did the Republicans, whose only major success was the election of Chase as Governor of Ohio.

A third competitor for liberal support appeared in a movement backed by the old Blair-Benton Jacksonian Democrats. Quick to see in the Nebraska bill a complete fulfillment of all their dire prophecies regarding the slave power and the apostasy of the Democratic Party, they renewed their activities to establish influence in party affairs. Since the days of Polk, they insisted, false leaders had controlled the Democracy. Now the principles of Andrew Jackson ought to return to power. Benton, Blair, and Van Buren had attempted such a move in 1852, with William O. Butler of Kentucky as their candidate, but had failed. Now they began to see another Old Hickory in Sam. Houston, who had opposed the Nebraska bill so valiantly. With new enthusiasm, they set about to stir revolt in Democratic ranks and to bring the old party back to its first principles.[27]

Great difficulties must admittedly be overcome if the local groups of 1854 were to be welded into a national Republican Party. Chase and Greeley, nevertheless, were hopeful. In March, 1855, the New York *Tribune* admonished "the friends of freedom" that the time had come to "be girding up their loins for future contests." It insisted that the only substantial and widespread basis for an enduring and successful party in the free states was that on which they "reposed." The Republicans had "the heart, the conscience and the understanding of the people with them. Every motive that [could] sway the action of independent liberty-loving, moral, or religious. men" drew the voters to their ranks. "All that is noble," it said, "all that is true, all that is pure, all that is manly, and estimable in human character, goes to swell the power of the anti-slavery party of the North. That party is no longer the faction, the handful of men it once was, with designs misconceived, motives aspersed, and conduct decried. It now embraces every Northern man who does not want to see the government converted into a huge engine for the spread of slavery over the whole continent, every man who is and was opposed to the scandalous attempts to abridge the territory of freedom and enlarge that of servitude by the passage of the Kansas-Nebraska bill."[28]

Chase was likewise certain that a new national party was necessary. He had been defeated for re-election to the Senate but the new Republican Party in Ohio had made him governor. Return to national influence depended on the nationalizing of that party. He therefore proposed to make a demonstration in the West that would be "so hard, and vigorous, and united as to compel the assent of the foolish Whigs of New York and the East." From the vantage ground of his new state office, he secured the support of Governors Grimes of Iowa and Bingham of Michigan and made potent appeal to the Anti-Nebraska Know-Nothings everywhere. During the summer of 1855, he travelled in the East and soon had a committee of correspondence making contacts wherever local party units had been formed. Soon he was ready with plans for a national convention.[29]

While Chase labored in Ohio, a group of Washington politicians had organized a Republican Association to act as a central clearing house for all party interests and to forward the work of national organization. They did not, at first, accept Chase's program, but the chances for victory were too favorable to allow internal strife to develop. In January, they acquiesced. Then, as the Houston boom dwindled away and Benton took conservative grounds on slavery in Kansas, Francis Preston Blair, Sr., awkwardly brought the Jacksonian Democrats into line and accepted the permanent chairmanship of the preliminary convention held in Pittsburg, February 22, 1856, to organize a national Republican Party and plan its first convention. Meanwhile, after a bitter fight consuming nine weeks and requiring 133 ballots, the Republicans had elected Nathaniel P. Banks, Jr., Speaker of the House. With new confidence, they prepared to enter the presidential campaign of 1856. They had perfected a national organization. Whether they would be able to fuse the disjointed mass of Free Democrats, Whigs, and Free-Soilers into an effective party behind a satisfactory candidate for a great national campaign depended entirely on whether the resentments and fears produced by the Nebraska bill continued to agitate the public mind. That, in turn, depended largely upon what might occur, or what people could be made to believe had occurred, in the South and in Kansas.[30]

* * * *

The sudden collapse of the Southern movement in 1850 and the sharp reaction against further commotion left the South quite unprepared for the Nebraska controversy. Surprisingly little was said in the average Southern newspaper during the period when Douglas was introducing his bill and it was being discussed in Congress. As the Richmond *Enquirer* said, on March 2, 1854:

Throughout the South there prevails a repugnance to agitation. We had enough, and too much, excitement during the Compromise Controversy of 1850, and now there exists an indisposition to popular meetings and legislative resolves.

In July, six weeks after the bill had become law, J. L. M. Curry wrote from Alabama:[31]

It is difficult for us to comprehend, or credit the excitement, that is said to prevail in the North, on account of the Nebraska question . . . here . . . there is no excitement, no fever, on the subject. It is seldom alluded to in private or public and so far as the introduction of slavery is concerned, such a consummation is hardly hoped for.

As late as August 26, the New Orleans *Bee* reported that ". . . the South really manifests an astonishing indifference to the result. There is no excitement, no appearance of exultation, scarcely an evidence of passing interest."

South Carolina was just as uninterested. On June 21, the Charleston *Mercury* commented on the strange "spectacle presented by the North and South at the . . . moment." At the North society was "convulsed, all the slumbering elements of sectional bitterness roused, and slavery agitation awake again, after its brief and delusive sleep, strengthened by new accessions, and eager for the onset." The Northern press, Democrat and Whig alike, was united in war upon the South. At the South, on the other hand, all was calm and easy indifference. The thunders which came rolling from the North died away before they reached the Southern latitude, "or if heard at all, [were] scarcely heeded."[32]

Opinion developed slowly. Southern Senators and Representatives were, of course, forced to take positions as debate developed in Congress. Sometimes party affiliations caused division among them—the Whigs being less enthusiastic— but on the whole sectional interests dictated opinion. This opinion, however,

showed many shades and some sharp contrasts. A few favored
the bill because it seemed to open new territory for the expansion of slavery and the increase of Southern strength. More
approved the principle of sectional equality which the measure contained, but held no great hopes that either Kansas or
Nebraska would become a slave state. They differed among
themselves as to whether the squatter-sovereignty doctrine permitted action on slavery in territorial days or whether it implied that such action came only with statehood. Some supported the bill because Northern radicals made it a sectional
issue; they would present a united Southern front against
aggression. Some openly opposed the whole movement as a
needless renewal of the slavery conflict from which the South
stood to gain nothing and suffer much.[33]

More than fifty Southern members of the two houses of
Congress made speeches on the Kansas-Nebraska bill. Only
two of these, both Representatives, expressed any confidence
that slavery would be established in the territories. Zollicoffer
of Tennessee said: "I have strong faith that Kansas will become a slave state."[34] Goode of Virginia said that he saw no
reason why slavery should not go to Kansas and that he would
consider that he had failed in duty if he did not "make a determined, yet honorable effort, to secure it for the South."[35]
All other speakers were either doubtful whether slavery would
be extended by the act or sure that their section would derive
no material gain by its passage. More than half of all who spoke,
whether they favored the bill or not, were emphatic in their
declaration that the region was unadapted to slave labor and
that "on the bleak hills of Nebraska and the barren plains of
Kansas slavery [would] never exist." A few, like Franklin of
Maryland and Millson of Virginia, went so far as to declare
that the Douglas bill was an aggressive free-soil move, intended to wipe out all traces of slavery from Nebraska and
Kansas and to multiply the numbers of free-soil and non-slaveholding communities. Franklin anticipated Douglas by insisting that slavery could not exist without positive local law,
something that could never be secured. Some who were less
certain about its effect upon slavery questioned the expediency

of the bill. Preston Brooks of South Carolina thought the effort to organize Nebraska was premature, and Hunt of Louisiana insisted that the repeal of the Missouri Compromise was a violation of good faith, engendering discord and dissension among the people of the different sections. The majority, however, professed to believe that the North now offered the South justice and the end of sectional strife. Only two Southern Senators and nine Southern Representatives voted against the bill. The almost unanimous reason given by those who approved was their long-held and firm belief in the unconstitutionality and the unfair character of the Missouri Compromise. They had simply fallen into sectional line, regardless of parties, because the Nebraska bill, on its face, seemed to recognize Southern rights.[36]

Back in the Southern states quiet continued. As Benton said at the end of April:[37]

It is now four months since this movement for the abrogation of the Missouri Compromise commenced in this Congress. It began without a memorial, without a petition, without a request from a human being. It has labored long and hard in those Halls, and to this hour there is not a petition for it from the class of States for whose benefit the movement professes to have been made!—not a word in its favor from the smallest public meeting or private assemblage of any Slave State. This is the response of the South to this boon tendered to it by northern members under a Northern President. It is the response of silence—more emphatic than words. . . .

Editorial comment was brief and for the most part reflected opinions generated in Washington. Whig papers in some localities showed less enthusiasm than did their Democratic neighbors who often felt under obligation to support the Administration. But, even within these limits, there was, as the Charleston *Mercury* observed, great variance. "By many," that paper said, "it [the Nebraska bill] is regarded with indifference; by some, openly opposed; while the mass look upon it as a thing of so little practical good, that it is certainly not worth the labor of an active struggle to maintain it. . . ."[38] Editors, nevertheless, believed with their Congressmen that they should support the principle of sectional equality implied in the effort to repeal the Missouri Compromise even though they entertained little hope for the addition of new slave states. Both the Richmond *Enquirer* and the Richmond *Whig* denied the constitutionality of the Missouri Compromise and the South's original interest in it; neither expected slavery to expand. As the *Enquirer* said:[39]

. . . The Nebraska bill contemplates only the recognition of a principle. All agree that slavery cannot exist in the territories of Kansas and Nebraska. . . . It is not, therefore, because of its effect in extending the sphere of slavery that the South advocates the repeal of the Missouri restriction, but solely for the reason that it would indicate the equality and sovereignty of the States. The single aim of the Nebraska bill is to establish the principle of *Federal non-intervention* in regard to slavery. . . .

The *Enquirer* would have been filled with astonishment and indignation at the violent opposition in the North to "a measure so just in regard to the rights of the South," if it had not understood "the arrogant and aggressive character," the "grasping and ferocious nature of the anti-slavery fanaticism."[40]

In North Carolina, the Raleigh *Register* (Whig) regretted that the Missouri Compromise should have been disturbed. Repeal would be "the rallying cry for another anti-slavery agitation which [would] throw all that had preceded it in the shade." That editor thought the probability of establishing slavery in the territory was exceedingly remote. He contended, however, that, since the issue had been raised, the South should unite to carry it through. The Democratic *North Carolina Standard* denounced the *Register* for its lack of enthusiasm and its hostility to Douglas. It supported the bill as an effort to establish equality in the territories, and remove an unconstitutional restriction. It asserted that a great principle was involved and, although slavery was not likely to go there, that principle should be upheld by one voice—a Southern voice.[41]

The South Carolina press was slow to react. Papers like the *Black River Watchman* and the *Sumter Banner*, which had been almost rabidly sectional in the 1850 controversy, scarcely mentioned the Nebraska bill in the year 1854. *The Daily South Carolinian,* of Columbia, early noted Northern excitement and urged the South to stand firm. "The Nebraska bill," said one of its editorials, "was no measure of hers; it brought her no practical benefits; it was only the perfection of a sentiment of justice; but that sentiment having been molded into action . . . it becomes her in point of honor and for her own future peace to stand for it." The *Charleston Mercury* and the *Charleston Daily Courier* both approved the act in a moderate way. They viewed it as a move to put the South on an equal footing with the North and to carry out the Compromise of 1850. It would do something towards restoring the South to the position of equality in the Union even though no one supposed that slave states would spring up in Nebraska. Yet support was lukewarm enough to permit the publication of letters from subscribers who called the bill "a cheat and fraud on the South," and "a mere nonentity—absolutely worthless to the South."[42]

Editorial opinion in Georgia followed the same general pattern. The legislature approved Douglas's bill and took its stand on the principles of 1850 but many prominent spokesmen considered it an unnecessary reopening of sectional agitation, an "endeavor to carry slavery where nature's laws prohibit[ed] its entrance" and where a solemn faith was pledged that it should not go. In a short time, however, general approval of the Missouri Compromise repeal came, first from hesitating Democrats and then from the Whigs. On that issue there could be but one sentiment, as the Savannah *Republican* observed. On the matter of material benefits to the South, however, there could be, and was, disagreement. The Columbus *Enquirer* admitted that it had "never . . . entertained any settled opinion relative to the probability of slavery being introduced into this region . . ." and the Macon *Telegraph* bluntly stated that the bill did not give the South a single inch of slave territory. The *Southern Recorder,* of Milledgeville, denounced it as a measure ostensibly adopted as an act of justice to the South, but one which contained, in its squatter-sovereignty principles, "as subtle a poison as the fatal gift which prostrated the fabled strength of Hercules." The Augusta papers were, as usual, moderate in their statements. The *Constitutionalist and Republic*, a staunch Democratic sheet, made only a few references to the struggle. Its support of the measure was strictly on party grounds. It referred to Douglas as a man of peerless moral courage and to his action as having planted the Democracy of this country upon true constitutional ground, but it made no reference to the extension of slavery. The *Chronicle and Sentinel* (Whig) was skeptical from the beginning. It disliked sectional agitation and declared that the squatter-sovereignty feature of the bill meant free territory. It was soon referring to "the Kansas swindle."[43]

The reactions of the newspapers in the Lower South showed just as much variance. The Whig attitude was well expressed by the Mobile *Advertiser*: ". . . we are distinctly in favor of the measure . . . but we must be permitted to doubt the policy of so soon reopening the slavery excitement." As to any real gain for the South, this paper could only say that many of her most astute and devoted sons were greatly in doubt. At least Kansas should not be yielded up without a decent struggle. The Natchez *Courier* was less friendly. It felt that the defeat of the bill would be a subject of national felicitation. Its passage would only afford abundant material for Northern agitation; the South had no real interest in the passage of the bill—not even on the score of principle. Squatter sovereignty in Kansas destroyed every Southern opportunity. Property, always timid, would move slowly. "Before the first five hundred slave-holders reach[ed] those regions, fifty thousand Northern men and foreign emigrants—all opposed to slavery . . . [would] have flocked there [and] formed territorial law for [Southern] exclusion." Nevertheless the *Courier* approved of the principle of equal rights and asked for a united South.[44] Both the New Orleans *Bee* and the *Daily Crescent* criticized the introduction of the measure and doubted whether it would prove of any use to the South. They were sure that the practical value of the bill was exceedingly small. The masses, said the *Bee*, were and would remain in a condition not very far removed from indifference toward it; the issue was too purely abstract to agitate the minds of the community. All the fuss in relation to it was confined to the North, while the South, "though bearing the daily brunt of the fiercest objurgations, could not be driven into wrath and retaliation" because it "cared too little for the result. . . ." The *Crescent* could see only "a vast turmoil about nothing; and aggravation of abundant ill blood. . . ." "Victory would produce only a barren sceptre. . . ." Slavery could never prevail in Nebraska. The measure had been forced down the throats of a large portion of the confederacy by "the sneaking aspirant to the Presidency from Illinois. . . ." It was not just worthless to the South; it was injurious.[45] Memphis and Nashville Whig papers were in accord with these sentiments. The Memphis *Eagle and Enquirer* rebuked Douglas for reopening the slavery agitation, even though it approved of the principle of equality embodied in his bill. It later referred to the unwise and unnecessary legislation of 1854 and insisted that it was an anti-slavery measure under which a "hundred thousand foreign abolitionists . . . can proceed to Kansas and vote it a free state the moment they touch the soil!" The *Republican Banner and Nashville Whig* condemned the measure as "but . . . the ashes and cinders of Sodom's apples" to the South—a mockery and humbug. Yet, worthless as it was to the South, it furnished to "the anti-slavery fanatics of the *North a pretext* for agitating." Douglas might just as well have attached the Wilmot Proviso to his bill as to have inserted popular sovereignty. Either would produce precisely the same result. "Before *we* could get up in the morning, eat our breakfast, yoke the oxen and get off the darkies," said a correspondent, "the Yankees, with the assistance of the squatters, would possess the land and have their quarantines established."[46]

Democratic comment in the Lower South differed from Whig only in so far as lip service to the national administration required. Almost unanimously, Democratic editors approved of the introduction of the bill and justified it on the ground that it carried out the principles of 1850. Few went farther than to assert that Southern institutions were being placed theoretically on an equal footing in the territories with those of the North. The Mobile *Register* accepted the right and justice of the measure and resented the "new ordeal to which the government and institutions of the Union" were about "to be subjected by the mad zealots of Anti-slavery." Northern reactions were nothing but "damnable villainy." The Montgomery *Advertiser and Gazette* paid scant attention to the bill until it became law. It accepted the principle of equality but clearly stated that the act was not designed to make Kansas a slave state. It, too, was alarmed by Northern "anti-slavery madness." The *Mississippi Free Trader* hailed the bill as "a triumph of the territorial principles for which the great majority of the people of the South [had] contended," and denied emphatically that the squatter-sovereignty doctrine was included in it. If the handful of adventurers who happened to be upon the ground to elect the first territorial legislature could abolish slavery, then indeed was the bill "a mere snare for the South. . . ."[47] The New Orleans *Daily Delta* could see no practical advantage for the South in the bill, but thought the principle valuable. The Memphis *Appeal* was equally moderate, advising the South to keep quiet and sober, but to be firm in the stand she had taken. It defended Douglas as one of the best and wisest statesmen of the Republic, and asserted that, if Northern fanaticism, which had refused to hear him in his own city, were to succeed, then the Union would go to pieces. The *Union and American* of Nashville was more positive than its neighbors that slavery would triumph in Kansas. The Nebraska bill, regardless of what some might say about the squatter-sovereignty principles, gave the South "its *Constitutional* rights in the territory" and that meant freedom to take and hold slaves there. The passage of this bill was "an earnest that a majority of the people's representatives [were] national in their sentiments, and resolved to 'crush out' . . . the fanatical spirit of Abolitionism." Kansas would be a "slave state."[48]

This survey of Southern reactions to Kansas-Nebraska developments makes it quite clear that there was little to justify Northern excitement and anti-Southern resentment, or to prolong such attitudes through the next few years as the driving force behind the Republican Party. The bitterness of the Northern assault did now and then produce a sharp sectional reply and talk of the impending dissolution of the Union. But the Charleston *Mercury* was right in its declaration that there was no compact sectional sentiment at the South in favor of the Nebraska and Kansas bill. As long as the North was intensely hostile to it, the South could not stand listlessly by and see the bill repealed. But she was not in an aggressive mood nor had she advanced beyond her 1850 position in regard to the extension of slavery.[49] This was strictly a Northern upheaval. It would have to generate its own power if it were to keep its momentum. Therefore, Kansas had to be cast for a tragic rôle.

The idea that North and South were to wage a battle for the possession of Kansas developed in the North as soon as the terms of the Kansas-Nebraska bill were known. The application of popular sovereignty promised control to the party first on the ground with a majority. It suggested the strategy of artificial stimulation of settlement. As early as March, 1854, the enthusiastic mind of Eli Thayer of Worcester, Massachusetts, was busy on a scheme for saving Kansas. Out of his planning ultimately came the New England Emigrant Aid Company, incorporated for the purpose of assisting free-soil emigration to Kansas and making profits out of the rapid development of this new western area. Some eight or ten other organizations for forwarding settlers to Kansas soon appeared in Connecticut, New York, Ohio, and Washington, D. C. The New England Company, however, with Thayer as its chief promoter and Amos Lawrence as its treasurer, attracted the most attention and did the most effective work. The New England clergy were assiduously canvassed for funds and members. Agents and speakers travelled about stirring enthusiasm and taking subscriptions. But success was small. In the year 1854–55, only 1240 settlers were dispatched to Kansas and among these, said the *Liberator*, "hardly a single abolitionist can be found. . . ." Financial success was equally small. In October, 1855, Lawrence, the treasurer, wrote: "So far as paying our debts goes, we are a bankrupt corporation, and have been."[50]

From this plight a band of well-meaning Missouri citizens unintentionally rescued the Emigrant Aid Companies, and, at the same time, supplied the emotional impetus to the Republican Party which the South had failed to give it. Missourians had genuine and traditional interests in Kansas. The old Santa Fé trail from Franklin and Independence to New Mexico had played an important part both in the material and spiritual development of Missouri. The Kansas plains had linked market and supply and the wheels of heavily laden Missouri wagons had left deep scars upon those plains to witness possession by the right of conquest. Service to Indian missions across the border and trade with the tribes and military posts had strengthened the claim. Rightly the Missouri farmer, with the usual Western restlessness, looked across the border and dreamed of the day when he might move again into fresh new lands. Kansas was his particular domain. It belonged to him as new lands had traditionally belonged to the settlers nearest their borders. Long before Douglas made his move, Missourians had been drifting, "Sooner"-like, into the forbidden region. The opening of the territory and the arrival of the newly appointed governor, Andrew H. Reeder, in October, 1854, was the signal for accelerated action by all those who dreamed of cheap government lands, boom profits in town sites, public offices, and fair American frontier excitement. An old story was being repeated. In perfectly normal American fashion, plain men from the Ohio Valley world, Missourians rightly predominating, began the settlement of Kansas. Disorder and even lawlessness were inevitable. Land surveys had not been completed. Rumors of the activities of the Emigrant Aid companies and soon the arrival of their settlers, hurried local groups into action. Force was used to meet force. Claim jumping and bitter conflicts over prospective town sites led to assaults and even murders. The desire for public office and the material advantages such office would give encouraged corruption of every sort in the formation of government.[51] Consequently, when, on November 29, an election to choose a delegate to Congress from the territory was held, and again, in March, 1855, when a territorial legislature was to be elected, Missourians in considerable numbers crossed the border and cast their votes for candidates satisfactory to themselves.

How much the determination to make Kansas a slave state had to do with this action we do not know. Unquestionably Missouri slaveholders resented the free-soil efforts, and the idea of slavery defense had entered into some of their preliminary meetings and plans. Yet their conduct was so much like that of Iowans in Nebraska at the very same time that serious doubts arise as to whether the slavery issue did anything more than to furnish an excuse for perfectly normal action.

Iowa men padded the first Nebraska census for the purpose of influencing the location of the capital. The canvass for Nebraska's territorial offices was carried on east of the Missouri River and the man chosen as territorial representative was an Iowan who, at best, was only "an occasional squatter in Nebraska City."[52] In the election of the territorial legislature, Iowans again poured across the border and chose their fellow citizens to that body. One group left Council Bluffs to vote in Burt County, which did not have a single white resident; they stopped in Washington County and elected a member for Burt. In Washington County, sixty-five or seventy votes were polled from ten or twelve voters. Iowans voted *en masse* in Nebraska City and many citizens of western Iowa visited Nebraska for the first time, as did James Magrath, for the purpose of voting. Almost half of the first Nebraska legislature was from Iowa. That legislature spent its early sessions, held in a building donated by Iowa speculators, voting charters and other favors to Iowa citizens who were just moving in or planning to do so. Some of these prospective residents, it must be added, never acted on their intentions.[53]

But realities were one thing now; the reactions they produced, quite another. Iowa and Nebraska were not related to the slavery controversy; Missouri and Kansas were. What happened in Nebraska was not news; events in Kansas were front-page material. Nebraska was just another frontier; Kansas was the battleground of freedom! Irregularities had occurred in Kansas where squatter sovereignty was being worked out, and these irregularities had been committed by Missouri slaveholders. That was a challenge to free men. Those who had charged "the slave power" with a black scheme to expand slavery by the Douglas Kansas-Nebraska bill now had positive proof of all their contentions. A wave of deep emotion swept eastward. Republicans in Congress began to speak. The weakening Emigrant Aid Company found new strength. John Brown, the hapless failure in business, turned westward toward Kansas. The Republican Party could move forward toward success.

CHAPTER FIFTEEN

BUILDING THE REPUBLICAN PARTY

M Y knowledge of facts is imperfect," wrote President Pierce in May, 1856, regarding affairs in Kansas. He spoke for his own generation and for ours as well. Exactly what occurred in Kansas in the period 1854–60, and why it occurred, will probably never be known. Like so many other things in that day, Kansas became a symbol, and realities lost their significance. "Bleeding Kansas" became more important in American life than Kansas, the territory and state.

The larger facts are more or less clear. In the elections held to choose a Congressional delegate and a legislature, some Missourians crossed the border and voted. How much their votes influenced the final outcome of the elections we do not know. Alexander H. Stephens, after a careful check of the census taken only thirty days before the second election, found that settlers from the Southern states outnumbered those from the entire North by more than six hundred. On the doubtful assumption that all Southerners were pro-slavery, he concluded that the outcome represented the will of the majority.[1] This opinion was strengthened after Governor Reeder had canvassed the vote, had declared it void in eight districts, and had ordered new elections.[2] Under normal conditions, that would have been the end of the story. In the case of Kansas, it was the signal for local strife and national excitement. The Missourians had committed a fatal blunder in invading Kansas. Opponents, led by Emigrant Aid settlers, attributed the outcome of both elections to Missouri votes and when the legislature adopted Missouri's laws and enacted a slave code, they refused to recognize either the legislature or its laws. In September, 1855, they held a convention at Topeka, elected Reeder, who had broken with the first government, delegate to Congress, and Robinson, of the Emigrant Aid Society, governor, They then framed a constitution and asked Congress to admit Kansas as a free state. One group, at least, sought in this way to make Kansas affairs contribute to the national conflict. "If they give us occasion to settle the question of slavery in this country with the bayonet," wrote the newly elected Kansas governor, "let us improve it. What way can bring the slave's redemption more speedily? Wouldn't it be rich to march an army through the slaveholding states & roll up a *black cloud* that would spread dismay & terror to the ranks of the oppressor?"[3] The House, under Republican control, voted in favor of admitting Kansas under this revolutionary group, but the Senate checked the movement. Thereupon the free-soilers proceeded to organize secret military companies to resist the forces of law and order.

The lawlessness and brutality which immediately developed in Kansas were not wholly the result of a simple struggle between freedom and slavery for the possession of the territory. Some of the disorder went with the frontier as such, some of it grew out of conflicting land titles and rivalry between localities for political and railroad advantages, some of it existed only in the reports which newspaper correspondents sent back East.[4]

Kansas settlers, like other frontiersmen, usually found their funds exhausted before their new land began to yield a surplus. The control of government and the salaries from public office often measured the difference between failure and holding on. Control of government also gave the power to locate county seats, to determine the location of the territorial capitals, and to influence the lines along which the railroads would run. The Kansas struggle was, to some extent, a conflict between two frontier groups for just such advantages. Slavery differences aggravated but did not produce the interests involved. Disputes over lands contributed even more to the struggle. Unlike other territories, Kansas, when opened to settlement, had little land available for entry. Indian reservations occupied the greater part of the most desirable tracts. Some of these lands had been ceded in trust to the United States Government, but were not as yet part of the Public Domain subject to pre-emption by settlers.

Land surveys in Kansas moved slowly. Not until the fall of 1856 were enough surveys completed so that the first public-land sales could be held and settlers permitted to know where their lines ran. Up to that time they had not been able to hold legal title. The rush of settlement, however, had not been delayed because of these conditions. Settlers "squatted hither and yon, completely disregarding Indian rights and government rules." They set up squatter courts to give "a form of community sanction to their rights" and to permit "title registration and transfer in the absence of legal titles." Professor Malin has shown that the Kansas struggle invariably reached a crisis in different neighborhoods just as the surveys were being completed and men were finding out where their land lines conflicted. He has also noted that, under the town-site act of 1844, companies incorporated by the legislature could make their entry at the regular land office, but companies not so incorporated had to apply to the judge of the county court, who would enter and hold the town site in trust for them. Control of the territorial government under such conditions gave solid economic advantage. "There is room to question sometimes," says Malin, "whether [the] concern [of free-state men] was greater over their possible defeat on the slave issue or over their loss of opportunity for town-lot speculation."[5]

The speculations of Governor Reeder and their relation to his attitudes on the slavery question were open gossip. Early in 1855, the Atchison *Squatter Sovereign* declared that no sooner had Reeder arrived in the territory than he "immediately entered into land speculations. . . ." His "tour of observation" to obtain information necessary to the organization of government was nothing but a tour of speculation, the buying of Indian lands for a song. Later the same paper charged that he manipulated the judicial districts and delayed their organization in the interests of his holdings at Pawnee, Tecumseh, and Leavenworth. "Since his advent among us," it grumbled, "his only aim has been to 'get money' by fair means or foul. . . ." Some districts were denied their just share of representation in the legislature because the governor "owns no land in this section of the country. . . ." The selection of Pawnee, where Reeder's holdings were large, as the site of the state capital and the delay in calling the legislature until he and his "partners" had completed a hotel in which to accommodate the members were denounced as deliberate efforts at personal gain.[6] The governor's leanings toward free soil were believed to have no better foundations. Toombs of Georgia charged, on the floor of Congress, that Reeder's later break with the legislature was due to their removal from Reeder's town to somebody else's town. The fact that Congress recalled him for speculation in Indian lands adds strength to all the charges made against him.[7]

The famous war on the Wakarusa began as a land-claim dispute. It amounted to little more than a show of force by rival groups formed as much to protect their material interests as to influence the question of slavery. The killing of Samuel Collins by Patrick Laughlin, which became one of the most famous of the "crimes committed by the slavery party," has now been shown to have been nothing but a personal quarrel between two settlers *both* of whom were free-soil men.[8] The "sacking of Lawrence," which consisted largely of the destruction of a newspaper plant and a hotel, is so thoroughly tangled up with the personal squabbles of one Sheriff Jones and the struggles of rival political elements that no fair historian can possibly accept it as a simon-pure slavery affair. Even the *Herald of Freedom* attributed the hostility against Lawrence to the fact that "it is a rival town and in the way of their advancement."[9] Its report of proslavery activities in the vicinity of Douglas on June 2, 1855, went on to say that "a gang of twenty-five or thirty land pirates," had driven one "Mr. Honwick" and one "Mr. Ockley" from their claims which others pretended to own. This statement makes one suspect that the affair may have been like that of a "Mr. Emerson," reported by the *Kansas Tribune* to have been an instance of proslavery violence but which, on investigation, turned out to be a case of deliberate claim jumping by Emerson himself.[10] Genuine free-state and proslavery attitudes unquestionably contributed to the troubles of the new territory, but a surprising number of personal and interest difficulties were elevated to the dignity of battles for principle. Unquestionably also many men made the slavery issue a pretext for violence in the interest of personal gain.[11] John Brown himself seems to have gone to Kansas in the beginning for purely economic reasons; there was certainly much of personal bitterness over land titles as well as hatred of slavery in his later violent conduct. Many Kansas contemporaries viewed him, on good evidence, as little better than a thieving ruffian.

Kansas leaders quickly saw opportunities for material gain from the spreading of lurid tales about a slavery war in the territory; politicians outside of Kansas as quickly discovered the uses to which a "Bleeding Kansas" might be put. On January 25, 1856, Robinson wrote A. A. Lawrence, "that extensive preparations are being made for the destruction of Lawrence and all of the free-state settlements. You can have no idea of the character of the men with whom we have to deal. . . ." A few days before, a group of six speakers had been dispatched on a mission of explanation and appeal to the North. With consummate skill they made use of the wild threats of such Missouri extremists as B. F. Stringfellow and the wilder rumors of a great mass movement in the South about to overrun Kansas.[12] Newspapers, such as the New York *Tribune,* the St. Louis *Democrat,* and the Chicago *Tribune,* provided their readers with a steady stream of atrocity stories from Kansas correspondents. Every act of violence occurring in the territory was twisted into a proslavery attack on freedom, and when real happenings were lacking imaginary ones were concocted. The victim was always "one of our most intelligent, energetic and respectable citizens," and the aggressors always, the Missouri brigands, these ruffians, these bloodthirsty savages maddened with whiskey. Day after day, these papers reported murders, lynchings, robberies, and violence. One ambush shooting of a "law abiding citizen" was said to have ended with "a hellish ha! ha! and the remark: 'There is more d----d abolition bait for the wolves.' " One writer declared that:[13]

It is the Southern hive from which the barbarous hordes are to swarm that are to make a desert out of our paradise unless they are repulsed at once. They are already making incursions into our borders, marked with all the cruelties and ferocities of the Goths and Vandals of old time. . . . Unless we can put down the Barbarians, the Barbarians will most certainly put us down.

The effects of these appeals were immediate. Interest in Emigrant Aid revived and funds poured in. New committees were organized to "concert such measures as may be deemed expedient for the protection of the citizens of Kansas from the ruffian incursions of the Missouri Barbarians." A New York State Kansas Aid meeting in Albany appointed a committee to raise money and encourage emigration so that Kansas might resist "the insolent attempts of a foreign people to impose upon them the despotism of laws which would be a disgrace to the most savage people." Gerrit Smith told a Buffalo convention that, "You are looking to ballots, when you should be looking to bayonets; counting up voters, when you should be mustering arms and none but armed emigrants; electioneering for candidates for civil rulers, when you should be inquiring for military rulers. . . . Political action is our greatest hindrance, because it delays the only remedy for the wrongs of Kansas . . . the action of armed men. . . . If all manhood has not departed from us, we will not consent to leave our Kansas brethren to be butchered." He would have the convention "look to the protection of Kansas by physical force, and against whatever foe, Federal troops or any other troops. If our brethren in Kansas can be protected only by the shedding of blood, then blood must be shed."[14]

With the presidential election approaching, politicians in Congress were quick to make capital out of Kansas. President Pierce in his first message had recognized the existence of disorder but had denied that it justified the interposition of the Federal executive. He had blamed organized meddling for the difficulties and, in a second message, had accepted the Kansas legislature and refused to go behind its election. In the Senate, Douglas attempted to secure an enabling act and Seward urged admission as a free state. Toombs tried to secure a non-partisan commission to settle the whole affair. Republican control of the House, however, checked conservative moves and turned

Kansas into a political football. Efforts were made to repeal acts of the Kansas legislature, then to unseat Whitfield, the regular territorial delegate, and put Reeder in his place. With this as a point of departure, members took extreme partisan ground and realized all the political possibilities in tangled Kansas affairs. At length, on March 19, the Republicans were able to put through a measure for the sending of an investigating committee to Kansas.[15] "Official" distortion was to be added to an already adequate domestic supply.

The beating up of excitement and the statement of extreme partisan attitudes reached its climax in the speech of Charles Sumner on "The Crime against Kansas" delivered in the Senate on the 19th and 20th of May. It was a masterly tirade such as only Sumner could have given. Even today it has not lost its fire. Its very brilliance emphasized its disregard of truth and sportsmanship. It assumed the unquestioned soundness of every charge made against the slave power in Kansas, and poured appropriate disdain and abuse upon the unoffending head of the aged Senator Butler of South Carolina. "The most un-American and unpatriotic speech that ever grated on the ears" of Congress, said Senator Cass. ". . . Is it his object to provoke some one of us to kick him as one would a dog in the street, that he may get sympathy upon the just chastisement?" asked the more volatile Stephen A. Douglas. Sumner is "essentially a man of emotions and sentiments," said one of his Boston friends, "it is very easy for him to believe anything to be true that he wishes to. . . . I do not think he has a truthful mind."[16]

Preston S. Brooks, representative from South Carolina and relative of Senator Butler, quickly put Douglas's suggestion to practice. Two days after the offensive speech, while Sumner sat at his desk after the adjournment of the Senate, Brooks expressed his contempt for both the man and his words by beating him over the head with a gutta-percha walking stick. His object was insult as much as injury. Gentlemen would understand the significance of a caning.[17]

How severely Sumner was injured we shall never know. Scalp wounds bleed freely and later physical infirmities may easily and honestly be ascribed to some well-remembered injury. On the other hand, the full extent of an injury is not always immediately apparent. The physician who first attended Sumner found three wounds, one requiring no attention, and two which had to be closed with two stitches each. After a few days, he declared his patient able to return to duty. The doctor was thereupon promptly dismissed by Francis Preston Blair, Sr., who carried Sumner to his country home, Silver Springs, and took charge of all future information given the public. From that time until December, 1859, Sumner remained out of public life—a "martyr to Southern brutality," his seat in the Senate eloquently vacant. When he was able to go to Europe in March, 1857, and engage "in a continuous round of social engagements . . . and a sight-seeing program . . . strenuous enough to reduce an ordinary traveler to a state of complete exhaustion," Southern skeptics charged him with shamming, but this did not weaken the great effect on the public mind which the assault had created.[18]

Coming as it did at the time when Kansas affairs were contributing mightily to the rounding out of sectional stereotypes, the Brooks-Sumner affair fell directly into pattern. The reactions of men, North and South, were far more important than the realities in the case; the uses to which it could be put were not dependent upon the facts in the case. "As you may suppose," wrote G. S. Hilliard from Boston, on May 28, 1856, "our community talks of nothing and thinks of nothing but the recent assault upon Sumner."[19]

Nothing ever was so unlucky—not merely in itself but in its circumstances. Providence itself seems to be on the side of the Republican party. Sumner is now not merely their champion but their martyr, and his election for the next six years is now certain. Such events entirely destroy the influence of any reasonable and reflecting man in Massachusetts. The most vehement passions are now sweeping over the state like a prairie fire, and the people will no more listen to a calm examination of the tendency of Sumner's principles and doctrines than would a Methodist campmeeting to a legal discussion of the doctrine of contingent remainders.

The New York *Tribune* took the lead in asserting that "Bully

Brooks" had "sneaked and lain in wait" for Sumner with the intention of murdering him. The affair would have ended "with drawing a bowie-knife and stabbing his insensible victim to the heart had not two New York gentlemen . . . come to the rescue [and] seized the assassin. . . ." The *Tribune* took for granted unanimous Southern approval of the deed and pictured it as a typical expression of normal Southern attitudes and character. It was "an illustration of the ferocious Southern spirit"; Brooks was "that almost sainted champion of slaveholding dominance. . . ." "A thorough-going and consistent" advocate of slavery could not "scruple at a lie or false oath" or hesitate "at an assault or a murder." Before it had finished, the *Tribune* had augmented the affair into an aggressive attack by the whole slaveholding South upon the North and democracy— the forerunner of other attacks already being prepared. "The scepter of the self-appointed oligarchy," it warned, "is a gutta-percha cane, backed by pistols and bowie knives under the flap of the coat, and its patron saint . . . is Bully Brooks."[20]

"Bleeding Kansas" and "bleeding Sumner" were thus made to serve the cause of the Republican Party in its first national campaign. Throughout the summer and fall, they constituted the emotional forces which made Fremont its candidate, fashioned its platform, and carried its campaign toward the November election. Never has a party been so fortunate in the sequence of events. Never has one made better use of the materials provided.[21] "The Black Republicans," charged the Lecompton *Union* (Kansas), "have all along shown their determination to keep up the excitement in Kansas in order to have some hobby out of which to manufacture political capital to carry them through the approaching Presidential election. . . ." Tales of butchery, massacre, and murder, "furnished by lying correspondents and telegraphic reporters," it said, "were going the rounds of the Northern abolition press." These were "falsehoods too palpable to be believed even by the vilest abolition fanatics," yet their flow went on unchecked as a means of creating political capital. "Kansas was made to bleed for the benefit of Northern politicians in their pursuit of popular favor," said the *Union* after the election was over.[22]

It was distant from the ordinary travel of the country and there was no small difficulty in ascertaining the truth. The Republicans had their agents in Kansas, who furnished accounts of horrible occurrences, as required, to meet the necessities of their employers. Many who had no such agents manufactured news to suit the occasion in their own offices. Poor, Kansas was made to bleed to order.

To which comment, the *Kansas Weekly Herald* added one of its own: "the leaders . . . do not want the Kansas question settled. They want to keep up the cry of 'bleeding Kansas,' and delude the ignorant into the embraces of black republicanism, by the cry of outrages in Kansas, in the hope that it may enable them to ride into power upon its dangerous wave in 1860."[23]

Results justified the means. When the November election returns were in the Republican candidate had polled the astonishing total of 1,341,264 votes. The Democrats had placed James Buchanan in the White House but the Republican Party had established itself in two short years as a major national party whose success could not be far off.

*   *   *   *

Reactions in the South to Kansas and the rise of the Republican Party were far from uniform, but they tended to become increasingly violent. Most writers agreed that a new and unprovoked attack had been launched against the South. "The course of events has made it clear as light," said the Richmond *Enquirer,* "that the South stands upon the defensive, and that the whole responsibility of the present turmoil, and threatened disaster, rests upon Northern aggressors on Southern rights."[24] The Montgomery *Mail* took the same attitude. "The issues soon to be met," it declared, "are none of our seeking. We are stationary and entirely tranquil. The masses of abolition are moving forward to attack us."[25] In the same spirit, the Mobile *Register* indignantly asked:[26]

Do we demand that no more *free* States shall be admitted to the Union? Do we ask to be permitted officiously to intermeddle with the domestic polity of the free States? Do we claim that the common territory shall be given up exclusively to the use, occupation and enjoyment of the people and institutions of the South? Nothing of the kind. We simply say to the North, we are your equals in the Union, attend to your affairs and leave us quietly to manage ours.

The New York *Tribune* was especially blamed for fomenting the new outbreak. "Its aim," said the New Orleans *Bee*, "is persistently and unweariedly to stir up the embers of fanaticism; to maintain them at a glowing red heat; to defame the South; to disparage her institutions; to establish invidious contrasts between her material and intellectual progress and that of the North; to ascribe, by cunning distortion of facts and plausible sophisms of argument, Northern superiority exclusively to its exemption from slavery; to treat the South as a decaying—almost effete—community; . . . to inculcate in the minds of the ignorant and prejudiced the most monstrous and unfounded ideas touching the treatment of slaves; . . . in fine, to create amongst its readers, a large majority of whom have never set their feet in the South, or beheld a slave, the immutable conviction that the slaveowner is a barbarian and brute, whose delight is to torture suffering humanity, and to whose ears the wail of his victim and the crack of the whip are the choicest music. . . ." Such tactics, thought the *Bee*, would "at no very distant day compel the South to assume an attitude hostile to the stability of the Union. . . ."[27]

The struggle for Kansas was viewed as but one phase of this aggression. The utterly false charge that by the Nebraska bill a "vast territory consecrated to the genius of freedom was transferred to the cruel Moloch of the slave power" had set a group "of deluded fanatics" to preparing an army for "an invasion of an enemy's country." "It was, in fact, a crusade, preached by the St. Bernards of an unholy and impure fanaticism to conquer the New Territories from the participation of the Slave States of the Union. This design was loudly, vauntingly, insultingly proclaimed, and to this attempt to carry their point by means outside and beyond the limits of the law, [was] to be attributed the acerbity of feeling which now threatened to break into the bitterest feud. Had the Missourians submitted unresistingly to the consummation of this scheme, they would have deserved the imputations of the most degrading cowardice. . . . They did not make the issue, it was forced upon them. . . ." Kansas lay directly west of Missouri. Missourians went there because it was the nearest unoccupied territory.[28] They were "willing that things should take their natural course, but they [had] no intention of being made the victims of a deliberate Abolition conspiracy." They would not "have an Abolition State, got up by subscription, in their very sight." It was a "struggle of fanaticism and rancor on one side, and of plain self-defense on the other."[29]

Under such circumstances, force had to be met with force. Missouri had become the outpost against an assault which, if not resisted, would subject the whole South to "the fate of Jamaica." "The cause of that state," said the Jacksonville (Ala.) *Republican,* "is the common cause of all the Southern States. She must not be permitted to be overthrown."[30] The "bloody deeds" committed in Kansas were but "the first step . . . in the black program" which the now dominant Northern radicals were preparing and which would reach its climax, as Wilson of Massachusetts boasted, when "the Southern mother shall clasp her babe with wilder fondness to her bosom when she hears at her door at midnight the tramp and the voice of the black avenger."[31] The South must be united. Southern emigrants must be hurried off to Kansas.

The emigrant-aid movement which now developed in the South was a weak and inefficient affair. It was anything but the great outpouring pictured by the Northern anti-slavery leaders. The meetings and resolutions which launched it were vigorous enough, but planters with slaves could not move easily nor could they take chances with the squatter-sovereignty doctrine. These and other difficulties were suggested by R. G. Earle of Jacksonville, Alabama, who, when urged to lead a group, declared that "if a party of one hundred or more *gentlemen* who have the good of their country at heart" were "willing to remove to Kansas" he would go with them, but that he was "unwilling equally to assume command of any company formed without the direction of law . . . and bound by the responsibilities incident to legal authority." To this appeal he received no response.[32] Immigration societies were formed in nearly all the Southern States; funds were raised; local leaders issued spasmodic calls for volunteers; editors proclaimed the cause in Kansas to be the cause of the South and talked of the thousands of men who would go.[33] Only one expedition, however, came out of the "laboring." Early in 1856, a few hundred young men, without slaves or families, "rendezvoused" at various points in Alabama and Georgia and then set out under Jefferson Buford for Kansas. The effect of their departure on Northern emotions far exceeded any contribution they were to make to the winning of Kansas. The move, however, exhausted Southern enthusiasm for material aid.[34] Soon its conservatives were questioning the wisdom of precipitating a physical struggle in the territory. The Charleston *Standard* deplored the whole matter and advised the South to abandon the contest. Slavery was not to be strengthened by extension. Disunion would be the only result attained.[35] The Charleston *Patriot* and the Winnsboro *Register* both objected to further efforts at emigration as a waste of effort and money.[36] J. H. Hammond was confident that the South "did not want another foot of slave territory"; she should consolidate and improve what she already had.[37] Others seized the occasion to denounce Stephen A. Douglas for reopening the issue. They talked of the Kansas struggle as the work of designing politicians, North and South, and absolved the people from the guilt of raising and continuing the slavery controversy. Such "misguided men" would bring irreparable woes upon the country and plunge it at last "in fratricidal war from which both sections, at best, would emerge so prostrated, ruined and impoverished, that a third of a century of unabated peace and prosperity would not suffice to restore them. . . ."[38]

A radical element, on the other hand, talked of disunion. "Unless . . . some unexpected change takes place in the general sentiment of the North," said the *Daily South Carolinian*, "a dissolution of the present Union must ultimately take place." "The differences between the North and the South," observed one of its readers, "are not temporary and accidental but continuous and unavoidable." "Stripped of all its surroundings of forms" what was happening in Kansas was "simply a war between the North and the South." It was time to face realities and to accept the battle.[39]

Southern reactions to the Brooks-Sumner episode varied as greatly as did their reactions to Kansas. They ranged from outright approval of the attack to an equally open denunciation of it. Fellow South Carolinians generally approved. The *Southron* of Orangeburg Court House expressed its high appreciation and hearty approval of "the caning of the HONORABLE charles sumner" but would "have been better pleased if Mr. B. had used a cow-hide instead of a cane."[40] The *Daily South Carolinian* thought Sumner had not gotten "a lick more than he deserved." The expression of Northern opinion brought out by the event clearly showed that "the days of the Union [were] numbered."[41] The Sumter *Watchman* thought "the chastisement . . . suited to and but the legitimate desert of the uncalled for outrage." Brooks had "truthfully carried out the will of the State, and probably the South."[42] Charleston papers were less emphatic. The *Mercury* was at first disposed to condemn the act in the most unmeasured terms as a "plain violation of the right of speech guaranteed by the Constitution" and by "the sacredness of the Senate Chamber." Upon further consideration, however, the *Mercury* remembered that Massachusetts had placed herself "above the Constitution" and had become "a state of outlawry." Sumner as "the High Priest of this lawlessness" had no right to claim the protection of the law. He had to be dealt with outside of the law. Brooks had "simply done his duty—nothing more, nothing less."[43] A writer in the *Evening News*, on the other hand, declared that Brooks was "wrong in chastising Sumner, wrong in method, and wrong in place." "What has Mr. Butler, or Mr. Brooks, or South Carolina gained by the thrashing of that man? Just nothing."[44] The *Courier*, at first, was silent. It neither approved nor condemned. Not until Brooks returned home and the people of Columbia, including the Negro slaves, welcomed him with hearty speeches of approval and gifts of a pitcher, a goblet and a cane, and the Edgefield district committee planned a great dinner in his honor, did it take positive ground. Then it followed the lead of the *Mercury*, which viewed these demonstrations not as simply honors for one who had justly chastised "an insolent defamer of the South" but rather as public recognition for one whose "act represented a bold feature in the great sectional controversy, long standing, and now more threatening than ever." The Brooks dinner was "an assemblage of Disunionists," already convinced that "the preservation of this Union, without the extremest dishonor to the South, [was] impossible."[45]

Outside of South Carolina, opinion was generally temperate and sane. Hotheads here and there approved of Brooks's course, but the dominant sentiment was against it. No sympathy was wasted on Sumner and most people agreed that he had gotten less than he deserved. They also agreed that no other method would have been suitable or effective in dealing with such a man. But they questioned the time and place chosen for chastisement and were doubtful as to its wisdom from the larger sectional point of view.

The comments of the Richmond *Enquirer* and the Nashville *Union and American* were typical of those which approved. The *Enquirer* insisted that Southern Representatives had either to accept habitual insolence and insult or seek some appropriate and adequate redress. Since a gentleman could not retaliate in kind, Brooks had chosen the only course open.[46] The *Union and American*, while it regretted that the attack was made in the Senate chamber, insisted that the halls of Congress did not give refuge for criminals and that not until the voice of abolitionism ceased "to war upon our constitutional rights, and its echoes no longer vibrate[d] in the halls of Congress, . . . [could abolitionists] claim those halls as a place of refuge when they fly from the spirit of insulted honor and slandered manhood they have invoked."[47]

The majority, however, condemned the choice of time and place. The Georgia *Telegraph* (Macon) confessed to a deep mortification and chagrin over the occurrence. The fact that punishment was inflicted in the Senate chamber excited "an unfeigned sorrow and mortification." "It will be worth a thousand speeches and arguments to abolitionism," the *Telegraph* continued, "and has well nigh undone all that the gallant and talented representatives have accomplished this session to give weight to the position of the South. Our unwise friend is more terrible than a score of enemies. . . . The venom of such a speech as Sumner's could hurt nobody but the author of it."[48] The Mobile papers spoke in the same vein. The *Advertiser* thought the assault admitted of no justification. Its chief effect would be to create a demand for a speech which otherwise would have fallen dead upon the public ear. This ill advised and rash act would do the South more harm "than the combined skill, talent, diligence and malignity of the whole abolition crew could have effected in a twelve-month. . . ."[49]

> Every sound thinking unprejudiced man in the country knows and feels that the personalities in Sumner's speech were abominable, despite all the white-washing resolutions Massachusetts may pass, and that, considering the time and place and manner of Mr. Brooks' assault it was rash, unwise and utterly indefensible, no matter how many "gold-headed canes" Columbia, Charleston or any other town may send him.

The Mobile *Daily Register* judged both Brooks and Sumner guilty of misconduct and deeply regretted the way in which rabid spokesmen had seized upon the assault to excite public passion. "To these dealers in garbage," it said, "Mr. Brooks is a benefactor. And if it be a good thing to lay the foundations for a dissolution of the Union in a sentiment of extreme malevolence . . . then must Brooks and Sumner both be regarded as patriots of a very high order. . . ." Bitterly it noted that the Southern States in a body were being "made responsible for the untoward occasion . . ." and the whole affair "charged directly upon slavery, which is represented as 'the prolific and necessary parent of every species of ruffianism, brutality, and blackguardism.' "[50] The New Orleans press was also generally moderate. The *Bee* had no sympathy to waste on Sumner but was "sincerely grieved at an event which beyond all doubt . . . [had] quickened into redoubled activity the smouldering fires of Abolition zeal" and had detached from the South many warm friends.

Brooks should have foreseen such consequences and reserved his practical rebuke of Mr. Sumner for a more appropriate time and place.[51] The *Picayune* thought Brooks's act should be deeply deplored and severely reprehended. It infringed on "Senatorial privileges, the immunity of Senatorial character, and the freedom of speech, where reply is as free as attack." Thus a "good cause suffer[ed] from the heat and haste of its indiscrete friends."[52] The *Daily Crescent* made light of the whole affair but saw the tempest that had come of it. "The Type-batteries, North and South, glisten[ed] in fearful array, and belligerent newspapers invade[d] each other's territories like the locusts of Egypt!"[53]

Both the *Republican Banner and Nashville Whig* and the *Hinds County* (Miss.) *Gazette* condemned Brooks's choice of time and place. The former paper hoped that Southern men of all parties would raise "their voices in strong and earnest rebuke and condemnation of the desecration, by such brutality, of the Halls of the National Legislature." The Memphis *Daily Appeal* took the same view, but indignantly asked which was more seditious, "Sharpe's Rifle Sumner, or Belligerent Brooks?" G. B. Lamar, writing to Howell Cobb, expressed the extreme attitude:[54]

Viewed dispassionately in every light, the assault was unquestionably unjustifiable, unmanly, ill-timed, ill-advised, injudicious to the cause of the South, and totally indefensible as to time, place, and manner. . . .

The political campaign and election of 1856 did more to reawaken Southern fears and develop Southern unity than any other event since the introduction of the Wilmot Proviso. The Whig Party in the South was gone and the Know-Nothings, after early rapid gains, had reached and passed their peak in the local elections of the preceding year. They were still to be reckoned with in Louisiana, Tennessee, and Georgia, but the drift of former state rights Whigs toward the Democratic Party was already great enough to give that party something more of a Southern flavor. This fact, together with the purely Northern character of the Republican Party, turned the campaign of 1856 into a sectional struggle. "For the first time since the adoption of the Federal Constitution," said the New Orleans *Daily Crescent*, "a Presidential canvass is being conducted on purely geographical grounds. For the first time, an important party in the North has arrayed itself under sectional banners and is striving to elevate a man to the Presidency on the one simple, exclusive, distinct idea of hostility to the South." It was "not a duel between sections on a point of punctilious honor"; but rather an "internecine war—war to the knife and to the hilt." "The Roman battle cry has gone forth against us," declared the Mobile *Daily Register*, "and we of the South are summoned to our defensive arms and walls with 'delenda est Carthago' ringing in our ears. . . ."[55]

The only issue involved in the campaign, asserted the Southern leaders, was the existence of slavery. It was on trial for its very life. The Republicans were "the mortal enemies of every man, woman and child in the Southern States. . . . If they should succeed in this contest . . . they would repeal the fugitive slave law . . . they would create insurrection and servile war in the South . . . they would put the torch to our dwellings and the knife to our throats. . . ." "Obsolete land distribution, bank and tariff questions" should "be eschewed and ignored. . . ." The paramount issue was slavery.[56]

Convinced of the danger thus threatened, the radical element insisted that the election of Frémont should work the end of the Union. He was a strictly sectional candidate. He represented a spirit of hostility to the South. As Judge P. J. Scruggs of Mississippi put it:[57]

. . . The election of Frémont would present, at once, to the people of the South, the question whether they would tamely crouch at the feet of their despoilers, or like their ancient forefathers, openly defy their enemies, and assert their independence. In my judgement, anything short of immediate, prompt, and unhesitating secession, would be an act of servility that would seal our doom for all time to come.

Others suggested delay. Even if Frémont were elected, they would wait for some overt act before resorting to disunion. Perhaps even the fanatical Frémont might repudiate the Black Republican platform altogether and become the champion of

Southern Rights! Not more than a fourth of the Republicans believed what they said. The remainder were engaged in "a wild, heartless and unprincipled hunt after office."[58]

A foolish delusion, retorted the radicals. "We style it warfare," opined the Augusta *Daily Constitutionalist*.[59]

Abolition is not simple, quiet, erroneous, *unobtrusive* opinion, but aggressive, loud-mouthed meddlesome action. . . . It is today stronger and more intolerant than ever before. Some may satisfy themselves with the general phrase, *reaction*. Oh, there will be no reaction. . . . Abolitionism is but just coming of age. It has not reached its majority. The children who were born at its inception in 1835, are just now taking rank among the voters of the North. The generation now rising has known no political Josephs, no ancient hand of gratitude and Union. The men who are now coming onto the stage, who are beginning to replace their fathers, and clutch the reins of government, are men who sucked in Abolition opinions with their mother's milk. . . . They were taught them at the fireside, listening to tales of terror through the long winter evenings. Pictures addressed eyes yet untaught to read. The Sabbath school and the day school taught on this subject the same unvarying lesson. The press and the pulpit, the lecture room and lyceum, the stump and forum, every avenue of mind and heart has been steadily at work completing the impression, until we now begin to awake to some small sense of its generality and depth. But we see now only the beginning of the end. The seed is beginning to ripen, but the harvest time is not yet.

The election of Buchanan quieted the fears of the majority, but the heavy vote for Frémont in the North and West gravely alarmed the more thoughtful element. "The strength developed by Frémont portends the continued agitation of slavery," said the New Orleans *Bee* on November 8. "Had he been badly beaten, his partisans would have been discouraged, and the prestige of their doctrines would have been lost; but having made so respectable a run, they will perceive every inducement . . . to renew their exertions, to organize their forces for another contest, and to keep up the struggle with energy and perseverance. . . ."[60] The fight would, therefore, go on to the bitter end. North and South had been revealed as enemies; they were "countrymen only in name." Already the Republicans were preparing for the next campaign by invoking anew Bleeding Kansas and spreading false tales of new aggressions. The Democrats had won, but Buchanan had been supported at the North and at the South on "directly opposite grounds" in regard to the extension of slavery. Any effort he might make to settle the Kansas question would bring "shadows, clouds and darkness, surcharged with storm and tempest," to his party. The country was drifting toward sectional political division. Middle ground was disappearing. Northern Democrats, with a few exceptions, were holding "that the people, while in a Territorial condition" could exclude slaveowners and their property. Southern Democrats, almost unanimously, were of the opposite opinion. They were, in general, willing to leave the issue to the Courts. The Republicans, on the other hand, would "absolutely refuse to accept the decision of a Case, as the settlement of the Principle. . . ." That attitude made necessary "a Southern party in self-defense"—a party "or resistance" because the South was "openly attacked. . . ."[61]

The New Orleans *Daily Crescent* best expressed the conservative reaction to the election:[62]

We are among those who have never allowed a thought to harbor in their bosoms for a moment that, by any contingent or remote chance, the Union of these States could be brought into jeopardy. We have cherished that idea with a singleness of heart, a fervency of purpose, and devotion of soul, as strong and all-pervading as our natures are capable of. And until within a very few days, we laughed at those who hinted at the bare possibility of disunion.

We are sorry to say that the settled convictions of a life-time have received a stunning shock and that we have no laughter now to tender as answer to the disunion pronunciamentos of the more impulsive among our Southern brethren. . . . It is evident . . . that Col. John C. Fremont, the candidate for the Presidency of the freesoilers, abolitionists and haters of the South generally, has received the electoral votes of a large majority of the Northern people! Almost as a mass, the North has gone for him, and gone for him too on a platform the carrying out of the principles of which would inflict immeasurable degradation upon the Southern people—would reduce them to the level of serfs—would deprive them of every real vestige of manly equality, strip them of respect at home and abroad and render them the laughing stock of the governments of the old world. . . .

This was the work of four short years. What could the South expect at the end of another four years! Union for disunion was becoming a Southern necessity.

* * * *

James Buchanan's inaugural address was a labored affair. He spoke with some confidence about the solution of the controversy over slavery in the territories. The simple rule that the will of the majority should govern was a happy conception. Nothing could be fairer than to allow the people of a territory to decide their own destiny for themselves. True, a difference of opinion as to the point of time at which the people of the territory might accept or exclude slavery had developed, but the Supreme Court of the United States was speedily and finally about to settle it. Cheerful submission to this decision would bring to an end the long and bitter controversy and would destroy, at the same time, the sectional parties which that controversy had created. Buchanan then took the oath to preserve, protect, and defend the Constitution. A few days later the Court handed down its decision in the case of Dred Scott of Missouri.[63]

The basic facts regarding the Dred Scott case can be stated with reasonable accuracy. It developed about the person of "a shiftless" St. Louis Negro sold, in 1833, by one Elizabeth Blow to Doctor John Emerson, a surgeon in the United States Army. Emerson carried the Negro first to Fort Armstrong in Illinois and then to Fort Snelling in Wisconsin Territory—regions made free-soil by the Compromise of 1820 and the Northwest Ordinance. Here Scott was married and became the father of two children. In 1838, Emerson returned to St. Louis, where he died in 1843, leaving his property to his wife and daughter. Scott, who was part of the estate, was out of work much of the time and soon fell back on Henry Blow, son of his former owner, for the support of himself and family. To escape this burden and to turn whatever Scott might earn to his own support, Blow, in April, 1846, financed Scott in a suit for his freedom on the grounds that residence in free territory had made him a free man.

This action was not unusual. Already, between 1822 and 1837, eight cases of similar character had been decided in favor of Negroes. That, however, was before the question of slavery in the territories had entered politics. Now everything was different. Scott's case in the state courts dragged through six years. In the first trial, judgment was against Scott. In the second, it was in his favor. Then followed a series of appeals through various state courts and, finally, an agreement to carry the case to the federal courts.

Mrs. Emerson had, in the meantime, moved to Massachusetts and married one Doctor Chaffee, an ardent anti-slavery man. She now transferred Scott to her brother, John F. A. San[d]ford, by fictitious sale, and a group of anti-slavery lawyers engineered a suit for Scott as a citizen of Missouri against Sanford, a citizen of New York, in the United States Circuit Court of Missouri. Sanford, in answer to the suit, denied the jurisdiction of the court on the grounds that Scott was a Negro and therefore not a citizen of Missouri nor entitled to sue in federal courts. This was the celebrated plea in abatement.[64]

In March, 1854, the Missouri court found for Sanford and the case was appealed to the United States Supreme Court on writ of error. The case came up for conference in May. A sharp division of opinion developed at once "upon the point whether the question of the jurisdiction of the lower court could be raised after Sanford had accepted its jurisdiction by pleading over the facts and [after] the case had come to the Supreme Court upon an exception taken in the instructions of the lower court on the facts." A deadlock resulted. Then Justice Nelson suggested a compromise—the case should be reargued "upon the question whether or not the jurisdiction of the lower court was subject to review and, if so, whether or not Scott was a citizen of Missouri." On these terms, the case was argued in December, 1856, and a majority of the Supreme Court agreed to dispose of the case without raising the question of jurisdiction and without discussing the territorial question. Nelson was then asked to prepare the Court's opinion on this basis.

Such an opinion would have removed the case from politics and would have left the status of a slave returned to a slave state to be determined by the courts of that state.[65] At this point, however, Justices McLean and Curtis decided to submit a dissenting opinion covering the whole territorial question. As a result, under pressure from the Southern members, the majority also decided to speak more broadly. Nelson and Greer held back, but Buchanan then brought Greer into line, and the result was the famous Dred Scott decision, delivered by Chief Justice Taney on March 6, 1857.

Taney began with an effort to show that no Negro could be a citizen.[66] To do this, he maintained that citizenship was derived from the federal government. It had never belonged to Negroes, who had been regarded "as beings of an inferior order and altogether unfit to associate with the white race, either in social or political relations." This contention of Taney's was both unsound and unnecessary. The Constitution, inferentially, had left it to the states themselves to determine citizenship; even the right to sue in federal courts on grounds of diverse citizenship depended solely upon state citizenship. Furthermore, the question whether any Negro could be a citizen was not properly before the Court, but only the question whether this particular Negro was a citizen. The Missouri Supreme Court, as the proper body to do so, had already decided that he was not.

The second part of Taney's argument was designed to prove the Court's right to discuss the merits of the case after it had decided that it had no jurisdiction. It is now generally agreed that he succeeded in showing that this was the accepted practice of the Court at that time; but it is also generally agreed that the Court's opinion was nothing more than *obiter dicta* and that to give such an opinion when the public mind was so stirred over the slavery issue showed deplorably bad judgment.

In the third part of his opinion, the Chief Justice insisted that the power of Congress to govern acquired territory was derived from the treaty-making power, not from the power to "make needful rules and regulations respecting the territory and other property of the United States." This power, said

Taney, must be exercised with due respect to the Constitution, which clearly forbids the taking of life, liberty or property without due process of law. Since slaves were property, *in a national* sense, they were automatically protected in the territories. The Missouri Compromise had never been constitutional.

This was flimsy reasoning. Property is whatever the law protects as such and all private property is based upon local law. Slaves were, therefore, property only where the state laws made them so. They carried this status into other states only as interstate reciprocity granted it; and, *vice versa*, slaves made free by residence in other states retained that freedom only as the same interstate reciprocity permitted it. If Illinois and Wisconsin refused interstate comity to Missouri law, then their own laws had no bearing on Dred Scott's condition after he entered the state of Missouri.

To Taney's opinion, McLean and Curtis dissented. They differed in their approach but generally held for Scott's citizenship and the application of Illinois and Wisconsin law in Missouri. Neither rose above the moral or intellectual level set by the Chief Justice. Curtis's assumption that the recognition of Negro citizenship by some states gave the Negro the right to sue in all states was as unsound as Taney's attempt to make slaves nationally property. McLean's denial that the jurisdiction of the lower court was in question was only a clever way of avoiding his own acquiescence in an earlier decision against the right of Negroes to sue in the courts for freedom in a slave state by reason of residence in a free state. (Strader *v.* Graham.) Both parties were intent on arguments, not on truth. Both were supporting positions already assumed. Both saw larger ends to be served than those of the humble Dred Scott. So that when all the verbiage, clustered about the case, is removed, says Professor Hodder, "the only point decided by the judgement of the Court was that the status of a slave, leaving a slave state and subsequently returning to it, was determinable by the courts of that state."

Viewed from the vantage ground of the present, the decision seems to contain little to excite public passions. It had been ren-

dered against the wishes of a reluctant majority which had been
forced to act because McLean and Curtis were determined to
speak at all cost. Why these two insisted on forcing the slavery
question we do not know. Professor Hodder has made bold to
suggest that self-interest dictated the move. McLean was attempting to make political capital out of his opportunity and to
further his chances for the Republican nomination in 1860.
Curtis expected soon to retire to private practice in Boston,
where he had fallen into disfavor by defending the fugitive
slave act of 1850 and calling resistance to it treason. He sought
to regain favor by a public statement on the slavery issue.
Whether these suggestions are valid or not does not matter.
They do help to contradict and disprove the old charge that the
Dred Scott decision was the work of a group of proslavery
men who sought to serve the South through the Court. Neither
Taney nor any of those who took his side was a slaveholder. The
Chief Justice had early freed the slaves he had inherited, and
had, on more than one occasion, expressed his grave condemnation of human bondage. His Southern colleagues on the bench
showed little more of enthusiasm for the institution of slavery.
Their sectional bias stemmed from attachment to state rights.
At its worst the Dred Scott decision was nothing more than "a
fatal error of judgment"—an error for which more than one
group was responsible. As Charles Warren has so aptly said:
"The whirlwind of abuse which swept upon the Court ... [was]
due more largely to misunderstandings of the decision, and to
falsehoods spread relative to Taney's opinion, than to the actual
opinion itself."[67]

Once more facts yielded to passions. Republican newspapers,
led by the New York *Tribune*, turned on Taney and the Court
with distortion and abuse. They declared that the decision was
"entitled to just as much moral weight as would be the judgment of a majority of those congregated in any Washington
bar-room. . . ." "This wicked and false judgment" was the
work of "five slaveholders and two doughfaces" and rendered
the "Constitution of the United States . . . nothing better than
the bulwark of inhumanity and oppression." The Court had at
last completed "the utter subjugation and extermination of all

that remained of the protesting voice of liberty. . . ." It had become "the Court of a political party, and not of the United States." Its decisions had ceased to be binding and "impeachment, not obedience, belong[ed] to it."[68] Western papers took up the cry. "Where will the aggressions of slavery cease?" asked the *Illinois State Journal.* "Freedom and white men are no longer safe," it concluded. The Cincinnati *Daily Commercial* saw slavery advancing on Ohio and "all that [had] been established by legislation or compact since the American Revolution" undone. "There is such a thing as THE SLAVE POWER," it said. "It has marched over and annihilated the boundaries of the States. We are now one great homogeneous slaveholding community."[69]

Not all the press lost its head. A few New York papers, especially the *Times* and the *Herald,* took a conservative stand and deplored the violence of the *Tribune.* Democratic newspapers, as a rule, everywhere defended both the intelligence and the integrity of the Court. But the damage had been done. Republican politicians, even Seward and Lincoln, went on repeating the false charges of a slave-power conspiracy and arousing the fears of common men against insidious foes. Taney and his Court suffered heavily "in the loss of confidence in [their] sound judicial integrity and strictly legal character." Stephen A. Douglas lost even more by the damage done to squatter sovereignty.[70]

* * * *

The practical import of the Dred Scott decision was that any citizen had a right to take his property with him to any territory and to have it protected there. This seemingly ended the controversy over the question raised by the Kansas-Nebraska Act as to whether the people of a territory could limit or prohibit slavery before statehood days. It constituted a body blow at popular sovereignty. What could Stephen A. Douglas say to his Northwestern followers? How could he reconcile the law as interpreted by the Court and his own ardent insistence on the right of the people to rule? On June 12, 1857, he gave his answer. In a speech delivered in Springfield,

Illinois, at the request of the Federal Grand Jury, he frankly accepted the right of the Court to pass on the powers of Congress over slavery in the territories and urged all good citizens to heed its decision. Then, with equal frankness, he insisted that, in a practical sense, the right of Popular Sovereignty had not been impaired. Any citizen had the right to carry his slaves to a territory, but that right necessarily remained "a barren and worthless right unless sustained, protected, and enforced by appropriate police regulations and local legislation, prescribing adequate remedies for its violation. These regulations and remedies . . . necessarily depend[ed] entirely upon the will and wishes of the people of the territory, as they . . . [could] only be prescribed by the local legislatures." Popular Sovereignty and self-government, he therefore concluded, had been sustained and more firmly established by the Court's decision![71]

Such an explanation might have satisfied devoted followers in Illinois and have kept political fences in good order had not affairs in Kansas required a practical trial of conflicting doctrines. Conditions there had become quieter as political necessity for disorder waned, and steps were being taken toward the registration of voters preparatory to the election of a constitutional convention. Buchanan was exceedingly anxious to prevent further conflict or to give Republicans new political ammunition. After much effort, he persuaded Robert J. Walker, born in Pennsylvania but politically seasoned in Mississippi, to accept the governorship. He pledged him unwavering support in securing a fair and honest settlement of all problems. Kansas could be saved for the Democratic Party even though everything indicated that it would become a free state.

Walker found conditions in Kansas highly unfavorable to a quick and satisfactory passage to statehood. Free-state men, under the leadership of Jim Lane and "Governor" Robinson, refused to cooperate either in completing the census or in conducting the election of delegates to the constitutional convention. Their refusal to participate, and a goodly amount of the usual kind of Kansas corrupt voting, resulted in the choice of a proslavery convention and the formation of the notorious Lecomp-

ton Constitution which declared that the "right of property is
. . . higher than any constitutional sanction, and the right of
the owner of a slave . . . is . . . as inviolable as the right of the
owner of any property whatever." The convention then decided
to permit the people to vote only for the constitution with slavery or for the constitution with no slavery. The outcome, as
announced in December, was a triumph for the slavery party
by a vote of over six thousand to less than six hundred. Free-
state men had again refused to act. Bleeding Kansas was still
worth more to Republican politicians than a free state won in
open contest.

President Buchanan, smarting under Southern criticism incident to Walker's meddling in the affairs of the Kansas legislature, and justly skeptical of ever securing a Kansas settlement through the cooperation of all parties, now urged the
admission of Kansas under the Lecompton Constitution.
Roundly he denounced those who had resisted the authority
of the government authorized by Congress. He insisted that
they would have voted against the constitution in whatever
form submitted, "not upon a consideration of merits . . ., but
simply because they have ever resisted the authority of the
government authorized by Congress." By the Dred Scott decision, Kansas was "at this moment as much a slave state as
Georgia or South Carolina." The only way to peace and quiet
was a speedy admission to statehood.[72]

Such a course of action Stephen A. Douglas, now about to
begin a campaign for re-election to the Senate, could not support. The steady rise of northern Illinois to political strength
and the settled opposition to slavery expansion thoroughout
the whole Northwest made it impossible for him to go beyond
the popular-sovereignty doctrine which, in practice, was making free territory. He must hold to the right of the people to
settle their own problems; he might profess indifference as to
how they settled them; but he knew what his constituency had
willed without knowing it: *that the decision must be for freedom.* Douglas had to choose between political suicide in Illinois
and the possibility of political assassination by the administration. He did not hesitate. As soon as he "discovered the trick

by which the people were to be cheated," he took his stand firmly against the President's course. "By God, Sir," he is reported to have said, "I made James Buchanan, and by God, Sir, I will unmake him." Back in Washington he quickly completed the break and joined hands with his late Republican foes to check the admission of Kansas under the Lecompton Constitution.[73]

The bitter struggle of the ensuing weeks saw all the force of party control turned against Douglas. The personnel of the Committee on Territories of which he was chairman was so changed as to leave him in a minority; the Democratic newspapers of Illinois which supported him were deprived of official advertising and post-office printing; pressure was brought on local officeholders to denounce him and foster meetings for the same purpose. He was to be read out of the party. He was to be destroyed politically. But Douglas more than held his own in Congressional debate. The doctrine of self-government was still a force to be reckoned with.[74] As politicians hesitated, local Democrats in the Northwest rallied to Douglas's support.[75] Republicans gave reluctant praise and sufficient votes to check the Administration's plans and to carry a compromise measure by which the people of Kansas were permitted the following August to reject the whole scheme. Buchanan was furious. Douglas spoke confidently of his re-election in the coming Senatorial contest in Illinois. But those who thought back over the strange political disorders of the past twelve years must have trembled a bit as they remembered the death of the Whig Party, the rapid rise and fall of the Liberty, the Free-Soil, and the Know-Nothing Parties, and the mushroom-like growth of Republican strength on emotional issues. They must have realized that a new political crisis was at hand.

When Kansas rejected the Lecompton Constitution in August, 1857, the danger of slavery expansion into the territories was at an end. The original reason for the creation and maintenance of the Republican Party no longer existed. The Douglas popular-sovereignty doctrine, if applied as he insisted it should be, meant free territory and free states. Kansas had proven that beyond question. Already some Republican leaders had begun to realize that the party must have a broader base and a new leadership if it were to survive. Thousands with no other political roof over their heads and no other hope for the spoils of office were vitally concerned. It was becoming more difficult every day to maintain the emotional tension on which the party had been built. Bleeding Kansas was losing its appeal. Reaction was about due. The rift in the Democratic Party, therefore, had been a veritable godsend. Even the New York *Tribune* lauded Douglas to the skies. Anson Burlingame and Schuyler Colfax called on him and boldly hinted at Republican support for the presidency in 1860. Others, including Greeley, insisted that Douglas should not be opposed for re-election to the Senate. By proper treatment he might be brought into the Republican fold. The leadership and program so necessary for Republican existence and expansion might thus be secured.[76]

For Illinois Republicans the situation was serious. It was, as J. K. Dubois wrote Lyman Trumbull, "asking too much for human nature to bear, to now surrender to Judge Douglas . . ., to quietly let him step foremost in our ranks and make us all take back seats. . . . When Judge D. is made our Leader, with all his sins yet unrepented for, the party is scattered and disbanded in Illinois." They were willing and anxious for Douglas to split his own party, but they wanted to reap the benefits, not leave them to the Little Giant. Their leaders, therefore, were greatly alarmed lest they should be obliged to receive Douglas into the Republican Party. It was discouraging, wrote C. H. Ray from Chicago, to see all their hard work resulting only "in keeping a warm place for him whom we all hate." It was a matter of party, not just one of principles. Slavery in Kansas was no longer the major interest. J. D. Carton told Trumbull just that in so many words:[77]

Now I do not think that any sane man on earth thinks that all the presidents and all the coherents and all the Congresses, and all the supreme courts and all the slave holders on earth, with all the constitutions which could be drawn, can ever make Kansas a slave state. No, there has been no such expectation and I do not believe desire on the part of the President to make it a slave state, but as he had already been pestered to death with it, he resolved to make it a state as soon as possible and thus be rid of it and let them fight it out as they like. . . . Now I expect they will carry the abominable thing but it wont make it a slave state, nor will one fifth of the Democratic party in the Northwest ever support it. [But] there will not be a disposition with those who oppose it to affiliate with the Republican party. . . . The Republican party wont let them if they would. See the course pursued by the Republican papers in Chicago & elsewhere denouncing Douglas & all his friends . . . for fear they may be left without a party. . . . To talk of such men being anxious to defeat the measure above all things is a mockery. They would sacrifice it a thousand times rather than forget a party advantage. . . .

Against such a background, Abraham Lincoln, on June 17, 1858, arose to address the Illinois State Republican Convention which had that day named him as its candidate for the Senate to oppose Stephen A. Douglas. His speech was largely an attempt to justify the action of his party in putting forward a candidate. He began with what he always insisted was a prophecy:

"A house divided against itself cannot stand." I believe this government cannot endure permanently half slave and half free. I do not expect the Union to be dissolved; I do not expect the house to fall; but I do expect it will cease to be divided. It will become all one thing, or all the other. Either the opponents of slavery will arrest the further spread of it, and place it where the public mind shall rest in the belief that it is in the course of ultimate extinction, or its advocates will push it forward till it shall become alike lawful in all the States, old as well as new, North as well as South.

Then followed a brief recital of events, beginning with the Nebraska bill and ending with the Dred Scott decision, which, as Lincoln interpreted them, indicated the steady encroachment of slavery on free territory—events so neatly spaced and so cleverly fitting into each other that all seemed to be the result of a common plan or draft drawn up before the first blow was struck. It was, therefore, reasonable to conclude that "we may, ere long, see . . . another Supreme Court decision, declaring that the Constitution of the United States does not permit a *State* to exclude slavery from its limits." That was all slavery now lacked "of being alike lawful in all the states."

"Unless the power of the present political dynasty" was broken that Court decision was "probably coming." The issue was a practical one. The question was whether a right system or a wrong one should triumph. The people of Illinois could not leave such a decision in the hands of a man who did not care whether slavery be voted down or voted up. The divided house would become all free only by giving over government to a party and to leaders who believed that slavery was wrong and should be put on the road to ultimate extinction.

Here was a clear justification, on purely moral grounds, for the continued existence of the Republican Party under its own leadership. Here was an anti-slavery program vague and elastic enough to satisfy every element in a party which contained all degrees of opinion from abolitionism to simple non-extension. Here was the extreme partisan appeal to un-founded fears clothed in dignified legal and Scriptural language and softened with homely humor. Here was a political contest being elevated to the eternal conflict between right and wrong. Compromise on either party or issues was unthinkable. The Republicans would be in at the kill.

In the speech-making which followed and which culminated in the now famous Lincoln-Douglas debates, Lincoln added little to his original positions. Under Douglas's prodding, he "explained" the meaning of his words, but in such ways as always to require further "explanation" and to leave generations of biographers still "explaining." He denounced the Dred Scott decision for declaring that a Negro could not be a citizen, yet declared that he himself was not in favor of Negro citizenship. He insisted on equal rights for all, yet bluntly disclaimed the doctrine of social equality for the races. He constantly raised the moral issue but refused to assume any responsibility for practical action. He would leave things as they were. His real purpose and accomplishment was to lay bare the fundamental inconsistency of Douglas's position as a sound exponent of Western political and moral opinion and as a loyal member of the existing Democratic Party! He forced Douglas, at Freeport, to repeat his formula for upholding the Dred Scott decision and, at the same time, preventing slavery in the territories through unfriendly legislation. He made him appear thoroughly indifferent to great moral issues.

For all this Greeley and his Eastern friends were quite unappreciative. To Joseph Medill, Greeley wrote:[78]

You have repelled Douglas, who might have been conciliated and attached to our side . . . and instead of helping us in other states, you have thrown a load upon us that may probably break us down. . . . Now go ahead and fight it through. . . . [Lincoln's] first Springfield speech (at the Convention) was in the right key; his Chicago speech was bad; and I fear his new Springfield speech is worse. . . . You have got your Elephant—you would have him—now shoulder him! He is not very heavy after all. . . .

But Greeley, as usual, had missed the true measure of the man and of events. The ability to match strength with Douglas, whose fight was a national event, made Lincoln also a national figure. It supplied the Republican Party with a new leadership, uncontaminated by participation in earlier struggles tainted by fanaticism—a leadership resident in the greater Northwest where the party's real strength was to be found. A new slavery formula, conservative in wording, deadly in its implications, had been given that party. A voice, capable of expressing the common man's moral convictions without demanding from him the action necessary for reform, had spoken. An old-line Whig, praising Henry Clay and opening the way for the adoption of a hard-headed capitalistic program on lands and internal improvements and tariffs, had appeared in Douglas's own neighborhood and had proven himself worthy of the Little Giant's steel. The Republican Party was making substantial progress.

CHAPTER SIXTEEN

THE LAST CRISIS

T
HE people of the South had not been indifferent to Douglas's conduct. He represented in many ways what they considered the fair and sound Northern element in the Democratic Party. Many of them had favored him as the presidential candidate in 1856 and, after his failure, had been looking forward to his success in 1860. His break with the Administration over the Lecompton Constitution and the clearer statement of his principles in the Illinois senatorial campaign had left them in a more or less confused state of mind. Many denounced him as a slinking traitor; a few approved his course; others sadly regretted the whole affair but were willing, for party reasons, to forgive and forget. In the main, Lincoln had guessed correctly. Democrats, North and South, were no longer of one mind. If Democratic politicians could be forced to talk, they would quickly uncover the widening rifts in their party.

When Alexander H. Stephens urged his colleague, Howell Cobb, to sustain Douglas, Cobb indignantly refused and insisted that this was a deeper and more important question than the election of Douglas.[1] It was a question of maintaining the Democratic Party upon its true principles. "Whilst upon some of the old issues," he said, Douglas made strong professions, he, Cobb, could "see nothing in his course upon new issues to inspire hope and confidence in him. . . ." He wished that both Douglas and Lincoln could be beaten. The Richmond *Enquirer*, on the other hand, did not think that Douglas's defection amounted to much.[2] He was honest but mistaken in his break with the Administration. It would have been vastly wiser, of course, to have admitted Kansas under the Lecompton Constitution and then to have allowed her to abolish slavery, but Douglas had in the past "borne the brunt of many battles and struggled manfully in the cause of [the] party and in defense of the rights of the South." He deserved re-election to the Senate. Contrary to all Lincoln lore, the *Enquirer* staunchly defended Douglas's Freeport speech and the doctrine of unfriendly local legislation as a means by which the people of a territory could prevent the introduction of slavery:[3]

> The Illinois statesman never did better service to the constitutional rights of the South, than will be effected by following up the frank and manly suggestion of that speech. It repeats, from an authoritative source, what the "Enquirer" has persistently held up to the attention of Southern men—viz.: that the present state of Federal legislation is entirely inadequate for the thorough and effectual protection of slave property in the Territories.

This, however, it declared, was not new doctrine. Orr of South Carolina had stated it in even greater detail in the debates on the question.[4] Slavery, he had asserted, was dependent on friendly local legislation. It could not exist without it. And what if the people of a territory refused to pass such legislation? What was the remedy? "None, sir," Orr answered. "If the majority of the people are opposed to the institution, and if they do not desire it engrafted upon their territory, all they have to do is simply to decline to pass laws in the territorial legislation for its protection, and then it is as well excluded as if the power was invested in the territorial legislature, and exercised by them, to prohibit it. . . ." Jefferson Davis, in his Bangor speech, had taken the same position:[5]

> If the inhabitants of any Territory should refuse to enact such laws and police regulations as would give security to their property . . . it would be rendered more or less valueless. . . . In the case of property in the labor of man . . . the insecurity would be so great that the owner could not ordinarily retain it. . . . The owner would be practically debarred . . . from taking slave property into a Territory. . . . So much for the oft-repeated fallacy of forcing slavery upon any community. . . .

Not until Douglas explained his views more fully in an article in *Harper's Magazine*, September, 1859, did the *Enquirer* part ways with him.[6] His insistence that a territorial legislature could "rightfully and legally . . . exclude the introduction of slave property . . . or abrogate the right to hold slaves already introduced; and that neither the Congress, the Executive or the Judiciary of the United States can rightfully intervene to protect slave property . . .," was too much for that newspaper. Then his doctrines became much worse than even those of Seward.[7] His essay was "an incendiary document, calculated to produce nothing less than a repetition of the anarchy and bloodshed which has lately disgraced the soil of our territories."

Many newspapers in other parts of the South took similar positions. The New Orleans *Daily Delta* came to Douglas's support because he was a Democrat.[8] It sided with him, *not* against the Administration but against the Black Republicans. In his Freeport doctrine, it declared, his views "of fact and practicability singularly coincide[d] with those expressed by Mr. Calhoun and some other extreme Southern statesmen, Jeff Davis among them. . . ." The *Delta* denied that Douglas had enunciated any doctrine inconsistent with the principles of the Dred Scott decision. What Senator Douglas had said did not express a new principle, or any principle at all, as a rule of action, either in Congress or the territories.[9] It was "simply the statement of a legal position which [could] not be controverted, and which was long ago enunciated by leading Southern men, as the basis of their demands for affirmative legislation on the part of Congress, for the protection of the rights of slaveholders in the Territories." The *Daily Crescent* and the New Orleans *Bee* both infinitely preferred Douglas to Lincoln—"an out-and-out Black Republican and Sewardite."[10] The Democratic Party could not afford to shelve Douglas. Should he fall, he would not fall alone, "but like Samson of old" would "pull down his enemies with him." Other leading papers of the section, including the Mississippi *Free Trader*, the Hinds County *Gazette* (Miss.), the Memphis *Ledger*, the Montgomery (Ala.) *Confederation*, the *Southern Advocate* (Ala.), the Augusta (Ga.) *Daily Constitutionalist*, and the Georgia *Telegraph*, stood by Douglas for the sake of party harmony. They were sick of Kansas and the strife it had been used to produce. They were in the same mood as J. H. Hammond, who wrote: "Damn Kansas forever and ever. I hope never to come within minie rifle range of the infernal thing again."[11] But most of them also wavered a bit, not at Douglas's answer to Lincoln at Freeport, but at the *Harper's Magazine* article.[12] Even the loyal New Orleans *Daily Delta* considered his doctrine as there developed only a short cut to all the ends of Black Republicanism.[13] The time had come to think first of sectional interests and then of party.

Sympathy with Douglas, however, was only one part of the Southern story. Many editors and leaders, who might claim equal attachment to the Democratic Party, broke definitely and permanently with him when the Lecompton issue first arose. The Freeport doctrine added to their number. Some of them fondly hoped for his destruction in Illinois. The Charleston *Mercury* announced that it considered him the great leader in Congress of the Black Republican cause in Kansas.[14] His speeches in the Senate were "the clap-trap of a demagogue"; he himself was "a self-seeking renegade, truckling to the anti-slavery sentiments of his people." The South had been betrayed; it could no longer count on Northern Democrats. It must find some remedy outside the Democratic Party. The *Southern Reveille* (Miss.) was even more violent.[15] Douglas's defection "was so gross, so shameful a betrayal of confidence and the trust of his friends, that though he should wash in the waters of the Jordan" he could not cleanse himself of suspicion. He was to be feared "ten thousand times more . . . than a thousand Lincolns." "Apostate" and "traitor" cried the Montgomery *Advertiser and Gazette;*[16] "Prince of Demagogues," snarled Benjamin H. Hill.[17] If Douglas was to be received back into the Democratic fold and foisted upon the South as the only man who could be elected in 1860, then, said the Columbus (Ga.) *Sun,*[18] "give us Know-Nothingism, Black Republicanism —anything before Democracy. If we are to have a Republican President, let us have an out and out 'dyed in the wool' one, that we may know and prepare to fend off the blow . . . rather than one who, while he holds out the hand of pretended friendship, stabs us to the heart with a dagger which he has concealed beneath the cloak of his hypocrisy."

The deeper significance of what was at stake in the turmoil which Douglas had raised was suggested now and then by some more thoughtful editor. John Forsyth of the Mobile *Daily Register* warned his readers that:[19]

> The inevitable consequence of the triumph of Mr. Douglas will be, either that the political character of the Democratic party as the great conservator of the constitutional rights of the South will be essentially demoralized, or that the party will be completely broken up and denationalized.

He saw that Douglas was engaged in an attempt to modify the complexion of the Democratic Party so as to adapt it to the increasing intensity of the anti-slavery sentiment of the North. By defeating the Administration and the Southern Democrats in Congress on a question directly involving the rights of the South, Douglas had won his re-election in Illinois and made his doctrines those of the Northwestern Democracy. This had placed him in a position where he could offer his party, in the next presidential campaign, the alternative of probable success by accepting him and his platform and abandoning the South, or destruction as a national party. The South could either yield for the sake of a party victory or resolve herself into a minority sectional party! Either choice would mark the beginning of the end!

*   *   *   *

Southern state rights men who had already decided that secession was inevitable took new heart as Democratic troubles increased. Since the disastrous movement of 1850, they had been unable to recover lost ground. The effort to stir disunion sentiment in the campaign of 1856 had failed. Even in South Carolina the threat lacked something of the ring of reality and the National Democrats under Orr's leadership kept control.[20] Rhett and the *Mercury*, meanwhile, had fallen on evil days. To political rejection had been added financial difficulties which restrained the expression of unpopular opinions and soon put the paper on the market. The demand for the reopening of the African slave trade, fostered by L. W. Spratt of the Charleston *Standard*, brought further confusion to the state.[21] The argument that more and cheaper Negroes would "diffuse the slave population as much as possible and thus secure in the whole community the motives of self-interest for its support" fitted the logic employed by the advocates of Southern unity, but it did not coincide with the interests of the border states or the moral concepts of all those who upheld state rights. The radicals were, therefore, badly divided on the issue and their leaders as badly confused. Rhett at first approved, then drew back as division developed. Governor James H. Adams fell in with the movement, but James H. Hammond, newly elected senator, joined the opposition. The conflict spread to other states. Spratt carried his program to the Southern Commercial Conventions of the next few years and forced the issue and the cleavage it produced, upon the whole South. William L. Yancey and James D. B. DeBow became ardent supporters of the movement; Roger Pryor and Edmund Ruffin opposed. The New Orleans *Daily Delta* "would reopen the African slave trade that every white man might have a chance to make himself owner of one or more negroes," but the Richmond *Enquirer* declared that "if a dissolution of the Union is to be followed by the revival of the slave trade, Virginia had better consider whether the South of a Northern Confederacy would not be far more preferable for her than the North of a Southern Confederacy."[22]

While these distractions were at their height, Douglas began his revolt against Buchanan. Southern radicals sensed their opportunity. Strife among those who still adhered to the national parties promised sectional gains. Almost with one accord, those who were calculating the value of the Union turned toward Montgomery, Alabama, where the Commercial Convention of 1858 was to meet. When that body assembled, it was not a commercial convention at all; it was a gathering of disunionists. The *Daily Confederation* declared that "every form and shape of political malcontent was there present, ready to assent to any project having for its end a dissolution of the Union, immediate, unconditional, final."[23] United action failed because of division over the reopening of the African slave trade, but Yancey, Rhett, and Ruffin there caught the vision of a United South and a divided Democracy. A few weeks later Ruffin and Yancey launched their *League of United Southerners,* which was to be composed of committees of safety organized all over the cotton states to "fire the Southern heart, instruct the Southern mind, give courage to each other, and at the proper moment, by one organized concert action, . . . precipitate the cotton states into a revolution."[24] Then, in July, 1859, Yancey and Rhett began a joint speaking campaign in South Carolina to unite the South on a platform of action announced in the *Mercury* in October:[25]

1. The next legislature should issue a declaration of rights of the South, and announce its decision to vote for no candidate for president who did not distinctly affirm them.

2. If the Charleston Convention affirmed these unequivocally, it should be supported.

3. If the Democratic candidate on such a platform should be defeated, the legislature at its regular session following the election, should recall its members of Congress and invite the cooperation of its sister states looking to their common safety.

4. If the Charleston Convention should refuse to grant the explicit recognition demanded, the Southern delegates should withdraw and have a convention and candidate of their own.

5. If such candidate was elected the South was safe.

6. If he was defeated, the course outlined under (3) should be followed.

Economic factors aided the radicals. The growing demand of the North and Northwest for homestead legislation, internal improvements, and protective tariffs, more and more assumed the form of a sectional program. Northerners spoke of Southern opposition to these demands as interference with the people's rights and evidence of slave-power conspiracy. "It will be seen with what hostility and contempt Southern Democrats treat the project of giving a portion of the public lands, belonging to the people, to the people," growled the Illinois *State Journal.*[26] "Mr. Grow's amendment," it said in speaking of the same legislative effort,[27] "looks for the basis of the government to a yeomanry, and not to a landed aristocracy. It prefers the farmer to the planter. . . ." Every human being has "an inalienable right to a reasonable share and a proportionate part" of the public land, declared an Ohio Congressman, "as much as he has a right to inflate his lungs with . . . air . . . or to drink . . . water. . . ." The action of "the bogus Democracy" in denying Northwestern men this "innate privilege" was nothing short of tyranny. When President Buchanan later checked the effort with his veto, the Dubuque (Iowa) *Herald* blurted out: "Last Saturday the old reprobate, who sits in the Presidential Chair at Washington, *vetoed the Homestead Bill.* . . . The slave propagandists demanded that the bill should be vetoed, and their pliant tool was swift to obey them. Let the pimps and hirelings of the old sinner defend this last act of his, if they dare."[28]

Southern spokesmen held their own in the controversy. "Congress has no more right to give away the public property than it has to set fire to the Capitol," retorted the Georgia *Telegraph*.[29] The cry for the "landless" came from the same throats that "bawled" for legislation against slavery. Both demands were at war "with sound general policy" and the "true spirit and genius of a free republican government." This Northern drive for "LAND—LAND, honestly acquired if possible,—if not, LAND!" said the Richmond *Enquirer*, was simply the old vandal spirit of ambition and avarice inherited from our Anglo-Germanic forefathers, and it constituted the real motive back of the desire to destroy slavery and to achieve a purely political sectional predominance.[30] Free homesteads meant only homes for abolitionists. Better that the "territories should remain a waste, a howling wilderness" than that they should be so settled.[31]

The growing Northern demand for increased tariffs, accentuated by the panic of 1857 and the hard times thereafter, brought like reactions. The Charleston *Mercury* reminded its readers that the South had been paying tribute to the North for thirty years.[32] Patriots who had thrown off the British yoke had tamely submitted to the impositions of their associates in a common government. Slavery agitation was the inevitable sequence of such submission. "Let the South rise up in her majesty and vindicate her right to her property from uncon-

stitutional exactions of the North. . . ." The appeal met with
less response than such appeals had met in earlier time. Diversification of economic effort had weakened the free-trade element. But the Commercial Convention at Knoxville in 1857
saw the tariff issue again brought forward and Southerners
like James H. Hammond resorting to the sectional appeal
when new measures were suggested. The move for direct trade
with Europe gained strength from the revival of the issue.

River and harbor improvements and railway routes to the
Pacific also provided subjects for sectional antagonisms. Northwestern papers blamed the South for all of Buchanan's unfavorable acts. "The President has finally followed the example of his master, and shown his cloven foot," railed the
Sandusky *Commercial Register*,[33] when Buchanan declared his
intention to veto all river and harbor appropriations. "Millions to subjugate Kansas," it concluded, "but not one cent to
relieve the internal necessities of the country." This same paper insisted that the President's movements in regard to the
Pacific Railroads showed "an uncompromising and exclusive
committal to Southern interests. . . ." It was certain that the
North would never assist in building "a mammoth national
work" from "whose benefits" it would be excluded.[34]

Southerners countered with the assertion that the North
showed its lack of respect for the provisions of the Constitution
by its demands for unauthorized internal improvements and
by its "disgraceful" attacks on statesmen for their "manly and
unselfish" votes against such measures.[35] They charged that
the South paid more than her share of taxes and received less
than her share of disbursements.[36] The North had an annual
advantage of more than forty million dollars. Its plan was to
reduce the South to a mere colony—dependent and suppliant.[37]
Some writers went so far as to declare that the effects of secession would be to transfer the energies of industry, population,
commerce and wealth, from the North to the South. They saw
Northern wealth to depend largely on its union with the
wealth-producing states. These extremists believed "the whole
government . . . drifting fast upon the rocks of Disunion."[38]
The last vestiges of sympathy between the sections were dis-

appearing. North and South had already become emphatically two peoples.[39] The interests of the two sections were antagonistic. Southern men could have no confidence in any man north of Mason and Dixon's line.[40] A dissolution of the Union was inevitable. "The battle between the North and South," wrote Samuel C. Elam to J. H. Hammond, "has [already] been fought, and the North is the victor. . . . A few more years and the preponderance of power in the Senate and House will be so greatly in favor of the non-slaveholding interests that the Federal legislation between West and East on protective tariffs and internal improvements will bear insupportably heavy upon the cotton growing states. . . . I see no escape then but *independence out of the Union*."[41] "When the curtain falls over the campaign of 1860," prophesied the Mississippi *Free Trader*, "it will hide only the victor and the dead."[42]

The radicals, however, were ahead of the main current. Union sentiment was still strong among the rank and file. In July, 1859, the New Orleans *Daily Crescent* commented on the "queer fashion now in vogue, and followed by quite a large and respectable class of Southern men generally and Southern journalists"—the fashion "of deprecating the agitation of the slavery issues, and proscribing the discussion of these vital questions as being mischievous and injurious policy. . . ."[43] Others testified to the fact that the noisy advocates of disunion were few and feeble in comparison with the overpowering odds against them.[44] Edmund Ruffin bitterly complained, in August, 1858, that "scarcely a dozen men in Virginia . . . will now even speak openly, much less act, in defense of the South to the extent that was avowed very generally a year or two ago." Under existing circumstances, he saw "no use in attempting to collect auxiliaries or to make any arrangement for action."[45] Even Jefferson Davis was sure that this great country would continue united. He compared the "trifling politicians" who talked of disunion to the mosquitoes "around the ox," able to annoy but never to wound or kill. He praised "the common interests" and the "common sentiment of nationality which beat in every American bosom" and was certain that the good sense and good feeling of the people would avert any catastrophe.[46]

The reasons for union sentiment were quite apparent. In the first place, few Southerners had any genuine material interest in whether Kansas became a free or a slave state.[47] Careful observers testified to the indifference of the people and the feeling that Southern politicians were fighting for a shadow. Kansas could not possibly be made a slave state.[48] Secondly, most Southerners were heartily sick of the constant turmoil and agitation. The Southern fire-eater was a false prophet. His only service was to nourish Northern extremists. "Not an extravagant, foolish sentiment uttered in the delirium of passion, by some half-witted, crack-brained politician in the slave states," said the Tuscaloosa (Ala.) *Monitor*, "but it is eagerly caught up by the whole pack of yelping screamers of the North and paraded forth in staring capitals as the sentiments of the South!"[49] Thus sectionalism North was strengthened by sectionalism South; the designing demagogues were given powerful weapons for mischief. The time had come to refute the false notion that only those who always denounced the North and urged the South to resent insults were loyal Southerners. "No sadder mistake was ever made," said the *Republican Banner and Nashville Whig*, "than that of the Southern people who place their reliance in the fire-eating, disunion-plotting demagogues.[50] No more terrible calamity could befall the South than the rupture with the North." The true test of Southern devotion was not hatred of the North but devotion to the Union.

In the third place, many prominent Southern leaders had become convinced that the South could best achieve her great purposes within the Union. "The South is & will be henceforth nearly united & we can always divide the North & govern it essentially," declared James H. Hammond.[51] ". . . we can whip them *in the Union* & the attempt to do it, will only the better prepare us to kick them out of it, if we fail."[52] His idea was "to avoid faction language & extremeism." Nine hundred and ninety nine out of every thousand of the voters and "49 in every 50 of the substantial & influential men of the South," he insisted, were "for the Union until it pinches."[53] The Richmond *Enquirer* supported Hammond's position and pointed out that *independence* from the present government meant only *dependence* on European governments for protection and prosperity. The Southern states would become mere "cotton" colonies of European nations. If her interests were regarded and her institutions respected, the South would do well to remain in the Union.[54]

A fourth reason for the conservative temper of the South was the fact that the region was prosperous. Crops generally were good and prices satisfactory. The panic of 1857 did not affect the planters except as New York banks were unable to honor sterling bills or New York drafts drawn in payment for cotton.[55] In spite of supposed wrongs, the "Southern people . . . still enjoy[ed] their lands and negroes." "For ten years," said the Dallas *Gazette*, "their produce has commanded higher and more regular prices than they ever did before. . . ."[56] "Could any sane man believe," it asked, "[that] they will risk the blessings they enjoy for the purpose of encouraging measures that may lead to civil war, because enthusiasts or demagogues tell them to gird up their armour and fight against anticipated evils, or in favor of a string of abstractions so contradictory and impracticable that it would puzzle the shrewdest metaphysician of the age to expound them?" The Mobile *Daily Register* took a like view. If the South would present a solid front, one determined will, it could force new and stronger guarantees for slavery. "But will any sensible man undertake to tell us," it asked, "that the South can be aroused upon any existing issue, with cotton at 13 cents, and negroes at $1,500, with lands rising in value, planters with pockets full of money and merchants prospering?"[57]

Perhaps also the very lack of unity among the Southern States themselves had something to do with their staunch adherence to the Union. Division over the question of reopening the African slave trade was only the latest manifestation of a growing difference in attitude toward slavery between the cotton states and the border states.[58] Have "the old States of the South," asked the New Orleans *Daily Delta*, "manifested the same broad, earnest and reliable devotion to slavery, to the increase of the power, resources and defensive means of this institution, to the enlargement and grandeur of the South, that should invite our cordial confidence and co-operation, and enlist that ardent fraternity and congeniality of purpose and feeling which should animate those who fight under the same flag and for the same cause?"[59] The *Delta* charged those states, instead, with having opposed and prevented the annexation of Cuba and the passage of protective duties for sugar. It denounced South Carolina, in particular, for having nullified the tariff laws and for now attempting to protect her own poor cotton lands from competition with those of the Southwest by the exclusion of additional slave labor from the country. Its neighbor, the *Daily Crescent*, called attention to the fact that slavery was rapidly passing in the border states.[60] Delaware was little more a slave state than Vermont; Maryland was "well nigh abolitionized"; St. Louis was in the hands of Free-Soilers; the anti-slavery forces had elected John Letcher governor of Virginia; the strength of slavery was gradually but surely being sapped in Kentucky. These states were rapidly selling their slaves to the Lower South and becoming Northern in their outlook. The *Crescent* would, therefore, forbid further interstate slave trade. It would drop the squabbles over worthless territorial abstractions and concentrate the efforts of the cotton South on holding the border states to Southern institutions and values. The South would be wiser if it secured what it had and recognized the cold fact that the territories were lost. Yet here they were, divided upon impractical issues, denouncing Douglas, the only man in the nation friendly to the South who stood anything like a good chance of beating Seward in 1860; here they were permitting the border states to become slaveless areas through sales to the lower South. Mere party designations should be dropped. The abolition threat suggested unity for a people who, in the end, would all float or all sink in the same boat.

As the summer of 1859 wore on, it became increasingly apparent that conservative men and attitudes dominated the South. Bitter opposition had already developed to the *League of United Southerners* and it had made little headway; praise of the union was growing bolder and more frequent.[61] A few writers had even begun to question whether the Republican Party was an abolition party and carried a direct threat to the South.[62] They were thoroughly cognizant of the new conservative trend in Republican thinking. The prospect for committing the South to positive action in 1860 appeared to be steadily on the wane. Yancey and Rhett and Ruffin were justifiably discouraged. The people were not awake to their danger.

Then, on October 16, the whole situation began suddenly to change. When darkness settled down on the quiet Maryland hills that night, a little band of silent, determined men left the farmhouse at which they had been secretly gathering for the past few weeks and turned down the road toward Harpers Ferry. Under the long gray shawls which they wore, they carried rifles, christened in Kansas, "Beecher's Bibles." Ahead of them went an old farm wagon loaded with hand pikes recently fashioned in New England blacksmith shops. Their leader was the grim avenger, John Brown, Kansas battle-scarred, who carried according to Wendell Phillips, "letters of marque from God." They had come with vague plans for seizing the government arsenal at the Ferry and stirring the Negro slaves of the surrounding countryside to rebellion against their "hated" masters. Abolitionists had talked long enough. The hour for action had struck.

The effort was a pitiful failure. The sleepy little village of Harpers Ferry was thrown into turmoil for a day; a few unoffending citizens lost their lives; most of the invaders were killed or captured; Brown himself, critically wounded, was seized, tried, and hanged for treason, murder, and inciting slaves to rebellion. The slaves of Virginia and of the farther South remained quietly at their tasks.

The importance of John Brown's raid—a mere fiasco—however, cannot be measured in terms of its childish conception and its hopelessly inadequate execution. More important than anything which happened at Harpers Ferry were the reactions of men, North and South, to what they read into the events there. In the North the almost necessary first reaction, among all but fanatics, was disapproval. Brown's action was too extreme, too violent. The more conservative spokesmen were quick to see the relation between the talk of Seward and Greeley and Lincoln and the action of Brown. The doctrines of the irrepressible conflict and the higher law led inevitably to violence. Brown was a "madman," but the irresponsible orators were traitors.[63] Republican leaders also drew back. The growing hope for success in 1860 must not be jeopardized by such actions. The attempt to connect their party "with Old Brown's mad outbreak" was "a necessity of the slave Democracy"; but the real responsibility, insisted the New York *Tribune*, belonged to those who "sustained the Border Ruffian Pro-Slavery war against Free labor in Kansas." Brown was the fruit of the violence and injustice of Bleeding Kansas.[64]

Northern radicals, on the other hand, did not hesitate to put their stamp of approval on Brown's efforts. Emerson wished that men had "health enough to know virtue" when they saw it and "not cry with the fools, 'madman,' when a hero pass[ed]." He referred to Brown as a "new saint awaiting his martyrdom, and who, if he shall suffer, will make the gallows glorious like the cross." Thoreau saw Brown as "an angel of light" and foretold the day when poets and painters and historians would record his deed as one to be set alongside the Landing of the Pilgrims and the signing of the Declaration of Independence. "Saint John the Just," Louisa May Alcott called him! "The noble John Brown's example," the Reverend George B. Cheever labelled his act.[65]

Gradually also the real attitude of the anti-slavery man and the more advanced Republican began to emerge. Hatred of slavery and slaveholders unconsciously altered opinions and drew a sharp line between what Brown had tried to do and the way in which he had done it. Ultimate approval of purpose and motives was inevitable. The New York *Tribune* was not inclined "by one reproachful word [to] disturb the bloody shrouds wherein John Brown and his compatriots [were] sleeping. They dared and died for what they felt to be right. . . . Let their epitaphs remain unwritten until the not distant day when no slave shall clank his chains in the shades of Monticello or the graves of Mount Vernon."[66] The inference was clear. John Brown had had the courage to do what weaker men wanted to do but dared not. The "disinterestedness and consistent devotion to the rights of human nature" which had "prompted his . . . desperate undertaking" had elevated him to the position of a hero.[67] The results would be good. John Brown had "loosened the roots of the slave system."[68] "The end of slavery in Virginia and the Union [was] ten years nearer than it seemed a few weeks ago."[69] Yes, John Brown dead was verily a power. Men should be "reverently grateful for the privilege of living in a world rendered noble by the daring of heroes, the suffering of martyrs,—among whom let none doubt that History will accord an honored niche to Old John Brown."[70]

The Harpers Ferry Insurrection stirred the South even more violently than it did the North. Reactions were not uniform, but they did reveal new depths. Something more vital, more basic, had been touched. Physical invasion and the stirring of servile insurrection, even when attempted by a handful of men, were no trivial matters in the setting of the past few years.[71] "The public mind" rolled and tossed "like the storm-whipped billows of an enraged sea." Men wanted to know who was behind the movement. Who supplied the money with which the guns and ammunitions were purchased?[72] The South had "heretofore disregarded the raving of Northern fanatics because they believed such madness to be merely a pecuniary speculation." Harpers Ferry, however, proved that fanaticism meant more than words. The irrepressible conflict was to be waged to its bitter end. The people of the South could now see "the destiny which await[ed] them in this Union, under the control of a sectional anti-slavery party in the free states."[73] If Brown had succeeded, "out of the ashes of our fair Republic would have risen another Saint Domingo." Virginia's "soil would have reeked with human gore . . . and the torch [would have been] applied . . . in the numerous and well worked mines of the entire South."[74] No one should be surprised at Brown's act; it was a logical step in a developing program.

Reaction to Northern comment was equally sharp. Unfortunately, it was the extreme opinion which attracted attention and was widely quoted. The Richmond *Enquirer* justified this

on the grounds that while only the few blurted out such sentiments, thousands of others applauded or sat silent. It cited
the crowds that listened to Wendell Phillips and gave their
approbation. It warned its readers that these people were far
more important to the South than the conservatives, for they
were the ones who were "fanning the flame of civil discord,
which, in an unlooked for hour, [would] burst forth into a
consuming conflagration." "We shall feed the now smouldering embers with every particle of fuel furnished by the Northern fanatics," it said. "As long as conservatism sits silent, and
listens coward-like to such treason, we shall inform our readers of public sentiment at the North, and if the information
inflames, why let the consequence fall upon the authors and
abettors." "The conservatives of the North [were] cowed and
trampled under foot by the impudent, blatant Abolitionism. . . ." A few more Phillips meetings and the South might
well ask: *"Is this the Government of two peoples as different
in our sentiments of right and wrong as we are in our institutions?"* If what took place at Harpers Ferry could take place
in the Union, what worse could happen *out of it?*[75]

When Northerners suggested that Brown be dealt with
gently because of the effect of severe action on *Northern public opinion,* Southerners were quick to note the absence of
Northern public opinion against thrusting a pike into the heart
of a Southern planter. Was Brown less a murderer because
the men he killed at Harpers Ferry held slaves? Was his invasion of Virginia less treason because she was a slaveholding
state? Northern attitudes seemed to imply as much. "Our connection with the North is a standing instigation of insurrection
in the South," said the Charleston *Mercury.* "The Union itself [has become] a powerful organization by which domestic
disquietude is created and the mightiest dangers impend over
the South." The action of Brown and his men was nothing compared with the fanaticism of hatred against slavery which the
event had shown to exist throughout the North.[76] "It is Brown's
treason without his courage," said the New Orleans *Picayune,*
"his frenzy without his nerve, with even greater malice, because safe from the penalties he was daring enough to brave

in his own person—for we have no statutes against moral treason, the treason of disloyalty in the heart, to the peace and union
of the confederacy. . . ."[77]

Nor did the Republican effort to minimize the Harpers
Ferry episode and to laugh at the consternation it had caused
in the South, help matters. The "insane character of the undertaking" and its "prompt and easy suppression" did not less-
en the importance of the move *as a symbol*. "The Harpers
Ferry tragedy," said the Mobile *Register*, "is like a meteor
disclosing in its lurid flash the width and depth of that abyss
which rends asunder two nations, apparently one."[78] Brown's
raid should have sobered the loose-talking Republican politicians who had falsely taught the Northern people that slavery was an explosive to which the application of a torch would
bring swift destruction. But instead it had brought only ridicule
and further abuse. Few Northern spokesmen had faced the
cold fact that Brown's intention was to start a servile war with
its attendant horrors. Blame had been pushed about and at
last thrown back on Douglas and the South itself. The only
lesson Republicans were willing to draw from the affair was
that those who held slaves exposed themselves to constant
danger.[79]

Southerners did, indeed, learn this lesson from John Brown,
but in quite a different way from that suggested by the Republican press. Here for the first time the race question was
thrust, stark naked, into the struggle of sections. The common white man who held few or no slaves was brought face to
face with the fact that some Northern men were determined to
set the Negro free just as the fire-eaters had foretold. Coming
at a time when their ownership of land was steadily increasing
and talk of reopening the African slave trade for the benefit of
lesser men was popular, Brown's raid touched both their fears
and their avarice. That class, which in 1850 had wrecked the
Southern Movement, now took the lead. The cause of disunion
became the poor man's cause. Albert Gallatin Brown spoke for
them when he described the effects of emancipation by saying:[80]

. . . the rich will flee the country. . . . They will see the danger

afar off and will prepare to meet it. . . . But the poor who are doomed
to toil . . . they have no time to watch the storm or to mark its coming. . . . The poor will have to bear its fury . . . [they] alone will be
left to await whatever fate betides them. What will that fate be? It
will be found that millions of negroes, now held in subjection by masters, who restrain their licentiousness, have been set at liberty to
maraud, and plunder and steal. . . . Then the non-slaveholder will
begin to see what his real fate is. The negro will intrude into his
presence—insist on being treated as an equal—that he shall go to the
white man's table, and the white man to his—that he shall share the
white man's bed, and the white man his—that his son shall marry the
white man's daughter, and the white man's daughter his son. In short,
they shall live on terms of perfect social equality. The non-slaveholder
will, of course, reject the terms. Then will commence a war of races
such as has marked the history of San Domingo. . . .

* * * *

The presidential campaign of 1860 brought the sectional conflict to its final crisis. Political campaigns in the United States
incline to exaggeration and distortion. Opponents are vilified
and, on all occasions, the impression given that the destiny of
national ideals and human progress is at stake. Passions are
aroused, and only the fact that the people have come to understand that they are being lied to prevents dangerous reactions.
Generally, therefore, life resumes its normal course after each
election and no harm is done. Now and then, however, in American history, the campaign issues themselves have been vital ones.
Fundamental differences of opinion and interest have stirred
emotions; party lines have weakened or strengthened. The
people have come up to a campaign in a serious frame of mind.
Then resort to the usual political clap-trap has brought genuine peril and critical national situations have resulted. That
happened in 1860.

The campaign opened before the bitterness evoked by John
Brown had softened and while Southern legislatures were still
voting military supplies, and public leaders were urging a
Southern convention to demand equality in the Union or an
INDEPENDENT SOUTHERN CONFEDERACY.[81] The
revival of interest in Helper's *Impending Crisis*, published in

1857, and Northern approval of the work added to the unsettled state of emotions. Helper's thesis, that slavery was harmful to the South, especially to her white workers, smacked of abolitionism of the school of John Brown. The book preached in a fiery strain what John Brown undertook to put into practice. "A more vile, slanderous, seditious, unprincipled work never was published."[82]

The opening of Congress on December 5, 1859, provided a convenient focus for sectional strife. For eight weeks the House was deadlocked in the effort to elect a speaker. Congressmen, nevertheless, insisted on discussing the sectional issues and on fastening guilt for recent disturbances on their opponents. Men went armed and physical violence broke out on more than one occasion.[83] Threats to withdraw from Congress or to eject by force any Black Republican chosen Speaker were freely tossed about and Governor Gist, of South Carolina, offered troops to assist. "I will have a Regiment in or near Washington, in the shortest possible time," he assured Representative William Porcher Miles.[84] Southern nationalists in the Senate, under the lead of Jefferson Davis, meanwhile, introduced resolutions embodying the extreme Southern position on slavery and its rights in the territories for the avowed purpose of embarrassing Douglas and preventing his nomination by the coming Democratic Convention.[85] Southern moderates, like James H. Hammond, began to feel that the windowless walls of the Senate chamber shut out all air, all light, all reality!

Back in the cotton states radicals and conservatives struggled to direct the course of events. In December, 1859, the legislature of South Carolina proposed a convention of delegates from the slave states and sent spokesmen out to urge acceptance. Mississippi fell into line, but Virginia was silent and Alabama, under Yancey's influence, resolved to stand alone, declaring that if a Republican President were elected in 1860, the governor should call upon "the qualified voters . . . to elect delegates to a convention of the State to consider, determine, and do whatever . . . the rights, interests, and honor of the State of Alabama require[d] to be done for their protection."[86] Yancey was later able to carry through the state Democratic convention a platform denying the right of Congress or a territorial legislature to prohibit the introduction of slavery into a territory and demanding protection for slavery *in all territories*. The platform also required the Alabama delegates to the coming national convention to vote as a unit and to withdraw unless their principles were accepted before a candidate was named. The regular Democrats of South Carolina, Florida, Mississippi, Louisiana, Texas, and Arkansas endorsed the *Alabama platform* and prepared to force the issue on the Charleston convention.

The excited state of the public mind gave the radicals a decided advantage. On the surface they seemed to be in complete control. Yet the undercurrents were conservative. Union sentiment had not been completely destroyed and many Democrats were still willing to accept Douglas. As a citizen of Jackson County, Alabama, wrote his local editor, the people of the upper creeks were generally against "the ultras." Others reported like conditions in North Carolina, Georgia, Louisiana, and Tennessee.[87] Even Rhett was of the opinion that few public men of the South had a "stomach for the fight" which lay ahead. He bluntly admitted that there was no hope of the state rights men controlling the Charleston convention and therefore stressed the importance of obtaining the secession of Alabama and Mississippi delegations on the issue of squatter sovereignty and the construction of the Dred Scott decision. "As to uniting the whole South on any measure of resistance worth a fig," he wrote, "the idea is absurd as it is unnecessary. . . . It is useless to talk about checking the North or dissolving the Union with unanimity and without division of the South. . . . The South must go through a trying ordeal before she will ever achieve her deliverance, and men having both nerve and self-sacrificing patriotism must head the movement and shape its course, controlling and compelling their inferior contemporaries." He felt, however, that the people were now well ahead of their leaders.[88]

Rhett's doubts were justified even as his plans were bold. He could not be certain that South Carolina herself would choose delegates to the Democratic Convention who would support Alabama and Mississippi.[89] They would not dare vote for Douglas, he said, but would they encourage Alabama to obey her instructions? He feared not. His friend D. H. Hamilton was confident that there was a strong Douglas party in Charleston and that the convention would develop a pretty strong party in the state in favor of Douglas.[90] I. W. Hayne agreed with him regarding Douglas's strength in the state but hoped that, under the excitement of a convention, the men of South Carolina would not be behind the general sentiments of the South.[91] Events proved these analyses accurate. The South Carolina delegation, like those from the other Southern states which now turned toward Charleston and the National Democratic Convention, contained many men who were anxious for compromise to save party and Union.

Northern Democrats were as determined to uphold Douglas and his interpretation of squatter sovereignty as were Southern radicals to repudiate both. They had to be. No other candidate or platform could possibly gain support in the North. Their numerical majority in the convention must be uncompromisingly employed. Consequently, when, on April 23, the delegates assembled, Northern members quickly made certain of control by seating the contested New York delegation favorable to Douglas and by declaring that the convention would recognize the right of each delegate to cast his individual vote unless his state convention had instructed for the unit rule. This decision kept irregulars in Northern instructed delegations in line and permitted Southern irregulars in uninstructed delegations to break away. Thus fortified, the Douglas forces, which could cast only a minority Democratic vote in the coming election, rejected the platform embodying the Alabama principles and substituted those of Douglas. A bitter debate ensued. Northern spokesmen defended the principle of Popular Sovereignty and insisted that the South put no additional weights upon them in the coming campaign. "Are you, for a very abstraction, going to yield the chance of success," one of them asked. Yancey answered for his section. He demanded the "benefit of the Constitution" for the protection of the minority. That was no abstraction. He charged all difficulties to the refusal of Northern men to defend slavery. "If you had taken the position directly that slavery was right," he shouted, ". . . you would have triumphed, and anti-slavery would now have been dead in your midst." Pugh, of Ohio, was on his feet in an instant. Solemnly he thanked God "that a bold and honest man from the South had spoken and revealed the full measure of Southern demands." "Gentlemen of the South," he cried, "you mistake us—you mistake us—we will not do it." Whereupon Yancey and his Southern group bolted the convention and rendered further action impossible. The great Democratic Party, one of the last truly national institutions in a dividing nation, had split. A sectional party for the South, comparable to the Republican Party at the North, was now possible.

The tragic movement reached completion a few weeks later when the Northern wing of the party assembled at Baltimore to make Douglas its leader and his doctrines its platform, and the Southern wing met in Richmond to nominate John C. Breckinridge on the *Alabama platform*. The presidential contest of 1860 was thereby reduced to the terms which John Taylor had said, back in the 1830's, would bring on a Civil War![92]

A few days after the break-up of the Charleston convention, Robert Barnwell Rhett wrote a tragically revealing letter to his friend, William Porcher Miles:[93]

> I suppose you have heard and understood that the withdrawal of the South Carolina delegation was brought about by the outside pressure and indignation expressed at the course of the Columbia Convention [which had elected South Carolina's delegates]. Their spirit rose from the time they got to Charleston until they went out of the Convention. When they came, they had no more idea of going out than of flying. They would not even go to the Southern Caucus. If they had not retired, they would have been mobbed, I believe, but let all this pass now!

While the Democrats were demonstrating the effects of Bleeding Kansas, Bully Brooks, the great debates, and "the madman," John Brown, on their party, Southern conservatives had joined with moderates from the North in a *Constitutional Union* convention and named Bell of Tennessee and Everett of Massachusetts to lead them on a platform which recognized no principles other than the Constitution of the country, the Union of the States, the enforcement of the laws. They assumed that the country was weary of the slavery controversy with its "miserable abstractions" and its effort to "establish uniformity of opinion . . . where every man ought to be free to think and feel according to his own judgement." The party was composed largely of the survivors of the defunct Whig and American Parties, but it was to form the center about which conservative planters and union men of the Border States and the cotton South, who could not accept Douglas, would gather. It was another manifestation of the thoroughly upset state of emotions and opinions which existed in the nation.

The Republicans, meeting in Chicago on the 16th of May, rejected Seward and Chase and Bates, who had borne the brunt of earlier conflicts, and chose Abraham Lincoln of Illinois, old-line Whig, as their leader. The platform adopted was as Northwestern as the candidate. Fittingly enough, it began by asserting that the perpetuation of the party was necessary, paid its respects to the principles of the Declaration of Independence, recognized the right of the states to control their domestic institutions, and elaborated the usual Republican doctrine regarding slavery in the territories, including a rejection of the Dred Scott decision. Then, with high ideals out of the way, it advocated a protective tariff, a homestead act, appropriations for river and harbor improvements, liberal naturalization laws, and a railroad to the Pacific! Here was the old Free-Soil platform of 1848 come of age! Here was the Whig program of the 1840's anti-slaveryized! Here was that political maturity which blends ideals and materialism without conscious effort. The break of home markets on the prairies and the development of industry in Pennsylvania and the Northeast had brought a new fusion of interests; the calls for foreign labor and for foreign settlers had come to balance; the value of Western raw materials and markets had offset Eastern losses from homesteads and internal improvements. The Republican Party had achieved a base broad enough to satisfy the Old Whigs, catch its share of the foreign element, attract the eager forces of a new expanding economic order, and yet hold its original members who had enlisted in a great moral crusade.[94]

* * * *

The campaign which occupied the summer and early autumn of 1860 was notable because it developed largely into an inter-party struggle in each section rather than into a conflict of sections. In the North, it became primarily a contest between Douglas and Lincoln; in the South, a struggle between Breckinridge and Bell. As the Nashville *Banner and Whig* said in August:[95]

> Here in the South it is a waste of labor to fight Republicanism, or its representative, Abe Lincoln. There is but one opinion here in regard to that party—and that is that it is sectional, aggressive upon the South, and founded upon an idea to resist the triumph of which every South-ern man should be willing to sacrifice all other political issues, and make common enemy. We have not, therefore, in this canvass, de-voted much of our space to an exposition of the position and purpose of the Republican party, preferring rather to leave that duty to our gallant Northern Union men, who have the enemy in their midst, while we, meanwhile, turn our attention to the sectional spirit which infests the Southern states, and which, under the lead of such restless and dangerous spirits as Yancey, Keitt, Rhett, Spratt, and their fel-low disunionists threaten, equally with Republicanism North, to prove a wedge to split the Union in twain.

The Illinois *State Journal* reduced the Northern struggle to the same proportions. The Constitutional Union Party, it said, could not muster more than a corporal's guard in the North. "The people are determined that this time there shall be a clean, fair contest between conservative Republicanism on one side, and fire-eating, slavery-extending Democracy," which, of course, meant Douglas![96]

This was an unfortunate development. Unconsciously Re-publicans saw the campaign as a continuation of their fight against the Democratic Party which both Douglas and the Buchanan administration represented. It was an effort to achieve full and permanent party status and success. Douglas, as he had in the Senatorial campaign of 1858, symbolized the opposition. The struggle was still for free territory; for legis-lation favorable to the welfare of free common men. It was the same old battle for democracy against privilege and corruption. It still had the flavor of a crusade acquired from long subsistence on the one idea of the Wilmot Proviso, as Caleb Cushing put it. ". . . The political stock in trade of the Republican Party," he added, was "the insolent assumption, in some of them, perhaps, the stupid mental delusion, that whatever view they take of the measures of government is the only moral side of public questions."[97]

The problem which Republican politicians faced in waging their campaign in 1860 was simply one of completing the job already under way since 1854 and earlier. They had only to go on with the old weapons used in building the party and to broaden their appeal as circumstances favored and new recruits required. It was not even necessary for their candidate to make speeches or to enlarge on his own personal points of view. The most significant feature of Republican activity was, in fact, a revival of the Old Whig "hurrah" methods of 1840 in which the young Wide-awakes substituted marching in uniforms with torchlights and fence rails and songs and cheers, for sober discussion. The non-extension of slavery issue was now, of course, rather threadbare and hollow. No one really expected slavery to expand farther into the territories. Press and orator, however, made use of it from habit and the masses gave it whatever turn they wished. Abolitionists, like George W. Julian, believed that the Republican program clearly contemplated the *extinction* of slavery in all the states and that the party "(whatever pretended leaders or organs may say) [stood] firmly committed to the policy of divorcing the Federal Government from slavery, and to the prosecution of this policy as an unmistakeable protest against its existence." "I am for the Union," he added, "simply as the servant of Liberty, and I shall go for its dissolution the moment I become convinced that it can be preserved only through the perpetual enslavement of four millions of people and their descendants. We of the free states . . . have the power to settle the slavery question wisely and justly."[98] The campaign speeches of Sumner and Seward, while avoiding open aggression, invariably cast the issue in terms of slavery. Sumner indulged in "ringing pronouncements of 'a new order': the people had declared that freedom was national, that there was no protection for slavery in the Constitution 'which could not contain the idea of property in man.' " Seward told a Boston audience that Lincoln's sole claim to election was that "he confesses the obligation to the higher law . . . and avows himself, for weal or woe, for life or death, a soldier on the side of freedom in the irrepressible conflict between freedom and slavery."[99] So many Republicans actually believed the same thing, while still talking non-extension, that the American Anti-Slavery Society was not far wrong when it summed up the campaign by saying that, while the Republican position had not been all that they might have wished,[100]

Still it would be an injustice to the party not to say, that all through the campaign its presses and its speakers uttered many noble sentiments; exposed, with many words of earnest reprobation, the folly and wrong of slavery; and, with unanswerable arguments, from which they only drew modest inferences that it ought to be allowed to spread no further, proved really that it ought not to be tolerated anywhere. We think, too, that, however they might deem it prudent to invite "conservative" support, the party's clearest-sighted advocates were conscious that its most trustworthy strength lay in its anti-slavery element; and its best hope for victory in the enthusiasm and determination which appeals to that would best awaken. . . .

Others broadened the anti-slavery appeal along lines suggested by Lincoln. The Southern doctrines of a stratified society and an inferior laboring class endangered the white worker as well as the Negro. Southerners, they charged, looked down on all those who toiled. When James H. Hammond and Herschel V. Johnson, Douglas's running mate, surveyed Northern conditions and asserted that the free laborer was, in fact, a slave, these Republican spokesmen accepted the statements as insinuating inferiority. To Johnson's remarks the Illinois *State Journal* replied: "The workingmen of the North have now learned in person what a slaveholding aristocrat thinks of them. . . . The haughty, insulting, overbearing of this aristocratic slaveholding nabob . . . is a fair example of the ruling element of the Democratic party."[101] An Ohio editor declared that Hammond's reference to "the mudsills of Society" revealed his "cordial and intense hatred of laboring men and free labor" which characterized "the boasted National Democracy." This attitude explained the bitter opposition of the Democratic Party to the homestead law which "preserves our Western domain for free homes for free men." The Republicans were "not willing that the free white laborers . . . should be compelled to labor by the side of Negro slaves . . . that the degradation of the compelled and enforced labor of the slave should be suffered to fall upon the honest toil of free white men and women."[102] The Democratic Party, on the other hand, was "the true 'nigger' party" and was, therefore, opposed to free homesteads, improvements of harbors and rivers, protection to American industry and the organization of new free territories and free states. The struggle was between democracy and aristocracy! The foreign element could be won over by such appeals![103]

To the slavery issue was added, on occasion, a slur on Southern character and the charge of bluster and swagger. When a quarrel in Congress led Pryor of Virginia to challenge Potter of Wisconsin to a duel and the latter named bowie-knives as the weapons, Republicans thought it a grand joke. The Northern press was hilarious at the indignant refusal of Pryor's second to permit him to engage in combat by "this vulgar, barbarous, and inhuman mode."[104] One newspaper humorously remarked that Northern people had "long been deluded with the notion that every Southerner was a walking, pent-up volcano, ready to belch forth fire and death at a touch; that he was the embodiment of courage and high-strung fortitude; and to cross his path was as good as death." But now the sham had been exposed and "the chivalric, ferocious ogres" had been revealed as "a very harmless set of blusterers who are brave only when they have a very decided advantage. . . ."[105] Southern threats of secession in the event of Lincoln's election were considered of the same material. They were "almost too absurd either for discussion or ridicule." They were only "windy bombast."[106] The non-slaveholding white of the South made secession a humbug.

For the strong conservative element in such centers as New York City, the Republican appeal took quite a different form. Much was made of the corruption of the Buchanan administration. Lincoln's election was urged as the only way to end all slavery conflict. The idea that the West was a better market than the South was coupled with the suggestion of profits to be gained from the Republican program of internal improvements, tariffs, etc. Southern extravagance and the economic weaknesses of slavery were contrasted with the solid qualities of the Republican regions. In fact, said Samuel B. Crittenden, the Republican Party is "the only conservative party existing in the country."

Such a campaign left Republicans totally unprepared for the realities which were to follow the election. Victory would be largely a party triumph—a triumph over Douglas as the symbol of the hated Democracy and the fantastic slave power which had long stood behind him. It would make party and the salvation of party the paramount interest in the confusion of realities ahead!

The campaign of 1860 in the South was a far more serious affair. The fight there was for and against a movement which aimed at Southern independence. The little band of "men with both nerve and self-sacrificing patriotism" of which Rhett had spoken, were determined to make this crisis the last one. Their main stock in trade was the charge that the North had steadily encroached on Southern constitutional rights and was determined to destroy slavery. Northern motives were selfish and material. The South had been and would be increasingly plundered in the interests of Northern gain. A crisis had been reached. The alternatives were independence or humble submission. The Charleston *Mercury* summed up the situation in this way:[107]

If this were the beginning of our difficulties in the South—if our present position of embarrassment and danger were not the result of years of accumulated aggression and wrong, there might be some hope of a favorable change in the improved nature of things, and that the parties of the country, like a spent flood, might return to their wonted channels of peace and usefulness. But the distemper of the times has been gathering virulence through twenty years of progress and agitation. It has been fed by the strongest passions of our nature, and nurtured by the meanest. It has obliterated all the old party lines, which stood for a half century dividing the opinion of the country. The last to perish, as the first to arise with the strength of the Union, built on principles of justice and the Constitution, was the Democratic party. That too has fallen. One by one all its cardinal principles have been surrendered in the North to an absorbing sectionalism. And now the South stands alone behind her broken pledges, useless surrenders, disappointed hopes and sacrifices; before her, a united North banded together against her rights and interests, threatening dangers. Her deliverance cannot be accomplished by the aid of "national" parties, —nor by her old sentimentality for the Union, which has been used against her as all generous emotions are used by the base and selfish —nor by further surrenders—nor by party trickery—nor by fears and prayers. The Northern people have forced upon us the conviction, reluctantly and slowly attained, that no submission on our part can win their forbearance, and no rights escape their violation, and that our safety rests in ourselves. . . .

The North was bent on carrying the irrepressible conflict to a finish. The Republicans had turned against Seward because he was disposed to temporize with the South and lacked the necessary nerve to carry through measures of Southern subjugation. But Lincoln was a "proper tool" to do the job—"the *beau ideal,* of a relentless, dogged freesoil-border-ruffian . . . a vulgar mobocrat and Southern hater [who would] neither turn back from his work nor do it by halves. . . ."[108] He had already "pointed his hungry hordes to the fertile and smiling fields of the South, and told them the day would come when they would own them. . . ." For a generation Northern men had been taught that it was legitimate to plunder slaveholders. The only real issues in the election, therefore, were whether the people of the slaveholding states would be permitted to hold their slave property undisturbed; whether Southern "social security or financial prosperity [could] withstand Northern Republican license."[109]

The stirring up of race fears also constituted a prominent part of the radical campaign. Over and over again the press and the orator asserted that a Republican triumph meant more John Browns and the ultimate freeing of the slaves.[110] "Their aim is to free the negroes and force amalgamation between them and the children of the poor men of the South," charged C. C. Clay. "If Lincoln . . . shall be elected," said the Montgomery *Mail*, "every postmaster will be a tamperer with slaves, every marshal and other Federal functionary, a promoter of rebellion."[111] The non-slaveholder especially would suffer. Rich men might escape. But the poor white man—what an appalling fate would be his! "I shudder to contemplate it!" wrote Daniel R. Hundley. "What social monstrosities, what desolated fields, what civil broils, what robberies, rapes and murders of the poorer whites by the emancipated blacks would then disfigure the whole fair face of this prosperous, smiling and happy Southern land." It would produce a war of extermination marked by such atrocities and crimes as to make ordinary wars seem like peace itself![112]

The final appeal was to sectional pride and interest. Scorned and humiliated and defeated *in* the Union, the South was still the master of the world! Cotton was King! "Across the waters of the Atlantic the two great powers of Europe, with boundless military resources, and millions of golden peacemakers lying idle in their vaults," stood ready to bid for a Southern alliance. The South had the cotton which these "foreign friends" had to have or their "thrones [would] crumble to dust."[113] "We can dictate to Christendom," cried the Montgomery *Advertiser!* Self-interest, if not every impulse of freedom and honor, compelled the South to dissolve its connection with abolitionism! An independent South would be a prosperous South. Why strive longer to hold together two distinct civilizations, as separated and hostile as were "Carthage & Rome, England & France." The two sections did not longer understand each other. The Pryor-Potter affair proved that. Northerners viewed the duel but as a simple proposal of one man to kill another. The challenged man was in their eyes justified in employing all means and taking all advantages to prevent it. Potter, "a large, brawny Hercules of a man," had, according to Northern opinion, pulled "quite a smart dodge" in proposing bowie-knives as weapons against the "narrow-breasted" Mr. Pryor! And a smart dodge was always in order in the North. "That man gains a great deal of credit who eludes a bargain, a pledge, or gets out of any sort of scrape by a quibble ... such as men in the North wink their eyes at and say, 'devilish clever, isn't it?' and such as men in the South blush at, and are tabooed by all honorable men." To the North Potter was a hero; to the South he was a coward. Values and standards of conduct revealed two nations.[114] Lincoln's election would be the signal for action!

Southern conservatives met the sectional movement squarely and fearlessly. "Why the hot haste, excitement and precipitation?" they asked. "If there ever was a time to move coolly and carefully," it was just now.[115] Yancey and his group were not the whole South even though they talked as if they were. The planters, farmers, working and business men would think for themselves. The surface current might run toward secession, but the masses had not yet spoken.[116] Even Yancey had not been able to stir the common people of his own city on his return from Charleston. They sensed the danger to the country too much to be swayed by the ordinary arts of the politician.[117] And besides, just where, anyway, had the South as yet suffered any "real detriment, loss or humiliation from the fanatical doctrines" of the North? The South had triumphed "nine cases out of ten in all the geographical and sectional conflicts" which had arisen. Only in Kansas had she failed, and that failure was due to soil and climate, not to Free-Soilers. The radical position was based on apprehensions, not on actual harm already done. The Republican bark would be found to be far more dangerous than the bite. The election of Lincoln "would certainly be considered a catastrophe by every patriot in the land," but it could furnish "no possible excuse for hasty and precipitate action on the part of the South."[118] Southern rights could be maintained within the Union. The power to impeach, the independence of the courts, even the loyalty of many Northern friends of the Constitution, were bars against any illegal acts by Republican officials. Furthermore, secession was nothing but revolution. "The Constitutional right of peaceable secession is the most senseless of things ever discussed by wise men," said a Georgia editor. "Everyone knows," he continued, "that while a State, and indeed every Citizen of that State, may hold the opinion that such State has the right to secede when it pleases, it being the sole judge for itself of infraction of the Compact of Union, yet if the other states happen to think that there has been no violation of the organic law, except by the attempt at secession, and choose to attempt coercion, it brings the seceding party face to face with revolution, and to the final test of *all right, might.* The right of secession is not worth a fig, as long as others choose to test that right by force."[119] "Revolution is the word and not secession," wrote Judge Sharkey of Mississippi. "If we are suffering from evils and those evils are intolerable, we must prepare to beat our plows into swords and plunge them deep into the breasts of our fellow-citizens. That is the only way of getting out of the Union."[120]

Economic interest also favored the conservative appeal. The strength of both the Douglas and Bell groups in the South lay in the planting regions along the Mississippi River; in the border states, where rivers and canals tied interests to the Northwest; on the coast and in the back country of North Carolina which had given so much to the Ohio Valley; in middle Georgia and in the coastal towns of both the Gulf and the Atlantic. A break with the North would cut ties social and economic as well. Markets would be lost and supplies and capital cut off. As the Memphis *Appeal* told its readers, profits for the merchant who distributed Northern goods to the country round about had never been as high as they were in 1860. In spite of the loss of a few slaves, lured away by deluded fanatics, the South profited by its relations with the people of Illinois and Indiana, "vast numbers" of whom were "as sound on the negro question as the secessionists themselves." If the cotton states withdrew from the Union, the enormous profits of Northern trade would go to Memphis and other cities on the border. Wealthy men of the South, the conservative taxpaying citizens, would flee the whirlwind and "crowd into Tennessee and the Middle States and their cities. . . . Charleston, instead of becoming the great political and commercial capital of a Southern Confederacy, would dwindle into utter insignificance, while Memphis [and other towns just outside the confederacy] would grow apace in wealth and population. . . ." Loyalty to the Union would pay dividends![121]

Thus did the Southern factions wage their campaign against each other with little regard for what was taking place across the Mason and Dixon line to the north. Not until the last few weeks of the campaign did it dawn upon them that, regardless of which group triumphed in the South, the Republican Party would triumph in the nation. Some even accused the radicals of fostering division in the interests of Lincoln's election and the opportunity to secure secession thereby. They urged those who loved the Union to agree upon one of the three candidates, Breckinridge, Bell, or Douglas, and unite the solid vote of the South with that of conservative Northern men in one grand effort to turn back the exultant Republicans. But the lack of clear-cut understanding and the rancor of personal and party conflict checked all efforts and brought the great majority of Southern men to the end of the campaign as much in confusion, division, and uncertainty as they had been from the start. They too were unfitted to face the harsh realities of the days ahead.[122]

* * * *

The vote of 1860 proved only one thing—that the majority of the people were still conservative. Lincoln polled 1,866,452 votes, against 2,815,617 for all his opponents (Douglas, 1,376,957; Breckinridge, 849,781; Bell, 588,879). His vote was highly sectional. In ten Southern states he did not receive a single popular vote. Breckinridge, the States'-rights candidate, on the other hand, carried the South, but failed to secure a majority of its popular vote. His vote, while heavier in the North than Lincoln's was in the South, was also largely sectional. He was primarily the candidate of the cotton area. Thus had a divided opposition and a fortunate distribution of votes given the Republican Party a victory and the nation a minority President. The major parties, like most other institutions and values, had become thoroughly sectional.

CHAPTER SEVENTEEN

THE BREAKUP OF THE UNION

WHAT happened in the next few months before the guns began their fire on Sumter was in reality only anticlimax. When the excitement of the campaign was over, thousands North and South drew back with the realization that their votes in the late election had not been intended to say what the results of that election seemed to portend. Men had voted the Republican ticket for many different reasons. Opposition to slavery was only one of them. Foreign groups, whose votes, one historian has said, accounted for Lincoln's majority in the Northwest, had been greatly influenced by their interest in homesteads;[1] Pennsylvanians had been attracted by the tariff promises; others, disgusted with Buchanan's administration, had identified the Democratic Party with the slaveholding interests and had voted Republican as a protest.[2] Now that the issue had to do only with the South, many hesitated. Opinion was uncertain and confused. "The North has been growing more and more conservative since Dec[r] & the South has nothing to fear, absolutely nothing," wrote one who had voted for Lincoln.[3] Thurlow Weed and William H. Seward were for conciliation—Weed even talking of restoring the Missouri Compromise line; Greeley and Sumner were for letting the disgruntled states secede if they wished; Preston King thought that the Southern movement amounted to little and that a slight show of force would bring it to an end; Wade began to talk about annexing Canada to offset the loss of the Deep South.[4]

City elections, meanwhile, showed an alarming drift back to the Democrats; by January newspapers as ardent as the Springfield *Republican* were prophesying a reorganization of parties in the North in which one wing of the Republican Party would separate from the other to engage in more decided antislavery work. "If the South show any liberal spirit," wrote Henry Adams, "the reaction will sweep us out dreadfully and thin our ranks to a skeleton." In Congress committees and individuals set themselves at the task of finding compromises along lines which had been rejected years before. Everywhere men seemed appalled at the situation they had brought upon themselves. Business interests quailed at the approaching storm. Politicians grew uneasy. "We have it from Conservative Republicans," said the Boston *Courier*, "that this is a favorable moment to move off from the abolitionists who have control of the party." A Boston citizen warned Sumner that men who passed for Republicans but had no sympathy with Republican principles were gaining great power in Massachusetts affairs.[5]

In Washington Seward soon took charge of Republican interests and labored almost as fervidly as Buchanan himself for the preservation of the *status quo*. Even after secession had begun and the Confederate States had been formed he continued his labors for a peaceful settlement. Slyly he established contacts with Southern agents in Washington and gave solemn assurances of the good intentions of his party in regard to slavery in the territories and states and even of the willingness to abandon the forts in Southern areas. He urged the border states to remain calm and loyal. He cultivated Union sentiment in the cotton states. He was evidently sincere in his belief that war was not imminent, that the Southern States were not lost to the Union. But his efforts only added to the uncertainty and the confusion. In his hands the Republican program became no clearer.

Buchanan likewise sought peace. Studiously he avoided any act that might precipitate conflict. He was no Jackson and he knew it. While men labored for compromise the North should not commit an overt act which might lead to war. Yet he would not admit the right of secession. The framers of this government "never intended to implant in its bosom the seeds of its own destruction, nor were they at its creation guilty of the absurdity of providing for its own destruction." Nor would he hand over the forts in Charleston harbor to the state of South Carolina. He would only avoid every act which would needlessly tend to provoke aggression. All of which permitted a certain amount of drifting, of uncertainty, without giving a program for action.

Amid this growing confusion one firm and positive force began to make itself felt. Those who had toiled through the years to build a new party—a better party, of morals and democracy—could not now stand aside and see the fruits of hard-earned victory slip from their hands. Long they had waited for offices; longer had they waited for an administration which would look after the interests of the common man of the North and West. Into their party had gone their faith in democracy and Christianity as the enemies of aristocrats who lived by the sweat of other men's faces and whose self-indulgence embraced the whole of sin. Compromise, the breakup of the Union, a fusion government—these were not to be thought of. True Republicans could not yield an inch. Lincoln understood, even if others did not. Out of his Springfield office came the flat refusal to accept the compromises which Crittenden and others offered; on the basic Republican issues no yielding of any kind could be expected.[6] A man who had accepted the cause of party as the cause of *right* and *democracy* could not sacrifice the principles of that party's platform. A union descended from the Holy Commonwealth of colonial days—God's great experiment in government by and for a people—could not be broken to pieces without a struggle.

Southern men were as confused and uncertain after the November election as were their fellows at the North. Many there had voted for Breckinridge for reasons other than the wish to secede. The larger number were simply weary of the constant strife and they wanted the slavery issue settled. Some had felt that they must stand by their section as the only way of showing their dislike for the Republican threat. They had no idea of forming a new nation. Some thought that the only way to bring Northern conservatives to their senses and to check abolition sentiment was to go as far as necessary along the road to separation. They loved the Union—but it was the Union under the Constitution interpreted as they knew it should be.

The election of Lincoln sobered the more conservative elements in the Breckinridge party just as it alarmed the Douglas and Constitutional Union groups. None of them were quite prepared to face the facts of Republican domination, in spite of the frequent declaration that Lincoln's election was not a cause for breaking up the Union. What should be done? "Well, in the first place," answered the Augusta *Chronicle and Sentinel*, "the times require that we should be perfectly cool, or as cool as we can be, and that we proceed in this business with due deliberation, putting aside rashness and passion as far as possible, and that we take no step that is not marked and pointed out by a due regard to all the interests, the vast interests, of this section of the Confederacy. The greatest danger . . . is that men under the strong excitement of the moment may not act either justly or wisely, towards themselves, and toward their brethren around them."[7] To act calmly and wisely was, indeed, difficult in an atmosphere of tension and alarm. It was even more difficult for men who were disorganized and scattered by defeat. The Constitutional Union Party had been organized on the spur of the moment to face an emergency. It was of little use now in giving direction to conservative action.

The forces of opposition were thus destined to drift with the current and never to reveal their true strength. They did, however, begin nobly. In every state, they spoke their minds, pointing out the legality of Lincoln's election and demanding to know just how the South would be injured by Lincoln's administration.[8] They denied the right of secession and questioned its wisdom. "It is no remedy for Southern wrongs, or it is only a mad-man's remedy," said the Memphis *Enquirer*.[9] They charged their opponents with plotting rebellion all along and using favorable circumstances to accomplish deep-laid schemes. They asked just what could be gained by breaking up a Union which had given so much of benefit.[10] A few, in the Border

States, suggested the formation of A Border State Confederation, composed of Maryland, Virginia, Kentucky, Missouri,
Arkansas, Tennessee, and North Carolina, by which the sane
people of the South could escape the extremists of both sections.[11]

But the advantages were all on the side of those who had
determined on secession. Fears and uncertainty played into their
hands. "Black Republicanism" was as powerful a weapon in the
South as the "Slave Power" was in the North, and apprehension
of the dire things it might do carried lesser men along with the
current and rendered greater men silent. Lincoln's refusal to
compromise gave strength to the blackest charges made against
the intentions of his administration. As the Louisville *Journal*
said:[12]

> The unconciliatory and defiant course of the Republican leaders
> has rendered the advocates of patience and steadiness in the South all
> but powerless. Beyond dispute, it is the principal cause of the fearful
> distrust of the North which now possesses and inflames the Southern
> breast.

The wild talk of Republican newspapers also weakened the
Southern conservative and strengthened his foes. It was useless
to talk about the protection afforded Southern rights by the
Constitution and the courts while the Chicago *Tribune* was
insisting that:[13]

> The Republican victory would be incomplete if it did not promise
> sooner or later to reform the United States Supreme Court. That
> bench full of Southern lawyers, which gentlemen of a political tem-
> perament call an "august tribunal," is the last entrenchment behind
> which despotism is sheltered; and until a national convention amends
> the Constitution so as to defeat the usurpations of that body, or until
> the Court itself is reconstructed by the dropping off of a few of its
> members and the appointment of better men in their places, we have
> little hope for Congressional action in the way of restricting slavery.

It was even more difficult to urge the cause of loyalty when
Northern editors talked of the hated "Slave Power" and boasted
of the ease with which secession would be crushed.[14] As a

Georgia editor said, there was something besides Southern
Equality needed to preserve the Union:[15]

> We have heard a great deal about rights, wrongs, remedies,—but
> all this talk is mere delusion. Georgia, today, would not give a penny-
> whistle for the Fugitive Slave law of 1850, or all the fugitive slave
> laws Congress could pass. She cares absolutely nothing at all about the
> Personal Liberty Bills of the North considered as a matter of inter-
> est; for since the formation of the government she has not lost in
> fugitives as much as she has lost on her cotton crop within ten days
> by reason of the excitement of the times. Neither is it Lincoln that
> Georgia would resist—there is no degradation or dishonor to any of
> her sons, that Lincoln gets a majority of the electoral vote, unless
> he got them by some act of ours. Our opposition is to the *animus* of
> the North, as exhibited in the passage of Liberty Bills, and finally in
> the election of an irrepressible conflict representative as the Chief
> Executive of the States.

These things revealed "the absolute and apparently irreconcil-
able incompatibility of temper, character, interest and feeling
between the Northern and the Southern sections of the Confederacy."

Under such circumstances, the radical group easily moved
from defeat in the campaign of 1860 to secession as the only
alternative left. They fought delay. Many of the leaders had
long believed the Union a curse to the South and they feared
that if they moved too deliberately the North might offer
favorable terms. Others urged quick action lest the people cool
off and accept less than justice. They must strike while the iron
was hot. Delay was their worst enemy.

By December 17, 1860, Rhett and his followers had secured
a convention in South Carolina, composed of those who were
ready to stand alone, if necessary, in defense of Southern rights.
The next day an ordinance of secession was adopted. Within
six weeks, Mississippi, Florida, Alabama, Georgia, Louisiana,
and Texas had followed South Carolina's example. The Cotton
Kingdom was ready to form itself into the Confederate States
of America.

Secession, however, had been accomplished only after a hard
fight, often against the will of a majority which was unable

to stem the emotional tide. Bitterly the conservatives surrendered, many of them with the praise of Union on their lips.
"My heart has been rent by . . . the destruction of my country—the dismemberment of that great & glorious Union, cemented by the blood of our fathers," wrote Benjamin F. Perry
of South Carolina in his Diary. "The American people seem
demented. . . . They are exulting over the destruction of the
best and wisest form of government ever sacrificed by God to
man. Fools & wicked fools, they know not what they do &
may God forgive them. . . ."[16] A more poised and judicious
Georgia editor accepted the secession of his state by declaring
that he could not rejoice in the event. "We have loved the
Union with an affection pure and unselfish," he said, "not for
any blessing it conferred, but because no pulsation of our heart
ever beat that was not loyal to the *great* idea of our ancestors
—Union, Liberty, and Fraternity. . . . We would cheerfully,
as ever we lay down to childhood's slumber, lay down our life,
to have preserved the Union, as our fathers made it. . . ."[17]

The next day a rival paper in his own city reported the wild
and noisy celebration with which the people had received the
news:[18]

Just such a crowd will not perhaps be seen again in this generation,
for the blacks, in blessed ignorance that all this fuss was about them,
entered into the rejoicing, and almost forgot that the whites have the
best right to the sidewalk.

The secession of the Cotton Kingdom and the formation of
the Confederate States of America left the Border States suspended geographically, and emotionally as well, between two
uncertain extremes. Powerful forces pulled in each direction.
The last decade had seen a rapid increase of economic ties with
the North and a slow but sure altering of slave relations which
bound them to the South. Union sentiment was strong among
the masses; a realization that a clash between the North and
the South as sections would expose the Border States to the
gravest dangers, internal and external, had slowly dawned with
the presidential campaign. Cotton-States men were already raising the question whether the Border States would make safe

companions in a Southern confederacy. These states were gradually disposing of their surplus slaves to the farther South;
they were not as sound on tariff as they might be. Would not
a Confederacy of which they were members soon face again
the same situation the United States now faced? "Will the
interests of Baltimore, Richmond, Louisville, St. Louis or
Memphis be identical with ours?" asked a Mississippian. Would
not these cities tend more and more toward manufacturing?
Would they accept the free-trade program so dear to the cotton interests? Would they continue to support slavery when
their economic interests were on the side of free labor?[19] But
there was another side to the picture. Abolition efforts had most
seriously affected the Border States. Their slaves were the ones
who had taken passage on the underground railway. John
Brown's invasion had been launched against Virginia. And, what
was most important, Mason and Dixon's line ran to the north
of them. They were by tradition and blood as Southern as
the men of the Southwest. They stood to lose by any change
of present conditions which did not give greater understanding and peace. What could they do other than wait and hope?
The failure of the Peace Convention in February definitely
ended the hope of settlement by mutual sectional effort. Which
way should they turn? The answer lay largely with Abraham
Lincoln. Uncompromisingly, he answered it for them.

When Lincoln left Springfield to take over the presidency
of a crumbling republic, three courses of action were open to
him. He might continue the watchful-waiting policy of his
predecessor, hold the Border States, and hope for a reaction
which would bring the "erring sisters" back to the Union and
the nation to peace. It would not be a popular or a promising
way. It would require withdrawal from the forts in Confederate
territory and a gradual, if not admitted, yielding of Republican
principles. It might end only in the permanent establishment
of the new Confederate government. It had already ruined
James Buchanan. It might destroy Lincoln and his party. Yet,
if the nation were saved and a civil war averted, it might be
worth the trial and the cost.

A second course was that of complete surrender by compromises sweeping enough to satisfy the now aggressive South. That would immediately wreck the Republican Party and sacrifice all that the campaign and the years behind it meant. Even if the South accepted, all the problems and sentiments which had produced this crisis would remain. Yet who could say that these problems were not gradually solving themselves? The territorial conflict was certainly over; even slavery might, from natural causes, be on its way out. Who was wise enough to forecast the future?

The third course was that of action. Lincoln could refuse to accept the fact of secession, hold the forts, collect the revenues, and enforce the law. Andrew Jackson had succeeded with such a policy. The strong conservative element in the Lower South would assent; the Border States would approve. The only difficulty was one of managing public opinion so as to keep it on the government's side. An appeal to Union sentiments, to the old national traditions, would prepare the way. The rash actions of the hotheads in the seceded states would furnish the excuse for action. The same vague talk which permitted listeners to understand what it suited them to understand would accomplish the rest. Party and nation—now one in values—might be saved at a minimum cost of force.

Whether Lincoln thought all this out or not we do not know. Some things indicate that he did. Yet his talk and his actions were not always concise and direct. He hesitated and fumbled to a degree, but he did act, and action quickly set him along the third course. As he turned eastward, he stated a program, in questions at Indianapolis, which seemed harmless to the North, but which instantly alarmed the South. ". . . Whatever may have been the motive which suggested the Indianapolis harangues," said the Nashville *Patriot*, "there can be no mistake as to one thing, and that is they prove him to be a narrow-minded Republican partisan incapable apparently of rising to the attitude of statesmanship necessary to a thorough comprehension of the national crisis, and the remedies demanded by patriotism to preserve the government he has been selected to administer. . . ."[20] ". . . It is a war proposition couched in language intended to conceal the enormity of the crime beneath pretexts too absurd to require exposure and fallacies too flimsy to deceive the most stupid," commented the Louisville *Daily Courier*.[21] In Washington, he launched a series of secret intrigues for the holding of the Southern forts which staggered the staid and careful navy and military men who had been in charge. Agreements between local officials and garrisons were ignored. Ships, disguised and sometimes flying the British flag, were dispatched on secret missions with men and supplies. The unofficial assurances given to Southern agents by Seward were repudiated and a set of conditions created which made the actual firing on Fort Sumter by alarmed and enraged Southerners almost a foregone conclusion.[22]

Whether these acts were part of a well-worked-out policy of accepting what seemed to be an irrepressible conflict, and cleverly throwing the responsibility for beginning the war onto the South for the psychological advantage, or whether they were the result of blundering along with the sweep of events, we cannot say with complete assurance. We do know that, with Lincoln's assumption of control, a firmer, uncompromising temper marked the policy of the Federal government. There was constant talk of yielding after a respectable show of force, but no definite assurance of action. Fort Sumter, in the harbor of Charleston, South Carolina, the most dangerous spot in all the troubled nation, was made the point of decision. Acting under orders directly from the President, in the face of sound warnings that such a move meant war, Captain Fox, one April day, set out from New York harbor with ships and provisions for the relief of the Federal troops still holding that fort. On April 12, the Confederate troops stationed about the harbor opened fire, thereby "forcing" Lincoln to call for troops for the suppression of rebellion.

A few days later, Lincoln consoled Captain Fox for his failure to reach and relieve the fort, by writing: "You and I both anticipated that the course of the country would be advanced by making the attempt to provision Fort Sumter, even if it should fail; and it is no small consolation now to feel that our anticipation is justified by the result."[23] Not long after this letter was written, he boasted to his friend Orville H.

Browning that: ". . . He himself conceived the idea, and proposed sending supplies, without an attempt to reinforce giving notice to Gov. Pickens of S. C. The plan succeeded. They attack Sumter—it fell, and thus, did more service than it otherwise could."[24]

With the call for troops to subdue their fellow Southerners, the conservative element in the Border States lost their hold. Two days later, Virginia went out, then North Carolina, Arkansas, and Tennessee, leaving Maryland, Kentucky, and Missouri divided into local warring factions. As those who had refused to allow emotions to overrule their minds gave way, one of them spoke for the sanity of his age and of all time: "I am impotent to do anything which my judgment and conscience approve. I cannot avert the war, consistent with the re-establishment of a government so good as that we pull down. Whilst I cannot hesitate where no choice is left, only to fight for the South and home, or for the North, if I should fall in such a contest, I would find in a dying hour no comfort in the conviction that I had sacrificed my life in a *just* cause. It is true that I believe that Lincoln had no right to call out the militia, make War and blockade the ports. . . . If the restoration of the Union was his object, which I believe was his object, then he is a fool. If his purpose was to drive off all the Slave states, in order to make war on them and annihilate Slavery, then he is a Devil and in the latter supposition I could fight with a hearty good will. . . . My maxim has always been to choose among the evils around me and do the best I can. I think the annals of the world furnish no instance of so groundless a war—but as our nation will have it—if no peace can be made—let us fight like men for our own firesides."[25]

The well-meaning but bewildered Lincoln would have been pained by such comment had it come to his ears. He was, however, too much occupied by crowding events to explain his motives and his plans. Not until the blood and tears of war had cleared men's vision would his patience and his good intentions become clear to his fellow Americans.

The Lincoln call for troops ended the long years of sectional debate. A North and a South, each conscious of its superior ways

and each certain of the depravity of the other, now stood ready
to give all "in self-defense" and in defense of God's interests.
The politician and the pious reformer were through; the soldier was about to take charge. "The voice of reason is stilled,"
again wrote the old conservative Southerner. "Furious passion
and thirst for blood consume the air. . . . Nobody is allowed
to retain and assert his reason. . . . The very women and children are for war."

A few days later, Jefferson Davis, president of the new-born
Confederate States of America, set aside June 13 as a day of
fasting and praying. In response an obscure overseer on a
Louisiana sugar plantation scrawled a pencilled prayer to his
God "that every black Republican in the Hole combined whorl
either man woman o chile that is opposed to negro slavery . . .
shal be trubled with pestilents and calamitys of all Kinds and
Drag out the Balance of there existance in Misray and Degradation with scarsely food and rayment enughf to keep sole
and Body to gather and o God I pray the to Direct a bullet
or a bayonet to pirce the Hart of every northern soldier that
invades southern soile and after the Body has rendered up its
traterish sole gave it a trators reward a Birth In the Lake of
Fires and Brimstone. . . ."

Months later from the battlefield of Bull Run a correspondent for the New York *Herald* reported to his paper and its
credulous readers that "the barbarities practiced by the rebels
at the battle . . . [were] unparalleled." He related how a
Northern private had found a wounded Southerner lying in
the sun and had carried him to the shade "where he gently
layed him down and gave him a drink from his canteen. Revived by the drink, the ingrate drew his pistol and shot his
benefactor through the heart." "Rebel" cannoneers, he said,
had deliberately trained their guns on groups of wounded men,
and "rebel fiends in human shape" had taken "the bayonets
and knives of our wounded and dying soldiers and thrust them
into their hearts and left them sticking there." Others had
severed the heads of the dead and had amused themselves by
"kicking them about as footballs." The bodies of Union officers had been "literally cut to pieces," and prisoners had

"been pinioned to trees and tortured by bayonets thrust at them." Such barbarities, concluded the reporter, were "unworthy of the Christian era," but were fair samples of the "boasted chivalry of these worse than fiends."[26]

The distortions and the hatreds of the years had flowered in open battle. The irrepressible conflict of the politician had been reduced to the struggle of armies. The disillusioned old Confederate soldier at Appomattox, looking back across the years which held Shiloh and Gettysburg and Cold Harbor, might well question the wisdom of "loving another country."

NOTES

NOTES

CHAPTER ONE

1. *The Georgia Telegraph* (Macon, Georgia), April 13, 1858; *Ibid.*, May 12, 1860.

2. See Frederick Jackson Turner, *The Frontier in American History; Sections in American History; The United States, 1830–1850.*

3. James Truslow Adams, *New England in the Republic;* Caroline Ware, *The Early New England Cotton Manufacture.*

4. H. C. Hubbart, *The Older Middle West.*

5. Joseph Schafer, *Four Wisconsin Counties.*

6. Ulrich Bonnell Phillips, *Life and Labor in the Old South.*

7. Avery Craven, *Soil Exhaustion . . . in Virginia and Maryland.*

8. Avery Craven, "The Turner Theories and the South," *Journal of Southern Hist.*, V, 291–314.

9. T. P. Abernethy, *From Frontier to Plantation in Tennessee;* Wendell Holmes Stephenson, *Isaac Franklin, Slave Trader and Planter of the Old South;* Charles S. Sydnor, *A Gentleman of the Old Natchez Region.*

10. R. G. Wellington, *The Political and Sectional Influence of the Public Lands, 1828–1842.*

11. V. L. Parrington, *The Romantic Revolution in America, 1800–1860,* 271–460.

12. Marquis James, *Andrew Jackson, Portrait of a President.*

13. Each of these movements has its own bibliography. The following are suggested as typical: M. E. Curti, *The American Peace Crusade;* J. A. Krout, *Origins of Prohibition;* Helen Marshall, *Dorothea Dix;* D. B. Frothingham, *Transcendentalism in New England;* Henry Canby, *Henry Thoreau;* C. Sears, *Fruitlands;* R. W. Leopold, *Robert Dale Owen;* Lindsay Swift, *Brook Farm.*

14. Gilbert H. Barnes, *The Anti-Slavery Impulse.*

15. B. M. Palmer, *Life and Letters of James Henley Thornwell;* Dumas Malone, *The Public Life of Thomas Cooper.*

CHAPTER TWO

1. Rupert B. Vance, *Human Geography of the South;* Clarence Cason, *90° in the Shade;* H. H. Bennett, *The Soils and Agriculture of the Southern States.*

2. Charles Henry Ambler, *Sectionalism in Virginia from 1776 to 1861;* T. J. Wertenbaker, *Torchbearer of the Revolution.*

3. William A. Schaper, *Sectionalism and Representation in South Carolina, Rept. of the American Historical Ass'n.*, 1900, I, 230–463.

4. J. S. Bassett, "The Regulators of North Carolina," *Annual Rept. of the Am. Hist. Ass'n.*, 1894, 141–212.

5. J. L. M. Curry to C. C. Clay, Talladega, Ala., July 11, 1854 (Clay MSS.); *The Southern Planter* (Natchez, Miss.), Jan., 1842; *Mississippi Free Trader*, Nov. 1, 1858.

6. T. J. Wertenbaker, *The Planters of Colonial Virginia*, especially 183–247.

7. J. D. Butler, "British Convicts Shipped to American Colonies," *Am. Hist. Rev.*, II, 12–33.

8. *Life of the Reverend Devereux Jarratt, by himself . . . in a series of letters addressed to Reverend John Calmon . . .* (Baltimore, 1806).

9. *Henrico County Minute Book*, 1682–1701, 107–108; *York County Records*, Vol. 1671–1694, 34. (Both quoted in Bruce, *Social Life in Virginia in the Seventeenth Century*, 133, 194.)

10. R. D. W. Connor, *Cornelius Harnett*; Guion Johnson, *Ante-Bellum North Carolina*, 52–79; William Byrd, *Histories of the Dividing Line Betwixt Virginia and North Carolina* (W. K. Boyd, ed.), 92.

11. D. H. Bacot, "South Carolina Upcountry at the End of the Eighteenth Century," *Am. Hist. Rev.*, XXVIII, 682–698; Edward McCrady, *South Carolina Under Royal Government*, 373–375; U. B. Phillips, "South Carolina Federalists," *Am. Hist. Rev.*, XIV, 529–543; 731–743; Ralph Izard to Thomas Jefferson, June 10, 1785, quoted U. B. Phillips, *op. cit.*, 537.

12. U. B. Phillips, *Georgia and States Rights*, 15–112; E. M. Coulter, *A History of Georgia*, 178–222, 249–266; Avery Craven, "Georgia and the Union," *The Georgia Historical Quarterly*, XXIII, 219–235.

13. J. G. Baldwin, *Flush Times in Alabama and Mississippi*; T. P. Abernethy, *The Formative Period in Alabama*; T. H. Jacks, *Sectionalism and Party Politics in Alabama, 1819–1842*.

14. T. B. Thorpe, "Sugar and the Sugar Region of Louisiana," *Harper's Magazine*, VII, 758–759; Louise L. Harper, "Le Patriarche de St. Jacques," in *Le Currier des États-Unis*; C. Gayarre, "A Louisiana Sugar Plantation of the Old Regime," *Harper's Magazine*, LXXIV, 606–621; Lyle Saxon, *Old Louisiana*.

15. D. R. Hundley, *Social Relations in Our Southern States*, 193. On slave ownership, see *U. S. Census, 1860*.

16. A. N. J. Den Hollander, "The Tradition of 'Poor Whites,' " in *Culture in the South* (W. T. Couch, ed.), 403–431.

17. Frank L. and Harriet C. Owsley, "The Economic Basis of Society in the Late Ante-Bellum South," *Journal of Southern History*, VI, 24–45.

18. William A. Corrigan to Robert Corrigan, January 19, 1851; William A. Corrigan to William F. Corrigan, April 28, 1851; William A. Corrigan to William F. Corrigan, Feb. 2, 1842. (Corrigan MS.)

19. M. W. Leckey to James Walker, Jan. 19, 1850 (Walker MS. U. of Ill. Library); F. L. Olmsted, *Journey in the Back Country*, 160; J. H. Ingraham; *The South-West*, II, 26; Preston Brooks, *Cong. Globe, 33 Cong. 1 Sess.* Appx. 374.

20. Edward J. Hales in *Fayetteville Observer*, Feb. 28, 1853; Ebenezer Pettigrew to J. H. Bryan, Oct. 26, 1847, *John H. Bryant Papers*, IV.

21. The story of the Southern professional classes has not yet been written. There are a few sketches of "bench and bar" in the different states, but otherwise one must rely largely on individual biographies. See, however, T. C.

Johnson, *Scientific Interests in the Old South;* R. H. Shyrock, *Selections from Letters of Richard D. Arnold, M.D.;* W. L. Holt, "Josiah Clark Nott of Mobile," *Medical Life,* XXXV, 485–504; J. H. Easterby, *A History of the College of Charleston* (for Mitchell King); William E. Wightman, *Life of William Capers;* William E. Hatcher, *Life of J. B. Jeter, D.D.;* B. M. Palmer, *Life and Letters of . . . Thornwell;* J. P. Carson, *Life, Letters and Speeches of James Louis Petigru.*

22. Horace Kephart, *Our Southern Highlanders.*

23. J. P. Carson, *Life, Letters and Speeches of James Louis Petigru,* 227.

24. Joseph Lesesne to Francis Lieber, Sept. 20, 1846 (Lieber MS.).

25. *Vicksburg Sun,* April 9, 1860.

26. Ulrich B. Phillips, "The Central Theme of Southern History," *Am. Hist. Rev.,* XXXIV, 30–43.

CHAPTER THREE

1. *Writings of Thomas Jefferson* (Memorial Edition), II, 329; John Taylor, *Arator* (4th ed.), 188–189; Jefferson, *Notes on the State of Virginia* (1787), 274.

2. Avery Craven, *Soil Exhaustion . . . in Virginia and Maryland.*

3. F. in *Farmers' Register,* I, 552; Jefferson Papers (MS.), Vol. CXCVIII, Jefferson to Mr. Gibson, April 16, May 2, 1813; *American Farmer,* I, 99, 330; *Farmers' Register,* III, 619–626.

4. Avery Craven, *op. cit.,* 72–121; William Strickland, *Observations on the Agriculture of the United States of America,* 49.

5. John Taylor, *Tyranny Unmasked; New Views of the Constitution of the United States* (1823), 50–83; *Construction Construed and Constitutions Vindicated.*

6. Avery Craven, "John Taylor and Southern Agriculture," *The Journal of Southern History,* IV, 137–147.

7. *Arator,* 31–33; 17–26; Bernard Drell, "John Taylor of Caroline and the Preservation of an Old Social Order," *Virginia Magazine of History and Biography,* XLVI, 285–298.

8. *Ibid.,* 31.

9. *Ibid.,* 36–37.

10. Chas. M. Wiltse, *The Jeffersonian Tradition in American Democracy.*

11. John Taylor, *New Views of the Constitution of the United States,* 50–83; *Arator,* 42–46.

12. W. E. Dodd, "Chief Justice Marshall and Virginia," *Am. Hist. Rev.,* XII, 776–787; D. R. Anderson, *William Branch Giles,* 212–223.

13. Andrew C. McLaughlin, *A Constitutional History of the United States,* 394–396; Henry H. Simms, *Life of John Taylor.*

14. John Taylor, *Construction Construed . . .,* 27, 42–48, 140.

15. *Ibid.,* 83, 84, 108.

16. *Ibid.,* 125–127, 147.

17. D. R. Anderson, *William Branch Giles,* 223.

18. *American Farmer,* II, 57–58; III, 320–325; IV, 41.

19. John Taylor, *New Views* . . ., 248–249; *Constitution Construed* . . ., 291 301.

20. *Proceedings and Debates of the Virginia State Convention of 1829–30.* (Richmond, 1830.)

21. *Ibid.*, 65–76.

22. *Ibid.*, 316, 858.

23. *Ibid.*, 389 (Mr. Campbell).

24. *Ibid.*, 55–59 (Mr. Cook).

25. *Ibid.*, 28.

26. *Ibid.*, 63.

27. *Ibid.*, 149, 133, 282–283.

28. *Richmond Enquirer*, Jan. 7, 1832; *Ibid.*, Jan. 19, May 4, 1832. C. H. Ambler, *Sectionalism in Virginia*, 191–199; Joseph Clarke Robert, *The Road from Monticello; Constitutional Whig*, Jan. 13, 17, 21, 24.

29. *The Speeches of Philip A. Bolling in the House of Delegates of Virginia on the Policy of the State in Relation to Her Colored Population* . . .; *The Speech of Thomas Marshall (of Farquier) in the House of Delegates of Virginia, on the Policy of the State in Relation to Her Colored Population* . . .; *The Speech of Charles Jas. Faulkner (of Berkeley) in the House of Delegates of Virginia on the Policy of the State with Respect to Her Slave Population* . . .; *Richmond Enquirer*, March 30, 1832.

30. *Speech of James M'Dowell, Jr. (of Rockbridge) in the House of Delegates of Virginia, on the Slave Question.* . . .

31. Thomas Roderick Dew, *Review of the Debate in the Virginia Legislature of 1831 and 1832* (Richmond, 1832).

32. Ulrich Bonnell Phillips, *A History of Transportation in the Eastern Cotton Belt to 1860*; Ulrich Bonnell Phillips, "The South Carolina Federalists," *Am. Hist. Rev.*, XIV, 537–539; James H. Birche to Frederika Bremer, April 19, 1837 (Bremer MS., Huntington Library); T. D. Jervey, *Robert Y. Hayne and His Times*, 223; J. G. de R. Hamilton, "James Hamilton, Jr." (MS.); *Register of Debates in Congress*, VIII, Pt. I, 80–81; Hugh S. Legaré to A. Huger, Dec. 15, 1834; Nov. 21, 1835.

33. D. F. Houston, *A Critical Study of Nullification in South Carolina*, 53–54; J. G. Van Deusen, *Economic Basis of Disunion in South Carolina*, 40–41.

34. Gaillard Hunt, *John C. Calhoun*, 1–98; D. F. Houston, *op. cit.*, 7, 12.

35. Edwin L. Green, *George McDuffie*, 76–119; *Annals of Congress, 18 Cong. 1 Sess. II*, 2400 *et seq.*; 2423; Ames, *State Documents on Federal Relations*, No. 4, 6.

36. *The Crisis or Essays on the Usurpation of the Federal Government, by Brutus* (Charleston, 1827).

37. Laura A. White, *Robert Barnwell Rhett*, 15.

38. Chauncey Samuel Boucher, *The Nullification Controversy in South Carolina*, 223, 229, 271.

39. *Richmond Enquirer*, July 24, Aug. 10, Aug. 14, Aug. 28, 1832.

40. Quoted in *Richmond Enquirer*, Aug. 14, Aug. 28, 1832.

CHAPTER FOUR

1. J. C. Ballagh, *White Servitude in the Colony of Virginia* (Johns Hopkins Univ., *Studies*, XIII, Nos. 6–7).

2. *Ibid.*, 45–49; P. A. Bruce, *Economic History of Virginia in the Seventeenth Century*, II, 1–130.

3. *Hening's Statutes*, I, 254, 440, 517–518, 483; II, 187; H. F. McIlwaine, ed., *Journals of the House of Burgesses of Virginia, 1693–1702*, 188.

4. J. H. Russell, *The Free Negro in Virginia, 1619–1865*, *Johns Hopkins Studies in History and Political Science*, 31 Ser. No. 3, 23–25, 29–30, 32–33.

5. *Hening's Statutes*, I, 146.

6. *Journal of the House of Burgesses of Virginia*, 1772, 131; *Huguenot Family*, 352; Ballagh, *op. cit.*, 21ʳ.

7. Edward B. Bryan, *Letters to the Southern People*, 10; J. H. Thornwell, *Fast Day Sermons, or the Pulpit on the State of the Country*, 16, 46; A. T. Bledsoe, *An Essay on Liberty and Slavery*; T. R. R. Cobb, *An Inquiry into the Law of Negro Slavery in the United States of America*, 83–84; *Jacksonville Republican* (Ala.), June 20, 1854; *Richmond Enquirer*, Aug. 14, 1855.

8. Mrs. Rachel O'Connor to David Weeks, July 11, 1829 (Weeks Hall MS.); Jessie W. Parkhurst, "The Role of the Black Mammy in the Plantation Household," *Journal of Negro History*, XXIII, 349–369.

9. Luther P. Jackson, *Free Negro Labor and Property Holding in Virginia, 1830–1860* (MS. Thesis, U. of Chicago); *Memphis Whig*, June 8, 1854 (rape and lynching); *Advertiser and Gazette* (Ala.), July 26, 1858 (rape and lynching); Rachel O'Connor to Mary C. Weeks, Jan. 11, 1830 (Weeks Hall MS.).

10. B. Garland to his "Brother," Barrens, Mississippi, July 18, 1852 (MS.).

11. William Jacobs to Mary C. Weeks, Nov. 29, 1837 (Weeks Hall MS.).

12. Rachel O'Connor to A. T. Conrad, May 26, 1836 (Weeks Hall MS.); *Baton Rouge Gazette*, Jan. 30, 1830; *Mississippi Free Trader*, Oct. 17, 1854; May 22, 1852; *Columbia Enquirer*, May 27, 1856.

13. Vera Shlakman, *Economic History of a Factory Town*, *Smith College Studies in History*, XX, Nos. 1–4, 98–150.

14. Term "slave breeding" has been used in very loose fashion and applied to the rearing of slaves, the selling of slaves, and the rewarding of mothers. Actual mating of selected individuals is what men understand when the term is used regardless of what is being described. "No man in the South, we are sure," said the *Richmond Enquirer*, Aug. 14, 1855, "ever bred slaves for sale. . . . Will some Yankee or Englishman, ere the charge is repeated that slaves are bred to be sold like horses, when they are old enough for market, point out a single instance in the present or the past of a Southerner's pursuing such a business?" The challenge was never answered, nor has any historian since that day produced one single document to answer it.

15. Frances Butler Leigh, *Ten Years on a Georgia Plantation*, 233.

16. W. E. B. DuBois, *Black Reconstruction*, 35, 43; Frederic Bancroft, *Slave-Trading in the Old South*, 67–87; John Bernard, *Retrospects of America, 1797–1811*, 204.

17. *Public Documents of Massachusetts, Annual Report of Public Offices and Institutions,* 1857, 1858, 1859; *Manuscript Census,* 1850 (Mississippi State Archives).

18. Guion Griffis Johnson, *A Social History of the Sea Islands,* 101; J. W. Fowler Plantation Records; Wm. F. Palfrey Plantation Records; John B. Miller Plantation Records; F. W. Pickens Plantation Records. (MSS. in Duke University and Louisiana State University Libraries.)

19. *New Orleans Daily Picayune,* 1855–1858.

20. Vera Shlakman, *op. cit.,* 54–55; C. L. Green, *Holyoke, Massachusetts,* 45.

21. *DeBow's Review,* X, 623–625; *Southern Agriculturalist,* 1842.

22. *Ibid.,* X, 325–328; R. H. Taylor, *Slaveholding in North Carolina* (Sprunt Hist. Pub.), No. 18, 1–2, 89–92; Ulrich B. Phillips, *American Negro Slavery,* 261–290.

23. Vera Shlakman, *op. cit.,* 53–54; *Holyoke Town Records,* 1857, 11, quoted, C. M. Green, *op. cit.,* 43–44.

24. *DeBow's Review,* XXII, 38–44; X, 325–328.

25. John W. Savage in *Southern Planter,* 1842, 19–21; *DeBow's Review,* X, 325–328; S. A. Cartwright in *DeBow's Review,* XI, 335; *DeBow's Review,* X, 623–625.

26. H. M. Henry, *The Police Control of the Slave in South Carolina.*

27. Ulrich B. Phillips, "Plantations with Slave Labor and Free," *Am. Hist. Rev.,* XXX, 738–753.

28. Alfred H. Stone, "Problems of Southern Economic History," *Am. Hist. Rev.,* XIII, 779–797; Louis Hacker, *Triumph of American Capitalism;* C. S. Sydnor, *Slavery in Mississippi,* 181–202; R. H. Taylor, *Slaveholding in North Carolina,* 93–96; J. S. Bassett, *The Plantation Overseer,* 276.

29. Avery Craven, *Soil Exhaustion in . . . Virginia and Maryland,* 122–161.

CHAPTER FIVE

1. H. C. Hubbart, *The Older Middle West, 1840–1880,* 3–72; J. D. Barnhart, "Sources of Southern Migration into the Old Northwest," *Miss. Valley Hist. Rev.,* XXII, 49–62; S. B. Weeks, *Southern Quakers and Slavery.*

2. Avery Craven, *Soil Exhaustion in . . . Virginia and Maryland.*

3. *Charleston Mercury,* Aug. 23, 1828.

4. *North Carolina Hist. Rev.,* VI, 140–142; *Papers of Thomas Ruffin* (Hamilton, ed.), I, 278; Bernard, *South Atlantic States in 1833,* 321–322; *Legislative Documents* (N. C.), 1833.

5. Avery Craven, "The 'Turner Theories' and the South," *Journal of Southern History,* V, 291–314.

6. Fletcher Melvin Green, "Gold Mining: a Forgotten Industry of Ante-Bellum North Carolina," *The North Carolina Historical Review,* XIV, 1–40.

7. A. P. Usher, *An Introduction to the Industrial History of England,* 276–313; Henri Pirenne, "The Stages in the Social History of Capitalism," *Am. Hist. Rev.,* XIX, 494–515.

8. M. B. Hammond, *The Cotton Industry,* Pt. I, 3–33; Ulrich Bonnell Phillips, *American Negro Slavery,* 150–186; R. H. Taylor, *op. cit.,* 32–38.

9. F. L. Riley, ed., "The Autobiography of Gideon Lincecum," *Mississippi Historical Society Publications*, VIII, 443–519; T. P. Abernethy, *The Formative Period in Alabama, 1815–1828; Seventh Census . . . 1850*, 333 ff., 353 ff.; *Cong. Debates, 22 Cong., 1 Sess.*, 80–81; Ulrich B. Phillips, *Plantation and Frontier*, II, 197–208.

10. Thomas H. Benton, *Cong. Globe, 25 Cong., 3d Sess.*, Appx. 30–31.

11. Marquis James, *Andrew Jackson*, II, 304; Ulrich B. Phillips, *Georgia and State Rights*, 39–86.

12. T. P. Abernethy, *Formative Period in Alabama*, 24–30.

13. *Papers of Thomas Ruffin* (Hamilton, ed.), I, 193–197; *Raleigh Register*, March 16, 1827; R. H. Taylor, *op. cit.*, 60.

14. F. L. Riley, ed., "The Autobiography of Gideon Lincecum," *Mississippi Historical Society Publications*, VIII, 443–519.

15. Susan D. Smedes, *Memorials of a Southern Planter*, 42–83.

16. M. W. Philips, "Diary" (F. L. Riley, ed.), *Mississippi Historical Society Publications*, X, 305–481.

17. F. L. Olmsted, *Seaboard Slave States*, 329–330; 576–577; R. P. Brooks, *History of Georgia*, 213–215; Ulrich B. Phillips, "Origin and Growth of the Southern Black Belts," *Am. Hist. Rev.*, XI, 798–816.

18. F. J. Turner, *Rise of the New West*, 47.

19. L. C. Gray, *History of Agriculture in the Southern United States to 1860*, II, 673–720.

20. J. G. Baldwin, *Flush Times in Alabama and Mississippi*, 81.

21. Augusta *Georgia Courier*, Oct. 11, 1827, quoted, *Plantation and Frontier* (U. B. Phillips, ed.), I, 283–284; Benj. Parke to Lewis Hill, July 8, 1835.

22. *American State Papers*, Land, II, 479, 490–495.

23. *The Daily True Delta*, Feb. 6, 1850.

24. *Columbus Democrat*, Feb. 20, 1841; quoted by R. C. McGrare, "Apologia of American Debtor States," *Dodd Essays*, 93.

25. Charles S. Sydnor, *A Gentleman of the Old Natchez Region: Benjamin L. C. Wailes*, 6.

26. *Dallas Gazette*, March 21, 1856.

27. Susan D. Smedes, *op. cit.*, 67; J. D. Wade, *Augustus Baldwin Longstreet*, 5, 59, 61–64.

28. *Cong. Debates*, VI, Pt. I, 415 (1830); *American State Papers*, Land, IV, 529; VIII, 435; VI, 608–609.

29. *Baton Rouge Gazette*, April 28, May 5, 12, 30; Sept. 15, 1827; Feb. 2, 1828; Sept. 18, 1830 (advertisements of branded and maimed slaves); F. L. Olmsted, *A Journey in the Back Country*, 81; A. Hodgson, *Letters from North America*, I, 153; H. W. Vick, *Southern Planter*, Sept.–Dec., 1842, 17–18.

30. Based on runaway advertisements in Baton Rouge, Natchez, and New Orleans newspapers.

31. W. C. Whitaker, *History of Protestant Episcopal Church in Alabama*, 17–92; A. West, *History of Methodism in Alabama*, 29–127; William E. Wightman, *Life of William Capers, D.D.*, 446, 471–472; B. F. Riley, *A Memorial History of the Baptists in Alabama*, 5, 40–41, 53–77; *The Life, Travels, Labors and Writings of Lorenzo Dow*, 289–296.

CHAPTER SIX

1. For a discussion of these early moves, see William Sumner Jenkins, *Pro-Slavery Thought in the Old South*, 7–47.

2. E. L. Fox, *The American Colonization Society, 1817–1840*.

3. Asa Martin, "Pioneer Anti-Slavery Press," *Miss. Valley Hist. Rev.*, II, 509–528.

4. *Colonizationist and Journal of Freedom*, II, 47–48; Francis Lieber to Charles Sumner, Oct. 27, 1835 (Lieber MS.); *Address to the People of West Virginia shewing that Slavery is injurious to the public welfare and that it may be gradually abolished without detriment to the rights and interests of Slaveholders, By a Slaveholder of West Virginia (Ruffner)*.

5. Reported in George H. Moore, *Notes on the History of Slavery in Massachusetts*, 83–87.

6. Reported in Moore, *op. cit.*, 251–256.

7. *Annals of Congress, 16 Cong., 1 Sess.*, 314–335, 338, 372, 1023; John W. Walker to Charles Tait, Feb. 11, 1820 (Tait MS.); Ulrich Bonnell Phillips, *The Course of the South to Secession*, 96 (Livermore).

8. "Let us hear no more of humanity—it is profaning the term. Their object is power . . .," *Annals of Congress, 16 Cong., 1 Sess.*, 329.

9. V. S. Clark, *History of Manufactures in the United States, 1607–1860*; Blanche Hazard, *Organization of Boot and Shoe Industry in Massachusetts before 1875*.

10. P. W. Bidwell and J. I. Falconer, *History of Agriculture in Northern United States, 1620–1860*, 203; *New England Farmer*, XI, 293; Percy W. Bidwell, "The Agricultural Revolution in New England," *Am. Hist. Rev.*, XXVI, 688–702.

11. *New England Farmer*, IV, 212–213.

12. *Farmers' Register*, VII, 237–238.

13. Lois Kimball Mathews, *The Expansion of New England*, 171–194; A. B. Darling, *Political Changes in Massachusetts, 1824–1848*; Frederick Jackson Turner, *The United States, 1830–1850*, 39–91.

14. Caroline Ware, *The Early New England Cotton Manufacture*.

15. H. F. Wilson, *The Hill Country of Northern New England*, 1–57; Avery Craven, "The Abandoned Farms of New England," *Annual Rept. of the Am. Hist. Ass'n.*, 1922, I, 353–354; *New England Farmer*, X, 1; *Mass. Rept. on Statistics of Labor*, 1890. Introduction, ". . . where are the once prosperous families that occupied the farms above the foundry village? . . . Except now and then a single family, holding on like a ship-wrecked mariner to a lonely rock in the great ocean, all are gone. . . ."

16. Russel H. Anderson, "New York Agriculture meets the West," *Wis. Magazine of History*, XVI, 163–198; 285–296.

17. See R. W. Emerson's essay on "New England Reformers" and James Russell Lowell, "Thoreau" (*My Study Windows*).

18. H. C. Goddard, *Studies in New England Transcendentalism*; Henry Canby, *Thoreau*; M. E. Curti, *The American Peace Crusade*; Susan B. Anthony [and others], *History of Woman Suffrage*; Henry Steele Commager, *Theodore Parker*; Vernon Louis Parrington, *The Romantic Revolution in*

America, 1800–1860, 271–426; Van Wyck Brooks, *The Flowering of New England*; S. E. Morison, *Maritime History of Massachusetts.*

19. Ralph Volney Harlow, *Gerrit Smith*; H. D. A. Donovan, *The Barnburners*; J. B. McMaster, *Life and Letters of Stephen Girard*, II, 402–406; D. R. Fox, *Decline of Aristocracy in Politics of New York*, 198–262, 381–408; A. B. Darling, *op. cit.*, 17–18; F. Byrdsall, *History of the Loco Foco Party . . .*; Wm. Trimble, "Diverging Tendencies in New York Democracy in the Period of the Loco Focos," *Am. Hist. Rev.*, XXIV, 396–421.

20. *The New England Farmer*, X, 18–19; T. W. Carter to Thomas Walker, July 12, 1851 (Walker MS.); *Niles Weekly Register*, LI, 116.

21. Arthur B. Darling, *Political Changes in Massachusetts, 1824–1848*, 1–39, 130–250; A. B. Darling, "Workingmen's Party in Massachusetts," *Am. Hist. Rev.*, XXIX, 81–86; *A Documentary History of American Industrial Society* (John R. Commons and others, eds.), V, 84–90; 146–148 (Labor Movement, 1820–1840).

22. D. R. Fox, *Decline of Aristocracy in the Politics of New York*, 387.

23. F. Byrdsall, *History of the Loco Foco Party*, 68–69, 168.

24. *Ibid.*, see preface and dedication.

25. Octavius B. Frothingham, *Gerrit Smith, a Biography*, 62, 72, 148–149, 157.

26. *American State Papers, Public Lands*, V, 36; *Documentary History of American Industrial Society* (John R. Commons and others, ed.), VIII, 44–45 (Labor Movement, 1840–1860); George M. Stephenson, *The Political History of the Public Lands from 1840 to 1862*, 102; *Cong. Globe, 33 Cong., 1 Sess.*, Appx., 956.

27. W. P. and F. J. Garrison, *William Lloyd Garrison*, III, 22–23.

28. Quoted by Gilbert H. Barnes, *The Anti-Slavery Impulse*, 101. For facts on Garrison, see W. P. and F. J. Garrison, *op. cit.*, I, 80, 140; *The Liberator*, 1 January, 1831.

29. Garrison, *op. cit.*, I, 74–76, 100.

30. *Ibid.*, I, 140.

31. *Ibid.*, III, 32–33; Address before the Free People of Color, April, 1833, 11: ". . . The English language is lamentably weak and deficient in regard to this matter (strength of denunciation). I wish its epithets were heavier. . . . I wish I could denounce slavery and all its abettors in terms equal to their infamy. . . ."

32. William Lloyd Garrison to Susan B. Anthony, Jan. 4, 1877. (In Harper MS.)

33. *Letters of Theodore Dwight Weld, Angeline Grimké Weld, and Sarah Grimké, 1822–1844* (2 vols.), Weld to C. G. Finney, April 22, 1828, I, 14–18; Weld to Angelina Grimké, March 1, 1838, March 12, 1838, II, 575–585, 592–603.

34. Quoted in Gilbert H. Barnes, *op. cit.*, 104.

35. *Ibid.*, 64–108.

36. *Ibid.*, 109–152; B. C. Clark, *John Quincy Adams*, 359–407; *Cong. Globe, 24 Cong., 1 Sess.*, Appx. 221, 333, 402; *Ibid., 26 Cong., 1 Sess.*, 122–123, 251, 764.

37. Julian P. Bretz, "The Economic Background of the Liberty Party," *Am. Hist. Rev.*, XXXIV, 250–264; *Free American*, Aug. 19, 1841; Thomas

P. Martin, "The Upper Mississippi Valley in Anglo-American Anti-Slavery and Free Trade Relations, 1837–1842," *Miss. Valley Hist. Rev.*, XV, 204–220.

38. *Letters of James Gillespie Birney* (Dumond, ed.), I, 562–574.

39. Thomas P. Martin, *op. cit.*

40. *Letters of Theodore Dwight Weld . . . Sarah Grimké*, I, 880.

41. *The Anti-Slavery Alphabet* ("In the morning sow thy seed"), Philadelphia, 1847.

42. Booklet of Anti-slavery Children's Poems in Huntington Library.

43. *Ibid.* This booklet is evidently the one purchased by the editor of the *Mississippi Free Trader* in Buffalo and discussed by him in an editorial, Sept. 14, 1854.

44. *Anti-Slavery Hymns for the New England Anti-Slavery Convention, Wednesday and Thursday, May 25–26, 1859.*

45. *Abolitionist's Library . . . No. 1, January, 1834. The Despotism of Freedom*, by David Lee Child. Reproduced in *Anti-Slavery Almanac* for different years.

46. Henry H. Simms, "A Critical Analysis of Abolition Literature, 1830–1840," *Journal of Southern History*, VI, 368–382; Dwight L. Dumond, *Anti-Slavery Origins of the Civil War in the United States*; Arthur Young Lloyd, *The Slavery Controversy.*

47. H. B. Stowe to Lord ——, Jan. 20, 1853 (MS. in Huntington Library).

48. *Our World: or the Slaveholder's Daughter* (New York and Auburn: Miller, Orton & Mulligan, 1855).

49. *A Chapter of American History. Five Years' Progress of the Slave Power . . . by John Gorham Palfrey* (Boston, 1852), 61–66.

50. *Letters of James Gillespie Birney* (Dumond, ed.), I, 568.

51. Quoted by Julian P. Bretz, *op. cit.*

52. *Annual Report of the American Foreign Anti-Slavery Society*, 1850, 150.

53. *Ball's Splendid Mammouth Pictorial Tour of the United States, . . . Compiled for the Panorama* (Cincinnati, 1855), No. 13, 26–29; *Anti-Slavery Tracts*, No. 7, "Revolution the only Remedy for Slavery," 1855.

54. *American Slavery as It Is: Testimony of a Thousand Witnesses* (New York, 1839).

55. *Ibid.*, 60; 90, "An honorable friend . . . was *present at the* burial of a female slave in Mississippi who *had been whipped to death* at the stake by her master, because she was gone longer of an errand to the neighboring town than her master thought necessary. . . . To complete the climax of horror, she was delivered of a dead infant while undergoing the punishment." David L. Child, *Despotism of Freedom.*

CHAPTER SEVEN

1. *An Essay in Vindication of the Continental Colonies from a Censure of Mr. Adam Smith, in His Theory of Moral Sentiments. . . . By an American*, 42; "A Summary View of the Rights of British America," *American*

Archives, Ser. IV, I, 696; *Writings of Thomas Paine* (Conway, ed.), I, 7 (quoted, Wm. S. Jenkins, *Pro-Slavery Thought in the Old South,* 27–31).

2. *Annals of Congress, 15 Cong., 1 Sess.,* 234.

3. *Review of the debate in the Virginia Legislature of 1831 and 1832. By Thomas R. Dew; Review of the Slave Question. By a Virginian.*

4. Guion Griffis Johnson, *Ante-Bellum North Carolina,* 560–572.

5. T. D. Jervey, *The Slave Trade,* 20–23; C. S. Boucher, *The Nullification Controversy in South Carolina,* 107 n.

6. Ulrich Bonnell Phillips, *Georgia and States Rights,* 158–159.

7. *Annals of Congress, 16 Cong., 1 Sess.,* I, 92, 116, 259–275, 374–387.

8. *A Refutation of the Calumnies Circulated against the Southern and Western States, Respecting the Institution and Existence of Slavery Among Them. To which is added, A Minute and Particular Account of the Actual State and Condition of their Negro Population. Together with Historical Notices of all the Insurrections that have taken place since the Settlement of the Country. By a South Carolinian.* (Charleston, 1822.)

9. *Richard Furman's Exposition of the Views of the Baptists, Relative to the Coloured Population of the United States, in Communication to the Governor of South-Caroline, 1832.* (3d ed. 1835.)

10. Edward Brown, *Notes on the Origin and Necessity of Slavery;* Thomas Cooper, *On the Constitution of the United States, and the Questions that have arisen under it;* C. C. Pinckney, "Address to the South Carolina Agricultural Society" (Pamphlet); Charleston *Courier,* Nov. 28, 1829 (Miller); Whitmarsh B. Seabrook, *A Concise View of the Critical Situation, and Future Prospects of the Slave Holding States, in relation to their Colored Population.*

11. Thomas R. Dew, *Review of the Debates in the Virginia Legislature of 1831 and 1832;* Pro-Slavery Argument, 287–490.

12. *The Works of John C. Calhoun* (Crallé ed.), II, 625–633; *Cong. Globe, 25 Cong., 2 Sess.,* Appx., 61–62.

13. Laura A. White, *Robert Barnwell Rhett;* Avery Craven, *Edmund Ruffin, Southerner;* Harvey Wish, "George Fitzhugh, Conservative of the Old South," *Southern Sketches,* II, 1 Series.

14. John Fletcher, *Studies on Slavery;* Josiah Priest, *Bible Defense of Slavery . . .;* Reverend Thornton Stringfellow, *Slavery, Its Origin, Nature and History. Its Relation to Society, to Government, and to True Religion;* Reverend Fred A. Ross, *Slavery Ordained of God;* Richard Fuller, *Our Duty to the African Race;* George D. Armstrong, *A Discourse on Slaveholding; The Christian Doctrine of Slavery. Duties of Masters to Servants.* (McTyeire, Sturgis, Holmes.)

15. J. H. Thornwell, *Report on the Subject of Slavery Presented to the Synod of South Carolina at their sessions in Winnsboro, November 6th, 1851;* "An Address," *Southern Presbyterian Review,* 541.

16. *Pro-Slavery Argument,* 14, 109–110.

17. Edmund Ruffin, *Political Economy of Slavery; Slavery and Free Labor Compared;* Fred A. Ross, *Slavery Ordained of God.* (Letter to Albert Barnes.)

18. "A Vindication of Secession and the South from the Strictures of Rev. R. J. Breckenridge, D.D., LL.D., in the Danville Quarterly Review" (Co-

lumbia, 1861), 14; "Defense of Southern Slavery against the Attacks of Henry Clay and Alexander Campbell," 44.

19. B. M. Palmer, "A Discourse before the General Assembly of South Carolina on December 10, 1863, appointed by the Legislature as a Day of Fasting, Humiliation, and Prayer," 11–12.

20. G. S. Sawyer, *Southern Institutes*, 192; J. R. R. Cobb, *An Inquiry into the Law of Slavery in the United States of America*, I, 23–24, 35–40; Richard Fuller, *Our Duty to the African Race* . . ., 136.

21. Samuel B. How, *Slaveholding Not Sinful*, 80 ff.; Edmund Ruffin, "African Colonization Unveiled"; "Defense of Southern Slavery by a Southern Clergyman," 38; George Fitzhugh, *Cannibals All*, 30–36, 43, 163.

22. Richard H. Colfax, *Evidence against the Views of the Abolitionists, Consisting of Physical and Moral Proofs of the Natural Inferiority of the Negroes*; John J. Flournoy, *An Essay on the Origin, Habits, etc., of the African Race, Incidental to the Propriety of Having Nothing to Do with Negroes.*

23. Josiah C. Nott, M.D., "Two Lectures on the Natural History of the Caucasian and Negro Races. Mobile, 1844"; J. C. Nott, M.D., and Geo. R. Glidden, *Types of Mankind* . . .; J. H. Van Evrie, M.D., *Negroes and Negro "Slavery": The First an Inferior Race: The Latter Its Normal Condition* (N. Y., 1863).

24. *Richmond Enquirer*, July 6, 1854; April 29, 1854.

25. *The Works of Calhoun* (Crallé ed.), II, 630; Edmund Ruffin, *Political Economy of Slavery*, 8–10; Reverend N. L. Rice, *Ten Letters on the Subject of Slavery* . . ., Letter I; Thornton Stringfellow, "Scriptural and Statistical View in Favor of Slavery," 144; F. A. Ross, *Position of the Southern Church in Relation to Slavery* . . ., 68.

26. *The Works of Calhoun* (Crallé ed.), II, 630–631.

27. For George Fitzhugh see: *Cannibals All; A Sociology for the South;* "What Shall be done with the Free Negroes, Essays written for the Fredericksburg Recorder, By George Fitzhugh, of Port Royal" (1851); "Slavery Justified, By a Southerner"; Harvey Wish, *George Fitzhugh, Conservative of the Old South* (*Southern Sketches*, No. 11 Series).

28. Avery Craven, *Edmund Ruffin, Southerner*, 127–142.

29. Elwood Fisher, "Lecture on the North and South Before the Young Men's Merchantile Library Association of Cincinnati, January 16, 1849," 38; see also *Southern Literary Messenger*, XXV, 81; New Orleans *Daily Crescent*, Nov. 30, 1855; Henry Hughes, *A Treatise on Sociology, Theoretical and Practical.*

30. "Memoirs of a Nullifier, written by Himself" (Columbia, 1832).

CHAPTER EIGHT

1. For discussion of "gag rule" anti-slavery methods see: Gilbert H. Barnes, *The Anti-Slavery Impulse*, 109–145.

2. James Petigru Carson, *Life, Letters and Speeches of James Louis Petigru*, 125 (Petigru to Hugh S. Legaré, July 15, 1833).

3. *The Works of John C. Calhoun* (Crallé ed.), III, 140–202.

4. George W. Julian, *The Life of Joshua R. Giddings*, 102–140.

5. Gaillard Hunt, *John C. Calhoun*, 199.

6. *The Works of John C. Calhoun* (Crallé ed.), III, 140–142; Laura A. White, *Robert Barnwell Rhett*, 32–50; James Petigru Carson, *op. cit.*, 195.

7. Justin H. Smith, *The Annexation of Texas*, 1–33; Eugene C. Barker, "Slavery and the Colonization of Texas," *Miss. Valley Hist. Rev.*, XI, 3–36; "Stephen F. Austin," *Ibid.*, V, 20–35; "Notes on the Colonization of Texas," *Ibid.*, X, 141–152; C. S. Boucher, "In Re that Aggressive Slavocracy," *Ibid.*, VIII, 13–79.

8. *The Commerce of the Prairies by Josiah Gregg* (Milo Milton Quaife, ed.); Henry C. Hubbart, *The Older Middle West, 1840–1880*, 3–87; Cardinal Goodwin, *The Trans-Mississippi West*, 114–274; Dan E. Clark, *The West in American History*, 442–466.

9. Ralph C. H. Catterall, *The Second Bank of the United States*, 22–92.

10. *Western Intelligencer*, Feb. 5, Oct. 23, 1817; Nov. 10, 1819 (quoted in E. C. Barker, "The Colonization of Texas," *Miss. Valley Hist. Rev.*, X, 143).

11. *Missouri Advocate*, Aug. 27, Oct. 15, 1825 (Barker, *op. cit.*).

12. *The Austin Papers* (Eugene C. Barker, ed.), *Annual Report of the Am. Hist. Ass'n.*, 1919, I, Pt. I, 1–6, 395–396.

13. Eugene C. Barker, "The Colonization of Texas," *Miss. Valley Hist. Rev.*, X, 144–145.

14. Justin H. Smith, *The Annexation of Texas*, 1–51.

15. Joseph Schafer, *A History of the Pacific Northwest*; William J. Marshall, *Acquisition of Oregon* (2 vols.); Fred W. Powell, *Hall J. Kelley on Oregon*; Cornelius J. Brosnan, *Jason Lee, Prophet of the New Oregon*.

16. G. L. Rives, *The United States and Mexico, 1821–1848* (2 vols.); Eugene C. Barker, *The Life of Stephen F. Austin, Founder of Texas, 1793–1836*.

17. Gerald W. Johnson, *America's Silver Age*; Glyndon G. Van Deusen, *The Life of Henry Clay*; Claude M. Fuess, *Daniel Webster* (2 vols.); Gaillard Hunt, *John C. Calhoun*; R. G. Wellington, *The Political and Sectional Influence of the Public Lands, 1828–1842*.

18. B. H. Hibbard, *A History of the Public Lands*, 193–194; R. G. Wellington, *op. cit.*, 111–112; Laura A. White, *Robert Barnwell Rhett*, 51–84.

19. Virgil Maxcy to J. C. Calhoun, Nov. 6, 1843, *Annual Rept. of the Am. Hist. Ass'n.*, 1929, 190–191. "Wherever in fine the friends of M. V. B. have come to act on the Presidential question, their whole conduct is marked by trick and deception and every body now begins to think in this part of the world, that V. B. will out manoeuvre you and certainly get the nomination whether the delegates to Convention be appointed one way or the other."

20. R. M. T. Hunter to John C. Calhoun, Oct. 10, 1843, *Annual Rept. of the Am. Hist. Ass'n.*, 1929, 186–188.

21. Maxcy to Calhoun, Dec. 10, 1843, *Annual Rept. Am. Hist. Ass'n.*, 1899, II, 902–903.

22. John C. Calhoun to F. W. Pickens, Nov. 24, 1843, *Annual Rept. Am. Hist. Ass'n.*, 1929, 191.

23. John C. Calhoun to Geo. McDuffie, Dec. 4, 1843, *Annual Rept. Am. Hist. Ass'n.*, 1899, II, 552–555.

24. *Ibid.*, 559–560.

25. *Ibid.*, 841, 846.

26. Gaillard Hunt, *John C. Calhoun*, 260; Calhoun to R. B. Rhett, Sept. 13, 1838, *Annual Rept. Am. Hist. Ass'n.*, 1899, II, 399; Calhoun to James Edward Calhoun, Dec. 20 and Dec. 24, 1837, *Ibid.*, 386.

27. Eugene C. Barker, "The Influence of Slavery on the Colonization of Texas," *The Mississippi Valley Hist. Rev.*, XI, 3–36; R. M. T. Hunter to John C. Calhoun, Dec. 19, 1843, *Annual Rept. Am. Hist. Ass'n.*, 1899, II, 906.

28. *Jacksonville Republican*, Dec. 13, 1843; W. D. Lyles to Levi Woodbury, May 24, 1844 (Woodbury MS.).

29. Jesse S. Reeves, *American Diplomacy under Tyler and Polk*, 89–113.

30. *Ibid.*, 114–137; Justin H. Smith, *op. cit.*, 116–129.

31. John C. Calhoun to James Edward Calhoun, Feb. 7, 1844; to ——, March 9, 1844; to Mrs. T. G. Clemson, March 15, 1844, *Annual Rept. Am. Hist. Ass'n.*, 1899, II, 567, 574–576; *Ibid.*, 556, 567 (to R. M. T. Hunter).

32. Jesse S. Reeves, *op. cit.*, 138–161.

33. Silas Wright to Martin Van Buren, April 14, 1844 (Van Buren MS.); J. M. Niles to Martin Van Buren, Dec. 30, 1844; F. P. Blair, Sr., to Martin Van Buren, March 18, 1844 (Van Buren MS.).

34. Holmes Alexander, *The American Talleyrand*, 396–398; Glyndon G. Van Deusen, *The Life of Henry Clay*, 368–378.

35. "Letters of Gideon J. Pillow to James K. Polk, 1844," *Am. Hist. Rev.*, XI, 832–843.

CHAPTER NINE

1. J. N. Norwood, *The Schism in the Methodist Episcopal Church*, 1844; Mary Burnham Putnam, *The Baptists and Slavery, 1840–1845*.

2. W. E. Smith, *The Francis Preston Blair Family in Politics*, I, 175–176; Marquis James, *Andrew Jackson, Portrait of a President*, 266–268; 279–284; 334–338.

3. Francis Preston Blair, Sr., to Martin Van Buren, May 30, Dec. 24, 1844; Jan. 20, July 9, Feb. 28, April 9, April 16, 1845 (Van Buren MS.).

4. Herbert D. A. Donovan, *The Barnburners*, 52–60.

5. Wright to Flagg, March 12, 1847 (quoted in Donovan, *op. cit.*), 63 n.; Donovan, *op. cit.*, 60–84.

6. W. M. Meigs, *Thomas Hart Benton*, 225–275.

7. See *Cong. Globe*, Vol. 13 (1843–44), 474–497; Clarence Henry McClure, *Opposition in Missouri to Thomas Hart Benton*, 82.

8. *The Diary of James K. Polk During His Presidency, 1845–1849*, Dec. 24, 1845. "Col. Benton spoke," he said, "of the Baltimore Convention of 1844 and charged corruption upon them." *The Cong. Globe, 28 Cong. 1 Sess.*, Appx. 568, 607, June 13, 1844; E. J. McCormac, *James K. Polk, A Political Biography*, 257; Benton, *Thirty Years' View*, II, 614–615.

9. Francis Wharton to John C. Calhoun, *Annual Rept. Am. Hist. Ass'n.*, 1929, 263.

10. *Missouri Register*, May 21, 1844; see Clarence Henry McClure, *op. cit.*

11. Isaac Hill and Blair had broken during the Tyler Administration. See W. E. Smith, *op. cit.*, I, 151–152.

12. Blair to Van Buren, March 18, 1844 (Van Buren MS.).

13. Blair to Van Buren, May 20, 1844 (Van Buren MS.); Van Buren to Blair, Oct. 5, 1844 (Blair MS.); Blair to Van Buren, July 9, 1845 (Van Buren MS.); H. M. Judge to J. C. Calhoun, Dec. 9, 1844, *Am. Hist. Ass'n. Rept.* 1929, 268–269; J. H. Pacddey to M. Van Buren, May 31, 1844 (Van Buren MS.); Andrew Jackson to Francis Preston Blair, Sr., Feb. (?), 1845 (Blair MS.).

14. *Republican Banner and Nashville Whig*, May 11, 1856; W. E. Smith, *op. cit.*, I, 144–181.

15. Blair to Van Buren, Feb. 29, 1848 (Van Buren MS.); Benton later charged that Calhoun had required Blair's dismissal as price for South Carolina's vote in 1844, T. H. Benton, *Thirty Years' View*.

16. T. H. Benton, *Thirty Years' View*, II, 647.

17. *Ibid.*, II, 678–679.

18. *Jefferson Inquirer*, Sept. 8, 1849 (quoted in McClure, *op. cit.*, 142).

19. Duff Green to John C. Calhoun, March 26, 1845; Lewis S. Coryell to John C. Calhoun, April 6, 1845; Duff Green to John C. Calhoun, June 1, 1845, *Annual Rept. Am. Hist. Ass'n.*, 1929.

20. Calhoun to T. G. Clemson, April 25, 1845, *Annual Rept. Am. Hist. Ass'n.*, 1899, II, 652–653; Calhoun to T. G. Clemson, April 25, 1845, *ibid.*, 652–653.

21. J. D. Richardson, *Messages and Papers of the Presidents*, IV, 381.

22. Frederick Jackson Turner, *The United States, 1830–1850*, 543–544.

23. John C. Calhoun to John Y. Mason, May 30, 1845, *Annual Rept. Am. Hist. Ass'n.*, 1899, II, 660–661; *The Diary of James K. Polk During His Presidency, 1845–1849* (Milo Milton Quaife, ed.), I, 155; John C. Calhoun to Mrs. T. G. Clemson, Jan. 11, 1845, *Annual Rept. Am. Hist. Ass'n.*, 1899, II, 695.

24. Duff Green to John C. Calhoun, Sept. 24, 1845, *Annual Rept. Am. Hist. Ass'n.*, 1899, II, 1055.

25. *Cong. Globe, 29 Cong., 1 Sess.*, 1028; *Charleston Mercury*, quoted, *Niles' Register*, Dec. 6, 1845, 214; *The New York Evening Express*, Nov. 27, 1845.

26. John C. Calhoun to James Edward Calhoun, July 2, 1846, *Annual Rept. Am. Hist. Ass'n.*, 1899, II, 698.

27. Laura A. White, *Robert Barnwell Rhett*, 88.

28. Clark E. Persinger, "The 'Bargain of 1844' as the Origin of the Wilmot Proviso," *Annual Rept. Am. Hist. Ass'n.*, 1911, I, 189–195.

29. *Cong. Globe, 29 Cong., 1 Sess.*, 15, 110.

30. *Niles' Weekly Register*, LXIX, 289–290.

31. Speech in House of Representatives, Jan. 5, 1846, *Cong. Globe, 29 Cong. 1 Sess.*, 139–142; *Speeches in Congress*, 150–151; *Ibid.*, 98, 101, 151.

32. *Ibid.*, 104; *Cong. Globe, 28 Cong., 1 Sess.*, 613, Speech of May 21, 1844.

33. F. W. Taussig, *The Tariff History of the United States*, 114–115.

34. M. R. Eiselen, *The Rise of Pennsylvania Protectionism*, 199–208; for vote see Frederick Jackson Turner, *The United States, 1830–1850*, 556–559.

35. The *Chicago Democrat*, April 7, 1846; April 3, April 25, June 13, Aug. 10, Aug. 25, Sept. 1, Sept. 2, Oct. 30, 1846.

36. *Ibid.*, Nov. 10, 1846; July 6, 1847.

37. Mahlon D. Ogden to John A. Rockwell, Dec. 21, 1847 (Rockwell MS.).

38. *Chicago Daily Journal*, Nov. 19, 1846, Aug. 19, 1846; *Tri-Weekly Quincy* (Ill.) *Whig*, Jan. 24, 1846.

CHAPTER TEN

1. *The Diary of James K. Polk During His Presidency, 1845–1849.* (Milo Milton Quaife, ed.)

2. C. B. Going, *David Wilmot*, 35–36. G. W. Julian wrote: "I would like him better if he did not swear so much in conversation." (Julian MS.)

3. C. B. Going, *op. cit.*, 51.

4. Clark E. Persinger, "The 'Bargain of 1844' as the Origin of the Wilmot Proviso," *Annual Rept. Am. Ass'n.*, 1911, I, 189–195; R. R. Stenberg, "The Motivation of the Wilmot Proviso," *Miss. Valley Hist. Rev.*, XVIII, 535–541; Manuscript Diary of Gideon Wells in Huntington Library; *Cong. Globe, 29 Cong., 1 Sess.*, 1185, 1186: On Monday, Aug. 3, the day of the River and Harbor Bill veto, Brinkerhoff reproached his friends for voting for the tariff before the "Harbor Bills" were passed. "Had my friends postponed the vote on the tariff bill one week, as I advised them to do, this bill [R. & H.] would have become a law." A Pennsylvania Democrat, Richard Broadhead, advised Western men "to cut loose from what is called Southern domocracy, and go with their true friends from the Northern and Middle States."

5. C. B. Going, *op. cit.*, 51, 65; *Cong. Globe, 29 Cong., 1 Sess.*, 1204.

6. R. R. Stenberg, "The Motivation of the Wilmot Proviso," *Miss. Valley Hist. Rev.*, XVIII, 535–541; see also *Chicago Democrat* (weekly), Jan. 30, 1849, for Wentworth's story of the Proviso.

7. H. R. Mueller, *The Whig Party in Pennsylvania*, 133; Harrisburg *Telegraph*, July 8, 1846; *Pennsylvanian*, July 22, 24, 1846, quoted by Malcolm Rogers Eiselen, *The Rise of Pennsylvania Protectionism*, 193 n.

8. See Wentworth's statement that it was agreed to by Democrats to prevent Whigs from doing it. *Chicago Democrat* (weekly), Nov. 17, 1849.

9. Going, *op. cit.*, 145–146.

10. David Wilmot to Preston King, Sept. 25, 1847 (copy in Van Buren MS.); Wilmot to Victor E. Piollet, July 4, 1846.

11. Johnson and Brown, *A. H. Stephens*, 218.

12. *Cong. Globe, 29 Cong., 2 Sess.*, Appx., 244; R. B. Rhett to John C. Calhoun, Sept. 8, 1847, *Annual Rept. Am. Hist. Ass'n.*, 1899, II, 1132–1133; H. W. Conner to John C. Calhoun, Sept. 28, 1848, *ibid.*, 1182–1184.

13. *Cincinnati Gazette*, Oct. 7, 1847.

14. *Cleveland Plain Dealer*, quoted in *New York Tribune*, June 29, 1846. On Aug. 8, before news of Wilmot Proviso had reached it, this paper had said: "Another four years will add slave territory enough to the South to forever overbalance the free representation from the North.—Let the boundaries of Slavery be set!" Quoted *Detroit Daily Advertiser*, Aug. 11, 1846.

15. *True Democrat*, quoted in *National Era*, Dec. 9, 1847; *Daily Sanduskian*, Feb. 26, 1850; *Chicago Democrat*, Jan. 30, 1847.

16. Theodore C. Smith, *The Liberty and Free Soil Parties in the Northwest*, 121; Salmon P. Chase to Joshua Giddings, Aug. 15, 1846.

17. *Detroit Daily Advertiser*, Aug. 8, 1846. Western resentment against the duties on tea and coffee and Polk's pocket veto of the River and Harbor Bill of 1847 should also be noted. Wentworth went so far as to say: "Had Mr. Clay been for free tea and coffee and Mr. Polk against it, who doubts but the election of 1844 would have differently resulted?" *Cong. Globe, 29 Cong., 2 Sess.*, 311. *Chicago Daily Journal*, Nov. 1, 1848, speaks of a vessel grounded in Chicago harbor by striking "Mr. Polk's farm."

18. *The Chicago Journal*, Aug. 10, 1846; *The Daily Sanduskian*, June 1, 1848; see also, B. H. Payne, "Contest for the Trade of the Mississippi Valley," *DeBow's Review*, III, 98.

19. T. C. Smith, *op. cit.*, 99–100, 129.

20. Salmon P. Chase to Joshua Giddings, Feb. 9, 1843; January 21, Feb. 15, 1842 (Giddings-Julian MS.).

21. Helen Cavanagh, *Anti-Slavery Sentiment and Politics in the Old Northwest, 1844–1860*, 31–39 (Manuscript Thesis, University of Chicago).

22. Herbert D. A. Donovan, *The Barnburners*, 60–83.

23. *Ibid.*, 90–96.

24. P. M. Hamer, *The Secession Movement in South Carolina*, 1–3; John C. Calhoun to —— ——, Nov. 7, 1846, *Annual Rept. Am. Hist. Ass'n.*, 1899, II, 710–711; John C. Calhoun to Mrs. T. G. Clemson, *ibid.*, 716; *Cong. Globe, 29 Cong., 2 Sess.*, Appx., 244 (for Rhett).

25. *The Works of John C. Calhoun* (Crallé ed.), IV, 339–349.

26. *Richmond Enquirer*, Feb. 18, 1847.

27. Virginia's Resolutions were adopted on March 8; see H. V. Ames, *State Documents on Federal Relations*, 245–247; *Niles' Weekly Register*, LXXV, 73.

28. *Niles' Weekly Register*, LXXII, 178; James Byrne Ranck, *Albert Gallatin Brown*, 48–56.

29. A. B. Moore, *History of Alabama and Her People*, 259–260; *Acts of Alabama, 1847–48*, 450–451; Clarence Phillips Denman, *The Secession Movement in Alabama*, 3–13; Richard Harrison Shryock, *Georgia and the Union in 1850*, 132–141; Texas Legislature, March 18, 1848, quoted, H. V. Ames, *op. cit.*, 245; Joseph Carlyle Sitterson, *The Secession Movement in North Carolina*, 38–53.

30. John C. Calhoun to Mrs. T. G. Clemson, 19th March, 1847, *Annual Rept. Am. Hist. Ass'n.*, 1899, II, 720; Philip M. Hamer, *The Secession Movement in South Carolina*, 11–12, 13–14.

31. William E. Smith, *The Francis Preston Blair Family in Politics*, I, 222–225.

32. Committee report to Martin Van Buren, June 16, 1848, telling of their "arbitrary and insulting exclusion" (Van Buren MS.); Roy Franklin Nichols, *The Democratic Machine, 1850–1854*, 15–29; Reginald Charles McGrane, *William Allen, A Study in Western Democracy*, 126–137.

33. *The Life of Thurlow Weed, Including His Autobiography and a Memoir* (Harriet A. Weed, ed.), I, 571–583.

34. Quoted, G. G. Van Deusen, *The Life of Henry Clay*, 391.

35. William H. Bennet to Caleb B. Smith, Feb. 8, 1848 (Caleb Smith MS.); E. W. McGoughy to Caleb Smith, March 15, 1848 (*ibid.*).

36. *Lafayette Journal*, quoted in Theodore C. Smith, *op. cit.*, 128; J. A. Lazall to Caleb Smith, Dec. 20, 1848 (Caleb Smith MS.).

37. *Cleveland American*, May 26, 1847.

38. John C. Calhoun to Andrew Pickens Calhoun, April 16, 1848; to Thom G. Clemson, July 23, 1848; Laura A. White, *Robert Barnwell Rhett*, 96–98.

39. *Chicago Democrat*, July 7, Nov. 13, 14, 1848; *Milwaukee Sentinel*, June 5, 15, 1848.

40. Committee to Van Buren, June 16, 1848 (Van Buren MS.); Francis Preston Blair, Sr. to Martin Van Buren, Feb. 29, 1848; *ibid.*, Dec. 9, 1847 (Van Buren MS.).

41. *Ibid.*, Blair to Van Buren, June 11, 1848 (Van Buren MS.).

42. James Cooper to Howell Cobb, *Am. Hist. Ass'n. Rept.*, 1911, II, 137. In twelve Southern States Democrats lost 14,000 votes from 1844 and Whigs gained 39,000. *Raleigh Standard*, Nov. 15, 1848.

43. *Illinois State Register*, Dec. 1, 1848; *Chicago Democrat*, Nov. 14, Dec. 1, 1848; *Indiana Sentinel*, June 2, 1849. See also speech of John L. Robinson in the House of Representatives, Dec. 18, 1848, *Cong. Globe, 30 Cong., 2 Sess.*, 54: ". . . The fact that General Taylor was a Southern man, owning a large number of slaves, identified in feeling and interests with them upon the institution of slavery, had a powerful influence in bringing about this result. . . . Are all the great questions which naturally divide the two parties to be swallowed up by this one?"

44. Francis Preston Blair, Sr. to Martin Van Buren, Nov. 30, 1848 (Van Buren MS.); Martin Van Buren to Francis Preston Blair, Dec. 11, 1848 (Blair MS.).

CHAPTER ELEVEN

1. *Cong. Globe, 30 Cong., 2 Sess.*, Appx., 80, 309.

2. *Ibid.*, 54–55 (Robinson); 123 (Brown).

3. *Ibid.*, 38 (Root); 55 (Giddings); 83 (Gott).

4. To Charles J. Faulkner, Aug. 1, 1847 (MS. Huntington Library); *Thirty Years' View*, II, 694–700.

5. *Charleston Mercury*, Aug. 21, 1848; Laura A. White, *Robert Barnwell Rhett*, 98–99.

6. *Works of John C. Calhoun* [Crallé ed.], VI, 290–313.

7. *Cong. Globe, 30 Cong., 2 Sess.*, p. 440; *Richmond Enquirer*, Dec. 25, 1848.

8. Chauncey Samuel Boucher, "The Secession and Cooperation Movements in South Carolina, 1848–1852," *Washington University Studies*, Vol. V, No. 2;

Clarence P. Denman, *The Secession Movement in Alabama*, 1–13; J. C. Sitterson, *The Secession Movement in North Carolina*, 38–53; Dorothy Dodd, "The Secession Movement in Florida," *Florida Hist. Soc. Quarterly*, XII, 3–19; Richard H. Shryock, *Georgia and the Union in 1850*, 178–216; Cleo Hearon, *Mississippi and the Compromise of 1850*, 16–90.

9. John C. Calhoun to John H. Means, April 13, 1849, *Annual Rept. Am. Hist. Ass'n.*, 1899, II, 764–766; to J. H. Hammond, Jan. 4, 1850, *ibid.*, 779, 781; James H. Hammond to John C. Calhoun, *ibid.*, 1193; *The Mississippi Free Trader*, Feb. 10, 1849; *The Sumter Banner*, March 21, 1849.

10. Richard H. Shryock, *op. cit.*, 179.

11. Feb. 8, 1849. "Cobb Papers," *Ga. Hist. Quarterly*, V, No. 2, 38.

12. *Perry Journal* (MS.), entry Aug. 6, 1849 (U. of North Carolina); quoted in Augusta (*Daily*) *Chronicle & Sentinel*, Jan. 10, 1849; *Savannah Republican*, Jan. 1, 1849.

13. Blair to Van Buren, Dec. 3, 1849 (Van Buren MS.).

14. Quoted from *Cincinnati Globe*, Nov. 17, 1848, by Theodore C. Smith, *Liberty and Free Soil Parties in the Northwest*, 179.

15. G. M. Mathews to Caleb Smith, June 7, 1849; J. Yarland to Caleb Smith, July 3, 1849; C. H. Hunt to C. Smith, July 14, 1849 (Smith MS.).

16. *Cong. Globe, 29 Cong., 2 Sess.*, Appx., 316–317.

17. *Mississippi Free Trader*, Oct. 10, 1849.

18. *Daily Sanduskian*, Feb. 26, 1850.

19. Quoted by K. Coman, *Economic Beginnings of the Far West*, II, 255.

20. H. H. Bancroft, *History of the Pacific States*, XVIII, 159.

21. John C. Calhoun to Charles J. Faulkner, Aug. 1, 1847; C. J. Faulkner to John C. Calhoun, June 15, 1847, *Annual Rept. Am. Hist. Ass'n.*, 1929, 385–387; *Annual Report of the American and Foreign Anti-Slavery Society*, 1849, 13.

22. *Annual Rept. Am. Hist. Ass'n.*, 1911, II, 141; *Cong. Globe, 31 Cong., 1 Sess.*, 1–27, quotes on pages 26, 27; Benjamin Perley Poore, *Perley's Reminiscences*, I, 360.

23. *Cong. Globe, 31 Cong., 1 Sess.*, 27–28.

24. *Ibid.*, 66.

25. *Cong. Globe, 31 Cong., 1 Sess.*, 51–59; 119–123; John C. Calhoun to Andrew Pickens Calhoun, Jan. 12, 1850, *Annual Rept. Am. Hist. Ass'n.*, 1899, II, 780; *Cong. Globe, 31 Cong., 2 Sess.*, 133.

26. Glyndon G. Van Deusen, *The Life of Henry Clay*, 399.

27. *Cong. Globe, 31 Cong., 1 Sess.*, 244.

28. *Ibid.*, 1 Sess., Appx., 117–127; 567–573.

29. *The Works of John C. Calhoun* (Crallé ed.), IV, 542–578; *Cong. Globe, 31 Cong., 1 Sess.*, Pt. I, 451–455.

30. *Cong. Globe, 31 Cong., 1 Sess.*, Appx., 269–276. For Douglas, Chase, Davis and Seward, *ibid.*, 364, 486, 149, 260.

31. See H. D. Foster, "Webster's Seventh of March Speech and the Secession Movement, 1850," *Am. Hist. Rev.*, XXVII, 255–264; J. R. Tucker to James H. Hammond, March 26, 1850 (Hammond MS.); Robert Toombs to Linton Stephens, March 22, 1850, *Annual Rept. Am. Hist. Ass'n.*, 1911, II, 188.

32. *Cong. Globe, 31 Cong., 1 Sess.*, Appx., 260–269.

33. Francis Preston Blair, Sr., to Martin Van Buren, March 24, 26, 1850 (Van Buren MS.).

34. Francis Preston Blair, Sr., to Martin Van Buren, March 26, 1850 (Van Buren MS.); Journal of B. F. Perry, entries for April 28, May 19, June 16 (MS. University of North Carolina).

35. William E. Dodd, *Jefferson Davis*, 118; *Memoirs of Thurlow Weed*, 176–177.

36. Benjamin Perley Poore, *Perley's Reminiscences*, I, 378.

37. *Richmond Enquirer*, Jan. 10, 1850; Dec. 25, 1849; Jan. 21, 1850; *National Intelligencer*, Feb. 16, 1850.

38. New Orleans *Daily True Delta*, Dec. 30, 1849; Jan. 12, 1850; Jan. 30, 1850.

39. Richard H. Shryock, *Georgia and the Union in 1850*, 245; *North Carolina Standard*, Jan. 16, 1850; Feb. 13, 1850.

40. *Alabama Beacon*, Dec. 22, 1848; The Montgomery *Advertiser and Gazette*, Nov. 20, 1849; The *Mobile Daily Register*, Jan. 9, 1850.

41. South Carolina had sent General Daniel Wallace to Jackson as a personal representative during the Mississippi Convention in October, *The Spartan*, Feb. 21, 1850, quoted in Hamer, *op. cit.*, 47.

42. Richmond *Republican and General Advertiser*, Jan. 15, Jan. 28, March 1, May 13, 1850; Lynchburg *Virginian*, quoted in Richmond *Whig*, Jan. 25, 1850; *New Orleans Daily Crescent*, Feb. 23, 1850; *New Orleans Daily Bee*, Feb. 25, March 5, April 5, 1850.

43. *North Carolina Standard*, March 27, 1850; Richard H. Shryock, *op. cit.*, 254–256; Clarence P. Denman, *The Secession Movement in Alabama*, 47–64; Letter of Hilliard in Montgomery *Advertiser and State Gazette*, April 24, 1850.

44. *Richmond Enquirer*, April 16, 17, 1850; *ibid.*, April 20; *The New Orleans Daily Delta*, March 3, 1850; Daily *Nashville Union*, Feb. 27; March 12, 1850; Mobile *Daily Register*, March 4, 1850; Montgomery *Advertiser and State Gazette*, March 6, 1850; Cleo Hearon, *Mississippi and the Compromise of 1850*, 123 n.

45. Richard H. Shryock, *op. cit.*, 257–260; *Richmond Enquirer*, March 12, 1850; March 19, 1850; see Resolutions of Limestone County Meeting, Mobile meeting, etc., Montgomery *Advertiser and State Gazette*, April 13, 23, 1850; *ibid.*, April 24, 1850; *Alabama Journal*, May 22, 1850; *New Orleans Daily Delta*, March 16, 1850; *New Orleans Daily Crescent*, May 27, 1850.

46. *Columbus Whig*, quoted in *Hinds County Gazette*, April 19, 1850.

47. *Resolutions, Addresses and Journal of Proceedings of the Southern Convention . . . in the Year 1850*; *National Intelligencer*, July 13, 1850; *Charleston Mercury*, June 15, 17, 20, 1850.

48. F. H. Hodder, "Authorship of the Compromise of 1850," *Miss. Valley Hist. Rev.*, XXII, 525–536.

49. *Richmond Enquirer*, Oct. 15, 1850.

50. Richard H. Shryock, *op. cit.*, 319.

51. Rhett had said that Georgia would "lead off," *Charleston Mercury*, Sept. 12, 1850; *Acts of General Assembly of Virginia, 1850–51*, 201;

Raleigh Register, Nov. 13, 1850; Salisbury *Carolina Watchman*, Nov. 14; *North Carolina Standard*, May 3, 1851; New Orleans *Daily True Delta*, Sept. 4, Sept. 8, Sept. 25, 1850; *The New Orleans Bee*, Feb. 8, 1850; Mobile *Daily Advertiser*, Oct. 25, 1850; see Resolutions of meetings, *Jacksonville Republican*, Oct. 22, 1850; Mobile *Daily Register*, March 21, 1851; Mobile *Daily Register*, Nov. 14, 19, 1850; Jan. 7, 1851; Mobile *Daily Advertiser*, July 2, 1851.

52. Cleo Hearon, *op. cit.*, 159–210; J. F. H. Claiborne, *Life and Correspondence of John A. Quitman*, II, 44–45, 46–51; *Vicksburg Whig*, Nov. 27, 1850.

53. *Mississippi Free Trader*, Oct. 9, 1850; *Woodville Republican*, Sept. 4, 1850; Aug. 26, 1851; *Natchez Courier*, Aug. 13, Sept. 11, 17; Oct. 1; *Port Gibson Herald*, quoted in *Mississippi Free Trader*, Oct. 19, 1850.

54. *Charleston Mercury* (Country Edition), Oct. 1, 1850.

55. *Black River Watchman*, Sept. 28, 1850.—"Every man who is capable of reflection knows that the hour of Southern destiny has come. . . . The South cannot retreat." Oct. 19, 1850; Philip M. Hamer, *The Secession Movement in South Carolina*, 66–67; Francis Lieber wrote Dec. 8, 1850, that he knew only four men including himself who were not secessionists (Lieber MS., Huntington Library); see also Resolutions of Southern Rights Conventions, *Charleston Mercury*, Sept. 26, 28; Oct. 2, 4, 5, 21, 22, 24, 30, 1850.

56. See Benjamin F. Perry's *Journal*, Nov. 7, 17, 20, 29.

57. *Journals of the Conventions of the People of South Carolina Held in 1832, 1833, 1852*, 150; Francis Lieber to G. S. Hilliard, Oct. 18, 1851 (Lieber MS.); Philip M. Hamer, *op. cit.*

58. *Black River Watchman*, Nov. 8, 1851.

59. A. H. Stephens to James Thomas, *Annual Rept. Am. Hist. Ass'n.*, 1911, II, 184.

60. James A. Seddon to R. M. T. Hunter, Feb. 7, 1852, "Correspondence of R. M. T. Hunter," *Annual Rept. Am. Hist. Ass'n.*, 1916, II, 137; Arthur C. Cole, *The Whig Party in the South*, 135–211.

61. Richard H. Shryock, *op. cit.*, 290; Governor Seabrook to Governor John Quitman, July 15, 1851 (Seabrook MS.); *Spirit of the South*, Oct. 22, 1850.

62. *Annual Rept. Am. Hist. Ass'n.*, 1899, II, 1189 (New Orleans); *Black River Watchman*, Aug. 2, 1850 (Charleston); Shryock, *op. cit.*, 321 (Savannah); *Mississippi Free Trader*, Aug. 20, 1851 (Natchez); *Mobile Daily Advertiser*, July 11, Nov. 11, 1850 (Mobile, etc.); Shanks, *The Secession Movement in Virginia*, 44 (Richmond).

63. J. H. Lumpkin to Howell Cobb, Oct. 5, 1850, *Annual Rept. Am. Hist. Ass'n.*, 1911, II, 214; James A. Meriwether to Howell Cobb, Aug. 24, 1850; *ibid.*, 211; M. C. Fulton to Howell Cobb, Nov. 6, 1850; *ibid.*, 217–218; Francis Lieber to George S. Hilliard, Oct. 18, 1851 (Lieber MS. Huntington Library); Herschel V. Johnson to John C. Calhoun, July 20, 1849, *Annual Rept. Am. Hist. Ass'n.*, 1899, II, 1196.

64. Henry L. Benning to Howell Cobb, Sept. 2, 1852, *Annual Rept. Am. Hist. Ass'n.*, 1911, II, 318–319.

CHAPTER TWELVE

1. *Columbus Sentinel* in the *Charleston Mercury*, Jan. 23, 1851. Quoted by Shryock, *Georgia and the Union in 1850*, 344.
2. Howell Cobb to Absolom H. Chappell and Others, Feb. 7, 1851, *Annual Rept. Am. Hist. Ass'n.*, 1911, II, 225.
3. Mobile *Daily Register*, Feb. 8, 1850; *ibid.*, March 1, 1850.
4. Laura A. White, *Robert Barnwell Rhett*, 15–17, 24, 39.
5. *Ibid.*, 68–84.
6. *Ibid.*, 109.
7. See biographical sketch by Dwight L. Dumond, *Dictionary American Biography*, XX, 592–595; J. W. DuBose, *Life and Times of Yancey*.
8. *Ibid.*, 76, 362; *Eufaula Democrat*, Sept. 10, 1850; *Huntsville Democrat*, Oct. 17, 1850, quoted by Clarence P. Denman, *op. cit.*, 47 n.
9. Avery Craven, *Edmund Ruffin, Southerner*.
10. W. P. Cutter, *Yearbook of the United States Department of Agriculture, 1895*, 493.
11. Broadus Mitchell, *William Gregg, Factory Master of the Old South*.
12. E. Merritt, *James Henry Hammond*; J. H. Hammond to J. C. Calhoun, March 5, 1850, *Annual Rept. Am. Hist. Ass'n.*, 1899, II, 1210–1211; *DeBow's Review*, IX, 20, 120–124.
13. *Ibid.*, X, 106–107; see also program suggested by an Alabama paper in *DeBow's Review*, IX, 22.
14. *Richmond Enquirer*, Sept. 1, 1855; also Dec. 17, 1855.
15. *Southern Dial*, I, No. 2, 79.
16. See Avery Craven, *Soil Exhaustion in the Agricultural History of Virginia and Maryland*; *Edmund Ruffin, Southerner*, 49–72; McCormick and Hussy both developed their reapers in this section.
17. Lewis Cecil Gray, *History of Agriculture in the Southern United States to 1860*, II, 779–857.
18. Edmund Ruffin, *An Address on the Opposite Results of Exhausting and Fertilizing Systems of Agriculture*.
19. *DeBow's Review*, XIV, 34–46; I, 436; see Avery Craven, "Agricultural Reform of the Ante-Bellum South," *Am. Hist. Rev.*, XXXIII, 302–314; *Soil Exhaustion in the Agricultural History of Virginia and Maryland*, 152–159.
20. *DeBow's Review*, XX, 58.
21. The *Sumter Banner*, April 18, May 30, 1849.
22. Augusta *Chronicle and Sentinel*, Jan. 14, 1857; *New Orleans Daily Crescent*, April 20, 1857; *New Orleans Daily Crescent*, Feb. 11, April 7, April 14, May 11, 1857; July 20, 1855; Nov. 12, 1856; Augusta *Chronicle and Sentinel*, Jan. 14, 1857.
23. *New Orleans Daily Crescent*, Nov. 12, 1856; *The Southern Literary Messenger*, XVII, 178, March, 1851.
24. *Charleston Mercury*, Sept., 1850; *Southern Advocate* (Huntsville, Ala.), Aug. 8, 1855; Petersburg *Intelligencer*, Aug. 22, 1855; *Daily Crescent* (New Orleans), March 6, 1850, April 12, 1850.

25. See R. R. Russel, *Economic Aspects of Southern Sectionalism, 1840–1861*, 226–229; Kathleén Bruce, *Virginia Iron Manufactures in the Slave Era*, 275–324; T. J. Wertenbaker, *Norfolk*, 182–205.

26. *Niles' Weekly Register*, LII, 369; Col. Memminger's speech at Second Convention, 1838, *Charleston Courier*, April 11, 1838; see *DeBow's Review*, I, 17, for Memphis Convention resolutions.

27. *DeBow's Review*, XXIII, 36–59; XI, 154; XXIII, 193; *Louisville Journal*, quoted *Richmond Enquirer*, Dec. 11, 1856.

28. See map in Ulrich Bonnell Phillips, *History of Transportation in the Eastern Cotton Belt*; R. S. Cotterill, "Beginning of Railroads in the Southwest," *Miss. Valley Hist. Rev.*, VIII, 318–326; "Southern Railroads," *ibid.*, X, 396–405.

29. *DeBow's Review*, X, 362, 363. For like articles, see *Southern Dial*, I, No. 2, p. 1; *Richmond Enquirer*, Sept. 9, 1859; June 14, 1854; *Memphis Daily Avalanche*, Aug. 6, 1859.

30. *Kanawha Valley Star*, Dec. 2, 1856; *DeBow's Review*, XIII, 258–260; Augusta *Daily Constitutionalist*, Dec. 18, 1856; Mobile *Daily Register*, Aug. 26, 1856.

31. *Mississippi Free Trader*, July 31, 1857; *Southern Advocate*, Sept. 5, 1855; *Richmond Enquirer*, June 19, 1854; *Advertiser and Gazette* (Montgomery, Ala.), Nov. 18, 1854; Montgomery *Daily Mail*, May 9, 1855.

32. *Kanawha Valley Star*, Dec. 2, 1856.

33. Francis Lieber hesitated to leave South Carolina for Harvard because his salary there was larger. To Charles Sumner, Dec. 27, 1850 (Lieber MS.). Catalogue of University of Virginia, 1859–60; E. M. Coulter, *College Life in the Old South*.

34. For general review of Southern education, see *DeBow's Review*, X, 1851, 476; see also *Statistics*, XX, 389–390; G. R. Fairbanks, *History of the University of the South at Sewanee, Tennessee*.

35. *The Advertiser and Gazette*, Montgomery, Ala., June 21, 1856; quote is from Preface of Hubbard's book.

36. Note furnished to the author by the late Ulrich Bonnell Phillips.

37. Copy in author's possession.

38. F. L. Mott, *A History of American Magazines* (N. Y., 1930), I, 626–657.

39. See Avery Craven, *Edmund Ruffin, Southerner*, p. 12; also F. L. Mott, *op. cit.*, 653.

40. The *New Orleans Daily Crescent*, June 27, 1855; May 29, 1852; the New Orleans *Daily Picayune*, May 18, 1856; the *Montgomery Mail*, March 29, 1855.

41. New York *Evening Mirror*, quoted *Jacksonville* (Ala.) *Republican*, Oct. 23, 1855.

42. *Charleston Mercury*, July 27, 1857. See also Jan. 7, 1860.

43. *Ibid.*, Sept. 16, 1850.

44. *Richmond Enquirer*, Aug. 18, 1855; *ibid.*, Nov. 13, Dec. 15, Dec. 28, 1855.

45. *Richmond Enquirer*, Jan. 17, 1860; *Raleigh Standard*, Nov. 5, 1859; *Charleston Mercury*, May 27, 1857; *New Orleans Daily Crescent*, May 9, 1859; Feb. 19, 1857; *Georgia Telegraph*, March 1, 1859.

46. New Orleans *Daily Crescent*, May 26, 1859.

47. *Southern Press*, quoted in *Jacksonville Republican* (Ala.), Oct. 5, 1852.

CHAPTER THIRTEEN

1. Daily *Chronicle and Sentinel* (Augusta, Ga.), Jan. 10, 1849.

2. Joseph Clarke Robert, *The Tobacco Kingdom*, 203–205; for a full statement of the improved condition of free Negroes see Luther P. Jackson, *Free Negro Labor and Property Holding in Virginia, 1830–1860* (Manuscript Thesis, University of Chicago).

3. Henry Clay to the Committee, Macon Union Celebration, Feb. 13, 1850, quoted Shryock, *op. cit.*, 339; the Augusta (Daily) *Chronicle and Sentinel*, March 19, 1849, insisted that "a cart load of good manure was worth more for the state than a thousand anti-abolition resolutions, no matter how eloquently they are expressed."

4. *Edmund Ruffin Diary*, Aug. 16, 1858 (Ruffin MS.): Henry T. Shanks, *The Secession Movement in Virginia, 1847–1861*, 46–84.

5. *The Spirit of the South*, June 17, 1851, Oct. 16, 1851; Lewy Dorman, *Party Politics in Alabama from 1850 through 1860*, 65–76.

6. Cleo Hearon, *Mississippi and the Compromise of 1850*, 224; James Byrne Ranck, *Albert Gallatin Brown*, 100–105; Henry S. Foote to Howell Cobb, July 9, 1851, *Annual Rept. Am. Hist. Ass'n.*, 1911, II, 242.

7. John N. Williams to Benjamin F. Perry, April 1, 1851 (Perry MS.); W. W. Boyce to Benjamin F. Perry, March 17, 1851 (Perry MS.); Laura A. White, "The National Democrats in South Carolina, 1852 to 1860," *South Atlantic Quarterly*, XXVII, 371, 375.

8. *The Savannah Republican*, April 9, 1852.

9. Said Doctor Henry Bowditch: "I should be ashamed of myself, and traitor to my highest principles, if I did not spend every leisure hour in plotting how that infamous law, prepared by the late Congress, can be defeated. I go, if need be, for open resistance; and for my support I appeal to that God to whom our fathers appealed in the dark hour of the Revolution." V. Y. Bowditch, *Life and Correspondence of Henry Ingersoll Bowditch*, I, 209; *Annual Report of the American and Foreign Anti-Slavery Society*, 1851, 3; Whittier announced himself to be a nullifier, *William Lloyd Garrison* (Garrison ed.), III, 303.

10. Henry S. Commager, *Theodore Parker, Yankee Crusader*, 214–219; Wendell Phillips to Elizabeth Pease, March 9, 1851, see *William Lloyd Garrison* (Garrison ed.), III, 324.

11. The quote is Charles Sumner's comment on Parker's sermon against Judge Curtis; Gerrit Smith called Webster "the base and infamous enemy of the human race," Ralph Volney Harlow, *Gerrit Smith, Philanthropist and Reformer*, 298; Claude M. Fuess, *Life of Caleb Cushing*, II, 103.

12. Ralph Volney Harlow, *op. cit.*, 289–290.

13. *Ibid.*, 299.

14. Claude M. Fuess, *op. cit.*, II, 107.

15. *A Memoir of Benjamin Robbins Curtis* (R. B. Curtis ed.), I, 122, 136.

16. Roy Franklin Nichols, *Franklin Pierce*, 189–204.

17. Henry Clyde Hubbart, *The Older Middle West,* 81; A. L. Kohlmeier, *The Old Northwest as the Keystone of the Arch of American Federal Union,* 53.

18. Lois Kimball Mathews, *The Expansion of New England,* 171–272; Avery Craven, "The Advance of Civilization into the Middle West in the Period of Settlement," in *Sources of Culture in the Middle West* (D. R. Fox ed.).

19. Joseph Schafer, *Four Wisconsin Counties.*

20. A. L. Kohlmeier, *op. cit.,* 191–192.

21. Joseph Schafer, *op. cit.,* 192; Arthur C. Cole, *The Era of the Civil War,* 205–210 (*Centennial History of Illinois,* III); H. C. Hubbart, *op. cit.,* 97–98, 102.

22. See Henry Clyde Hubbart, "Pro-Southern Influences in the Free West, 1840–1865," *Miss. Valley Hist. Rev.,* XX, 45–62.

23. *Cincinnati Daily Enquirer,* Jan. 6, April 25, 1857, quoted Charles R. Wilson, "Cincinnati a Southern Outpost in 1860–1861?" *Miss. Valley Hist. Rev.,* XXIV, 473–482.

24. *Cong. Globe, 29 Cong., 1 Sess.,* Appx., 258.

25. *Cong. Globe, 30 Cong., 1 Sess.,* Appx., 506–507.

26. Henry Clyde Hubbart, *The Older Middle West,* 1–29.

27. H. Rutherford to J. J. Bowman, July 31, 1843 (Rutherford MS.): *Prairie Farmer,* Nov., 1848. The best study of this economic situation is Madison Kuhn, *Economic Factors in the Development of the Republican Party, 1852–1860* (MS. Thesis, University of Chicago); Senator Breese's speech was delivered on July 21, 1843; *Lancaster* (Wis.) *Herald,* June 10, 1848.

28. *Chicago Democrat* (Weekly), June 30, 1846 (Wentworth); *Cong. Globe, 29 Cong., 1 Sess.,* Appx., 784–785 (Brinkerhoff); *Quarterly Publication of the Historical and Philosophical Society of Ohio,* XIII (1918), 15; *Chicago Democrat* (Weekly), Dec. 18, 1850; *Detroit Daily Advertiser,* July 31, 1846.

29. *Chicago Democrat* (Weekly), Jan. 30, 1849; Feb. 22, 23; July 13, 1850; James E. Boyle, *Chicago Wheat Prices for Eighty-one Years,* 69; *Chicago Daily Democrat,* Oct. 11, 1850; "It is due to truth to say that the prohibition of slavery has been little discussed save in the north part of our State, whilst in the South part of the State, the Wilmot Proviso is denounced as an incendiary, treasonable and abolition measure. . . . A large proportion of the emigrants of the South part of this State are from the slave States, where men are educated to believe that manual labor is disgraceful and that slave labor is the only honorable means of cultivating the soil. . . ." *Chicago* (Weekly) *Democrat,* Jan. 19, 1850.

30. *Western Citizen,* Dec. 30, 1850; *Watchman of the Prairies,* June 11, 1850; *Indiana True Democrat,* Nov. 15, 1850; *Detroit Tribune,* Oct. 15, 1850.

31. See Theodore C. Smith, *op. cit.,* 227–228.

32. The *New York Tribune,* Oct. 23, 1850; *Ravenna* (Ohio) *Liberator,* April 11, 1851; *National Era,* Dec. 5, 1850.

33. Theodore C. Smith, *op. cit.,* 226–244; W. H. Siebert, *The Underground Railroad.*

34. *Ibid.*, 262; Andrew Wallace Crandall, *The Early History of the Republican Party*, 1854–1856, 1–26.

35. *Cong. Globe, 33 Cong., 1 Sess.*, Pt. I, 175, 221–222.

36. Salmon P. Chase to Hannibal Hamlin, Feb. 4, 1853 (Chase MS.); *ibid.*, Dec. 31, 1853.

37. *Cong. Globe, 33 Cong., 1 Sess.*, 281; Salmon P. Chase to Hannibal Hamlin, Jan. 23, 1854 (Chase MS.).

38. Frank H. Hodder, "The Railroad Background of the Kansas-Nebraska Act," *Miss. Valley Hist. Rev.*, XII, 3–22; see Salmon P. Chase's own statement regarding Marsh of Virginia, Chase to Hannibal Hamlin, Jan. 24, 1854 (Chase MS.). See also clippings from Southern newspapers in *National Intelligencer*, June 24, 1854; Albert J. Beveridge, *Abraham Lincoln* (Standard ed.), III, 199 n.

39. George Fort Milton, *The Eve of Conflict*, 121; Douglas to *State Capitol Reporter* (N. H.), Feb. 16, 1854, quoted in George Fort Milton, *op. cit.*, 129; *Washington Union*, Feb. 2, 1854.

40. Frank H. Hodder, "Genesis of the Kansas-Nebraska Act," State Historical Society of Wisconsin, *Proceedings*, 1912; "Railroad Background of the Kansas-Nebraska Act," *Miss. Valley Hist. Rev.*, XII, 3–22.

41. P. Orman Ray, *The Repeal of the Missouri Compromise; Cong. Globe, 29 Cong., 2 Sess.*, 470, 625.

42. See Frank H. Hodder, *op. cit.*, *Miss. Valley Hist. Rev.*, XII, 3–22.

43. Mrs. S. B. Dixon, *A True History of the Missouri Compromise and Its Repeal*, 445–448.

CHAPTER FOURTEEN

1. *Battle Creek Weekly Journal*, March 3, 1854.

2. The Sandusky (Ohio) *Commercial Register*, May 27, 1854.

3. The *Free West*, April 6, 1854.

4. *Ohio State Journal*, July 17, 1854; the *Free West*, Feb. 2, 9, 1854; *Alton Telegraph*, Jan. 21, 1854.

5. *Cong. Globe, 33 Cong., 1 Sess.*, 617, 636; the *Free West*, March 30, 1854; Cincinnati *Christian Press*, quoted in *Free West*, March 2, 1854.

6. The *Free West*, Jan. 19, 1854; the *New York Tribune*, Sept. 6, 1854; *St. Louis Intelligencer*, copied in *Illinois Daily Journal*, Sept. 23, 1854; *Illinois Journal*, June 21, 1854.

7. *Cong. Globe, 33 Cong., 1 Sess.*, Appx., 134.

8. *Ibid.*, 151.

9. *Ibid.*, 263–269.

10. *Ibid.*, 275.

11. *Ibid.*, 328.

12. *Ibid.*, 339–340.

13. Roy F. Nichols, *Franklin Pierce*, 336–337; see speeches of English, Taylor, Allen, Bell, *Cong. Globe, 33 Cong., 1 Sess.*, Appx., 619, 598, 255, 414.

14. The *New York Tribune*, July 6, 1854; Sandusky *Commercial Register*, Aug. 1, May 25, 27, Nov. 17, 1854; see also *Battle Creek Weekly Journal*, March 17, 1854; Alton *Daily Telegraph*, March 9, 1854; Daily *Chicago Journal*, June 6, 1854; *Ohio State Journal*, June 5, 1854.

15. *Cong. Globe, 33 Cong., 1 Sess.,* 648.

16. "No legislation on River and Harbor appropriations, so much needed by the North—no legislation on the Pacific Railroad, so vital to the interests of our great Commercial States and Atlantic Cities—no Niagara Ship Canal, but Nebraska—enforcing the Fugitive Slave law—filibustering for Cuba and her slaves—increasing the rates of postage is all that the present Administration has at heart. . . ." *Commercial Register* (Sandusky, Ohio), June 22, 1854; *Cong. Globe, 33 Cong., 1 Sess.,* 222.

17. Ralph H. Gabriel, *The Course of American Democratic Thought,* 12–25.

18. Dwight L. Dumond, *Anti-Slavery Origins of the Civil War in the United States;* A. C. Cole and J. G. de R. Hamilton, *Am. Hist. Rev.,* XXXVI, 740, XXXVII, 700.

19. The *New York Tribune,* June 3, 1854; Oct. 20, 1854; July 21, 1854.

20. The *New York Tribune,* May 26, 1855; Sept. 23, 1854; Sept. 21, 1854; Aug. 18, 1854; Sept. 21, 1854.

21. The *New York Tribune,* June 22, 1855; Aug. 3, 1854; July 11, 1854.

22. *Commercial Register,* Sandusky, Ohio, Aug. 5, 1854; *New York Examiner,* quoted in *Liberator,* Jan. 7, 1853.

23. The *Quincy* (Ill.) *Whig,* Aug. 12, 1854.

24. The *Chicago Democrat,* Sept. 2, 1854; the *Free West,* Aug. 21, 1854; *National Era,* March 23, 1854; "They have cried out abolition so much that if I was really a Garrison or a Phillips they could not think worse of me than they do." Lyman Trumbull to Palmer, Nov. 23, 1854, *Ill. State Hist. Soc. Journal,* XVI, 22.

25. *Alton Weekly Courier,* Sept. 20, 1854; clipping from *Missouri Democrat* in Blair manuscripts; *Free West,* Aug. 31, 1854, quoting *Lacona Gazette* (Ill.).

26. Andrew Wallace Crandall, *The Early History of the Republican Party, 1854–1856,* 20–26; Howell Cobb to James Buchanan, Dec. 5, 1854, *Annual Rept. Am. Hist. Ass'n.,* 1911, II, 348. Desertions in Douglas's state included such key men as Wentworth, Trumbull, and Palmer.

27. Blair to Van Buren, Jan. 25, 1856 (Van Buren MS.). When Houston weakened Blair thought of Frémont as the Jacksonian candidate.

28. Greeley had now broken with Weed, Seward; *New York Tribune,* March 6, 1855.

29. Joshua Leavitt to Chase, March 13, 14, 1855 (Chase MS.).

30. In one of his speeches Benton opposed restoring the Compromise line and insisted that under the Louisiana Treaty masters had a right to enter with slaves. That immediately ruined him as Blair's candidate. William E. Smith, *The Francis Preston Blair Family in Politics,* I, 326–327.

31. J. L. M. Curry to C. C. Clay, Jr., Talladega, Ala., July 5, 1854 (Clay MS.); see also *Republican Banner and Nashville Whig* (Tenn.), April 7, 1854. Editor interviews cotton planter and finds "no anxiety whatever" over the Kansas-Nebraska Bill.

32. *Charleston Mercury* (Tri-Weekly edition), June 21, 1854.

33. Arthur C. Cole, *The Whig Party in the South,* 285–295.

34. *Cong. Globe, 33 Cong., 1 Sess.,* Appx., 586.

35. *Ibid.*, 904.

36. Cullom of Tennessee, *ibid.*, 901; Franklin of Maryland, *ibid.*, 419; Millson of Virginia, *ibid.*, 426; Etheridge of Tennessee objected to being turned over to the "tender mercies of squatter sovereignty," *ibid.*, 586; Brooks of South Carolina, *ibid.*, 371; Hunt of Louisiana, *ibid.*, 437.

37. *Ibid.*, 561.

38. *Charleston Mercury* (Tri-Weekly edition), June 21, 1854.

39. *Richmond Whig*, Feb. 10, 1854; *Richmond Enquirer*, March 9, 1854.

40. *Richmond Enquirer*, Feb. 2, 1854; John Minor Botts said he would "like to see this misshapen and ill-begotten monster killed." *Washington Union*, Feb. 17, 1854.

41. *Wilmington Journal* said that the Whigs were indifferent, Feb. 14, 1854; *ibid.*, Feb. 1, 1854; Feb. 11, 1854; *Wilmington Commercial* took same position; *North Carolina Standard*, Jan. 11, 14, 28; Feb. 4, 11; March 8, 1854.

42. The *Daily South Carolinian* (Columbia), Feb. 21, June 1, 9, 24, Aug. 21, Oct. 12, 17, 1854; *Charleston Mercury*, Jan. 20, 1850; *Charleston Courier*, May 17; *Charleston Mercury*, Feb. 10, 1854; March 16, 1854; for Florida, see Dorothy Dodd, "The Secession Movement in Florida," *Fla. Hist. Soc. Quarterly*, XII, 19–21.

43. Benjamin H. Hill in *Columbus* (Ga.) *Sun*, Feb. 25, 1856; *Savannah Republican*, Feb. 25, 1854; *Columbus Enquirer*, June 13, 1854; *Macon Telegraph*, June 6, March 7, 1854; *The Southern Recorder*, July 15, 1856; The Augusta *Constitutionalist and Republic*, Aug. 24, Sept. 1, 1854; the Augusta *Chronicle and Sentinel*, Oct. 16, 1856, condemns the introduction of the Bill as a useless reawakening of strife.

44. The *Mobile Advertiser*, Feb. 18, May 10, June 4, 1854; the *Natchez Courier*, April 4, May 11, June 15, June 20, 1854.

45. *New Orleans Bee*, Feb. 4, 11; March 11, 24; May 17, 29; Sept. 7; Aug. 26, 1854; The *New Orleans Daily Crescent*, March 3, June 3, Nov. 14, 1854.

46. The Memphis *Eagle and Enquirer*, Aug. 3, 1854; *ibid.*, quoted *Memphis Appeal*, April 25, 1856; the *Republican Banner and Nashville Whig*, March 4, March 9, Jan. 31, May 25.

47. The *Mobile Register*, Jan. 16, 1854; the *Montgomery Advertiser and Gazette*, Feb. 1, 7; March 14, 16, 23; July 27, Nov. 18, 1854; Aug. 8, 1857; the *Mississippi Free Trader*, March 21, 1854.

48. The New Orleans *Daily Delta*, May 30, 1854; the *Memphis Appeal*, July 21, May 1, 13; Sept. 7, 16, 1854; the *Union and American*, July 28, March 18, 1854.

49. The *Charleston Mercury*, June 21, 1854.

50. Ralph V. Harlow, "The Rise and Fall of the Kansas Aid Movement," *Am. Hist. Rev.*, XLI, 1–25; *The Liberator*, June 1, 1855; statement of Lawrence is quoted by Harlow, *op. cit.*, 7.

51. Paul Wallace Gates, "A Fragment of Kansas Land History," *Kansas Historical Quarterly*, VI, 227–240; William O. Lynch, "Population Movements in Relation to the Struggle for Kansas," *Studies in American History Inscribed to James Albert Woodburn*.

52. F. J. Burkley, *The Faded Frontier*, 58, 61; D. M. Johnson, "Nebraska in the Fifties," *Publications of Neb. State Hist. Soc.*, XIX, 186–196; Hadley Johnson, *Proceedings and Collections of Neb. State Hist. Soc.*, V, 51–58.

53. *Journal of the Council of Second Regular Session of General Assembly of Nebraska*; *The Palladium*, Feb. 28, 1855; March 28, 1854; see Lorraine Watson, *The Influence of Iowans and Railroad Interests on the Development of Nebraska* (MS. Thesis, University of Chicago); Savage and Bell, *History of Omaha*, 141.

CHAPTER FIFTEEN

1. Alexander H. Stephens, Speech in House of Representatives, July 31, 1856, *Cong. Globe, 34 Cong., 1 Sess.*, 1855–1856, Appx., 1070–1076.
2. L. W. Spring, *Kansas*, 51.
3. Robinson to Thayer, April 2, 1855.
4. Paul Wallace Gates, "A Fragment of Kansas Land History," *The Kansas Historical Quarterly*, VI, 227–240.
5. James C. Malin in personal letter to the Author. Professor Malin has made an exhaustive study of Kansas history in John Brown's period.
6. Atchison *Squatter Sovereign*, Feb. 3, 1855; April 17, 1855; March 20, 1855; May 1, 1855; *Kansas Weekly Herald*, April 27, 1855.
7. L. W. Spring, *Kansas*, 56.
8. Kansas Historical Society *Collections*, XIII, 188.
9. *Herald of Freedom*, April 21, 1855.
10. W. L. Fleming, "The Buford Expedition to Kansas," *Transactions of the Alabama Historical Society*, I, 188–189.
11. See speech of acting Governor, *Council Journal of Legislative Assembly of Kansas Territory*, 1858, 7.
12. Quoted in L. W. Spring, *op. cit.*, 104; Kansas Hist. Soc. *Collections*, XIII, 148.
13. *New York Tribune*, May 29, 1855, case of Wm. Phillips; *ibid.*, April 28, 1855, case of George Parks; *ibid.*, March 24, 1856; May 13, 1856; June 27, 1856.
14. Quoted from Ralph V. Harlow, "The Rise and Fall of the Kansas Aid Movement," *Am. Hist. Rev.*, XLI, 1–25.
15. James D. Richardson, *Messages and Papers of the Presidents*, V, 327–350, 352–360; *Cong. Globe, 34 Cong., 1–2 Sess.*, 691; Andrew Wallace Crandall, *The Early History of the Republican Party*, 111–126. The Kansas question was thrust forward at the very opening of Congress. On December 5, before the Senate was fairly organized, Senator Hale introduced a resolution requesting the President to inform the Senate whether he had received evidence of resistance to the execution of the laws in Kansas which required the interposition of military force. From that time on, Kansas was always "on tap" for party use.
16. *Cong. Globe, 34 Cong., 1 Sess.*, Appx., 529–544; for Cass's statement, *ibid.*, 544; for Douglas's reply, *ibid.*, 544–546; G. S. Hilliard to F. Lieber, Dec. 8, 1854 (Lieber MS.).
17. Personal reminiscences of James Simons, who heard conversations between Brooks and his father on the subject. (MS. letter in private hands.)

18. Statement of Doctor Cornelius Boyle, *Richmond Enquirer*, June 6, 1856; Wm. E. Smith, *The Francis Preston Blair Family in Politics*, I, 346–347; Laura A. White, *op. cit.*, in *Wm. E. Dodd Essays*, 133–134.

19. G. S. Hilliard to F. Lieber, May 28, 1856 (Lieber MS.).

20. *New York Tribune*, May 27, May 24, Oct. 29, May 23, Oct. 4, May 31, Oct. 11, 1856.

21. Andrew Wallace Crandall, *Early History of the Republican Party, 1854–1856*, 203–271.

22. *Lecompton Union*, Aug. 30, Oct. 2, 1856; April 27, 1857.

23. *Kansas Weekly Herald*, May 2, 1857.

24. *Richmond Enquirer*, Oct. 11, 1854.

25. *Montgomery Mail*, May 25, 1855.

26. *Mobile Daily Register*, Feb. 1, 1856.

27. *New Orleans Bee*, Nov. 7, 1856.

28. *Montgomery Mail*, May 5, 1855.

29. *The Tri-Weekly Charleston Mercury*, June 24, 1854.

30. *Jacksonville Republican*, May 29, 1855.

31. *Mississippi Free Trader*, Dec. 7, 1855; see also Jefferson Davis to W. L. Connor, Dec. 7, 1855, "We should not allow the abolitionists to colonize Kansas by emigrant Societies without making an effort to counteract by throwing in a Southern population. . . ." (Davis MS.)

32. *Republican Banner and Nashville Whig*, Aug. 9, 1856; Jacksonville (Ala.) *Republican*, March 11, 1856.

33. *Dallas Gazette*, Nov. 2, Nov. 9, Nov. 29, 1856; *Advertiser and Gazette*, Jan. 5, June 14, 1856; *Charleston Mercury*, Feb. 4, 22, 1856. Note also action of a few Southern legislatures.

34. *Mobile Daily Register*, April 9, 1856; *Transactions of the Alabama Hist. Soc.*, IV, 167 ff.; *Mobile Daily Advertiser*, Nov. 4, 1855.

35. Quoted in *Charleston Mercury*, Feb. 16, 19, 1856.

36. Both of these papers objected to further efforts at emigration as a waste of effort and money; quoted in *Republican Banner and Nashville Whig*, May 3, 1856.

37. J. H. Hammond to George Douglas, June 21, 1856; J. H. Hammond to W. G. Simms, Jan. 20, 1855 (Hammond MS.).

38. *Prattville Statesman*, quoted in *Southern Advocate*, June 18, 1856; Augusta Daily *Chronicle and Sentinel*, Oct. 16, 1856; Mobile *Daily Register*, Sept. 16, 1856; *Republican Banner and Nashville Whig*, April 27, 1856; *New Orleans Daily Crescent*, Oct. 8, 1856.

39. *Daily South Carolinian*, Feb. 8, 1856; Nov. 15, 1855; *Baton Rouge Advocate*, Jan. 8, 1856; *Charleston Mercury*, Feb. 22, 23, 1856.

40. *The Southron*, May 28, 1856.

41. *The Daily South Carolinian*, July 30, Sept. 20, 1856.

42. *Sumter Watchman*, June 4, 18, 1856.

43. *Charleston Mercury*, June 13, 1856.

44. *Charleston Evening News*, June 10, 1856.

45. *Charleston Courier*, Aug. 29, Sept. 1, 1856; *Charleston Mercury*, Oct. 7, 1856.

46. *Richmond Enquirer*, June 4, 1856.

47. *Nashville Union and American*, June 3, 1856.

48. *Georgia Telegraph*, May 27, 1856.

49. *Mobile Advertiser*, June 7, 1856.

50. *Mobile Daily Register*, June 5, 1856.

51. *New Orleans Bee*, June 3, 1856.

52. *New Orleans Picayune*, May 27, 28, 1856.

53. *New Orleans Daily Crescent*, July 31, 1856.

54. *Republican Banner and Nashville Whig*, May 27, 1856; *Hinds County Gazette*, June 4, 1856; *Memphis Daily Appeal*, May 31, June 21, 1856; Gazaway B. Lamar to Howell Cobb, May 31, 1856, *Annual Rept. Am. Hist. Ass'n.*, 1911, II, 365–366.

55. *New Orleans Daily Crescent*, Oct. 7, 1856; *New Orleans Picayune*, Oct. 7, Nov. 2, 1856; *Mobile Daily Register*, April 19, 1856.

56. *Southern Advocate*, April 30, 1856; *New Orleans Daily Crescent*, June 19, 1856; *North Carolina Standard*, Sept. 24, 1856.

57. *Daily Constitutionalist* (Ga.), Sept. 20, 1856; *Daily South Carolinian*, Oct. 3, 22, 1856; *Port Gibson Reveille*, Oct. 30, 1856.

58. R. Ridgeway to Wyndham Robertson, Sept. 9, 1856 (Robertson MS.); *Daily Chronicle and Sentinel* (Ga.), Oct. 9, 1856; Jeremiah S. Black to Howell Cobb, Sept. 22, 1856, *Annual Rept. Am. Hist. Ass'n.*, 1911, II, 382–383.

59. Augusta *Daily Constitutionalist*, Sept. 20, 1856.

60. *New Orleans Bee*, Nov. 8, 1856; *Daily Constitutionalist*, Nov. 8, 1856.

61. *New Orleans Daily Crescent*, Nov. 17, 1856; *Republican Banner and Nashville Whig*, Nov. 13, 1856; *Charleston Mercury*, Dec. 25, 1856.

62. *New Orleans Daily Crescent*, Nov. 11, 1856.

63. J. D. Richardson, *Messages and Papers of the Presidents*, V, 429–436.

64. Benjamin C. Howard, *Report of the Decision of the Supreme Court . . . in the Case of Dred Scott versus John F. A. Sanford;* Carl Brent Swisher, *Roger B. Taney*, 476–523.

65. Charles Warren, *The Supreme Court in United States History*, III, 2–41.

66. F. H. Hodder, "Some Phases of the Dred Scott Case," *Miss. Valley Hist. Rev.*, XVI, 3–22. I have followed this article rather closely in my discussion of the case. Quotes are from it.

67. Charles Warren, *The Supreme Court in United States History*, III, 25.

68. Quoted by Warren, *op. cit.*, III, 26–41.

69. *Illinois State Journal*, March 9, 1857; *Cincinnati Daily Commercial*, March 12, 1857.

70. Warren, *op. cit.*, III, 31–37; *North American Review*, Oct., 1857.

71. George Fort Milton, *The Eve of Conflict*, 260.

72. J. B. Moore, *Works of Buchanan*, X, 183, 190–192.

73. For Douglas's break with Buchanan, see George Fort Milton, *op. cit.*, 261–273.

74. *Cong. Globe, 35 Cong., 1 Sess.*, 14–18, 24, 47, 117, 140.

75. Douglas manuscripts contain many letters approving his course. Those from following persons are typical: Wm. Hull (Wis.), Dec. 5; N. B. Baker (Ia.), Dec. 7; W. J. Elliott (Ind.), Dec. 7; Thos. McNamarer (Ohio), Dec. 7; J. Logan Chipman (Mich.), Dec. 8; John Wyatt (Ill.), Dec. 8; Jervis

Spencer (Md.), Dec. 10. "I thank God, for your own sake as well as that of my country, that you have taken the impregnable position you have . . . ," Geo. M. Davis (N. Y.), Dec. 10, 1857.

76. George Fort Milton, *op. cit.*, 280–283.

77. J. K. Dubois to Lyman Trumbull, April 8, 1858; Geo. A. Nourse to Lyman Trumbull, April 27, 1858; C. H. Ray to Lyman Trumbull, March 9, 1858; J. D. Caton to Lyman Trumbull, March (?), 1858 (Trumbull MS.).

78. July 24, 1858. Nicolay and Hay, *Abraham Lincoln, a History*, II, 140.

CHAPTER SIXTEEN

1. *Annual Rept. Am. Hist. Ass'n.*, 1911, II, 443.

2. *Richmond Enquirer*, Jan. 7, 30; Feb. 11, 26; March 1; June 15, 1858.

3. *Ibid.*, Sept. 10, 1858.

4. *Ibid.*, Sept. 30, 1858.

5. *Ibid.*, Oct. 15, 21, 1858.

6. *Ibid.*, Aug. 30, 1859.

7. *Ibid.*, Sept. 7, 1859.

8. New Orleans *Daily Delta*, July 20, 23, 28; Aug. 14, 19, 20, 1858.

9. *Ibid.*, Sept. 10, 11, 22; Oct. 6, 16, 27, 1858.

10. *New Orleans Daily Crescent*, Aug. 17, Sept. 11, Sept. 21, Oct. 2, 1858; Jan. 20, 1859; *New Orleans Bee*, July 19, 26; Aug. 13, Sept. 17, 1858. See also M. J. Crawford to Alexander H. Stephens, Sept. 8, 1858 (Stephens MS.).

11. To Wm. Porcher Miles, Nov. 17, 1858 (Miles MS.).

12. *Nashville Patriot*, Oct. 13, 1858; *Nashville Union and American*, Sept. 7, 8, 9, 1859.

13. *New Orleans Daily Delta*, Sept. 15, 1859.

14. *Charleston Mercury*, Dec. 12, 28, 1857; April 12, 1858; Aug. 10, 1858.

15. *Southern Reveille*, Dec. 29, 1858.

16. *Montgomery Advertiser*, Feb. 13, Oct. 23, 1858.

17. *Daily Chronicle and Sentinel*, Oct. 21, 1858.

18. *Columbus Sun*, Oct. 6, 1858.

19. *Mobile Daily Register*, Nov. 12, 1858; see also Dec. 13, 1857.

20. Laura A. White, *Robert Barnwell Rhett*, 37–38.

21. See Harvey Wish, "The Revival of the African Slave Trade in the United States, 1856–1860," *Miss. Valley Hist. Rev.*, XXVII, 569–588.

22. *Richmond Enquirer*, June 4, 1858.

23. *Daily Confederation*, May 18, 1858 (Montgomery, Ala.).

24. *Daily Confederation*, May 26, 1860. Yancey to James S. Slaughter, June 15, 1858. Avery Craven, *Edmund Ruffin, Southerner*, 162–163; 167–168.

25. *Charleston Mercury*, Oct. 13, 1859, quoted in Laura A. White, *op. cit.*, 157.

26. *Illinois State Journal*, March 9, 1859.

27. *Ibid.*, Feb. 2, 1859.

28. Quoted by G. M. Stephenson, *A Political History of the Public Lands,* 217.

29. *Georgia Telegraph,* March 1, 1859.

30. *Richmond Enquirer,* Dec. 30, 1859.

31. *Columbus* (Miss.) *Democrat,* quoted in *Cong. Globe, 35 Cong., 1 Sess.,* Pt. III, 2304.

32. *Charleston Mercury,* Nov. 1, 1858.

33. *Sandusky* (Ohio) *Commercial Register,* June 7, 1858.

34. *Ibid.,* March 3, 1858.

35. *Richmond Enquirer,* Sept. 7, 1858.

36. *DeBow's Review,* XVII, 368–378.

37. *New Orleans Daily Crescent,* July 3, 1857.

38. *Mississippi Free Trader,* Feb. 17, 1857.

39. *Montgomery Advertiser and Gazette,* Feb. 17, 1857; *Southern Recorder,* Jan. 13, 1857.

40. *Republican Banner and Nashville Whig,* Aug. 14, 1858; July 30, 1859.

41. April 7, 1858. Hammond Papers, MS.

42. *Mississippi Free Trader,* July 14, 1857.

43. *New Orleans Daily Crescent,* July 28, 1859.

44. *Richmond Enquirer,* March 2, 1858.

45. Avery Craven, *Edmund Ruffin, Southerner,* 168.

46. Speech at sea, in *Daily Confederation,* July 20, 1858. See also the harsh criticism of Davis for his friendly attitudes toward Northerners, etc., *Charleston Mercury,* Aug. 10, 1858; for receiving degree at Bowdoin; *ibid.,* Oct. 16, 1858, calls him a "Union Mormon"; *Advertiser and Gazette,* Nov. 25, 1858, "Kind hospitalities" of North have blinded him; *Republican Banner and Nashville Whig,* Aug. 12, 1858, notes the "fiercely denunciatory" character of all comments on him.

47. For typical statement see: Benj. Fitzpatrick to C. C. Clay, Aug. 30, 1859 (Clay MS.).

48. Jonathan Worth to John A. Gilmer, March 9, 1858. *Correspondence of Jonathan Worth,* I, 55; Josiah Evons to B. F. Perry, Jan. 19, 1858 (Perry MS.); P. B. Sweatt to A. H. Stephens, April 6, 1858 (Stephens MS.); *New Orleans Daily Crescent,* July 28, 1859; *Richmond Enquirer,* March 2, 1858; Benj. Fitzpatrick to C. C. Clay, Aug. 30, 1859 (Clay MS.).

49. *Tuscaloosa Monitor,* May 28, 1858.

50. *Republican Banner and Nashville Whig,* Feb. 7, 1858.

51. To Wm. Gilmore Simms, March 26, 1858 (Hammond Papers, U. of N. C.).

52. To Edmund Ruffin, Aug. 17, 1858 (Ruffin MS.).

53. To Wm. Porcher Miles, Nov. 23, 1858.

54. *Richmond Enquirer,* June 18, 1854.

55. R. R. Russel, *Economic Aspects of Southern Sectionalism,* 102–103.

56. *Dallas Gazette,* May 13, 1859.

57. *Mobile Daily Register,* May 3, 1859.

58. See *Richmond Enquirer,* June 4, 1858.

59. New Orleans *Daily Delta,* Aug. 28, 1858.

60. *New Orleans Daily Crescent,* July 20, 1859; May 18, June 16, 1857; Dec. 1, 1859.

61. The *Daily Confederation,* July 31, 1858; *Auburn Gazette,* Sept. 19, 1858; Avery Craven, *Edmund Ruffin, Southerner,* 168.

62. *Nashville Patriot,* Sept. 21, 1859; *Republican Banner and Nashville Whig,* Oct. 16, 1859; *Richmond Enquirer,* June 13, 1859.

63. *New York Herald,* Oct. 19, 1859.

64. *New York Daily Tribune,* Oct. 19, 20, 21, 22, 26, 31; Nov. 12, 1859; *Sandusky Commercial Register,* Oct. 19, 20, 29; Nov. 4, 15, 1859; *Illinois State Journal,* Oct. 26; Nov. 2, 9, 30; Dec. 14, 1859; Jan. 11, 1860; *Buffalo Commercial Advertiser,* Oct. 29, 1859; *Boston Journal,* Oct. 29, 1859.

65. J. F. Rhodes, *History of the United States,* III, 383–416; George B. Cheever to Susan B. Anthony, Dec. 9, 1859 (MS., Harper Collection, Huntington Library).

66. *New York Daily Tribune,* Oct. 19, 1859.

67. *Ibid.,* Oct. 31, 1859.

68. R. P. Warren, *John Brown,* 431; *Boston Journal* (Supplement), Oct. 29, 1859.

69. Horace Greeley, quoted in Rhodes, *op. cit.,* III, 403.

70. *New York Daily Tribune,* Dec. 3, 1859.

71. *Mobile Daily Register,* Oct. 25, 1859; *Memphis Morning Bulletin,* Oct. 20, 21, 25, 1859; *Memphis Avalanche,* Oct. 22, 1859; *Georgia Telegraph,* Oct. 25, 1859.

72. *Richmond Enquirer,* Jan. 21, 1860; Oct. 20, 1859; *Daily Constitutionalist* (Augusta, Ga.), Nov. 3, 18; Dec. 7, 1859.

73. *Charleston Mercury,* Oct. 31, 1859; *Daily Enquirer* (Ga.), Oct. 21, 25; Nov. 2, 5, 11, 30, 1859.

74. *Mississippi Free Trader,* Dec. 1, 1859.

75. *Richmond Enquirer,* Nov. 5, 1859; *Raleigh Standard,* Oct. 26, 29; Nov. 12, 1859; *Mississippi Free Trader,* Dec. 24, 1859.

76. *Charleston Mercury,* Oct. 31, 1859; Nov. 1, 2, 5, 26; Dec. 10, 1859.

77. *New Orleans Daily Picayune,* Dec. 2, 1859.

78. *Mobile Daily Register,* Oct. 25, 1859; *Sandusky Commercial Register,* Oct. 20; Nov. 4, 15; *Illinois State Journal,* Nov. 2; Dec. 14, 1859.

79. *New Orleans Daily Picayune,* Oct. 22; Nov. 3, 1859; *Memphis Morning Bulletin,* Oct. 20, 21, 1859; *Nashville Patriot,* Oct. 20, 1859; *Wilmington Daily Journal,* Oct. 19, 28, 1859.

80. *Mississippian,* Oct. 10, 1860. Quoted in P. L. Rainwater, *Mississippi, Storm Center of Secession,* 147.

81. *Mississippi Free Trader,* Dec. 24, 1859. On effects of Helper's book on South, see: *Nashville Union and American,* Feb. 10, 1860; *New Orleans Picayune,* Dec. 16, 1859; A. B. Crork to B. F. Perry (undated, in B. F. Perry MS.); Gilbert J. Beebe, *A Review and Refutation of Helper's Impending Crisis.*

82. *New Orleans Daily Picayune,* Dec. 15, 1859; *Nashville Union and American,* Feb. 10, 1860.

83. *Cong. Globe,* 36 Cong., 1 Sess., 1–656; Martin J. Crawford to Alexander H. Stephens, April 8, 1860 (Stephens MS.).

84. D. H. Hamilton to Wm. Porcher Miles, Dec. 9, 1859 (Miles MS.); Gov. Gist. to Wm. Porcher Miles, Dec. 9, 1859.

85. *Cong. Globe, 36 Cong., 1 Sess.,* Pt. I, 658–935.

86. C. G. Memminger to Wm. Porcher Miles, Jan. 16, 1860 (Miles MS.); *Acts of Alabama,* 1859–60, 658–697; C. P. Denman, *The Secession Movement in Alabama.*

87. *Republican Banner and Nashville Whig,* Jan. 8, 13, 21; Feb. 1, 17; *Houston* (Texas) *Weekly Telegraph,* Jan. 18; *Memphis Daily Morning Bulletin,* Jan. 28; *Southern Advocate* (Huntsville, Ala.), Feb. 8, 15; *Raleigh Standard,* March 17 (1860); A. H. Stephens to *Macon Banner,* March 25 (Stephens MS.); Wm. K. Kearney to L. O. B. Branch, Jan. 27, 1860; W. H. Miller to L. O. B. Branch, May 11, 1860 (Branch MS.).

88. R. B. Rhett to Wm. Porcher Miles, Jan. 29, 1860 (Miles MS.).

89. R. B. Rhett to Wm. Porcher Miles, March 28, 1860; April 11, 1860 (Miles MS.).

90. D. H. Hamilton to Wm. Porcher Miles, April 4, 1860 (Miles MS.).

91. I. W. Hayne to Wm. Porcher Miles, April 15, 1860 (Miles MS.).

92. D. L. Dumond, *The Secession Movement.*

93. Robert Barnwell Rhett to Wm. Porcher Miles, May 12, 1860 (Miles MS.); See also Lillian A. Kibler, "Union Sentiment in South Carolina in 1860," *Journal of Southern History,* IV, 346–366.

94. See also suggestion that Southern support was hoped for, *Richmond Enquirer,* Jan. 13, 1860. Declaration of Independence section was inserted only after Giddings had threatened to bolt the Convention. On Republican move to new base, see Seward's speech in Congress, Feb. 29, 1860, *Cong. Globe, 36 Cong., 1 Sess.,* Pt. 2, 910–914.

95. *Republican Banner and Nashville Whig,* Aug. 30, 1860.

96. *Illinois State Journal,* May 16, 1860.

97. C. M. Fuess, *The Life of Caleb Cushing,* II, 207–208 n.

98. G. W. Julian to T. W. Higginson, Oct. 24, 1857 (Giddings-Julian MS. Collection).

99. Laura White, "Sumner and the Crisis of 1860–1861," in *Wm. E. Dodd Essays;* D. L. Dumond, "Issues involved in the Movement for Conciliation, 1860–1861," *Michigan Academy of Science, Arts and Letters,* XVI, 455; Seward's speeches showed a complete lack of understanding of seriousness of issues involved and belittled secession danger.

100. *Annual Report of Am. Anti-Slavery Society,* 1860, 33–34, 43–44.

101. *Illinois State Journal,* Sept. 26; Oct. 3, 1860.

102. *Sandusky Commercial Register,* July 20; Aug. 13, 1860; *New York Tribune,* Nov. 7, 1859; June 25; July 20, 1860; James R. Baxter to John Sherman, April 26, 1860 (Sherman MS.): "We have only one hope of success in our State, that is the Homestead Bill."

103. *New York Tribune,* Aug. 15, 1860.

104. *Ibid.,* April 17, 1860.

105. *Sandusky Commercial Register,* April 15, 1860.

106. *New York Tribune,* Oct. 22, Nov. 3, 1860.

107. *Charleston Mercury,* June 13, 1860.

108. *Ibid.,* Oct. 15, 1860; see also J. D. Ashmore to B. F. Perry, Nov. 19, 1860 (Perry MS.).

109. *Mississippi Free Trader*, June 13, 1860; *Raleigh Standard*, June 9, 1860; Lawrence Keitt to Wm. Porcher Miles, Oct. 3, 1860 (Miles MS.).

110. *Nashville Union and American*, Oct. 28, 1859; *Kiowee Courier*, Aug. 3, 1860; *Richmond Enquirer*, Jan. 18, 1860; *Weekly Advertiser*, Sept. 12, Dec. 12, 1860; *Charleston Mercury*, Nov. 3, 1860; *Montgomery Mail*, Aug. 18, 1860.

111. *Montgomery Mail*, Dec. 1, 1860; Aug. 18, 1860.

112. *Southern Advocate*, Dec. 12, 1860; *Charleston Mercury*, Oct. 31, 1860; James P. Holcome, Speech before people of Albemarle, Jan. 2, 1860; Wm. H. Holcombe, *The Alternative, a Separate Nationality or Africanization of the South. A Southern Document* (Wytheville, Va., 1860).

113. *Montgomery Weekly Advertiser*, Oct. 17, 1860.

114. New Orleans *Daily Delta*, April 26, 1860; *Houston* (Texas) *Tri-Weekly Telegraph*, Oct. 4, Nov. 10, 1860.

115. *Weekly Georgia Telegraph*, May 12, 1860.

116. *Southern Advocate*, June 13, 1860.

117. L. W. P. Blair to B. F. Perry, June 4, 1860 (Perry MS.); *The Confederation* (Montgomery), May 19, 1860.

118. *New Orleans Bee*, May 8, June 25, July 27, Sept. 3, Nov. 8, 1860.

119. Augusta *Chronicle and Sentinel*, Sept. 18, Oct. 9, 1860.

120. In *Natchez Courier*, Oct. 25, 1860.

121. *Memphis Appeal*, Oct. 24, 1860.

122. *Southern Recorder*, Oct. 23, 1860; *Nashville Union and American*, Oct. 14, 1860; Augusta *Chronicle and Sentinel*, Oct. 2, 1860; Israel B. Bigelow to Stephen A. Douglas, Brownsville, Texas, July 20, 1860 (Douglas MS.).

CHAPTER SEVENTEEN

1. "The Fight for the Old Northwest, 1860," *Am. Hist. Rev.*, XVI, 774–788.

2. Wyndham Robertson, "Speech . . . on the state of the Country"; Samuel J. Tilden to Wyndham Robertson, March 18, 1861 (Robertson MS.).

3. A. A. Lawrence to R. J. Breckinridge, quoted by Laura White in *Dodd Essays*, 185 n.; Belmont wrote to John Forsyth in November: ". . . I meet daily now with men who confess the error they have been led into, and almost with tears in their eyes wish they could undo what they helped to do." *Letters of Belmont*, 6, 21.

4. T. W. Barnes, *Memoirs of Thurlow Weed*, 308–309; Laura White in *Dodd Essays*, 148–149; *Cong. Globe, 36 Cong., 2 Sess.*, 103–104; *New York Herald*, Dec. 24, 1860, Report of Seward's speech to New England Society in which he plainly showed that he did not understand the seriousness of the situation. He talked of "all the hills of South Carolina" pouring forth their population to protect New York if a foreign foe should attack. He expected, as did Lincoln, a sharp reaction in the South which would check secession or return seceded states to the Union. His policy was to hold the border states and yet show enough federal strength to encourage the cotton-state conservatives. See Lincoln's memorandum for Trumbull's Springfield Speech, Nov. 20, 1860, in *Uncollected Lincoln Letters* (Tracy ed.), 168. Also letter to John

B. Fry, Aug. 15, 1860. Nicolay and Hay, VI, 50. Greeley's attitude conditional on free approval of majority in South.

5. R. L. Allen to J. R. Breckinridge, Jan. 21, 1861; R. B. Curtis to Wyndham Robertson, Dec. 24, 1860; *Boston Courier*, Jan. 7, 1861; Laura White in *Dodd Essays*, 165 n. Crittenden manuscripts are filled with letters approving compromise and showing conservative trend. See also *Chicago Tribune*, Dec. 13; *Philadelphia Daily News*, Aug. 20; Speeches of Sen. Pugh in Congress, Dec. 10, 1860; August Belmont to Herschel V. Johnson, *Belmont Letters*, 42; E. L. Pierce, *Memoir and Letters of Charles Sumner*, IV, 18; F. Bancroft, *Seward*, II, 532–533. Yet Trumbull manuscripts and Washburn manuscripts are as full of letters urging firmness and no compromise; C. M. Pemberton to Washburn, Feb. 1, 1860; Philip S. Foner, *Business and Slavery*.

6. *Complete Works of Abraham Lincoln* (Nicolay and Hay ed.), III, 258–259; VI, 112–115. Lincoln was as confused as Seward and expected a quick Southern reaction.

7. Augusta *Chronicle and Sentinel*, Nov. 8, 1860; Montgomery *Confederation*, Nov. 23, 1860; *The North Alabamian*, Dec. 21, 1860; for idea of secession and later conciliation, see P. L. Rainwater, *op. cit.*, 170–171.

8. *Memphis Daily Morning Bulletin*, Nov. 8, 1860; *Natchez Daily Courier*, Nov. 17, Nov. 24, 1860.

9. *Memphis Enquirer*, Nov. 13, 1860; *North Alabamian*, Nov. 16, 1860.

10. D. G. Cotting to Alexander H. Stephens, Nov. 22, 1860 (Stephens MS.); *Raleigh Standard*, Nov. 27, 1860.

11. Z. B. Vance to W. W. Lenoir, Dec. 26, 1860 (Lenoir MS.); *Nashville Union and American*, Dec. 20, 1860; John H. Kennedy, *The Border States. Their Power and Duty in the Present Disordered Condition of the Country.*

12. *Louisville Journal*, Dec. 31, 1860.

13. *Chicago Tribune*, March 4, 1861.

14. *Illinois Weekly State Journal*, Dec. 26, 1860; *New York Tribune*, Feb. 8, 1861: "Will Abraham Lincoln stand firm in this trying hour? We answer: 'He will!' " There was also a feeling that Republicans could not be relied on. A few had talked generously, but their fellows had given no assurances by action in Congress and one element was always uncompromising. Some refused to take secession seriously; *Boston Atlas and Bee*, March 27, 1861: "People have never been able to believe that the secessionists were in downright earnest in their avowed purpose to make a new nation by cutting a few blocks out of the American Union. . . . The unconditional surrender of the Republican Party is required." "If our members of Congress give one principle which the Republican Party stands upon, we are gone, hook and line," Wood to Washburn, Dec. 20, 1860 (Washburn MS.); "This Union cannot be saved by compromising principle," Thos. H. Dudley to J. E. Haney, Dec. 8, 1860 (Dudley MS.); "This thing slavery must be met and finally squelched," Herndon to Trumbull, Dec. 21, 1860 (Trumbull MS.); *ibid.*, Feb. 9, 1861, "Before I would buy the South by compromises and concessions to get what is the people's due, I would die and be forgotten, willingly."

15. Augusta *Chronicle and Sentinel*, Dec. 12, 1860; Dec. 1, 1860.

16. Diary of Benjamin F. Perry, MS.

17. Augusta *Chronicle and Sentinel,* Jan. 20, 1861.

18. Augusta *Daily Constitutionalist,* Jan. 22, 1861.

19. *New Orleans Daily Picayune,* Dec. 8, 1860.

20. *Nashville Patriot,* Feb. 15, 1861.

21. *Louisville Daily Courier,* Feb. 13, 1861.

22. Charles W. Ramsdell, "Lincoln and Fort Sumter," *Journal of Southern History,* III, 259–288; John S. Tilley, *Lincoln Takes Command.* The influence of the Blair family on Lincoln's course was ever of major importance.

23. Crawford, *Genesis of the Civil War,* 404. It should be clearly understood that Lincoln did not deliberately choose to plunge the nation into such a war as resulted from his acts. He simply did not understand the situation. He overestimated the strength of the union forces in the South under existing conditions; he counted too certainly on controlling the Border States. He most certainly felt the pressure of radical Republican opinion for firm action, but hoped both to escape war and save his party. He suffered heavily, however, from his bad habit of "double talk," such as appeared in his Inaugural, where he insisted that he would enforce the law and hold government property but also assured the South that he would maintain inviolate the rights of the states and denounced the invasion by armed force of the soil of any state or territory. He was going both to coerce and to conciliate! An excellent case, on supportable evidence, can be made out for Lincoln, either as an aggressor or as a conciliator. My own conclusions are that he did not see clearly, had no clear-cut program, and was swept along, trying to hold both his party and the South, to a point where he had to take a chance at Sumter which might demonstrate his strength or produce an explosion.

24. *The Diary of Orville H. Browning* (Pease and Randall ed.), I, 475–476.

25. Jonathan Worth to T. C. & B. G. Worth, April 13, 1861, May 15, 1861, *The Correspondence of Jonathan Worth* (J. G. R. Hamilton ed.), 142, 149.

26. The overseer's prayer was first published by Ulrich Bonnell Phillips in an article in the *American Historical Review,* XXXIV, 32. The original is now in the Library of the University of North Carolina. *The New York Herald,* July 24, 1861.

INDEX

INDEX

Abolition (*see also* Anti-slavery), Quakers and, 118; early periodicals, 120; in the South, 119–120; in New England, 121; in Missouri Compromise struggle, 122–123; Garrison and, 134–138; Weld and, 138–140; propaganda, 142–150; publications, 145; revival of charges by Republicans, 341–344

Adams, Henry, 429

Adams, Gov. James H., 399

Adams, John Quincy, 140; 176–177; 186, 191, 204

Address of the Southern Delegates in Congress to Their Constituents, 234

African Slave Trade, effort to reopen, 398–400; 411

Agriculture, condition in South, 1800–1832, 40–42; Taylor on, 44; depression in South after 1812, 95–97; in New England, 125–127; in New York, 1840, 127–128; Ruffin's work for, 279; reform in South, 284–285

Alabama, 105–106; 233; and crisis of 1850, 260; Whigs, 262; and Nashville Convention, 263; and Compromise of 1850, 265; manufacturing in, 288; Union party in, 306; emigration to Kansas, 373; decides to stand alone, 413; 415

"Alabama Platform," 413–414; 416

Alcott, Louisa May, 408

Allen, William, 235, 245, 321

Alton Telegraph, quoted, 333

American Colonization Society, 119, 157

American Farmer, The, 286

American Slavery As It Is, 148–149

Ann Arbor *True Democrat*, quoted, 228

Anthony, Susan B., 138

Anti-Corn League, in United States, 141–142

Anti-Slavery, in Virginia, 54–58; in the South, 153–154; becomes anti-extension, 339–341; New York *Tribune* gives abolition twist, 341–344. (*See* Abolition.)

"Appeal of the Independent Democrats in Congress to the People of the United States," 326–327, 333–335

Arator, 45

Armstrong, George D., 163

Arnold, Richard D., 31

Astor, John Jacob, 185

Astoria, 185

Atchison *Squatter Sovereign*, quoted, 363

Athens (Ga.), 288

Augusta *Chronicle and Sentinel*, quoted, 287, 354, 431

Augusta *Constitutionalist and Republic*, quoted, 354, 379, 396

Austin, Moses, 182

Austin, Stephen, 183

Bacon's Rebellion, 20, 24

Balch, Benjamin, 84

Balch, John, 84

Bancroft, Frederick, 83

Bancroft, George, 198

Banking, in Mississippi, 112

Banks, Nathaniel P., 348

Baptists, and slavery, 156–157, 201

Barbour, James, 123

Barnburners, 203, 231, 235, 237

Barnwell, Robert, 154

"Beecher's Bibles," 407

Bell, John, 257, 416

Belle Grove, 27

Beman, Nathan, 276

Benning, Henry L., 270–271, 281

Benton, Thomas Hart, 203–206; blames Calhoun, 208–210; 234, 242, 245, 249, 319; on South and Kansas-Nebraska Bill, 351

Berrien, J. M., 233, 244

Birney, James G., 140, 141–142, 147, 197

Black Belts, 109

Black Codes, 89

"Black Republicanism," 272, 369, 396, 397, 413, 432

Black River Watchman, quoted, 268–269, 352

Blair, Francis Preston, Sr., 201–202; blames Calhoun, 207–210, 234; urges Van Buren to revolt, 237; 240, 257–258, 348

Blair, Frank, Jr., 345

Bledsoe, Albert T., 294

"Bleeding Kansas," 361, 365, 369, 388, 408

Blow, Elizabeth, 381

Blow, Henry, 381

Border State Confederation, proposed, 431–432

Boston, 124–126; 308, 309

Boston *Courier*, 429

Breckinridge, John C., 416

Brief and Candid Answer, A, 121–122

Brinkerhoff, Jacob, 214, 222, 322

Brooks, Preston, 351; assault on Sumner, 367–368; 369; Southern reaction to, 374–377
Brown, Albert Gallatin, 233, 241, 257, 306, 411–412
Brown, A. V., 204
Brown, Edmund, 158
Brown, Joe, 31
Brown, John, 84, 280, 360; raid on Harpers Ferry, 407; execution, 407
Browning, Orville H., 437–438
Bryan, Edward B., 268
Bryan, J. H., 154
Buchanan, James, 225, 370; effect of election on South, 379; inaugural, 381; 388, 400, 429–430
Buffalo Convention, 238
Buford, Jefferson, 373
Burlingame, Anson, 390
Burns, Anthony, 312
Butler, William O., 347
Byrd, William, 25

Calhoun, John C., 62, 63, 64–65; and defense of slavery, 161; 169, 177, 178–179; and Texas, 187–199; description of, 194–195; Sec'y of State, 194–196; annexation of Texas, 198–199; 201, 202; and Benton, 204–205; charged with causing trouble, 206–210; and Oregon, 212; and Memphis Convention, 212–213; resolutions in Congress, 232; and presidential nomination, 234; 236; and crisis of 1850, 242–244; 249, 250; compromise of 1850, 251–255; 257; death, 258–259; denunciation of Douglas, 320
California, 220, 242, 244; gold discovered, 245–246; 250
Camak, James, 285
Cameron, Simon, 225, 235
Campaign of 1860, 412, 418–427
Campbell, Lewis D., 339
Cannibals All, 170
Carrigan, William, 31
Carroll, G. R., 285
Carter, John, 84
Casor, John, 71
Cass, Lewis, 134, 202, 235, 236, 249, 320
Catholic Church, in Northwest, 316
Cavaliers, 22–24
Charleston, 20–21; 270, 290, 303, 415, 416
Charleston Daily Courier, quoted, 353, 374–375
Charleston Evening News, quoted, 374
Charleston Mercury, quoted, 213, 261, 275, 298–299, 349, 351, 352, 353, 357, 374, 397, 398, 400, 401, 410, 422
Charleston Patriot, quoted, 373
Charleston Standard, quoted, 373, 398

Chase, Salmon P., 140, 229–230; elected governor, 245; 257, 323, 324, 326, 333; defends Appeal, 334; and origins of Republican Party, 347–348
Cheever, George B., 408
Cherokee Indians, 96, 103–104
Chicago, 218, 316; and fugitive slave law, 322–323
Chicago Democrat, quoted, 228, 239, 322
Chicago Daily Journal, quoted, 218, 228
Chicago River and Harbor Convention, 236
Chicago Tribune, quoted, 365, 432
Chicopee (Mass.), Mills, 86
Child, David L., 149
Church, The, in Southwest, 114–115
Cincinnati, 314
Cincinnati Gazette, quoted, 227
Clay, C. C., 424
Clay, C. M., 246
Clay, Henry, 7, 187–188, 197–198, 235, 249; Compromise of 1850, 250–251; 258; West and American System, 315
Clayton Compromise, 236
Clemens, Jere, 250
Clergy, place in Southern society, 31
Cleveland Plain Dealer, quoted, 227, 244
Cleveland True Democrat, quoted, 236
Climate, of South, 35–36
Cloud, N. B., 286
Cobb, Howell, 239, 244, 247, 249, 305, 377, 394
Cohens vs. Virginia, 47
Colfax, Richard, 167
Colfax, Schuyler, 390
College of South Carolina, 14
Collier, Henry W., Gov., 260–261
Columbus, Ga., 288, 353
Columbus Whig, quoted, 263
Compromise of 1850, Clay starts move, 250–252; Calhoun's speech on, 252–254; Webster's speech on, 255–256; Seward's speech on, 256–257; favoring factors, 258–259; growing sentiment for, 260–263; completion of, 264; Southern reaction to, 264–271
Constitutional Union Party, 416–417, 418
Cooper, James, 239
Cooper, Thomas, 13, 158, 301
Corwin, Thomas, 322
Cotton, beginnings in Europe, 99–101; beginnings in United States, 101–102; the gin, 101; increase, 110–112; shipments to England and to New England, 110; dominance in Southwest, 111–112
Cotton Kingdom, 95; geography of, 97–98; basis for, 102–103; character of, 111–116; 304

Council Bluffs, 359
Craft, Ellen and William, 309
Crisis or Essays on the Usurpations of the Federal Government (Turnbull), *The*, 63
Crittenden, J. J., 235
Crittenden, Samuel B., 422
Cuba, 339, 406
Curry, J. L. M., 349
Curtis, B. R., 310, 311, 383
Cushing, Caleb, 310, 311, 419

Dabney, Thomas, 84, 108, 113
Daily Sanduskian, quoted, 228
Dallas *Gazette*, 405
Dana, R. H., 312
Darling, Arthur B., quoted, 131–132
Davis, Jefferson, defense of slavery, 162; 227, 235, 250, 257, 258, 263, 266, 306–307; and unfriendly legislation doctrine, 395; 403, 413, 439
Dawson, William C., 28, 289
DeBow, James D. B., 281, 286, 289, 290, 399
DeBow's Review, 282, 296
Delano, Columbus, 245
Democratic Party, split in New York, 230–231; in South in 1850, 262; in Georgia after 1850, 305; after 1856, 379–380; affected by Lincoln-Douglas Debates, 393; and Alabama Platform, 414; Convention of 1860, 415–416
Detroit *Daily Advertiser*, quoted, 228, 322
Dew, Thomas R., 57, 153; defense of slavery, 159–160
Dixon, Archibald, 326
Doctors, place in Southern society, 31–32
Dodge, A. C., 321, 339
Douglas, Stephen A., 214, 250, 264, 318, 319, 320, 321; introduces Kansas-Nebraska Bill, 325; and slavery, 328; motives in Kansas-Nebraska effort, 328–331; 366, 386; and Dred Scott decision, 388–390; break with administration, 390–391; campaign for Senate, 390–393; debate with Lincoln, 391–392; effect of break with administration, 394–395; Freeport doctrine, 394–395; 396, 406; Northern demand for nomination, 415
Douglass, Frederick, 146
DuBois, W. E. B., 83
Dubuque (Ia.) *Herald*, 401
Duer, William A., 247

Edgewood Plantation, 84
Education, in South, 292–293
Edwards, Jonathan, 12, 130

Elam, Samuel C., 403
Election, of 1848, 234–240; of 1852, 312; of 1856, 370; of 1860, 427
Emerson, John, 381, 382
Emerson, Ralph W., 12, 309, 408
Emigration, from Old South, 41; to Cotton Kingdom, 95; to Northwest, 95; to Texas, 181–183; from Europe, 316; to Kansas, 357; 361–362, 373
Erie Canal, 376
Essay on Calcareous Manures, 279
Evans, J. J., 307
Everett, Edward, 193
Expansion, 3, 26, 94, 182; of New England, 315–316; of South to Northwest, 313–314; into Cotton Kingdom, 97–98, 102–110
Exposition, The, South Carolina, 64

Fallon, James, 25
Farmers' Register, 279
Ficklin, Orlando B., 214
Fillmore, Millard, 259
Finney, Charles G., 12, 130, 277
Fisher, Elwood, 172
Fitch, Doctor Graham, 239
Fitzhugh, George, 162, 166, 170–172
Florida, 243
Flournoy, J. J., 167
Floyd, John B., 259
Flush times (in Southwest), 111–115
Foote, Henry, 258, 266
Foote, H. S., 31, 320
Forsyth, John, 398
Fort Sumter, 437
Fowler, J. W., 85
Fox, Capt. Gustavus, 437–438
Franklin, John R., 350
Free Soil Party, 238; platform in 1848, 238; 240, 247; combines with Democrats in Massachusetts, 310; in Northwest, 322, 324
Free West, The, 333
Frémont, John C., 209, 369, 374
Fripp, John E., 85
Frontier, 3, 5; character in Southwest, 112–115
Fugitive Slave Law, 230, 251, 265; 322–324
Fuller, Richard, 163
Furman, Richard, 156–157

Gadsden, Christopher, 25
Gag Rule, 176, 178
Garnett, James M., 50
Garrison, William Lloyd, 120, 131, 135–138, 319
Gaston, William, 153
Genius of Universal Emancipation, 137
Georgia, settlement, 26; anti-slavery in, 154; opposition to Wilmot Proviso in,

233; election of 1848, 236; in crisis of 1850, 262; and Compromise of 1850, 264–265; manufacturing in, 288–289; reaction after 1850, 304–305; and Kansas-Nebraska, 353; emigration to Kansas, 373; conservative flavor, 414
Georgia Constitutional Union Party, 304–305
Georgia Platform, The, 265, 306
Georgia *Sentinel,* quoted, 272
Germans, in Northwest, 315
Giddings, Joshua, 140, 142, 176, 178; on Oregon, 215; on Wilmot Proviso, 229; 230, 242, 326
Gildersleeve, Basil L., 294
Gillon, Alexander, 25
Gilmer, Thomas W., 190
Gist, Gov. W. H., 413
Globe, The, 201, 202, 208
Gold, in South, 98; in California, 245–246
Gott, Daniel, 242
Graniteville (S. C.), 288
Grayson, William J., 268
Greater New England, 5, 12, 249
Greeley, Horace, 293, 347, 408, 428
Green, Beriah, 140
Green, Duff, 190, 212
Greenwood, 27
Gregg, William, 280–281
Grimes, James W., 345, 348
Grimké Sisters, 146

Hamilton, James, Jr., 59, 64, 269
Hammond, James H., 165, 243–244, 281, 286, 373, 396, 399, 402, 403, 404, 413, 420
Hannegan, E. A., 212, 214, 321
Harper, Chancellor, 66
Harper, William, 169
Harpers Ferry, 280; raid on, 407, 409
Harper's Magazine, 293, 296, 395, 397
Harvard University, 294
Hayne, I. W., 415
Hayne, Robert Y., 6, 59, 62, 84
Hazelwood, 46
Heartt, Dennis, 153
Hedrick, B. S., 301
Helme, Doctor R. H., 153
Henry, Patrick, 24
Higginson, Stephen, 84
Hill, Benjamin H., 397
Hill, D. H., 295
Hilliard, Henry W., 263
Hinds County, Mississippi, 83; *Gazette,* 377, 396
Hodder, Professor F. H., 384–385
Holcombe, James P., 294
Holland, Edwin C., 155–156
Holley, Horace, 301
Holmes, George F., 294

Holt, Edwin, 84
Holyoke Mills, 86
Homestead Bills, 339, 400–401
Houston, Sam, 193; repudiates Kansas-Nebraska Bill, 336–337; 347
Hubbard, F. M., 295
Huguenots, in South Carolina, 25
Humanitarian movements, 11
Hundley, D. R., 424
Hunkers, 203, 231
Hunter, R. M. T., 186, 189, 192, 305

Illinois State Journal, quoted, 334, 386, 400, 418, 420–421
Illinois *State Register,* quoted, 239
Indentured servants, 68–70; laws governing, 69–70
Industrial Revolution, in New England, 124–126
Industry, compared with plantation, 110
Internal improvements, 217–218, 321–322, 402
Inquiry into Principles and Tendencies of Certain Public Measures (Taylor, J.), 45
Iowa, 359
Irish, in Northwest, 316

Jackson, Andrew, 11, 61, 64–65; relation to Cotton Kingdom, 103; 186, 196, 201, 202, 204, 314
Jackson (Mich.), 344
Jacksonian Democrats, 346–347
Jacksonville *Republican,* quoted, 372
Jarratt, Devereaux, 23
Jefferson, Thomas, 24, 40, 42–44, 118, 123, 152, 223
"Jerry," rescue of, 310
Jervey, Theodore D., 154
Johnson, Anthony, 71
Johnson, Herschel V., 270, 420
Jones, George W., 321
Jones, J. W., 285
Jones, Sheriff, 364
Journeymen Mechanics of Philadelphia, 132
Julian, George W., 419

Kansas, 338; struggle for, 357–359; "Bleeding Kansas," 361; conditions in, 362–365. (*See* "Bleeding Kansas.")
Kansas-Nebraska Bill, introduced, 325–326; reaction to, 326; motive for introduction, 329–331; 332; distortion of, 331–335; Douglas defends, 335–336; passes, 337; and the extension of slavery, 350–351; Southern press on, 351–357
Kansas Tribune, quoted, 364
Kansas Weekly Herald, quoted, 370

Kelley, Hall Jackson, 185
King, Preston, 220, 225, 230–231 ; 428
King, Rufus, 123
Know-Nothing Party, 346, 377, 397
Knoxville Commercial Convention, 289, 402

Lamar, G. B., 377
Lamar, M. B., 193
Land ownership, North and South compared, 301
Lands, public, 181 ; in Kansas, 363–364 ; 401
Lane, Jim, 387
Lane Theological Seminary, 139–140
Lawrence, Amos, 357, 365
Lawrence (Kansas), 364
Lawrence (Mass.), 124, 288
"League of United Southerners," 278, 400, 406
Leavitt, Joshua, 142, 147, 277
Lecompton Constitution, 387–388, 389
Lecompton *Union*, quoted, 369
Lee, Daniel, 285
Legaré, H. S., 193
Legaré, J. D., 285
Lewis, Liburn, 145
Liberator, The, 135, 357
Liberia, 166
Liberty Party, 141, 197–198, 226, 230
Lieber, Francis, 34, 268
Lincecum, Gideon, 106–107
Lincoln, Abraham, 312, 314, 318, 319, 386 ; House Divided Speech, 391 ; debate with Douglas, 391–392 ; and Dred Scott decision, 392 ; nominated in 1860, 417 ; Southern picture of, 423 ; refusal to compromise, 430 ; possible courses, 435–436 ; and Fort Sumter, 437
Linn, Lewis F., 186
Livermore, Representative, 122
Locofoco, 132–134
Louisiana, sectionalism in, 22 ; crisis of 1850, 260, 261 ; Nashville Convention, 263 ; attitude toward Kansas-Nebraska Bill, 354–355 ; 356 ; conservative flavor, 414
Louisville *Daily Courier*, quoted, 437
Louisville *Journal*, 432
Lowell, James Russell, quoted, 128, 219
Lowell (Mass.), 124, 288
Lundy, Benjamin, 137, 138, 191
Lyell, Sir Charles, 86

Macon, Nathaniel, 184
Macon *Telegraph*, quoted, 353, 375–376, 396, 400
Malin, James C., quoted, 363
Manufactures, move for, in South, 286–288 ; statistics for South, 288

Marcy, William L., 203
Marshall, John, 42–43, 47, 52
Marshall, Thomas, 246
Martin, Martha, 333, 334
Martin vs. Hunter's Lessee, 47
Martinez, Don Antonia, 183
Maryland, 68, 70
Mason, George, 84
Mason, James M., 252
Massachusetts, 83, 121 ; industrial revolution, 124 ; 126, 131–132 ; opposition to fugitive slave laws, 309–311 ; Know-Nothing success in, 346
Maxcy, Virgil, 189
May, Samuel J., 310
McCulloch vs. Maryland, 47
McDowell, James, Jr., 57
McDowell, Joseph J., 214
McDuffie, George, 59–60, 62, 190
McGuffey, William H., 297
McLean, Justice John, 383, 385
Meade, R. K., 247
Medill, Joseph, 393
Memoirs of a Nullifier by Himself, 173
Memphis, 270, 303
Memphis *Appeal*, quoted, 356, 377, 426–427
Memphis Convention, 188, 212–213, 217
Memphis *Eagle and Enquirer*, quoted, 355, 431
Memphis *Ledger*, 396
Methodist Church, 115, 169 ; and slavery, 200–201 ; in Northwest, 313
Mexican War, 211
Miles, William Porcher, 413, 416
Miller, Stephen D., 158
Millison, John S., 350
Minor, John B., 294
Mississippi, 243 ; call for Nashville convention, 245 ; and crisis of 1850, 261 ; Whigs and crisis, 262 ; and Compromise of 1850, 266 ; Union Democrats in, 306 ; and Kansas-Nebraska, 356 ; follows South Carolina, 413
Mississippi *Free Trader*, quoted, 244, 266, 281, 356, 396, 403
Mississippi River Trade, 314, 317
Missouri, conditions in, 182–183 ; politics, 205 ; interest in Kansas, 358 ; courts and Dred Scott, 282
Missouri Compromise, 50–51, 73, 122–124, 152 ; repeal, 325–326
Mobile, 270, 290
Mobile *Advertiser*, quoted, 354
Mobile *Daily Register*, quoted, 261, 273, 355–356, 370, 376, 378, 398, 405, 411
Monroe, James, 54
Montgomery, proposed convention, 268 ; 399

Montgomery *Advertiser and Gazette,* quoted, 261, 306, 356, 424
Montgomery *Confederation,* quoted, 396
Montgomery *Mail,* 370, 424
Morton, Samuel G., 167
Murphy, William S., 193–194

Nashville Convention, called, 245; meeting, 259, 261, 262, 264
Nashville *Republican Banner and Nashville Whig,* quoted, 355, 377, 404, 418
Nashville *Union and American,* 356, 375
Nashville *Patriot,* 436
Natchez, 105, 113, 270
Natchez *Courier,* quoted, 267, 334
Natchez *Free Trader,* quoted, 261
Nebraska, settlement, 359
Negro, the number in South, 36; influence on South, 37; comes to America, 70–72; opposition to, 72; and plantation system, 72; growth in numbers to Revolution, 73; as a laborer, 74–76; effects of slavery on, 76–79; child-bearing, 84–85; effects of plantation on, 89–90; growth of black belts, 109; Calhoun's attitude towards, 253–254; domestic surplus, 303; race issue in campaign of 1860, 423–424
New England, industrial development, 124–126; expansion of, 315–316; revolt against fugitive slave law, 322–324; and Kansas-Nebraska Act, 335
New England Emigrant Aid Company, 357, 361–362
New Mexico, 220, 242–244, 246, 250
New Orleans, 27, 85, 270; commercial convention, 289; 290, 314
New Orleans *Bee,* quoted, 262, 349, 354, 371, 376, 379, 396
New Orleans *Daily Crescent,* quoted, 260, 261–262, 263, 281, 287, 354–355, 377, 378, 380, 396, 403, 406
New Orleans *Daily Delta,* quoted, 260, 263, 356, 396, 397, 399, 405–406
New Orleans *Picayune,* quoted, 377, 410–411
New Orleans *True Delta,* quoted, 260
New York, settlement, 127; depression, 128; revivals, 130; locofocos, 132–133; anti-slavery, 138; political division, 202–203, 230–231, 235, 237; New York City and South, 291; trade with South, 308–309; campaign of 1860 in, 422
New York *Evening Express,* quoted, 213
New York *Herald,* quoted, 386, 439

New York State Kansas Aid Society, 366
New York *Times,* 386
New York *Tribune,* quoted, 334, 337, 341–344, 347, 365, 369, 408
Nicholson Letter, 235
Norfolk, 96
North Carolina, 21–22; Constitutional Convention of 1835, 21; society in, 24–25; conditions in 1820's, 58, 96; and anti-slavery, 153–154; legislature acts in 1849, 243; and crisis of 1850, 262; and Nashville Convention, 263; and Compromise of 1850, 265, 270; and Kansas-Nebraska, 352; conservative flavor, 414
North Carolina *Standard,* quoted, 260, 265
Northeast, 6, 124–126, 216
Northwest (Old), 5, 6–7; interest in Oregon, 186; anger over Oregon, 214; and internal improvements, 217–218; revolt under Polk, 313; settlement in Ohio Valley, 313–314; social-economic development, 313–314; settlement of Lake area, 315–316; social-economic development of Lake area, 316–319; cleavage and unity in region, 319–325; Kansas-Nebraska, 336; politics, 400–401
Nott, Josiah, 31, 167–168
Nullification Controversy, 60–66

Oak Alley, 27
Ohio, early anti-slavery in, 120, 130, 140; Texas-Oregon dispute, 214; political revolt, 229–230; and Wilmot Proviso, 242–245 (Chase governor); settlement, 315; economic-social development, 316; and fugitive slaves, 323; Chase sees revolt, 326; Kansas-Nebraska, 345; Chase and Republican Party, 347–348; 401; Pugh defies South, 416
Ohio State Journal, quoted, 333
Ohio Valley, 5, 6–7, 313–315, 318
Olmsted, Frederick Law, 31
Orangeburg (S. C.), 25
Oregon, 180, 182, 185–187, 192, 211; Calhoun and, 212; Northwest and, 214; organization, 227, 252, 322
Orr, James L., 276, 308, 309, 395, 398
Osborne, Charles, 120
Our World: or the Slaveholder's Daughter, 146

Page, Thomas Nelson, 18
Pakenham Letter, 195–196
Palfrey, William F., 85
Palmer, Reverend B. M., 165

Parker, Reverend Theodore, 293, 309, 310, 312
Peace Convention, 435
Pennsylvania, and tariff, 1846, 216–217; and Wilmot, 224
Perry, B. F., 31, 234, 244, 258–259, 268, 277, 434
Petigru, James L., 177, 179
Petition Struggle, 176–177
Pettigrew, Ebenezer, 31
Philadelphia, merchants and South, 291
Philips, M. W., 286
Phillips, Philip, 330
Phillips, Wendell, 310, 312, 407
Pickens, F. W., 84
Pierce, Franklin, 312, 337, 361, 366
Pillow, Gideon J., 198
Pinckney, C. C., 158
Pinckney, Henry L., 176
Plantation system, 89–90
Poinsett, Joel, 65, 259, 268
Polk, James K., 198–199; and *The Globe*, 202; administration and parties, 206–207; and expansion, 211; and Mexico, 211; and Oregon, 211–212; and internal improvements, 217; quoted, 220; and renomination, 234
Poor whites, 28–29
Port Gibson *Herald*, quoted, 267
Port Royal (S. C.,), 25
Prairie Farmer, quoted, 321
Pratt, Daniel, 289
Prattville (Ala.), 288
Preston, William C., 64, 139, 259
Priest, Josiah, 163
Prigg vs. Pennsylvania, 230
Pro-Slavery argument, 153–174; in South Carolina, 155–159; Dew's argument, 159–160; agents of, 161; from Bible, 162–164; slavery and American ideals, 164–165; benefits to Negro, 165–166; from science, 167–169; and a superior civilization, 169–172
Providence (R. I.), 124
Pryor, Roger, 281, 289, 399, 421
Pryor-Potter challenge, 421, 424–425
Pugh, George E., 416
Purrysburg (S. C.), 25
Putnam's Magazine, 293, 296

Quakers, and slavery, 120, 153; and petitions, 175; in Northwest, 313
Quitman, John A., 261, 266, 306

Railroads, in South, 290–291; and Kansas-Nebraska Bill, 329–330, 402
Raleigh Letter, 197
Raleigh *Register*, quoted, 352
Raleigh *Standard*, quoted, 239, 281, 352
Randolph, John, 53–54, 62

Randolph, Thomas Jefferson, 55
Rankin, John, 149
Ray, C. H., 390
Redmond, D., 285
Reeder, Andrew, 258, 361–364
Reid, Robert W., 123
Republican Party, origins, 206–210, 312; birth of, 344–345; use "Bleeding Kansas," 388; and senatorship in Illinois, 389–391; and John Brown, 408–409; Convention of 1860, 417–418; campaign of 1860, 419–422
Review of Debates in the Virginia Legislature, 57
Rhett, Robert Barnwell, 64, 84, 179, 189, 202, 213, 214, 227, 231, 236, 242, 264; sketch of, 274–276; 398, 414, 416
Rhode Island, 83, 345
Rice planting, in Carolinas, 40
Richardson, W. A., 337
Richmond, 270, 290, 303
Richmond *Enquirer*, quoted, 232, 259–260, 263, 281, 283, 301, 349, 370, 375, 394–395, 396, 399, 404
Richmond *Republican and General Advertiser*, quoted, 261
Richmond *Times*, quoted, 244
Richmond *Whig*, quoted, 352
Ripon (Wis.), 344
Ritchie, Thomas, 202, 234, 263
Roane, Spencer, 42, 47
Robinson, Charles, 365, 387
Robinson, John L., 24
Robinson, Stuart, 163
Rockwell, Julius, 221
Root, Joseph M., 242
Rosedown, 27
Ross, Reverend Fred A., 164
Ross, John, 97
Ruffin, Edmund, 50, 162, 164, 172, 259; sketch of, 278–280; 289, 305, 399, 400, 403
Ruffin, Thomas, 84
Ruffner, Henry, 246
Russell's Magazine, 296

Saffin, John, 121
St. Louis, 303, 314, 381
St. Louis *Democrat*, quoted, 365
St. Louis Intelligencer, quoted, 334
St. Louis Railroad Convention, 1849, 329
Sandusky *Commercial Register*, quoted, 332, 338, 343, 402
Sanford, John F. A., 382
Santa Fé Trail, 181, 358
Saturday Evening Post, 293
Savannah, 270; convention of 1856, 289
Savannah *Republican*, quoted, 244, 353
Scotch-Irish, 25

Scott, Dred, 312; case, 381–386; facts of, 381–382; Taney's opinion, 383–384; Curtis and McLean, 383, 384; import of decision, 386–387

Scruggs, P. J., 378

Seabrook, Whitemarsh, 157, 268, 269

Sectionalism, 2, 4, 10; in Virginia, 20, 51–57; in South Carolina, 20–21; in North Carolina, 21–22; in Lower South, 22; in Louisiana, 22; in Tennessee, 22

Sedden, James A., 269

Selling of Joseph, The, 121

Sewall, Samuel, 121

Seward, William H., 249; on Compromise of 1850, 256–257; 311, 326, 386, 408, 428, 429

Shadows, The, 27

Shadrach, 309–310

Sharkey, Judge, 426

Shaw, Robert, 84

Simms, William Gilmore, 296

"Slave Power," 2, 227, 272, 386, 432

Slave trade, domestic, 304

Slaveholding, numbers of slaveholders, 27–28; advantages and disadvantages, 80–83; justification of, 151–152. (See Slavery.)

Slavery, debates over, in Virginia, 52–57; Dew's defense of, 57–58; emergence from indenture, 70–71; character of, in South, 75–76; advantages and disadvantages, 80–83; effects on size of families, 83–85; slave breeding, 83, 304; working hours, 85–86; quarters, 86–87; food, clothing, 87–88; did it pay?, 90–91; effects on South, 91–93; slaves in cotton, 110; effects of frontier on, 113–114; evils of, 146–149; justification, 151–152; defense of, 152–174; in Texas, 184–185; in District of Columbia, 242; weakening in Border States, 406; issue in campaign of 1860, 419, 420–421

Smith, Gerrit, 131, 133, 162, 310, 366

South, the, geography, 19–20; distribution of population, 92; reaction to Wilmot Proviso, 231–234; reaction to Kansas, 370–371; and Douglas, 394–398; Union sentiment in, 403–407; reaction to John Brown, 409–413; campaign of 1860, 422–427

South Carolina, geography, 20–21; early society, 25; conditions in 1820's in, 58–60; depression in agriculture in, 96–97; anti-slavery in, 154; opposition to Wilmot Proviso in, 233–234; reactions to anti-slavery, 1849–1850, 243; and Crisis of 1850, 261; and Compromise of 1850, 266–268;

reaction after 1850 effort, 307–308; Kansas-Nebraska Act, 349; 352–353; Brooks-Sumner affair, 374–375; proposes convention, 413; conservative flavor, 414; secession, 433

South Carolinian, Daily, quoted, 353, 373–374

Southern Advocate, 396

Southern Agriculturalist, 285

Southern Commercial Conventions, 289–290, 399, 402

Southern Cultivator, 285

Southern Dial, 283

Southern Literary Messenger, 281; quoted, 287–288, 296

Southern Quarterly Review, 296

Southern Recorder, quoted, 353–354

Southern Reveille, 397

Southern Rights Association, 265, 266, 278

Southron, The, quoted, 374

Southwest, 5, 8–9; flush times in, 26–27; rise of Cotton Kingdom, 95–99; Indian removal, 102–103; growth, 105–110; spirit of, 111–112; churches in, 114–115; speculation in, 112. (See Cotton Kingdom.)

Spratt, L. W., 398–399

Springfield Republican, 428–429

Stanly, Edward, 262

Stanton, Edwin M., 140

Stanton Hall, 27

Stephens, Alexander H., 226, 233, 262, 337, 361, 394

Stowe, Harriet Beecher, 18, 323

Strickland, William, 42

Stringfellow, B. F., 365

Stringfellow, Thornton, 163

Strong, Selah B., 231

Sturges, Russel, 84

Sumner, Charles, 310, 326, 335; speech on "The Crime against Kansas," 367; assaulted, 367–368; Southern reaction to assault, 374–377; 419–420, 428

Sumter Banner, quoted, 244, 352

Sumter Watchman, quoted, 374

Taney, Roger, 383–384, 385

Tappan, Arthur, 277

Tariff, 216, 224, 321, 401

Taylor, John, of Caroline, 40, 42–51; and states' rights, 47–48; on Supreme Court, 48–49; 253, 416

Taylor, Zachary, 234, 236; and Compromise of 1850, 259; death, 259

Temperance, 129, 317

Tennessee, 26, 263, 270; manufactures, 288; attitude towards Kansas-Nebraska, 355; conservative flavor, 414

Texas, 180, 183–185; and politics, 189–199; senators and tariff, 216
Thayer, Eli, 357
Thompson, Waddy, 234, 268
Thomson, James, 223
Thoreau, Henry D., 408
Thornwell, J. H., 14, 163
Tobacco, planting in Virginia, 40
Toombs, Robert, 233, 248–249, 262, 364, 366
Towns, George W., 260
Trade, on Mississippi, 314, 317; of Northwest, on Lakes, 317; by railroads, 317
Truck gardening, 285
Trumbull, Lyman, 345, 390
Tucker, Beverley, 259
Turnbull, Robert, 63, 157
Turner, Nat, 55, 120
Tuscaloosa *Monitor*, 404
Twain, Mark, 314
Tyler, John, 188–189, 192–193, 198–199
Types of Mankind, 168
Tyranny Unmasked, 50

Uncle Tom's Cabin, 144, 145–146, 293, 323–324
Union sentiment, in South, 403–407
University of Alabama, 294
University of Mississippi, 294
University of North Carolina, 294, 295
University of the South, 294
University of Virginia, 283, 294, 302
Upshur, Judge Abel P., 53, 193–194
Utica Convention, 237

Vallandigham, C., 318, 320–321
Van Buren, John, 237
Van Buren, Martin, 179, 189, 197, 201, 202–203; and Calhoun, 206–210, 221; and Wilmot Proviso, 231, 234; and New York factions, 237; bolts party, 237, 240
Van Evrie, Doctor J. H., 168
Van Zandt, John, 230
Vance, Zebulon, 31
Vesey, Denmark, 120, 152
Virginia, sectionalism in, 20, 51–57; growth of aristocracy, 23–24; Convention of 1829–1830, 51–55; anti-slavery in, 54–58, 153; reaction to anti-slavery, 243; and crisis of 1850, 259–260; and Nashville Convention, 263; and Compromise of 1850, 265; reaction after 1850, 305; conservative in 1860, 413
Virginia and Kentucky Resolutions, 44

Wade, Benjamin F., 323, 326, 335

Wakarusa War, 364
Walker, Robert J., 111, 216, 387
Walterboro (S. C.), 63
Waltham (Mass.), 124
Warren, Charles, quoted, 383
Washburne, E. B., 333
Washington *Union*, 263
Webster, Daniel, 6, 187, 192, 193; and Compromise of 1850, 250, 255–256; 257, 305
Webster-Ashburton Treaty, 186–187
Weed, Thurlow, 235, 428
Weld, Theodore, 138–140, 148–149, 175, 277
Welles, Gideon, 222
Wentworth, John, 214, 236, 238, 239, 322
Western Journal, quoted, 321
Whig Party, 175–176, 192, 261; in Georgia, 1850, 305; in Alabama after 1850, 306; "Cotton Whigs," 309; rise in Northwest, 322, 325; anti-Nebraska Whigs, 345–346; Southern Whigs and Kansas-Nebraska, 349; ends in South, 377
White, Elijah, 187
"Wide-Awakes," 419
Williams College, 276, 277
Wilmington *Commercial*, quoted, 260
Wilmot, David, 221; and Proviso, 223–227, 257
Wilmot Proviso, origins, 222–226; reactions to, in North, 227–228; Southern reactions to, 231–234, 241, 244, 279; in Northwest, 322
Wilson, Henry, 223, 372
Wilson's History of the United States, 295
Winnsboro *Register*, quoted, 373
Winthrop, R. C., 247
Winthrop, Thomas, 84
Wisconsin, 237
Wise, Henry A., 305
Woodville *Republican*, quoted, 267
Woodward, George W., 225
Workingmen's movement, in Massachusetts, 132
Worth, Jonathan, 438, 439
Wright, Elizur, 140
Wright, Silas, 203, 231
Wyeth, Nathaniel, 186

Yale University, 294; model for West, 315
Yancey, William L., 214, 235, 265; sketch of, 276–278; 289, 306, 399, 400; Alabama Platform, 413–414; 415–416; 425
Yeomen farmers, in South, 29–32